*Marriage of
Inconvenience*

Marriage of Inconvenience

*Euphemia Chalmers Gray
and John Ruskin:
the secret history of the most
notorious marital failure
of the Victorian era*

ROBERT BROWNELL

PALLAS ATHENE

CONTENTS

INTRODUCTION P. 9

CHAPTER I: **SCOTTISH ROOTS** P. 21

CHAPTER II: **THE BOY JOHN** P. 31

CHAPTER III: **FIRST LOVES** P. 50

CHAPTER IV: **THE DARK SHADOW** P. 56

CHAPTER V: **THE FAIR MAID OF PERTH** P. 67

CHAPTER VI: **STRANGE COURTSHIP** P. 92

CHAPTER VII: **THE PROPOSAL** P. 105

CHAPTER VIII: **A VERY SUFFICIENT AND ENTIRE MAN-TRAP** P. 115

CHAPTER IX: **A SPECULATIVE MAN** P. 144

CHAPTER X: **THE WEDDING** P. 167

CHAPTER XI: **THE NEWLY-WEDS** P. 181

CHAPTER XII: **KEEPING HOUSE** P. 211

CHAPTER XIII: **OCEAN'S LOVELY DAUGHTER** P. 257

Opposite: Euphemia Ruskin, *by Thomas Richmond, 1851*
Frontispiece: The Order of Release, 1746, *by J. E. Millais, 1852-3*

CHAPTER XIV: **HIATUS** P. 284

CHAPTER XV: **QUEEN OF MARBLE AND OF MUD** P. 300

CHAPTER XVI: **DANCING WITH DANGER** P. 315

CHAPTER XVII: **SCANDAL** P. 332

CHAPTER XVIII: **UNTYING THE KNOT** P. 352

CHAPTER XIX: **A HIGHLAND HOLIDAY** P. 373

CHAPTER XX: **POETIC JUSTICE** P. 406

CHAPTER XXI: **THE TRAP SPRUNG** P. 425

CHAPTER XXII: **A MEDIÆVAL PANTOMIME** P. 451

CHAPTER XXIII: **AFTERMATH** P. 473

CHAPTER XXIV: **ROSE LA TOUCHE** P. 500

EPILOGUE P. 519

APPENDIX P. 523

ACKNOWLEDGEMENTS P. 537

ILLUSTRATIONS P. 539

NOTES P. 542

INDEX P. 590

Sketch of Ruskin for the Glenfinlas portrait, *by J. E. Millais, 1853*

John Ruskin *by George Richmond, c. 1857*

INTRODUCTION

❧

On the 10th of April 1848 the marriage took place between John Ruskin and Euphemia Chalmers Gray in her father's house in Perth, Scotland. The bride was nineteen years old and the daughter of a provincial Scottish lawyer. The bridegroom was twenty-nine years old, wealthy and a literary celebrity. His reputation had been established by two volumes of art theory and criticism published in 1843 and 1846 under the series title *Modern Painters*. There was to be a ten-year interval before two further volumes in the series appeared. By the time of his marriage to Miss Gray, John Ruskin's formidable intellectual powers had been re-directed into the politically sensitive field of architecture. He was already at work on *The Seven Lamps of Architecture* which was to be published in 1849, and it was followed by the three volumes of *The Stones of Venice* in 1851 and 1853. The index to the third and final volume of *The Stones of Venice* was finished on the same Scottish holiday that precipitated the end of his ill-fated marriage.

Within months of the holiday the marriage was annulled in circumstances which gave rise to a storm of scandal and gossip. The Gray and Ruskin families, their heirs and trustees attempted to smother the scandal but this only served to heighten public interest in the case. There has been speculation and public fascination with regard to the marriage ever since – usually salacious and usually hostile to Ruskin. The seemingly endless procession of films, plays, an opera, novels and 'factional' accounts produced to service this prurient demand have done little to uncover the truth, but much to obscure the importance of Ruskin's ideas. This book is an attempt to provide the first plausible evidence-based account of the Ruskin/Gray marriage – an account which will be seen to have little in common with received opinion.

Although the story has usually been told in terms of personalities and intimate psychologies, it is also important to understand the turbulent political background to the marriage. The proposal was accepted during the most critical phase of the greatest financial crisis of the nineteenth century. On the day of the wedding the Chartists marched on London. The first year of the marriage was the European 'year of revolutions'. The newly-weds' European tour had to be postponed due to fighting in the streets of France in which the archbishop of Paris was shot dead and the Bourbon monarchy fell. Their first trip to Venice was to a city that had been besieged, bombarded, starved into submission and disease, then put under martial law by an Austrian army of occupation. These events inevitably played a part in shaping both Ruskin's personal and his intellectual life.

The publication of *The Stones of Venice* and the annulment of his marriage had exactly opposite effects upon his reputation. *The Stones of Venice* established him as the pre-eminent architectural theorist of his age and would secure his position as a writer of historical and international importance. The scandal which surrounded the ending of his marriage resulted in his ostracism by 'Society' and consequently his alienation from many of the very people of wealth and power he had been seeking to influence by his writing. The marriage and its annulment should have been a private affair affecting only himself, his wife and their families. A pact of silence had been agreed between the main protagonists and annulments, unlike divorces,

Euphemia Ruskin, *by John Ruskin, 1848 or 1850*

were not usually reported in the press. However, instead of being just a minor social scandal, it developed into a concerted public campaign against Ruskin fomented by an establishment that believed that their political and vested interests were directly threatened by his uncensored eloquence.[1] This more widespread campaign against him was intended to encourage general public resistance to his ideas. With regard to 'Society' in the latter half of the nineteenth century it proved largely successful in its aim. The Gray family, finding themselves suddenly embroiled in a very public scandal, and having good reason to defend their own version of events, were almost compelled to adopt an extremely hostile posture with regard to their former son-in-law. From the outset members of both families continued to assert opposite views of what had happened. It was in the tradition of eminent Victorians to draw a veil over unpleasant events by suppressing or destroying relevant documentation. The Gray/Millais side was both more thorough and more persistent in this respect for two reasons. Firstly they had, as I shall show, more to lose by the truth coming to light, and secondly, as a family of lawyers they were familiar with what constituted documentary evidence and where it was to be found.[2] They also eventually became wealthy enough to acquire any relevant correspondence that went through the sale rooms. Moreover, where evidence was not backed by written proof, for example in memoirs or academic works, they were also prepared to threaten authors with legal action in order to suppress any uncomfortable revelations. The Gray/Millais family had yet another advantage in that John Ruskin left no children to protect his interests. Hence the bonfires of personal letters and papers after his death.

Readers should however, beware of attributing malicious

intentions to all those involved in this tragedy. This is essentially a story of respectable, decent people who found themselves in impossibly difficult situations. These were people who would not set out to tell deliberate lies but who, because of the censorious nature of the times in which they lived, felt compelled to go to great lengths to prevent the truth being known. I have therefore assumed that everything written by the main protagonists was true except where it could be suspected of being otherwise because they themselves contradicted it or because facts, dates or events suggested a different explanation.

The problem that began with an understandable desire of both sides to suppress the facts, was compounded by a deliberate campaign of rumour, gossip and innuendo that affected both families. As a result, even Ruskin's early literary executors conspired with the Gray family to keep the whole issue from the public. Early Ruskin biographers made only the briefest of references to the marriage and subsequent authors were reluctant to trawl through the masses of widely dispersed uncensored material for the truth about what was after all an event which seemed only marginally relevant to the man's ideas. The widespread willingness of researchers to accept unproven or tendentious statements uncritically as 'given,' has created an unwitting consensus of error even amongst Ruskin enthusiasts. As a result twentieth century accounts of John Ruskin's failed marriage to Euphemia Chalmers Gray have remained inextricably entangled in authorial fantasies of pubic hair and personal hygiene. The manner in which his private life has been interpreted has been a constant embarrassment to his supporters and for his many detractors a stick with which to beat him. This nexus of disinformation has continued to affect the attitude of the reading public to John Ruskin.

The situation has been compounded by unfettered speculation about what actually did happen in this unfortunate marriage, much of which is endlessly repeated despite there being little or no evidence in support of it. The gaps in the account have often been filled with ludicrous speculations of dubious evidential quality. Unfortunately the misleading and partisan versions of events presented in the latter half of the twentieth century by Admiral Sir William James and Mary Lutyens were uncritically adopted by many writers as a convenient paradigm of Victorian patriarchal oppression and marital dysfunction. John Ruskin's pioneering rôle in women's education, artistic expression and political activism was conveniently forgotten in the general rush to promote the folk-myth of John as abuser and Effie as victim turned victor.[3] Thus it is that at the start of the twenty-first century the work of one of the most influential social critics this country has ever produced still languishes in the shadow of public ignorance, calumny and ridicule.

The amount of myth, legend and folklore which has built up around John Ruskin's private life would have been of great interest to the man himself. The relationship between myth and fact was a preoccupation of the culture in which he moved. There can be no doubt that, as with the Christians in Rome, or of the Gothic style in the eighteenth century, all the attempts to demonise John Ruskin and mislead the public about his ideas have only served to create a deep and abiding fascination with the man. After all, how many people today remember Kugler, or Waagen, or Eastlake?

Although I have attempted to concentrate on what was actually said or written, readers must bear in mind that the vast majority of the letters bearing on the subject came from the Gray family archive and with the potential for scandal in mind were carefully selected and vetted over several generations before being released into the public domain. The Bowerswell Papers, as they became known, consist mainly of Euphemia Gray's letters to her mother and family, supplemented by the letters of others addressed to the Gray family home. The bulk of Mr. and Mrs. Gray's letters to their daughter are absent because Euphemia destroyed all of them shortly after she received them so that her husband John would not read them. All but three of Euphemia's sixty-odd so-called 'love letters' to John are missing and the Morgan's holdings also include letters with leaves missing or torn out, blacked-out passages and some wrongly attributed dates. More correspondence, and particularly Euphemia's Venetian diaries, may yet come to light. There are also significant gaps in the correspondence and journals, not only of the Gray family but of other protagonists, including Ruskin himself.

If John Ruskin's private life remains in contention, his works remain as controversial and enigmatic today as they were in his own time. The sometimes wilful misinterpretation of his ideas by his contemporary critics can be explained to some extent by the religious and philosophical revolution then in progress. Amongst the Protestant élite of London Society the feeling in religious matters was such that perhaps one of the most damaging lies spread about him at the time of the annulment was that he was about to become a Roman Catholic, since Catholicism was regarded as unpatriotic as well as heterodox. Later on his unconventional religious beliefs proved to be a major obstacle to his marrying Rose La Touche. Ruskin's own personal standpoint in the religious controversy at any given time, as far as it can be understood, contributes in no mean degree to an understanding of his life and works. At a time when Puritanism and anti-intellectualism were on the increase and when Christianity

Flos Florum Rosa:
Portrait of Rose La Touche
by John Ruskin c. 1872-4

was on the defensive against scientific advance, John Ruskin proposed a renewed harmony between art, religion and philosophy as a means of maintaining spiritual values against a destructive tide of scepticism and materialism. He was never, at any time in his life, the puritan prig his detractors accuse him of being. In fact even from his youth he violently opposed the puritan tendency in the Evangelical sect and stridently contradicted their anti-intellectualism and their philistinism. He was a competent geologist, author of published scientific articles, knew Charles Darwin personally from when he was at Oxford and championed the study of natural history for those about to take religious orders.

My intention in studying the period of the marriage was twofold. Firstly I intended to look at this most notorious marriage of the nineteenth century and to try to sort out the fact from the fiction. Despite, and in many cases because of the concerted campaign by the Gray/Millais family to acquire and vet all the relevant documents, some revealing factual evidence about the marriage has survived because, on their own admission, they never knew what might be in the possession of what they always referred to as 'the other side' and what evidence might be needed to counter it. Put into its proper context alongside the legal facts and a substantial amount of circumstantial evidence, the true nature of the marriage and its end can be surmised with reasonable certainty. Secondly I intended to show that the intellectual environment in which John Ruskin's architectural books were produced, influenced his moral, personal and political development to such an extent that he adopted similar strategies in both his writing and his personal relations. This would serve to counter accusations that it would have been out of character for him to have acted in the marriage as I describe below. In fact one has only to read periodical reviews of his books written even before the scandal broke to see that speculation about his professed and actual meanings and motives preoccupied both his supporters and his detractors. This second aim became my book *A Torch at Midnight* which is now published as a separate volume.

Because of a deliberate intention on Ruskin's part to 'veil' his message in allegorical 'draperies', even his supporters had difficulty ascertaining the precise nature of what they were reading. He did this partly because of the censorious atmosphere of the times, partly because of his religious apostasy, and partly because of his conviction that art should ideally be allegorical or symbolical in the highest degree: that it should literally 'tell stories'. Bound up in the allegory of *The Seven Lamps* and its successor were 'stories' about the origins of Christian art and theology in pagan antiquity and a demonstration of the symbiotic relationship between politics, art and the moral welfare of states: highly controversial notions both then and now. Indeed, throughout the nineteenth century, allegory itself was regarded with deep moral suspicion, a persistent prejudice which even the present author has experienced. John Ruskin believed that he had to dedicate his life to the task of warning society about the nightmare into which it was plunging headlong and from which he alone could save it. Our present popular culture would regard as absurd the very idea that a handsome and talented young man possessed of a vast fortune and a celebrity lifestyle should choose a life of difficulty and sustained hard work for the public good, rather than a selfish life of leisure, luxury and sexual relations with a pretty young wife who had no real interest either in him or his work. That perhaps only demonstrates how right John Ruskin was, and how misshapen our culture has become partly as a result of neglecting his warnings.

This book is essentially the history of a marriage that failed before it began. Modern readers should beware of assuming that social and sexual relations in the first half of the nineteenth century in England were similar in all respects to those of modern times. Romantic love was not considered to be an invariable precursor to marriage nor was sexual intercourse. In Evangelical households like the Ruskin's and the Gray's the children obeyed their parents and followed parental orders with regard to prospective partners. Many marriages were arranged between families for any number of pressing reasons which might have little to do with mutual affection. Nor did this necessarily prevent these marriages developing into stable loving relationships. Present-day notions of a decent age for marriage are also modern developments. Many women younger than Euphemia Gray made successful marriages to men much older

than John Ruskin without any social stigma attaching to either
of them. Although the age of consent was twelve, most respectable
men and women, if not totally ignorant of sexual matters, were
probably virgins when they married. Once the wedding was
over, the law of the land was quite clear: marriage was an indissoluble contract terminated only by death. On becoming married
the wife ceased to exist as an independent legal entity and her
financial resources passed into the absolute possession of her
husband.[4] If she ran away from her husband he could use the law
to bring her back. Although a wife in extreme circumstances
might possibly obtain a separation enabling her to live apart from
her husband, she could not then re-marry and would be financially dependent upon her husband. The fact that her husband
virtually owned any children of the marriage prevented many
wives from choosing to live separately.[5] There was effectively no
possibility of divorce for respectable women. Wives in bad
marriages would endure almost any amount of neglect and
cruelty to avoid ending the marriage since some blame always
attached itself to the woman. A woman's reputation was not
merely a social necessity; the loss of it could result in social
banishment, poverty, and inability to survive. Women mostly kept
their bodies clothed from head to foot and respectable married
women did not wear their hair loose and uncovered in public.
Wives went to great lengths to avoid any suspicion of loose
morals or illicit connections. In a legal atmosphere where adultery could be deduced from over-familiarity with a member of
the opposite sex or being together in a private place, it was not
necessary for accusers to determine the time and place of the
carnal act. Even gossip could create guilt. Carnal relations outside
wedlock could have catastrophic consequences for women. Artificial birth control was virtually unknown and would anyway have

been shunned by women concerned about their reputations. However, it should not be assumed that great numbers of women passed their lives in a living hell of domination and suppression. The fact that families were involved in the setting up of the marriage meant there was always support at hand. Because the bond was indissoluble there was a greater effort by all involved to make the thing work. Neither should the ability of women to manage their menfolk to the advantage of all concerned be underestimated. Marriage was still regarded as having a civilizing effect upon men, bringing out their natural instincts to provide, protect and nurture. Men, then as now, were not all cruel, unfeeling tyrants, nor had fathers yet been turned into folk demons by the followers of Freud or radical feminism. Men too valued their reputations. If, however, marital relations turned sour and the partners could not find a *modus vivendi*, then a bad marriage in early Victorian England might become a very unpleasant situation in which to find oneself. In such circumstances, finding a way to end the marriage without irreparably damaging the other partner's reputation could be an act of great humanity.

Finally it should be noted that although the Victorian age began with an inherited, oppressive and obdurate matrimonial legal framework, by its end the laws relating to marriage, divorce and custody of children had been significantly reformed, to the great relief of women in particular. This reflected the increasing acceptance of women in many other aspects of society and culture. Modern writers would do well to remember that, like the many other great social reforms of the period, this was achieved not in spite of the Victorians but by them.

CHAPTER I

SCOTTISH ROOTS

‹›

In 1809 John Ruskin's grandparents arrived in the small Scottish town of Perth. John Thomas Ruskin and his wife Catherine had been forced to leave Edinburgh when their grocery business collapsed, and probably chose Perth because their daughter Janet (known as Jessie) already lived there. They rented a substantial property, Bowerswell House, which stood, and still stands, on the Hill of Kinnoull overlooking the town. It was 'lately' built according to the 'for sale' notice in the Perth Courier of 24th August 1809. The builder, John McEwen (1753-1813),[1] a baillie of Perth Town Council in 1803 and 1807, seems to have put it up for sale immediately. The house was therefore only about five years old when John Ruskin's grandparents arrived. They rented the property from Margaret McEwen, who had inherited it, and later from Patrick Taylor who must have bought it with sitting tenants. At one stage Taylor used it as security for a £6400 loan. The Ruskins never owned the house and do not appear in the records of Saisines as a consequence. Ownership of the house changed hands in 1816, 1817, 1820 and 1821, before Patrick Small Keir sold it to George Gray, writer (lawyer) of Perth and future father of Euphemia, in 1827.[2]

In 1801 John James, the Ruskins' sixteen year old son and the man who would be John Ruskin's father, had been sent to London to supplement the family income. For the next three years one of the few family connections he had there was his cousin Margaret Cock (later changed to Cox). In 1804 she entered the

Bowerswell House as originally built (after a watercolour formerly at Bowerswell)

Ruskin household in Scotland as a companion for her aunt and stayed for thirteen years. She became engaged to John James in 1809, when he was 24 and she 28. Grandpa Ruskin was opposed to the match. Cousin marriages were not strictly respectable and Margaret was an older woman. John James was handsome, educated and hardworking; Margaret, though educated and clever, was only a publican's daughter. Grandpa Ruskin's parlous finances and increasing mental instability not only made her daily life a trial, but kept John James working away from Perth to support his family. The result was an interminable engagement of eight years which threatened Margaret's prospects, since she was by then getting past her child-bearing prime.

That was the situation when the horrible events of the year 1817 unfolded. Margaret's mother died on September 24th and on returning from the funeral in London she discovered that Grandma Ruskin had died of a stroke during an emergency christening of her daughter Janet's sickly new-born baby. Two of Janet Richardson's children had already died that year; then on October 30th Grandpa Ruskin 'died suddenly' in mysterious circumstances, probably having killed himself. For Margaret, Grandpa Ruskin's death was only one of five deaths in this thirteenth year with the family. Nevertheless it freed her from a nightmare existence as sole carer of a mentally troubled man who had dammed up her life and driven his family to the brink of ruin. Interestingly, three days after he died Grandpa Ruskin was buried in consecrated ground in Greyfriars churchyard. The cause of death was recorded simply as 'sudden'.[3] On 2nd February 1818, his son John James married Margaret Cox in the evening after supper, 'in the old Scotch fashion', and they left Perth for London the next morning. Their son John Ruskin was born there on 8th February 1819.

In his autobiography John baldly stated that his grandfather 'at last effectually ruined, and killed, himself.'[4] A recent Ruskin biographer states that most of the sources agree that Ruskin's grandfather cut his throat in the bedroom of Bowerswell House in Perth. However, beyond John's simple statement of fact, most of the circumstantial detail surrounding this event has only one source: Albert Gray (later Sir Albert). He was a younger brother of Euphemia Chalmers Gray, the woman who was to be the other partner in the most notorious marital failure of the Victorian era. Albert produced two 'transcriptions' of statements claimed to be by other Gray family members. Albert Gray used all this family gossip to produce his account of John Ruskin's marriage to Euphemia Gray, even adding further details himself after the old lady died.[5] Albert himself was only three years old at the time the marriage ended. The first transcription was of a purported statement by his 'grand-aunt' Mrs. Andrew Gray. This is supposed to be a statement by a ninety-one year old woman, made shortly before she died, concerning events sixty years previously at which she herself had not even been present.[6] Albert Gray claimed that her account was based on talks with 'her best friend' Jessie Richardson who had died fifty years previously in 1828. This makes his account of *The Marriage of John Ruskin* third-hand hearsay and extremely suspect. Neither is there any firm evidence that Andrew Gray himself was present at any of the events of that terrible autumn. It is possible that he was involved in the funeral with Peter Richardson. Nor have I been able to discover where exactly George Gray lived in Perth, before he moved into Bowerswell House. The Grays might possibly have been neighbours, since the saisine document for George Gray's purchase of Bowerswell House was signed next door at Annat Lodge, but that could also have been because it was another of the vendor's properties. According to Albert Gray, John Thomas Ruskin lived next door to his mother's grandfather during a brief sojourn in Dysart but there was no connection.[7]

Even a cursory reading of Albert Gray's transcription reveals extreme bias and antipathy to the Ruskin family. Grandpa Ruskin is described as tall, moody and subject to fits of anger. The Richardsons (Jessie's family at Perth) are described as coarse and ugly. Jessie's sister-in-law Moll is nevertheless vain and wears her petticoats too short. Ruskin's father-to-be, John James, is scrofulous and sickly, whilst his mother-to-be Margaret is of 'curious character', a 'commanding, self-willed temper', determined and tall and with a squint. We read that whilst John James was seriously ill, his future wife 'slept in the same room', as she did later when he was convalescing in Dunkeld, conduct which 'gave rise to many rumours and scandals.' Ruskin's mother Margaret is then accused of blackmailing his father John James into marriage by saying that she had forfeited her reputation for him. This she did according to Mrs. Andrew Gray by writing letters to him in London. Of course there was no way that Mrs. Gray or any one else could have known the contents of such an intimate, private correspondence and this is typical of the tendentious nature of this purported 'evidence'. The surviving letters between John James and Margaret are of two people deeply in love both before and after the marriage. As for his being blackmailed into marriage, a letter sent to his mother in April 1815 contradicts this assertion most emphatically. He refers to Margaret as 'her on whom my life depends' and asks his mother to remember that 'Mrgts fate & mine are one'.

> Oh my own Mother as you have always loved me will you & my dear Father assure Margt that you have both become reconciled to our union & be happy – or will you see her & me both fall sacrifices to this anxiety. Neither her constitution nor mine are fit for a long struggle. I have already said that if it leads to eternal Ruin I will fulfill my engagement with Margt. I hope my Dr. Father will therefore no longer cause us any uneasiness.[8]

He was still writing embarrassingly passionate love letters to his wife ten years after they were married.

It is also from Albert Gray's transcription that we have the vignette of Margaret with her hands clasped around Grandpa Ruskin's throat, holding the wound closed whilst the doctor sews it up. She is described as being so cool and calm that we are left with the impression of a woman preternaturally hard, unwomanly and without feelings. The transcription of Mrs. Andrew Gray's account also includes a description of Margaret and John James shutting themselves in the drawing room downstairs away from Grandpa Ruskin just before he died, the suggestion being that their behaviour caused Grandpa Ruskin's terminal depression. In reality, John James was in London at the time. Quite how

Mrs. Andrew Gray would in any case have known any of these details is uncertain. Shortly after Grandpa Ruskin first fell ill, John's father wrote that 'It appeared that my Father's despondency was occasioned by the state of his affairs & I fondly hoped when an arrangement of these was completed that his mind would have recovered its natural strength.'[9] Apart from his parlous finances, if anything pushed Grandpa Ruskin to the brink it would have been the recent death of his wife.[10]

There are so many proveable errors in Albert Gray's transcript of Mrs. Andrew Gray's account that it is difficult to take the remainder as any kind of reliable evidence. Aunt Jessie lived at a different address. Margaret was thirty-eight not 'over forty' when she married and her husband was as determined as she was that they should marry. The Ruskins married in Perth not London. The servants may have been taken by surprise by the wedding but not in the way she suggested. Despite all this, biographers continue to treat everything not proveably wrong as probably if not definitely true, rather than as malicious gossip coloured by twenty-eight years of fear of scandal and ongoing family acrimony. The question is not just 'why would an old lady at the end of her life give a biased account of such distant events?' but 'why was it necessary to record these reminiscences at all?' I believe that the answer to both these questions is relevant to the whole sequence of events. In the introduction to his account of the marriage Albert Gray asserts that his account is a response to Collingwood's biography of John Ruskin, published in 1893, which in his view had broken a pact of silence agreed between the families, a pact to which Collingwood was never a party. Even this was untrue: Albert Gray had interviewed Mrs. Andrew Gray in 1877 when he had been prompted by quite another situation. This discrepancy is yet another inconsistency in a tale full of inconsistencies.

The second 'source' for the throat-cutting incident is another Albert Gray transcript, this time 'based on' the undated reminiscences of Effie's niece, Eliza Tucket Jameson. This transcript asserts that in 1827 shortly after George Gray acquired Bowerswell House, Effie's mother not only spent her wedding night in the room where Grandpa Ruskin allegedly cut his throat, but later gave birth to Effie there too. This source is even more distant from the events since Eliza was not born until 1843, twenty-six years after Grandpa Ruskin's death, sixteen years after George Gray's marriage and fifteen years after Effie was born. In this case too it is important to know why it was necessary for Albert Gray to record these details. If Albert wanted to know the facts why did he not ask his father George at any time before he died in that year, or his mother Sophia who lived until 1894? Was the 'pact of silence' observed even within the family? Liza Jameson's 'reminiscences' also appear in Clare Stuart Wortley's notes to her transcripts of the Bowerswell letters. Once more there is significant inaccuracy and bias. According to Wortley, Jameson claimed that Margaret (b. 1781) was twelve years older than John James (b. 1785) instead of four, and described Margaret, whom she never met or even saw, as a 'strong minded and wilful woman [...] she was the evil influence in her son's life and her interference between him and Effie was unbearable.'[11] These were not reminiscences but family gossip.

John James Ruskin married Margaret Cock in Perth on February 2nd 1818. The marriage may have been 'quiet' but it was not secret. The couple waited three months after Grandpa Ruskin died, the normal banns were observed, the couple lived at different addresses and the Rev. John Findlay, Minister of St. Paul's Parish Church officiated. Afterwards the married couple left for

London where John James had been working for nine years. Prior to his father's death he had been sending £200 a year home to his parents but now he was able to use this money for his own family and to start clearing his father's substantial debts. John James was a hard worker and an astute businessman. He had risen to be head clerk of Gordon, Murphy & Co, wine importers, but had realised that the company was being badly run. When he was offered a partnership in a rival venture, he took it. Pedro Domecq provided the Spanish vineyards, Henry Telford the capital and premises, John James Ruskin put in the business acumen and took on the sheer hard work of being the firm's only commercial traveller. Ruskin, Telford and Domecq became a runaway success and gradually made Mr. Ruskin a very wealthy man indeed.

The Ruskins and their son John continued to visit Perth every summer for the next ten years until his aunt Jessie died in May 1828. John thought it curious that his mother never took the children for walks but stayed indoors with Jessie.[12] His mother would never set foot in Bowerswell House again, although on her final visit she did call on the Grays who had by that time made Bowerswell their new home but, according to the Grays at least, she refused to cross the threshold. By 1847 she had an 'insuperable dislike' to Perth and a 'superstitious dread of her son connecting himself in the most remote degree with the place.'[13] John noted that the servants shared this dread of Bowerswell House whenever they walked near it.[14] Nor did the house fail to live up to its fatal reputation. In the thirteen years subsequent to the Grays moving in, seven of their children died. Effie only survived because she was at school in England during the scarlet fever outbreak that killed her sisters. The remaining children also survived both whooping cough and smallpox. John's father had good reason to think the place a fever trap. Even without the

Bowerswell House as rebuilt by George Gray

horrific memories of her time shut up in Bowerswell with Grandpa Ruskin, Margaret had a strong disincentive to taking her precious only son there.

Bowerswell House was only about forty years old in 1842-4 when George Gray undertook an expensive rebuilding in that neo-Renaissance style which John was to assault so comprehensively in his books. There has been some confusion about the nature of this work but there can be no doubt that this was a remodelling of the original building. The steeply sloping site would have precluded major relocation, which would have required either large scale excavation or embanking to create a new terrace. The terrace is in fact the same one visible on the water colour of the original building reproduced by Lutyens (version on p. 22).[15] Abutments have been added to the terrace wall, but not keyed into the original masonry, clear evidence that they are later additions. The positions of the chimney stacks seem also to have been retained. The cellars of the original building are still in situ and, as they were also the foundation walls of the original house, must follow the original plan. One consequence of the new building on the old foundations is that the window of the room which contains the entrance to the cellar is most awkwardly incorporated into the new façade. It would never have been so positioned in a new building. The remarks which Effie made about the 'old' and 'new' house were therefore simple references to the old and new built parts of Bowerswell. Mrs. Andrew Gray's 'reminiscences' of the new house constructed behind the old and Sophia Gray's mention of 'the upper story at the back of the house'[16] are perfectly understandable since the major extension work was on the south-west or Tay frontage and the original entrance to Bowerswell was on the west or Rosebank side via what is now the back entrance. Anyone approaching the building from the original entrance (still extant) would see the new (higher) extension rising 'behind' the old house. The new front drive was part of the remodelling work.[17] Thus the house which had such terrible memories for John's mother, and such fatal consequences for children who lived in it, was to all intents and purposes still there.

It should be noted that the horror stories which later came to be attached to Bowerswell – the gory details of Grandpa Ruskin's purported madness and suicide, his coarse and immoral relatives, his scrofulous son and the strange and scandalous behaviour of John's mother – did not prevent the Grays from moving into the house themselves, spending their wedding night in the very room where the suicide was alleged to have happened, arranging for Effie to be born in the same room, keeping close and friendly relations with the Ruskins over many years, and looking upon John as a suitable partner for their daughter. Indeed these lurid stories only seem to have entered the public domain at the time of the marriage breakdown.

CHAPTER II

THE BOY JOHN

ༀ

John Ruskin was born on 8th February 1819 at 54 Hunter Street, Brunswick Square, in London. John's poignant account of his childhood in his autobiography, *Præterita*, has coloured most perceptions of him as a repressed or psychologically damaged child with one or both of his parents as the culprits. Even though he wrote later that 'I think the treatment, or accidental conditions, of my childhood, entirely right, for a child of my temperament,' readers of his autobiography might demur. It is however important to realise that *Præterita* was the musing of an old man, repeatedly disappointed in love, pondering the cruelty of a Fate that had ultimately deprived him of the intimate human warmth and affection that he longed for. The surviving Ruskin family letters tend to contradict as much of his early autobiography as they confirm. However the inaccuracies and exaggerations sometimes speak volumes about his perception of a childhood which he described as being both monastic and luxurious at the same time.

John was an only child born to a woman who was by contemporary standards well past her prime. After nine years of being engaged, she must have almost despaired of ever having a husband, never mind a family. She regarded her child, it would seem, as a gift from Heaven:

My mother had, as she afterwards told me, solemnly 'devoted me to God' before I was born; in imitation of Hannah. Very good women are remarkably apt to make away with their

The house at 54 Hunter Street where John Ruskin was born; subsequently demolished

children prematurely, in this manner: [...] 'Devoting me to God,' meant, as far as my mother knew herself what she meant, that she would try to send me to college and make a clergyman of me: and I was accordingly bred for 'the Church.'[1]

His mother took him to church from a very early age. 'I do not conceive she at all furthered her purposes by taking me to church at an age when I didn't understand English,' he wrote.[2] Presumably this was to instil an habitual reverence and godliness in the little fellow. However it had the opposite effect since it was an activity he loathed. 'Luckily for me,' he wrote later, since it caused him to develop 'an early disgust for Sunday, and church' that was to shape his future development,

I found the bottom of the pew so extremely dull a place to keep quiet in, (my best storybooks being also taken away from me in the morning,) that, as I have somewhere said before, the horror of Sunday used even to cast its prescient gloom as far back in the week as Friday – and the glory of Monday, with church seven days removed again, was no equivalent for it.[3]

He later wrote of his childish 'dread of ill-keeping the Sunday' as being 'mere fear after all; no real feeling – a childish terror – induced by whipping and sermonizing.'[4]

His mother took upon herself the responsibility of educating her son. She compelled him to read two to three chapters of the Bible every day of his young life:

As soon as I was able to read with fluency, she began a course of Bible work with me, which never ceased until I went to Oxford. She read alternate verses with me, watching, at first, every intonation of my voice, and correcting the false ones, till she made me understand the verse, if within my reach, rightly, and energetically. It might be beyond me altogether; that she did not care about; but she made sure that as soon as I got hold of it at all, I should get hold of it by the right end.

In this way she began with the first verse of Genesis, and went straight through, to the last verse of the Apocalypse; hard names, numbers, Levitical law, and all; and began again at Genesis the next day. If a name was hard, the better the exercise in pronunciation, – if a chapter was tiresome, the better lesson in patience, – if loathsome, the better lesson in faith that there was some use in its being outspoken.[5]

Modern readers might suppose that John would have resented this daily toil just as much as he did going to church. However

Margaret Ruskin *by*
James Northcote 1825.
The only known image
of John's mother

this was one aspect of his upbringing that he came to appreciate in later years:

> this maternal installation of my mind in that property of chap-
> ters, I count very confidently the most precious, and, on the
> whole, the one essential part of all my education.[6]

Being devoted to God and bred for the Church had other
implications. The young boy had to learn how to resist the
temptations of the world. According to his own account his
early life was particularly ascetic:

> I was never allowed to come down to dessert, until much later
> in life – when I was able to crack nuts neatly. I was then
> permitted to come down to crack other people's nuts for them

John James Ruskin
by George Richmond, 1848.
John's father had this
portrait of himself done
in the same year his
son was married and
gave it to him as a
wedding present

– (I hope they liked the ministration) – but never to have any
myself; nor anything else of dainty kind, either then or at other
times. Once at Hunter Street, I recollect my mother giving
me three raisins, in the forenoon, out of the store cabinet; and
I remember perfectly the first time I tasted custard, in our
lodgings in Norfolk Street – where we had gone while the
house was being painted, or cleaned, or something. My
father was dining in the front room, and did not finish his
custard; and my mother brought me the bottom of it into the
back room.[7]

Their next house at Herne Hill had a large back garden,
'renowned over all the hill for its pears and apples'. There were
also cherries, mulberries, gooseberries and redcurrant bushes:

decked in due season, (for the ground was wholly beneficent,) with magical splendour of abundant fruit: fresh green, soft amber, and rough bristled crimson bending the spinous branches; clustered pearl and pendant ruby joyfully discoverable under the large leaves that looked like vine.

And yet even this natural bounty was made an exercise in self-sacrifice and obedience for young John, since:

> The differences of primal importance which I observed between the nature of this garden, and that of Eden, as I had imagined it, were, that, in this one, all the fruit was forbidden; and there were no companionable beasts: in other respects the little domain answered every purpose of Paradise to me; and the climate, in that cycle of our years, allowed me to pass most of my life in it.[8]

At the end of the chapter he explained that in saying 'all the fruit was forbidden' he only 'meant, of course, forbidden unless under definite restriction'. He nevertheless let the original statement stand rather than changing it. He came later to regard his youthful diet in a positive light, claiming to have:

> an extreme perfection in palate and all other bodily senses, given by utter prohibition of cake, wine, comfits, or, except in carefullest restriction, fruit; and by fine preparation of what food was given to me.[9]

Temptation was not confined to the bodily appetites:

> My mother's general principles of first treatment were, to guard me with steady watchfulness from all avoidable pain or danger; and for the rest, to let me amuse myself as I liked, provided I was neither fretful nor troublesome. But the law

was, that I should find my own amusement. No toys of any kind were at first allowed; – and the pity of my Croydon aunt for my monastic poverty in this respect was boundless. On one of my birthdays, thinking to overcome my mother's resolution by splendour of temptation, she bought the most radiant Punch and Judy she could find in all the Soho bazaar – as big as a real Punch and Judy, all dressed in scarlet and gold, and that would dance, tied to the leg of a chair. I must have been greatly impressed, for I well remember the look of the two figures, as my aunt herself exhibited their virtues. My mother was obliged to accept them; but afterwards quietly told me it was not right that I should have them; and I never saw them again.

Nor did I painfully wish, what I was never permitted for an instant to hope, or even imagine, the possession of such things as one saw in toy-shops. I had a bunch of keys to play with, as long as I was capable only of pleasure in what glittered and jingled; as I grew older, I had a cart, and a ball; and when I was five or six years old, two boxes of well-cut wooden bricks. With these modest, but, I still think, entirely sufficient possessions, and being always summarily whipped if I cried, did not do as I was bid, or tumbled on the stairs, I soon attained serene and secure methods of life and motion; and could pass my days contentedly in tracing the squares and comparing the colours of my carpet; – examining the knots in the wood of the floor, or counting the bricks in the opposite houses; with rapturous intervals of excitement during the filling of the water cart, through its leathern pipe, from the dripping iron post at the pavement edge.[10]

Whatever the situation when he was very small, other toys did come later; he mentioned a silver-mounted postillion's whip given by his father[11] and a two-arched bridge construction kit, (which he suspected was also a present from his aunt Bridget).[12] From the letters we also know that he was given a compass and that he had boats and a ship to sail in the pond at Croydon.[13] After his aunt died, he and his cousin Mary played shuttlecock and battledore.[14] His father bought him a dog and a sheep when he was four, and a Shetland pony later![15] Books of all kinds were of course provided as a matter of course and regardless of expense. If there was any real deprivation it would seem to have been not of toys but of a normal childhood and particularly the normal social activities of children.

In his autobiography there are chapters headed 'The Springs of Wandel' and 'The Banks of Tay', both of which refer to places where his relatives and their children lived (both coincidentally called Richardson but not directly related) and where his strict and solitary regime was mitigated by their warm humanity. John described his visits to his kindly aunt Bridget's house over their baker's shop in Market St., Croydon as 'occasional glimpses of the rivers of Paradise';[16] and whilst his parents took him on tours to see castles and large country houses, he claimed that it was 'under the low red roofs of Croydon, and by the cress-set rivulets in which the sand danced and the minnows darted above the Springs of Wandel' that his true sympathies had been formed.[17] His sojourn with his widowed aunt Jessie Richardson in Perth was of a similar paradisiacal nature:

> And my readers may trust me when I tell them that, in now remembering my dreams in the house of the entirely honest chief baker of Market St., Croydon, and of Peter – not Simon – the tanner, whose house was by the riverside of

Perth, I would not change the dreams, far less the tender realities, of those early days, for anything I hear now remembered by lords and dames, of their days of childhood in castle halls, and by sweet lawns and lakes in park-walled forest.[18]

After her husband's death in 1824 auntie Jessie, 'a pure dove priestess, if ever there was one, of Highland Dodona', lived at Rose Terrace, in a suburb of Perth facing the River Tay over a greensward known as the North Inch.[19] She had nine children, three of whom had already died before their father passed away. Four older boys were nearly always away at school or college and so, for several summers, whilst Mr. Ruskin travelled on his Scottish business, John and his mother stayed with aunt Jessie and her two daughters; Mary 'ascending towards twelve', and Jessie 'between her sixth and ninth year'. Even John's mother became 'a curiously unimportant figure at Rose Terrace', being nearly always in close conversation with her sister-in-law. As a result:

> Mary, Jessie, and I were allowed to do what we liked on the Inch: and I don't remember doing any lessons in these Perth times.[20]

The Scottish holidays ended when his eight year old playmate Jessie 'died slowly, of water on the brain' and his aunt died 'of decline' shortly afterwards in 1828. The Ruskins adopted the orphaned Mary, then aged fourteen and brought her to live with them at Herne Hill. It is worth pointing out that this meant that ten-year-old John effectively had an elder sister from this time onwards. She was to marry within twelve months of John.

When he was three years old his Croydon relations came over for his birthday. Even his mother admitted that: 'John never spent such a birthday you know how bridget [sic] loves him she even put a stop to the cleaning that the servants might enjoy themselves and every one of the children brought him something he was particularly cheerful himself too.'[21] However, if *Præterita* is to be believed, John, even at four years old, had already detected 'just the least possible shade of shyness on the part of Hunter Street, Brunswick Square, towards Market Street, Croydon.'[22] After the Ruskins became wealthier, and despite having moved to a larger house closer to their relatives at 26 Herne Hill, Camberwell, the visits to Croydon became less frequent owing to his mother's 'fixed purpose of making an ecclesiastical gentleman of me, with the superfinest of manners, and access to the highest circles of fleshly and spiritual society'.[23] When John was eight his mother wrote to her husband that she was going to visit the Richardsons at Croydon but 'I do not like to be more than a day or two at a time on John's account he observes so closely and left were he any time there together the ways and manners might effect [sic] him.'[24]

After his aunt Bridget died when he was ten, the visits to Croydon ended and 'an exclusively Herne Hill-top life set in.'[25] Subsequently only the most socially acceptable of the cousins were welcomed at Herne Hill. His mother's desire to avoid commonplace connections was complicated by her own sense of inferiority which also prevented her from socializing normally with those of more obvious wealth or of a higher class. The combination of his mother's old-fashioned Puritanism and his father's cultured Romanticism also meant that they had little in common with their immediate neighbours. John described the 'monastic severities and aristocratic dignities' of their life at the time:

> My parents lived with strict economy, kept only female

The house at 28 Herne Hill where the Ruskins lived from 1823 to 1842,
Pencil and ink drawing probably by Ruskin

servants, used only tallow candles in plated candlesticks, were content with the leasehold territory of their front and back gardens, – scarce an acre altogether, – and kept neither horse nor carriage. Our shop-keeping neighbours, on the contrary, had usually great cortège of footmen and glitter of plate, extensive pleasure grounds, costly hot-houses, and carriages driven by coachmen in wigs. It may perhaps be doubted by some of my readers whether the coldness of acquaintanceship was altogether on our side; but assuredly my father was too proud to join entertainments for which he could give no like return, and my mother did not care to leave her card on foot at the doors of ladies who dashed up to hers in their barouche.[26]

John cited the example of his father's best friend and business partner, Henry Telford:

All the family at Widmore would have been limitlessly kind to my mother and me, if they had been permitted any opportunity; but my mother always felt, in cultivated society, – and was too proud to feel with patience, – the defects of her own early education; and therefore (which was the true and fatal sign of such defect) never familiarly visited any one whom she did not feel to be, in some sort, her inferior.[27]

The relations with the Grays of Camberwell (neighbours unrelated to the Grays of Perth) were similarly complicated. Despite the warm friendship between Mr. Gray and Mr. Ruskin, despite the fact that the couple were entirely respectable and pious, despite the fact that

> Mr. Gray's house was always the same to us as our own at any time of day or night, [the Ruskin house was] not at all so to the Grays, having its formalities inviolable; so that during the whole of my childhood I had the sense that we were, in some way or other, always above our friends and relations, – more or less patronizing everybody, favouring them by our advice, instructing them by our example, and called upon, by what was due both to ourselves, and the constitution of society, to keep them at a distance.[28]

Society at that time was quite severely stratified according to class; thus, despite his intelligence, education and increasing wealth, even John's father was excluded from the higher social circles by both his social background and his occupation. As a result of his parents' social prejudices, John grew up with a deep aversion to and an inability to cope with formal social occasions:

> I was taught no precision nor etiquette of manners; it was

enough if, in the little society we saw, I remained unobtrusive, and replied to a question without shyness: but the shyness came later, and increased as I grew conscious of the rudeness arising from the want of social discipline, and found it impossible to acquire, in advanced life, dexterity in any bodily exercise, skill in any pleasing accompaniment, or ease and tact in ordinary behaviour.[29]

John claimed that the family 'seldom had company, even on week days', and as a child he would often be excluded from such visits as did occur. Similarly

the society of our neighbours on the hill could not be had without breaking up our regular and sweetly selfish manner of living; and on the whole, I had nothing animate to care for, in a childish way, but myself, some nests of ants, which the gardener would never leave undisturbed for me, and a sociable bird or two; though I never had the sense or perseverance to make one tame.[30]

In fact he had a complete menagerie of animals. Beginning when he was four, the family letters mention a sheep, a dog, a kitten and the Shetland pony. He also inherited 'Dash', the Richardsons' spaniel. John was however in no doubt that beside the blessings of his upbringing there were 'equally dominant calamities'. In *Præterita* the 'chief of evils' was his parents' unremitting care and discipline. He claimed that up until the age of seven he had never heard either of his parents raise their voice in anger or disagreement to each other, to him or to the servants. He had never felt anxiety or seen any grief. Likewise he never thought to question their authority:

I obeyed word, or lifted finger of father or mother, simply as a ship her helm; not only without resistance, but receiving the direction as a part of my own life and force, a helpful law, as necessary to me in every moral action as the law of gravity in leaping. And my practice in Faith was soon complete: nothing was ever promised me that was not given; nothing ever threatened me that was not inflicted, and nothing ever told me that was not true.[31]

This was not quite the way his mother saw it at the time. At three years old he was already causing some consternation:

Were he Son to a King, more care could not be taken of him and he every day gives proof of possessing quickness memory and observation not quite common at his age with this however I fear he will be very self-willed and passionate – he has twice alarmed me a good deal by getting into such a passion that I feared he would have thrown himself into a fit this will be I trust be cured by a good whipping when he can understand what it is for properly at present I am compelled to give way more than I like for fear of baiting it.[32]

This behaviour would have future consequences. In a later letter she remarks: 'I never met with any child so sensible to praise or blame [–] this would be dangerous without strong right principles.'[33] The problem was that his mother in particular was over-protective of him and consequently stifled vital aspects of his development. Even when he visited Croydon he was never allowed to go out with his cousins 'lest they should lead me into mischief; and no more adventurous joys were ever possible to me there, than my walks with Anne or my mother.' This led to more calamity:

My judgement of right and wrong, and powers of independent

action, were left entirely undeveloped; because the bridle and
blinkers were never taken off me. Children should have their
times of being off duty, like soldiers; and when once the obedience, if required, is certain, the little creature should be very
early put for periods of practice in complete command of itself;
set on a bare-backed horse of its own will, and left to break
it by its own strength. But the ceaseless authority exercised
over my youth left me, when cast out at last into the world,
unable for some time to do more than drift with its vortices.[34]

The equine metaphor is quite apt here since his mother
'in her own son's education [...] had sacrificed her pride in his
heroism to her anxiety for his safety; and never allowed me to
go to the edge of a pond, or be in the same field with a pony.'[35]
Likewise on a trip to Wales:

> And if only my father and mother had seen the real strengths
> and weaknesses of their little John; – if they had given me but
> a shaggy scrap of a Welsh pony, and left me in charge of a
> good Welsh guide, and of his wife, if I had needed any
> coddling, they would have made a man of me there and
> then [...] If only! But they could no more have done it than
> thrown me like my cousin Charles into Croydon Canal,
> trusting me to find my way out by the laws of nature.[36]

Instead, the Shetland, well broken, was bought in London and
the same obsessive attention paid to John's safety and progress
in riding as in his moral welfare. The pony was always on a lead
rein. He never learned to ride properly, but whether this was
because he was too closely supervised is not clear. It may have been
simple lack of physical aptitude as a result of his cosseted childhood. Never being able to trip on the stairs or engage in the rough

and tumble of children's games would not have given him much confidence in his own physical prowess. As he got older he was given dancing and fencing lessons but these too seem to have come to nothing.[37]

In retrospect the first calamity of his upbringing to spring to his mind was 'that I had nothing to love'. It is perhaps the most surprising thing about his autobiography that it contains a specific denial that he loved his parents:

> My parents were – in a sort – visible powers of nature to me,
> no more loved than the sun and the moon: only I should have
> been annoyed and puzzled if either of them had gone out.[38]

This is made all the more significant by his parallel declaration that 'I entirely loved my aunt, and young baker-cousins'. That the Croydon Richardsons were a sort of surrogate family for him is confirmed by his remark that he had 'a kind of brotherly, rather than cousinly, affection' for the Richardson children.[39] Charles Richardson indeed became a sort of admired older brother to him. The family letters seem to paint a slightly different picture. A very early letter dictated for his mother to write, opens with a forthright declaration: 'My Dear Papa I love you' although this is somewhat devalued by his subsequent 'I love Mrs. Gray and Mr. Gray'. (These were the Camberwell Grays, who were childless and and who, like his aunt Bridget, fussed over John and gave him treats denied to him by his parents).[40] It has to be said that the letters he wrote to his father which, as his mother noted several times, particularly in his very early childhood, were entirely unsupervised and uncorrected, seem full of high spirits and genuine affection. She noted John's 'exuberant mirth so common with him' when his father was home. His father once complained that a letter from a thirteen years old John did not have 'that Buoyancy of spirit that airy lightness, that easy vein that overflowing of a fountain of clear waters that your former letter does.'[41]

In *Præterita* John connected the obstruction of his loving feelings at Herne Hill with his mother's puritanical regime; a regime which extended to all the members of the household:

> Not a servant was ever allowed to do anything for me, but what it was their duty to do; and why should I have been grateful to the cook for cooking, or the gardener for garden-ing, – when the one dared not give me a baked potato without asking leave, and the other would not let my ants' nests alone because they made the walks untidy? The evil consequences of all this was not, however, what might have perhaps been expected, that I grew up selfish or unaffectionate; but that, when affection did come, it came with a violence utterly rampant and unmanageable, at least by me, who never before had anything to manage.[42]

It is clear that by the end of his life John believed the main responsibility for the tragedy of his personal life lay with his parents. Anyone who reads *Præterita* must see that by that time he thought that his mother in particular had behaved very unwisely. However, before we judge her too harshly, it is impor-tant to acknowledge what she achieved. John at least survived childhood. Victorian England was a dangerous place for infant children. Scrapes, cuts or fractures often proved fatal in that era before antibiotics. When she was only seven or eight years old, Margaret Ruskin's father, 'got his leg crushed by his horse against a wall and died of the hurt's mortifying.'[43] This would explain her carefulness with horses. The Grays and the Richardsons in Perth seem also to have been kind and loving parents, yet lost a dozen children between them. Most of the diseases that killed them were of the sort picked up from playmates or from the damp and dirty places where ordinary children love to play. The Grays had fifteen children and lost seven. Margaret Ruskin was thirty-nine when she had John and she did not conceive again. He was not just an only child; he was also irreplaceable. Who is to say that Margaret Ruskin's obsessive over-protection of her child did not save his young life? Given the social conditions in Victorian Britain, particularly during the hungry forties, John, for all his 'calamities', was a privileged child. His mother's religiosity was not extreme enough to prevent him reading Byron, and at twelve years old he was allowed to drink wine and visit the theatre with his father.

The other point to remember is that this was no ordinary child. John's parents recognized and nurtured a precocious intellect. John Ruskin was the creation of the unstinting efforts of his parents in educating and guiding their gifted son. He was educated at home by his mother until he was ten, and privately until he was fourteen. His mother's regime was fairly demanding. This was a typical day when he was twelve:

> the weather has been uncertain but I have had him out as much as possible and having every day gone regularly through his latin exercise and grammar an hour of Greek some of prosody and the bible got by heart he has not had time to get a letter ready for today but intends writing for tomorrow.[44]

John's own account of a typical day might seem even more onerous but perhaps not when compared with the seven hour curriculum of a modern thirteen year old:

> I should have written you before, but have been so completely occupied in the hours commonly known as morning, noon

and night with those destroyers of time, those lessons, that it was totally and altogether out of my power; notwithstanding I have found time for translating forty lines of Homer per day most regularly [...] I believe you will find in most of my former letters, the great subject is want of time. I find it now still more scarce than ever for what with Livy, and Lucian, Homer, French, Drawing, Arithmetic, globe work & mineralogical dictionary, I positively am all flurry, all hurry, never a moment in which there is not something that ought to be done. Mr. Rowbotham [his tutor] comes to night, & it is 12 O'Clock, & I have a walk to take, and four sums to do, & to translate 40 lines of Homer, & learn a verb or two, (besides the time taken up by dinner) all before 6 O'Clock.[45]

Many of the activities described in the letters were actually his hobbies and interests. One of the recurring themes in his mother's letters is how to stop him overtaxing his brain, particularly with constant poetry writing. By the time he was five years old John was devouring books, having learned to read by his own idiosyncratic method. At six he began to imitate the books he had read. His first dated poem of seven octosyllabic couplets was written a month before he was seven. By the age of 12 he was working on the *Iteriad*, a 2212 line poem about a family tour of the Lake District. The child prodigy did not falter. By fifteen he had scientific articles published in the *Magazine of Natural History*. By eighteen he was publishing his first architectural articles. In 1839, at twenty, he won the Newdigate Poetry Prize at Oxford. By 1843 he had published his first book on art and shortly afterwards he was a literary celebrity.

CHAPTER III

FIRST LOVES

❦

When he was eight years old John had agreed with his little cousin Jessie that they 'would be married when they were a little older.' At that tender age they saw marriage mainly in terms of freedom from adult restriction. Mause, the Richardsons' old Scots puritan servant, had forbidden John and Jessie from jumping off their favourite box on Sunday:

> 'Never mind, John,' said Jessie to me, seeing me in an unchristian state of provocation on this subject, 'when we're married, we'll jump off boxes all day long if we like!'

John thought that this incident:

> may have been partly instrumental in giving me that slight bias against Evangelical religion, which I confess to be sometimes traceable in my later works.[1]

A more significant awakening came when he was eleven or twelve and made the acquaintance of the daughter of the Rev. E. Andrews, the preacher at the Ruskins' regular place of worship, the Beresford Chapel, Walworth:

> Miss Andrews, the eldest sister of the 'Angel in the House,' was an extremely beautiful girl of seventeen; she sang 'Tambourgi, Tambourgi' with great spirit and a rich voice, went at blackberry time on rambles with us at the Norwood spa, and made me feel generally that there was something in girls that I did not understand, and that was curiously agreeable.[2]

Given his age it seems fairly probable that this was some sort of sexual awakening, and would suggest that John was developing quite normally. His housekeeper cousin Joan Severn later confirmed that:

> his old nurse's evidence <u>was</u> that from a baby he always seemed exactly like other <u>children</u>/boys – up to 12 when she had constant care of him.[3]

It would be reasonable to assume that the services of a nurse would be dispensed with at the onset of puberty.

In 1836, when he was only seventeen, four of the five pretty young daughters of his father's business partner Pedro Domecq came to stay at Herne Hill. They had been educated in Paris, spoke French, dressed in the height of fashion and possessed all the social graces that John lacked. In *Præterita* John describes the experience as being 'thrown, bound hand and foot, in my unaccomplished simplicity, into a fiery furnace, or fiery cross, of these four girls, – who of course reduced me to a mere heap of white ashes in four days.'[4] His helpless teenage passion settled on fifteen year old Adèle Clotilde, the eldest of the four. Although there was never any suggestion that his love was requited, this would not necessarily have been an obstacle to marriage. Adèle's father was favourably disposed to the arrangement which would have made excellent sense from both a business and a personal point of view. Mr. Ruskin wrote later: 'Her father was full of affection for his own child and for mine and expressed entire approval of their being united, even offering to make his Daughter a protestant.' It was however not to be. Any possibility of a match had been thwarted by Mrs. Ruskin, for whom Adèle's Roman Catholic religion and continental education proved too much of a challenge. According to Mr. Ruskin 'the character of the young Lady's mother was also objectionable.'⁵ The girls continued on their way to their convent education at New Hall in Chelmsford but John's agony was prolonged when his mother not only took him there to visit them, but invited the girls to spend their holidays at Herne Hill. The four or five weeks they spent with the Ruskins at Christmas did nothing to further John's suit.

John remained besotted despite his mother's assurances that Adèle was not the only girl in the world. In 1838 he was introduced to Charlotte Withers, a 'fragile, fair, freckled, sensitive slip of a girl about sixteen; graceful in an unfinished and small wild-flower sort of way, extremely intelligent, affectionate, wholly right-minded, and mild in piety. An altogether sweet and delicate creature of ordinary sort, not pretty, but quite pleasant to see, especially if her eyes were looking your way, and her mind with them.' John spent a week with her and later claimed that if she'd stayed a month he might very well have fallen 'melodiously and quietly in love' with her. Unfortunately her father was a failed coal merchant and this meant that, despite her musical accomplishments, she was not the kind of person the Ruskin parents thought suitable and so she was allowed to leave. According to *Præterita*, 'A little while afterwards, her father "negotiated" a marriage for her with a well-to-do Newcastle trader, whom she took because she was bid. He treated her pretty much as one of his coal sacks, and in a year or two she died.'⁶ In another attempt to divert his son's thoughts away from Adèle, Mr. Ruskin next sent him off to Hampstead to meet the rich, beautiful and intellectual Miss Wardell, the only daughter of an extremely wealthy business neighbour of Ruskin, Telford and Domecq. Once again 'the two fathers agreed that nothing could be more fit, rational, and desirable, than such an arrangement.' Once again 'the negotiations went no further' but this time it was because of John who decided she was not his type.⁷ Miss Wardell was also to meet a tragically early death.

When a year later in 1840 Adèle married the Baron Duquesne, John was badly affected and became seriously ill shortly afterwards. That Easter he hæmorrhaged blood and had to interrupt his university studies. This was to become a significant pattern in his life: extreme emotional stress provoked severe illness. He claimed it took four years to mend his broken heart. However, whilst in Rome that year travelling for his health, John spotted the 18-year-old Georgiana Tollemache in the church of Santa Maria Ara Coeli. He later described her as:

> A fair English girl who was not only the admitted Queen of
> beauty in the English circle of that winter in Rome, but was
> so, in the kind of beauty which I had only hitherto dreamed
> of as possible, but never yet seen living: statuesque severity
> with womanly sweetness joined.[8]

Admiring her only from afar, he did not speak to Georgiana until 1854, by which time she was married to the Hon. William Cowper (later Lord Mount-Temple); but particularly from 1863 until John died in 1900 she was his close friend.

Meanwhile Pedro Domecq died, and in June 1843 his brother John Pedro offered Mr. Ruskin his niece Caroline, at eighteen the youngest Domecq daughter, as a wife for his son; but this seemed also to have been unacceptable.

A more sustained romantic entanglement involved Charlotte Lockhart whose father, John, was the editor of the *Quarterly Review,* the biographer of Sir Walter Scott, and heir to Scott's home at Abbotsford by virtue of his marriage to Scott's daughter Sophia. John first met Lockhart through one of his father's connections and in 1839 he had been introduced to Lockhart's 'little harebell-like daintiness of a daughter' when he was twenty and she was only

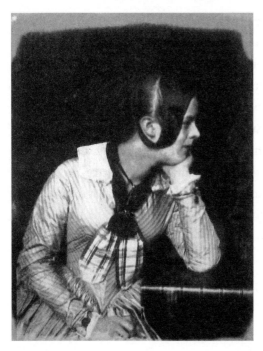

Charlotte Lockhart, *c. 1846,*
by David Hill and
Robert Adamson

ten. By 1846-7 John had earned his own entrée into the elevated
London society in which Lockhart moved and 'the little high fore-
headed Charlotte' had grown into an eighteen-year-old 'Scottish
fairy, White Lady, and witch of the fatallest sort, looking as if she
had just risen out of the stream in Rhymer's Glen, and could only
be seen by favouring glance of moonlight over the Eildons.'[9]
Several authors have seen this description as revealing John's early
nympholeptic tendencies. However it should be borne in mind
firstly, that Charlotte was eighteen and John did not write this at
the time, but in old age; secondly, that Rhymer's Glen, also the
subject of a watercolour by Turner, is on Sir Walter Scott's Abbotsford estate which was Charlotte's family property. There was
therefore a factual basis for the image and an irresistible apposite-
ness in using it. Thomas the Rhymer was supposed to have been
seduced there by the Queen of the Fairies with whom he lived for

seven years until her spell broke. With a lifetime's hindsight this would have been yet another, and ironic, reason for John to use the image. Whatever the actual relationship between John and Charlotte, he seems to have made some sort of declaration to her before Euphemia Gray came to visit in 1847.

It is worth noting at this point that John had had three major infatuations: the first when he was seventeen with fifteen-year-old Adèle Domecq (the eldest of the four visiting sisters); the second when he was twenty-eight with an eighteen-year-old Charlotte Lockhart, who then married a man seven years older than John; and the third, at the same age, was to be with Euphemia Gray who was nineteen. Indeed because of the way she had been brought up Euphemia was probably much more emotionally mature for her age than he was. I would suggest that despite John's sheltered and religious upbringing this was fairly normal behaviour for a young man of his age and in his position and does not support in any way a view that he was unhealthily attracted to young girls. He was in fact exactly the same age as his future wife's father had been when he married his nineteen-year-old bride Sophia in June 1827. In the meantime John's father had discussed the marriage of his son to a fifteen-year-old and an eighteen-year-old with perfect equanimity. Even after her marriage to John, Euphemia herself had no obvious moral qualms in discussing the putative marriage of a sixteen-year-old heiress to a Polish Count old enough to be her father.[10]

CHAPTER IV

THE DARK SHADOW

୧୬

At the time of the annulment Mr. Ruskin explained the effect of John's disappointment over Adèle Domecq to his friend William Alexander:

> my Son had in 1840 nearly died of a Broken heart from attachment to a French young Lady whom he resigned in obedience to his mother who objected to the Roman Catholic faith.[1]

Normal healthy people do not 'nearly die' of disappointment in love. Nor do broken hearts hæmorrhage blood. Certain of John Ruskin's biographers have tended to regard the blood spitting incident as a Romantic detail and his subsequent attention to his health as hypochondria. Collingwood offered a more prosaic explanation of John's coughing up blood by pointing out that John was declared consumptive in May 1840.[2] Consumption was the contemporary term for tuberculosis, a potentially fatal myco-bacterial infection that primarily affects the lungs. There was, and is, nothing remotely Romantic or psychosomatic about the disease. The most common form of human tuberculosis usually begins with flu-like symptoms which progress to a persistent cough, the spitting of blood caused by lesion of the lung tissue, and consequent weight-loss or general wasting of the muscles. The primary lesion of the lung can sometimes heal and the infection be contained within a protective tubercle. If this does not happen, the disease begins to consume the organ in which it has lodged, usually the lung, and the illness progresses to a fatal conclusion. This can sometimes be a protracted process with periods of remission or latency. Human tuberculosis is usually spread when ærosol droplets of infected sputum ejected by the coughing of the infected person are inhaled by those in prolonged and close contact. This means that the disease often spreads within families: hence its description as 'the family attendant'.

The classic case was that of the Brontë family, seven of whom died from the disease, but other notable Victorian families such as the Trollopes and the Oliphants also suffered. John was later (1863) to become a close friend of George MacDonald the writer. MacDonald's mother had died of the disease in 1833 when he was eight and George himself survived repeated attacks of consumption starting in 1850. He lost his fourteen year-old half sister Isabella in 1855 and his father and brother John to the disease in 1858. Four of MacDonald's own children died later; two of them within a year of each other. Another child, Grace, survived childhood but died in 1884 after giving birth to a baby who also died of the same disease. Although tuberculosis is environmentally transmitted, susceptibility may also be inherited. The micro-organism that causes it was identified in 1865, but the pathology of the disease, and particularly of the secondary infections it causes, was not properly understood until much later. Even today tuberculosis can be a very difficult disease to identify and treat. It is not always confined to the lungs; indeed in some cases the lungs can be unaffected. Almost any organ in the body can be infected. Tuberculosis of the larynx is perhaps the most infectious form, whereas something like tuberculosis of the kidneys would be the least. The disease can often lodge in the lymph glands in the neck, resulting in 'scrofula', or lymphatic tuberculosis, the disease that John's father was said to have suffered in his youth. Throughout the forties and fifties John was treated in various ways for 'sore throats' including by 'massage'. As scrofula can cause an ulcerous discharge from the infected glands through the skin of the neck it may even account for the old-fashioned high stock that he habitually wore. Although it seems that his father's tuberculosis was 'closed' and therefore not infectious, there is a possibility that John was inadvertently infected by his father coughing or sneezing.

From the Ruskin family letters we can see that John had regular bouts of childhood illness. However his mother seemed most concerned by his sore throats, coughs or fevers. In 1826 Jessie Richardson's son James was taken ill with consumption while staying at Croydon and Herne Hill. In a letter Margaret Ruskin wrote in May of that year she tried desperately to reassure her husband who seems to have feared not only that he himself was consumptive, but that he might also have had something to do with James having contracted the disease. Margaret mentioned that the consumptive symptoms of John Tweedale (another relative) were the same as those which were at that very moment ending the life of James Richardson at Perth. Mrs. Ruskin, no doubt with Grandpa Ruskin in mind, was particularly disturbed by the fact that James' symptoms included depression and delirium and that the disease seemed to affect the mind. For his part Mr. Ruskin was not only concerned for himself; his precious son had been in contact with both James himself and with the Croydon children. Margaret reassured her husband that she had prevented his son from mingling with her sister's children 'for fear of infection'.[3] Later in the same month, David Blaikie, (another Richardson relative) contracted the disease and called at Herne Hill. Margaret commented: 'never I think was consumption so prevalent or so rapid as it has been this spring [–] it appears as a sort of plague this season.'[4]

James Richardson died on 8th May 1826. His little sister, John's playmate Jessie, died the following year from 'water on the brain', suggesting the hydrocephalic effects of a tubercular infection of the meninges. Her mother Jessie died a year later from 'decline', a word often used to describe the effects of tubercular phthisis, phthisis being the clinical term for the depression, fatigue and muscle wasting effects of pulmonary consumption. James' father Patrick Richardson had already died in 1824 'briefly apoplectic'[5] but his trade might well hold the clue to the demise of his family. He was a tanner or skinner, with a leather shop and was thus exposed to the bovine variant of this dreadful disease which often affected abattoir workers. What seems fairly probable is that much of the extended Ruskin family circle was riddled with tuberculosis of one form or another. Mary Richardson, another potential carrier of the disease, became part of the Ruskin household in 1828. She spent nineteen years with the Ruskins without more than a day's illness before succumbing to 'cold' and 'decline' after returning to her new marital home after a trip to Scotland. John Richardson noted in May 1830 that the Ruskins were 'travelling through England on acct. of Uncles and Johns health'.[6] This was the Lake District tour when John was eleven. The first clear indication of John having a pulmonary disease seems to have been in 1835 when he was removed from the Rev. Thomas Dale's school after an attack of 'pleurisy', a likely early symptom of tuberculosis, which also raises the possibility of his having been infected by a fellow pupil.

Having consumption in the family was not something you would have wanted to advertise. In June 1835 Mr. Ruskin wrote to George Gray from Vevay:

I am going about with my Son whose health threatens to give

way from remains of whooping cough and over growth – Since we came to France and this country his cough has entirely ceased + and his recovery proceeds rapidly.[7]

Whilst on the 1840 European tour, and after his son's consumption had been diagnosed, Mr. Ruskin explained away John's illness as 'my son having injured his health by over Study'.[8] It was true that John seriously weakened his constitution by overwork on classical texts for his degree. He wrote in his diary that 'university had nearly floored me, but it had other things allied with it.'[9] One of these was the emotional shock of hearing of the marriage of Adèle:

> that evening in Ch.[rist] Ch.[urch] when I first knew of it – oddly enough on the 12th. – and went staggering down the dark passage through the howling wind, to Child's room, and sat there with him working through long interminable problems, for what seemed an infinite time, without error, without thought, all confusion and horror in eyes and brain.[10]

His severe workload was his way of obliterating Adèle from his mind after her engagement. However, it wasn't until three weeks later that John developed a 'short tickling cough ... followed by a curious taste in the mouth, which I presently perceived to be blood.'[11] He walked round to the High Street to tell his parents what had happened. His mother, 'an entirely skilled physician in all forms of consumptive disease', arranged for him to sleep out of college. The next day he was with the doctors in London who all gave gloomy prognoses, except for Sir James Clark who recommended him to rest and spend the winter abroad: standard advice for consumptives.[12] In fact Sir James, physician in ordinary to the Queen, was an expert on the disease, having published a

Treatise on Pulmonary Consumption in 1835. Later Mr. Ruskin would also claim his son nearly died of a broken heart. Effie had obviously heard this version when she wrote after the annulment that John 'broke a blood vessel from disappointment.'[13] Although the 'disappointment' may well have triggered the attack, I would suggest that the chronology alone would show these statements to be nonsense. What had caused John to spit blood was tuberculosis.

The illness did not pass. The patient was not cured. Collingwood, John's first biographer, who knew him intimately over many years, pointed out that the 1840 illness had left John with a 'weakness of the spine, which during all the period of his early manhood gave him trouble, and finished by bending his tall and lithe figure into something that, were it not for his face, would be deformity.'[14] John's slight stoop and hunched shoulders do not appear in the Glenfinlas portrait but were noted by journalists and exaggerated by caricaturists.[15] This stoop was symptomatic of yet another common secondary tubercular infection, this time of the joints of the vertebræ which can cause them to collapse and deform. This used to be known as Pott's disease. This infection of the joints is a particular effect of bovine tuberculosis, which apart from infecting abattoir workers was, in that time before the invention and adoption of pasteurisation, more usually caught from infected milk. Even leaving aside the Richardson connection, the family letters show that young John was given fresh un-pasteurised milk twice a day at Herne Hill. His belief in fresh milk as a healthy alternative to tea and coffee appears several times in his letters home from Venice.

Under doctor's orders the Ruskins left England for the Continent in late September 1840. In Rome on December 18th John complained of his chest and had five days of fever, delirium and pain which he recorded on the 25th. On the 30th 'this confounded illness' was still there and by the 13th of January 1841 he was in Naples coughing up blood again. He hinted at the seriousness of the attack in *Præterita*:

> For some time back, the little cough bringing blood had not troubled me, and I had been taking longer walks and otherwise counting on comparative safety, when here, suddenly, in the gentle morning saunter through the shade, the cough came back – with a little darker stain on the handkerchief than usual. I sat down on a bank by the roadside, and my father's face was grave.
>
> We got quietly back to the inn, where he found some sort of light carriole disposable, and set out, himself, to fetch the doctor from Rome.[16]

The doctor's advice was that 'there was nothing new to be done, nor said. Such chance attack was natural in the spring [...] only I must be cautious for a while.'[17] John claimed in *Præterita* that this was the last time the cough ever troubled him. However his diary records that there was more blood on the 20th and the 22nd of March. On the 27th he was confined to the house 'for fear of bringing this thing back – tickling and plaguing all day.' From the 16th to the 24th of April he had more chest problems, fever and 'was ill, with threatening of blood and afraid to stir or sketch.' In a letter of May 16th from Venice he noted that 'I have not been particularly well. Things went wrong with me at Albano, two months ago, and I have been very lazy since – blood coming three days running, and once afterwards; better now, however.'[18] On 17th May he was again frightened at dinner by some threatening of blood but it went away.[19] His father told George Gray in a letter of 24th May 1841 that:

My son was extremely unwell after leaving Naples but at Venice recovered very fast and continues tolerable – though he gains no flesh and is in a precarious state – we trust however by care his life may be prolonged although he will never be fit for any arduous duties and this sits upon his mind and affects his health – We may be thankful he is no worse and that we had the power of withdrawing him from the severe winter of 1840/1 experienced in England.[20]

Effie's uncle Andrew Jameson, who had also been ordered abroad in 1840 on account of a chronic throat infection, bumped into the Ruskins at Turin on their way back home and commented 'Young Mr. R looks very delicate – His symptoms are the same as I had – but he appears to have naturally a much weaker frame.'[21] Mary Richardson also noted the meeting in her diary: 'his [Jameson's] health very delicate but the better for Italy, his attacks very like John's only more severe.'[22] Back in England Mr. Ruskin forced John to cancel a tour of Wales with a friend when the disease threatened to return. He was despatched to Dr. Jephson's clinic at Leamington to recuperate. His father asked anxiously 'Have you any return of blood or any threatenings?'[23] Collingwood noted that 'the malady had left traces' on John, 'which, in one way and another, haunted him ever after. One of the worst effects of consumption was to be thought consumptive, and marked down as an invalid.'[24] (Even as late as the 1940's, tuberculosis was associated with poverty, bad living conditions and dirt.) There was definitely a social stigma attached to this disease which both John and his father felt keenly. John subsequently developed a phobia about invalids. One of the least attractive revelations in *Præterita* concerns one of John's Croydon cousins:

Margaret, in early youth, met with some mischance that

twisted her spine, and hopelessly deformed her. She was clever and witty, like her mother; but never of any interest to me, though I gave a kind of brotherly, rather than cousinly, affection to all my Croydon cousins. But I never liked invalids, and don't to this day.[25]

This 'mischance' was almost certainly tuberculosis related. In 1849 John told Effie about 'my poor cousin Margaret – disturbed in the spine – and has lungs all disease – her cough continual.'[26] Margaret's mother, John's aunt Bridget in Croydon, had died in 1830 'of "cold" literally' according to John in *Præterita*.[27] Although there are a multitude of diseases which might have accounted for her death, a fatal 'cold' strongly suggests the extreme respiratory symptoms of tuberculosis. Once again this terrible disease might have been implicated, a disease that seemed to haunt John's life. Much later there was the strange case of the pre-Raphaelite painting *Too Late* by William Lindsay Windus. The subject is a young woman whose lover returns after a long absence only to find her dying of consumption. John gave such a damning criticism of this painting in his *Academy Notes* for 1859 that it may well have ended the artist's career. Could it be that the painting had touched a raw nerve?

One very serious form of tubercular infection occurs when the infection spreads generally throughout the body and seeds itself in many different locations. This is known as miliary tuberculosis because the multitudes of tubercles resemble millet seeds. If miliary tuberculomas form within the brain the resulting cognitive and behavioural changes can in rare cases be mistaken for mental illness. Psychosis, hallucinations and hearing voices have all been documented.[28] Perhaps this might be a more than plausible explanation for John's grandfather's reputed madness.

Furthermore if Grandpa Ruskin had also had lymphatic tubercules we may even have an explanation for his throat wound. It may have been a desperate attempt by a disturbed mind to lance the perceived source of his infection. Before the development of functional chemotherapy, scrofula was often treated by surgery. This might possibly account for the various inconsistencies in the facts surrounding the case. He would have cut his throat and thereby killed himself, but without intending suicide. A suicide does not usually go seeking help having once embarked upon the attempt, but Grandpa Ruskin did. It would also explain the entry on the death certificate: 'Sudden'; and the fact that he was subsequently buried in consecrated ground. He had technically killed himself but was not therefore a suicide. The social stigma attached to consumption, scrofula, madness and suicide would however have ensured that the whole incident would never be discussed.

Perhaps even more tragically, the love of John's later life, Rose La Touche, died of a non-specific wasting disease with mental perturbation, described at the time as 'neurasthenia', then a recently invented word often used on the medical certificates of women in the late nineteenth century to avoid the social stigma of madness. Some authors have suspected anorexia nervosa as a more modern prognosis: I would suggest that tuberculosis, perhaps even a miliary variant affecting the brain, is another possible alternative, since Rose presented with a range of symptoms. Olive Mackenzie's grandparents were servants at Rosie's Harristown home and her mother was even named after her. She told her daughter that, 'Rose was an unusually lovely girl – pink-cheeked and frail. My mother's opinion was that Rose probably suffered from tuberculosis which was prevalent and fatal in those times.'[29] How she caught it does not bear thinking about. She and her mother were regular visitors to the home of George MacDonald, who suffered repeated bouts of the disease and whose immediate and extended family had been devastated by it. John, as well as being close to Rose also became a close friend of MacDonald. John's 'madness' in later life might even have had a similar physical explanation since latent tuberculosis can revive at any time: five, ten or even fifty years after the initial infection. The degradation of the immune system associated with old age often allows a resurgence of the disease.

Modern research has shown that severe emotional states can cause the effectiveness of the immune system to dip. John's disease always worsened when he was emotionally traumatised.[30] The prime example was the Adèle Domecq affair. In 1847 John's consumption flared up again. He had just become romantically involved with Euphemia Gray and the emotional turmoil of his parents' opposition threatened to cause a relapse.[31]

CHAPTER V

THE FAIR MAID OF PERTH

εⱭ

The connection between the Ruskin and Gray families dated back to the earliest days in Perth and continued after John's parents moved away to London. Patrick Richardson had been the link which first brought the two families together. As skinners and tanners the Richardsons were already connected to the Gray family in their original trade as glovers, long before Patrick joined George Gray in a fishing and shipping enterprise. Mr. Ruskin's gentle sister Jessie had been forced by Grandpa Ruskin to marry the 'rough tanner' Patrick Richardson. Patrick, corpulent and unhealthy, died in July 1824, leaving Jessie with four boys and two girls to bring up alone. Richardson's business partner George Gray had married Sophia Jameson in 1827 and their first child, Euphemia, was born on 7th May 1828. Although the Ruskins ended their regular visits to Perth after John's aunt Jessie died in 1828, Mr. Gray and Mr. Ruskin together managed the trust fund they had set up for Jessie's surviving children and the Grays visited their now wealthy friends, the Ruskins, in London. Thus it was that John first knew Euphemia Chalmers Gray as a child. Mr. Ruskin later wrote:

> I had known Mr. + Mrs. Gray of Perth many years when they sent their daughter to School in England they asked us to receive her during vacations.[1]

Phemy, as her family called her, started her education at the fashionable Avonbank School near Stratford-on-Avon in August 1840 when she was twelve. Her parents did not accompany her

Avonbank School at Stratford-upon-Avon

to school that first time but dropped her off at the Ruskins' home at Herne Hill in Camberwell and went off on a European tour. This was the first time she met John, who was then twenty-one. She was escorted to the school either by the junior school mistress or a family friend depending on which account you read.[2]

Her early letters home from Avonbank reveal an interest in fashionable clothes and trimmings, a crush on the natural history teacher, Mr. Walker, and an aversion to being called 'Miss Effie' by Mr. Packer. Elizabeth Gaskell had also started at Avonbank in 1821 when she was eleven and her recent biographer Jenny Uglow has written at length about the school. It was founded and run by the three eldest Byerley sisters, using a legacy from a relative in the Wedgwood family. Although the sisters were Dissenters, the school was run on Anglican lines for reasons of respectability and commerce.

The school was to have many well-connected pupils including Harriet Martineau's niece and Joseph Priestley's grand-daughters. Other pupils included Julia Leigh Smith, Barbara Bodichon's aunt, and Jessie Boucheret, both connected to later libertarian feminist movements. It should not however be assumed that the school was a hotbed of feminism but, as Uglow has pointed out, neither did the school encourage the passive obedience of the wife to the husband. The basic curriculum seems to have been fairly uncontroversial: 'Reading, Spelling, Grammar and Composition, Geography and the use of the Globes, Ancient and Modern History'. Later on it was expanded with Italian, French, Dancing, Drawing, Writing and Arithmetic, Music and Needlework on offer, mostly for extra payment. Judging by Effie's subsequent appalling handwriting, bad spelling, almost total absence of punctuation and lack of interest in things historical, it can only be assumed that she found the accomplishments more to her taste than the academic achievements.[3] The purpose of the school seems to have been to produce educated respectable wives who would rise to the challenges of Victorian marriage.

Euphemia visited the Ruskins at Herne Hill in 1841 and, after they moved into their grand new home at Denmark Hill, she became a regular visitor. She was there in 1843 when she was fifteen, in 1846 when she was eighteen, and then again in 1847, by which time she was nineteen years old and mature enough for John to develop a serious infatuation with her. John was twenty-eight, the author of *Modern Painters* and a rising literary star. The girl who stayed at Denmark Hill that spring and summer of 1847 was however no ordinary nineteen-year old. She was extremely pretty, of a good average height and well dressed. She was lively, flirtatious and good in company. Her Scottish accent would not have concerned the Ruskins since even John had a hint of his father's Scots brogue. Euphemia was also a bright girl and had at least been given some education. She had won school prizes, including one for History, and could speak French and German.

Even by 1841 her uncle Melville Jameson had noticed 'how far already she is before her old Perth schoolmates.'[4] He was also amused at:

> Phemy's experience – She has made I think the most grati-
> fying progress, not only in her mere school knowledge but
> what is of more importance, in her observation of men and
> things – her remarks are really excellent on many subjects.[5]

This education was however a mixed blessing. The amount of time that she spent away from home did not go uncriticised. The Jamesons exchanged the opinion that home was the best place for her in the holidays as 'she would have got too far for her age had she remained' at school.[6] Mr. Ruskin later expressed his dislike of 'the restless undomestic character of the Girl'[7] and believed that 'Phemy has been allowed to go too much about ever to become domestic.'[8] When the marriage got into difficulties he wrote scathingly to her father:

> If she had when young got the household tastes of her Mother
> and her domestic turn – her character would have been differ-
> ent but you sent her about visiting and thinking of Dress till
> she became unsettled and restless, and then to these Board-
> ing Schools where mistresses pilfer parents and teach Daughters
> the most approved mode of ruining Husbands.[9]

Phemy does indeed dwell on 'Dress' a good deal in her early letters; perhaps this was not unusual for a pretty teenage girl at a fashionable school. Both description and expenditure were to increase as she matured.[10] Just before the marriage John quoted from one of her letters in which she had said that she did feel happier when she was nicely dressed.[11]

One unfortunate consequence of her upbringing may have been that her teeth were neglected. She retained several milk teeth and she seems to have considered them as rather unattractive. However given the rudimentary nature of dentistry at that time she most probably had no remedy. Her mother also had bad teeth. In addition Phemy suffered from insomnia and painful feet but this latter may have had more to do with her fashionable footwear than lack of parental oversight.

The long periods of time spent away from her home and parents also meant that she had to deal with the most awful circumstances alone. From the summer of 1840 to the autumn of 1841 she did not return home at all. During this time, whilst not at Avonbank School, she stayed with a school friend near Stratford-on-Avon and with the Ruskins. It was whilst with the Ruskins that she had to cope with the news that first one and then the other two of her younger sisters had died of scarlet fever. Her two younger brothers had already died. John, having to cope with serious illness himself, wrote his only fairytale, *The King of the Golden River*, for her at this difficult time. His diary for September 15th 1841 reads: 'Not much done today … a little of Phemy Gray's fairy tale. Poor thing – she wants something to amuse her now.' Eventually she went back to Perth: her father had insisted on her being withdrawn from school to help at home. Her sisters' governess took up her education until she returned to Avonbank, again via the Ruskins' house, in December 1843. Mr. Ruskin was under the impression that when she visited in 1846 she had come from Avonbank. Phemy's brother Albert also thought that his 'sister remained at the Stratford School until she was 16 or 17, while she was there she paid further visits to the Ruskins.'[12] Her grandson Admiral Sir William James too wrote that the last time her father came south to take her home from

Euphemia Chalmers Gray in 1847, aged 19, *by George Richmond R.A.*

school was in October 1846.[13] Lutyens was therefore probably mistaken when she wrote that Phemy left Avonbank for good in June 1844. Either way Phemy missed several years of her education. At some stage the Ruskins changed her pet name from Phemy to Effie, a name she always hated. John later recalled the first time she had permitted him to call her Effie:

*John Ruskin in
1843, aged 24,
by George
Richmond R.A.*

Do you recollect the first time I ever called you 'Effie' –
when I was frightened at finding you practising in the cold
drawingroom and stopped and begged pardon – and your
giving me leave an evening or two afterwards – What a
luxury it was to call you Effie – and is.[14]

The result of this upbringing was a naturally clever girl proficient in languages and conversation, skills honed during long spells alone in the company of affluent strangers. She was a good dancer and could also play the piano well enough to give her listeners pleasure. But although she was of above average intelligence, lively and entertaining, she lacked educational depth and breadth. Mrs. Gaskell, who admired John greatly and may not have been entirely impartial, described another aspect of Effie's character in a letter she wrote at the time of the marriage breakdown:

> I have known Mrs. Ruskin for some time, – she was at the same school as I was – though of course \^{she was}/ much younger. Still we had the bond of many mutual schoolfellows. Now don't think me hard upon her if I tell you what I have <u>known</u> of her. She is very pretty very clever, – and very vain. As a girl when she was staying in Manchester her delight was to add to the list of her offers (27 I think she was <u>at</u>, then;) but she never cared for any one of them. It was her boast to add to this list in every town she visited just like somebody in the Arabian Nights, who was making up her list of 1000 lovers.[15]

Mr. Ruskin later wrote that 'In 1846 Miss Gray was rather forced upon us',[16] and there was talk both of a cold reception on the part of the Ruskins,[17] and of their fleeing from the Grays. This was only partly because her visit clashed with the start of their European tour of that year. There had been no previous evidence that they resented her presence. At that time John was still in the shadow of Adèle, and Effie must at first have been regarded as a welcome distraction. However it is clear from subsequent letters that John's parents were seriously alarmed by the growing intimacy between the two young people and were relieved to be able to carry him off to the Continent and out of her reach. With a

The house at 163 Denmark Hill where the Ruskins lived after 1842,
by Arthur Severn

year's hindsight John wrote to Effie that:

> When my mother said to me in October last year [1846] –
> Only wait this winter John – and then you shall see her – I
> consented (though sulkily) because I thought you were only
> seventeen; you know you corrected me on your birthday. –
> if I had known – or thought – of the truth – I wouldn't have
> waited an hour – and much suffering I should have saved to
> myself and a little perhaps to you – for I don't know if you
> were or not – but you really looked distressed the night you
> left Denmark Hill.[18]

On her next visit to Denmark Hill, Effie's behaviour with John
made his father even more concerned. Effie arrived in April
1847 and very soon afterwards Mr. Ruskin was complaining
about her to her father. In his letter of April 28th to George Gray,
Mr. Ruskin alerted him to the undesirable consequences of
Effie's flirtatious behaviour at Denmark Hill:

My Dear Sir,

We have been friends for so many years standing that I hope our communications with each other may assume a more frank and easy and confidential form than those betwixt ordinary acquaintances usually do – We have had the very great pleasure of your Daughter's company for these few days past and what we think of her will best appear from the subject of this letter. – You know that my Son is at home – I cannot arrive at the purpose of this letter than by giving you a short sketch of his past life –

In 1835 when he was 16 I happened to have my Partner the late Mr. Domecq residing with two of his Daughters for three months in my house – I believe I have already told you that most unexpectedly to us my son became strongly attached to the youngest Daughter of Mr. Domecq. [This was Adèle, Mr. Domecq's second daughter, and the younger of the two then visiting, the elder was already engaged.] Her father was full of affection for his own child and for mine and expressed entire approval of their being united, offering to make his Daughter a protestant. I felt this a great kindness and concession but we could not sanction a union with Romanism even tho professing to cease to be so and the ample fortune belonging to the Lady though always an agreeable an accompaniment was no inducement to run such a risk as his Mother thought existed of her Son becoming a Roman Catholic, the character of the young Lady's mother was also objectionable – The passion however was powerful and almost threatened my son's life – various journies abroad have scarcely dissipated his chagrin nor repaired his health – The only young Lady we have had about us since from whom any thing was to be feared I will admit was your own Daughter and because Mrs. Ruskin and myself were persuaded that no young man of taste and feeling could long look upon her with indifference we felt called upon immediately to consider all consequences. For myself I am of course most deeply anxious for my son's happiness but whether it was derived from Paris or from Perth, from small fortune or from great, I was disposed to let matters take their course trusting that my son would not commit any very fatal mistake if left to his own guidance in such an affair – I ascertained however that not only to Romanism but to Scotland and most especially to Perth Mrs. Ruskin had an insuperable dislike – she has had so much misery herself in Perth that she has quite a superstitious dread of her son connecting himself in the most remote degree with the place – With knowledge of these objections in his Mother's mind and of the power of the presence of such a young creature as Miss Gray I felt there was no safety but in flight – We did not fly from you last year but we gave you I fear a very cold reception and your stay was very short – Since you took Miss Gray to Scotland last year my son has been abroad and since his return he has in the society he has fallen into found a young Lady who has engaged his affections and to whom he has made proposals the result of which is not yet known – To you as a father I make such disclosures as under similar circumstances I should desire to be made to me. – I would not presume to say that Miss Gray cannot be daily with my son without the smallest danger to herself but I deem it more than possible from what I already see that both may fall into some danger and that very great embarrassment might arise to all of us should the favourable impression which each may be already making on the other proceed to take a more definite form – I repeat that as far as I am concerned I lay no restraint nor prescribe any course to my son – He may follow his own inclinations but as he has committed himself for the present and as his Mother if he had not seems so averse to Scottish alliances I cannot help giving expressions to my apprehensions that both you and I are placing our young people in danger and that we should at least adopt every measure of caution and safety in our power.

I beg to apologise for this long letter and for saying any thing you may consider uncalled for but I might have saved my son from many a pang had I once been as early in my fears and precautions. We join in kindest regards to you and Mrs. Gray.

I am My Dear Sir
Yours very truly
John James Ruskin

I wish in place of burning you would return me this letter in case of my son asking at any time if a Letter were written.[19]

Mr. Ruskin was nothing if not straightforward. However, if Mr. Gray had but known that the Lady in question was also of Scottish extraction he might not have been quite so restrained in his reply. Of course a famous heiress was a different thing from a lawyer's daughter from Perth. Even so, there is a hint of prickliness in Mr. Gray's reply. He was after all being asked to rein in his daughter, who apparently knew nothing about the engagement, when it was clearly John, the older of the two, and whose sense of honour alone should have held him back, to whom Mr. Ruskin should have spoken. To add insult to injury Effie was declared unsuitable solely on the grounds of being from Perth! Mr. Gray acted immediately.

Perth 1 May 1847
Believe me that I fully appreciate the kind feeling which

has induced you to enter so frankly into your family matters with the view of preventing an unhappy attachment arising betwixt your son and my Daughter and you may be assured that knowing as I now do the position in which your son stands with respect to another Lady and, irrespective of this, the feeling of Mrs. Ruskin to a Scotch alliance, and particularly with a native of Perth, I shall use such means and influences as is within my power immediately to separate the parties which I trust will be quite sufficient to prevent the renewal of any penchant the one may have ever felt for the other – Accordingly by this post I have written my friend Mr. Gadesden who kindly requests me to allow Phemy to pay him a visit asking whether it would be convenient for him to receive her now and I have no doubt he will send for her directly – On the 18th I believe it is arranged she goes to Mrs. Paget who is then to be in London –

It strikes me forcibly that Mrs Ruskin could have quietly given Phemy a hint that John was under engagement, that this would have completely served every purpose we have in view – If I know anything of Phemy at all I think she would at once have acted on such a hint and without betraying confidence kept her affections disengaged on (as the case might be) any advance from the other side. [In fact Mrs. Ruskin had told Effie the very first night she arrived.]

I know well that Phemy has always expressed herself favourably of John as a person for whom she had a high respect as a man of talent and refined manners, but I know also that she has a great deal of good sense and maidenly pride and is the very last person in the world that would either give her affections to one in John's present position or, were he entirely free, accept him at the expense of wounding his mother's feelings – No happiness could ensue from such a connection and therefore do I feel the more obliged to you for the unreserved communication you have made me which I sincerely hope may be the means of putting an end to all our fears – I have considered it my duty to shew your letter to Mrs. Gray and she intends when writing to Phemy to touch upon the subject very gently as we are both persuaded that it is all we require to do –

I return your letter as desired.[20]

Effie was duly made aware of the situation by her mother in a letter which has not surfaced. It is worth noting that particularly after the marriage the greater number of her letters home are to her mother rather than her father. Only one of the many letters which Mrs. Gray wrote to Effie appears to have survived. Effie refers more than once to her mother's fear that her letters might be seen by others and almost invariably destroyed them. In addition to this, Effie's normal handwriting was absolutely appalling, a fact often regretted by her father. Even Millais later noted: 'I remember she told me that he was disgusted with that part of her education.'[21] Add to this the fact that Effie began to 'cross' overwrite her letters and it becomes hardly surprising that Mr. Gray seems to have relied on his wife to read Effie's letters to him.[22] I believe anyone who works on Effie's letters must also suspect that her mother was living her life vicariously through her daughter and took great delight in her social escapades, unlike her father who only seems to have known what was in the letters from what his wife chose to tell him. Thus it was that instead of being chastened by her mother 'gently touching upon the subject' of Mr. Ruskin's concern, Effie seems to have viewed the whole situation as a great lark and reported back enthusiastically to her mother:

Mrs Ruskin told me of John's affaire the first night I came but I did not tell you as I thought she perhaps did not wish it to be known but she did not tell me who the Lady is and John never hints of her. He is the strangest being I ever saw, for a lover, he never goes out without grumbling and I fancy the young lady cannot be in London. Mrs. R says 'if my John gets her he will have a treasure as she is very elegant and highbred'. Mrs. R tells me she has never seen her and that she is in a higher walk of life than they are but she knows her well by character.[23]

Effie was naturally interested in John's love life and happy to gossip to her mother on the subject in a letter sent on May 8th:

I have not yet had the courage to ask John who his Lady-love is, of the last syllable I suspect there is little. It is an extra-ordinary affair and I could astonish you were I at home to tell you about them. I suspect from what is said that the lady has a fortune and that love must come after marriage. Mr. and Mrs. R. are always talking about marrying for reason, rather odd, isn't it? I much doubt whether John will ever marry her as he has not asked her yet but is bound to marry her. I cannot understand the affair nor I suppose can you but at any rate if I tell you anything about them I trust you will keep it entirely to yourselves as Mr. Ruskin never told me he had written to Papa about it. In fact Mrs. Ruskin tells me that nobody knows and she only told me in case, as she says, that John and I should <u>love each other</u>, wasn't it good, I could not help laughing but thanked her for her caution which however I <u>did</u> not <u>require</u> as I consider him the same as married and should never think of such a thing. However I think this little gossip will amuse you but be sure it goes no further as I should dislike it exceedingly and <u>Papa</u> must be particular in writing or saying nothing that I write.[24]

A week later she had found out more about the affair:

What you say about J's affaire is very true, if he marry it is from prudence and a false notion of duty, he has only seen the young Lady six times at parties in his whole life and does not love her a bit, but believes they have each qualities to make the other happy were they married. Did you ever hear such philosophy? I think Mr. and Mrs. R. are doing wrong, at least they are wishing for their son's happiness and going the wrong way to work. He adores them and will sacrifice himself for them, as I see too easily. Private![25]

By the end of the month she had radically altered her judgment of the Ruskins:

Bye the bye, I have heard a little more about John Ruskin's affair and if he has got into a mess it is his own fault as Mr. and Mrs. Rn only wish for his happiness, a fact which is proved by their refusing a lady with £30,000 but then she was a catholic, but I have not yet found out who the present lady is as they don't talk about it.[26]

Whilst John had been on the Continent with his parents, *Modern Painters II* had been published and had proved a great success, selling three times as many copies as the first volume. On his return John found himself lionised by Society. Mr. Ruskin was well aware that being a writer on art gave John a special status: 'I have not named to anyone, what Company he has kept since leaving College – but I was gratified to find him admitted to

Tables of Ministers, Ambassadors and Bishops but I was aware this arose from his having shown some knowledge in the fine Arts, a subject chiefly interesting to the higher Classes.'[27] John's celebrity as a writer on the fine arts gave him access to the kind of society from which even his father was excluded. In fact the 'society' John had 'fallen into' was primarily that of the 'old Scott and John Murray circle' centred on the house of Lady Davy in Park Street. This was where he had met Charlotte Lockhart, grand-daughter of Sir Walter Scott, heiress to Abbotsford and, to a young man brought up on Scott's writing, impossibly glamorous. As we have seen, Mr. Ruskin was under the distinct impression that there was some kind of formal understanding between John and Charlotte. This impression must have been from what John told him since neither of the Ruskin parents ever met her.[28] Any suggestion of Mr. Ruskin matchmaking here would therefore be simply wrong.

In *Præterita* John commented laconically of Charlotte: 'I never could contrive to come to any serious speech with her'.[29] The last time he saw her was at Lady Davy's where the hostess had given him Charlotte to take down to dinner:

> but I found she didn't care for a word I said; and Mr. Glad-
> stone was on the other side of her – and the precious moments
> were all thrown away in quarrelling across her, with him, about
> Neapolitan prisons.[30]

John was someone to be seen with that season. Did Charlotte collect John's declaration in the way that Effie collected 'offers', or was it more serious? Did Charlotte misunderstand John's intentions with regard to her? Given John's social naïvety, the ending of the affair, such as it was, was bound to be rather untidy. He seems to have omitted to inform his father that it was over; hence John's behaviour with Effie continued to cause his father some concern. One event in particular caused him real anguish. On the 13th of June Effie wrote to her mother that 'Mr. Ruskin took a box at the French theatre on Thursday night John and I went with him. We enjoyed it very much I did much more than the [former?] time.'[31] Effie was obviously at her flirtatious best, revelling in being on the arm of the literary celebrity of the season. John was 'as all the world saw [...] over head and Ears' besotted with Effie.[32] However Charlotte's father was also in the audience and as a consequence Mr. Ruskin suffered 'almost agony in the French Theatre for fear Lockhart or any of his party by chance could see what no human Being could mistake.' Mr. Ruskin's fears were not simply that John was still informally engaged but also that by flirting with Effie under the very nose of Lockhart he would 'let him fancy that your affections were not at all concerned in your proposal to his Child.'[33] Whatever the consequences, soon afterwards Charlotte announced her engagement to a much older man, the wealthy barrister James Hope, whom she was to marry on the 19th August.

Whatever really happened, John's relations with Lockhart, the Murrays and Lady Davy seemed unaffected, but on 13th August 1847 John had to write a cryptic explanatory letter to a puzzled Lady Davy:

> my <u>own</u> hope – never entertained but in foolish moments – and those – (though I do not say that all such are so with me) few and far between – had been for some time entirely extinguished by Miss Lockhart's manner when I last saw her. And it is with real pleasure that I hear of the approach of an event which cannot but, I think be the forerunner of as much happiness to her and to you all who love her as we may dare to hope for in this life. I should myself have often

spoken more openly – and perhaps once or twice have asked more distinct questions – had I not imagined it possible that ~~Miss Lockhart~~ [sic] you might still suppose Miss Lockhart to entertain feelings connected with the subject which caused her some annoyance towards the close of last year which might render if not your answer difficult, at least my enquiry improper.[34]

This is interesting for the mention of a subject involving John which annoyed Charlotte in late 1846 and probably led to either his or her hopes being dashed. This could not therefore have involved Effie and was certainly not the French Theatre incident which took place in June of the following year and just before Charlotte announced her engagement to Hope. However a letter from Charlotte's father to John Murray reveals that his daughter had already been firmly engaged to someone else in November 1846:

My dear Murray, I am sure you will be happy my girl is to be married (probably at Easter) to a wealthy young friend of ours, whom I think you saw here – Mr. Nisbett of Cairn Hill. He is the son of an old friend of ours and the heir of a fair estate about 15 miles off, of which he takes possession in Feby. [probably?] [illeg.] 10,000 a year and all the relations are pleased at the affair. Missy will remain in Scotland till Xmas dividing her time between the [McNeils?] + the mother of the intended [...] Your visitors will be pleased on Charlotte's part of this Epistle.[35]

This sounds like a very firm engagement indeed, but in the light of what followed, it must have been broken off at some stage. Given the acquiescence of all the relations, this must have caused a fair degree of family drama. A letter to Charlotte from her father on December 30th seems to indicate that wedding presents were already being received.[36] There is however a significant gap in the surviving correspondence of Mr. Lockhart and his daughter between December 1846 and August 1847. That is, between Mr. Lockhart relaying to Charlotte the congratulations on her engagement to Nesbitt (including one from William Wordsworth on the 14th November) and the discussion of her wedding to James Hope. This hints at something so dark that the family wanted it erased from the record. John was certainly involved in this unfortunate situation since he had provoked some sort of 'annoyance' at the close of the year and was courting Charlotte in the spring. John's good friend Charles Eliot Norton later described Charlotte as John's first love, and noted that as a result of his infatuation John had been in a 'grievous' and 'stupid' state all winter and then spent some weeks in Ambleside, in Cumberland, in spring 1847 in order to be near her: all to no avail.[37] This was not a trivial crush. He was still upset in August. There was yet another aspect to this story. Charlotte's father John Lockhart, the editor of Murray's *Quarterly Review*, had asked John to write a review for the magazine. John's reviewing Lindsay's *Sketches of the History of Christian Art* was to be a life changing experience for him in two ways. Firstly the book itself 'unsealed his eyes' with regard to the pagan origins of Christian art in a way that was to affect his whole career. Secondly Lockhart edited John's review severely, and in a way that made John permanently distrustful of both bookselling and reviewing.[38] He wrote one further review for the same magazine and then no more. According to John, Charlotte was unimpressed and uninterested in his article. Whether this experience caused any further difficulties for his attachment to Charlotte is not clear.

John's reaction on discovering that his father had arranged for Effie to be removed from Denmark Hill can be imagined. Mr. Ruskin, terrified that the emotional upset of being thwarted in yet another affair might make John ill again, wrote a hasty letter to George Gray begging him to let Effie stay. What he wrote is interesting because it supports Effie's own statement that the very idea of her being in love with John was laughable:

> we had no grounds whatever to think that Miss Gray was in the least interested about my son beyond the interest of one young person for another on a renewed acquaintance – If it entirely depended on the Lady I think much of her judgement and womanly discretion that my fears would be few, but my son's poetical temperament comes rather in abatement of his Discretion.[39]

The last phrase was a cryptic way of saying that John was of course completely besotted with Effie.

Effie meanwhile was having the time of her life. At first she was treated as almost a member of the family at Denmark Hill and got on very well with Mr. and Mrs. Ruskin. Mr. Ruskin she wrote was 'as kind as ever and as droll' and as for Mrs. Ruskin 'we get on admirably':

> John I see very little of excepting in the evening as he is much engaged but he seems I think to be getting very celebrated in the literary world and be taken much notice of.[40]

Effie practised piano and knitted most mornings whilst John seems to have kept to his work regime by sketching and reading. Afternoons were for exercise and fresh air, either walking or driving. In the evening John would wait outside her room and take her down to dinner on his arm. Afterwards she played on the piano till the old folks dozed off. She was naively impressed by the affluence of the Ruskin household, sending her mother details of expensive grocery lists, servants' wages and expensive art acquisitions. 'They have got home a very fine picture by the above artist [Turner] of Venice which is the largest they have and which must have cost <u>something</u>.'[41] She had also been instructed to try and secure her brother a position at Ruskin, Telford and Domecq but had no success. She wrote to him that 'I am afraid I can do little or nothing for you in the way of business with Mr. R. as he gives me no encouragement when I say you would be a better merchant than a writer.'[42] George was at that time training to be a 'writer' or lawyer with his father, so this attempt to get a better paid job may be the first sign of impending financial problems at Bowerswell. Effie's letters home are filled with descriptions of fashions, public events, encounters with celebrities, and of course young men. This extract is fairly typical:

> Talking of geniuses Mr. and Mrs. Liddell came the other day, she a lovely girl of 19 with sparkling black eyes + hair dressed in a black + blue checked silk, a beautiful upper dress of Polka form of blue velvet fitting to her figure trimmed with rich black lace and large buttons, a gray chip bonnet lined with pink crape and pink ribbon outside and in yellow kid gloves etc. etc. she is very fashionable and dines often with her Majesty. Mr. L is headmaster of Westminster School and one of the Queen's chaplains. I don't like Mrs. L's manner and she has not a sweet voice.

So much for genius! The letter ends with more comments on fashion:

The bonnets this season are quite round in front and not at all at the ears. I see a great many cloaks of pale glace silk with ruched frills around them.[43]

It seems plain enough from this short history that in the Ruskin social circles marriage was regarded as a family enterprise. However, the Wardell, Withers and Lockhart affairs showed that John was far from being in thrall to his parents' ambitions. In fact, in the following October, Mr. Ruskin would admit as much by apologising to John over the affair with Charlotte: 'I felt half ashamed of having got you into difficulty with Miss L.'[44] John's father was ambitious for his gifted son in the way that only a man who has known the abyss of poverty and dysfunctional parenting could be. Having worked his whole life away in an effort to lift his entire family out of all danger of want, he simply wished his son to take advantage of the high connections made possible by the family wealth, and marry into the social élite. 'I expected you to marry rather high from opportunities given,' he told him later.[45]

By abandoning Effie to the hospitality of her school friends and 'forcing her' on the Ruskins, George Gray was involved in a similar game: Effie was to receive a fashionable education and make social connections with a view to marrying well. When she came to stay with the Ruskins in 1847 it was high time for Effie's expensive education at Avonbank School to bear fruit. There can be little doubt that she was on the hunt for potential suitors and that she had little trouble collecting them. But whether she considered John as one of them is another matter. Nothing in her letters gives any impression of her being in love with John at this time. She regarded the very idea as laughable. She regarded John as 'a queer being, he hates going out and likes painting all day.'[46]

We have seen that her father asserted that she was 'the very last person' who would, 'were he entirely free, accept him at the expense of wounding his mother's feelings – No happiness could ensue from such a connection'. Even Mr. Ruskin didn't believe that Effie was in love with John.

John may have been a wealthy celebrity but he was also a recurrent consumptive. As we have seen 'the malady had left traces on him'. His father believed he would never be fit for any arduous duties. Although fine-featured, with startling eyes, he was delicate if not gaunt, weak-framed and slightly stooped. Between attacks of illness John recovered some strength but never full health. Quite apart from his consumption, his personality was also fairly unusual. Because as a child he had been kept from mingling with his peers and never allowed any freedom, because his parents had never left him alone, he had grown up a bookish recluse, unable to ride, a bad dancer and awkward in fashionable society. He did however have a personal charm that operated strongly on people he liked. Mary Russell Mitford found the young Ruskin 'very eloquent and distinguished-looking, tall fair, and slender, with a gentle playfulness, and a sort of pretty waywardness that was quite charming.'[47]

Effie, on the other hand, had been away from her parents and in fashionable society for virtually the whole of her teenage years. She had developed from a child to a woman largely without the restraining influence of her family. She was sophisticated and fashion-conscious with highly developed social skills and a penchant for flirtation. She lived for dressing up, gossiping, dancing, flirting, balls and young men. She was also a fearless and stylish horse rider. In short: the way these two young people had been brought up had made them almost precise opposites. Quite apart from all this, Effie had collected a train of young men with whom she had various degrees of 'understanding' and was, most probably, already formally engaged to at least one of them. Even at Denmark Hill there were constant visits from young men clearly infatuated with her: 'Prizie' Tasker, young six-foot William 'Snob' Gardner, 'Brooks' and Parker Howell 'a very good dancer' with whom Effie had been 'dancing and going about with' to the extent that even her parents in Perth had heard gossip.[48]

CHAPTER VI

STRANGE COURTSHIP

ભ

Before Effie left Denmark Hill on June 15th to stay with the Gardners at Sussex Gardens, she and John seem to have had some sort of romantic farewell in her room. John declared his feelings for her and she allowed him to assume that she reciprocated. It must have been a scene she had played often. John, as the Charlotte Lockhart business would seem to show, was not so familiar with the game of flirtation and courtship. It would also seem from later letters that Effie had allowed things to go a little too far and John had assumed a little too much. A letter he sent to her eight months later shows that John clearly dated the beginning of their intimate relationship from that day:

> your Father and Mother might remember that since we have been engaged – and of course before that – June 15th now 8 months.[1]

It had been arranged that after leaving the Ruskins, Effie would stay with her friends the Gardners for a fortnight and then move on to friends in Leicestershire. In the event, on the very first evening she was with the Gardners, she suddenly begged her father to allow her to cut short her stay:

> You will I doubt not think this is a strange request but I have <u>many reasons</u> for writing it, one of which is the <u>extreme</u> impropriety of my travelling alone homewards from Leicestershire and down to Mrs. Paget's.[2]

When she wrote to her brother she did not mention travelling alone but gave other rather unconvincing reasons: although she liked the Gardners, they were 'not of so refined a class as the Ruskins,' they were too fond of good dinners, there were too many stairs to her room, she was sleeping badly and she hinted at illness. She was so desperate to return home that she offered to take the steamer to Dundee, a 'sea voyage which of all things on Earth I consider most insufferable.' She was always very prone to sea-sickness. Her father gave his permission and she sailed on June 30th. It has been assumed that she wished to prepare her father for John's proposal but, in the light of what was to happen, it would seem that her real purpose was almost certainly to forestall any such thing.

After Effie left Denmark Hill, John was so naïvely confident that he and Effie had an understanding that he spoke about his feelings with his parents. They objected strongly to his being engaged to her. On June 22nd John travelled to Oxford but was again taken ill and sent yet again to Dr. Jephson's clinic in Leamington. John later told Effie that the illness was a result of his parent's opposition:

> I hardly know how great a misfortune it may yet turn out
> to be – that I was not permitted to engage myself to you long
> ago – it would at any rate have saved me from much loss of
> health – a loss which I think it unlikely I shall ever recover
> from.[3]

When John arrived at Dr. Jephson's, William Macdonald, a recent visitor to Denmark Hill, was also there. John writes of him with some affection in *Præterita*. He is described as a youth 'of perhaps two or three and twenty' and 'the son of an old friend, perhaps flame, of my father's' who 'had come to see us once or

93

twice with his mother' and 'took a true liking to me'.[4] As a member of an old Perth family, he was also acquainted with the Grays and the Jamesons. Effie, on the lookout for eligible young men, met him and mentioned him to her mother in a letter of the 3rd of June: 'I like him very much what I have seen of him'. On further acquaintance she seems to have been even more impressed by young William:

> Did I tell you in my last how delighted I was with Mr. MacDonald. I never met anyone so good in fact we all think he is too good to live I had a great deal of conversation with him on Thursday night and Friday forenoon we all think if he is spared he will do an immense deal of good on his estates he is coming out hear [sic] to stay on the 16th. and I am sorry I shall not be here. But he appears delicate and had a bad cough.[5]

Macdonald in turn seems also to have been strongly attracted to Effie; most young men were.[6] Macdonald had also been angling for John to visit him in Scotland since at least 1845.[7] John had already arranged to visit him that autumn at Crossmount, the Macdonald hunting lodge near Pitlochrie.[8] Effie knew about the trip by the 12th but on the 18th told her mother that she was certain that John would not visit the Grays:

> John Ruskin will certainly be in Scotland to stay with Mr. MacDonald but you need not expect to see him at Bowerswell he cannot come for various reasons and as you know Mrs. Ruskin would be miserable every moment he was in Perth or under our roof which would be much worse it is extraordinary to me how a woman of her powers of mind and extreme clearness of understanding can be so superstitious.[9]

John's trip must therefore have already been planned before Effie left Denmark Hill. That, and what had happened on her last evening with John, meant that suddenly she had urgent reasons to be at home.

Effie dined with the Ruskins on 25th June on her way to the boat but did not see John who only returned from his Oxford trip on 3rd July. This Scottish jaunt was to be only the second full trip John had ever made without his parents and both he and Effie knew he would have to pass through Effie's home town and the place of which his mother had developed an almost superstitious dread. John's visit to Perth on the way to Pitlochrie was the first time he had been there in twenty years. He spoke to Effie's father in the town whilst the post horses on his carriage were being changed but he did not visit Bowerswell up on the hill of Kinnoull; nor did Effie come down to meet him. His visit to Perth on that particular day was apparently not as unexpected as Effie's return home had been. If he knew she was there he did not try to see her. He certainly did not make any proposals or declarations, most probably because his parents were opposed to it.

John later endowed this trip with enormous symbolical significance. Crossmount becomes a chapter heading in his autobiography; the last before the ominous elision that represents his marriage. He writes of the owls in the pines there as the birds of the Scottish Athena (Edinburgh was known as the Scottish Athens) and their cries as prophetic of mischief, the first symptom of which was his loss of Miss Lockhart.[10] He uses Turner's paintings of the contest of Apollo with the female Python, and the dragon above the Garden of the Hesperides as foreshadowings of his own impending struggle with a 'nearer Python, as might wreathe itself against my own now gathering strength' and for which he 'was yet wholly unprepared'. This was almost certainly an allegorization of his marriage.

It would seem that John hardly knew Macdonald before the month he spent at Crossmount. In *Præterita* he expressed thankfulness for Macdonald's company the once or twice he visited Denmark Hill but immediately told of the difficulty he had with the word 'friendship'. At Crossmount John found that Macdonald had recovered quickly from his illness. To Mrs. Gray John wrote that 'he looks so well after his rough Highland life' and in the letter to Lady Davy he was 'stronger than his gamekeeper'.[11] John was however out of sympathy with William's bloodsports, later referring to his 'evangelical duty to do some shooting in due season'. John was always opposed to cruelty to animals and forty years later when he wrote his autobiography he recalled the 'mewing and shrieking of some seventy or eighty hares brought down in bags' for the poor of Pitlochrie.[12] That it should be the hares that stuck in his mind is significant. They are after all an ancient symbol of lust because, unlike rabbits, they always mate in the open.

On the way to Crossmount John had stopped at Dunkeld, from where he wrote to his father. Although the general tone of the letter is rather neutral, the opening lines may have alarmed his parents:

> I feel so utterly downhearted to-night that I must get away tomorrow without going out again, for I am afraid of something seizing me in the state of depression.[13]

There can be no doubt about what kind of seizure he meant. This caused his parents to be concerned about his emotional state in case it provoked another resurgence of his illness.[14] From Crossmount John wrote to Mrs. Gray to explain why he had not visited Bowerswell. His explanation seems to have been that he had had to leave because he was so depressed because of all the unfortunate associations that Perth had for him personally. There is no hint in the letter that he has any intention of proposing to Effie, or indeed that he had any kind of special interest in her. Nor did he intend to visit Bowerswell on the way back. He was, as ever, obedient to his parents' wishes. Did Effie breathe a sigh of relief?

Unfortunately his parents, in a panic about his health, had begun to reconsider their opposition to his proposal:

Denmark Hill Augt. 29th. 1847

My dearest John

Confused as my yesterday's letter was I think you could not fail to understand that your father and I have but one wish, one desire, that of seeing you in health and capable of enjoying the infinite blessings placed within your reach, and that whatever you may judge necessary to promote your happiness will not merely be acceded to but acceded to with thankfulness and joy both by your father and me. I shall say nothing more of Effie until I know what your plans and wishes are. I am more than thankful you have left Dunkeld, I have felt anxious and uncomfortable about you for these few days more so than during any time of your absence and could not help wishing, either that we were with you or you home again. I feel much sorrow at knowing how much you suffer at times and in particular scenes but be assured my love there is no radical or permanent change in yourself, many causes have been in operation for many years producing by degrees the distressing effects you at times labour under – these causes I trust soon to see removed, and depend upon it my Dear John you will then find yourself capable of infinitely higher enjoyment in the greater part of those things which constituted the happiness of your childhood [...] I hope to have better accounts of you on Monday and that your spirits and health will strengthen daily among the mountains, need I my Dear John say take care of yourself and run no risks which may be avoided, the Scotch Lakes are not to be trusted any more than the English with Sails, you know what you owe to your father and me, our dearest treasure our blessing beyond all value, God preserve you my Dear John and give you all He knows to be needful to make and keep you what he would have you to be, ever

my Love

Your affect Mother Mrgt. Ruskin[15]

This letter was followed a few days later by one from his father that John inscribed 'extremely important and beautiful':

In regard to E.G. – you have taken more objection out of my manner than I had in my mind – Be sure of this that all hesitation or pause on my part is for fear of you – Vanity does mingle a little – but mortification I should have had double in the L.[ockhart] union I always knew this – but we had kept you to ourselves till marriage and I expected you might marry rather high from opportunities given and that then we must give you up – now with E.G.[ray] I gain much – I escape also from painful communications even for a short time with people out of my sphere – as for the opinion of G. Richmond and Acland, I think E.G.[ray] superior to Mrs. R [ichmond], Mrs A [cland], and from all I know to the two Mrs. Liddells – but for you I fear a little worldly trouble of affairs and I dread any future discovery of what you seem to fear – motives of ambition more than Love – or of tutored affection or semblance of it, though I only do so from the knowledge of the desirability of the union to the Father not as you do from supposing you not to be lovable – I reckon there are not Mr. Dales number 74 but 174 in Love with you at this date 2 Sepr 1847 – I cannot deliberate in an hour but in a moment I say – go on with E.G. but not precipitately – If her <u>health</u> is good and she suffers little watch her but do not <u>shun</u> her for 6 or 8 or 12 months – I do not ask you to do this if you prefer marrying at once but as I want you to stand well with Lockhart and the Intellectuals I should be sorry to let him fancy that your affections were not at all concerned in your proposals to his Child – as to your fears and opinions of wedded Life – the unhappiness is generally in the Individual – the Ladies only draw out a Temper which exists – make their husbands show their paces. A man cannot be very unhappy that in the greatest difference with a Wife never for a moment wished himself unmarried.[16]

In his letter to John of September 5th Mr. Ruskin enclosed a letter that Mrs. Ruskin had received from Effie. It would seem that although she was still writing to Mr. and Mrs. Ruskin, she was not writing to John. This was strange behaviour indeed for two people about to be engaged. The debate about Effie continued. Neither Mr. Ruskin nor John seemed to have any doubt that Effie was willing to accept John, but then again Mr. Ruskin would have assumed as much from John's attitude:

We are rejoiced to have your Mondays letter – never before having had two blank days as Pitlochrie gives us – for Sunday here and Sunday there make Fry and Tuesday no days here.

It is soon explained about E. In comparing her with Mrs. A[cland] and R[ichmond] and I mean as her Looks, presence and fair common sense – youth and Gaiety would place her before the World – but here I was behind the scenes and full of fears for her and y [torn] suspicious of her and her family [torn] of which the World knew nothing [torn] your chance good and [torn] binding with Miss L. and the conduct of E. while she believed you engaged with another, seemed like an attempt to break it for her own purposes or else a sort of abandonment of self and duty and Character to the pleasure of the moment come what would of it. If anything of this existed – she would not compare with Mrs A. but I am endeavouring now to think that you considered the Lockhart affair hopeless, and so allowed yourself to be with E in a way which if not off the other, was in my eye wrong and I now wish to believe that E. saw there was not great chance [torn] than had the other Engagement been as I thought – it would have been delicate to do – I now wish to believe they were my Suspicions only which made me think E. acting under Orders – and staying here to create confusion and displeasure to accomplish what her family were bent upon – If her Father and Mother are good honest people and she entirely sim[torn] hearted you need not be ashamed of [torn] your Choice – I wanted a [torn] to pass to see if any light [torn] would come upon the affair but having seen great Injury done your health by former French affair and seeing you at a time of Life to be married and not likely to be better suited and Mama now reconciled – I am quite agreeable to any step you take – I would give a good deal however if E. had nobly left the House the moment the other affair was named – Now that it is done with I should have rushed with great eagerness to have brought her back [torn] – She is a sweet [torn] Friends about as unobjectionable as [torn] I felt and spoke severely because I would still give much if I could obliterate from my mind that passage of the history of both of you – but I repeat I may be entirely wrong and I am not willing again from suspicions [torn] to subject you to a second [torn] too much for your frame to bear. [torn][17]

Mr. Ruskin's main worry was that Effie was being 'tutored' in her affection, and 'acting under Orders' from her father and family. This was because he had begun to hear disturbing reports about her father's finances. There was a further letter on September 13th in which we learn that John had finally admitted that he had been refused by Charlotte before taking up Effie:

I fear you are annoyed at my alluding to E's visit. I cannot help my opinions – they are often wrong – but I am glad to exhaust a subject and to get to the end of trouble because reserve, closeness – on either side – begets continued mis-understanding. It is I assure you no easy matter to draw you out and I am rather slow – what may be called thick headed – bull-headed – obstinately blind perhaps – Until I drew from you this last Letter – I could not see that you had been acting and I have been judging under entirely different circumstances – You acted as if you had finally done with Miss L. – and Miss G acted upon an idea got from you that you were no longer engaged. Now I judged you as pledged to another and likely to get another and I judged E as one knowing only this – Your argument would be right as of Miss G's leaving the House, even if you had been engaged, being uncalled for, if you had been to her as to Miss Sidney or any other Visitor, but as all the world saw you were over head and

Ears – and she was aware of our fears – it totally altered the case – When you saw me so angry under false impressions – suffering almost agony in the French Theatre for fear Lock-hart or any of his party by chance could see what no human being could mistake – in place of letting me alone & only thinking me unkind – I wish you had done me the honour & justice or say flattered me so far as to have reasoned thus

"My Father has not been generally harsh

"or unkind or non-indulgent – what can be

"the matter now? He must be under some

"grievous error or delusion to be in such

"a fury – I will enlighten him."

Had you openly and jocosely said 'Oh as to that affair L it is done with – and E knows better than to suppose I am engaged' – for you tell me for the first time in your last Letter – 'Knowing as she did that I had been refused by another' – I see my dearest John that I should have changed my tone & very interesting novels are composed out of the misunderstandings that compose the web or woof of Human Life – Why we might have gone on – doubting, wondering – regretting, blaming – It is arguing about the colours of the Cameleon – It is the White Shield & the Black. Let us be done with it. I have your happiness at heart & I think for me – you might have had French, Scotch or English – but I daresay Mama judges best – Only trust to my Love, give me your Love & pursue your Happiness & your duty. I am even now assuming too much when I think that my opinion would have been entirely changed had I known that E knew your first affair was done with – She knew & was distressed at know-ing Mama & I had objections. I cannot persuade myself that she should not have gone, but I have been too much with

Sir W Scott lately to make large allowances for human frail-
ties. But let these matters past sleep – Mama has changed her
objections into approval – I give mine and moreover add that
I deem it more likely to secure your happiness to be a married
man than a single, and that I know no young Lady I should
myself so much like for your wife <u>now</u> as Miss Gray.[18]

In a letter of October 4th, besides telling John more about Mr.
Gray's financial difficulties, Mr. Ruskin revealed that he had
finally told John the reason for Mrs. Ruskin's aversion to Perth:

> In one of these letters that affected me you say had we told
> you all about Perth so + so, I believe Mama never would but
> I felt half ashamed of having got you into difficulty with Miss
> L. and I felt it due to myself and mama also to show you that
> we had some reasons for opposing your wishes, beyond mere
> vanity and ambition.[19]

In the event, Mr. Ruskin's earlier advice to John to delay
proposing for several months would have been sound advice to
follow. Mr. Ruskin doubted Effie because of what he now knew
about Mr. Gray's finances; John was not sure that Effie truly
loved him because he thought he was not loveable. John suggested
that an unmarried Effie should go with them to Switzerland the
following year. Mr. Gray objected to this admirable plan.[20] John's
mother also objected to the plan for reasons of her own. Without a female chaperone it would not appear quite respectable nor
would it be 'proper or wise'.[21] More than this, like her husband she
feared the effect that disappointment and happiness deferred
might have on John. By praising the Grays and encouraging
John to visit them on his way home, she effectively gave her
permission to the proposal. John immediately wrote to Mrs.

Gray asking if he could call 'for a day in the course of the week after next.'[22] The letter contained many asides to Effie who it seems had taken offence at his criticism of her native land and of her riband. Thus it was that after the 'hunting' at Crossmount, (he had spent most of the time sketching and thrashing at a field of thistles) and after a short stay at Pitlochrie, John and his man-servant Hobbs (John Hobbs, called George to avoid confusion) finally arrived at Bowerswell on the 2nd of October 1847.

CHAPTER VII

THE PROPOSAL

သာ

There can be absolutely no doubt that John visited Bowerswell with the intention of proposing to Effie. In a letter to Macdonald of 5th October he wrote:

> I love Miss Gray very much and therefore cannot tell what to think of her – only this I know that in many respects she is unfitted to be my wife unless she also loved me exceedingly. She is surrounded by people who pay her attentions, and though I believe most of them inferior in some points to myself, far more calculated to catch a girl's fancy. Still – Miss Gray and I are old friends, I have every reason to think that if I were to try – I could make her more than a friend – and if after I leave here this time – she holds out for six months more I believe I shall ask her to come to Switzerland with me next year – and if she will not – or if she takes anybody else in the meantime – I am really afraid I shall enjoy my tour much less than usual – though no disappointment of this kind would affect me as the first did.[1]

Effie's response to his arrival was not however the one he had hoped for and not the one that the romantic final scene at Denmark Hill had led him to expect. Something went catastrophically wrong with his proposal and he was not engaged when he left Bowerswell. The letter he wrote to Mrs. Gray on 10th October from Berwick, was certainly not what might be expected from a young man who has just found his heart's desire:

My Dear Mrs. Gray,

I am in a sad way this morning – making myself as miserable as can be – in a little dark room looking out into a <u>great</u> dark, shut up – blank square windows and horrible street – wind howling down it most pitifully – just about to find my lonely way to church – I would put up with Mr. A and Mr. G again (and be thankful) – to have somebody to go with me – I can't read nor write – for pure vexation – except to inflict myself on you at Bower's Well and try to fancy myself talking to you. I got a letter from my father yesterday forwarded from George to Mr. Jameson – there were many kind messages in it to you all – I got early into Edinburgh – the carriage was light – and I came fast – much regretting that I had not seen Mr. Melville Jameson – but I thought I should be too late at Edinburgh – and as I knew strangers had been asked to dinner – it would not have done to have been after my time. I met some very agreeable persons at Mr. Jameson's – but they feted me terribly – I made a round next morning among the artists – liked the men better than their things – except Harvey's – he is both a good man – and a good painter. (One o'clock) Everything wrong together – Pouring rain – melancholy old English church – about one fifth full – nobody joining in service – fat old rector who could not speak but in gasps – so that it was well he had not got much to say. Filthy streets – filthy ramparts – No letters at post office – All dreary and hopeless – and I can't fasten my mind upon anything to make me forget myself – I am going to try the Scotch church in the afternoon.

Pray send me a single line – post office Leeds, to say you missed me a little at Bower's Well – if any letters come to Perth, they may be sent to Leeds on Tuesday – but after that to

Denmark Hill – where – God willing I hope to arrive on
Thursday. I will write then – I hope more cheerfully.

That he wrote to Mrs. Gray rather than Effie herself is one
clue, but there is another in the regards at the end:

> Kind love to all – best to Alice and Effie – (Alice may have
> it all if Effie does not want any)

and yet another in the postscript scrawled across the front of the
letter:

> I suppose I may be permitted to say 'Effie' in writing to you
> – I pray pardon for my impertinent message. I am sure she
> is a great deal kinder to everybody than they deserve.[2]

I believe that the simple interpretation of this letter is that John
had been rebuffed by Effie, who did not want any of his 'kind
love'; did not, it seems, even want him to call her 'Effie'. It
would seem that Effie had indeed rushed back to Perth to forestall John and had enlisted her mother's aid in doing so. The very
fact that the letter to Mrs. Gray was written at all suggests that
she had perhaps been more receptive to John than was her
daughter. For her part, Effie was being entirely consistent with
her position back in May when she thought the very idea of a relationship with John was a joke: 'that John and I should love each
other wasn't it good, I could not help laughing'.[3] There is in fact
no evidence whatever that Effie had any particularly strong feelings for John before this time. Even Admiral James wrote that:

> there is nothing in her letters up to the time she returned home
> to suggest that she and John were anything more than good
> friends.[4]

This makes it all the more curious when we discover that Effie, after spending the week at Bowerswell making it very plain to John that she was not interested, then wrote not one but two letters to John which he received, not at Denmark Hill on his return, but at Leeds where he had to change trains on his way back home. Suggestions that Effie had been playing 'hard to get' are therefore absurd. The degree of urgency in these letters is indicated by the fact that the Grays knew that he would be home with his parents in London only two days later. Significantly the first letter was signed 'E.C.G.', the second 'Effie'. Neither of them has come to light. His reply to these has also disappeared and several of the succeeding letters have missing sheets. What we do know is that he answered her letters whilst at Leeds but only after he received the second:

> You know I couldn't possibly help answering your letters to me – received at Leeds – though I felt as you do about the place – but though I had got one before, with E.C.G. this one was 'Effie' – and I could never have borne to receive two without answering.[5]

He was certainly engaged by the time he wrote to Effie on November 2nd and this letter also shows that his first proposal had been refused:

> It would be doing dishonour to my own love – to think that – when I had leave to express it – it was not intense enough to deserve – to compel – a return – No – I cannot doubt you any more – I feel that God has given you to me – and he gives no imperfect gifts – He will give me also the power to keep your heart – to fill it – to make it joyful – Oh my treasure – how shall I thank <u>Him</u>?[6]

John later stated that he had 'offered marriage by letter, to Miss Gray, in the autumn of 1847, and was accepted'.[7] This would tend to exclude the possibility that he had proposed and been accepted on his visit to Bowerswell. Quite when this proposal was sent, and if written why it was not preserved, as the prime evidence of betrothal, in that letter-hoarding family of lawyers is a mystery. Even Effie's own brother Albert Gray admitted that he could not say 'when precisely the engagement took place: it was some time in September or October of 1847 when Ruskin was in Scotland on a visit to Macdonald of Crossmount.'[8] James too skipped over the actual engagement (and the October 10th letter), despite presumably having the whole of the Bowerswell Papers at his disposal. Indeed, from the surviving correspondence it is difficult to ascertain what were the causes of Effie's sudden changes of heart.

John referred to the events at Perth in later letters. The first was on December 9th from Folkestone. John wrote to congratulate Mrs. Gray who had just had a baby. Given John's professed aversion to babies at that time the discussion of that happy event was brief and he moved on quickly to the subject of the engagement. This was apparently the first time he had written to Mrs. Gray on the subject since the engagement and he seems anxious both to reassure a mother worried that her daughter is to be married and also to explain his behaviour at Bowerswell:

> I have often been thinking of writing to you before now, though not in the vain idea of <u>thanking</u> you for what you have entrusted to me, Effie's happiness, and your's in her. How <u>could</u> I? or what could I say, that would render your parting with her less painful. You cannot but have <u>seen</u> how much I loved her, and you know that with one like her, to love her

once is to love ever, and that the <u>much</u> love, which is the end with others, is but the beginning of Love, with her. Nay – the more pain you – and all her fond relations, feel, in the loss of her, the more trust you must have in her future happiness – knowing by what a close chain of affection she is ever bound to all around her. And although I do not like to speak confidently of myself, yet in this I may – I am sure if she can but love me half as well as I do her, and if she can put up, therefore – with what might otherwise prove a source of discomfort to her, her being almost <u>too necessary</u> to me – she must be happy. But it was my sense that her happiness must depend upon the degree of her regard for me, and that in the retired life which it may be necessary for me to lead, there must be much that would be irksome to her, unless rendered tolerable by strength of affection; which <u>in part</u> occasioned the singularity of my conduct at Bowers Well, a conduct which probably occasioned you much concern, and appeared as unjustifiable as strange. Believe me, I have none of that false and selfish pride, which would prevent a man from coming frankly forward through mere fear of exposing himself to the chance of a refusal. But I felt that to Miss Gray's open and kind heart there might be a severe trial in the seclusion from society which my health or my pursuits might often render necessary, I wished to be certain that I <u>could</u> be to her in some degree, at least, the World that she will be to me; and I was the less ready to admit the evidence I could perceive of her affection, because I could not understand how she <u>could</u> love me. (I think, always, that if I had been a woman, I never should have loved the kind of person that I am). And although you might think that she gave me as much encouragement, when I was at Bowers Well, as I had the slightest right to hope for – and although – had I been more a stranger – this would have been so, still, she had until then been so frank and open with me, and her manner had been so different – (I cannot tell you how but it was), only four months before, that I felt it severely, the more so from the few words you said to me on the Monday [he had arrived on the Saturday], for I was grieved alike at the idea of <u>your</u> not being entirely in her confidence – or – if you were – at her feelings being so changed towards me as your expressions tended to make me believe – and – if they had been, in so short a time, whatever reasons she might have for regarding me with coldness, I could never have hoped to have attained such a place in her affections, as I felt it necessary I should possess, both for her happiness and mine. I think, if she had not spoken a word or two to me that night, in her old way, I should have left Perth the following morning. Thank God that she had not <u>quite</u> cast me off, and that now, I have hardly any fear but that my love for her, constant and grateful as I am sure it will be – will be able to balance to her the cruel sacrifices she must make in yielding to it.[9]

This letter makes it very clear that when John had arrived at Bowerswell to propose marriage it was to discover that Effie's manner had changed from what it had been at Denmark Hill four months before. She was now regarding John 'with coldness'. If she was in love with John or had encouraged his advances then she had certainly not confided in her mother sufficiently to tell her. Consequently Mrs. Gray had not been sympathetic to John's behaviour which seemed sudden, strange and unjustifiable. Mrs. Gray had told John on the Monday in a few words that Effie had no feelings for him. He felt this severely. Moreover although he had come with the idea of proposing he had held back, not for fear of being rejected, but because he knew the relationship would not work if Effie didn't love him as much as he did her.

I believe that this is what John was thinking about in the letter of 10th October when he wrote:

> Kind compliments to Dr. P. I am thinking of sending him a little drawing – in order to show Effie that I repent of my rudeness – nearly as sincerely & thoroughly as she of her kindness.

He repented of the rudeness of his clearly unexpected and unwelcome proposal; she repented of the 'kindness' she had shown him at Denmark Hill and which he had misconstrued. His letter of 19th December was a reply to Effie, not to Mrs. Gray, but the subject was the same. John was still trying to sort out what had happened at Bowerswell. Effie had obviously been defending her decision not to confide in her mother about what had been going on at Denmark Hill. John replied:

> still I am ready to admit that – not having been in the habit of being communicative – you might have felt no need of support or of confidence last autumn – and I believe it is only selfishness on my part which makes me wish you had told, not indeed <u>all</u> that passed between us – for that I agree with you in thinking should be sacred between us two – but something of what I had <u>said</u> – and something – or all – of what you had <u>felt</u>. But it wasn't 'temporary insanity', was it love? That's what I want to know.[10]

I would suggest that the most plausible reading of these lines is that Effie's flirting with John had led to a situation where he had in fact already *declared* his feelings for Effie before she left Denmark Hill, and that she had allowed him to assume that she *felt* the same. She had not however taken the situation so seriously as John and had not therefore troubled to consult her parents on the subject. We are reminded of Mrs. Gaskell's account of Effie adding to her list of suitors. Consequently Effie must have been appalled when he arrived at Bowerswell to propose. Her sudden coldness towards him came as a great shock:

> Ah – cruel Effie – how I bore with your treatment of me on Kinnoul I can't conceive – I really think I must be a good creature. Not to take my arm – and I to walk on quietly and bear it – I ought to have turned back at once and said I would go back to mama [Mrs. Gray] – and done it too, and told her plainly what was the matter."

The letter then moves on to a more general discussion of women's tastes in men and the failure of suitors. John quotes 'a poem to a discarded bouquet'; an allegory of a discarded suitor that he regarded as

> rightly expressive of the feelings of bouquets on such occasions – My bouquet was not discarded – you know – but received again into favour – and thus twice honoured – and ever since, beloved; – it would have been a weak and base bouquet to have thought of dying. Its colours are quite bright still.

In summary it is clear that at the time of John's visit, despite having had her daughter with her for some time, Mrs. Gray acted as if she knew nothing about any previous 'understanding' between John and Effie and, after a difficult two days, she told him that her daughter had no feelings for him. Effie behaved coldly towards John and seems to have pleaded 'temporary insanity' for what had happened at Denmark Hill. She paraded her admirers before him and flirted with them. She also claimed to be already promised to someone else and asked John to address her formally. As a result John had left Bowerswell disappointed and not engaged. After he had gone Effie apparently had a very sudden change of heart which resulted in her sending not one but two letters intended to intercept him at Leeds en route to London and before he was back home with his parents. Despite her forbidding him to use the name, the second letter was signed 'Effie'.

In the absence of both these letters and the first sheet of the next known letter, what had happened to Effie in the meantime is not clear, but by the time of this undated letter he had been accepted. The result was an engagement kept secret on Effie's insistence since she was almost certainly already engaged in some way or other to someone else.[12] When he was eventually told about it, Effie's Uncle Andrew Jameson commented circumspectly on 'so sudden a denouement' and 'losing Phemy so soon' but was happy to think that she and John had already seen so much of one another and had a tolerably good knowledge of each other.[13] John commented that Uncle Andrew 'seems never to have thought I should <u>stay away</u> from you – though he <u>did</u> think the <u>marriage soon</u>.'[14] The chapter in Admiral James's book covering the engagement is entitled 'Strange Wooing'. The least that can be said about the proposal was that it was so odd and confused that it was still being discussed between the engaged couple nine weeks later. The other remarkable aspect of this engagement is that, after leaving Bowerswell on the 9th October 1847 after his proposal had been refused, John did not see Effie again until he arrived in Edinburgh in the second week of March 1848 – a period of over five months![15] On the 29th the couple travelled to Perth for the wedding on the 10th April. These were not to be the only strange circumstances attending these nuptials.

CHAPTER VIII

A VERY SUFFICIENT AND ENTIRE MAN-TRAP

☙

Besides claiming that what happened at Denmark Hill with John was 'temporary insanity' on her part, Effie had also tried to fend him off by claiming a prior suitor. John wrote many years later that 'She married me for money, breaking her faith to a poor lover.'[1] Mrs. Gaskell wrote that 'Effie Grey [sic] <u>was engaged at the very time she accepted Mr. Ruskin</u> he did not know of it until after their marriage'.[2] Joan Severn, John's cousin who looked after him in old age, also noted that 'at the time E. made love to him (to save her father from disgrace) she was already engaged to another man in India, (who was broken-hearted by her desertion of him).'[3] Violet Hunt even suggested that 'the lover she threw over to comply with her parents' wishes and save the family fortune committed suicide.'[4] Lutyens has identified Effie's betrothed as William Kelty MacLeod, the son of one of their neighbours on the Hill of Kinnoull.[5] According-ing to her source, Effie became officially engaged to him in 1845 or 1846 before he went out to India with the 74th Highlanders. He and Effie were to have been married on his return. If this is true then Effie was indeed in an awkward position. This was probably the reason that Effie begged John to keep the engagement a secret from close relatives and even from their future best man. John reas-sured her on November 11th 'Don't be anxious about secret – I have not even told Macdonald. Be assured it will be safe.'[6] William MacLeod may well have heard about the secret engagement, perhaps even from Effie herself, because by the end of November 1847 he was back in Perth. She met him again at a ball in November and told John about it. With hindsight there is more than a touch of dramatic irony in John's reply:

> You cruel, cruel girl – now that was just like you – to poor William at the Ball. I can see you at this moment – hear you. 'If you wanted to dance with me, William!' If!! You saucy – wicked – witching – malicious – merciless mischief loving – torturing – martyrising – unspeakable to be feared and fled – mountain nymph that you are – 'If!' When you knew that he would have given a year of his life for a touch of your hand. Ah's me – what a world this is, when its best creatures and kindest – will do such things. What a sad world. Poor fellow, – How the lights of the ballroom would darken and its floor sink beneath him – Earthquake and eclipse at once, and to be 'if'd' at by you too; Now – I'll take up his injured cause – I'll punish you for that – Effie – some time – see if I don't – If I don't. It deserves – oh – I don't know what it doesn't deserve – nor what I can do. As for poor William – you can do him none now – there is but the coup de grace to be given – the sooner the better – and the flower of Love lies Bleeding: to be borne in his bright plume – How long? [...] But I comfort myself – not only by thinking how far more fortunate I am than thousands – (think of poor William losing you altogether, and that for no fault of his own – no folly either – but because he cannot ask you.)[7]

If William was indeed her sweetheart and she had been forced to give him up for a marriage of convenience, then John's flippant tone would have twisted a dagger in her heart. The reason that William could not ask Effie to marry him may well have been that he could not afford to. A soldier's pay was not great and by this time the rumours that John's father had already heard in

London about Mr. Gray's financial difficulties must have been common knowledge at Perth. Given the increasingly apparent extent of his problems, many of her suitors and their parents would have been having second thoughts. In John's letter of December 19th the subject was again William. Effie had received a letter from him:

> Well now about poor William – As I think confidence so desirable between parent and child – much more between husband and wife – in fact if <u>they</u> have secrets from each other, except of things in which others are concerned independently – I do not think they are husband and wife properly they are not One – And so – I won't thank you for showing me the letter (!!) for it would have been wrong of you not to have told me – though – as to <u>my</u> being a judge of the propriety of the step – I of course have neither knowledge to go upon – nor am I a fit person to judge. Everything depends on your knowledge of him – and on what you thought it necessary to tell him – and what he said on the Sunday (which pray tell me as soon as you can) But I have not the least doubt that it was perfectly right it certainly was as kind, and good or you would not have done it.[8]

The *coup de grâce* was eventually delivered to poor William's chances when Effie wrote him a final letter some weeks later.

John had already told Macdonald that at Bowerswell Effie was 'surrounded by people who pay her attentions ... far more calculated to catch a girl's fancy' than himself. William was not the only young man with whom Effie was involved. Her favourite polka partner, James 'Prizie' Tasker, seems also to have had an understanding with her. Admiral James for one seems to have thought that Tasker was more problematical than William since he elided all reference to him from his book *The Order of Release*.[9] John felt that there was even more to the relationship with Tasker than Effie admitted:

> I have been looking at your accounts of Mr. Tasker again –
> I feel sure he was feeling his way that night of the <u>West</u> – and
> if you had not walked so fast, he would have spoken plainly
> – but you acted rightly and like yourself – and saved him the
> mortification of a direct refusal. But I have no patience with
> these cautious men.[10]

John was still exploring the subject in January:

> Your parents were very right in all they did. They must have
> wanted you to marry Mr. T when they made you what you
> used to be with him.[11]

There was also an understanding with a 'Captn. C.' mentioned in a letter written either on 21st November or 9th December 1847:

> By the bye you haven't told me anything about Captn. C. –
> and the happiness he looked forward to – grant him that –
> but – I'm very sorry I can't help it don't be angry with me –
> I would rather he didn't call you Effie any more![12]

This was probably 'my old friend the Handsome Capt. Campbell' who she mentioned in a letter of May 1850.[13] The emotional carnage did not end there. John's letters reveal that Effie had also broken the hearts of her aunt Jessie Jameson's three brothers:

> And so poor Harvey Duncan is really gone – now are you not
> a terrible creature, Effie – to serve Aunt Jessie's three broth-
> ers so – one after another – Kill them off by computation! –

I don't know anything dreadful enough to liken you to – You are like a sweet forest of pleasant glades and whispering branches – where people wander on and on in its playing shadows they know not how far – and when they come near the centre of it, it is all cold and impenetrable – and when they would fain turn, lo – they are hedged with briars and thorns and cannot escape, but all torn and bleeding – You are like a wrecker on a rocky coast – luring vessels to their fate – Every flower that you set in your hair – every smile that you bestow – nay – every gentle frown even – is a false light lighted on the misty coast of a merciless gulph – Once let the ships get fairly <u>embayed</u> and they are all to pieces in no time – You are like a fair mirage in the desert – which people follow with weary feet and longing eyes – until they faint on the burning sands – or come to some dark salt lake of tears – You are like the bright, – soft – swelling – lovely fields of a high glacier covered with fresh morning snow – which is heavenly to the eye – and soft and winning on the foot – but beneath, there are winding clefts and dark places in its cold – cold ice – where men fall, and rise not again – And then you say you 'don't know how it is' – No – there's the dreadfulness of it, – there's the danger – Ah, Effie – you have such sad, wicked ways without knowing it – Such sweet silver under-tones of innocent voice – that when one hears, one is lost – such slight – short – inevitable – arrowy glances from under bent eyelashes – such gentle changes of sunny and shadowy expression about the lovely lips – such desperate ways of doing the most innocent things – Mercy on us – to hear you ask anybody 'whether they take sugar with their peaches'? – don't you recollect my being 'temporarily insane' for all the day afterwards – after hearing you ask such a thing – and then all <u>that</u> is the least of it – but you are such a good girl, too – and so sorry for all the harm you do – and so ready to like everybody, in reason, – and so surprised when you find they don't understand reason – and so ready to promise after you've half-killed them or driven them mad, that if they won't mind that once, you 'won't do it again', and so everything that you ought to be, and can be –, that I think you ought to be shut up in an iron cage – or in one of those things which you have got in the Perth Tolbooth – and not allowed to speak to or see anybody – until you are married. A strict convent might do – bye-the-bye – if there are any near Perth.[14]

John probably intended this letter to be humorous, but the jealous undertone is unmistakable. John had admitted that jealousy was a problem for him in the first dated letter after the engagement:

My own Effie – my kind Effie – my mistress – my friend – my queen – my darling – my only love – how good of you – and I can't answer you a word today. I am going into town with my mother in half an hour – and have all manner of things to do, first – but I am so glad that you have my letter speaking about this very thing – Indeed I <u>never</u> will be jealous of you – and I will keep that purer form of jealousy – that longing for more love – within proper limits – and you will soon find out how to manage this weakness – and perhaps to conquer it altogether; I can't enter into details today – but indeed it was anxiety and weakness of nerve which made me so fretful when you were here [at Denmark Hill] – natural enough I think – and even then, I was only jealous of <u>some</u> people – and that because I was hurt by your <u>condescension</u> – it was, I think – at the root – more pride than jealousy –

> I was speaking of large parties to my mother yesterday for you
> – she said 'You wouldn't like to see her surrounded by a circle
> of gentlemen like Mrs. Liddell?' 'Indeed I should,' I said.[15]

The subject of jealousy was still in Effie's thoughts in February 1848:

> I told Papa the other day that you said you never would be
> jealous without cause and he says unfortunately jealous
> people always <u>find cause</u> which I think quite true but I hope
> at heart you are really not a jealous being, and the absurdity
> of your giving as a reason that my manner to you and other
> people was quite the same is really the most preposterous
> thing I ever heard. You must have been thinking of something
> else when you wrote that! But really John I love you so much
> that I don't think much about the jealous part of you for
> I do not believe you will be at all so after we are married and
> I daresay you will allow me to ask anybody I like to take
> some pudding without behaving afterwards as madly as Mr.
> Munn.[16]

John's early love letters to Effie were very much concerned with her effect on other men and her behaviour with them. Her sudden disconnection from her other suitors and wooers seems to have so devastated the young men involved that John was prompted to write:

> you may think yourself happy if you get out of Perth with-
> out doing any more mischief – and really, now, it is <u>not fair</u>.
> So long as a young lady has her hand free, if people run the
> risk of coming near her – she cannot help it – they have their
> chance, – and have no right to complain if they lose it. But
> you know, <u>now</u>, my sweet, you are neither more or less – stay

– I don't mean that – for more you are – and a great deal more – but still you are a very sufficient and entire <u>man trap</u> – you are a pitfall – a snare – an ignis-fatuus – a beautiful destruction – a Medusa – I am sorry to think of anything so dreadful in association with such a dear creature – but indeed – people ought to approach Bowers Well now as Dante did the Tower at the gate of the city of Dis.

They should never venture, unless they have a friend to put his hand over their eyes or they are lost men –To be blindfolded at the bottom of the hill is their last chance, – their only one. I would not jest with you, but that I think you have had quite enough sorrow lately – believe me I feel for you – you must have suffered very much in being compelled to give so much pain and in parting from your old friends – and I feel for <u>them</u> still more – you may well say how much some people have to suffer in comparison with others. Still, I believe that most people have their share some time – if not in privation or bodily suffering, it comes in discomfort or discontent – or in sorrows of the affections –. How enviable most people would think <u>me</u> – yet you know I have had some share of acute pain, and in general feeling, <u>before</u> you took pity on me – my boy George [his man-servant] was the happier of the two. It made me question myself very seriously when I heard of these two grieved hearts – whether it was in my power to trust that the one which you had chosen was worth the sacrifice – I wonder if you will ever look back – and think that –. No – that you will not, I am sure – and it needs nothing to make me try to be all that I can be to you and for you – indeed I will do my best.[17]

John was not the only man who Effie had led on: far from it.

Here are at least six in Scotland alone; and these were just the ones that John knew about. He was however, as events unfolded, the only one with both the finance and the means of persuading his parents to allow him to marry into a family doomed to financial ruin.

To modern readers, John's surviving love letters to Effie appear alternately self-doubting, adolescently passionate, condescending and wisely prophetic. There are some excruciatingly embarrassing passages, but one thing is certain: he was absolutely besotted with Effie. On a Thursday afternoon in November John wrote to Effie from Denmark Hill; this is the full text of the letter:

My Dearest Euphemia,

What a pretty name you have – I like to write it in full, sometimes, it puts me in mind of old times – Do you recollect the first time I ever called you 'Effie' – when I was frightened at finding you practising in the cold drawingroom and stopped, and begged pardon – and your giving me leave an evening or two afterwards – What a luxury it was to call you Effie – and is – By the bye – you haven't told me anything about Captn. C. – and the happiness he looked forward to – Grant him that – but – I'm very sorry – I can't help it – don't be angry with me – I <u>would</u> rather he didn't call you Effie any more! <u>please</u>!

How difficult it is to be quite true – There was I, yesterday – making a great <u>merit</u> of telling you all that you asked – and pretending that I ought to be rewarded for it – as if I were not dying all day long to tell you everything I am doing and thinking – and only too happy to be asked or to be listened to! My Mother bade me say – last night – when I read her the passage in your letter about her coming – that you would not have to wait so long for her blessing – for she blesses you and prays for you every day of her life.

I think fortune is in my favour. You know we cannot be married in Lent – and Lent begins 8th. March – or thereabouts – So that – don't think me selfish or without a conscience – You know I can't help Lent's coming in the way – nor the necessity for our leaving England in April – It's very terrible – but indeed you will have to fix some day before the 8th. March – and I shall have to come to Scotland in February. My own love – Only two whole – unbroken – interminable months between us – if God permit. – I have been looking at your accounts of Mr. Tasker again – I feel sure he was feeling his way that night of the <u>West</u> – and if you had not walked so fast he would have spoken plainly – but you acted rightly & like yourself & saved him the mortification of direct refusal. But I have no patience with these cautious men.

You know – I often speak depreciatingly of myself. To show you this is not affectation – I will tell you that – as I was talking with Sir W. Ross in the Academy – last Tuesday – I came to the conclusion that I was worth <u>three</u> of him – both in sense and feeling – only he is a good natured person – and I like him, in a general way.

That's all I can tell you today – I have letters to answer by the dozen – but I shan't answer them, except by sixes and sevens.

Evening. My Mother gave me a message for you yesterday – which I forgot! an important one, too, that you must not – though – of course – you will know this without her telling you – but it may be as well to remind you – that any dresses you may be buying for next year, had better be of the plainest kind – for travelling – of stuffs that will not crush –

nor spoil, nor be bulky in a carriage – for you know we shall be <u>four</u> – and very simply made – you will only want one of any more visible or exhibitable kind – in case we might go to opera at Paris – or be seen a day or two here, before leaving. You may guess there is no <u>dressing</u> at Chamouni – the higher the rank commonly the plainer the dress – and it would be no use to leave handsome dresses behind you here, merely to find them out of fashion when you come back. You will not need them very warm – the climate of Chamouni is much about the same as that of Perth – morning and evening – but with hotter sun in the middle of the day – but have them close up to the throat – for fear of ice chills – <u>notice</u> this – which is <u>my</u> advice especially – and also – not to have the flounces <u>too</u> full – nor too <u>long</u> – it will not do to be exposed to chance of treading continually on your dress in going up hill – and the Swiss hills are steep, mind; – you had better have one dress quite cool – Geneva and Vevay are often as hot as Italy. For the rest – I need not say to you – knowing your good taste – not to have your best dresses <u>fine</u> or expensive – Your beauty is conspicuous without the slightest adornment – and the least <u>over</u> dress would appear as if you <u>wished</u> to draw all eyes to you – it should be your study to dress if possible – so as to <u>escape unobserved</u> – while yet the dress – when it <u>was</u> observed – should be perfect of its kind – becoming – graceful – perhaps even – now and then – a little piquant – but never conspicuous. I don't know – but I have a great fancy that I shall ask you sometimes to put on your finest dresses when we are alone – and always your simplest when we are going into public.

When we are <u>alone</u> –You and I – together – Mais – c'est inconcevable – I was just trying – this evening after dinner

– to imagine our sitting after dinner at Keswick – vous et moi. – I couldn't do it – it seemed so impossible that I should ever get you all to myself – and then I said to myself "If she should be dull – if she should not be able to think but of her sweet sisters – her deserted home – her parents giving up their chief joy – if she should be sad – what <u>shall</u> I do – either – how shall I ever tell her my gladness – Oh – my own Love – what shall I do indeed – I shall not be able to speak a word – I shall be running round you – and kneeling to you – and holding up my hands to you as Dinah does her paws – speechless – I shan't do it so well as Dinah though – I shall be clumsy and mute – at once perfectly oppressed with delight – if you speak to me I shall not know what you say – you will have to pat me – and point to something for me to fetch and carry for you – or make me lie down on the rug and be quiet – or send me out of the room until I promise to be a good dog; and when you let me in again – I shall be worse – What <u>shall</u> I do?

Friday evening. I have been correcting the last sheets of M.S. and am so tired. I couldn't do anything – except write to you – I feel quite rested directly.

I read the last page – no – stop – the one about the dress – to my mother – and quite got into disgrace – she asked me how I could possibly be so impertinent as to think you didn't know everything you ought to get – that she only meant me to hint that you needn't get dresses to be left at home – and that she begged pardon for hinting so much that – She said 'you would be thinking that we were afraid of your dressing too highly' – and that it was very wrong of me to say anything – But I don't think it was. I don't see how you could get your dresses with comfort to yourself – unless you had some idea of what I should like – and as you knew that I always <u>liked</u> to see you in full dress – it was just possible that you might have indulged me in this a little, contrary to your own taste – yet now that I read it over – it does read abominably impudent – I beg your pardon a thousand times, dear Effie: dress as you think best – I never saw you but well dressed, yet – though – for best of all bests – I am divided between the velvet knots, and the plaid over the head, – and in the garden, you know – when you first came – No – the best of all bests was – that night – the <u>wave</u> – but that won't do on all occasions.

Mama desires me to say that, far from being able to tell you how to dress, she wants you to come and tell her. She can't please herself, and she wants you for a thousand things besides.

We are all going to Folkestone for a week – I shall hardly be able to write you a word tomorrow – though I hope for a letter – but after this – I trust I shall be free.

I am a little ashamed of speaking so much of your fair face – Effie – but, indeed when I search into my heart – it is not the features that I care for – it is the sweet – kind – half pensive – depth of expression which is the great charm. I have been intending a long time to tell you this – but reserved it for the philosophical letter – only I am afraid of your again beginning to think that I only love you 'because you are pretty'.

Saturday. I have your precious letter – my love – I will write about March from Folkestone – D.V. – when I have thought over the matter a little to find out all that may be said in its favour – But how can you think of our 'quarrelling' – or make resolutions in case of such a contingency.

I am sure it is <u>physically impossible</u> – and this I say seriously. Fools may quarrel even when they love each other

– or wise people quarrel, when they don't; – but we are not fools – : I think we are both reasonable people – with something more than the average of sense – and then we love each other – how deeply? Tell mama she may just as well think of our quarrelling <u>before</u> marriage – as after it. – I expect it is the likelier – or rather the less inconceivable – and I think we are just as likely to give each other up altogether, as to do <u>that</u> – Ever my dearest – fairest – kindest Effie. Yours beyond all telling.[18]

John's overblown romantic style is highly reminiscent of his father's letters to his mother, which he had probably read since messages from John James to his son were regularly appended to them. They elicited a similar response from Mrs. Ruskin. In 1831 she had begged her husband to moderate his praise of her:

[I a]m always afraid when you have been away any time and your imagination painting visions of me that the reality may disappoint you [–] I beg my own you will not expect you will not fancy that which is not.[19]

In 1847 it was her son who received the warning:

you say you love her more the oftener you write to her may you not be in some degree surrounding her with imaginary charms – take care of this.[20]

Mr. Ruskin finally congratulated Effie on the engagement on 21st November 1847. It was a generally positive letter but he could not keep his fears hidden. The italics are the present author's.

My dear Effie
I do not write letters generally on a Sunday but I think I

cannot do better than to perform an omitted duty in writing a few lines to you on such a day. I have not had the
pleasure of addressing you since my son has obtained your
consent to a Union, on which I feel very sincerely convinced
(take place when it may) I shall have good reason to congratulate both myself and him – I have never yet seen the young
Lady nor should I know where to go in search of one more
likely in my mind to make my Son entirely happy or as
reasonably so, as a Wise man ought in this world to expect
– I only trust he may prove as well adapted for you as you seem
to be for him – you have both fine qualities and good talents
and your tastes and dispositions are sufficiently alike, differ-
ing only enough to make an agreeable variety, to prevent the
monotony perhaps Insipidity of entire agreement.

Mrs. Ruskin had various opportunities of sending pretty
messages – by your late intimation, I have been somewhat
remiss – but you have been no less in my thoughts – and my
Son and his Mother both knew that my Silence might be
taken as entire acquiescence in plans so promising of happiness to my Son. *From all you saw, or might guess at here, you
may fancy that my opinions have not always been what I now
express and that my approval comes late* – but dearest Effie –
my objections were never to <u>one</u> but to <u>two</u> – I cannot
perhaps correctly say two – my son never had two Loves but
he certainly during your visit to London had fully one and
a half and I was kept extremely uncomfortable with a double
source of anxiety – my son's happiness and Honour –

The young Lady that caused my uneasiness had, happily
penetration enough to see that my Son only offered her half
a heart and another Swain having fortunately brought her an
entire one, the affair terminated <u>en regle</u> and agreeable to all

parties – Whatever encouragement Circumstances led me to give my Son in his other pursuit, I can truly say that I am much more satisfied now that his success has been at Perth – I never saw the young Lady in question, I cannot therefore say I admired her – now I am only restrained from declaring myself your most devoted admirer by knowing that you have much more of this stile of Phraseology than you care for and that my son's letters may at present be suspected to run a good deal in the same strain –

It is very pleasant for all parties that there are as far as you yet discovered, no dissentients to this union, a point of some importance to the chief actors for it is lamentable to witness how often the happiness of the young is interrupted or marred by the contentions among their elders, always ready on occasions matrimonial, to come forth with bundles of objections, misunderstandings, whims and eccentricities, so that in a party of perhaps forty the only contents are the two carried off in the post Chaise – I earnestly hope that you will neither be visited by trouble before nor by regrets after the Ceremony, I cannot express a higher opinion of your merits and Character than by at once most readily entrusting my Son's future happiness in your Keeping – *I humbly trust that this union will have not only the approval of friends on Earth but of Heaven* and that under the happiest and holiest Influences you will both long live to enjoy each other's Society so living as to lay the foundation of a happiness that may be eternal. Give my kindest regards to your Mama and Papa George &c Accept of the same yourself – in all which Mrs Ruskin joins me.[21]

The reference to his silence and that his approval came late is an important indicator for his attitude to the marriage. He had obviously been cajoled into writing, 'an omitted duty', since his opinion had not always been approving and he still suspected Effie's motives. I would agree with Lady Eastlake that this letter is quite extraordinary as a potential father-in-law's letter to his son's intended. It seems calculated to raise in Effie's mind every-thing that could be wrong about it in this world and the next. The idea that there might be 'dissentients to this union' is surely a veiled reference to her other suitors. Likewise the 'trouble before' the ceremony, which could have been either to do with jilted suitors, or with Mr. Gray's imminent bankruptcy, or indeed both. The 'regrets after' needs no explanation in the light of what was to follow.

By 21st November John had received nineteen letters from Effie. According to John, letters passed between the couple daily for at least six months before the wedding. Only three of Effie's have ever come to light. Judging by the numbers written by John on the envelopes of these letters, the couple seem to have exchanged at least sixty letters during the engagement. In my own opinion none of Effie's remaining three are entirely convincing as love letters. I include them in their entirety for readers to make up their own minds.

> 8th February
>
> Again I do wish you many many happy birthdays my dear-est John. I should think you would experience a melancholy kind of feeling in thinking that this is the last birthday you will have in a Batchelor state. I hope you have the sun shin-ing on you in greater abundance than we have for rain here is the order of the day and very disagreeable it is, the damp weather is so relaxing that it quite glues me to the fire. Mama seems to be more fortunate in Edinburgh for she writes to me

of having called here and there and every place. I do not think I have yet answered your questions about stripes and spots but I have not forgotten it and I shall tell you what I think when I am more at leisure but at present I have not time to think about it. You see the children are all confined to the house yet with colds and when they are always in the nursery they weary, besides it is not good for them to be in one room for so long a time and when they come downstairs I have to amuse them. We are to have some gentlemen at dinner tomorrow and a party is always a consideration to me, not accustomed to the regulation of dinners excepting for ourselves, but I do not trouble myself much about it although I must see that everything is right, for Papa always says, 'My dear, you always give us a very good dinner, I don't understand these things you know!' I just wish the rain would stop and let me into town. I suppose you will say the same to me: 'Effie! I am particularly engaged with my third volume, and the one is a thing of very minor importance to the other. By-the-bye, Effie, you will oblige me by mending this box of pens.' Then you will put the pens into my hand and proceed with your writing, I will probably put the pens down, go and order the dinner myself and come back again and mend them, that is after I learn how! I hope, though, seriously, that your book will get on well and I will not tease you nor come near your study wherever that be while you are engaged in it unless you bid me. I told Papa the other day that you said you never would be jealous of me without cause and he says unfortunately jealous people always <u>find cause</u> which I think quite true but I hope at heart you are not really a jealous being, and the absurdity of your giving as a reason that my manner to you and with other people was quite the same is really the most preposterous thing I ever heard. You must have been thinking of something else when you wrote that! but really John I love you so very much that I do not think about <u>the</u> jealous part of you for I do not believe you will be at all so after we are married and I daresay you will allow me to ask any body I like to take some pudding without behaving afterwards as madly as Mr. Munn. Pray forgive me for this scrawl, I have a pen that won't write. Give my love to Mr. and Mrs. Ruskin and my devoted love to you, my dearest from Your

    Effie Gray[22]

9th February

My Dearest John,

I hope you enjoyed yourself yesterday with your friends, you would have I think a very agreeable party, we did not forget you, I am sure because after dinner Papa made quite a long speech in honor [sic] of the day as if you had been here, and again at night he had some negus before going to bed and he repeated the wish for your happiness. I am sorry to hear of Mrs. Moore being so poorly – what a fine expression she has! I am very glad that Mr. Moore gave you that sermon. I think you are coming round by degrees to the point I want you to arrive [at] but as all great changes are – not sudden but the work of time and affected by slow degrees – I care not how long you are in coming to his way of thinking so that you do arrive at the desired end – you will only become the more steady and certain in your conversion. So you are pleased with my attempts at adornment on Blucher [her pony]. Papa, barbarous man! had him shot one day privately and buried under the Beech tree; he said he had sent it out to grass for the winter. I suspected something wrong and by various entreaties I got so far into the Gardener's good graces that he told me he had shot it the savage! I mourned for it most bitterly. But you promise me some rides, now that is very good of you but I am afraid you will get nervous about me and say 'now my dear Effie don't go there you really will be off' and Mrs Ruskin will say I am sure the very first day after we have been out, she will tell you that my neck is in danger and that she wonders how you can allow me to do such a madlike thing but perhaps when she sees how blooming and healthy we look after it she may gradually begin to think that there cannot be so much danger in the thing after all. I shall be so glad to get into practice again in an exercise I am so fond of, I have not been on horseback for two years now but when one has been trained to it from childhood it is a thing you never can forget and I never was frightened. Robert [her brother] is quite well and has been feasting for the last few days on mutton chops, I could no longer stand his reproaches on soup-maigre. My wishing to see a Stork will quite come up to your first notion of having me all to yourself shut up in an old Tower where you would fly up and visit me! Papa says he cannot understand your wishing not to be married before going abroad. I quite think with you, but it would interfere terribly with modern propriety not to speak of the pleasure. No it wouldn't do at all! Your father is very kind, it is certainly very delightful to feel oneself loved. I hope he arrived in good health. Poor Mama is getting dreadful weather, it is pouring again but I hope that as we have had so much of it now the remainder of the Spring may be dry. I am much pleased with your description of your visit to Mrs. Bolding [Mary

Richardson], I shall write to her as I do not imagine she will think of writing to me. You will indeed like Mr. Macduff. Mr. MacDonald and he might be taken for brothers they are so much alike in general appearance. If it were not too absurd in me speaking of any body's writing but my own I should like to imitate your writing the word under-currents which I have just been able to decipher – it is so 12345678910

unduuuuuuuuu uts

all the same

Good bye and believe me

Ever entirely Your

Effie Gray[23]

10th February

My dearest John,

I do not know how I can sufficiently thank you for your estimable letter this morning so full of tenderness and affection almost too kind and good, you will quite spoil me, my love, it almost made me weep with joy to think myself so beloved, not but that I was fully impressed with that before, but this morning's letter almost made me rejoice too much in thinking that so much happiness was permitted to me who am so unworthy of it. I am indeed happy beyond telling in thinking you love me so much and truly glad am I if by expressing my earnest desires for continued happiness on your part I added one moment of pleasure on your birthday to you – I wish I could have added my thoughts more fully to my wishes for you and was much dissatisfied that my letter was so unexpressive of my feelings for had you been here much more should I have said to what I wrote. Many trials we shall probably have but not from want of love on either part, that must be the greatest trial I think in married life, finding that the only being perhaps in the world whose affection is necessary to you as a part of your being not loving and assisting you in all your joys and cares, leaving you with the utmost indifference when you are in trouble to get out of it the best you can, and in Joy not partaking the feeling but perhaps trying to subdue it if not in a similar mood, this would be I think the summit of wretchedness and misery. You who are so kind as a son will be a perfect lover as a husband. I meant by saying that we had much to find out in each [other] was not that I expected to find great faults in you, I think I know all that I have to expect and I shall see your coat brushed and mend your gloves and especially keep you from wearing white hats, and in order to compromise the matter with you I shall promise never to wear an <u>excessively</u> Pink Bonnet which can be seen all over the Exhibition although I suppose you have not particular objection to one of a paler hue. Pink is a very favourite colour of mine but I will subdue the shade out of respect to your superior discernment in these matters. I did not think your cousin Mary would consider it necessary to write to me so I wrote to her a few lines yesterday just to say I hoped she had no objections to the approaching relationship between us. I have numerous letters of congratulation now from all my lady acquaintances, all saying nearly the same thing, thinking I have bright prospects before me and much happiness but expressive of great disgust at you for taking me away from them all. My dinner party went off very well yesterday. Bobbie says Mr. Ruskin is a very good gentleman, why can't he always stay here with you, I'll give it to him when he comes if he says he will

take you away, you are never to go away (suiting the action
to the word he lays on the whip to the chair with no small
force, as if you were the chair or rather the chair you).

Goodbye my dearest love

Ever Yours in all sincerity

Euphemia C Gray[24]

There is no telling how representative these letters were of the
scores of other letters she wrote. A couple of weeks previous to
this, John's mother, who had obviously not seen John's more unrestrained correspondence with Effie, noted that: 'very few what
are called love letters are so purely affectionate as John and
Effie's, hers so loving yet so free from passion as well as John's.'[25]
Passionless love letters seem a contradiction in terms. Likewise
Effie expressing her delight that John loves her is not quite the
same as expressing her love for him. On Effie's own admission
John later used one of her letters written to him before the
marriage as an example of her duplicity.[26] At the time of the annulment he gave several to his proctor as evidence, letters which Effie's
brother Albert seems later to have acquired illegally and burnt.
We must also take into account that these are letters written by
a nineteen-year-old with a lot on her mind. She was worrying
about her father's financial affairs, her mother's pregnancy, the
impending marriage and her former suitors. One of her very first
letters to John had mentioned that her hair was falling out to the
extent that she might need artificial aids. For at least some of the
engagement period she was looking after her poorly siblings
confined to the house, and eventually she herself took to her bed.
She also claimed to be suffering severe letter fatigue after all the
letters she had written in reply to the relentless stream of correspondence from her intended and blamed the constant letter

writing for her weakness, a point that her mother took up with the Ruskins. John, who back in January had naively harboured hopes of Effie helping him in his work, complained about her handwriting: 'As you say – your hand might conceivably be better; considered as an MS and notebook hand – and though I am the last in the world who has any business to talk about writing – yet for that very reason, it may be in your power to do me much service by writing legibly.'[27] By the 23rd of February and obviously sceptical about the letter-fatigue, he protested that he did not detect any evidence of either labour or effort in her letters to him, in fact they had been written easily and rapidly and were not overlong. By this time he had also detected a distinct lack of enthusiasm in the constant complaints: 'I do think that ever since you left us last summer you have been managing yourself very ill – and I think it a little hard that your father and mother should lay all the blame on your writing to me.'[28] If Effie found letter writing a trial, John pestered Effie for letters, made a ceremony out of reading them and could hardly finish them before he was scribbling his grateful responses. He re-read them avidly:

> I have been reviewing your letters tonight – I have got one, already – for every year of your life – and that's a great many, you know my love – ! though you are not so very old, I will allow. [...] I have been thinking how long it will be before I know all your letters by heart. Not long – Yet I should so like to have them printed, in a little pocket volume – to carry about with me always.[29]

It wasn't only the letter writing that irked Effie. From John's replies we can see that she seems to have had a more general problem with keeping up her enthusiasm for the engagement. With her hair falling out she suggested hopefully that people don't care for looks after marriage. She worried about John being jealous of her with other men and accused him of only loving her 'because she was pretty'. She assumed that he would be melancholy at the prospect of no longer being single because she herself was so. She thought about them quarrelling after they were married and made resolutions about what she should do. She wished she could make him more happy. She strongly resisted the idea of bringing the marriage forward to February when John suggested it in November and repeatedly told him how sad she was. 'My Dear Euphemia – your's would not have been the first letter that expressed sad thoughts in its joy' he wrote to her in response to her complaining:

> And so – love – you did not know how to tell me how heartsick you were! Do you not think that for once you might have told me to judge you by <u>myself</u>. Think – my Effie – what a difference between you – with brother and sisters – and many many – countless friends about you – not to speak of Papa and Mama; – and me – alone here on the sea beach –. May not you – when you are heartsick another time tell me that you feel a little – a very little – as I do?[30]

She had written him a letter after a long sleepless night:

> What can keep you from sleeping my pet – All night – too! Now pray – pray don't – it is very bad indeed of you – what are you so anxious about – one would think you were <u>miserable</u> at the thought of April. But do not write me long letters after sleepless nights.

The suspicion that she was having second thoughts re-appeared in the postscript: 'You are not thinking of saying that you have "been thinking about it" or "writing to a friend" – and won't have me now! Are you?'[31] And again in his letter of 15th December he wondered about her other lovers: 'when I heard of those two grieved hearts – whether it was in my power to trust that the one you had chosen was worth the sacrifice – I wonder if you will ever look back – and think that – No – that you will not I am sure.'[32] John's concern at Effie's lack of enthusiasm seems also to have provoked a reassuring letter from Mrs. Gray which John mentioned:

> It says you are looking so well – and so happy, – and that you love me very much; and it says that mama has no fear for you in giving you to me, and that she would let you come and visit us now – if it were right![33]

Unfortunately, and even before he had finished his reply, a 'little note' arrived from Effie that 'put me so out of heart that I can't write any more'. This time she was suffering from a headache which by 18th December had caused her to take to her bed. Her brother George took over the letter writing until the following Monday. John helpfully promised her a letter every day.

By February 23rd John was again anxious about her health. She had complained of losing her youthful spirit, being nervous, despondent, 'outwearied', weak, miserable and was constantly playing piano in a minor key. He sympathised with her position:

> That you have had charge of an household – anxiety about your mother's health, agitation respecting ~~pain unavoidably given to~~ your lovers has all been unavoidable – but it has been most unfortunate.[34]

He tactfully suggested that she should avoid all 'excitement of society – or of music', concentrate on 'healthful and unexciting studies', such as Botany, and go to bed early:

> I don't believe myself, that the going to Edinburgh will do
> you much good but anything is better than the way you are
> going on now.[35]

On 28th February Effie finally wrote a happy letter to John describing how she had been dancing madly at a party at Bowerswell. Even so John felt it necessary to chide her for her negative attitude to the wedding: 'Distressed Love I know no cure for, but I think promised love ought to make people more industrious and happy – and not "fit for nothing all day".'[36] On March 1st Effie travelled to Edinburgh where she was to attend the marriage of a friend from Avonbank school and then meet John. Apart from the opportunity to see his future wife, John did not think Edinburgh was a good idea. He begged her not to write to him whilst she was there lest it made him more anxious. Whilst in Edinburgh and before John arrived Effie stayed at the home of Lord Cockburn, the father of yet another Avonbank girl. Being back in society effected a miracle cure on Effie. From being unable to stir a limb or lift a pen, Effie not only regained her liveliness and stamina but wrote at least three letters home about what she was getting up to. Of a party at Lady Murray's which she attended before her future husband arrived she told her mother that 'the ladies are all perfectly dressed, a great many <u>nobs</u> and Dragoons + fine uniforms, great flirtations, and splendid music [...] the music lasted till twelve then we had dancing till three in the morning. I got introduced to good partners and got some good polking.'[37] The half-page immediately before this revealing snippet has been torn out. It was perhaps as well that Effie did not write to John in this vein; it would certainly have given him cause for concern. Effie also attended a party at Lord Jeffrey's arriving on the arm of the aged Lord Cockburn. On being asked their names in order to be announced Lord Cockburn told the flunkey 'say, Lord Cockburn and his second wife'! Effie reported this incident with great glee to her mother, but it was not the sort of remark any father would appreciate in connection with his daughter; particularly when she was due to be married. John was delighted with the version of the story he heard: 'But you must not only be a very happy creature – but a very clever creature or the old Judges would not give you whole hours of tête-à-têtes.'[38]

On the 6th of March John told Effie not to tell anyone when he was coming to Edinburgh:

> There are moments when I think you have been a foolish girl to marry me – I am so nervous, and weak, and – dreamy – and really ill & broken down – compared to most men of my age, that you will have much to bear with and to dispense with – my father was for many years in the same state, and it ended in his secluding himself from all society but that which he sees in his own house. I inherit his disposition – his infirmities, but not his power – while the morbid part of the feeling has been increased in me by the very solitude necessary to my father. At this moment, the dread I have of the bustle of Edinburgh is almost neutralizing the pleasure I have in the hope of being with you – it amounts to absolute <u>panic</u>. And – above all – in speaking of me to your friends, remember that I am really not well. Do not speak of me as able (though un-willing) to do this or that – but remember the real frets – that late hours – & excitement of all kinds are just as direct and certain <u>poison</u> to me as so much arsenic or hemlock and that the <u>least</u> thing excites me. From a child, if I turned from one side to another as I slept, the pulse was quickened instantly

and this condition has of late years been aggravated by over work – and vexation. I have been four years doing the mischief – and it will be two or three at any rate, before, even with the strictest care it can be remedied. – Take care that you make people understand this as clearly as possible.[39]

The contrast between the two letters is most marked. Effie revelled in social occasions, dancing and late nights. Wherever she went she was surrounded by fit young men. At Perth, William was a soldier back from India; James 'Prizie' Tasker was her vigorous polka partner; 'Captn. C.' seems also to have held a position of physical responsibility, either as a military man or on a ship. John himself told Macdonald that Effie was 'surrounded by people who pay her attentions, and though I believe most of them inferior in some points to myself, far more calculated to catch a girl's fancy.' To Mrs. Gray he admitted: 'I think, always, that if I had been a woman, I never should have loved the kind of person that I am.' Whether or not she loved John, Effie must have known that she was going to be married to a husband whose personality was the complete opposite to her own, and who was not in good health. Not only that, but his health was made worse by the very things that Effie so loved to do.

CHAPTER IX

A SPECULATIVE MAN

❧

If John was worried that he might not be as attractive or loveable as Effie's other admirers, Mr. Ruskin's letters to John had expressed his deep concern that Effie might be 'acting under Orders',[1] have 'motives of ambition more than Love' and that her affection might be 'tutored' knowing how desirable the union was to her father.[2] He was implying that Mr. Gray might be attempting to arrange a marriage of convenience for Effie because of his financial difficulties. In a letter of March 1848 to Mr. Gray, Mr. Ruskin told him he had already been told that he, Gray, was financially ruined six months previously.[3] If the six months is an accurate period, and where time and money were concerned Mr. Ruskin was generally accurate, this was in late September 1847: just before John called at Bowerswell.

Perth was a town of speculators and Mr. Gray was an inveterate speculator. He had travelled to the United States in 1843 in order, according to his son, to see about land speculation;[4] he speculated heavily in the previous phase of the railway share bubble and was subsequently excited both by 'Australasian Banks'[5] and California gold mines.[6] Mr. Ruskin later told Mr. Gray that:

> long since indeed I used to say jocularly that from speculative propensities I believed to prevail in Perth. I did not in a business point of view value any gentleman there as to property at 3 months purchase.[7]

Just before John went to Bowerswell, Mrs. Ruskin wrote to him about Mr. Gray:

The Gray family, *by J. E. Millais. This is an imaginary sketch of a party at Bowerswell in 1853. George Gray, whom Millais had met briefly, is at the far left. Effie, is playing the piano and her mother is at the far right. Millais had not met her, but Ruskin commented on the likeness. George Gray Jnr. is dancing at the centre*

He has I believe at present been over persuaded by friends and brought himself into some difficulties with railroads but he is prompt, knows business, and I have great hopes will see his way and pursue it with Steadiness, and may not be so great a loser in the end. I am led to hope this because many years ago he came to London in a great hurry about some business he with some friends had entered into and which though promising at first threatened in the end to involve them in difficulty and hazard.[8]

Like thousands of other provincial middle class investors (including the Brontë sisters, Thackeray, Darwin, J. S. Mill and Charles Babbage), George Gray had put his money and property into buying shares in the new railway lines that were being built. Successive bouts of this railway investment mania had occurred in 1824-5 and 1835-7 and another had culminated in 1845. Railway share prices had begun to rise as early as 1843, just before Mr. Gray began the expensive rebuild of Bowerswell House. Several soundly based schemes had given high returns on the investment and share prices rose steadily until 1845. By 1846 this had resulted in a fever of railway speculation with many more lines being floated than were feasible. One third of the total mileage of railways authorized between 1844 and 1847 was never built. Some schemes were undoubtedly fraudulent, others merely well advertised. Government legislation did nothing to dampen the mania. The 1844 Railway Bill had not capped dividends at 10% and had allowed some railway companies to submit accounts which did not allow for depreciation on fixed assets. This resulted in continued public expectation of inflated profits and the promise of high dividends on shares, which in turn lifted share prices even higher. Railway Bills were rushed through Parliament in 1846 much faster than was sensible. Famously, the Board of Trade offices were besieged by railway scheme promoters on the last day for the submission of plans for the 1846 Parliamentary session. The share price bubble attracted thousands of new investors. Investment in the railways rose from less than £4m per year in the early forties to over £30m in 1847: a sum so staggering that it has been represented as 45% of total domestic capital investment.

The railway companies had adopted as standard practice the issuing of shares for a small deposit, only calling up the remainder of the value of the share as the company progressed. Different types of investor would join the scheme at different stages. A person wishing to earn a regular dividend for his investment would be more interested in a fully paid-up share. The get-rich-quick investor, anxious to make big money fast, would be more interested in rises in share prices than regular dividends. He would therefore be more tempted by the original issue which could be acquired for as little as £1 called, and sold at a profit later.

Mr. Gray, at one time worth £25,000 in property giving 5% interest plus £3,000-4,000 a year from his legal business, had invested heavily in both British and continental railway shares.[9] Like thousands of other investors he had acquired shares for a small deposit and had only seen them increase in value. The Railway Share Price Index rose from 93.3 in February 1843 to 167 in July 1845. However, after this peak in late summer 1845, shares began to plunge in value; and between 1846 and 1850 the value of railway stocks collapsed by 50%. The railway companies had begun to call in the balances on deposit shares. To most investors the collapse would only have become really apparent in mid 1846.[10] Wise investors would have sold out then. Wealthy investors such as Mr. Ruskin could hope to ride out the crash. George Gray was neither of these. With hindsight the first inkling of her father's impending difficulty was undoubtedly Effie's repeated attempts beginning in April 1847 to get a job for her brother George at Ruskin, Telford and Domecq.[11] A letter of the following month also noted gloomily that:

> Mrs. Gardner told me yesterday that their next door neighbour + tenant Mr. Webster had been speaking about Papa to Mr. G and saying he knew him. The Railway I suppose.[12]

The situation for holders of railway shares deteriorated rapidly in the autumn. A severe financial crisis had developed owing to the failure of the British and Irish harvests two years running and the general necessity of importing food. Imports such as Russian wheat had to be paid for in bullion, which depleted the Bank of England reserves. This in turn severely limited the amount of cash in circulation because this was linked to the gold reserves by an Act of Parliament specifically designed to prevent speculative bubbles. The result was that interest rates began to rise to unprecedented heights and, starved of credit, the railway companies called in the remaining balance on their shares. The repeal of the Corn Laws and the prospect of a good harvest resulted in the Corn Bubble collapsing which caused mass failures of corn speculators and in the general scramble for currency, commercial failures rocketed, leading to the threat that financial institutions would default. Four banks failed. Bullion ships still at sea were turned round and returned to England to take advantage of soaring interest rates. This crisis would come to be known as the 'October Panic' or 'the week of terror', when the entire financial system came close to meltdown. George Gray was one of thousands caught up in the devastating financial distress that followed. This, then, was the background to John's proposal to Effie Gray in the second and third weeks of October 1847.

When Mr. Ruskin wrote to George Gray in February 1848 he began: 'I lose not a day in replying to your kind letter of 21st inst. I will begin at the end of it.' This meant that the first topic of concern to George Gray in his (missing) letter was 'Railroads' with remarks on his daughter's marriage added at the end. Mr. Ruskin's priorities were precisely the opposite.

> You expect that Mrs. Ruskin and I should come to Perth and nothing can be more reasonable – I at once acknowledge, we ought to come; but with Mrs. Ruskin's feelings and prejudices I scarcely dare contend – for my own part, I am sincerely desirous of coming, but on the best consideration I can give the subject – I have decided to keep away – I cannot possibly tell any person – who, most happily like yourself – may be ignorant of all nervous affections, what uncertain poor

Creatures we are who once have been brought under the sway of such feelings – Were I like others – well and accustomed to visit and take up my abode in friends Houses, assuredly I should find myself at Perth towards the end of April – but having run the gauntlet of most of the disorders human nature is exposed to, and having my frame weakened and my nerves unstrung by the consequences, I can only exist in the absence of all excitement – that is by leading a quiet life – It is just 30 years this 1848 since I slept in a friend's house. I take mine ease at an Inn continually and I go on with my business pretty well – I have thought I might come to Perth but if I were unwell – I should only be in the way – a marplot and a nuisance.

I might merely say that if we are to go abroad with the young people I require every previous hour here that I can get – and besides I deemed it would be as pleasant for my son to be at Perth for a week or two and then in place of having an assemblage beforehand like the British Association – to get quietly married and steal away and leave the good folks to talk over it the next day – but my notions follow my nature which has always been rather retiring.

I can only assure you that though I may not appear at the Ceremony I shall not be absent nor wanting in giving my Daughter in Law a warm Welcome here – We anticipate (I mean Mrs. R. and myself) the greatest pleasure and nothing else than pleasure in the meeting and all that may follow that event – I fear I shall not stand excused in your eyes, nor in Mrs. Gray's but indeed my dear Sir – there is prudence at my time of life and with my temperament in not exposing oneself to more excitement than duty renders imperative.

I will now come to Railroads ...[13]

Mr. Ruskin's excuses for not attending the wedding might seem quite flimsy. This was after all the marriage of his only son and heir. He may well not have made a habit of staying at friend's houses, but he had spent a good part of his life travelling and staying in hotels. There was nothing to stop him booking into an hotel. It could even have been outside Perth if he was worried about Mrs. Ruskin's 'feelings and prejudices' arising from the horrific events of 1817 at Bowerswell House. In one of his first letters to Effie after the engagement John told her he did not expect his mother to attend the wedding because 'she would feel too much.'[14] Mr. Ruskin mentioned his health but this generally did not interfere with his travels for his business or the extensive Continental journeys he chose for relaxation. He twice mentions the wish to avoid the kind of excitement that weakens the frame and unstrings the nerves, the solution for which was that John and Effie should marry quietly, steal away and let the gossips do their worst the next day. Clearly it was this fear of 'excitement' that worried him most and, in discussing it, his mind slid naturally into the subject of Railroads.

In France the February Revolution had culminated in two days of street fighting in Paris in the course of which cries for reform changed into cries for a republic. On the second day, February the 24th, Louis-Philippe abdicated and fled to England. Mr. Ruskin's change of mind thus occurred on the day before the fall of the Bourbon Monarchy in France. This was the event that rendered Gray's shares in the Boulogne-Amiens Railway worthless and made his financial situation all but irrecoverable. Investment in France had collapsed by 15% since 1847 and railway stock was particularly implicated. By 1850 the volume of investment was down 27%. If George Gray had already been in deep trouble before, it was now even worse. The Ruskin parents' absence from the wedding would seem therefore to have been clearly linked to George Gray's financial situation and John's father's understanding of the nature of the marriage in that light. At that late stage he may not have been able to prevent the wedding but he could at least show his disapproval by not attending what had become for him a potential public humiliation in his home town.

By March 10th Mr. Ruskin had a draft marriage settlement prepared for George Gray to peruse. When he read Mr. Gray's reply he discovered that Effie would not be bringing a dowry with her. In the light of what he already knew of Gray's financial position this was not unexpected:

> I have recd. safely the Dft of Settlement and your Letter of 15 Mch which I am greatly obliged by – It is <u>not</u> likely to make the smallest difference with us – indeed if you do not, as often happens in such cases, deceive yourself or are led to plunge farther into Railroads – your situation is much better than I expected – I had no right to conclude you were without property and I therefore asked what you inclined to do for Phemy but my disposition is to look to the worst side of things, and my son already knows that I feared you were entirely ruined [...] I thought it best to prepare my son for the worst that the Information you now so kindly give me might not poison the cup of happiness I trust they are about to taste –
>
> If you can avoid a public breaking up and continue a business of £800 a year – you are just so much better than I led John to expect but for Godsake be done with Rails and Shares – or you will not have a Business, for who will confide in Railroad people I am not clear – if it affords you any

Consolation – I may lose £2000 – I hope not – but I give it up and neither I nor my son are likely to touch any speculative property – I don't think so much of my own commercial Character since I touched these Trash – You say <u>you may still lose</u> a large sum by Investments – have you yet calls to meet? I am awfully suspicious in mercantile affairs I may as well be frank with you and say I do not believe you can recover yourself – but you must keep a good heart and if you and George keep close to Business I don't think you or Mrs. Gray should fret about past losses – I could do very well at Perth now with £500 a year – all beyond brings turmoil and slavery but you enjoy society and feel differently – I am not well from politics and disgust at the French and greatly disappointed about our tour abroad.[15]

John meanwhile was in Edinburgh where he met Effie at her uncle's home. What she told him prompted him to write a letter to Mr. Gray.

17th. March

As we were returning yesterday – together from Craigmillar Castle (a fourteenth century ruin) she touched upon a subject which has (most unnecessarily as far as I am concerned) – caused of late such uneasiness to both her and you. Had even the communication which she made to me, been entirely unexpected by me, it would have produced no other impression upon me than one of gratitude for the candour and courage of the avowal – (accompanied of course – by such concern as I must ever feel for whatever cause of anxiety may occur to you or Mrs. Gray), but it was fortunate, as it happened, that I was able to set Effie's heart at rest at once, by assuring her that I had known of the unfavourable posture of your affairs at the time of my first proposals to her: and even previously, and although not certain of the extent of your losses – I had always been prepared for, and partly believed the worst.

I cannot state to you the exact time at which reports on this subject first reached my father: but he immediately warned me that they were such as he could not distrust, and this before my visit to you last Autumn. It was partly owing to this information that I departed from my first intention of not visiting Perth at that time, – and I find that I was right in attributing as I did, Effie's change of manner to me, in some degree to this cause, though, not knowing how far she was acquainted with the state of your affairs I could not venture to question her, or endeavour to arrive at any certain conclusion on the subject – My offer to her was however made sooner, on this ground, than it would otherwise have been.

Permit me however to assure you that – with whatever indifference – as far as they regard myself – I may look upon these unfortunate circumstances, believing as I do, that my dear Effie's comfort may be secured – and I trust – your hopes for her not disappointed, by the resources which my fathers kindness has put in our power; it is not without deep concern that I can think of the distress they may cause to you and to Mrs. Gray, – nor without much regret that I hear it is not yet in your power to extricate yourself from a position the anxiety of which must be even more grievous than the actual losses it may still necessitate. I am too well aware of your judgement – and decision of character – to venture even to hint an opinion to you on such subjects: but I may perhaps permit myself to express my own <u>feeling</u>, that loss is better than entanglement; and sacrifice than anxiety; and that impatience which makes an <u>end</u> of evil is often a truer friend to us than the patience which makes the best of it. The opinion of the world in such matters is, I have heard, little to be dreaded, because it is commonly right, and grants more respect to the confession of an error, than was lost by its commission.

For the present it grieves me much that I can be of so little service to you –; there are however modes in which hereafter I may be able to relieve you from some anxiety. This may perhaps be especially the case with respect to your two youngest daughters – it is fortunate that they are still so young: as, before you can have any cause for care respecting them, Effie and I shall – I hope have become settled and sage people – quite fit to be trusted with one or both – if you can spare them – and should then think it desirable that they should see something of such English society as we may be able to command – I should have looked forward at any rate to this plan – as both delightful for Effie and me – and not disadvantageous for <u>them.</u> For the rest, I hope that your energy and high standing in your profession may soon be the means of extricating you from all painful embarrassment, – and at all events, I trust that both Mrs. Gray and you will believe that these, in other respects unfortunate, circumstances have caused to me, selfishly and personally, no feeling but one of gladness at being enabled in any way to assure you or prove to you how priceless a treasure I count myself to possess in the hand of your daughter.[16]

Note that John suggested to Mr. Gray that he now believed that Effie's manner towards him had changed at Bowerswell back in October partly because she had learned of her father's financial situation. Lutyens inferred that Effie, knowing her father had financial problems, was too proud to continue with John. The two urgent letters Effie sent to John at Leeds absolutely contradict this supposition. I firmly believe that Effie's manner towards John had changed at Bowerswell because she did not love him and knowing about her father's financial problems she feared that if John spoke with her father she might be coerced into a marriage of convenience. Her manner changed again after she discovered that her father was not merely temporarily embarrassed but in fact feared absolute ruin. She then either wrote or was persuaded to write the two letters to Leeds that led to the engagement.

By March 1848 both John and his father were proceeding on information supplied by the Grays. John, who admitted in a postscript that he had not spoken to his father on the subject since before he saw Mr. Gray at Perth in October, naïvely supposed that, whatever happened, George Gray would be able to continue to earn a living as a lawyer. In fact if he went bankrupt ('a public breaking up') his reputation and his business would also have suffered badly. Mr. Ruskin, ever suspicious of Gray's motives, was right to ask Mr. Gray about the true extent of his losses. When the reply came it made him very angry with Mr. Gray:

22nd. March

I have your kind letter of 20 Inst. and have consulted a person of very sound Judgement on Railroad Shares – He considers Boulogne as mere Lottery tickets – as total Blanks on prizes of perhaps £10 each – To holders he says – if they have no other means of making Calls – sell – 200 shares may give £1000 – To those who can Keep – Keep. Everything depends on the individual having power to hold Railroad Property by settling all calls without selling them – at this period they should hold on for no doubt all Railroad Property is below its value – from the circumstances of your having bought 200 shares in Boulogne in which I thought myself venturous to take 25 and from your saying you have heavy calls to meet I have no hope of your getting clear – my Son seems to have gleaned as much at Edin. – you desired me to keep your situation private – now – my dear Sir it may do good to tell you that six months ago when you were far better than you are now – you were publicly reported to me as a ruined man we cannot mishear the world in these things long and it is ill natured enough to anticipate any fall. I knew your engagements which are publicly reported and you will I fear find its report true in the end – What distresses me is not your having nothing but your having to go to Bankruptcy and so losing confidence of the County of Perth and perhaps 2/3ds of your Business.

I am also sorely vexed at your just taking this time to disturb the young people who cannot pay your Calls – for John knows my Severity in money matters – that though I give where I can – were he to be Security for a Single hundred for the best friend he has – he should never see a shilling more of my money – I am so upset myself at hearing of any speculation that I would almost beg the great Kindness of you neither to tell me nor John and, if I dare presume, nor Phemy anything about such affairs – I am as I told you nervous and easily made ill and my health is of some Consequence of John and Phemy yet. I should be greatly obliged if you could postpone any winding up – for a few months, after that I shall be prepared for the worst.

I conclude your House is already as good as gone – I am happy to see my son's Letter pleased you – He will write in a very different strain and feeling – but I am naturally annoyed at all this coming on the young people – Had you frankly told me in Octr. or Novr. it would surely have been better than just at the consummation – Excuse all this plain speaking, or say writing. I had the same sort of thing with my Brother in Law whom I used to tell when he [wasted?] of his property that I did not value any man in Perth at fifty shillings. I ought not with such opinions ever show my face there.[17]

By February 1848, Mr. Gray's continental railway shares had become virtually worthless, but he still had to meet his instalment payments on these and his other shares. He only told Mr. Ruskin about this new position towards the end of March. This was what John was talking about when he later stated that two weeks before they were married, Effie had told him that her father 'had lost immense sums by railroads', and that George Gray himself had said that he was entirely ruined and must leave his house immediately.[18] Remember that Mr. Gray was a lawyer, a professional expert in bankruptcy proceedings. John later stated that this revelation 'entirely destroyed the immediate happiness of my marriage'.[19] One reason for this was that even if Mrs. Ruskin had not absolutely decided not to travel to Perth for the wedding in November 1847,[20] by the 23rd of February 1848 Mr. Ruskin had decided that neither of them should attend the ceremony.[21] Not wanting to worry the youngsters, Mr. Ruskin had not told them anything about the latest calamities. John only found out about the latest situation from Effie in late March just before she left Edinburgh for Perth to help with the preparations for the wedding.

By March 28th Mr. Gray was proposing that the ceremony, which the Ruskin parents had wanted to be in May and the Grays had fixed for April 23rd to avoid Lent, be brought forward into

Lent itself; very unusual for a marriage and specifically against Mrs. Ruskin's original wishes. Since invitations may already have been sent out for the original date, the reason for this late change must have seemed pressing indeed. In the event the date was still uncertain four days before the actual marriage! On 6th April Effie explained to Pauline Trevelyan that this may have prevented:

> these few lines in compliance with your kind wish to know our marriage day from reaching you in time, but I could not tell you the exact time as it was only fixed this morning owing to some arrangements of our mutual friends not being able to come at the same time; but we now intend that the ceremony shall take place on Monday afternoon [the 10th April] at four o'clock.[22]

This is a most unconvincing excuse, particularly since in the same letter Effie wrote that John had rushed off to Rossie Castle, one of Macdonald's places near Montrose, obviously to tell the best man about the change.

Effie's uncle Andrew Jameson was so shocked by the new financial revelations that he wrote to his sister Mrs. Gray on the 30th March: 'I am much distressed about you all and cannot think about anything else. I need not say how much we feel for you in this calamity.'[23] The reason for these sudden shifts of dates so soon before the wedding can only have been that George Gray believed that Bowerswell House was about to be seized by his creditors. From his letters Mr. Ruskin certainly believed this to be the case and George Gray did not contradict him. John later mentioned that: 'Mr. Gray, coming over [to Edinburgh] himself, told me he was entirely ruined and must leave his house immediately. His distress appeared very great [...]'[24] According to the Scotch custom the marriage ceremony was of course going to be held in the drawing room of the house about to be seized. No wonder John's father feared 'excitement' at the wedding; no wonder John didn't invite any of his friends.

Although furious with George Gray for not admitting his true position, Mr. Ruskin was pragmatic. He found the financial problems worrying, but the money itself did not constitute a major problem, just so long as Effie loved John and John loved Effie. Remembering that John had almost died after being forbidden to marry Adèle, his parents did not want to risk his health again whatever the cost. In any case, by this time the wedding was a *fait accompli*. The only course now was to pull together and steady the ship, which was essentially the subject of Mr. Ruskin's letter to Gray of the 28th of March:

> I trust to you meeting the future difficulties of your situation with fortitude and for the sake of Mrs. Gray and your fine family, applying your great good sense and fine energies to the preservation of a property which can never leave you, if you give your whole attention to it – I mean your Business – as I have allowed myself the privilege of a friend, I may once for all mention that I have thought George's Education rather too much varied and interrupted with pleasure for a man of Business and his application and steadiness are now of immense importance – I see no reason for allowing your own powers to be lessened by suffering for the past, you are only in the position of thousands who have tried the speculations of the day. I have a customer who 15 years ago could have retired on £130,000 – and he can just pay everybody and not have a shilling left. Railroads – and concerns promising 30% Int.t have done this. The danger is not your being in vigour of mind and Body enough to prosecute your daily

affairs. – If you are, you are still in the prime of Life and may live to be a wealthy man – There is a proverb in Spain that <u>a man is never dead, till he gives himself up</u> – I should hope your friends who have given you funds will be lenient and not vindictive – If a public exposure could be avoided – their Interests would be greatly served for I know your genuine goodness of heart and uprightness and that if such a quiet arrangement could be arrived at as to leave you possessed of an undiminished Business – they, your Crs [creditors] would I believe profit by some sinking fund you would make from your spare profits – I speak from my notion that part of your good Business is being factor for Gentlemen of Landed property, – now half of this would go perhaps if the whole extent of your late Operations were known – Whereas if you can weather the storm although it is well known that you have touched Railroads, the Injury to your Business would be much less than a public exposure would inflict –

I do not blame you individually for bold speculation – you are in a speculative society – and country – my miscalled Cautious Countrymen are all speculative. They like amusement and getting rich without labour – but there is nothing like keeping to our <u>Shop</u> whatever it be – you are all right yet whichever way you close accounts of purchases already made if you have courage to shun any new attempt to retrieve your fortunes –

In your case I should never make but one experiment – namely – to try how much could be made out of a Law Business in the Town of Perth – Supposing your speculations had all succeeded – what would have been the mighty addition to your happiness? There is no slavery like the slavery of fashion and high life – Mrs. Gray's society is the same and your children smile as sweetly with £500 a year as £5000 – and you enjoy much more of the Society of both than if you had to enact the great man which is generally done before the world and at the expense of domestic Comfort.

I suppose you will have my Son at Perth directly. There is no objection to the marriage taking place before the end of Lent if more convenient for all parties although I wrote we should prefer the end of Lent, but we leave all to them and you and Mrs. Gray.[25]

John, besotted with Effie, had at first been glad to be the knight errant for the Grays in their financial dire straits, even if it was with his father's money. His 'offer' had, he said, been 'made sooner on this ground than it would otherwise have been' implying by this that the marriage would somehow alleviate the dire situation. He later described how at this time: 'The whole family rested on me for support and encouragement – Mr. Gray declaring I was their "sheet anchor".' Of course John could only take Effie off their hands, he had no independent means of helping the Grays financially. Thus: 'no effort whatever was made to involve me in their embarrassments – nor did I give the slightest hope of being able to assist Mr. Gray who, I believed must assuredly have become bankrupt.'[26] But John was their only hope. Whatever her real feelings for him, once Effie realised that the bankruptcy of her father would have a catastrophic effect, not just on her family, but also on her own marriage prospects and lifestyle, she would have been willing enough to make the sacrifice. Her other suitors might have backed off in the face of the impending family ruin, simply because they or their families did not have sufficient means to help out. However it is far more likely that Mr. Gray had already decided that the wealthy Ruskin connection was his best bet and refused to entertain any other proposals. Parental interference of this kind was considered quite normal. Even John would not have proposed without his parents' permission since this would have meant being financially cut off by his father.

Mr. Gray had not admitted to his full liabilities at once, but only revealed the true extent of his financial problems gradually. The critical date was not the wedding day, but the date the settlement was signed. Put simply, once the settlement had been signed the marriage was unstoppable. Thus the Gray family could later maintain the half-truth that the Ruskins knew about his financial difficulties before the marriage.[27] On the 22nd March 1848 Ruskin's father wrote to Mr. Gray castigating him for pestering John and Effie for money to meet his calls. By that time Gray's house was 'already as good as gone' and 'winding up' imminent.[28] He advised Gray that the winding up should be delayed for a few months so that 'I shall be prepared'. The following week he was still hoping that Gray's 'friends' who had given him funds would not be 'vindictive', but apparently the whole extent of his 'late Operations' was still unknown to them too. If this had become known Gray stood to lose much of his legal business.[29] Four months after the wedding the situation was still so serious that John was certain that Mr. Gray could not 'retrieve his fortunes – even to competency' in less than ten years.[30] Mr. Ruskin's letter of 17th March 1848 had referred to a 'large sum by investments' which Gray still anticipated losing. 'Have you yet calls to meet?' he asked him. The three-year £3000 loan at 3½% Gray took out twelve months after the wedding was doubtless to cover yet another call on his shares.[31] Lutyens has argued that George Gray managed to extricate himself from bankruptcy without any help from the Ruskins since (unsurprisingly) there is no proof that any money changed hands for this purpose: but money did change hands, not in the usual form of a dowry from the bride's father, but in the way of an extraordinary sum of ten thousand pounds settled on Effie by Mr. Ruskin.[32] It is always difficult to give modern equivalents for historical sums of money, but as far as I can work out this would be nearly three-quarters of a million pounds today, an 'immense sum' indeed. This sum may not have been in the original settlement which Mr. Ruskin had drafted at the beginning of March because when he sent it to Perth he had asked George Gray what he intended to do for Effie. Effie should have been the one to bring the dowry: that was the tradition. Had John been allowed to marry either of the exotic Domecq sisters she would have brought with her a dowry of £30,000.

There has been some confusion about the marriage settlement sum. There can be no doubt that the £10,000 was in 3¼% Consols 'given to John and by him settled in marriage J. C. Rutter and J. P. Bolding trustees' as is apparent from Mr. Ruskin's account books.[33] Although John's father talked of settling the money on Effie, it would have been in John's name and paid to her through him because at that time it was not usual for a wife to have an independent financial status.[34] Under the settlement the £10,000 remained entirely under the control of Mr. Ruskin, and Effie only had a right to the income from it which was paid to her by John. Given Mr. Ruskin's knowledge of George Gray's financial status in 1848, the settlement might have been drafted specifically to prevent him appropriating any of the principal sum to pay off his debts. Had it been phrased carefully enough George Gray might not even have realised this. John's own income had been arranged in a similar way. His East India stock and ¾% Consols were included in Mr. Ruskin's summaries of 'My entire Property on the 1st January' for every year until his death.[35] John continued to receive his £300 allowance in this way even after he was married. On May 1st 1854 the accounts record a payment of £100 with '£300 additions' to John for '4 months of Marriage' indicating that before she left John, Effie had not been paid all her £25 per month allowance since Christmas, that it was usually paid through John, and that Mr. Ruskin kept control of the £10,000 after Effie left John.

Furthermore in the outgoings for 1855 Mr. Ruskin notes 'paid John 1 yr. 8 months being from 1 May 1854 the same as agreed for Marriage Allowance being now wanted for Workmen £500'. (The 'workmen' here are probably the Working Men's College which John was helping to set up.) This entry is on the same ledger lines as the entry for 'To Recd. Divd. on 10,000 3¼% Consols 153.5' on the facing page.[36] This is also proof that the £10,000 3¼% was still with Mr. Ruskin at this time. After the marriage had been annulled John's solicitor Mr. Rutter mentioned not having had time to look into the Settlements or to consider the subject of the £10,000 3¼ percents.[37] This I believe conclusively solves the mystery of the capital sum involved in the settlement. After the annulment Effie neither kept the settlement sum nor returned it because she never actually had it under her control.[38]

Perhaps George Gray's hair's breadth escape from bankruptcy being simultaneous with the marriage settlement was only a coincidence, but written proof of £10,000 settled on his daughter must at least have given him a formidable credit-worthiness, and credit was in short supply in 1848. Interestingly, Joan Severn, Ruskin's cousin who looked after him at Brantwood, claimed that the 'twelve thousand pounds' which John's father had to pay for the father's debts a week before the wedding, first alerted John to the true nature of his marriage.[39] There can be no doubt that the sum settled on Effie was £10,000, so the other £2000, if it ever existed, remains a mystery. Throughout his entire life Mr. Ruskin kept scrupulous account books of every penny of family expenditure, but the £10,000 of the settlement does not seem to have been identified until now. Interestingly the income page for 1848, the year of the settlement, totals £12,319 mainly from a most untypical mass sale of railway shares, bank stock and long annuities. This might conceivably have been the source of Joan Severn's £12,000 figure. She was not a financial expert and the expenditure page which faces it shows how this sum had almost all been spent during the year. Another mystery is why Bowerswell house and its furniture were not sold up when even George Gray thought it was inevitable? Perhaps it is possible to put these two mysteries together and come up with a solution. Had Mr. Ruskin paid an extra £2,000 to secure the house so that at least the wedding could go ahead? Such a sum could well have been drawn on his income from Ruskin, Telford and Domecq which was kept separate from the daily accounts. This might go some way to explaining the generous bank loan of £3,000 to a self-confessed candidate for bankruptcy twelve months later by his bank manager Mr. Burns, who had been in danger of losing his job because of George Gray's gigantic debts. The bank already held Gray's shares as security pending the recovery of the market. The house could have also partly secured the loan and, along with the marriage settlement, would have made Gray an acceptable risk.

Whatever had happened, Mr. Gray's financial difficulties were not immediately ended by Effie's marriage. Whether or not, as the Grays maintained, he managed to stave off bankruptcy unaided is in any case not the most relevant question in assessing the motives behind the marriage. One thing indisputable from all the evidence is that at the time of the wedding George Gray believed himself to be an utterly ruined man whose house and furniture were about to be seized. He had at that time very little hope of being able to extricate himself. The actions of the Gray family which led up to the engagement and marriage should therefore be viewed in this light.[40] Once Effie was John's wife the Grays thought they would at least be able to depend on help from the Ruskins to save them from utter ruin. Ruskin senior's reputation would not survive allowing his in-laws to become beggars. John proposed sooner because of the Grays' financial problems and I cannot think of any reason why the wedding should have been brought forward into Lent against the original wishes of all concerned other than that George Gray feared the imminent loss of his house. The marriage did not immediately ease his situation. Money matters remained a constant undercurrent in Effie's letters throughout the marriage.

CHAPTER X

THE WEDDING

༄

John Ruskin married Euphemia Gray at four o'clock in the afternoon on Monday April 10th 1848 in the drawing room at Bowerswell House. The ceremony was conducted by the Rev. John Edward Touche, the Minister of Kinnoull. Evening weddings were a Scotch custom, and John and Effie left immediately after the ceremony just as Mr. Ruskin had advised. The guests then sat down to dinner and toasted the newly-weds.

The fact that the marriage was according to Scottish law and celebrated in Scotland would have consequences later on. There were some important differences between marriage according to the 'Scotch form' and the English institution. In Scotland the marriage laws had a reputation for being more lax because the English 1753 Marriage Act, designed to prevent entrapment and elopement, was not law there. Thus the ceremony did not have to be publicly celebrated in a church or chapel by a regular clergyman in the prescribed daylight hours, no banns needed to be called and no parental assent was necessary. In fact, 'An Act to amend the Law of Scotland affecting the constitution of Marriage' came into force on 1st January 1849 to remedy abuses of the situation.[1] There is no suggestion that the actual ceremony that John and Effie underwent was either unanticipated or anything but legal and proper but the strange circumstances of this wedding have not been given sufficient prominence in any biography.

The date of the marriage, repeatedly changed, was still uncertain four days before the actual wedding. None of John's

The marriage certificate

close friends attended the ceremony. More significantly, although they had not forbidden the marriage and indeed were ostensibly in favour of it, John's parents did not attend the ceremony either. Effie's close friend Lizzie Cockburn declined to be her bridesmaid, and did not even attend the wedding, probably on the orders of her father, a circuit judge.[2] No cards were sent out even after the couple returned to Denmark Hill.[3] Again after appointing William Macdonald to be best man at his wedding, John seems not to have maintained the friendship after the wedding ceremony.[4] John was also extremely reluctant to visit Scotland after the wedding, only doing so twice under protest until the fateful holiday at Glenfinlas that ended his marriage. Finally and notoriously the marriage was never consummated.

John was an only son, conceived late in life and doted upon by parents so concerned for his welfare that his mother even moved to Oxford to be with him whilst he attended university. That neither of his parents should attend his wedding is incomprehensible under normal circumstances. Similarly John's extreme reluctance to visit Scotland after the wedding, even to pick up his wife is significant. His aversion to Scotland before the union was well known,[5] but apart from two short trips to drop off and pick up his wife at Perth, a duty he tried his utmost to avoid and which caused much family friction, he was afterwards to avoid Scotland until the final Highland holiday.

Mr. Ruskin advised that the newlyweds should leave immediately after the ceremony and let the gossips do their worst: a very strange and significant piece of advice indeed. Admiral James also claimed that

> the carriage drove away under a shower of satin shoes. A few worldly wise elders were not quite happy. The bridegroom seemed to them rather a queer fellow and out of his proper element in such company, but Effie looked supremely happy, so perhaps their slight feeling of anxiety was unjustified.[6]

Albert Gray also wrote: 'My parents always regarded him as an oddity, but the long friendship with the elder Ruskins disarmed criticism.'[7] No-one on either side of this strange marriage ever ventured to suggest that Effie was head over heels in love with John. All the evidence suggests that Effie had been 'suddenly' married to a man who, though rich, was widely regarded as an odd choice for a young woman with a train of far more conventionally eligible suitors. Collingwood called it an 'ill-omened marriage' since John had recently been refused by another lady and was being treated for consumption. The Grays never made any reference to John's tuberculosis and Effie seemed to think the Ruskin parents made too much fuss over John's health. Was it possible that the Grays did not know?[8]

A curious postscript to this strange marriage ceremony appeared in the *Memoirs* of Sir Henry Newbolt who recollected the following conversation with William Holman Hunt which occurred in 1885. It should be stated at the outset that Hunt's whereabouts on this fateful day are well known: he and Millais were at the Chartist demonstration in London. The account is worth repeating however if only to show that 'Society' continued to feel that there was something not quite right about the nuptials and that all kinds of rumours were circulating:

> when we had turned to the fire Hunt began to relate in his longer and more thoughtful style the story of R's life as he had seen it. He told me of the extraordinary and fatal devotion of the old Ruskins to their only son: of his genius and self-will: of his parents' urgent wish that he should marry Effie Gray, the daughter of a former partner of Mr. Ruskin. Gray had been in some way unfortunate, and his marriage would, they hoped, be an acceptable way of restoring his child's fortune. John would not listen to the suggestion – his thoughts were elsewhere – but he was well pleased to take Effie around the picture galleries and lecture her on Art: till in the end some sort of consent was got from him. Then came the climax of the Tragedy – in the marriage, at which Hunt was the only witness present from outside the family. The ceremony took place in the drawing room of a country house in Scotland,

and the young couple drove away soon after it, in two carriages. The first carriage contained the bride and bride-groom: in the second were John R's valet and his wife's maid, in charge of the luggage. At a certain distance from the house both carriages were stopped: R. dismounted from the lead-ing one and went to the other, after informing Effie that he had now performed his promise and intended to recognize no further duties towards her as his wife: he then sent the maid to accompany her and travelled himself in the second carriage with his own servant.[9]

This is of the same questionable nature as evidence as the Albert Gray transcripts. But gossip and rumour will play a large part in this story as it unfolds, and even the most garbled hearsay might contain a grain of truth. Hunt was after all a very close friend of Millais and, since Millais was to become one of the protagonists, Hunt would most likely have pressed him for infor-mation. This account may reflect what Millais himself had been told by the Grays or by others. The Ruskins *did* have an urgent wish that their son be married, but not at first to Effie. They only agreed to it out of fear for his health. Mr. Gray, not a for-mer partner of Mr. Ruskin, had *indeed* been unfortunate, and the marriage was intended to be a way of restoring Effie's fortune. John was definitely well pleased to escort Effie around London, in fact he was totally besotted with her. The wedding *did* take place in the drawing room at Bowerswell House. As for the carriage inci-dent, that could only have been an eye-witness account, emanating either from Effie, John or a Perth bystander. It might be worth noting that when John and Effie travelled to Venice the first time, they did in fact travel in separate carriages and Effie wanted this kept quiet *so as not to provoke gossip in Perth*.[10] Effie herself later admitted that 'immediately after the ceremony he [John] proceeded to inform me that I was not his wife and he did not intend to marry me.'[11] The fact that Perth society viewed the marriage with deep suspicion from the outset might well have had something to do with such an incident as Hunt described.[12] We know that none of John's family or friends attended the wedding. This would not have escaped the notice of the Perth gossips. The added detail that according to this account the wedding was also entirely a Gray family affair with only one non-family witness might also be significant. Eliza Jameson stated that Effie was already known in Perth as 'the virgin wife' from the first year of her marriage.[13] Since John and Effie did not visit Perth between their wedding in April 1848 and Effie's return to Perth in February 1849, any such rumours must have originated from events at the wedding itself. The only other source would be the Gray family but we know from the letters that they took great pains to promote the contrary image.

It seems certain that Effie married John in order to save her family and herself from utter ruin. Marrying for money in this way was known politely as a marriage of convenience; when the man was gulled into it by the woman it was called entrapment. For their part the Grays and their supporters put forward the bizarre argument that the fact that John was head over heels in love with Effie constituted proof that no entrapment took place, when in fact he could not have been entrapped otherwise! After the marriage collapsed in 1854, Ruskin's father was immediately forthright in his declaration that his son was entrapped.[14] This was a view he forcefully maintained: 'My Son caught by a pretty face married contrary to his parents judgement but not to their commands – Miss G. concealed the embarrassed circumstances of her Father – courted my Son and was united in her Father's

House at Perth, none of his own Friends attending the Ceremony
– He found at once that the Woman had no Love for him and
he lived with her accordingly'.[15]

John later admitted that the first real insight he had into the
catastrophic nature of George Gray's financial affairs was when
he arrived in Edinburgh just before the wedding. Even if his father
knew the true state of affairs he would not have told John for
fear of provoking the same kind of emotional shock that had
caused the resurgence of tuberculosis at the time of his infatuation with Adèle Domecq. If John had any evidence of his future
bride's real motives it did not appear in his letters before the
marriage. John of course had not been in Perth since the previous October and only returned shortly before the wedding. In
such a close community as Perth it must have been common
knowledge that George Gray was ruined and Effie had jilted
another man, a man strongly attracted to her and to whom she
was strongly attracted. My own belief, and this is in the absence
of any firm evidence, is that comments about the nature of the
marriage must have been made to John after he arrived in Perth
for the wedding: perhaps even by one of her former suitors. If John
then went to Effie and asked her directly about her feelings it
would have been difficult for her to dissemble, particularly if a
Bible was produced. At such a late stage of the proceedings,
indeed at any time after the settlement had been signed, there
could be no question of withdrawing without serious legal and
financial consequences. The marriage would therefore have been
fatally undermined even before it began. At the time of the
annulment Effie circulated letters written by John's parents before
the marriage commenting naïvely: 'Is it not so fortunate that Papa
has kept all the letters in case they should give us trouble?'[16] The
two points to note here being that the use of 'they' and 'us'

shows that she saw the marriage as being between two families rather than two individuals, and that George Gray foresaw the need to keep not just the evidence of the contractual negotiations but also of the personal and emotional commitments.[17]

Why did John's parents not go to his wedding? The most plausible scenario seems to be that Mr. Ruskin, suspicious of Effie's motives from the outset, anticipated the event as a personal humiliation in his home town and it was pride that kept him away. If so then that same pride probably prevented him being present when his son discovered that the marriage, as his father had always suspected, was to be one of convenience on Effie's part. Had Mr. Ruskin been there he could have accepted the financial consequences and allowed his son to call it all off. As it was, John had to face the appalling situation without the support of family or friends, and totally in the hands of the Grays.

Arranged marriages and marriages of convenience were not uncommon at that time and amongst that class. Modern readers should not jump to the conclusion that such a marriage was a bad thing in all cases. Collingwood, who knew John for a quarter of a century and had unrestricted access to all the papers at Brantwood for his biography, came to the conclusion that Effie was 'a charming girl placed in difficult circumstances.'[18] The present author is of a similar opinion. Effie should not be judged too harshly for agreeing to this mismatch. It may even be possible to regard Effie's decision to marry John as a selfless act performed in order to save her family from very real suffering. Even without this pressing commitment Effie would not have been the first bride to trade her charms for wealth and a celebrity lifestyle; nor would she be the last. Marrying for reasons of physical attraction or sexual satisfaction is a rather modern notion and not even universally practised today. Nor should we assume that the marriage was bound to fail in the long term just because the attraction was not entirely mutual at the outset.

In a later statement John argued convincingly that his letters to Effie before the marriage would prove that he had no prior intention of not consummating the marriage.[19] Unfortunately the most important of these letters were almost certainly acquired illegally by Sir Albert Gray in 1925 and most probably burned.[20] However in a surviving letter of November 30th 1847 John was clearly anticipating the more physical pleasures of his honeymoon:

> But your letter of last night shook all the philosopher out of me. That little undress bit! Ah – my sweet Lady – What naughty thoughts had I. – Dare I say? I was thinking – thinking, naughty – happy thought, that you would soon have – some one's arms to keep you from being cold! Pray don't be angry with me. How could I help it? – how can I? I'm thinking so just now, even.[21]

The twelve days he spent at Bowerswell before the wedding seem to have quenched his ardour. It must have been a dreadful time for him. On March 2nd he had described his impending marriage as 'a dangerous adventure – even the carrying away of a bride, whom nobody is willing to part with – and I don't know but I may have to do it in Lochinvar fashion.'[22] First there was the impending bankruptcy of his in-laws, the fear of bailiffs arriving to possess the house, the chaotic last-minute changes of plan, the dash to inform the best man; then the interminable socialising and the knowing interrogations by Effie's neighbours, friends and relatives. Her jilted suitors were not far away. If there had indeed been unpleasant revelations about Effie's true feelings and ulterior motives then the ceremony would have been even more of a trial. Effie was weak and nervous and John had a cold. In a letter Mrs Gray wrote to Mrs Ruskin the day after the wedding she described how after 'a trying fortnight [...] both John and Phemy bore up with the greatest firmness throughout the trying ceremony and both looked <u>remarkably well</u>.'[23] This would suggest that it had not been an altogether happy occasion. After the wedding the couple took Mr. Ruskin's advice and left the gossips behind. The first night of the honeymoon was spent at Blair Atholl. They arrived at 10 pm after a thirty-four mile drive by carriage that must have left both bride and groom exhausted. The marriage was not consummated either then or later.

It has been suggested that consummation was delayed for religious reasons. John's mother seemed to hint at something of this sort in her letter to him of November 27th 1847.[24] However, sexual abstinence was never a traditional part of the observance of Lent for Protestants such as the Ruskins and the Grays. Even fasting and more general abstinence at Lent would have been regarded as papist rituals. For Evangelicals such as the Ruskins, Lent was essentially about reflection and repentance for sin and excess of pleasure but would not necessarily have prevented consummation. Six years later John and Effie each gave accounts of what had happened after the wedding. It is important to realise that both these accounts were given years later in the acrimonious and confrontational atmosphere of marriage breakdown and with the legal situation firmly in mind. At the time of the annulment John stated that it was the revelation of George Gray's financial affairs that entirely destroyed the immediate happiness of his marriage. On the wedding night Effie had been anxious about her father's problems. He added 'My own passion was also much subdued by anxiety; and I had no difficulty in refraining from consummation on the first night. On speaking to her on the subject the second night we agreed that it would be better to defer consummation for a little time.'[25] Because of the realisation that Effie's motive in marrying him was not what he had believed it to be, John had found himself in a moral dilemma after the wedding which he dealt with by simply postponing consummation until he could feel morally certain that it was justified. Effie too must have been apprehensive about the sacrifice she was about to make for her family. John claimed, plausibly in my opinion, that the couple had come to an agreement not to consummate. Eleven days after the wedding John wrote to his friend Miss Mitford in a state of depression and fever of spirit occasioned by 'events on the continent' and 'other circumstances nearer home' which denied him 'the heart to write cheerfully.' In the same letter he referred to Effie being 'under the shadow of her new and grievous lot.'[26] The plain truth would seem to be that John was suffering the natural reaction of a man who had discovered that he had been gulled into a marriage of convenience. This was the interpretation that most worried Albert Gray when the letter was later published.[27]

Effie's March 1854 version of what happened was more accusatory:

> To go back to the day of my marriage the 10th of April 1848. I went as you know away to the Highlands. I had never been told the duties of married persons to each other and knew little or nothing about their relations in the closest union on earth. For days John talked about this relation to me but avowed no intention of making me his Wife. He alleged various reasons, Hatred to children, religious motives, a desire to preserve my beauty [...] After I began to see things better I argued with him and took the Bible but he soon silenced me and I was not sufficiently awake to what

position I was in. Then he said after 6 years he would marry me, when I was 25.[28]

I have deliberately elided a sentence here in order to represent accurately what Effie recalled John saying to her *at the time*. The elided sentence, which has caused an extraordinary amount of lurid speculation, was her recollection of what John told her in 1853, when he was in an entirely different situation and will be fully examined in its proper context in a later chapter. The strange authorial fantasies that never having seen a naked woman he was repelled by her pubic hair, that she was menstruating, or that she suffered from body odour, all have no basis in what John and Effie actually wrote. As will appear, they also fly in the face of the clear evidence that in the first period of the marriage they slept together naked (confirmed by Effie under oath), that John still found her attractive and looked forward both to taking her clothes off and holding her naked in his arms.

Once the decision not to consummate had been made, it was easy to think up any number of reasons why it was a good idea, Effie was anxious about her family's finances, John was not a healthy man, the newly-weds intended to travel abroad, Effie might have to climb 'Swiss hills', John did not want babies because he had to work. Given the circumstances immediately after the wedding it was probably a relief to both of them. For Effie there would be time to come to terms with her new relationship with John. For his part John would have had time to register his disappointment over what had just happened to him and to ponder his moral response. The situation in which he found himself must have caused him to examine his true feelings. That John might not have wished to make love to a woman when he discovered she had married him primarily because of her father's impending bankruptcy could seem prosaic compared to the more lurid speculations of John's enemies, but at least there is evidence to support it. John later told George MacDonald that 'he was not the man to claim intimate relations, to him most sacred, without the only justification for them, namely that of loving the woman beyond anything in heaven and earth.'[29]

For most present day readers the whole idea of abstaining from sex is such an alien concept that this fact alone seems to label John as abnormal, and he is judged accordingly, as if it would have been more 'normal' if he had forced himself on a distraught and unwilling Effie. However, at that time abstinence, restraint and even celibacy were preached, and even practised in certain circles, as a matter of principle. The practice of restraint was not restricted to those Romantic survivors of the Eglinton Tournament who practised courtly love, there were also socio-economic reasons why the upper classes should set an example for the toiling masses. The current economic model was underpinned by Malthusian ideas about over-population and the subsistence wage. Sexual abstinence by the poor was regarded as a bulwark against a glut in the labour market and therefore in their own best interest. There were also practical reasons why women should wish to avoid childbirth. In the 1840's deaths in childbirth, though not as prevalent as once thought, were depressingly frequent. By the 1850's several aristocratic marriages – for example those of Lady Waterford and her nieces Lady Pembroke, Lady Brownlow and Lady Lothian – remained suspiciously childless.[30] Given the moral and religious character of these grand ladies, artificial birth control is ruled out and non-consummation must be concluded. The beautiful Louisa, Countess of Waterford conducted a lifelong correspondence with John. Yet another childless married aristocrat, Lady Mount Temple, was one of John's closest friends and staunchest supporters. There were of course several childless relationships amongst intellectuals in John's circle, including notably the marriage of the Carlyles.[31]

Modern readers should however realise that whatever the circumstances of the marriage, once it had become an established fact, all concerned would have exerted themselves to the utmost to make it work. From the moment John's proposal had been accepted, both families would have suppressed any misgivings or rancour they might have had towards each other in order to support the newly-weds, and this for a very good reason. For respectable people such as the Ruskins and the Grays, marriage was final and indissoluble other than by death. The surviving letters between the two families throughout the marriage are generally supportive and concerned. There are occasional lapses, but only what one would expect between in-laws who are also friends of long standing. The procedure for newly-weds in such circumstances was to hope that love would grow with time. John was sure that this would be the case even before the wedding.

> I have been thinking a good deal over that hard question of yours – whether I shall always love you as I do now – and I still have the same answer – it will depend upon yourself – a wife has it in her power to make her husband love her more and more daily, and so he, with her. and I do so thoroughly intend to do everything that I can do, for your good and happiness, that I do faithfully believe I shall gain your love more and more as we live on – and I hope deserve it more and more. and if you love me I am certain to continue to find all my happiness in you.[32]

CHAPTER XI

THE NEWLY-WEDS

ﾝ

This state of non-consumption would not necessarily have been uncomfortable for the newlyweds. Although Effie may not have been in love with John, the couple had already been good friends for many years and there can be no doubt that John had fallen in love with her. He had rescued her from a terrible situation and was now in a position to offer her celebrity, comfort and security on a lavish scale. His parents had told him that love was something that grew between married couples and on this assumption he seems to have given himself six years to win Effie's heart as well as her hand. Nor was there any immediate reason to fear failure. On the honeymoon Effie wrote 'John and I are as happy as two people can possibly be and he is exceedingly kind and thoughtful.'[1] She also told her brother George that: 'it is not at all bad being "one of the married class"'[2] and 'we are enjoying ourselves very much'.[3] After the wedding night at Blair Atholl there had been another long drive to Killin in black, thundery weather. John was however not as happy as Effie described him to her family. She told Pauline Trevelyan that:

> We were rather early on our Highland tour and John did nothing but abuse every place one after another when he was awake, for to ride out what he calls the most melancholy country in the world he slept most of the way which I am sure you will be most shocked at, and I had the poor advantage of having all the beauties to myself.[4]

For his part John was at first amused by Effie's compulsive socialising:

> I did not leave her to herself for ten minutes at Kenmore, and when I came back, I found her inside the Turnpike engaged in confidential conversation with the turnpike woman – and a gentleman smoking. Then at Killin, she got over an old man who showed us Finlanrig until she got into his cottage – and before I knew what she was about – she was sitting at the fire drinking the old gentleman's health in whisky – and paying him compliments on his clean butter tubs. We met some people on the road to-day, as we were walking – whom she addressed as if she had known them thirty years – and if I hadn't remonstrated, a little farther on, she would have been quite thick with a party of Tinkers: not to speak of various terriers and shepherds' dogs, and a lamb today – which she must needs have on her lap in the carriage.[5]

After spending a few days in the Highlands the newlyweds moved via Glasgow and Penrith to Keswick in Cumberland. There they sailed on Derwentwater and rode white ponies to the top of Cawsey Pike five miles away. On other days they climbed Skiddaw and John rowed Effie up and down the lake.

By the time the honeymoon was over, the couple had established a pattern of life together without sexual relations. Both John and Effie later confirmed that, after they had been living this way for some time, John suggested that they should not consummate the marriage until Effie was twenty-five. Whether Effie agreed or had no alternative but to agree is not clear. After the annulment her family denied the existence of such a pact but, given the legal implications of such an agreement, that was to be expected.[6] The honeymoon was shorter than had been planned because John was anxious to get home to finish work on a new edition of *Modern Painters*. They had planned to travel back with Mr. Ruskin who was in Liverpool on business, but in the event he declined. He was however on hand to pick them up from Euston Station. Effie noted that the Ruskins' carriage had been newly painted and lined and the coachman fitted out in a splendid new coat 'in honor [sic] of our arrival'. There was a warm welcome waiting for them when they finally arrived at Denmark Hill on the 27th April:

> Mr. Ruskin greeted us most warmly and when we arrived at the gate of the garden the carriage stopped and the Gardener presented me with the most splendid bouquet of geraniums, Orangeblossom, Heath of the most delicate kinds, myrtles, cineraria, etc., all tied in ornamental paper and with White Satin ribbon. When we came to the door the servants were all standing with Mrs. Ruskin to welcome us, the women looked so nice with their neat caps of white net and ribbon and green and stone coloured mousselines up to their neck with their muslin aprons. Mrs. Ruskin had on a most splendid rich drab or pale brown satin with rich fringe on the front and a white blonde cap. She and Mr. Ruskin never saw John looking half so well and are quite delighted to see him so happy – and she bids me say how happy she is to have me here and she hopes now I will feel quite a daughter to her, but to go on – When we had dressed and gone into dinner a band of Germans came and played delightful music before the windows all time of dinner and it was a great treat. We spent the evening very happily. I played to Mr. Ruskin and Mrs. R spoke to John and me and made kind speeches. Mrs. R has given us the top of the house and very comfortable it is.

Mr. Ruskin and I go tomorrow to the private view of the Academy where we shall see all the nobs.[7]

No matter what dire circumstances and unpleasant suspicions had attended the engagement and wedding, there can be no doubt whatsoever that once it had happened John, Effie and the Ruskin parents spared no effort or expense to make the marriage work. The day after the newly-weds arrived at Denmark Hill, Mr. Ruskin wrote to Mr. Gray:

> Phemy is a little thinner than when with us last year, but very well and in her usual spirits or way which we never wish to see changed. – my son is stouter and better than we have ever seen him in the whole course of his life – They are in appearance and I doubt not in reality extremely happy and I trust the union will prove not only a source of happiness to them but of satisfaction and comfort to us all.[8]

Effie confirmed to her mother that her in-laws were as good as their words:

> John congratulated me on what he terms my *grande succès* [sic] on my first appearance in public. I am sure you will relieve me of all charge of affection in telling you these compliments myself but it is only to show you how entirely pleased Mr. and Mrs. R. are with John's wife which I know will gratify you and which I am most thankful for. I never saw anything so kind as they are. Mrs. R. overwhelms me with presents and I do not know what to say or do [...] I entreat John not to let me have so much but he says it is all right and that his mother wishes it. She always says when I refuse, my dear child, what can I do with them? You know I may as well give them now with pleasure for they will all be yours when I am gone

and Mr. Ruskin is so proud of his daughter &c and if John
is not as kind as kind can be tell me! and won't I settle him!
I assure her there is no need of that at present.[9]

Two days later Effie noted that 'Mr. and Mrs. R. are as kind
as can be' and 'I never saw anything like John, he is just perfect!!!!'[10]
We might almost overlook her use of the third person to describe
the young woman who was 'John's wife' and Mr. Ruskin's 'daughter'. She must have had a strong feeling that she was acting a part
in a play.

Whilst Effie was being showered with jewellery, bracelets
and cameos by Mrs. Ruskin and John, Mr. Ruskin was looking
for a furnished house to rent for the newlyweds in the fashionable Mayfair area of town. Effie, at Denmark Hill, told her
mother: 'For my part I am very happy here and do not care where
we go or stay.'[11] 'Seeing all the nobs', to use Effie's phrase, was to
take up much of the next two months, which according to Effie's
letters home became a constant whirl of high society occasions
and visits. This would have been something John would have
hated under ordinary circumstances but he was obviously making
a special effort to please his new wife. Mr. Ruskin told Mr. Gray
how pleased he was with Effie:

> I am glad to see Effie gets John to go out a little. He has met
> with most of the first men for some years back but he is very
> indifferent to general Society and reluctantly acknowledges
> great attentions shown him and refuses one half – Seven
> years ago he refused to spend a month at the Duke of Lein-
> ster's – He has had many valuable Invitations and disregarded
> them – I got him to dine with Sir Stratford Canning with diffi-
> culty and to go to Sir Robert Peel's House Opening – I only
> discovered by chance two years ago that Lord John Russell

was one of his Party – I am glad to find his acquaintances, obtained merely by fair Talent and good Conduct, immediately took Phemy by the hand – John some months ago refused Mr. Blake of Portland Place's Invitation, but they both went on Saturday and met first rate people and on Monday they dine at Lansdowne House – by invitation from Marquis and Marchioness of Lansdowne – but John would rather be in Switzerland – I hope they will contrive to be happy and take a due share of Society and solitude – Effie is much better calculated for society than he is – He is best in print.[12]

In the first hectic weeks Effie also mingled with the three Dukes and Duchesses of Sutherland, Argyll and Northumberland, Lord Ravensworth's sons, the Marquis of Northampton, Lord and Lady Lyttelton, Lady Davy, Lord and Lady Murray, Lord and Lady Shelburn, Viscountess Palmerston, Lady Frances Hope, Sir Walter and Lady James, Sir James Wigram, 'and all the lords and ladies you can think of'. She also met the Turkish Minister, the Bishop of Norwich, the Liddells, Calderidge the second Master of Eton, John Gibson Lockhart editor of the *Quarterly Review* and father of Charlotte, Hallam the historian of the Middle Ages, Mr. and Mrs. Sartoris, Henry Oliphant and the poets Milman and Rogers. She was also introduced to the artists Copley Fielding, Stanfield, David Roberts, Landseer, Tayler, Cox, Prout and of course Turner. As well as the endless round of dinners and visits, Effie was taken to the opera, where Mr. Ruskin took a box for them in the grand tier opposite the Queen. They saw Jenny Lind in *Die Regiments Tochter*, Grisi in Bellini's *Norma* and Alboni in one scene of Rossini's *La Cenerentola*. They were also admitted inside the square of troops on Horse Guards Parade to see 'a fine review of cavalry and Infantry'. Besides the incessant name dropping, Effie's letters home included the usual extensive commentaries on fashion, dresses and bonnets.

This whirl of social activity had consequences. The Grays, whose financial problems were still extremely dire, wrote to Effie accusing her of forgetting the family at Perth, neglecting her brother George's interests and of being too grand to visit her old friends.[13] Her father was particularly concerned that she should visit the Gardners and the Gadesdens, not just because she had stayed with them before she was married, but also because he was hoping that they could find a job for young George with a Colonial broker. She must have shown the letters to John who on the 12th of May took it upon himself to answer for her:

My dear Mrs. Gray, I have indeed given you some cause to suppose I had in some measure forgotten Perth, and ceased to think of you. But you must not think this. I do not say that I have not been self indulgent occasionally – and that – to a walk in the garden – or an hours reading in the summerhouse with Effie, I have not sacrificed time which had been more dutifully employed in writing to you – but whatever my faults of this kind may be – they never extend to or involve any forgetfulness of you – and for the rest, I have not since my return – been able – in the time which my utmost self-denial could secure – to answer all the immediately pressing letters of neglected friends – or the still more imperatively pressing letters of kind and forgiving ones – But the notes which Effie has received from you and George today I must hasten to answer for her: I wish it were in my power to do so in a way that would relieve your minds from the anxiety which cannot but increase day by day – and still – all that I can yet say is that you must not think I forget you – or your wishes: You – my dear Mrs. Gray – cannot but see the danger that there would be not only diminishing the chance of success in Georges present object – but of involving also in no small degree – Effie's happiness – if any idea – however slight – arose in my father's mind that my affection for her was made in any – even the most unconscious way – a means of obtaining advantage or undue influence over me – and through me, over him, <u>at this time</u> – When that affection has been more prolonged on my part – and when my father and mother have had longer opportunity of discovering – what they perceive more and more day by day, how entirely the best affection that I or they can give is deserved by your daughter – and how much my happiness is involved in hers – and secured by her – it will become their natural wish to show you their sense of this by every means in their power. But whatever I at present asked or represented – could not but be looked upon by them as prompted by the excitement of strong – and perhaps transitory feeling – and the use of my influence by you at such a time would be the surest way to diminish it. You must remain for the present trusting in my earnest desire to replace to you in the duty of a son what you have parted with in the obedience of a daughter [...] George must not lose spirit – nor patience – nor above all admit the painful and wounding thought that I can be less mindful of him among the gaieties of London than among the pines of Kinnoull – there is nothing here that I enjoy except the society of your daughter in our home – and it is not at such times that I am likely to forget her brother – if I go into society it is for her sake, and to my infinite annoyance – except only as the pleasure I have in seeing her admired as by all she is – and as happy as with all she is – rewards me and more than rewards me for my own discomforts and discomfitures.[14]

As far as Effie's duty to visit old friends went, neither she nor John had any doubt that she was now moving in higher social circles and that John's friends came first. John took all the blame for this but Effie backed him up by arguing that no-one could accuse her of vanity in her choice of friends; she would always regard those who had shown her kindness: 'but a line must be drawn or else in John's position people will come in flocks not through regard to me but to get access to him, and the society in which we are placed and my conduct now must be regulated by his wishes and I am certain he will never ask me to do anything contrary to what is right.'[15] Effie, basking in John's reflected celebrity and applying her own formidable talent for socialising, seems to have been genuinely happy with her new life at this time. When the couple were alone and away from John's parents there were even glimpses of genuine mutual affection. On June 7th she told her mother how: 'You would have laughed last night to see John and I going to our garden with Mungo [the dog]. Coming to the Haystack we climbed up to the top of it and I sat on the wall but John going the wrong way slipped up to the chin in the straw which put us into fits of laughter and was a capital chance for Mungo who jumped over him and tried to annihilate him. However he at last got out of his hole, such a figure you never saw and his best clothes on, and he was so delighted with it.'[16]

This idyll was soon to be shattered. The gaiety and fashion of the London Season was interrupted by a short break with John's parents at the seaside whilst work was being done at Denmark Hill. In her letter to Pauline Trevelyan, Effie described John as 'truly happy' though 'longing to be on the other side of the

Channel.' From the chalk cliffs of Dover and Folkestone Effie caught her first glimpses of France where the newly-weds had planned a post-honeymoon tour together. However the same revolution which had nearly bankrupted Mr. Gray had also disrupted their wedding tour. A workers' revolt had just been bloodily suppressed and amongst the thousands of casualties was the Archbishop of Paris, shot whilst attempting to mediate. The violence affected the stock market and a slight rally in railway shares collapsed. Yet another gloomy letter arrived from Bowerswell with more entreaties to find a job for George. John's reply, written almost illegibly on the train from Folkestone to London, was not encouraging: he had asked his father about George without any success, but he was confident that railway shares would rise now that the revolution in Paris had been put down.

This letter was written whilst John and Effie were on their way back to London for a grand dinner at Lansdowne House in Berkeley Square. From there they travelled to Oxford to visit John's friend Dr. Henry Acland for Commemoration and 'a continual round of festivities' which included a performance of Haydn's *Creation*. Effie's report on the visit to her parents included the usual concern about the Gray family situation: 'Always tell me what goes on at home about money matters for I would be very uneasy if I thought you did not tell me.'[17] Things had not improved by July 10th: 'I am extremely sorry to hear how dull you have been and I do not hear anything here about funds or railways. [...] I am sorry for George for John can do nothing as yet and three months only are passed today, although it appears an age to you. I wish my father would try and keep like himself.'[18] The bad news from home may have contributed to Effie's becoming ill at Oxford. Her mother later described how John got Dr. Acland to see her: 'he asked her how she felt upon which tears welled down her cheeks and she could not answer – he enquired no further and said to John she [wants how to tell?] thinking I suppose it was some domestic [reflection?] which he did not like to enquire further into.' This diagnosis, Mrs. Gray implied, was not at all the case: Effie was really ill and got worse as time went by.[19]

John had by this time begun work on his new project involving Gothic architecture, the first fruit of which would be *The Seven Lamps of Architecture*. Because of the unrest on the Continent he had begun his work with a proposed tour of the English cathedrals. Leaving the socializing and entertainment behind, John and Effie started at Winchester and then moved on to Salisbury where Mr. and Mrs. Ruskin joined them. It was there that Effie had her first taste of the sort of life John had warned her he would have to lead in order to be able to write the books upon which his celebrity depended. Effie could never argue after the marriage that she had no previous idea of what her life with John might entail. The newly-weds had no means of support other than what Mr. Ruskin had very generously provided for them, and their position in high society depended entirely upon John's research and writing. Right from the start John had been well aware that unless Effie loved him 'exceedingly' she would be unfit to be his wife because it would be necessary for her to adjust her lifestyle to his. Shortly after the engagement he had spelled out exactly what he thought their life together would be like.

> I think I shall never be able to tell you what I intended – how I hoped you might find pleasure in helping me – I must tell you now [...] This then was my thought – Methought – that your exceeding fondness of, and acquaintance with, History, might lead you to take some interest in the histories and associations connected with the various edifices we

should see abroad, – or indeed anywhere. That, while I was drawing or measuring – or going up on leads or tiles – and such places where you couldn't come – (such scrambles as I have had – Effie – Next to an Alpine summit – an old church roof is the most exciting thing in the world.) you – in the aisle below – might be examining for me such written traditions of the place as were most interesting – and that from doing this – you would gradually come to take interest in the expression – style and sculptured histories, of the Architecture itself. Keen sighted as you are, I think you would soon find great delight in deciphering inscriptions – interpreting devices – and unravelling enigmas. – Gradually I think you might become far, far my superior in judging of dates and styles – and from your interest in these disputable questions – you would gradually be led to examine and to feel the relative beauty – propriety – or majesty of this or that manner. I think the pencil which would at first be in your hand to copy a broken letter – or note the order of a series of sculptures – would gradually come to make its own unpretending little memoranda of a capital here – an ornament there – a quaint piece of costume – or a graceful line of mosaic – I think you would probably see me take up these memoranda with avidity – carry them farther – and make use of them – that you would gradually be encouraged to carry them further yourself – and that in a little time – no very distant one – things might even come to such a pass as that I should be able to say to you – "Effie – I want those three capitals – and a bit of that frieze – will you, please, do them for me while I go up and examine the vaulting?" And that you would do them for me with great pleasure to yourself, and with more neatness and accuracy than any architect!

Now mind I do not <u>expect</u> this in the least – I do not wish you to try for it – nor do anything in the least painful or that costs you effort – In fact – if it were done with effort, it would be ill done – I shall not even be grateful to you – fancy! Not grateful! if it so happens – because I would not have it happen unless it gave you pleasure – But that if it should happen, you would be of the greatest service to me on a thousand occasions – and that we should have a subject on which our sympathy would procure us a thousand pleasures – is most certain, and I think it is <u>likely</u> to happen also – For you will have often to wait for me while I am examining cathedrals by the <u>hour</u> – you may do it at an Inn – but in most cases – when it is not cold, I imagine it will be in the church – that you may see what I am about – see me getting my coat all white over, and creeping into crypts on my hands and knees, and into rood lofts and turrets by inexplicable stairs etc. Well you will soon find – however much you may be delighted with the sensation of the thing at first – that one cathedral, carelessly seen – is much the same as another – you will be tired of sauntering up and down aisles – hearing fat priests chanting dull bass discords – or watching old women mutter over their beads. You will begin to ask me what I find so interesting to keep me all that time. I shall instantly stop and show you – as long as you attend – I shall give you something to find out or count – or to read for me – You will be interested – whether you will or no – you will notice the same thing when you see it in another church – you will find the other church more interesting in consequence – so the thing will go on – at least I think it most likely that it will. But if not – you will have to pass many an irksome hour – for you know I must go on with my <u>profession</u> and – while for a certain time of the day – I shall always be entirely <u>yours</u> – to go and be with you where you choose – yet for another part of the day, and that – usually the largest – you will have to be <u>mine</u> – or to sit at home. – So now you see what a thoroughly <u>selfish</u> motive – besides many an unselfish one, I had for asking you to take care of your sight.[20]

He had also thought that she could help him by copying notes and translating German texts. The section ended: 'Ah – how happy it will be.' Given Effie's personality this was a fond fantasy doomed to utter failure, the evidence for which, not least in Effie's atrocious handwriting and punctuation, was staring him in the face. Even by the February before the wedding he had realised that she had completely ignored his suggestions of how she might prepare herself to help him by studying French, Italian and Botany: 'you have not – so far as I know – except the writing of this last piece of French and the reading of the Misanthrope – done anything for me or with reference to my wishes – except only the writing of your letters.'[21] At that time Effie had seen her wifely rôle as leaving John alone when he was writing, mending his pens (when she had learned how), and ordering dinner.

John could and often did forget his troubles by working. Effie left her troubles behind by going out to balls and parties. Socialising made John ill: it cured Effie. Knowing how much she loved socialising, he had continually worried that she would find it difficult to adjust to her new life. Remember that as early as December 1847 he had warned her mother that:

in the retired life which it may perhaps be necessary for me to lead, there must be much that would be irksome to her, unless rendered tolerable by strength of affection; which <u>in part</u> occasioned the singularity of my conduct at Bowers

Well, a conduct which probably occasioned you much concern, and appeared as unjustifiable as strange. Believe me I have none of that false and selfish pride, which would prevent a man from coming frankly forward through mere fear of exposing himself to the chance of a refusal. But I felt that to Miss Gray's open and kind heart, there might be a severe trial in the seclusion from society which my health or my pursuits might often render necessary, I wished to be certain that I <u>could</u> be to her in some degree, at least, the World that she will be to me; and I was the less ready to admit the evidence I could perceive of her affection, because I could not understand how she <u>could</u> love me.[22]

Effie too seems to have been worried about her future husband's reclusive tendencies since the issue was still being negotiated in January when John explained the pitfalls of celebrity to her:

But I never answered your yesterday's letter about friends. Seriously, my love – I will grudge you <u>no</u> good friends: and I am really glad you have so affectionate a heart, but I must warn you against admitting the advances of every one who 'desires your further acquaintance' – Hundreds of people who have nothing to do but to amuse themselves – and can't do it – will be glad of your cheerful society, and others – out of mere idleness and curiosity desire to know <u>me</u> – and to talk nonsense about art – or pass their heavy time over my pictures – or sketches. Against their inroads nothing but the most rude firmness protects me – and the people who cannot get at me otherwise – will try to do so through you. I find myself so well and happy when I am quiet, and so miserable in general society that you will have to be very cautious as to the kind of persons and number, whom you admit to terms of familiarity – All this however we can talk over at our leisure – but in the meantime – don't make your heart a lodging house for every stray comer who will pay their two pence worth of fair speech – else I shall have to come and cut the 'twopenny rope' – and let them down anything but easily. (You know in the London old lodging houses the beds were hammocks – on ropes which were let go every morning at 6.) – but rather arrange your guests on the reformed lodging house principles – about which you can ask your Uncle Andrew – and have them in good order and give them fair entertainment – for indeed – if you don't look to it – your heart will soon be a mere caravanserai – or posada – where there is such a crowd, and it is so hot, that it is better to sleep out o' doors – And you know my love – that you said you liked to be called a Phoenix, but you must remember that there was but <u>one</u> Phoenix at once – whereas – if you bring your Friends upon me by Forty at a time – I shall be compelled to liken you to a Crane – who leads a Triangle with an illimitable base, – of Cranes behind her – so – or perhaps I shall begin to think of myself Alibaba – with a multiplying mirror among the Forty Thieves – or perhaps I shall be reminded rather of Milton's 'locusts warping on the eastern wind' – and shall come home expecting something nice for dinner – and a quiet chat across the table – and find six and twenty cousins or so in the pantry – and everything eaten up, and I shall be obliged if I can live like Mr. Jingle, on a pair of boots and a silk umbrella with an ivory handle! Or if I am reduced – as it seems likely – to live in the Cupboard – for the sake of a quiet life – on the top shelf.[23]

Even though she had been specifically warned about what it would be like, the interminable days spent in provincial towns whilst John examined, sketched and measured the cathedral architecture must have brought Effie down to earth with a bump. The three hours a day she spent trying to sketch in the chill, damp buildings would have been enough to test anybody's temper; even Mr. Ruskin found it slow.[24] Effie, still feeling unwell from Oxford, was given little sympathy or attention. This was not only because of Acland's opinion; John had picked up a cold at the seaside which turned into a cough at Salisbury. Given his medical history his parents were understandably alarmed. Mrs. Ruskin sent him to bed and Effie, mistakenly deemed to be partly responsible for exhausting him, was banished to another room. Effie later reminded Mrs. Ruskin of this incident:

> Whilst we were at Salisbury when you caused me to be put in another room on account of an illness, which he told me his father supposed to arise from his recent connection with me, he used to laugh and say his father was imagining things very different to what they were.[25]

After the marriage broke down, John wrote that he had begun to discover that he had been deceived in his wife's character 'before three months had passed'. This must have been the time to which he was referring. Effie was scathing about John's illness and very critical of Mr. and Mrs. Ruskin's reaction to it:

> John's cold is not away yet but it is not so bad as he had with us and I think it would go away with care if Mr. and Mrs. Ruskin would only let him alone, they are telling him 20 times a day that it is very slight and only nervous which I think it is, at the same time they talk constantly to him about

what he ought to do, and in the morning Mrs. Ruskin begins with 'don't sit near these towels John their [sic] damp' and in the forenoon 'John you must not read these papers till they are dried', and in this steaming weather George [Hobbs] has to take all his clothes to the kitchen fire to air them, and does not let him go out after dinner; we dine at half past four and from five to seven it is as warm as the hottest part of the day. John follows scarcely any of the directions and it would amuse me all this if I did not see that it makes John notwithstanding quite nervous and whenever they ask him how he is he begins to cough, then John coughs for a little and Mr. R says 'that cough is not going away I wish you would take care', and when I never speak of it I never hear him cough once; his pulse and general health are perfectly good. Whilst I am writing John is out of the room and Mr. and Mrs. R are concocting all sorts of remedies. Mrs. R is proposing tea-papers for his chest. They are most kind but I think all this does him harm.[26]

It would appear that Effie did not know that John had suffered from pulmonary tuberculosis or that it might return at any moment. Given the stigma attached to consumptives the Ruskins might not have wished to broadcast the information. Mr. Ruskin later told Mr. Gray that, after Dover, John 'got worse and at Salisbury was so ill that I thought he was going into a decline.'[27] Just such a nervous cough had led to pulmonary bleeding in Naples. With hindsight, removing Effie from John's room might even have been for her benefit rather than his since the disease was known to be infectious. Tragically this difference of opinion on his health led to a confrontation serious enough for John to remember it a year later as the beginning of a change in Effie's

attitude, which her family later attributed to an insidious physical illness. His letter is a remarkable account of the fault lines
opening up in this unfortunate marriage:

> I do not know when the complaint first showed itself – but
> the first that I saw of it was at Oxford after our journey to
> Dover: it showed itself then, as it does now in tears and
> depression: being probably a more acute manifestation, in
> consequence of fatigue and excitement – of disease under
> which she has long been labouring. I have my own opinion
> as to its principal cause – but it does not bear on the matter
> in hand.
>
> I was not however, at the time, at all prepared to allow as
> I should have done for her state of health – and in consequence
> – when, some week or so afterwards, she for the first time
> showed causeless petulance towards my mother, I reproved
> her when we were alone. The matter in question was one
> indeed of a very grave importance – being a wish on my
> mother's part that I should take a blue pill when I went to
> bed – the first use – as far as I remember of 'influence' on her
> part since our marriage – It was however also the first time
> that Effie had heard herself blamed: and the effects upon her
> otherwise excited feelings were permanent – and disposed her
> – as I think, to look with jealousy upon my mother's influ-
> ence over me, ever afterwards.
>
> I was at this time, very sufficiently vexed, for my own part
> – at not being able to get abroad – as well as labouring under
> severe cough – so that I was not able to cheer Effie or support
> her, just at the period when she first began to feel her changed
> position and lament her lost home – It was a sad time for her
> therefore altogether – and the mental and bodily illness were

continually increased. No further unpleasantness however took place between her and my mother.[28]

Effie's sudden removal from a glittering London social scene to sleepy Salisbury, the close and constant company of her in-laws, the tedium of her husband's working milieu, John's cough, the stifling atmosphere in the hotel, the constant bad news from Bowerswell; all conspired to bring home to her the reality of her situation. Since the marriage, the Gray family's financial difficulties had never been far from Effie's mind and money matters constantly surfaced in her letters home. She had been led to believe that her marriage would somehow alleviate her family's situation and had at first been optimistic about being able to help. Her first letter to her parents after the wedding had been intended to reassure them on this count, but also gives some idea of what the tense atmosphere at the wedding must have been like:

I hope we shall find a letter from you there telling us how the party went off after we left & how you feel now that it is all over. I wish for your sakes that other affairs would terminate favourably and I do hope that still things may not be as bad as you anticipate I will write often to you and I hope you will do so [openly] to me that I may have it in my power to be a source of some comfort to you both [...] Tell dear George I will not forget his interests and I think they are in no danger we plan to see about [illeg.] as soon as we possibly can he seemed to feel yesterday more than I thought he should he has a most tender heart. [...] I hope dearest Mama that you are no worse for your exertions now they are over & that you Papa will do your utmost to strengthen your trust in God and that all this present misery is sent by him to you for some wise purpose, do not despair, for what should it signify to you if

you lost the whole world whiles you have so many blessings
and a proper trust in your maker I only speak pardon me my
dear Father for touching on this but repining frets you and
breaks your health, and my mother who would do all for you
is undone when she sees you in such dejection.[29]

By the 22nd of April Effie was already trying out her power 'to
be a source of some comfort' to her family. She had received a
request from Mr. Gray for her to pay a dressmaker's bill which was
£9 larger than he could afford. This was presumably for her
wedding trousseau which was traditionally paid for by the bride's
father. Effie thought it would not be a good idea for her to start
paying her father's bills in such a blatant manner on her honeymoon: 'good as John is I do not think the idea would be agreeable
to anyone'. Mr. Gray was prevailed upon to pay the bill for which
Effie thanked him: 'I am especially grieved just now owing to your
present position but you will never have anything more to pay for
me and I shall endeavour to make it up to you some way at a future
time.' She explained that: 'If Mr. Ruskin had thought or known
that I had paid it, if you had not kindly consented to do so now,
it might have considerably added to the vexation of other matters
and I do hope that whenever we reach London that I may be able
to do something for George who if no longer with you and I also
gone would considerably lighten your mind.' Mr. Gray did not
however send the money directly to Miss Rutherford the dressmaker: Effie had had a better idea: 'instead of sending an order
to her for the money you should send it to me and I would pay
it all together which would be more [regular] way of doing business – be sure my dearest Father that I will do all in my power to
lighten your cares and had I not thought this against your interest I would have paid the account instantly without giving you

this care.'[30] In fact Miss Rutherford the dressmaker seems to have become one of the conduits by which Effie was able to support her family in their continuing financial dire straits. From her letters it is clear that she repeatedly provided clothing for the entire Gray family by combining the costs of their clothing with her own bill. However, by the time they reached Salisbury she had also finally realised that Mr. Ruskin's seemingly inflexible attitude in financial matters prevented her from being able to get her brother a job. She developed an unreasonable resentment towards Mr. Ruskin for not understanding her family's predicament. Probably she did not know that her father was still hiding the full extent of his problems from Mr. Ruskin. On the 23rd of July she wrote to her mother: 'I am glad to think you are comfortable at times but I cannot help being distressed about you all and I often cry at night when I think what a load hangs over you and that I cannot help you in the least degree, but it would be much worse if you did not tell me for then I would fancy things were worse than they are.'[31]

The several days John spent in bed at the White Hart Inn at Salisbury had the desired effect and by the 27th of July he was much better. However by this time Mr. and Mrs. Ruskin were both ill and so the tour of the English cathedrals was cancelled and a swift return to Denmark Hill was decided upon. Just before they left Salisbury Effie learned that she and John now had a house of their own at 31 Park Street off Grosvenor Square. Effie noted that 'Mr. Ruskin kindly pays the ground rent which is £300 and John and I the rent which is £200 a year.' Of course neither John nor Effie had any money of their own which did not derive ultimately from Mr. Ruskin's bank account. 'I am sure you will think this a great deal and so do I as the house is not large but extremely suitable for us and elegantly furnished, but it is the most fashionable place in London and it is Mr. Ruskin's desire that we take it for seeing John's friends and visiting with them it ought to be in a good situation and it is not as if we were making our home there permanently.'³² What the Grays thought about John and Effie's expensive lifestyle whilst contemplating their own desperate situation can only be imagined.

When the party arrived back at Denmark Hill, John was tucked up in bed, but already felt so much better that he started planning his next Continental tour. Effie also received some better news from home. Mr. Gadesden of Ewell Castle was at Bowerswell and lending a sympathetic ear to George's employment problems. She replied on August 3rd:

I hope through Mr. Gadesden you may get something for George. You see I would do anything for him and it seems very strange to me that Mr. Ruskin your oldest friend here should not offer to see if there are any vacant situations which George might fill but I see that both Mr. and Mrs. Ruskin will not and cannot see the use of him coming here or leaving Perth. They think that he could make a business in Perth as his father did before him. I also think there may be an under feeling as to not wishing to have him in London at all; they like to live by themselves and I think would dislike more relations coming about them for you see they are old now and cannot make changes or admit of new things without much trouble, and then they entirely treat me as John's wife and their daughter and indulge me in everything, but then it is a suspicion in Mr. Ruskin's mind I should think for fear I should influence John in the least, so I am obliged to be extremely careful in what I say regarding my own family at home for fear I should think I took

advantage in my present position, for you see he does everything for us, and it is delicate ground for us, especially me,
to speak to him on the subject for he is such a curious person
that you really do not know what he is meditating or devis-
ing. I think you are quite right not to send any letter to him
or rely in the least on him for help. I never speak to him
scarcely about George for I see that both he and Mrs. R. don't
approve of him doing anything but sticking to your desk, and
when they talk a little I always stop for fear of showing them
that I am angry for it does provoke me to hear them talking
of what they don't in the least feel or understand, and laying
down things about what he might do for himself in Perth
which I know to be perfectly impossible, so I just let them
have it all their own way as they say they know Perth much
better than I can do, and as we never have the slightest
dispute upon any subject I think you will agree it is better not
to begin with this one; but although Mr. Ruskin does this of
course John says this morning he, Mr. R. would be very
glad to hear of you getting anything for George through
other people so that although I am guarded in what I say to
him he has nothing to do with my actions and you may
command me in any way you please. I will see Mr. Gadesden and Mr. Ewart or any person in London that you think
could assist you and do what I can but I shall not be in our
house for six weeks yet and by that time perhaps you will have
thought of something I can do for you, and John says I may
do whatever I like.[33]

John and Effie planned to be away for six weeks in Normandy.
In the event they did not return for eleven weeks. Despite being
sick eight times on the boat, Effie, who had never been abroad

before, enjoyed the novelty of being in France. Because of the recent civil disorder they were sometimes the only guests in the hotels, but Effie chatted away to all and sundry, taking the opportunity to improve her French. John was working on his new project *The Seven Lamps of Architecture* which would require painstaking illustrations of Gothic architecture. He filled eight notebooks with sketches and observations as they progressed from Boulogne to Abbeville, Eu, Dieppe, Rouen, Falaise, Vire, Mortain, Avranches, Mont St. Michel, Coutances, St. Lô, Caen, Rouen again and back via Paris. Although Effie tried her best to participate in her husband's work, John realised that accommodating herself to his work was often tedious and unpleasant for her. He told his mother:

But poor Effie would be far better off with Papa and you than with me, for I go out on my own account and when I come in am often too tired or too late to take her out so that she likes to come with me, always to the same place, she sometimes does not go out all day – and I sometimes cannot – for fear of cold, and sometimes will not – for fear of losing time, stop with her to look at shops, the flowers, or the people – But she is very good and enjoys herself when she is out and is content to stop at home. Only you have certainly spoilt me, my dear mother, as far as expectations of walks are concerned – by your excellent walking – I had no idea of the effect of fatigue on women – Effie – if I take her, after she is once tired – half a mile, round – is reduced nearly to fainting and comes in with her eyes full of tears – if however I can once get her to any place where she can rest – she will <u>wait</u> for me three hours together – (and I certainly could not always say as much for you). So I carry my camp seat in my pocket – and when I want to make a note of anything – Effie sits down – n'importe ou – not in the cleanest places always – and is as quiet as a mouse. She is also a capital investigator, and I owe it to her determined perseverence – and fearlessness of dark passages and dirt in the cause of – philosophy – or curiosity – that I saw the other day the interior of the Abbaye St. Armande, certainly the most exquisite piece of wood painting for rooms I ever saw in any country. Her fatigue, too, depends more on the heat than the distance, and she has been up St. Catherine's with me this evening with great enjoyment – much increased by finding heather and bluebells in quantities at the top.[34]

Whilst they were in France John tried to keep to his usual regime. Up at six, working till lunchtime then 'I am at Effie's service till four', which essentially meant walking around the town for exercise and shopping, then more work till six, dinner and to bed at nine. Effie copied up his notes in the morning but not without some problems of legibility. On September 10th John told his father that 'Effie is sitting by my side just now writing out pages from the Proverbs for me – and printing them almost that they might be quite legible and she has written nearly all my diary for me from my dictation – saving my eyes for the present much, though if my eyes are to be saved eventually I am afraid she will have to write it over for me again.'[35] Whether she rewrote it or not, he later told her that he had made considerable use of the notes she helped him write in Normandy.[36]

By this time Effie was feeling the strain. More bad news about her family's health and finances had made her miserable. On the 28th August Mr. Gray wrote to 'Phemy' about trying to find a position in London for her brother George. The weather in England and Ireland had retarded the harvest yet again 'which must of necessity cause an efflux of bullion to America to purchase grain and make money scarce during next season – this will lower the value of all Railway property and produce much misery.' Mr Gray could not understand why his bank manager had not already foreclosed on him. By the 24th he had told Mr Ruskin that Mr. Burns stood to 'lose his situation' because of the Gray debt.[37] On September 3rd John had told his father that Effie was feeling very low the night before but:

> She has recovered to-day. Perhaps these matters are good for us – I am certainly terribly selfish and care little for anything so that I can get quiet – and a good pencil – and a Turner or two – it was and perhaps still is growing upon me – and it may be just as well that I am forced to think and feel a little for others – at least I may think – but I don't feel – even when poor Effie was crying last night I felt it by no means as a husband should – but rather a bore – however I comforted her in a very dutiful way – and it may be as well perhaps on the other hand that I am not easily worked upon by these things.[38]

By the 9th he was telling his father that: 'The only thing we can find to complain of is that Effie loses her hair continually; I wish you would ask my mother or William or Dr Grant why this is – it is really getting serious – and besides the thing itself, seems to be a sign of bad health – it comes out by handfuls when it is brushed in the morning. It has come out in the same way ever since she went to Dover.'[39] Effie thought that the proffered advice to shave her head was unhelpful and when the couple passed through Paris on their way home John paid 82 francs for 'Effie's hair'. This was almost certainly a false hair piece to replace the lost tresses which she had previously worn in braids around her head.

The hair loss may well have been related to the stress of her situation. George Gray had by this time addressed Mr. Ruskin directly about young George's prospects and told him that his legal business no longer produced enough income to employ George. Nor could he place him with lawyers in Edinburgh. Mr. Ruskin, who had always thought that George should continue with the law, now explained that when Ruskin, Telford and Domecq had been set up it had been decided that relations should not be employed by the firm. An exception had been made for William Richardson but after Mr. Ruskin had paid his keep for two years, he had proved useless and had then gone into decline and died. Their present clerks had been with them for 15 and 31 years and should any well-paid position fall vacant they would have a prior claim. Mr. Gray had also asked if George could stay with the Ruskins and try to find a position, with the inference that John and Effie's rich and powerful friends might help. Mr. Ruskin explained that although this had been possible for George as a schoolboy at Charterhouse, and might yet be possible for George as a professional man such as a lawyer, as a colonial broker he would be excluded from the society in which John and Effie moved; as indeed Mr. Ruskin himself, as a merchant, was excluded. This would put George in an intolerable position within the household and do nothing for his prospects. The debate rumbled on between the Ruskins and the Grays. John, under pressure both from his own conscience and from a distraught Effie, told his father that he felt it might be wrong to cut off his own relations in order to seek familiarity with strangers, but felt guilty enough that his father, now 63, was still working to provide a life of luxury for Effie and himself, without asking him to support George as well. The Grays had been offended by Mr. Ruskin's letter so he wrote another more emollient one.

John also wrote to both George and Mr. Gray. The problem was finally resolved when just before his nineteenth birthday George was found a position in a lawyers' office in Edinburgh. The Gray family however remained permanently resentful of the Ruskins for their intransigent attitude in the matter.

This was not all Effie had to worry about. Her father's railway shares had sunk again 'so as to destroy all hope.'[40] Scarlet fever had broken out at Bridgend and her siblings were confined to the house. Her aunt Jessie Jameson whom she loved 'exceedingly' was terminally ill and in fact died in September. Effie had been unwell even before all this; now she told her mother that: 'My distress will scarcely let me write and my tears blind me and have given me a severe headache.'[41] She told her father that: 'John sympathizes with me most kindly but he did not know her and could not be supposed to understand her as he only saw her a little last year and this. He like you Papa has a great dislike to mourning and did not wish me to wear more than half mourning' adding later on: 'we are extremely happy together and have been married half a year today.'[42]

The tour ended with a visit to Paris, which still bore the scars of the recent unrest. John and Effie found it melancholy despite visits to the Louvre and the theatre. From the window of the Hotel Meurice on the Rue de Rivoli, Effie gazed at the deserted Tuileries Gardens 'and only saw two people pass, a great many shops are shut and I did not see a single well-dressed man or woman the whole day above the rank of shop keepers [...] I saw no nice things, the people hanging about the streets have an air of distrust and vice plainly written. I never saw anything so triste but I am very glad to have seen it although I should rather not pass the winter there.'[43]

Just before they returned John noted that the continental tour had not been an unqualified success, at least as far as Effie was concerned:

> Effie – however much she has enjoyed herself – seems not to be quite so entrapped by the Continent, she says there is no place she has seen she would care to go back to, except Rouen. She seems to like the idea of keeping house.[44]

Looking back a year later he saw the tour as having been even more disastrous:

> we got abroad at last: I had hoped that this would put us all to rights –: but whether I over fatigued her in seeing cathedrals – or whether we drank too much coffee at night – her illness continued to increase – It was probably not much bettered by the necessarily distressing tone of her home letters at this period: (that of Mrs. Jameson's illness) but be this as it may, I ascribed her general depression to natural causes – and perhaps did more harm by endeavouring to distract when I ought to have soothed her – So she returned worse than she went: and I still in entire ignorance that there was anything particularly the matter with her.[45]

Their return to England was delayed because the Eleventh Legion of the French National Guard were embarking for England on an excursion. Effie, who had a *penchant* for men in uniform, enjoyed the spectacle and sent her mother a detailed description of their dress and appearance. It goes without saying that she found herself alone in the Ladies' Cabin chatting with four of them for an hour before the boat sailed at eleven o'clock that night.[46]

CHAPTER XII

KEEPING HOUSE

કર

John and Effie returned to Denmark Hill to find Caroline, Countess Béthune, Adèle Domecq's sister, in residence. John later described what happened:

> When we returned the Bethunes were staying at D. Hill: Effie wished excessively to avoid them – but this was not possible: nor was I at all sorry for this impossibility, for I wished Effie to know Mme de Bethune – and I thought she would be happy in doing so – I do not know whether she was or not – but doubtless the noise and excitement increased her illness – and it came to something like a crisis.[1]

In the event Effie quite enjoyed meeting the Béthunes. The Count made her laugh and she had much in common with the Countess. Effie found the lifestyle of the Béthunes in Paris interesting enough to relate it to her mother. It must have given her much pause for thought. The Countess, she wrote:

> speaks a great deal agreeably without saying anything that one can remember. At Paris she goes to a ball three times a week, the intervening nights to the <u>spectacle</u> but she seems happy here. Last night I would not dance [Effie was in mourning for aunt Jessie] but she and Mr. Watson [Mr. Ruskin's head clerk] were dancing. I asked the Count why he did not dance; he explained what is curious that in Paris the married men never dance, the married ladies always. The Count says what is the use of the young men but to amuse and be useful

to the Ladies. The young unmarried ladies, for there are hardly any they marry so young, are taken no notice of at all, and, says the Count, if the femmes had not some amusement they would get very triste and dull. She comes out twice a day in entirely new toilettes of which however she has no credit at all for her femme de chambre dresses her, buys everything, makes all her bonnets, caps, dresses, and treats her the same as a doll.[2]

Such candid talk may well have prompted Effie to reassess her first impressions of the Continent. It may have also given her insight into her own marriage. Was the Béthune marriage also one of convenience? Did Caroline Domecq bring her £30,000 dowry and the Count his title? Meanwhile Mr. Ruskin had given Effie a magnificent peace offering in the form of a dress-length of black velvet for Miss Rutherford to make up. The account book entry of 'Effie velvet gown £18-10' shows what a generous gift this was. By this time Effie was beginning to draw on her allowance, unspent whilst she was on the Continent, and as she became more confident in her manipulation of her finances there were also regular presents of money to her family. In the 27th October letter from Denmark Hill she told her mother:

I send you ten pounds, give £5 to George from me the other half is for you because I know at the end of the year you have many subscriptions for charity, missions and this should never be neglected and if you will accept this money from me and apply it to this purpose I shall be obliged to you to begin you can either give a little of it to [Rose Kitty Cock?] above the Park or buy some winter clothing for her, I have only one thing more to say that I − − [illeg. Private?] Remember! − <u>wish you only to speak to me about the money</u> John

<u>does not like to know anything about my money after he gives
it to me</u> which is very delicate in him because he knows very
well that I buy or send you a little present now and then he
says the money is entirely my own & he would be very sorry
if I had not a little over for anything I desired & you know
when I hadn't had always more pleasure in giving it away than
keeping it. I will send dear Papa something nice for winter
if you will tell me what he most wants the servants also in the
box. In haste.[3]

She wrote again the very next day but had already forgotten
the subterfuge of the money being for charitable donations. For
the Grays in 1848, charity began at home:

I hope you received the parcel and money quite safely yesterday. I did not like to send more in one parcel but I am very
happy to find from your note this morning that it will be
useful to George. I hope the enclosed ten pounds will be useful
to you in getting a few wants either for his needs or yours. I
am very glad that being so long away I am easily enabled to
send you this. Tell George when he is in Edinburgh by waiting a little I will be able again to send him a Christmas
present of money, which though a trifle he may like from me
better than anything else. John and I were talking of you this
morning and he wants me to send you what money I can but
does not wish you to know that he knows anything about it
which I think very delicate & kind but I think it right to tell
you to show you how good he is how liberal and that all that
I do is approved by [word missing] but as I said yesterday <u>you
must not appear in any letters excepting to me to mention
the subject</u> I think you very economical.[4]

From the postscript to this letter we discover that John was paying the postage on the Grays' letters. Three days later Effie was again reassuring her parents: 'I am very glad that the money was so a propos and you may be sure that I will not forget my promise and you may be sure that when I can give you shall never want and I will write to George as often as I can.'[5]

After George entered the lawyer's office in Edinburgh, John helped him out with his rent, giving him £2 monthly out of his own allowance.[6] Mr. Gray seems to have mentioned this inadvertently in a letter to Mr. Ruskin. For his part Mr. Ruskin was not unsympathetic. On hearing about George he wrote to Mr. Gray on the 6th November:

> I hope you do not think that because I said I could do nothing in the City for George that were you under a temporary cloud I should see him at a loss for a small sum to get him through his Law Studies. As to your position – I had no idea when I wrote of your House and Furniture being touched. I alluded to property generally, the reserve wherewith to continue Business, should include House and Furniture. I only regret you cannot by any cession of property of which the public generally can have no knowledge check or arrest the heavy Interest running which will eat you up as it did the Duke of Buckingham [...] but as I know nothing of your Liabilities and Shares I ought not to judge.[7]

Mr. Gray was still in trouble and Mr. Ruskin still didn't know the full story.

On November 2nd John and Effie moved out of Denmark Hill. Effie was delighted with their new home. 31 Park Street was 'a nice little box of a place' six stories high and with just about one room to a floor. There was a drawing room, large library with a small conservatory, a downstairs kitchen and a breakfast and dining room opening into each other. It had servants' quarters on the top floor and a spare room which Effie instantly earmarked for her brother George's use. This house in town was so fashionable that it made them close neighbours to Lady Davy. It had a specific purpose: to launch them into Society. Mr. Ruskin even bought them a visitors' book. He also provided them with a brougham carriage, painted in their own livery with intertwined rose and thistle on the door. The rose was emblematical of John's Englishness and the thistle of Effie's Scottishness. One wonders if they were depicted with their respective thorns and prickles.

By November 9th Effie was busy with the account books for the new establishment and discovered that it was four times more expensive to live in London than in Perth. However, interest rates had come down from 5% to 3% and she noted that the railway situation was improving.[8] On the twelfth she told her mother: 'anything else you want I shall be truly delighted to send you and wish you would just say anything you desire for I will not have another opportunity for some time likely.'[9] Effie had also been trying to persuade her parents to visit, even describing a typical Park Street meal to whet their appetites. By this time Effie and John were receiving Society visitors. Among the first were Murray the publisher, Lockhart and Lady Davy. On the 5th of December Effie recounted in a letter how Lady Davy had read extracts of her 1818 diary to her which included accounts of her time in Venice. Interestingly the same letter contained her reaction to some interesting news from Perth. Prizie Tasker and William were back in town. Of Prizie she wrote:

> [John] was wishing he was here so much today for he is very
> anxious for me to have some dancing. And the moment I

heard of his being in Perth I polkaed round the room by
instinct to a particular tune that I used to like. I would like
a polka with him so much for he really was my pet partner
or as the Countess talks of <u>mes danseurs</u>.[10]

The fascinating juxtaposition of thoughts in this letter united
Venice, young men, dancing and Countess Béthune's continental morality. Add to this John's apparent complicity and the
result was a dangerous and prescient mixture.

Effie must have found her new life not unpleasant. John's talent
and the Ruskin family wealth had catapulted her into a glittering world of travel, nobility, celebrity, art, fame and money not
commonly available to penniless lawyers' daughters from Perth.
If Ruskin's father is to be believed, the newly-weds had embarked
on a lifestyle which was to consume fifteen and a half thousand
pounds in six years.[11] In their first winter in Park Street they continued the social round. Effie's letters home are filled with 'nobs',
politicians and intellectuals. By December Effie was even worrying less about her father's finances. Mr. Ruskin had reassured her
that Mr. Gray's Boulogne and Amiens shares would improve
because France had stabilised under a new government and there
was increased confidence in the Railways. However the socialising seems to have taken its toll. By the time John and Effie went
to spend Christmas at Denmark Hill, they were both ill with a
cold and cough. John later described what happened:

> The depression gained upon her daily – and at last my
> mother – having done all she could to make her happy, in vain,
> was I suppose – partly piqued – and partly like myself –
> disposed to try some serious reason with her: finding her one
> day in tears when she ought to have been dressing for dinner,
> she gave her a scold – which if she had not been so ill she

would have deserved. Poor Effie dressed and came down –
looking very miserable – I had seen her look so too often to
take particular notice of it – and besides thought my mother
right: Unluckily Dr. Grant was with us – and seeing Effie look
ready to faint thought she must want his advice – I – being
thoroughly puzzled about the whole affair, thought so too –
and poor Effie, like a good girl as she is – took – to please me
– what Dr. Grant would have her – weakened herself more
– sank under the influenza – and frightened me at last very
sufficiently – and heaven only knows, now, when she will
forgive my mother. So far as I know them – these are the
causes – and this was the progress of her illness – and of her
change of feeling towards my parents.[12]

According to Effie, her cold turned to influenza, fever and loss
of appetite as a result of the change from their early hours and
moderate habits at Park Street to company every day, 'six o'clock
dinner and not in bed till between twelve and one.' However since
Effie had taken to her bed after only two days this was not a very
convincing explanation. There was plainly a distinct absence of
sympathy for her at Denmark Hill. John had a phobia about
invalids and Effie nurtured a continuing resentment of his
parents because of their intransigence over her brother George.
Dosing Effie indiscriminately with 'Epicacuahana' and laudanum
pills did not help and neither did being treated by two doctors
who disagreed with each other. She was however certain that she
would be cured within two days if she was allowed to go home
to Park Street. It is difficult not to suspect that, whatever the state
of her health, spending time with John's parents was the real reason
for her being miserable. In the event Mayfair didn't cure her,
although she certainly improved, particularly after her mother

arrived to visit her. Effie and her mother came to Denmark Hill with John on the 23rd but only John stayed to dinner. Mrs. Gray reported back to her husband that Effie was not sleeping and had lost weight. Mr. Gray after warning his wife: 'Do not spend sixpence you can avoid', also told her that the Share List was improving and, having brought his full business acumen to bear on the newly invented electric light, declared that it would never do for anything practical and that his gas shares were safe.[13] What he didn't tell her was that her children had all come down with whooping cough.

Effie's sudden decision to return with her mother to Perth at the beginning of February 1849 has never been properly explained. It may have been because of her ill-health, but Mrs. Ruskin for one was sceptical in a letter to her husband: 'I daresay she will very readily give you some account of the parties she was at after she gets to Perth.'[14] Even Mr. Gray's first thought was that it would do Effie good to see her old friends. Mrs. Gray and her daughter took the train to York and then onwards the next day to Edinburgh where, on February 6th, Mr. Gray told them how seriously ill the children were at Bowerswell. Mrs. Gray went straight home. Effie stayed in Edinburgh till the 10th before travelling home with her brother George to Perth. On the first of March her seven year-old brother Robert died of the whooping cough.

Effie was to remain in Perth for almost eight months. Given the appalling situation at home, Effie had ample reason to prolong her stay. There may however have been another reason why she stayed so long. Whilst she was at Bowerswell she could hand over the whole of her monthly allowance to her parents. Given that the cost of living was so low in Perth, a quarter of that in the metropolis, this would have helped the Grays avoid the worst consequences of their financial destitution. Significantly, it was whilst she was there that Mr. Gray was able to negotiate the loan that lifted him out of immediate danger of bankruptcy. On the 19th of May Mr. Ruskin wrote to congratulate Mr. Gray:

> I cannot delay replying to your kind letter of 9 May and expressing the great delight I feel and offering my sincere congratulations on your having emancipated yourself from the Thraldom in which you were held by Railroad and unsettled Bank Accounts. Nothing is so wearing as suspence and my former Letters would show you that I eagerly desired any kind of termination to your late troubles in preference to your hanging on, looking for what might never happen – to the entire discomfort of yourself and family – undermining your health and destroying half the powers and faculties of your mind [...] If I understand your arrangement, it is that you are left with a Debt to the Bank due in three years subject to Interest of 3½% till paid – but in no event with any other liability and entitled to any surplus that the Bank may realise over and above the £3000 should Shares recover themselves. I think it a far better settlement than the state of the market warranted and it gives me an Impression of great liberality on the part of the Bank and the friendly consideration shown by Mr. Burns. It speaks highly both for the Bank and for you, as I cannot believe the Bank would so treat persons generally. They know you and value you evidently and show judgement and discrimination in thus favouring you.[5]

Mr. Ruskin was genuinely pleased that Mr. Gray had solved his problems but, given the state of the market, he was baffled that such a generous loan could have been arranged by Mr. Burns who, several months previously, had almost lost his job at the bank because of Mr. Gray's debts. From the letter it is clear that the bank was holding Mr. Gray's shares as security and that at these rates it would cost Mr. Gray £105 a year to service the loan. Effie should have received about £200 from her allowance during the eight months she spent at Perth but John specifically told her:

> Take care my love that you be not cramped for want of money, you can always have anything paid in London by writing to Mr. Watson or Ritchie at Billiter St., indeed I left £40. with Ritchie for any occasions of the kind: but if you want more money at Perth and can let me know, I will tell them to send it.[16]

This indicates that John was wholly responsible for paying her allowance to her, but there is also a suggestion in one of Mrs. Ruskin's letters that Mr. Ruskin had asked Effie to give him accounts whilst she was at Perth. Whether these were accounts for the train journey or for her general expenditure is not certain from the context.[17]

The moment Effie left for Perth, John moved back into Denmark Hill. Except for a few days in the following autumn, the expensive house at Park Street was to remain empty for fifteen months. He was working hard to finish *The Seven Lamps of Architecture* before the traditional family tour and Effie's birthday on the 7th of May. After she reached Perth, Effie had decided not to accompany John and his parents on their trip to Switzerland. On April 18th the two horse-drawn carriages which had already been hired for the journey were tied onto a railway wagon at the back of the train to Folkestone where they were lashed to the deck of the boat for the Channel crossing to Boulogne. John was still scrambling the final pages of *The Seven Lamps* back to his proof reader and the 'final packet of revises' went to Smith and Elder as he waited in a snowstorm for the ferry to sail, which was not until the next day. He bit the final etching plate of 'Giotto's tower' in the wash hand basin of the hotel in Folkestone before crossing to Boulogne on the 23rd.[18] By this time the ill-fated Boulogne-Amiens Railway had finally been built but Mr. Gray, still a shareholder, received a depressing report that it was sleepy and slow when John, his parents, man-servant George, maid-servant Ann Strachan and the Ruskin carriages travelled the line on their way to Paris.

John wrote regularly to his wife during the eight months they were apart, but none of Effie's letters have come to light. John's surviving letters to her began with an affectionate, indeed loving tone, but ended with probably the nearest he had yet come to being angry with her. The Ruskin parents too started off with sympathetic and supportive messages but before long both sets of parents were exchanging increasingly testy opinions about her illness and her rôle. On the 4th of March Mr. Ruskin wrote a letter of condolence to Mr. Gray telling him how distressed they had been to hear of little Robert's death: 'You seem to be afflicted beyond the ordinary Lot of Man, in the Loss of so many sweet Children and the thoughts of these things darkens my very soul'. Unfortunately he then linked the child's death in a very insensitive way to Mr. Gray's financial problems:

> I daresay your greatest sufferings for the threatened diminution of your fortune have arisen not in fear of your own privations but on account of your family. I wish to God you could come to persuade yourself that it may be registered in Heaven, that on condition only of your ceasing to vex and disturb yourself about your worldly fortunes, will the health and Lives of your remaining children be preserved.

Mr. Ruskin was also not very happy about Effie being in Perth whilst John went abroad, but reasoned that John was not travelling for pleasure but for his work, just as he himself had always had to do; Effie had been bored in Normandy and since Christmas she had been too ill for 'Swiss Excursions.' John's work in the Alps was for what he then thought would be the final volume of *Modern Painters*, after which his father thought he would settle down to a more domestic existence:

> I hope my Son will accomplish all he wants this Summer to complete his work and become less of the Labouring Artist – in future – It may be his pleasure but to be with him is other peoples Toil – out of Doors at any rate – They must however arrange their comings and goings with each other – They will no doubt settle down very delightfully at last pleased with some house at Home and I hope allow you and me to come to hear them in chorus singing Dulce Dulce Domum.[19]

John seems to have genuinely missed his wife. Even before he left England he told her:

> My dearest Effie
>
> I am beginning to weary for a letter sadly: and I hardly know how I shall do at Boulogne tomorrow: for Boulogne is especially associated with my dearest wife, I having never gone there but that once with you: and it seems but a day since we were walking about the town in search of worsted: and choosing the pattern <u>the</u> pattern which cost us such worlds of trouble, afterwards.[20]

His following letters are interesting for the information they give about their physical relationship. Despite not having consummated the marriage, they had shared a bed and because the marriage was unconsummated it should not therefore be assumed that no physical intimacy took place. On the 24th of April he wrote:

> I expect a line from my dearest love to morrow at Sens: Do you know, pet, it seems almost a dream to me that we have been married: I look forward to meeting you: and to your next bridal night: and to the time when I shall again draw your dress from your snowy shoulders: and lean my cheek upon them, as if you were still my betrothed only: and I had never held you in my arms. God bless you, my dearest.
>
> Ever your devoted
>
> J Ruskin[21]

There are several points to be noted here. Firstly that he remembered the first night of the honeymoon with pleasure which would not have been the case if, as Admiral James suggested, he had been repelled by her body. Secondly that he was looking forward to experiencing her naked body again, which, again, would not have been the case if he had found her disgusting. Finally, he was still strongly attracted to her. From his next letter we learn that Effie replied to this letter at some length, referring specifically to their honeymoon:

> My Darling Effie
>
> I have your precious letter here: with the account so long and kind – of all your trial at Blair Athol – indeed it must have been cruel my dearest: I think it will be much nicer next time, we shall neither of us be frightened.[22]

This seems to be a direct reference to the arrangement between them that put off the consummation of the marriage until she was 25. Interestingly he ends the letter 'my dearest dearest bride' rather than 'my dearest dearest wife.'[23] Effie for her part seems to have been writing as a fond partner, asking if John was thinking about her, but the strained relations between the bride and her in-laws were never far from the surface:

> My dearest Wife –
>
> I did indeed think of you, both at Boulogne and at Paris as you will see by my letters: and much here today: walking in one of my favourite places, as you will see described as it appears now – (I came here to see it again), in the opening of the sixth chapter of the Seven Lamps – indeed we often and all think of you, and I often hear my mother or Father saying – 'poor child – if she <u>could</u> but have thrown herself openly upon us, and trusted us, and felt that we desired only her happiness, and would have made her ours, how happy she might have been: and how happy she might have made us all.'
>
> And indeed I long for you my pet: but I have much here to occupy me and keep me interested – and so I am able to bear the longing better perhaps than you, who have only the routine of home: I hope next summer I shall be able to make you happy in some way of your own.[24]

Effie was still suffering from her obstinate 'cold', which did not however prevent her from visiting friends and riding, and John, after travelling through foul and unseasonable weather to the Alps, also fell ill with a similar though more transient ailment. For her birthday, Effie received from her husband a bracelet by M. Bauttes of Geneva. He also promised her 'a <u>set</u> of Geneva ornaments' but those she would have to choose for herself. In his letter to his 'Darling Love' on the 2nd of May John described the family's gruelling itinerary so far with a view to persuading Effie, who slept badly, found early rising difficult and walking exhausting and sometimes painful, that this tour would not have been pleasant for her:

> But I am afraid my pet that you could not have managed to travel with us at the pace we have come, at all. Let me see: Monday, up at six, off at ½ past 8 – days rest at Boulogne. Tuesday, up at ½ past five, off at eight, get to Sens at six – evening – Thursday, off at ½ past eight, eleven hours to Mont Bard. Friday, off at 10, seven hours to Dijon. Saturday, off at eight, 10 hours to Champagnole. Monday off at ½ past eight and nine hours to Geneva – one whole day at Geneva – off today at eight. 9½ hours here.[25]

Back in Perth Effie, still apparently unwell, was struggling through Sismondi's *Histoire des Républiques Italiennes au Moyen Age* probably on John's behalf. He asked her to note all the references to Venetians. She was also 'plagued by the difficulty' of copying Raphael drawings. Having to explain the separation to her friends was even more trying. John was irritated by her comments:

> I cannot understand what it is that is now the matter with you: as you have everything to which you are accustomed, and have had, I should think, a good deal of pleasant society and excitement. Your friend Miss Boswell must be a nice clever creature: but it seems to me she has a good deal more cleverness than judgement or discretion, or she would understand the very simple truth that it was not <u>I</u> who had left <u>you</u> but <u>you</u> who had left <u>me</u> – Certainly I never wanted you to leave London, but you could not be happy unless you went to Perth: and away you went much more to the astonishment of <u>my</u>

friends in London than my departure to Switzerland can be to the surprise of yours in Scotland: I wonder whether they think that a husband is a kind of thing who is to be fastened to his wife's waist with her pincushion and to be taken about with her wherever she chooses to go. However, my love, never mind what they say or think: I shall always be glad when you can go with me and always take you with me wherever I think it is safe for your health that you should go, when it is not, you must be prepared to part with me for a month or two as I must either follow my present pursuits with the same zeal that I have hitherto followed them, or go into the church.[26]

Somehow it is difficult to imagine Effie in a country vicarage.

Effie's state of health became the main topic of the letters to and from Perth. John was not the only one mystified by her continuing complaint. On the 19th of May Mr. Ruskin wrote to Mr. Gray:

I am concerned to read your account of Phemy. By a few words, now and then read to us by John from her Letters, I should guess her to be full of Health and spirits of vigorous mind and Body and I cannot but hope that the sense of weakness felt by herself and apparent want of power to take Exercise as entirely nervous and so far a delusion as most nervous complaints are – though there must be some cause even to produce the feeling and conviction of weakness. There is always the comfort of knowing there is no great mischief doing – no permanent Injury to the frame. All these feelings may be dissipated in a day and I trust a Visit to Edinburgh and Ayr and Horse Exercise will come in aid of Recovery.[27]

Whilst in Edinburgh Effie saw Dr. James Simpson, the thirty-seven-year-old obstetrician and Professor of Midwifery at the University.[28] This did not necessarily indicate that Effie's problem was gynæcological; Simpson was later to treat Effie for an ordinary sore throat. Simpson was an early exponent of anæsthesia, and the discoverer of chloroform. He had recently published a riposte to supposed religious objections to the practice of anæsthesia in childbirth,[29] and had been appointed Physician Accoucher to Queen Victoria. He was not however responsible for the administration of chloroform to the head of the Church of England at the birth of her son Prince Leopold in 1857. This was because there were concerns about his partisan promotion of chloroform. It has been pointed out that he ignored warnings that chloroform could be extremely dangerous in certain circumstances and almost certainly suffered patient mortalities as a result. Lady Trevelyan noted a long conversation with him in 1853 in which his main topic seems to have been the high level of recreational use of anæsthetic drugs amongst Edinburgh Society.[30] Effie now told John what Simpson had said and Mrs. Gray wrote to Mrs. Ruskin on the same subject. Infuriatingly none of these letters have come to light and the actual illness was never specified in those that have. John replied:

> We have a line – my mother has at least – from Mrs. Gray –
> of which the contents might be summarily expressed in the
> sentence –'you see I was right' – it tells us what you told me
> of Dr Simpson's opinion: but does not so much as hint at any
> probable means of your recovery: However you may tell her
> when you write that she was right, and that now if she will
> give me any advice as to your management I shall receive it
> with respect: I should like to hear what she supposes brought
> it on in London – as it was not the influenza, and you had

it months before: I have been thinking over all you told me and it seems to me in the first place that your chief complaint is a nervous weakness preventing you from taking exercise enough to bring on perspiration – you would faint before you would perspire – you will not I think get out of this but by forced exercise to utmost of your strength every day: until you are able to take enough to put you into a heat: and then you will get well fast enough if you take it regularly: riding will I suppose be an intermediate means of gaining strength: spare no expence that may promote your recovery [...] your mother appears quite happy at discovering that you have a disease that may make you miserable for years. Your letter does not say a word of what Dr Simpson said was the cause of your complaint. I should like to write to him myself – what is his address? or if I write will you be in Edinburgh again so as to be able to send the letter with a fee?[31]

On the 4th of June Mr. Ruskin also wrote on the subject:

I wrote about fourteen days ago – I send a few lines now to beg of you to express for Mrs Ruskin, her best thanks to Mrs Gray for her kind letter giving an account of Phemy's visit to Dr Simpson and his opinion which was satisfactory and gave us hopes of speedy Improvement but we were greatly concerned to hear from John that by a letter just received no Improvement has taken place and that Mrs J.R returns to Perth scarcely so Well as when she left. It is the nature of these Complaints that whilst they are never Serious they are the most difficult to cure – because nervous patients never submit for a week together to either medical treatment or Control – It is impossible for Baths to effect any change on the functions of the System – instanter – Some regular course of Diet

– Baths – and Exercise will require to be persevered in for some time – It appeared that Phemy was best with the Horse Exercise at Perth, and I hope this will be resumed but always in moderation – overfatigue is Injurious – in task work or over Books or Drawing – a pleasing division of pursuits pursued with Interest – will be medicinal – however it is easy to advise – the difficulty is to make any one troubled with nervous weakness, persevere in any thing. I should be greatly obliged by your own opinion of Phemy's Health and how she appears compared with her appearance when she came down to Perth in Feby.[32]

From subsequent letters it is clear that Effie's 'nervous weakness' was somehow linked to her perception of her situation and that Mr. Gray was attempting to put her case to Mr. Ruskin as tactfully as he could. Mr. Ruskin was not one for subtle hints and pleaded for some plain speaking:

I have written you lately but I address you again to repeat the expression of my sincere regret at the continuance of our Daughters bad state of Health, and farther to inform you of the trouble we are all in from not knowing what should be done if anything can be done, on our part to bring about an amendment – It is evident to me that my Son also suffers from not being able to make out what his wifes entire feelings and wishes are. After all the encomiums heard about freedom, reserve and discretion I am of the opinion that much of the unhappiness of the World arises from persons not freely writing or speaking out their mind and this more especially with those Beings who are the most unlikely to cherish sentiments or feelings to which they would hesitate to give utterance.

It must be your desire as it is ours to see our Children as happy as the world can make them and I wish to God that we could at once learn or divine the cause of the least interruption of their peace or their enjoyment and that we could be the means of removing it. It is in part a consolation to me to be able to say that all our anxiety at present is on your Daughters account for except the uneasiness my Son experiences from Phemy's lingering state of health, I never saw him so well in his Life, nor so capable of following out his pursuits either independently, or with any share of sympathy that his nearest and dearest, or his friends and acquaintances may be kind enough to afford him. These pursuits are at least respectable and innocent, whether they be useful or not we must leave others who are better able to judge, to pronounce. About your Daughter both Mrs Ruskin and myself must continue to be anxious and as I use no reserve I will confess to you that the feeling is mingled with sorrow and disappointment: The chief aim of our Life when your Daughter became ours was to make her and my Son happy – all the young people that ever came about Mrs Ruskin have clung to her with Love and respect and I have heard from all of them, expressions of gratitude for kindness and advice received that have evinced the depth of Impression made. We have by chance met a Lady here, now above 40 years of age, that told me that she owed most of any good she had done to advice given to her when 16 years of age by Mrs Ruskin. We had fondly flattered ourselves that Phemy had some attachment to us all – I even thought as our House was agreeable to my Son that she might have stayed for a time with us, until they had formed some plan of a permanent residence – The Foreigners who were with us and who live much with their parents, expressed their surprise that she did not, but I quite approved of their taking the London House, because I wished them to be in the best Society. I mean best by Intellect and Birth, which if left alone they had opportunity of doing, but which with us they could not do to the same extent, but I could not be otherwise than surprised that before they had been three months settled, the arrangements of the House were changed, Mrs Gray sent for and a return to Scotland planned and executed and all the great expence of a Town Residence entirely thrown away. I could in no way account for this proceeding because I had seen no strong attachment to Perth in Phemy before, indeed one of my fears before the union was that from her so frequently leaving her home, her habits might be less domestic than might be desired – Her health was delicate but as the result has proved, I foresaw no great probability of that being much improved by a separation from her Husband and it was well known both before and after the union that my Son would not make Perth even a temporary Residence.

Phemy was prepared for this and indeed always knew he had no partiality for Scotland. I think much better of her than to believe that the country which she so often left before marriage, is now to be preferred to her Husband. I excuse her from not being able to sympathise in many of his local attachments, they come from early association and peculiar pursuits: ninety women out of a hundred would soon tire of this place and would prefer what I have heard Phemy say she would, the flying over a Desart on Horseback, but I would expect from her great good sense and talents that she would see that her ambition of which she has too much mind not to have a good share, could be little gratified by her Husband

abandoning the Haunts where his Genius finds food and occupation, to seek for stirring adventures which might end in
more mishap than profit. I am quite aware that his pursuits
to ordinary people may appear absurd but Phemy is not one
of these ordinary people. I fully expect her to comprehend
that however absurd or useless her Husband's present pursuits
or productions may appear to many around her, his being able
to follow them out and to complete them affords the best
chance of her ambition being gratified and his own character's aim and ends being established for he has the ambition
of working out some independence for himself. The few
who trouble themselves about him, are very much mistaken
if they think my Son is here for pleasure only or even to
accompany his Father and mother. He is here for hard work
and which it would be a great loss to him not to finish. In
fact my Business or the arrival of Mr. Domecq might bring
Mrs Ruskin and me home in a fortnight but we should not
think of letting him come with us unless his work were done
– and if Phemys Letters were to bring him home before his
time – the effect on her might not last a fortnight and she
would get worse by thinking that she had interrupted his
plans. You may tell her that Mrs Ruskin and I, though the
change was unexpected, can entirely forgive her rejection of
our kindness or good offices but we do expect from the Love
which we hope and believe, she bears my Son that she will
try to make his pleasures hers, to like what he likes, for his
sake, and to hear of the places which he loves with pleasure,
and if I might take the liberty of prescribing for her own
comfort and amendment, I should urge an effort to be made
to sacrifice every feeling to duty, to become interested and
delighted in what her Husband may be accomplishing by a

short absence, and to find a satisfaction in causing him no unnecessary anxiety, that his faculties may be in full force for the purpose to which they are devoted – I trust we may all yet understand one another and that there will be perfect love and happiness between our Children – I do not in the least wish to interfere – I studied to leave them when in their own House, entirely to their own guidance but now I speak to prevent misconceptions increasing and in the hope of your telling us what your own opinions are, or wherein you think we can do any good.[33]

Mr. Gray's draft version of his reply to Mr. Ruskin has survived, although it differed from the version he sent in at least one important respect. This was later to cause some friction between them and was only resolved when the line Mr. Gray denied ever having written was torn from his original letter and sent to him:

I was only favoured with yours of the 13th two days ago and as you may suppose the contents have given Mrs Gray and me very great pain and anxiety. I have not communicated the receipt of your Letter to Phemy as in the present delicate state of her health the consequences would I feel certain prove most injurious to her and I don't suppose you would willingly urge me to take any step likely to have that effect – In matters of this delicate nature Phemy is peculiarly reserved, so much so that altho' her health is suffering and her spirits depressed in consequence of the coldness and reserve which exists between her and your family she has never till within the last two days opened her mind to me on the subject – I have now taken the opportunity when alone with her in the garden, tho' without alluding to your Letter, of asking her how it was she never received any Letters from you or Mrs Ruskin as well as John and thereby drew her out upon the causes of misunderstanding which for some time past has alienated you from each other – I do not mean to repeat a word of what passed between us for the same reason that I have not told her a word of what you have stated to me – My object is solely and entirely to bring about a reconciliation in the best way I can and that will be accomplished more effectually by neither party being called upon to rise up and explain what had passed but by both endeavouring to conciliate the affection of each for the time to come – That you both misunderstand each others feelings and desires is as apparent to me as the sun at noon day – and that there is no substantial reason for this is equally clear – Phemy has the greatest affection for John – Her earnest wish is to have the same for you and Mrs. Ruskin – Do not then I most earnestly pray and beseech you continue for a moment to foster those opinions of her which you express in your Letter – I shall not allude to them further than to say that I am convinced you are mistaken as to her feelings and misinterpret her actions – You do not make allowance for her state of health which has had no small share I imagine in what may have been attributed to a wilful disposition, neither do you consider that her natural manners are thoroughly scotch by which I mean that she makes no display of feeling even to those to whom she is much attached – She hates hypocrisy and will never be tempted to practice it – I could write you as fully as you have done me in vindication of the particular charges you bring against her but I forbear to provoke a correspondence upon matters of so distressing a nature – If I may be permitted to hint a word by way of advice it would be simply that Mrs Ruskin and you should leave John and Phemy as much as possible to themselves – married people are rather restive under the control and supervision of Parents tho' proceeding from the kindest and most affectionate motives. Do not take amiss what I say for I have but one desire and that is to see you all happy and your minds disabused of hatred and uncharitableness towards each other – these feelings are too easily aroused and most difficult to allay – they embitter the cup of life even when it overflows with all other earthly blessings –

In my conversation with Phemy I have done all that a Parent can possibly do and I trust with good effect. Do let Mrs Ruskin and you meet her half way – forget and forgive.

I am afraid to trust myself writing upon this subject but before I close I can assure you that Phemy has no desire to disturb John in following out his pursuits neither does she in the very least sympathise with those persons to whom you refer as treating these with levity – Her pride in John's productions are precisely akin to your own and altho' she naturally feels his absence and may long for his return I am quite sure that no selfish desire on her part would induce her to wish him to return till he has accomplished the objects for which he went abroad.[34]

John meanwhile was attempting to cheer up Effie by looking to the future:

Have you any plans or thoughts for next year. I suppose not, for in your present state of mind you will be able to look at nothing with any pleasure. However, as, when we expected much – we were much disappointed, so now, when the future seems somewhat dark, we shall probably find it brighter as we advance. I have not the heart to write more till I know how you [are] – I cannot write cheerfully while I think you are ill, and I would not write sadly for that would do you no good – so I will only write that I love you, my dearest – and am your most devoted husband.[35]

Effie's reply would seem to have taken the discussion of future plans into a wholly unexpected direction:

> My darling Effie
>
>   I have been thinking of you a great deal in my walks today, as of course I always do when I am not busy, but when I am measuring or drawing mountains, I forget myself – and my wife both; if I did not I could not stop so long away from her; for I begin to wonder whether I am married at all – and to think of all my happy hours, and soft slumber in my dearest lady's arms, as a dream – However I feel – in such cases – for my last letter and look at the signature, and see that it is all right. I got one on Friday; that in which you tell me you are better – thank God; and that your father is so much happier, and that Alice is so winning and that you would like a little Alice of our own, so should I; a little Effie, at least. Only I wish they weren't so small at first that one hardly knows what one has got hold of:

This is an important paragraph because it provides evidence that at this stage of the marriage John normally slept in Effie's arms when they were together and he had even softened his attitude to babies sufficiently to contemplate having a little daughter. Later in the same letter he expressed more domestic sentiments. He and Effie had clearly been discussing where they wanted to settle. John had apparently suggested Vevay on Lake Geneva in Switzerland. Mr. Gray thought it would be not so nice in the winter. Effie was not enthusiastic either. John continued:

I have for seven years thought over the various topics of dissuasion which you mention – nor have I yet come to any conclusion – but I asked you for your own feelings, as their expression would in some sort turn the scale with me – not affirmatively indeed – but negatively: as, if you were to tell me that you would be unhappy, living in Switzerland, I should dismiss the subject from my mind; while if you told me you could be comfortable there, I should retain the thought for future consideration, as circumstances may turn out. I wanted therefore to know, not so much whether you thought you would like places of which you can at present form no conception, as whether you had any plans or visions of your own respecting this matter – any castles in the air which I could realise – or any yearnings which I could supply. I myself have for some time wished to have a <u>home</u> proper, where I could alter a room without asking leave – and without taking leave of it after it was altered – however we may as well wait a little and see what comes of the Russian descent on the south – and whether any body is to have a home anywhere [...] Poor Venice – I saw they were bombarding it last week. How all my visions about taking you there; and bringing you here, have been destroyed: Well it might have been too much happiness to be good for me.[36]

In the light of what was to happen when John returned from Switzerland, it would seem that Effie did indeed have some yearnings. She was sufficiently excited by John's extraordinary offer to write him 'two kind and cheerful letters' which he received at Chamouni on the 26th of June, unfortunately they arrived at the same time as the news that Mary Richardson, now Mary Bolding, had died. Even so, this exchange might still have led on to a happier relationship had not the two sets of parents involved themselves in more bickering and recrimination. Mr. Ruskin received Mr. Gray's letter on the last day of the month and replied four days later:

I have your esteemed Letter of 22nd June and am very sorry to cause you and Mrs. Gray a moments uneasiness – I never thought of troubling you till I saw there was something different from usual in Phemys Letters to my Son: you may suppose that very little of her correspondence escapes from my Son but he could not conceal his uneasiness in finding it arose to some allusions to feelings not at all explained but almost mysteriously pointed to, as causing suffering, and coupling this with the unaccountable estrangement of your Daughter to Denmark Hill – I wrote directly to you, entering my protest against Reserve merely to call your attention to the subject, for what with one thing and another I feared we were all getting into a Labyrinth of misunderstanding that though it might make a pretty subject for a Novel in three Volumes, was to be greatly dreaded as most disastrous to all the parties concerned in it – It just happened that the tone of Phemys Letters changed from the date of the last of a series that caused my writing to you, but though you and Mrs Gray have felt what I said too keenly, which I must always regret, I have at once gained a great deal by being open on the subject for you have done vast good by speaking to Phemy even to the limited extent you have, her Letters I believe are again all that my Son seems to wish and she has written a very sweet Letter to Mrs Ruskin, a perfect specimen of the sort of Correspondence that ought always to have existed between them. I get no praise however from you for the open system, for you reply to all my disclosures chiefly by an assurance that you mean to conceal everything – As I have told you that I believe concealment to be the very cause of any trouble arising amongst us, in fact it must be if none of us are evilly inclined, you cannot wonder at my preferring an opposite course. In my poor judgement your Letter itself proves that nothing short of the most perfect frankness and fullest explanation of feelings and wishes can entirely terminate all difficulties. You will say you will hint a word of advice, that Mrs R. and I should as much as possible leave John and Effie to themselves because married people are restive under the supervision and Control of parents and expect to be independent and feel chafed by the Curb – now what mischief does the concealment involved in this passage do – If there is one thing that I am duller at, than another, it is at taking a hint. For want of an explanation of any thing wherein I had interfered and which I should be rejoiced to avoid repeating, I am left hopeless of correcting myself from the simple unconsciousness of having in any instance sought to interfere or control or curb either my Son or his wife – I know only from your hint that all my endeavours to avoid this are fruitless. I thought I had even made it a study to ensure the Independence of both in a manner that not every Father likes to do, before his Death, and so far from thinking of their being restive (which by the bye is not a characteristic of well trained children like our Son and Daughter) I gave them credit for generosity enough to bear with me the more meekly in any humours and peculiarities of habit I may have – but your hints are enough to make me imagine that unless I mind more what I am about, we may have, besides the three Volume Novel – part of the Tragedy of King Lear acted in the family. Seriously,

my dear Sir, I wish you and Phemy to believe that wherever
I have erred in any way interfering – it has been in ignorance
– I am impressed with a wish to avoid it and I tried to do so
– I would not have gone to the expence I have done but to
place the young people beyond our Control – I do not think
I exercised my taste upon one single article they had occasion
to buy – I never dined or drank Tea in their House, adher-
ing pointedly to the non interference system – What Mrs
Ruskin has been about I cannot tell – we don't always know
what mischief our wives do – I saw Mrs Ruskin very much
put about on one occasion – but the Interference seemed to
be mutual – Mrs Ruskin had seen to a Dressing Room being
made comfortable for John having to leave his own Bedroom
in Winter – He was removed to one without a fireplace – in
order to turn the one prepared by his mother into a Room
for Visitors, although it was thought to be settled that they
could not afford to have a spare Bedroom. I daresay a little
previous explanation or a little more allowance for the anxiety of a Mother for the Safety of her Son, on Phemys part,
would have saved all misunderstanding – I cannot either
without further explanation guess where the Curb is felt – I
know of none at Denmark Hill except that we keep to our
old known ways – My son does not seem hurt by the Curb
for he brought us here against his Mothers intentions and to
my Inconvenience, and a more simple, happy, joyous Creature at the age of thirty I never saw – You say circumstances
have occurred to prevent Phemy as she said herself having
esteem and affection for Mrs Ruskin and me – now my
good Sir how in the world are these Circumstances ever to
be removed on the concealment System – I cannot guess or
dream of them. I desired to love Phemy – I sought to love her

– she seemed happy with us enough as Miss Gray. The time spent with us since the Marriage was not pleasant, but the causes of this were accidental – and not at all to be put to our account – We went on a most unfortunate Tour – at Dover my Son and I believe his Wife were out of humour at not getting abroad – this was partly our fault – we feared our Sons being in mobs and a creature like your Daughter being exposed to the gaze of Ruffians. My Son got cold at which my good humour vanished – they left us – he got worse and at Salisbury was so ill that I thought he was going into a decline – I was totally miserable and I daresay Phemy felt the whole Tour as I did, painful and unhappy. We got on pretty well on their return from France – They came to Denmark Hill about Xmas and Phemy being unwell, I daresay Mrs Ruskin wanted to exercise her Medical Skill – Phemy does not brook this and got out of humour so that other people than we expressed surprise and sorrow to see a change in her deportment from what it used to be – I am aware that Mrs Ruskin gives Lectures and being above 60 will speak to a very young person in a way that is not pleasant before others. I can fancy Phemy Schooled by some Worldly Wise people like the Boswells to be sure to assert at once the full authority of a married person and especially against that awful personage, a Mother in Law, to have been unusually sensitive and to have winced under some of Mrs R's plain speeches – but Mrs Ruskin hurts nobody – she often provokes me by making speeches to me that I am not flattered by but esteem remains the same on both sides – We were wrong in not making allowances enough for Phemys ill-health – but we thought with all that, a little more effort on her part to be pleased and happy with us, would have helped her Health – We wanted no display – and judged from neither English, nor French models, but judged Phemy as she was by Phemy as she had been – Mary Richardson never professed – but she was not an hours uncheerful in all the 19 years she lived in our House –

The whole purpose of this Letter is to show you that I have not the most distant idea of why we are not on far better terms with Phemy – and the tone of it is produced by the conviction that all the causes of the Estrangement must be utterly absurd – your Letter of reserve has let out much more than my most open confessions, for I did not think Mrs Ruskin and I had not still your Daughters Esteem and affection – we only knew some misunderstanding existed, somewhere – about something we knew not what – The Ideas you express about married peoples Love of Independence, makes me sore afraid that these very ideas, instilled into Phemy and encouraged, have been the cause of all the mischief – one thing I am sure of that had Phemy thrown herself entirely on our generosity and sought no independent authority, her Dominion over all our affections would have been greater at this day, and of all I know of my Son, her authority with him would have been great exactly in proportion as she had not sought to establish it on the exclusion of that of his parents – His love and esteem would have been enhanced by the Love he saw her bestow on those whom he regarded and the absence of the petty jealousies which so beset young married women in their struggles for a childish authority would have certainly increased his Respect for his wifes Character – As for Mrs R and me wanted an entire Daughter – Let Phemy come to us, as such, trusting, confiding and non exacting and see if she would not be far happier than in following the vulgar and worldly maxims which all her worldly wise friends can teach her – I send a separate Letter and one from Mrs R to Phemy.

I have every hope of seeing both the junior and senior branches of our family united and happy together and in Mrs Ruskin joining me sincerely in wishing such to be the Case and with kindest regards to Mrs Gray and you– I mean this letter for no more.[37]

It is difficult not to sympathise with Mr. Ruskin. He has been asked to take into account Effie's illness but told neither what caused it nor how it should be treated. Even if, as has been suggested, Effie's 'nervous' illness was caused by the non-consummation of her marriage, it is difficult to see how Effie could have held her in-laws accountable for this whilst maintaining such cordial relations with her husband. According to the Gray version of events even her own parents did not know at this time that the marriage was unconsummated. Simpson's diagnosis could not therefore have had anything to do with that situation. When later her health began to improve she said it was a strict diet, the warm climate and hot sun that had brought this about which 'showed how perfectly Simpson understood my state.'[38] The reason for Effie's coldness and reserve towards Mr. and Mrs. Ruskin must have been something else. Again, despite the fact that the married couple were wholly dependent upon Mr. Ruskin for their income, he has been told to give them their independence and stop interfering in their lives, and this by a man who has been pestering the newly-weds for money and moaning about his impending bankruptcy and ruin ever since they were engaged. Nor has Mr. Ruskin been given any inkling of what the nature of his interference might be. Having set up a £10,000 trust for Effie, provided a fashionable town house and super-fine carriage for the couple and not even visited them, he might well ask what more he could do. Mr. Ruskin was shrewd enough to suspect that Mr. Gray's constant avoidance of any specific complaint was a form of concealment. Perhaps Mr. Gray used more than his share of lawyer's reticence because he had something to hide. Mr. Ruskin focussed on the phrase in the letter of 22nd June that Mr. Gray denied ever having written: 'Phemy has the greatest esteem and affection for her Husband. She would wish to have the same for you and Mrs. Ruskin but hitherto circumstances have occurred to obstruct what she assures me is the ardent wish of her heart.'[39] What were the circumstances which had occurred? Did Effie bear a grudge against the Ruskins for not helping her brother to find a job and for keeping too close an eye on her finances? Did she hold them responsible not only for her parents continuing money problems but even for the death of her younger brother? Did her father want less 'interference' so that she would be able to send more money home? If so he could hardly have admitted that to Mr. Ruskin. No wonder he tried to deny ever having said it.

At this stage John most unwisely allowed himself to be drawn into the argument and wrote to Mr. Gray. After once again chronicling the course of Effie's illness, depression and estrangement from her in-laws he continued:

> So far as I know them – these are the causes – and this was the progress of her illness – and of her change of feeling towards my parents – you know better than I what is likely now to benefit her – but I look forward with confidence to her restoration to health by simply physical means – I am delighted to hear of the shower bath and the riding and the milk stead of tea – and the quiet: when I have her to manage again, I hope to do it better – and not to reason with – nor

blame, a physical weakness – which the course of time will, I doubt not, entirely cure.

In all this, however – you will perceive that I look upon the thing as a purely medical question – not a moral one. If Effie had <u>in sound mind</u> been annoyed by the contemptible trifles which <u>have</u> annoyed her; if she had cast back from her the kindness and the affection with which my parents received her, and refused to do her duty to them, under any circumstances whatever but those of an illness bordering in many of its features on incipient insanity, I should not now have written you this letter respecting her. I do so in order that you may not encourage her in those tones of feeling which are so likely to take a morbid form.

I dread your doing so – in consequence of the passage of your letter in which you deprecate my father's interference – God knows that <u>his</u> only interference from the beginning has been a constant endeavour to do Effie every kindness in his power – and that my mothers only interference except in the two above instances has been sometimes a successful endeavour to induce me to think more indulgently of Effie than I otherwise should have done – But grant that they <u>had</u> interfered – have they not every right? Having nourished and brought up their child with every care and thought and energy of their lives devoted to him – have they not a right to expect to be cherished by him in their old age – to be consulted in such matters as may interest them or please them? – to be obeyed in such as they may think it wise to command? – have they not every right also to expect that his wife should aid her husband in this, as in every other duty – and to be borne with by both if sometimes differences of temper should render that duty less than a delight? Or do you rather think that all this is to be done for a son – that all that is in the power of a father to do should be done for son and daughter – that this father should go on working into the after hours of life merely to provide them with more abundant means of happiness – and the only return for all this should be a demand that he should stand out of the way – that he should hint nothing – ask nothing – blame nothing – and expect nothing – and that a request to come down to dinner with a happy face should be considered a tyranny? I should indeed dread to think that such were the deliberate principles on which my wife intended to act – or was encouraged to act by her parents – and I hope to see her outgrow with her girls frocks – that contemptible dread of interference and petulant resistance of authority which begins in pride – and is nourished in folly – and ends in pain – 'Restiveness' I am accustomed to regard as unpromising character even in horses and asses – I look for meekness and gentleness in woman.

One other point startled me in your letter as it has grieved me in Effie, you speak of 'reserve' as a part of her character – If you mean absence of expression of affection – I have never seen it nor felt it in her – I have seen her face opening in the most radiant sunshine to those whom she loved: and I have only seen it clouded in the presence of those whom I had no reason to suppose she loved: But if you mean the deliberate reserve or non expression of thoughts – this is no part of character – it is a simple bad habit – partly owing in Effie to her not having been accustomed to take the trouble to arrange or to remember her thoughts – partly to their not having been enough enquired into – owing to her frequent residence among strangers during childhood: It is one of the parts of her educational character which gives me the most concern:

and which I should be most grieved to see encouraged.

You now know exactly how matters stand – and how I feel – I repeat that I do not blame Effie in the least: but I regret most deeply many of her feelings – and should do so more deeply still – if I did not think they were likely to pass away: if they should – and she can prevail upon herself without irritation, to bear what may be something irksome to her – or to cease to feel that irksome which affords her the only opportunity she has of proving the unselfishness of her love to her husband, she – and all in her, shall be most happy – if she cannot, she will be the chief sufferer. I do not know that she can ever now establish altogether the place she might have had in my parents affections – but I am sure that if she does not endeavour to do so, she will one day or other vainly and remorsefully feel its value. I was much gratified the other day by her letter to my mother, and by the tone of her letters to me – I am led to look for a speedy recovery of her health – and with her health, I doubt not also of her usual good temper – good sense – and cheerfulness – These are all that are needed – I would not have her an hypocrite. I would have her, if she cannot be more be at least what she used to be in my mothers house – when no duty called upon her to be either patient or cheerful.

With sincere regards to Mrs Gray – and (dearest) love to Effie, if at any time you think proper to show her this letter, which – for my part – you may read to the whole world – Ever, my dear Mr. Gray, very faithfully Yours[40]

Even though it was the Grays themselves who had described Effie's complaint as nervous in origin, references to 'incipient insanity' in this letter would not have helped John's marriage along.

Mrs. Gray later put this letter in a white envelope on which was written at some later date: 'Remarkable Letter of J. Ruskin's in which he artfully puts down his then so-called wife's unhappiness to any thing but the real cause which he himself only knew. S.M.G.' This implication that the non-consummation of her marriage was the cause of Effie's illness is not supported by any evidence. A few months later Effie told her mother that 'Charlotte [Ker] and John are very kind but know nothing about my complaint.'[41] Once again the question must be asked: if Effie was suffering from the non-consummation, why would she have fallen out with John's parents and not with John? If remaining in the same state as before the marriage was indeed making her so ill, why did she not confide in her own parents? Later on, when she was in Venice, her illness returned and Effie took a second opinion without John being present. Writing to her father she reported that the second doctor, a Dominican friar, mostly agreed with Dr. Simpson's diagnosis. 'Simpson always said it was an inflammation of the mucous membrane' of the throat. The Dominican told Effie that the 'irritation & blisters in the throat' were symptomatic of a 'slow inflammation of the intestines.'[42] This would tend to show that the non-consummation, troubling as it may have been to Effie, was not the 'real cause' of her illness. If this illness was anything more than merely physical it was far more likely to have been exacerbated by the strain of acting the part of the loving wife whilst being bombarded with bad news from home and being too closely supervised to help her family financially in the way she had planned. If she really loved John this would have been an impossible conflict of loyalties: if she didn't love him then it would have simply been an impossible conflict.

Predictably, John's letter caused more unpleasantness between the in-laws. When Mr. Ruskin suggested that Mr. Gray should bring Effie up to London rather than John travelling all the way to Perth to pick her up, Mr. Gray strongly disapproved. The gossip which had bedevilled the marriage from the very beginning had grown in volume since Effie's return. Effie being so long in Perth without her husband had led to more rumours of a rift in the marriage.[43] This was not merely embarrassing for the Grays, it also might have affected Mr. Gray's fragile financial position by undermining the new-found confidence in his ability to pay his debts. The Grays wanted to scotch the rumours by showing off John and Effie in Perth. From Mr. Ruskin's next letter it is plain that Mrs. Gray had naïvely linked the parlous state of her husband's finances to John's reluctance to come to Perth:

I cannot lose an hour in replying for Mrs Ruskin to your kind letter of 2 August as she is naturally anxious to remove from your mind any idea of our Son's reluctance to come to Scotland, at all arises from circumstances connected with Mr. Grays affairs: John has never expressed a word to us about the subject to lead us to suppose he was made a moments uncomfortable for himself, I am sure he was not: he was distressed I daresay at seeing Effie take these matters to heart. He seemed himself only pleased at the confidence Mr. Gray placed in him and you may rest satisfied that this and all troubles of the kind disturb him very little –

I believe if his Father and his Father in Law – in place of living in good Houses, were reduced to humble Cots his visits would be perhaps only the more frequent and paid with as heartfelt pleasure – In place of troubling himself about worldly affairs I think he only wonders at other people troubling themselves so much – I am quite sure that his dislike to Scotland is simply from finding he cannot be well in it and because he can do nothing there to any purpose.

I do not wonder at your being annoyed at his being so long away and you are right in expecting him to come immediately to Perth – it was wrong perhaps in me to suggest Phemys coming up with her Father and my error came of my hearing something said of her coming out to Switzerland with her Brother. I thought as this was an offer to leave Perth to come a long way, I might ask her to come a short way in her Fathers Company to save her Husband from Injury – for the probability is he will get a cold that will last him for the winter – I do not understand how this is so totally overlooked. It is nothing new – My Son was wretchedly ill at Edinburgh in October 1847 – He was ill at Crossmount with Mr. Macdonald – I might ask why he is expected to stay at Perth? are you or I to mind the idle talk of a set of silly people who sit in Judgement on peoples doings and think he ought to be sauntering up and down George Street and making forenoon Calls on them – I am sure when he comes to Perth that to all such people he will, from his habits, give ten times more offence than by staying away – I do myself think both John and Effie wrong in each going where the other could not come, but as I never was consulted – I neither give my opinion nor interfere – I see they are most attentive to each other in the frequency of their correspondence – I am sure my Son is very fond of his wife and I am sure he will not lose a moment he can help in coming to her – I hope you will make allowance for his Father and mothers fears about his health – we can never agree with other people on this point – John's Brain is too busy always to let his Body be strong – we know many say he ought to rough it more – He has tried this and failed – his last attempt at roughing it was at Oxford last summer and he joined us at Salisbury as if going into a decline – He must be taken as he is – we may be thankful to God that he is spared to us at all – He will do anything that strength permits to please Phemy and you and Mr. Gray but stay at Perth or in Scotland he cannot and I trust you will kindly resign all notion of it: but even here I keep to my plan of non interference – If he and Effie agree about it – Let him – try. I cannot promise to hear of his Health suffering with indifference but I impose no commands and trust to the good sense and affection of the young people determining this matter to the satisfaction of us all –

I am sorry you were not properly apprised of Mary Boldings Death – It was a strange neglect of her Brothers – My nieces Death came from severe cold caused by setting out in cold Weather causing internal inflamation and which none of her Doctors knew the exact nature of – She might however (even if they were not far wrong) have lived many years had not a second Cold brought on rapid decline which took us all by Surprise – Her first serious illness was got in Scotland, visiting her Brother at Glasgow – In all the 19 years she was in our House she was never for one entire day confined with Illness.[44]

Mr. and Mrs. Ruskin had a long-standing aversion to Perth arising from the events of 1817. Given the mortality rate amongst their Scottish relatives and John's latent tuberculosis, their fear for John's health hardly seems exaggerated. Mary (formerly Richardson) Bolding's death had given them even more reason to regard Scotland as a source of illness and disease. The circumstances of their son's marriage had also been embarrassing both for themselves and for John. On top of all this Effie had, in their view, more or less absented herself to Perth without consulting them. In the light of her constant social activity in Perth, Edinburgh and Ayr and expensive horse riding exercise, the incapacitating illness excuse was wearing a little thin. When Effie wrote to John in mid August demanding that he fetch her from Perth she received a scathing reply:

My dearest Effie,

I received about a fortnight ago at Chamouni a letter of yours – expressing your surprise at my having wished you to come to London with your father. There was much in the letter that would have displeased me, if I had not known that you were little used to weigh – or to consider, the true force of written phrases: and therefore – like my cousin Andrew's letters, yours sometimes take a tone and colour very different from that of your own mind when you wrote them, and bear a sense often quite different from that which you intended. However, putting the kindest interpretation I could upon it, there was still enough to cause me to delay my answer all this time, lest I should too hastily write what might give you pain: more especially your imputation of underhand dealing to me, as if I had expressed to you – as my own plan and wish, what was indeed a plan of my fathers. I never do anything of this kind – if it had been my fathers plan I should have told you so; – it was mine – and you supposing it to be anyone else's was doubly foolish – first because it imputed to me an artful conduct towards you: of which you have never found, and shall never find, the slightest vestige in me: and secondly, because it supposed my father and mother either had less sense, or were less disposed to be kind to you, than I am: the fact being that they are continually pleading with me in your favour – begging me to write to you – and reminding me of my duty to you: and it is in fact only in obedience to their instances that I am coming home just now, instead of staying a month longer, and perhaps going to Venice. I am indeed not a little struck with the contrast between their acting and feeling towards you – and yours towards them: as both have appeared lately – they are always doing all they can to increase my respect for you – dwelling on the best parts of your character – never speaking or thinking of you without affection, and often persuading me to write to you instead of to them, while you are watching their every word with jealousy, and suspecting their every act, of unkindness: All this however is natural enough – it is on your side at least what you very properly express as the 'Common feeling of Humanity', and I am not going to blame you for it – you can hardly help it at present, and suffer from it, as people always do from ungenerous feelings, quite enough without any addition of pain from me. As for your wish that I should come to Scotland – that is also perfectly natural – nor have I the smallest objection to come for you: only do not mistake womanly pride for womanly affection: You say that 'you should have thought the first thing I should have done after eight months absence, would have been to come for you.' Why, you foolish little puss, do you not see that part of my reason for wishing you to come to London was that I might get you a couple of days sooner; and do not you see also, that if love, instead of pride, had prompted your reply, you would never have thought of what I <u>ought</u> to do, or your <u>right</u> to ask, you would only have thought of being with me as soon as you could; and your answer would have been that of Imogen – 'oh, for a horse with wings' – Look at the passage.* Her husband sends a word he is to be at Milford on such a day – She does not 'think he might have come nearer' or think that she is a princess and ought not to go travelling about the country with a single servant. She only thinks – only asks – How far is't to this same <u>blessed</u> Milford and how far she can ride a day: Your feeling on the other hand, is some more of the <u>common</u> feeling of humanity, which I am perfectly willing to indulge: though I should have been much more so if it had been more temperately and modestly expressed: I once wrote to you that you 'would not have a <u>proud</u> husband' and on my word, you seem to have calculated thereupon to some extent; I have however at least so much pride that I do not intend to allow you to dictate to me what is right, nor even to take upon you the office of my mistress in knowledge of the world – If you knew a little more of it, you would be more cautious how you write impertinent letters to your Husband.

The whole affair however is too trivial to occupy me longer – and I am not going to treat you like a child, and refuse you your cake because you don't kiss your hand for it properly: I shall come to Perth for you as soon as I get home: only have your calls and ceremonies over, as I shall not stay there: I hope to be at Dijon tomorrow and home in about a fortnight – I am keeping my father out as long as I can – (and but for his feeling that I ought to be with you – I could keep him longer), for fear of the cholera – which I somewhat fear for him, as he is nervous and obliged to be in infected neighbourhoods; for myself – I would sleep in a cholera hospital

*Shakespeare, *Cymbeline*, III, ii

as fearlessly as at Denmark Hill. Write Hotel Meurice, Paris, I hope you have received my last letter from Chamouni, as it contains a curious story: by the bye – did you ever write to Thun: I sent to the post office there, but got no letter.

Evening. There are passages tonight in the journals about cholera in France, which make our movements somewhat doubtful – I am not sure whether we may not come direct home: at all events, it is of no use risking letters to Paris; you had better address anything you have now to say to Denmark Hill – I will write you the day after tomorrow from Dijon, D.V. – with more certain information – but at all events I trust to be with you soon – and that we shall not be again so long separated. I am

ever your most aff^e Husband

J Ruskin[45]

Having achieved her object Effie seems to have chosen not to react aggressively to John's rebuke. There is no way of knowing what her real feelings were at the time. But when the exchange of letters resumed it was as if John's rebuke had never happened. From the next letter of John's we have, we can deduce that she had written to ask him if he thought of her and the pleasures they had had in Normandy and could he buy her some bonnets and a 'Mantel' whilst he had nothing to do in Paris. Effie now believed that her depression had been the result of a stomach disorder. John expressed relief that it was nothing more serious, but pointed out that Effie lacked the constitution to cope with the disciplined diet and habits that could cure it quickly.

At this time John was planning a sustained twelve months of working in London and feared that Effie would be bored. Mrs. Ruskin had suggested that Effie should invite a companion to stay with her and John thought it a good idea:

> I have not the smallest objection to this – and if during the
> dull winter months you can get any one, whom you like, to
> live with you and keep you company in the middle of the day
> – and walk with you, it will perhaps save you from many
> moments of suffering – if not of illness: I feel just now – more
> decidedly adverse to all ordinary usages and customs of the
> Englyshe in 1849 than ever – and more misanthropical – and
> I will not see anybody when they call on me, nor call on
> anybody, I am going to do my own work in my own way in
> my own room, and I am afraid you will think me a more odd
> and tiresome creature than ever: so if you can prevail on any
> one to come and cheer you or amuse you, do: it will bore me
> a little in the evenings: but I don't care much about this as I
> shall generally be resting: and shall just lie back in my chair
> and hear you chat or read, or play.
>
> Only of course I trust to your judgement to choose some
> one whose ways of thinking will not worry me and who will
> not put me out of my way, or I shall put <u>them</u> out of my way.[46]

The idea of living in London unable to receive guests, unable
to visit anybody accompanied by her husband, and spending
endless evenings chatting, reading or playing piano would have
been a sort of living hell for Effie. Alternatives were quickly
devised. The first suggestion was a sojourn at an English spa town
probably for her health. She gave short shrift to the idea of six
months of foul drinks, extreme dieting and cold shower baths in
a provincial backwater. In fact she had probably decided where
she wanted to go even before John arrived at Bowerswell to
bring her home.

CHAPTER XIII

OCEAN'S LOVELY DAUGHTER

‎ℰℐ

When *The Seven Lamps of Architecture* was published in May 1849 it contained a publisher's slip advertising John's next architectural volume: *The Stones of Venice*. He had mentioned his need to visit Venice several times in his letters to Effie, but the trip had been postponed because of the 1848 Venetian Republican uprising, the subsequent siege and bombardment of the city by the Austrian Army and a serious outbreak of disease following the fall of the city to the Austrians. Back in late June, John had asked Effie if she had any plans or visions of her own about where she would like to live. By that time Lady Davy had read her Venetian diaries to Effie and she had been told all about Continental manners by the Béthunes. She had even been reading specifically about Venice in Sismondi. Venice had a reputation for intrigue, romance and sensuality. It was a city traditionally associated with masked balls, courtesans and loose morals. Of all the locations where her husband needed to work, Venice was by far the most exciting. Effie was on her own admission the sort of person who would prefer 'flying over a desart on horseback' to the solitude and grandeur of the Alps. There would be no horse riding in Venice but neither would there be any hikes up and down mountains or interminable afternoons in sleepy rural France. Of course by now the whole town was filled with young Austrian noblemen in uniform and John did not speak German: how lucky that Effie did.

Effie had already chosen Charlotte Ker as her companion for the

winter before John arrived at Bowerswell. Now Charlotte, whose
father was, coincidentally, Secretary of the Scottish Central Railway,
was asked to accompany them to Venice. It remained only for
John to ask his father's consent which he did in a letter sent from
Perth on September 22nd. Mr. Ruskin's reply missed them at Perth
and was forwarded to Park Street by which time John and Effie had
been able to speak to him in person at Denmark Hill. Mr. Ruskin
was entirely supportive:

> I quite approve of your going to Venice – to keep out of
> London till Feby but as both Cholera and Typhus have been
> horribly bad at Venice consequent on the sufferings and
> privations under Bombardment, allow me to suggest your
> going quickly over the Cholera French ground – Paris included
> – till you reach Montbard, shew your Wife Champagnole, and
> shew her at Chamouni to Coutet etc – for a few days so as to
> let Venice get cleansed, and then Novr to Feby would be
> delightful there – The only objection to your plan and pref-
> erence I should have given to Malvern arise from the regret
> of your not having rest to put down your Impressions of the
> Alps and the fear that carrying on these notes with the new
> and exciting work of gathering materials for the Stones of
> Venice may hurt your Brain and health – you better know your
> strength now and I must trust to your not letting the Fasci-
> nations of Venice (which will not die this year or for many to
> young people) draw you into a double task and an accumu-
> lation of Labour dangerously heavy. Think of it, both of you,
> and take your own way. Mama and I can bear any privation
> that your Happiness or your fame impose upon us. So let that
> consideration aside – I rejoice to hear of your both liking this
> plan and the person of a Companion – By your description

Miss Ker is just made for the occasion – I will attend to anything you require done here in your absence – so I beg of you to go where your Health and your work and pursuits lead you – If you are well and able to do for Venice what I think you will may I say Go where Glory waits thee – and now I am going to carry my feebleness to business for a few hours – I am like a person just out of fever – that means, however, I am better – What mama may have to say I must tell you tomorrow to Leeds unless you give another address – Mama would join her most affec love to mine to you and Effie – I am My dearest John

Yr most affect Father
J. J. Ruskin[1]

Even though John's parents would not be accompanying them on this tour, Mr. Ruskin would be footing the bill for it all, on top of the money he was paying for the expensive unoccupied house and servants at Park Street. If Effie was grateful to him it did not show in her letters at this time. Whatever the grudge she bore him, it had remained unaffected either by his letters or his generosity. Her letters home revealed her real sentiments and the complicity between mother and daughter. On September 30th she wrote:

Denmark Hill

My dear Mother

I received your kind note on my arrival in Park St last night we only arrived there then as Mr. Ruskin met us at the station We went or rather came out here and found Mrs Ruskin looking very well Mr. Ruskin very ill but both quite pleased to see us and to let us go to Italy and quite delighted that Charlotte was to go with us. Next morning we had some talk about our arrangements and I had some private conversation with Mr. Ruskin what an extraordinary man he is he was quite delighted that I spoke to him evidently and said he had nothing to blame me for and thought I had behaved beautifully I begged him to tell me what he was not pleased with he said there was nothing but that he thought sometimes John could not make me happy which was a new light certainly on the subject however we settled it all in the best possible manner but who can know what such a man thinks!! John and I then drove into town to look for a carriage, we concluded by fixing to take two, One for John George Stores and books, and an elegant [Phaeton?] for Charlotte and me. It is an open carriage but shuts very [tidy?] and large enough to hold John when he wants to come and Chat with us, it is rather heavy but very handsome and will require three horses we all think this a capitle arrangement for we shall be able to enjoy the country so much more but do not tell the gossips in case they think that although John and I intend going abroad we are not to travel together which would be a delightful catch for not the [Birrel?] but some others, bye the bye a capitle joke. Mr. Ruskin heard when he came home that a report was that I was so unhappy with John that proceedings were instituted for a separation he was fearfully angry and thinks less now of what the Farquesons said, bye the bye if I could only collect my ideas I could give you some brilliant hints, what do you think the great Philanthropist gave my servants when he went away I suppose to do them good. A volume of Pilgrims Progress. We found the house in beautiful order and everything just as I left it and the servants very well but very sorry that we are not to remain at home I was dreadfully tired I could not go on this way for many days longer and I was nearly obliged to come out of Church this morning I ought never to have been there for the heat and closeness of the air here is dreadful but Mr R wished us to be seen in Church and I could make no objection. Tomorrow will be another awful today but Tuesday I hope we shall be off.[2]

The Farquharsons were old friends of the Ruskins. Their son William Macdonald (a clan title) had been best man at John's wedding and thus privy to any scandal surrounding that event. They and William ('the great Philanthropist') had been staying in the empty house at Park Street and had relayed Perth gossip to the Ruskin elders: hence Effie's scathing remarks about someone she had previously described as 'too good to live'. Effie's sensitivity on the subject of the two carriages and the separate travelling arrangement also brings to mind the gossip that John had changed carriages for the honeymoon journey. More serious was the rumour that the couple were about to separate. No wonder Effie was anxious to get away. On their way back from Perth John had checked with Dr. Simpson at Edinburgh that his wife was fit to travel. Her illness seemed to come and go in her letter. It surfaced whenever she was describing time spent with Mr. and Mrs. Ruskin. It went away when she was talking about the plans for the tour. It also tended to be forgotten when she was writing about her favourite subjects:

the things John brought from Paris are beautiful, the bonnet crimson velvet with little feathers on one side and white flowers and ties inside very open in the front the cloak very thickly padded and quilted in a broad pattern all round, extremely warm and quite light two scarfs for evening one a white crape with blue the other rose and white checked silk very curious. He wants us to get our evening dress or so in Paris as he shall be visiting in Venice and Florence. John is in great spirits and quite delighted with the thought of going abroad and full of business.[3]

A letter John wrote in October to Lady Davy confirmed that the Venice trip was more because of Effie's needs than his:

> Nevertheless our sudden departure for the South was indeed in consequence of my wife's health – continued rather than alarming – which induced me – by Dr. Simpson's advice – to take her to Italy for the winter and in consequence to alter the present direction of my own pursuits – for I had been working the whole summer among the upper snows of the Alps – and intended to write something about their more divine architecture before pursuing any further inquiries into the measurable sublimities of man's raising.[4]

Effie, Charlotte Ker and John's man-servant George left for the Continent on October the 3rd, but the gossip did not abate. On the 20th Mr. Ruskin told Mr. Gray that he had received an anonymous letter posted in Scotland and formed by cutting letters and words out of books:

> There was no need for pretending bad health Miss Ker had plans, with flattering lips you see we shall keep him from the advice of his Mother + all shall be well – what a separation Father let me warn you, be separated no more from your only Son, your affectionate Son – he dearly loved by his Father + Mother I beseech you look after his health.

According to Mr. Ruskin all sorts of wild rumours were being spread 'One man comes to London and says there's a House building at Perth for the young people + much more nonsense'.[5] There were two other anonymous letters from Perth urging

John's parents 'to take care of our Son for the Gs only wanted his money.'[6]

John and Effie's party crossed from Folkestone to Boulogne, took the train to Paris and then travelled via Dijon and Champagnole to Geneva. John took the ladies shopping in Paris and Dijon. In Paris the plan had been for Effie to buy evening dresses, and she sent her mother lengthy descriptions of bonnets she bought. Both Effie and John were in great spirits and Effie wrote how they were mistaken for newly-weds.[7] Because it was late in the year, and bad weather might have closed the passes through the mountains, the pace of the journey was even more urgent than the usual Ruskin family tour. They even travelled on the Sunday. Effie, prone to sea-sickness, now discovered that the closed carriage also made her sick. The journey tired her out just as John had said it would when he wrote to her back in May. She was still suffering from her illness which now seemed to manifest itself in weakness and a sore throat. Switzerland however, which she had dismissed before she had seen it, lifted her spirits somewhat. She wrote to her father from Geneva:

> I got better towards the end of the days and enjoyed passing through the Jura from Champagnole exceedingly. I was very much delighted with the Pine forests and as the day could not have been finer the Autumn tints on the hills and the fall rushing torrents were exquisitely beautiful and the first view of the Alps the plain of Geneva and the Lake seen from an elevation of 3,000 feet the most striking Panorama I ever beheld but curious to say I was not in the least surprised by the magnificence of the view as it was exactly like what I had always supposed it would be. A very fine sunset illuminated Mont Blanc and the other hills to a great degree of beauty,

the gardens full of grapes and flowers and the people with the large round straw hats adding greatly to the picture. John was excessively delighted to see how happy we were and went jumping about and executing <u>pas</u> that George and I agreed Taglioni would have stared her widest at.[8]

It is fairly clear that John was in excellent spirits and, if Effie's letters are any guide, that whatever had put a strain on the relationship had apparently been left behind. John's letters from this time have disappeared but, according to Effie, he had received a 'nice letter from Mama [Gray] with which he is much pleased' and he was 'exceedingly thoughtful for my want of strength.' She had even been supplied with a 'nice fur foot bag' for her cold feet. At Chamouni they went hunting for ghosts and treasure and Effie discovered that she was an adept at dowsing. She gave French lessons to Charlotte Ker whilst John helped both the women with their Italian. The weather had turned mild so the urgency of making the Simplon Pass in time had abated somewhat. On the 17th Effie told her mother that she and John 'had a delightful walk this morning among the pine woods on the Brevon picking cloud berries and throwing the huge blocks of stone down seven hundred feet and watching them bounding from rock to rock'.[9]

In the surviving correspondence there are no complaints about John's behaviour or attitude and even though she was still unwell we must assume a benign relationship between them. Unfortunately Italy and particularly Venice was about to do its famous magic on the pair: a magic which brought out the extreme opposites in their characters. This stay in Venice allowed both of them to do what they did best to their heart's content. John fell under the spell of history, art and work; Effie was seduced by the sensual social culture. Though both were to be happier in Venice than ever before or afterwards, fissures were about to open up in this ill-omened marriage which would only widen as time went on.

When the Ruskin party descended from the Alps into the kingdom of Lombardy-Venetia, they found it under martial law and occupied by an Austrian army 75,000 strong. A major nationalist and republican insurrection had only recently been brutally suppressed and Venice itself had suffered an appalling siege. As recently as May 60,000 projectiles had been fired at the city and the siege only ended after starvation and cholera had weakened the defenders and they had run out of ammunition. Venice surrendered to Radetzky on the 27th of August, less than a month before John and Effie decided to travel there. When Effie wrote from Milan to her father on the 27th of October, the Austrian troops were much in evidence since the city was still under martial law. Effie also noted that the Milanese were refusing to mix socially with the occupying Austrians:

> This is a delightful place still in a state of siege and therefore melancholy full of Austrians + Croat Soldiery the best dressed and finest looking men I ever saw in their white coats and tight blue Italy trowzers. The people are very unhappy and complain dreadfully of the way in which they were betrayed to Radetsky by Charles Albert. We were at the Opera the other night it was full of Austrian Officers with a sprinkling of their wives and daughters but no Italian Ladies.[10]

John could and did speak to the oppressed Italians but Effie's Italian lessons had been a failure. Even by the 15th of November she only knew 'about a dozen words'. Although at first Effie affected her husband's scorn for the Austrian oppressors, her letters betray her blatant interest in the Austrian military. She was always impressed by young men in uniform and as the Austrians she met often had the added advantage of exotic and exalted nobility, her fascination with celebrity and status was also engaged:

My dearest Papa,

[...] John saw part of the old Visconti Palace being in course of removal the other day and the only reason they gave was that the modern Italian Piazza [she meant Palazzo] is much more comfortable to live in and that they were going to build one after their own mind instead. We are in great hopes of seeing Radetzky who is expected here every day from Vienna and we are determined to see him, as he is a <u>decided</u> Lion even if we should have to wait for him. Charlotte and I have a very nice open carriage, and with a valet-de-place on the box we drive out every forenoon and I assure you strike far more terror into the hearts of the Austrian Officers & Soldiers than Radetzky himself for such a thing as two Ladies has not been seen here for months and with the exception of young Lady Otway who is in the house here Charlotte and I reign supreme and many are the cigars that are taken out of the mouths as we pass and innumerable are the prancing of the horses trotting and galloping after us on the Corso but they are all Austrians or Croats and I am a thorough Italian here & hate oppression therefore wish them far enough.

Today we visited one of the galleries of art and saw amongst other curious things a letter from Lucrezia Borgia to Cardinal Bembo with a long lock of her hair which is very fair and fine tied with black, one splendid Fresco of Raphael and a great number of sketches of Leonardo da Vinci's. We went into the Refectory of a Monastery and saw his Fresco of the Last Supper which you know from prints. It is much faded and dimmed, but still the hand of the great master is visible throughout, and the centre figure, Our Lord, is full of dignity and Sweetness but the whole place was very sad to see, on the Entrance door the Large black Austrian Eagle painted, showing it was a Barrack, with soldiers looking out of every window, the Cloister full of them smoking and playing at dice and the centre a receptacle for all the refuse from the cavalry stables on one side.

This Milan is a most wonderful place for street organs and the Italians seem to do little else but sit at their doors, accompany the organs with their voices and eating hot chesnuts which are roasting in Bins on little wood fires in every part of the town and which are certainly very nice indeed for they roast them so well and they taste just like sweet Potatoes, but the Organs are delightful and we have a sort of continuous concert every evening John is very busy drawing an old Pulpit in St. Ambrogio full of grotesque monsters and most elegant devices of every kind of 9th century work. He is immensely pleased both with the work and the pulpit. I hope Melville is quite well again. These teething attacks must keep Mama very anxious about him and he is such a pale little thing but I hope he will soon recover his lost strength and play about with the others. I think we shall enjoy our stay at Venice very much and as they are doing all they can to propitiate the Austrians we may go out a little. Lady Otway tells me for she has just come from there that numbers of the refugee French and others, nobles, Spaniards etc, the Duc de Bordeaux, Conde Montemolin and others are crowding there and going to make it very gay so that we may meet some curious characters."

Their next stop was at Verona where Effie discovered that if her Italian was bad, her German, coupled with her natural sociability, was more than adequate to communicate with the Austrian military:

Just at this time a Band of 60 men in all entered the Square and set themselves in order to play by arranging a kind of trellis work all in a circle, putting candles and music thereupon, and with the bandmaster in the Centre began to play. We imagined that it was a compliment of Radetzky's sending this magnificent band to serenade the Princess, but we found out that they were the Band of a Regiment from the Grand Duke of Baden, and hearing that their former General, General Kolun, was in the Hotel they had come to Serenade him. His sons were chatting with us for an hour, talking English perfectly. The eldest, I should think about my age, already a Captain of Cuirassiers at Milan and very handsome, accosted us on the Balcony with his brother, a very lovely boy of about 14 also in his Father's Regiment. They informed us, taking off their hats and keeping them in their hands all the time they remained with us, that our servant had asked them some questions regarding the band and that they were afraid he had misunderstood them, which he had, and they had taken the liberty of answering them to us if they could be of any use. They gave us a great deal of information and appeared to reverence their Father extremely and I do not wonder for I never saw a finer man. They told us that no one could be a General with them unless he spoke five languages, and they both, I found out, spoke four. After the Princess left, their Father sent for them and they were off in a moment. Not to make us think them rude they returned again to make their adieus. The little one came first; I never saw such a face, so fine in features and so smooth a skin. He had talked with Charlotte and he came to bid us goodbye & tell us he was going next day to Trieste with his Father but he hoped we should come there and it would make him and his father much happiness. I said we could not have that pleasure. Then the elder one came. He said that he put himself entirely at our disposal whilst we remained and that he had only two field days with Radetsky to interfere and away he went cap in hands. Charlotte and I were perfectly charmed with their conversation and manners, so quiet and yet such high breeding. When we came into the room we found John deep in his books. I asked him why he had not come out to see the two Austrians. He said that he knew by the voices who we had with us and he was afraid if he came out that it would drive them away and he was very glad we had somebody to talk to like ourselves.[12]

A very definite pattern was emerging. Whilst Effie was promenading in the open carriage in front of the Austrian military in Milan, John was 'busy drawing an old pulpit in St. Ambrogio full of grotesque monsters and most elegant devices of every kind of 9th century work.' When Radetzky arrived at their hotel to meet their fellow guest Princess Samoilow, Effie abandoned her dinner to watch his arrival. Whilst she chatted with the youthful Austrians in his entourage, John remained 'deep in his books' and refused to come out. When 'Count Albert' (actually Alphonse), the son of Field Marshall Wimpffen, arrived with a very handsome carriage and pair, it was Effie and Charlotte who went to inspect the fortifications whilst John worked. Effie's comment was: 'Well, John, I don't think you would be understood by the world at all.' Another aspect of this pattern was that

John, so jealous before the marriage, now seemed to be completely unconcerned that Effie should entertain other men whilst he was busy. The first sign of this had been the little vignette in Park Street when Effie polka'd round the room after being told that Prizie Tasker was back in Perth. John's reaction, according to Effie, was to wish Prizie could be there to dance with her. Now he told her that it was 'very absurd that because I enjoy myself, you & Charlotte should be kept moping in the house.'[13] Even before the party arrived in Venice, John was making arrangements for the two women to go out into Society without him. Effie told her mother that: 'John has written to England to Lady Davy and others for some letters of introduction for us so that Charlotte and I may go out into a little Society in Venice and Florence, and as he is so busy he would like us to get acquainted with some English and amuse ourselves and during the Carnival we may have some amusement without troubling him.'[14]

They arrived in Venice by boat because the railway bridge had been partly demolished in the recent siege. Many of the palaces along the Grand Canal were pocked with shot damage but Effie did not notice. She told her mother that it was the most exquisite place she had ever seen and that they would not leave in a hurry. They stayed where John had always stayed before, at the Hotel Danieli: 'formerly a splendid Palace with marble staircase and doors and Balconies looking out on the sea covered with ships and churches and the Doge's Palace, the finest building in the world, with St. Mark's Place & Church 100 yards off.' In the evening they wandered around St. Mark's square, drank coffee under the arcade and listened to a sixty-strong Austrian military band playing under the stars. It was so warm that Effie discarded her bonnet, a breach of decorum which shocked Mr. Ruskin when he heard about it. Effie found travelling by gondola 'the most

The Riva degli Schiavoni in the third quarter of the 19th century,
showing the Hotel Danieli in the centre; the Doge's Palace barely
a hundred yards further, and the Campanile towering just behind

luxurious conveyance in the world if you can fancy yourself moved through canals of oil. There is no motion on the green canals and you lie all your length on soft cushions and pass other people in the same happy ease as yourself [...] nothing could be more enjoyable.'[15] In the following days Effie tried out her rudimentary Italian in the narrow shopping streets and John rowed her over to the Lido. Effie was so mollified by the atmosphere that she began to soften her attitude to John's father and even sent him letters. In the evenings when John was working on his book, Effie tried to make the best of the situation without her husband. She and Charlotte attended the evening Promenades with 'George who acts Duenna for us':[16]

> we have made no acquaintances as yet. We could easily amongst the Austrian Officers if we gave them the slightest encouragement, meeting them in scores every night at the Band or in the Cafés or Theatre, but as yet we have avoided

them as George only being with us I do not like to make acquaintance with every man with a moustache and sword who may choose to be civil to us, at night especially. John would like us to walk about chattering with some half dozen and amusing ourselves but we have some ideas of English propriety remaining and I tell him he must get us introduced in some other way as all our Austrian admirers might not turn out as well as Count Wimpffen. Accordingly he is going to ask his Banker to call on us, Mr Valentine, a young man and unfortunately unmarried.[17]

In Venice homeless people still huddled in the streets. There was also an undertow of random violence and lawlessness. Effie mentions several stabbings in her letters and the Ruskins also had their gondola stolen. Most of the Italian nobility had left the city for their country palazzi, and such women and men as remained were refusing to talk to the Austrians and boycotting any social events patronized by them. As the English community had also decamped and Effie being one of the very few non-native women in Venice, she revelled in the male attention she and Charlotte received. Her letters to her mother are full of shopping trips and handsome men. Mr. Ruskin commented wryly upon her sudden 'improved powers of locomotion' in a letter to her father and expressed his concern to John after he had daringly allowed her to row the gondola in the Grand Canal.[18] Effie had inexplicably and suddenly felt the need for violent exertion. Games of tig around the table gave way to shuttlecocks and battledores, and then to ball games.[19] She explained to her mother that 'I am however also looking well just now and don't want admirers either.' Amongst these were her *valet de place* who repeatedly told John she was 'jolie comme un ange,' her gondolier 'a very handsome fellow of the fine Giorgione red brown complexion' who 'pays me nice "piccolo complimento" in Italian which Charlotte thinks highly improper as she does not understand them,'[20] and Dr. Purvis from England, so handsome 'we could hardly keep from paying him compliments his face was so beautiful.' Dr. Purvis told her 'he had never seen so perfectly happy looking a person as I.' Austrian officers followed the two women back to their hotel and lounged around waiting for invitations. Then two 'Italian gentlemen' also followed them back to their hotel. She at first thought this hilarious if rather overdoing it, but when it continued she later told her mother that 'Charlotte and I are quite used to it now.' At the Opera she mentions that all the lorgnettes were turned to their box.[21] How her mother reacted to all this has to be imagined. Effie had told her 'You may say anything you like in your letters for I destroy every one after it is answered.'[22]

According to Effie, John also praised Dr. Purvis for his good looks, thought it delightful that men followed Effie back to the hotel, and seemed to take vicarious enjoyment in the attention Effie received at the Opera. Effie thought John 'the most extraordinary person, he does not mind us going with anyone we like.' 'We never saw anybody like him, so perfectly devoid of jealousy, and I am sure Papa will wonder at him as he thought at one time quite differently.' In the same letter she wrote that:

> Charlotte is just saying she thinks of writing a pamphlet on what a husband ought to be and giving John as a model, which he really is. I never saw any person so free from petty faults and narrow mindedness although peculiar in many ways. His gallantry of behavior to us both is most charming and he is so considerate and thoughtful for me that I am sure Papa would be quite delighted if he saw how kind he is.[23]

Charlotte had no aptitude for languages at all, which led to the interesting situation that neither of Effie's erstwhile chaperones understood a single word that was said to her or by her. Effie had engaged an Italian teacher to facilitate her shopping, but she worked much harder at her German, particularly after a 'tête à tête' with a handsome Austrian of John's age with 'white teeth' and 'very nice moustaches' had ended in mutual bafflement. This was Charles Paulizza, a first lieutenant of artillery in the Austrian army who was to become a devoted companion of both John and Effie. She also bumped into handsome, unmarried, young 'Count Albert' from Verona again. This was Count Alphonse Wimpffen; in Venice briefly with his family. Another admirer was Rawdon Lubbock Brown, a long term English resident of Venice. He had arrived in 1833 and spent the next fifty years trawling through the Venetian diplomatic archives, particularly as they had some bearing on English affairs. He was also unmarried and lived in a beautiful palace on the Grand Canal. With no obvious gainful employment, it is not difficult to imagine him engaged in some sort of clandestine diplomatic intelligence gathering on behalf of British interests.[24] Brown had an encyclopædic knowledge of Venetian history and, knowing everybody worth knowing amongst the Italians and English in Venice, was able to help John gain access to the library of St. Mark's. Brown was Effie's constant companion in Venice and became a lifelong acquaintance of both her and John. Effie's letters give the reader the impression of a much older man: in fact he was an extremely youthful-looking forty-three. When they eventually met Brown years later both Mrs. Gray and John Everett Millais were shocked at how young he appeared to be.[25] When the weather turned cold and Effie's illness returned, Brown suggested to her an all-over-rub with 'hair gloves morning and night' to improve her circulation. When that failed to have the necessary effect he sent her a 'hair strap which I use morning and night and which excites the skin.'[26] He baked her mince pies for Christmas, arranged for her to have fresh milk, and sent her a pot of Keiller's marmalade.[27] By late January Brown was sending her notes in the mornings and usually spent half his day with her on 'delightful walks.' By this time Charlotte had decided not to accompany Effie when she went visiting 'because for one thing she cannot speak a word and John prefers my going alone & she likes better not to go.'[28] Charlotte seems to have found herself in a very uncomfortable position with the Ruskins. According to Effie she spent most of her time darning stockings and put on a lot of weight. Despite the impression that Effie gives, it would seem that the male attention was both more welcomed by and focussed on Effie alone. Charlotte never married.

By the turn of the year the amount of male interest showed no sign of abating. She told her mother that 'We get plenty of admiration and attention, and the number of our admirers increases daily and they are extremely polite and don't make love to us which is a comfort.' Effie was plainly having the time of her life and related her adventures to her mother. 'Venice is such a capitle place for playing hide & seek in you see an immense way of[f] and if you don't want to meet any person who is looking for you, two turns down the cross lanes which inter- sect every corner [hide you?] at once from observation.' She then described how she and Charlotte had hid from Paulizza ('he & the Count are the most distinguished looking men we have seen but this man is the handsomest and about thirty') who was rushing about trying to stage an 'accidental' meeting with them. Other men sent books 'and things of that sort' prompting a rather ungrateful outburst:

Men are really great fools! And if you suppose that I ever forget my duty for an instant to my husband, you are not at all wrong in your remarks as to decorum! I hope I have inherited a little of my Father's sense and your discretion to some purpose. In fact John would require a wife who would take [care?] of her own character, for you know he is intensely occupied and never with us but at meal times, so that we can do anything we like and he does not care how much people are with us or what attention they pay us. I understand him perfectly and he is so kind and good when he is in the house that his gentle manners are quite refreshing after the indolent Italian and the calculating German, but we ladies like to see and know every thing and I find I am much happier following my own plans & pursuits and never troubling John, or he me.[29]

By this time even Mrs. Gray had begun to worry about Effie's behaviour. This letter reveals that her mother had made remarks on Effie's lack of decorum and probably called for some Gray family sense and discretion. She had also mentioned Effie's health, especially since their stay in Venice had now been extended to April and a return planned for the following year. Effie blamed John's work and was indignant that she should be recalled for such a flimsy reason. 'My health in this matter has not been at all consulted and I am astonished at your putting it on that head.' I leave it to the reader to decide whether or not Effie either wanted to return or was about to change her lifestyle. She later told her mother how John was 'greatly amused by how I thrive after dancing; he says I am a complete Salamander and thrive in destructive elements.'[30] Mrs. Gray's concern was no doubt lessened when Effie gave her a nice New Year's present of a black cloak and anything the children required: 'Name your own price to Mrs. Rutherford.'[31]

Paulizza having temporarily absented himself in order to learn English and John's banker Mr. Valentine being ill, Effie and Charlotte found themselves being escorted by the banker's assistant Mr. Blumenthal, who spoke English and Italian perfectly. His presence was much appreciated because by now the Italian men had begun to pester the women with compliments and by throwing bouquets of flowers at them as they passed, activities which Blumenthal's presence seems to have prevented. The weather continued cold. Blizzards swept the Lagoon and carpeted the city with snow. On the 29th December John 'more unsocial today than ever' shut himself up in his dressing room with a hot stove and worked through the day, and so the two women visited Brown as they often did.[32] Since John was looking for a house to rent, Brown had even suggested that Effie and John should move into the two lower floors of his palace and share his cook. The cold weather continued to cause Effie problems and, although she did not think it sufficient excuse to return to England, her illness still troubled her. Brown took a great interest in her physical condition and arranged for her to see one of the friars of the healing order of Dominicans who ran a hospital and asylum on the island of San Servolo. The good friar diagnosed a slow inflammation of the intestines and suggested a linseed and almond oil poultice and the application of eight leeches around the waist. Effie objected to being bled but after consulting John, wrote home for her father's advice. In the meantime Paulizza returned and informing Effie that he was also a medical man, offered to help:

> Paulizza my second doctor would also interest you. I have
> described his appearance before, but he seems to know as much
> of Physic as if he had lived in Hospitals & laboratories all his

Life. [...] when he comes he takes a spoon in a scientific way, examines my throat and feels my pulse at the hand which he says is steady enough but he pointed out to John that the pulse just under the ear told a different story and was much more excited. I always thought before that all pulses were the same but on feeling at the Throat the motion was distinct and nervous and at the hand steady and slow. The place is just under the jaw and must have sympathy with the state of my throat. He next explained to us that we had better allow him to come and put on the Leeches for me. I thought surely my ears had deceived me but now I am astonished at nothing foreigners do, for their life and education is so different from ours, and when he repeated his request, John & I could hardly help smiling when we looked at our handsome friend with his long curling moustaches and striking dress and I thought of the horror such a request would be listened to in our country and I said to him that, with us, women did these things and I could easily get a person here, but he said, 'No! No! I can't bear to think of you in such women's hands. I shall be as tender to you as any women. Do my dear little sick one let me come and wait upon you.' Nothing that I could say seemed to have the slightest weight in making him understand that it could not be done and John only laughed & seemed highly delighted with the novelty of the thing.[33]

In the event she was leeched on the 27th January by Brown's housekeeper Joan under the supervision of the friar. There was a last minute hitch. She had received an invitation to a military ball which she did not want the blood-letting to interfere with. If she had had to choose she would have chosen the ball. The friar reassured her. Paulizza arrived during the leeching but was refused entry because she was still undressed. Brown arrived later and was admitted. Paulizza had by this time become more than just a regular visitor. Effie wrote that 'his affection for us is something quite extraordinary.' He never went anywhere else in Venice but came continually to the Danieli. Whilst John always spent the evenings in his room working, Effie and Charlotte entertained Paulizza who joined them in chess games and polka practice.[34] Effie told her mother that Paulizza was to accompany her to a ball because he feared she might 'get into some scrape'. John had declared in advance that he would go but return early. From her next letter it is clear that her brother George, who knew his sister very well, had been furious with Paulizza both for the episode with the leeches and for his bringing her home from the ball. John and Effie both seemed to have found his concern amusing. Effie obliquely accused her brother of being jealous and terrified to trust her in other people's society and told her mother implausibly that Brown's housekeeper Joan had accompanied her to the ball. However, after waltzes with Paulizza and polkas with Prince Troubetzkoi, it was Paulizza whom she asked to take her home at 1.30 am. John had left at eleven.

George junior would not have been reassured, particularly when he read her next letter. 'I suppose that George would have considered the five hours [with Paulizza] speaking German & sailing in a Gondola improper and dangerous in the last degree.' The trip had been to St. Giuliano where Paulizza explained to her how during the siege he had according to Effie 'done something against Venice very wonderful with balloons but I could not exactly understand what.' (Paulizza's pioneering attempt at ærial warfare had not been entirely wonderful. Several of the balloon bombs had in fact fallen on his own position and he himself had been badly wounded.) At the next ball Paulizza and Prince

Troubetzkoi exchanged angry words about her dance card. Troubetzkoi, after becoming furious with another of her admirers for talking English to her, made a subtle pass at her causing her to flee the room. John had left at midnight. There was no mention of Joan this time. Effie left at 3 am with Paulizza. Now it was Rawdon Brown who warned her 'in the gravest colours' about her conduct. Brown lived in the Palazzo Businello whilst the owner, Mlle Taglioni the former dancer lived upstairs. Taglioni had separated from her French husband and had arrived in Venice with two children and Prince Troubetzkoi as her companion of six years. Troubetzkoi was to marry one of her teenage daughters two years later. In her letter Effie declared her intention to visit Taglioni. Her mother forbade it. In the event Effie became so familiar with Taglioni that she did not need to visit.

Her mother must have realised from Effie's letters that Paulizza was in love with Effie and have expressed some concern about whether Effie was telling her everything that was going on. Effie admitted to her mother that had John not been so kind amiable and good, 'excessive devotion from so handsome & gifted a man' would indeed be 'somewhat dangerous.' She also argued that she could be trusted to keep other people's secrets but was quite ingenuous about having none of her own. After describing herself as 'one of the odd of the earth' and having 'no talent whatever for intrigue as everything must be open as the day' she reassured her mother, without a trace of irony, that she had forbidden Charlotte ever to mention Paulizza in her letters home 'as one does not know, amongst so many, what construction might be put upon what she says, and she agrees with me that it is best not to speak about us.'[35] She then told her mother that she could forward all her letters to her brother George, who was seriously alarmed by her behaviour, but with a warning to use his good sense about what to keep private.[36] Her brother George remained very uneasy about what he was reading. Effie thought he would be 'dreadfully shocked.'[37] 'Tell George,' she asked her mother in February, 'that John is perfectly satisfied with my conduct in every particular and is kinder to me & fonder of me every day, and when I find a good husband I hope I know his value properly and appreciate him enough. John is particularly flattered with the attention they pay me, and when I go out would give me any thing I liked if he thought it would make me look better.' I am not sure that this would have reassured her brother. By the 11th of March she had decided that her mother ought to use her discretion about what George should be allowed to read.[38]

John meanwhile seems to have been perfectly amiable with all her admirers, at least according to Effie. He was content for her to be escorted all around the town and the lagoon by a number of handsome unmarried young men. He expressed no concern whatsoever about her visiting without Charlotte, indeed he preferred her to go alone. Effie could receive men friends at their rooms in the Hotel Danieli and John didn't even object to Effie practicing the polka with Paulizza whilst he worked in his closed room next door. His lack of jealousy was almost preternatural. He left Effie at parties and balls virtually unchaperoned to dance with whomsoever she chose and then be escorted home in the early hours by the 'handsomest man in Venice' who was besotted with her. When Rawdon Brown later warned her about this she claimed it had been 'by my husband's desire' that she did it. John did not even prevent her socializing with either Prince Troubetzkoi or Mme. Taglioni, both notoriously unrespectable at that time.[39] He allowed Effie and Charlotte to go to the Fenice scandalously unaccompanied. When Effie insisted on taking Domenico, their Italian speaking valet-de-place, to prevent men accosting her in her box, 'John laughed and said I was very cruel.' On the night Effie was able to enjoy listening to the constant attempts by her male admirers to gain admittance. According to Effie, John was never so happy as when men were paying attention to her and encouraged her to play the coquette.

However, and also according to Effie, John was totally engrossed in his work on *The Stones of Venice* and quite oblivious to the social scene. Effie quoted from one of his letters home:

> Operas, drawing rooms and living creatures have become alike nuisances to me. I go out to them as if I was to pass the time in the Stocks and when I am in the rooms, I say and do just what I must and no more: if people talk to me I answer them, looking all the while if there is any body else coming to take them away. As soon as they are gone I forget their names & their faces & what they said and when I meet them next day I don't see them. When I walk with Effie she is always touching me and saying that is so and so – now don't cut him or her as you did yesterday – Then I say Where? – like Mr. Winkle with the partridges. Then she says There – then I make a low bow to somebody whom I never saw before in my life, then they stare – and Effie assures me that so & so has gone away very offended.

Effie also described how astonished the inhabitants of Venice were at John's behaviour:

> Nothing interrupts him and whether the Square is crowded or empty he is either seen with a black cloth over his head taking Daguerrotypes or climbing about the capitals covered with dust, or else with cobwebs exactly as if he had just

arrived from taking a voyage with the old woman on her broomstick. Then when he comes down he stands very meekly to be brushed down by Domenico quite regardless of the scores of idlers who cannot understand him at all.[40]

Although at first John took them to the Opera whenever they wanted, his interest, according to Effie, was in the attention paid to her rather than the production. When they visited the Fenice for an opera John either fell asleep,[41] or sat at the back of the box writing a 'Chapter on Chamfered edges.'[42] There were however rare occasions when he left behind that 'certain green notebook without whose companionship I think it would be impossible for him to exist' and took a holiday.[43] He took Paulizza, Effie and Charlotte on a champagne picnic to Torcello after which John and Paulizza ran races around the buildings to prove they weren't tipsy. The same party had also gone to the Lido where they gathered shells, caught little crabs and raced them. John also accompanied Effie to the Cavalchina, an all night masked ball on the last night of Carnival.

By the end of February John's work was almost done and the Ruskins prepared to leave Venice. After a protracted and emotional send off involving just about everyone they had met or employed, they left Paulizza in floods of tears and were gondola'd to the railway station by Brown who had asked John's permission to present Effie with a precious red coral brooch.

CHAPTER XIV

HIATUS

☙

The stay in Venice seems to have been very much Effie's decision, although John had already planned to do some work there. What made up her mind? Was she intrigued by her conversation with Lady Davy about her Venetian escapades? Did Count Béthune's remarks on the mores of continental marriages make her want to experiment with living abroad? Whatever the case it would seem that, during their stay in Venice, John and Effie had conducted a very radical experiment in marital relations on the continental model. Whether this was by design or accident is not clear. What is certain is that for her part Effie found the experiment extremely rewarding and was reluctant to leave. No other conclusion can be drawn from her letters home. For most of the time in Venice she and John had indeed lived virtually separate lives. If her letters are anything to go by she had very little interest in her husband's work. She only referred to his book once and never mentioned its title. She assumed that John was also quite content with the way they were living and it would seem that she intended this lifestyle to continue after the couple returned to London. At the beginning of December she had told her father that 'He lets us go anywhere and do anything we like'[1], and later in the same month explained that John was so busy that he appreciated having a wife who could take care of herself, even to the extent of not caring who she associated with and for how long. For her part Effie was much happier planning her social life entirely independently of John.[2]

From Verona she wrote to her mother who had been preparing the ground for the impending reunion with John's parents. Effie had already written how grateful she was to Mr. Ruskin senior for having allowed her this extraordinary experience and now hoped that she and her parents-in-law would be better friends. She was no longer quite so possessive about John:

> For all I care they may have John as much with them as they please for I could hardly see less of him than I do at present with his work, and I think it is much better, for we follow our different occupations and never interfere with one another and are always happy, but I shall take care to let them be as little alone as possible together for they had far too much time for grumbling about nothing before.[3]

On their journey home they had stayed in Paris at the Hotel Meurice and Effie was able to meet all the Domecq sisters, now married into the French aristocracy. Diana had married the Comte Maison, Adèle the Baron Duquesne, Cécile the Comte de Chabrillan, Elise the Comte de Roys, and Caroline the Comte Béthune. There is every reason to believe that these were all *mariages de convenance* to which the girls brought their wealth and the husbands their titles. John displayed very little interest in his former flame Adèle, whom Effie thought was the plainest of them all. Effie got on best with Caroline and their acquaintance would even survive the annulment. As usual Effie's letters home are an inventory of expensive gastronomy, impressive real estate, precious gee-gaws and above all prolific fashion details. Effie described her visit to Cécile who had been the prettiest of them all and had married the richest husband:

Their house in the Place Vendôme is splendid and most

luxurious, all the furniture and walls covered with the richest satin, and statues, china & marbles of the finest kind everywhere. The rooms all opened into each other and at the end of the suite we found Cecile, the beauty, in a luxuriously furnished apartment lounging on the sofa. She always receives at four and there were several people there when we entered but they left. She is an exceedingly calm tranquil person looks younger than Madame Béthune & has not her mind at all. She was dressed à la Française in a sort of elegant dressing gown but tight to the waist of checked fawn & green glace silk trimmed richly with black lace, open at the neck showing an exquisite lace chemisette, and in front of the skirt a petticoat of white thick muslin with flounce of coarse work all the way down, long hanging sleeves showing her arms and hands like snow, with a scent bottle hanging from one finger, and a large coiffure of white lace with quantities of cerise satin ribbon & velvet mixed. She took us into her rooms which she had furnished according to her own taste. Her bedroom was one mass of crimson satin & Venice glass, the coverlet of the bed and curtains being rose silk covered with fine Lace, and on the wall a large crucifix in Ivory with a large Christ and other subjects from scripture of rare value. I never saw such a luxurious little creature. Of course her husband never enters these apartments excepting to dine with her, and take her out in the evening, but has his own rooms and servants at another part of the house. They are the best friends in the world & think highly of each other. I suppose most of the other sisters live in the same way.[4]

This final melancholy observation may have been a casual afterthought; she had however already mentioned at least five failed marriages in her letters home and seemed to be measuring her own against these. Remember that Effie too had only been seeing John at mealtimes and when he took her out in the evening. It may even have been that she was reconciling herself to her situation.

Unfortunately Effie did not only have her in-laws to worry about. Her own family had begun to pester her again, particularly about brother George. Already on the 7th April whilst she was still at Bourges she was having to explain both why she didn't want him at Park Street and why she would find it difficult to finance his stay in London.

> As to money I intended to save him what I could save off my own allowance to meet any expences he might have in London in going about but I am afraid I have not enough to do that and pay his expences up and down at the same time. I write this candidly because you know I would do everything I could to serve George or you but if I promised more than I could perform I would be doing wrong and I have no money lying by or he should have it at once.[5]

The reason she would have no money for George out of her allowance was perhaps because of the marathon shopping session she was about to have in Paris. After she arrived back in London on April 20th she wrote that 'I got all my things myself in Paris and a great deal of trouble and expence I was at, the Modiste only sent home my dresses at eleven at night when I was dreadfully tired with packing up [to go on my next] day and I had to settle her account afterwards.'[6] Readers will be spared the lengthy description of her purchases of dresses, bonnets and the rest.

On arriving back in England John and Effie spent a few days with Mr. and Mrs. Ruskin at Denmark Hill before finally settling back into Park Street. Luckily for her brother George, when Effie celebrated her birthday on May 7th the Ruskins were in a generous mood. Besides the cake as big as a wedding cake 'Each gave me a guinea and John ten, which was very kind of him as he knew I had rather spent my allowance in Paris but do not think this is all for I have some for George besides which is not my dress money at all.'[7] Relations between Effie and Mr. Ruskin seem to have been fairly cordial at this time. Perhaps she was finally showing some appreciation of the financial support he had provided and which had enabled her to live such an exciting and privileged existence in Venice.[8] No doubt his generosity on her birthday also helped, as did the staggering £20 he was later to pay for her Court dress.

Once back at Park Street Effie threw herself into the London Season with a vengeance. If John's literary fame and his father's wealth had been her initial springboard into Society, her well-honed social skills and flirtatious manner had helped her to exploit her position to the full. As a result she already had a substantial circle of acquaintance from the previous year. Now, dressed in the very height of French fashion, she would also have had a bulging store of exotic names to drop and a new found social aplomb from her sojourn in Venice. Besides being presented at Court by Lady Charlemont, she made many new contacts. There was however a familiar problem. Even before she had arrived home she wrote a letter to Rawdon Brown in which she explained that John, working on his book, was going to be even busier than he was in Venice, that he would sometimes go out with her in the evening but every morning after breakfast he would go to Denmark Hill to write and would only come back at six o'clock for dinner with her. She had tried to point out to John that if he worked in his study at Park Street she could at least see him during the day, but he claimed that Park Street was too dark to see his Turners, and that she would soon find acquaintances and could take care of herself:

> which I think you rather doubt. However so that he is satisfied and happy and gets on with his work to his own satisfaction I have always plenty to do and to interest me in my own pursuits if I never saw anybody.[9]

Effie seems at first to have been as delighted with London as she had been in the early days of their marriage; but London was not Venice. Amongst the titled and famous names in her letters were the inevitable young, and not so young men who clustered round her like wasps around an open jam pot. Certain names would continue to appear in her letters: Edward Cheney, whose house in Venice she had already visited in his absence, and the Fords, her neighbours in Park Street, whose daughters she chaperoned and whose only son Clare was soon to fall in love with her. John's absence from Park Street was to severely complicate her social life as a subsequent letter proved. On 15th May being in the rather unusual state of being all alone, (but only because the expected company had failed to show up) she wrote that on the previous day the young, unattached and handsome Mr. Newton, one of John's Christ Church friends, had sat with her until dinner time:

> in fact I think he came to dine but being alone I thought that the London convenances might be hurt whatever one might do at Venice by my asking him to dine with me alone when John was out of the house he is going to ride with me however when Mr. Liddell returns next week my coachman James will ride with us.[10]

There are several points to be made from this little anecdote. First, she had been in the habit of dining alone with men in Venice; secondly, even John's closest friends were in the habit of calling on Effie when he was not at home; and thirdly, John did not always come home to dinner if indeed he came home at all.

Riding in Hyde Park seems to have been one of the best ways to meet anyone who was in town. After Easter when the main Season began there could be as many as a thousand ladies on horseback on Rotten Row. Effie told her mother that the number of people riding in the Row was quite a spectacle. She and John sometimes promenaded in the carriage together. On one occasion she was recognised by her old friend 'the Handsome Capt. Campbell' but did not speak to him, an omission she intended to correct when next they met. This she thought not improbable since she had seen him riding there before. While John was at Denmark Hill, Effie would ride the carriage horse to the Park. When her brother George visited London he noted that 'all the ladies ride on horseback here, but badly.'[11] Being a little out of practice Effie at first rode at eleven in the morning when the Park was deserted, but later, accompanied by Mr. Gardner she was able to join the fashionable throng and show off her skills every day between five and six when there was a band playing. Inevitably on June 12th she and her brother George bumped into Capt. C whilst riding in the Row. Effie asked him to dinner the next day 'to meet Lord Eastnor.'[12] Eastnor cancelled. Later when Capt. C turned up with his wife, Effie was unfortunately not at home. Effie was forced to give up riding in July because of the heat and because work on the Great Exhibition was beginning to block the Row.

John meanwhile had been demonstrating his habitual aversion to social occasions by never telling Effie which people he had met, cutting everybody he could and never speaking to her about anybody.[13] In the same letter Effie described how John took her to a particularly crowded function at Grosvenor House but ran off and left her immediately: 'the crowds, the silk, and the lace, took away from all idea of individuality and I ceased to think those pretty who are the beauties of the present day and I was not sure whether I was myself or somebody else all the time.'[14] In August Effie wrote about an argument that she had had with John after she had pressured him into accompanying her to some social venue. He had called her a bad wife for taking him away from home and making him so uncomfortable.[15] Effie was beginning to find her situation in London rather disorienting. As well as men visiting her at home, she also had problems with visiting others and in a letter to Rawdon Brown she claimed only to accept if she had been given a proper invitation. She also confessed to him that she would much rather be in Venice and that she had been pestering John to fix a date for their return every day since they came back to England. John however, even busier than when he was in Venice, needed at least six months to write his book and had ruled out Italy for that year. Because of John's absence from home during the day and his reluctance to accompany her to parties and functions, Effie obviously felt constrained by the formality of London Society, preferring what she deemed to be the more relaxed continental attitude. Ominously Brown had already reported some malicious gossip to her involving her escapades with various young men in Venice and Effie was forced to defend her reputation. That she had to explain to Brown which particular incident with which particular young man was at issue gives some idea of the rather reckless social life she had been leading there. Brown had already pointed out to her 'in the gravest colours' the danger to her reputation of being taken home from a ball in her gondola by Paulizza in the early hours. This she put down to innocence and inexperience. It was she claimed because she had been brought up in that 'virtuous land Scotland' and had only attended two balls in her life. In any case it had been done by her husband's desire and he had been as unsuspecting of any harm as she was. She would never do it again and had 'learned a few things from my stay in Venice not to be forgotten.'[16]

As if that wasn't enough, in July the notorious Prince Troubetzkoi had arrived unexpectedly at Park Street whilst John was out and his presence had caused her great embarrassment. In Venice Effie had been on extremely friendly terms with the charming and gallant Troubetzkoi but in London his reputation was well known and not to be attached in any way to Effie's own.[17] He plainly felt a change in her manner towards him and called her a Puritan when she resisted his gallantries and who knows what else. In the moral atmosphere of London Society Effie had revised her opinion of him. The 'perfect Hercules' was now 'a bad man as ever I knew.'[18]

The Season ended in July when Parliament went into recess and its members returned to their country estates. In August John and Effie left London to visit various friends. On Effie's insistence these included the Cheney brothers, three perpetual bachelors who John found rather worldly and uninteresting. Effie was now close enough to Edward Cheney for him to bring her glass flowers from Venice for her hair.[19] The Cheneys were establishment classicists with a Georgian country seat in Shropshire stuffed with neo-classical mementoes. Given John's probable reaction to their provincial and orthodox taste, it is not surprising that Edward Cheney took an instant dislike to him. From the Cheneys John and Effie travelled to Effie's parents at Bowerswell. John returned almost immediately but Effie, who had already mentioned to Brown that her mother was in a delicate state of health, stayed on for another two months until Albert Gray was born on October 10th. The baby must have been conceived in February just as Effie was saying her farewells to her admirers in Venice. It would have been most reassuring for her mother at that time to know that Effie was coming home and she would be available to help her in the autumn. The topic of babies had already cropped up in an August letter to Brown who had apparently suggested that if Effie had children it might improve her health. Effie replied that 'I quite think with you that if I had children my health might be quite restored. Simpson and several of the best medical men have said so to me.' She claimed that the obstacle to this miracle cure was John who hated children and did not want children to interfere with his work. 'I often think I would be a much happier, better person if I was more like the rest of my sex in this respect.'[20]

After the birth Effie returned transformed to London on the 26th. She told her mother that:

> John was perfectly enchanted to see me again and said he never saw such a difference on any creature in two months he says my colour is so clear and healthy and I am stouter as well he thinks going home has done me a great deal of good and made me merrie again [...] he is in high spirits and as happy as possible to get me back.[21]

That autumn John seems to have made a special effort to accommodate Effie. He told her mother that they now usually walked together in the morning for exercise and Effie could walk fast and well. They visited second-hand bookshops on the Charing Cross Road, 'the only shops in London he ever goes in with me,'[22] and when John went off to Denmark Hill Effie took a cab home with the books. John thought she seemed better even than she had been in Venice the previous year, although she still longed to return there. John was not unaware of his wife's predicament. He told her mother that he hoped she would not want to spend another season in London, 'for it is assuredly bad for her: and all manner of difficulties are in the way of her walking or amusing herself without getting talked of. I think she will only be thoroughly well in a country home:– but I have no idea where my occupation may lead me, at present: and so let time pass on – until we shall be turned out of Park St. and then we must look about us.'[23] It has been suggested that Effie was suffering at this time because her marriage had not been consummated and she wanted to have children. If so then the prospect of a home in the country would surely have appealed to her. However it was Venice she was longing for and when she wrote to Brown on December 11th that she had been reading 'in my journal what I did these days last year,' it was 'an inexpressible enjoyment' to her. This author at least very much doubts that there was anything in her diary of that time to suggest that she was pining for maternal domesticity or had a great desire to get pregnant by John.

Although in that autumn of 1850 Effie attended several dinner parties without John, she seems not to have found this a very comfortable situation. She did however spend New Year alone with the family of an aristocratic acquaintance in Uxbridge and even managed a couple of balls. John was by this time working hard on *The Stones of Venice* and gave her instructions not to accept any invitations for him until the Season began.[24] Effie solved the problem by staging a series of social events at Park Street. Every Friday from February to March she invited about thirty of the clever and the nice (an Effie distinction) to visit her between 9 pm and 11 pm. They rarely cleared the house before midnight. She found playing the hostess at home very exhausting but even John seems to have enjoyed himself.

On the 3rd of April 1851 both John and Effie attended Court. This meant that as far as London society was concerned, they had arrived. From now on there was no society in the whole of Europe too high for them to attend. Another round of visits to friends outside London followed: Dr. Whewell at Cambridge, the Fawkes's near Leeds, a day with the Cheneys at Badger Hall in Shropshire, and on to the Pritchards at Brosely.[25] Relations between John and Edward Cheney remained cool. In August Cheney wrote that he thought Effie was a very pretty woman but that John neglected Effie in favour of literature, despite having neither talent nor knowledge. On the 1st of May, just after John and Effie returned to London, the Great Exhibition opened in the Park. Mr. Ruskin had paid for a season ticket for Effie which meant she could attend the opening ceremony. This she did in the company of three gentlemen, none of whom was her husband. Effie was pleased to note that most of the other ladies had to share one gentleman. Effie found herself in one of the best places to be in order to listen to the speeches. John was at home beginning volume two of *The Stones of Venice*. In his diary he wrote:

> All London is astir and some part of all the world and I am sitting in my quiet room, hearing the birds sing, and about to enter on the true beginning of the second part of my Venetian work. May God help me finish it – to His glory, and man's good.[26]

1851 was a momentous year in John's literary development but it would be impossible to discover this from Effie's letters. He published *Notes on the Construction of Sheepfolds*, *The King of the Golden River* (the fairy tale that he had written for Effie), and new editions of *Modern Painters* volumes I and II. Even the momentous publication of volume one of *The Stones of Venice* on 3rd March 1851 passed almost without a mention by Effie except that she thought it a handsome book.[27] She was obviously more preoccupied that month with her sittings for portraits by G. F. Watts and Thomas Richmond (reproduced p. 4), both paid for by Mr. Ruskin. These pictures of Effie were hung in the Royal Academy Exhibition of 1851, the opening of which signalled the start of the Season. The Academy Exhibition of that year also featured paintings by the Pre-Raphaelites Holman Hunt, John Everett Millais and Ford Madox Brown who, having been lambasted by the press for the unorthodoxy of their religious paintings of previous years, had by now largely reverted to literary subjects. The establishment press had however sensed radicalism and heresy and now planned a concerted ambush in an attempt to end their careers. John responded to the blatant bigotry of this critical assault by writing letters to *The Times* on May 13th and May 30th followed up by a pamphlet under the title *Pre-Raphaelitism*. Although John's intervention rescued the reputations of the Brotherhood, this episode began a new and controversial phase of his career. The press, thwarted in their vindictiveness, transferred their antipathy to John and his works. Henceforth John was 'that pre-Raffaelite fellow' to his enemies.

Effie's parents paid a visit to London at the end of May, bringing her brother George with them. They stayed with Effie in Park Street, which was rather cramped accommodation for so many. No doubt John spent this time with his parents. The Grays had come to see the Great Exhibition which was rapidly becoming the phenomenon of the age. According to Effie, John was much too busy to take her out into society: according to John it took him six months to recover from the late nights and hectic social life of that London season. In one of Effie's letters to Rawdon Brown there are hints of a kind of trade-off she had made with John. She would not complain so much about her restricted social life in London if John would take her back to Venice 'which I love a thousand times more than I ever could this place.'[28] Back in April Effie had written to Brown to ask him to find them a place to stay in Venice because John found the Danieli uncomfortable and expensive. The result was to be a six month let of rooms in the Casa Wetzlar from the Baroness Wetzlar. John, busy with his work, had left all the arrangements to Effie. In mid-July Rawdon Brown broke his self-imposed fourteen year exile in Venice and arrived in London, ostensibly to visit the Exhibition. He stayed with the Cheneys at their house in Audley Square and whilst John was in Malvern with his parents, Effie went with Brown to the Exhibition, to Kensington Gardens and even allowed him into Park Street.

On receiving a letter of thanks from the Pre-Raphaelites, John had taken Effie round to meet John Everett Millais at his parent's home on Gower Street. John had quickly recognised Millais as the most technically gifted member of the Brotherhood. At 22 years old, he was a year younger than Effie but seemed even younger. He was tall and strikingly handsome with curly blond hair and a noble profile. Over the following weeks Millais dined and took breakfast with John at Park Street. They got on so well that he was invited to accompany John and Effie to Switzerland but declined. He was also invited to dine at Denmark Hill three times in June. On the 24th Effie was also at the table. Meeting Effie again at this time must have been quite exciting for the young Millais since he was later to admit that even before he knew John he had heard scandalous rumours about her.

Effie for her part seems to have remained on good terms with Mr. Ruskin, who would after all be funding their next Venetian stay. He gave her presents, took her on outings and to concerts and was generally a proud father-in-law, only commenting on the flamboyance of her dress sense, which he probably thought was the main reason for all the male attention being paid to her. He was particularly proud of the high social circles in which Effie now moved, even without John, but from which he himself was barred by the way he earned his living. Effie's mother on the other hand, having now seen at first hand the rather informal social life of her daughter, seems to have been worried that it might cause tongues to wag. George had informed his mother that Clare Ford, a frequent visitor to Park Street, was almost certainly in love with Effie. Effie's attempt to reassure her mother speaks volumes about what was really going on:

> What you say is perfectly true and I am so peculiarly situated as a married woman that being much alone and most men thinking that I live quite alone I am more exposed to their attentions, but I assure you I never allow such people to enter the house and stop everything of the kind which might be hurtful to my reputation and I would not for the sake of improving any person destroy or impare the only fortune I possess, viz—a good name—which if you inquired here amongst the people calculated to know you would find that I had never been spoken about with anyone—if I was, the most respectable women in London would certainly not give me their daughters to Chaperone, and although you think me unsuspicious I am quite quick enough to see, observe or hear if anyone thought lightly of my conduct. I know well

that George has been gossiping to you about Clare [Ford] as Mr. Furnivall did to him. I soon got to the bottom of that & the result was nothing at all excepting that John got very angry with Mr. Furnivall for putting such ideas into George's head, merely thinking him jealous of Clare, whom he does not know and cannot indure. As for Clare I have shut him out and will not let anyone in whilst John is away but Mr. Brown. Clare goes abroad this week. What can I do more? I shall be quite as particular with Paulizza and never will encourage anything in my conduct but the most perfect propriety but if you think differently always write to me.[29]

Shutting out Clare Ford was a belated symbolic gesture. Within days of this letter not only would Clare be off abroad, but John and Effie would be on their way to Venice, leaving to Mr. Ruskin the task of clearing out the Park Street house. Mrs. Gray was no doubt mollified by the money order Effie sent to her in August. For his part young George was always to be suspicious of John's rôle in the ongoing Clare Ford affair and continued to believe John to be 'a proper scoundrel' as a result. He later told his niece that 'both in Italy and Venice & in Park St. with Clare Ford as a frequent visitor his [John's] schemes were very apparent & your mother was quite aware of them.'[30]

CHAPTER XV

QUEEN OF MARBLE AND OF MUD

⁊

John and Effie set out for the Continent on 4th August 1851 with Paris as their first stop. This time they did not take a carriage of their own nor was there a companion for Effie. Instead she had engaged a maid called Mary who she described to her mother as stupid, honest and faithful and incapable of telling a lie. More importantly, given the sensitive nature of Effie's correspondence and lifestyle, Mary could hardly read or write, knew no languages, did not like going out and sat sewing all day. The party arrived in Venice on September 1st to be met by Rawdon Brown and the sad news of the death of Paulizza who on July 11th had finally succumbed to the self-inflicted head wound he had received from his balloon bombs during the siege.

A few days later the couple moved into the Casa Wetzlar. The renting of the Baroness Wetzlar's first floor apartments, south-facing and on the Grand Canal nearly opposite the Salute, had not been entirely straightforward. John had wanted an extra room for him to write in and there had been 'a great fight' for this room. The other rooms consisted of a hall dining room; a beautiful drawing room; double-bedroom and dressing room—three servants rooms and kitchen: all for 'about 17 pounds a month'. By the 9th September John was able to describe to his father how he was 'writing with the green water of the Grand Canal shining through the openings of the golden marble balustrade of the balcony of my very comfortable room.'[1]

After some initial distractions from work due to sorting out the domestic arrangements in Italian, John handed the whole business over to Effie. Effie informed her brother George that: 'I have the entire charge of the accounts and John has nothing to do but go on with his work. I find that one can live here as comfortably and even luxuriously upon very much less than in London, and much better in every way.'[2] This probably caused her brother, who was still dependent upon her monetary gifts, to think twice about further criticising her lifestyle. In a subsequent letter to her mother she asked: 'Does he still think me badly treated?' On 26th September John told his father that Effie had estimated the household expenses at 800 francs per month.[3] This was more than John expected but still a substantial saving. The Danieli had cost them 53 francs a day which meant that even with the extra 4½ francs they would have had to pay for Mary they were now living more comfortably for half the price.

Life at Venice was indeed comfortable. Besides Effie's maid Mary and John's valet Hobbs, John and Effie had engaged a 'donna', two gondoliers and a cook. A typical day began at seven o'clock with Effie's Italian lessons. Breakfast at nine was prepared by Mary with fruit, milk and ice brought in by Beppo (Effie's 'servant, valet or anything') for a pittance and a dish prepared by the cook. After breakfast John would read and at ten there were prayers. At eleven Effie practised the clay modelling she learned at her thrice weekly classes, played on her 'beautiful piano' or did 'work'. Effie and Mary made curtains for the apartments and a coal fire (unheard of in Venice) was organised with Brown's help. John left the house after a two course lunch and was away till five researching for his book. Until then Effie was free to socialise, do shopping and generally be seen about the town. Dinner at five was a splendid affair of seven removes: macaroni soup, tuna, leg of mutton, cold veal in jelly, fried sweetbreads, roasted larks and blackbirds and then 'Spanish fritters'. This was followed by a 'desert' of figs, grapes and peaches. What was not eaten was fed to the servants or re-sold. At seven they went together to the Piazza San Marco where they sat or walked listened to the music and met Brown and Cheney.[4]

It would seem that Effie had initially made an effort to avoid the problems of being a woman alone which had tainted the previous Venetian stay. She was at first accompanied on her afternoon walks by Beppo, but being further from the public gardens than she had been at the Danieli, she soon tired and turned back. Gondola rides to the Lido and elsewhere seemed less exhausting. Most of her other problems were solved by an introduction which Lord Glenelg had given her to Lady Sorell, a gossipy amusing woman of impeccable lineage, unimpeachable reputation and reduced circumstances, who was delighted to chaperone Effie, help her with shopping and could introduce her to everybody worth knowing. Lady Sorell was indeed a godsend since she had been in Venice before the revolution and siege and knew all the residents who were now beginning to return. Even so, when John suggested she go to the Opera alone with Lady Sorell as her chaperone, Effie demurred.

In the first weeks Effie wrote to her mother about meeting Marshall Marmont, the Countess Esterhazy, Princess Hohenloe, the Infanta of Spain, Countess Pallavicini, Lord Dufferin, Marshall Falkenhayn, Baron Reischach and the Duchesses of Angoulême and Berry. John was baffled by the sudden arrival of such noble visitors at the Casa Wetzlar, putting it down to the fact that Effie was now regarded as a resident rather than a traveller. In reality it was all Lady Sorell's doing.

It might have seemed that once Effie and John had settled into their new domestic arrangements that their life together would

The Casa Wetzlar in 1852. The Ruskins rented the entire first (main) floor except for the room on the left. Effie's room had the little covered balcony on the right

proceed much as it had done during their first sojourn in Venice. This was not to be. A number of factors conspired to subvert their separate idylls. Nor can it be supposed that any of these were entirely unexpected. The perennial question of finances was the first cloud to cast its shadow over the brilliant Venetian stage. As early as mid November John was having to justify his expenses prior to the trip. He told his father:

> I do not consider myself economical – neither do I think myself extravagant. I placed no severe check on my expenses on the one hand – but I never bought anything idly.

His list of expenses included Liber Studiorum engravings, work by Albrecht Dürer, instruments for his research (probably photographic), an enormous collection of daguerreotypes and valuable minerals! Admitting their bad management and his careless accounting, he mistakenly believed that since his marriage he had only spent £100 more than he should have done.⁵ Mr. Ruskin knew better. Their expensive lifestyle was beginning to cause alarm at Denmark Hill. Just as he had paid for Park Street and their launch into society, this whole trip was of course also being paid for by Mr. Ruskin, who at sixty-seven was no longer a young man. He was getting tired and contemplating a retirement when he would no longer be able to generate the wealth needed to support his son and daughter-in-law in the manner to which they had become accustomed. Mr. Ruskin wrote that he had told John that 'I cannot leave Business & continue to give him such amounts of Revenue by a very great deal' and John had replied that 'he never would again live in such a fashion to require it'. His father was even thinking beyond that time: 'I was not blaming so much as I was cautioning for I have some fear that at my death they may go too fast.' Effie had found out about the letters to John and was not 'on quite gracious terms' with her father-in-law. Mr. Ruskin then wrote on 'this always disagreeable subject' to George Gray on 10th December:

> I have a very agreeable correspondence with my son with the exception of a few letters on finance, having taken the liberty of telling them that they much mistake their own character if the gentleman fancies himself economical or the lady fancies herself a manager. They have, like the soldier who spent half a crown out of sixpence a day, spent £1,670 out of £1074 per annum, for besides a large sum taken from publishers for my son's books being all gone – they have overdrawn above £1000. My son says they were unable to be in the circle they were at less and I confess I sent them there. [...] They have

many virtues and their faults may be ascribed more to their parents than themselves, and it is curious coincidence that for every fault on one side may be found a similar on the other. My son has been taken too much abroad ever to be quite content to live at home & Phemy has been allowed to go too much about ever to become domestic. My son is too fond of pictures and Effie is too fond of dress. They mean however to do right always [...] As I told my son, it makes little difference to me whether I die a thousand pounds richer or poorer but I should like to see them exercise some control over their expenditure.[6]

It was quite understandable that Mr. Ruskin should wrongly assume that Effie was overspending on dress, since her letters invariably dwell obsessively and at great length on fashion details. While John wrote to his father about his book, Effie thought his letters 'stupid' and regularly described her frills and flounces in her fashionable socialite 'news' which Mrs. Ruskin apparently enjoyed reading.[7] John wrote proudly from Venice on several occasions that Effie had been 'reine du bal'. To be queen of the ball in such high company required a serious trousseau. Both father and son were intensely proud of Effie's forays into the uppermost social circles and wanted her to be well dressed, Mr. Ruskin however consistently equated showiness with vulgar expenditure and repeatedly expressed an opinion that the top people should dress with restraint particularly if they were as attractive as Effie. Her little scheme to support her family through her dressmaker must have continued to exaggerate her dress bills in London and the marathon shopping spree in Paris would not have gone unnoticed.

Effie's 'entire charge of the accounts' proved much more

expensive for Mr. Ruskin than John had supposed. However neither Mr. Ruskin nor John suspected that Effie's 'management' of the household expenses was effectively doubling the cost of living in Venice. By 16th January John was complaining that the 'delightfully cheap' lodgings had turned out to be as expensive as Park Street! 'I am especially puzzled because it seems to cost nearly as much as when we had Miss Ker with us and two carriages and lived at an hotel.'[8] John was 'taken quite by surprise at the sums which go in candles and fuel and household expenses.' After calculating that the journey had already cost £800 by January 16th, John admitted being uncomfortable 'at the continual drain I am making on your purse – giving you no return.'[9] John was not being ironic when he told his father that he had also 'given a great deal in charity.'[10] Effie meanwhile had been keeping up her regular charitable donations. On the 17th November there was £5 to buy a Christmas present and an offer to pay for frocks for her little brothers Melville and Albert.[11] On the 30th of November Effie mentioned more money she had sent the previous week to her mother and Charlotte and yet more money 'for Christmas' enclosed in the present letter.[12] If Mr. Ruskin thought that Mr. Gray might help rein in his daughter's extravagance he was deluding himself. Mrs. Gray would probably have read the letter to her husband by the new gas lighting installed at Bowerswell which Effie mentioned on 25th November.[13] If she had difficulty with any of Effie's fashionable 'Frenchisms' she could perhaps have asked the Gray children's newly employed French governess for help.

Mr. Ruskin did not want to spoil the enjoyment that both John and Effie were experiencing and so relied on the 'good sense and kindness' of Mr. Gray to be circumspect in his dealings with Effie so as not to 'create dispeace.' Effie's antipathy to her financial benefactor did not need much stoking. John had written to his father from Venice on 26th September: 'Effie is getting so domestic that we really have no news for you.' Mr. Ruskin had innocuously passed this on to the Grays who immediately relayed it to their daughter, provoking her into an irrational attack on Mr. Ruskin's 'underhand manner' and 'duplicity.'

> What going out I had in London might be counted and was during May, June and July. What does he make of 13 months before during which time John was always with them and I at home alone many & many a day from morning till night and even last season?[14]

'Home', in this context, was of course mostly Perth where she had absented herself against Mr. Ruskin's express wishes for eight months! Both 'last season' and 'April, May and July' must refer to the 1851 Season. John however later admitted that he was ill that July and 'gave up all society – Effie knows that I positively refused to stir out – the last month that I was in London – and I would not do anything but rest.'[15] Readers must decide for themselves how domestic her life was at that time.

Of course Mr. Gray informed Effie immediately that old Mr. Ruskin was complaining about money again and the poisoned relations between the two families continued. George Gray had the same odd attitude to Mr. Ruskin's hard-earned money as his daughter, even to the extent of defending Effie's lifestyle whilst criticising John's expenses. He had to be reminded that although John did indeed acquire expensive pictures, it was Mr. Ruskin who bought them for him with his own money. George Gray of course was still unable to contribute a penny to the marriage and indeed was still receiving regular amounts of money from his daughter. Effie was sufficiently chastened by Mr. Ruskin's letters to do without half her £24 allowance for the first quarter of the year and give up her 'modelling master.'[16]

Another dark cloud hanging over the Casa Wetzlar was the knowledge that this sojourn in Venice would come to an end on 17th May next when the Casa Wetzlar lease expired and John would have finished the work he needed for his book. From the outset Effie knew for certain that her time in Venice was shortening fast and there would be no returning to the enchanted city in the sea. Just as she never quite grasped that their extravagant lifestyle was entirely dependent upon her aged father-in-law's hard work and generosity, Effie never quite came to terms with the fact that her husband's literary work was their only reason for being in Venice and his genius was their sole entrée into high society. John's father's wealth was certainly essential to launching and maintaining them, but Mr. Ruskin himself was barred from high social circles because men of trade, and indeed lawyer's daughters, had no place there in their own right. This meant that if John was to maintain his status, and Effie was to succeed in her social ambitions, then their married life had to be subordinated to John's work. John had made it quite clear to Effie before the marriage that in order to work he needed to be close to his source material and in a quiet and undisturbed environment.

In late December Mr. Ruskin began to ask about his son's plans for the future. John replied with details of his plans as they then stood:

> After I have been in Switzerland this summer – or if you and
> my mother change your minds and do not come, when I come
> home in June, I shall have six months work with engravers
> and printers before I issue 2nd. vol Stones: I then – God

willing shall do Modern Painters which will require a year, and a tour through England in search of Turners; on which if you and my mother could accompany me it would give me infinite pleasure: I must therefore, for my work, be two years at least in England after I come home.[17]

Note that at this stage *The Stones of Venice* and *Modern Painters* were still projected as two volume works. In the event, the third volume of *The Stones* would take up the rest of the two-year window, whilst *Modern Painters* would generate three more volumes and eight years of work! The two year timetable however remained remarkably constant suggesting that he was working to a self-imposed deadline which was not purely literary.

On December 22nd the first intimations of life after Venice began to appear in a letter to his father. Given that he would be returning to England for two years, the next question that arose was of somewhere to live. There would be no return to the expensive and abandoned Park Street house. John was quite explicit. He did not want to live far from his parents, but could not live in the same house as them because Effie and his mother would not get on. Mrs. Ruskin absolutely refused to have Effie at Denmark Hill. Living next door to them would also be absurd. 'About ½ a mile to ¾, away, is the proper distance.' 'And I must live verily economically – that is, by no means in style: I am obliged to spend – even here – twice what I intended, merely by being in too large a house, and being on visiting terms with the upper classes.' He was very clear that he wanted a small furnished house within walking distance of Denmark Hill. He preferred a house within sight of a field or two and with some sort of land-scape view, but even 'should not mind living in the Walworth Rd. – so that I could keep people out of the house – but in order to do that, one must be at least 3 or 4 miles in the country.' This meant that he would be living well outside London and well away from the social scene he so detested. 'But quiet, and therefore not London itself, – and economy – veritable economy – are both absolutely necessary.'[18]

John found Effie's many visitors very distracting. Part of the reason for a small house well out of London was to discourage them. 'As for visitors from London,' he told his father, 'I shall soon put an end to them: I don't care whom I displease.'[19] However, confident though he seemed of being able to achieve this, he still stipulated 'a comfortable room for me to escape into if people come whom I don't want to see – and Effie does'[20] otherwise he would have to go over to Denmark Hill to work.

John had not been entirely unappreciative of their expensive foray into high society. He told his father: 'I have seen what I could not have written generally of the world without seeing: but it does not in the least add to happiness, and I must now positively put an end to it.'[21] He later described how one day they had 'two generals and a commandant of a city – side by side on our sofa – and however the time might pass in badinage – things come out of the badinage of such men which are not to be had out of a decent teaparty in Camberwell.'[22] Society had however had such a negative effect upon him that it caused him to question his whole future. On the 28th of December he wrote a revealing letter to his father:

> Touching the houses – the question is especially difficult with me – because I never was so doubtful as to what the remainder of life would probably be devoted to: I always, before, had some faint idea of becoming a clergyman either abroad or at home: but after the experiences I have had of the

effects of my intercourse in a casual way with society for the last three years, I have given up all thoughts of it: I can do nothing right but when I am quiet and alone: But I still cannot settle my mind, because I always thought that though I am not fit to be a clergyman, it is my own fault that I am not: i.e. though I don't love people, and am made ill by being disturbed, and am over-excited in discussion and so on – I ought to love people more – and ought to like to see them – and to do them good – and I never can tell but some change might come over my religious feelings which would make What is now my poison become my food. [...] So that I have been putting off all thoughts about my future life until the works I have undertaken are done – but then this renders the question of taking a house still more awkward as every house I live in can only be looked upon as lodgings – and this is bad for Effie – uncomfortable for me – I have never the heart to arrange my room as I should like it – (and there is something for a studious person in the arrangement of his room) – because I have never thought of staying in it long, and have never cared to work in the garden, or attach myself to anything – because all was soon to be left. And for a man who has no attachments to living things – to have none to material things – leaves him very anchorless indeed.[23]

It would seem that he had been in a sort of limbo ever since he married Effie. As a result, all their marital homes had been merely temporary 'lodgings'. He could not attach himself to anything – 'because all was soon to be left.' Furthermore, he had been putting off all thoughts of his future life for two years until the 'works he had undertaken were done' and, coincidentally, the non-consummation agreement expired. The Herne Hill house he eventually settled on would be yet another temporary lodging. When he found out the enormous cost of furnishing it for two years he justified it on the grounds that if his parents left Denmark Hill, which they often talked about, they could use the house and furniture, or alternatively he could use some of it if he settled in 'Yorkshire or Switzerland.'[24] Quite what his father made of his married son's description of himself as 'a man who has no attachments to living things' can only be imagined. Was Effie not a living thing? Was this all a veiled discussion of his marital dilemma with the only person who might possibly owe him a sympathetic hearing?

In contrast to the renting of the Casa Wetzlar, Effie was told about the house hunting in England but not consulted:

> I do not speak of Effie in this arrangement – as it is a necessary one – and therefore I can give her no choice. She will be unhappy – that is her fault – not mine – the only regret I have, however is on her account – as I have pride in seeing her shining as she does in society – and pain in seeing her deprived, in her youth and beauty, of that which 10 years hence she cannot have – the Alps will not wrinkle – [...] but her cheeks will.[25]

When the house was finally acquired the subject of Effie resurfaced. She was not happy:

> As for poor Effie – I am rather afraid; her London Society will be out of her reach – and though we have worthy people in our neighbourhood – there is a wide difference between the society of the gentry of Camberwell – and the kind of companionship she has had – more especially lately [...] I don't wonder at her beginning to look a little melancholy at

the idea of the seclusions of Dulwich. [...] for Effie – who does not care for pictures – and dislikes quiet – and whose 'beaux jours' are just passing away, the trial is considerable. We must be as kind to her as we can.[26]

Effie mistakenly believed that Mr. Ruskin was constantly poisoning John's mind against her because of his continuing disappointment with the marriage. When she was told about the house she was convinced that he had somehow forced John to live close to Denmark Hill for selfish reasons.[27] This was clearly untrue. John needed to be near London for his work, had been very specific about the location and was happy and relieved when the house was settled. In fact Mr. Ruskin was not at all sure about the Herne Hill plan and after hearing that Effie was melancholy, he informed Mr. Gray on 30th March that he had 'great misgivings about the propriety of trying the scheme at all' and that he had 'great fears of Phemy being able contentedly to live at Herne Hill.'[28] On 2nd April he again told Mr. Gray 'I do myself think that the change will be a trying one – I wrote my Son sympathising in their having to leave the agreeable Society of Venice.' Mr. Gray seems to have denied there was any problem. This was a rather unhelpful point of view to which Mr. Ruskin responded:

> It is easy to tell me that it is all nonsense minding the change – & that a man should control & dictate to the wife – I do not believe that either you or John could make Phemy lead any Life but what she was herself disposed to lead – but I do think some effort may be gradually produced by the kindly given advice or remonstrances of her Mother & yourself.

Ominously the shrewd Mr. Ruskin then told Mr. Gray that

their married offspring 'never seemed to me to have more than a decent affection for each other.'[29]

By April John seemed much more certain about what came next. He wrote to his father of being settled in his mind 'as to what is right for me to do, and having made up my mind to do it.' The letter continued:

> For Effie, I believe she is in better health than she was, but I cannot say she is quite as happy as I am. She looks forward regretfully to leaving Venice – and with considerable dislike to Herne Hill, and for the present avoids the subject as much as possible – to which I have no objection – for if she cannot or will not make herself happy there, it is no reason why she should not be happy here.[30]

Effie meanwhile, knowing that her time in Venice was coming to an end and what awaited her back in England, threw herself with even more abandon into the pleasures of Venice. Her social life became more and more hectic as her time in Venice ran out. John made no attempt to restrict Effie's socialising, in fact he seemed to encourage her to take risks. He himself hated meeting people but in his letters to his parents he affected pride in seeing Effie ogled, fêted, and petted by her aristocratic acquaintances.

CHAPTER XVI

DANCING WITH DANGER

❦

As we have already seen, Effie was an habitual flirt. This was not something that arose entirely out of the peculiar circumstances of the marriage but which was in her character from the beginning. Mrs. Gaskell's description of the teenage Effie collecting 'offers' in every town she visited may have been hearsay but it does seem to contain an element of the truth. In order to marry John, Effie had to disentangle herself from at least six men in Perth alone. Lutyens believed that Effie was formally engaged to William Macleod, and that 'Prizie' Tasker was also on a hint and a promise; but what about the handsome Captain Campbell, Harvey Duncan and 'Aunt Jessie's three brothers'? John described her as being always 'surrounded by people who pay her attentions' and who were far more 'calculated to catch a girl's fancy' than he was. Effie also loved socialising, parties and dancing, activities which inevitably brought her into contact with numbers of eligible men. This does not in itself indicate any kind of character flaw or justify any moral opprobrium. She was a pretty and vivacious girl of marriageable age and extremely adept at playing the courtship game which was the prelude to making a good marriage.

However both John and Effie realised that her behaviour might cause problems after the marriage and Effie at least seemed realistic enough to know that she would not change into a domestic ornament overnight. Of her three surviving letters to John before the marriage, the first was clearly a response to a jealous outburst from John. 'I hope at heart you are really not a jealous being,' she wrote, responding to John's protest that her manner to him and to other people was quite the same.¹ Even her father had doubts on this count. Effie's later description of John as the perfect husband hinged almost entirely on his being 'so perfectly devoid of jealousy.'² If the marriage had been her free choice, or if John been more like William or Prizie, the constant presence of her husband at social occasions would have prevented any flirtatiousness being misunderstood or any gallantries getting out of hand. Unfortunately because of the contrived nature of the marriage, because of the extreme mismatch of their personalities, because of John's vocation, Effie did not merely find herself in compromising social situations, she was positively encouraged into them. What began as a generous impulse on John's part not to thwart her enjoyment of activities in which he himself had neither time nor inclination to indulge, soon turned into a very dangerous game indeed as they both realised that the marriage was never going to develop into a loving relationship.³

After the Gray family visited London in summer 1851, Mrs. Gray had felt compelled to offer Effie cautionary advice about her behaviour. Effie's brother George persistently expressed concern about Effie's relations with young men. He had been outraged about the liberties she allowed to Paulizza in Venice, and after he had stayed with Effie in London it was he who first raised the alarm about Clare Ford hanging around Park Street. Effie's reputation was not just a family concern. Rawdon Brown had written to Effie from Venice to warn her that she was being talked about even there. Effie however always had a plausible excuse and accused her critics of simply being jealous.

Effie must have thought that once she and John were on the continent, away from the censorious gaze of London society and back in Venice, she could resume her unconventional lifestyle and manage her critics. Although her letters to her mother were quite candid with regard to the life she was leading, Effie's normal handwriting and punctuation were so appalling that her father relied on his wife to read Effie's letters to him, and it is not entirely implausible that the more sensitive the subject matter the more indecipherable the letters became. Effie's letters from Venice were further encrypted by being 'crossed;' that is over-written at right-angles to the original text.[4] Her mother's letters, also crossed, might have made enlightening reading but very few have survived. Effie refers more than once to her mother's fear that her letters might be seen by others and invariably destroyed them so quickly that she sometimes had trouble remembering what her mother had asked in them.[5] I think it must be clear to anyone who works on Effie's letters that her mother was to a certain extent living her life vicariously through her daughter and took great delight in her social escapades, unlike her father who only seems to have known what his wife chose to tell him.[6] John later came to believe that Mrs. Gray was one of the most intriguing women he had ever known with Effie a close second.[7] The fact that Effie spoke good German and John did not, also added a whole extra level of encryption to her social relations with the Austrians. She must have felt even more secure because on this second stay in Venice she did not have Charlotte Ker with her, and she had replaced her clever and manipulative maid Melina with an illiterate stay-at-home menial who spoke no languages. Of course when they had stayed at the Danieli Hotel their comings and goings had been public knowledge; at the Casa Wetzlar no-one really knew who was visiting her.

Even during her first sojourn in Venice Effie had provoked jealousy and discord amongst her many admirers. In a letter of 9th February 1850 Effie described how at a ball she attended without John, Prince Troubetzkoi had exchanged angry words with

Paulizza in a dispute over Effie's dance card.[8] There may have been many other such incidents which passed unnoticed or unreported. Now, determined to squeeze the maximum amount of enjoyment out of what would almost certainly be her final performance on the Venetian stage, she seems to have raised her game to an entirely different level.

With the death of Paulizza she had lost her usual, if controversial, chaperone. Her new friends in Venice were the Countess Pallavicini (later 'Jane'), an Irish-Austrian married against her will to an Italian nobleman' who avoided his wife's acquaintances by staying in his room, and Lady Sorell, well-connected but on the verge of bankruptcy.[9] Effie's letters home were soon crowded with other men. Brown and Cheney paid their respects. Many English people were passing through. Frederick Gibbs, a lawyer recently appointed tutor to the royal children, was 'a good looking very nice man about 30 [...] I go about with him every day and he comes here to tea as well as young Brinsley Marlay who I may have mentioned to you in London.'[10] By 14th October these two had been 'almost living here for the last week.' When they left Venice for more distant parts they were replaced at Effie's dinner table by the young Lord Dufferin and Sir Francis Scott. Another Englishman who became a regular visitor to the Casa Wetzlar was Mr. Foster, a rather mysterious mercenary serving with the Austrian Army. The majority of Effie's acquaintances were however Austro-Hungarian military. Count Falkenhayn had six-inch handlebar moustaches, Count Festitics was a high-born and 'very handsome Colonel of Hussars commanding at Verona, a very young man to have so many orders and so high a position,'[11] Count Thun was Radetzky's ADC and Count Wrbna a General and ADC to the Emperor. Thirty-year-old Count Nugent, 'the handsome Count with his immense height, black eyes & hair

*Count Franz von Thun Hohenstein: left, lithograph after
painting of c. 1849. Right, photograph c. 1860*

and pale face,'[12] sang and played beautifully and was not averse
to a spur-of-the-moment polka with Effie in the palace of the
Governor. Three of these almost certainly accompanied Effie in
an incident she described on the 25th November:

> Last night I walked home from Mdme P's [Pallavicini] with
> the Princess Yablouknoffsky and three Austrian counts at
> midnight all talking German in the dark & lonely street
> with hardly any sky visible and no sound excepting their
> Lingua Brutto as the Italians say and the clinking of Sabres
> on the stone.[13]

As these were her main companions at this time it is reasonable to assume that they may have had something to do with the
sudden estrangement of Cheney and Brown which Effie
mentioned on the 30th.

> I see Mr. Cheney and Mr. Brown very seldom. I think they
> have got some idea about us that I can't make out. They always
> were satirical to John and laughed at him because they were

319

in reality angry to find he knew much better about art here than themselves and now they have a very queer manner to me. Mr. Brown never asks me to come and see him although I call regularly on them both as politeness requires but there is something about them both that I can't make out at all.[14]

This first estrangement of two of Effie's closest confidantes lasted for a couple of weeks. By the 14th December Effie had invited herself for tea with Brown but still found him rather touchy. Brown told Effie that she preferred bad company to his and he could not imagine how she could endure both. Lutyens suggested that Brown avoided Effie's company because he found Lady Sorell boring but it is clear from Effie's riposte to Brown that it was her general company he was criticising and not just poor old Lady Sorell who seems to have been more or less dropped after she had served her purpose. John later suggested that Brown had a jealous and irritable nature, but it would seem strange that it only manifested itself at this particular time.

Just after Christmas Effie went to the opera without John but with the Princess Jablonowska. Once there she was distracted in her box by a procession of male admirers including Wrbna, Nugent, Falkenhayn and General Duodo. A few days later the pro-Austrian British Consul invited her to a New Year's Ball at the Barbaro Palace where 'there was an especial want of Lady dancers, and as I made a point of dancing every turn with all the different gentlemen, who were numerous, so as not to let the party get dull, not having danced for some time I got such a pain in my side that I was glad to sit down.'[15] The following evening Princess Jablonowska, Jane Pallavicini, Nugent, Wrbna, Thun and Foster all came to tea at the Casa Wetzlar. Effie had organised a party for forty gondoliers in the kitchen and the evening ended with polka-ing till midnight. Even the handsome young Italian priest could not resist a polka with Effie.

Effie went to four balls in the new year of 1852. The first was on Monday 26th January and organised by Marshall Radetzky in Verona. John and Effie travelled there on the morning of the 26th by the ten o'clock train in the company of the garrulous Counts Nugent, Festitics and Wrbna. During the journey John left them to it and moved to another part of the train with his books. Thun met them at the station (John said at 2 pm, Effie 3 pm), and Foster brought a beautiful bouquet to their lodgings for Effie. At the ball in the evening Effie was presented to Radetzky and the Archduke Charles Ferdinand before Festitics and a half dozen other officers arrived and she 'was soon dancing away with people of all nations and tongues.'[16] John and Effie stayed in Verona all Tuesday 27th and travelled back to Venice on Wednesday 28th.[17] Foster, General Franco and Festitics were all on the same train. Count Thun and Baron Diller, Radetzky's ADCs, also followed Effie back to Venice in the same carriage. Back at the Casa Wetzlar, Falkenhayn and Wrbna called to see if she was back. Effie told John 'you had much better divide me into 20 pieces at once and give a bit to each of my Austrian acquaintances.' This perhaps gives some idea of how many male followers she had at this time. The situation was getting to be too much even for Effie. In a sudden change of heart, by 1st February she had instructed George not to admit anyone to the Casa Wetzlar for a month until the end of Carnival.[18]

In a letter to her mother sent on 8th February Effie had described herself with some hubris as the happiest person in Venice:

> For everybody is fond of me and pets me; I am the Belle at
> all the Balls and the people respect me for being virtuous and

occupied. The women are not jealous of me because I pay them all the politeness in my power and the men adore me, one & all, because, I suppose I like none better than the other and it flatters their vanity that being admired by Radetzky & the Arch Dukes, and complimented publicly by Gorzkowski, the Governor, on my looks and taste in wearing the Austrian colours, and dancing and talking with all and sundry without distinction, I have sufficient means and Liberty to do whatever I choose.[19]

However, rather like the 1852 Carnival itself, there was a rather unpleasant back story developing behind all the medals, uniforms, frills, flounces, velvet and glacé silk in Effie's letters. Since Christmas day Rawdon Brown had again sought to avoid her. Not only did he not return her calls but he was rude and insulting to her when he stumbled upon her in the Ducal Palace gallery. According to Effie she had taken to frequenting the upper gallery of the Palace in order that she might sunbathe and listen in peace and solitude to the military band playing in the Piazza San Marco. She claims to have been doing this 'for months'; so regularly in fact that the porter had taken to providing her with a chair and a mat. Brown flatly refused to believe her explanation. He was convinced that she was there with some ulterior motive, either an assignation or to catch the eye of someone on the square. He was convinced that he would soon find her out and began by questioning the porter after which he cut her once again.[20]

Brown was not the only man to fall out with Effie at this time. At a soirée at Countess Esterhazy's, Count Wrbna told her that he was 'dreadfully offended.' According to Effie's account this was because she hadn't let him into the Casa Wetzlar for over a week and he was simply jealous. He too seems to have been convinced that Effie was favouring someone. After claiming special privileges because 'I like you as much as all the rest put together' and being firmly refused, a furious Wrbna swore revenge upon Effie: 'I certainly will revenge myself for your injustice – and if any thing happens to you remember it is yr. own fault.'[21]

Effie invited Foster, Nugent, Thun, and Reischach to dinner before going to the Military Ball on the 18th of February. Thun brought her another bouquet. John accompanied her this time but she did not mention when either of them left. A day or two later John and Effie attempted to experience the last days of the Carnival in Venice even to the extent of wearing costumes and masks. Unfortunately because the whole thing had been organised by the Austrians in the face of a boycott by the better part of the Venetian population it was not only rather spiritless but there was an undercurrent of resentment and hostility. Effie went home early. For once John followed later.

It was at this point that Effie claimed to have learned that her independent lifestyle had begun to bear poisoned fruit. On the 23rd February they attended another ball organised by Radetzky in Verona. Thun presented Effie with yet another bouquet and claimed a dance with her. According to Effie, Thun was not his usual self. She asked why and was told that he was concerned about Baron Diller who was still unwell following what Effie had been told two weeks previously was a tumble down some stairs. Though not still confined to bed, Diller seemed anxious to avoid being seen and Thun 'turned off the conversation.' Back in Venice the following morning Effie discovered the true facts of the case:

> after we returned from Verona the first time George told his
> master that he had heard that a duel had been fought at

Verona about me, and an officer killed. I laughed at the thing as perfectly absurd. It is a point of honor amongst Austrians never to speak about affairs of that kind and probably every body knew but me. But it appears that Diller had some words in the ball room with another officer about dancing with me – who the other man was I do not know – but they lost their tempers, went out the next evening, and Diller got a very severe sabre wound all down the arm and cannot appear in the Marshall's presence until his arm is quite well. Did you ever know anything so foolish? I think these young men think as little of Duelling as they do of smoking a cigar and feel no responsibility in such behaviour. I am very glad I had nothing to do with it and that I neither said nor did anything to provoke such conduct.[22]

At best Effie is being naïve here; at worst she is being callous and duplicitous. That she could not see how her conduct could possibly have led to such a tragic outcome stretches belief. To laugh when told that someone has been brutally killed on your behalf is hardly a Christian reaction; nor is the description of the fatal duel as foolishness. Significantly the facts as she presents them do not seem coherent. She claims to have been told that the fatal duel had been fought on Tuesday 27th January, the evening after the first ball at Verona, and that the person involved was Baron Diller, 'as sweet, gentle, well-behaved a young man as can be.' The unfortunate dead man was never named. However she also told her mother that Diller and Thun had dinner with Radetzky on the Tuesday and both men travelled back to Venice on the Wednesday with the Ruskins in the same railway carriage in order to go to the Military Ball there. Diller was in 'such spirits that he talked all the way back to Venice.'[23] Since Effie did not mention any severe sabre wound, or even disarrangement of his splendid uniform, it must be assumed that either Diller had not been involved in a duel in Verona or he had emerged from it unscathed. On the evening of the 28th Diller was almost certainly in Venice in order to attend the Military Ball. So when did Diller receive his wound? On the 24th of February Effie mentioned that Thun had had double duty for three weeks, which suggests that Diller was out of action at the very beginning of February. In that same first week Effie mentioned for the first time that Brown was unfriendly and impertinent to her and that Wrbna was threatening her with revenge. This would tend to suggest that the duel came about after the Military Ball in Venice and that it was common knowledge in the city. Although the Ruskins missed the second ball at Verona on the 9th of February they did attend Radetzky's third ball at Verona on the 23rd of February. Effie did not see Diller, although Thun claimed he was spying on them from the musicians' gallery. On the 28th of February Effie heard that Diller had come to Venice with Thun and assumed that he had fully recovered. Once again she did not actually see him.[24]

Another curious aspect of this episode is that if Effie's account is to be believed, George, John's man-servant, had told his master about the duel after they returned from Verona the first time. John did not mention this dreadful occurrence to her until a month later and then only when she raised the subject. This is not credible. A man had died. Whatever nefarious motives John may or may not have had with regard to his wife he would certainly have warned her about her conduct in order to protect his own reputation. At some time before the Ruskins returned to England, Hobbs, who had been with the Ruskin family since 1841, decided that he did not want to continue to work for John and Effie. Effie was not sorry to lose him. She wrote that recently both she and John had trouble with his sulky temper and that he was reluctant to serve her. In fact Hobbs had been kept constantly at work for weeks on John's book, copying out manuscript sheets and taking daguerreotypes. He was after all John's personal servant and Effie had Beppo at her beck and call. Effie was also worried that when they got back home Hobbs would almost certainly gossip about 'everything' with the other Ruskin servants at Denmark Hill.[25] Effie certainly believed that Hobbs would have something to gossip about; and who was in a better position than her to know?

If Effie was indeed oblivious to what her behaviour was provoking, then it would seem that others were not. There would almost certainly have been gossip and social consequences. She described being 'instantly surrounded by Austrians and Ladies' in the Piazza San Marco. Her sudden desire for solitude in the week after the first Verona ball would also make much more sense if she was suffering the social repercussions of the duel. The increased hostility of both Brown and Wrbna in the period after the duel, which Effie again ascribed to simple jealousy, would seem much more justified in the light of the death and mutilation going on behind the scenes. Banning all the young officers from the Casa Wetzlar and the hours she spent alone in the gallery of the Ducal Palace would have been a quite understandable reaction to what had happened.

Effie had also fallen out with another of her admirers. Back in December Count Festitics, Governor of Vicenza and close friend of Wrbna, had offered to do a very worthwhile favour for one of Effie's Italian protégées but Effie felt that it would have put her under too much 'obligation to a stranger, especially to so young a man, so that the affair is finished.'[26] Festitics' visit to the

Casa Wetzlar described by Effie on 28th December seemed affable enough, but on February 24th Effie told her mother how she shared a seat in the train back to Venice with the 'handsome hussar' and how despite his 'detestation' of her they chatted agreeably. At Venice she accepted a lift in Festitics' coach and a rather extraordinary conversation followed:

> 'You know I can do anything I like here in my territory and it would give me great pleasure to order you to be hanged.'
> I said, 'In order I suppose to show the Vicentins what a fountain of justice and honor they have in their Governor?'
> He said, 'Yes, but you know I have motives of Hatred to you.'
> I said 'It is an honor sometimes to be disliked by certain people. I consider you and yr. friend Ct. Wrbna pay me a very high compliment.'27

Once again Lutyens ascribes Festitics' enmity to a trivial source, but simply turning down an offer of help does not inspire hatred nor is it a hanging offence. It could well be that this really was all merely the result of jealousy and wounded pride. But Festitics and Wrbna seem to have developed a much deeper enmity towards Effie. They confronted her again at a Soirée Poudrée at Mdme. Esterhazy's which Effie attended without John. This time Wrbna told her that

> their Vengeance wasn't quite ready but they were preparing it and it would fall on me all at once. I said I had plenty of friends. He said, 'Oh, none of them will be able to help you.' He said, 'You know the Barber of Seville?' I said no – He said, 'It shows what calumny can do, and already Gorzkowsky has a bad opinion of you. Both Festitics and I hate you but we have not confided to each other yet why'. Festitics joined in and said,

'Oh yes! Je vous dis tout bonnement que je vous déteste and
I only speak to you because you are pretty and à la mode.'[28]

Effie told her mother that Wrbna's enmity arose from the incident a month before and that Festitics' anger and hatred were
imaginary. Nevertheless she was worried enough to ask General
Falkenhayn if Wrbna and Festitics could really harm her. Falkenhayn laughed at the idea and suggested that they were only
piqued because she would not 'permit them to vous faire la
cour.' Even so, she kept the general by her side for the rest of the
evening. At Mme. Esterhazy's soirée these threats were issued in
front of witnesses: the witnesses did not spring to Effie's defence.
In fact this behaviour was entirely predictable since a duel fought
over a woman invariably cast doubt on her impeccable morality.
In the event of a duel ending in a fatality, she could expect to suffer
massive recriminations and in extreme circumstances social
ostracisation. Fatal duels involving a woman were invariably
associated with adultery and remained indelibly imprinted on the
collective memory as a social scandal. Women who culpably
provoked a duel were the target of particularly virulent public
condemnation. [29]

Falling out with influential members of the Austrian army was
not a wise move, especially since Effie had made sufficient
enemies on the other side. Being more interested in men and balls
than politics she, unlike John and his servant George, had always
been a great enthusiast for the Austrians. Whilst her husband
spoke Italian and kept his social contacts with the Austrians to
a minimum, she spoke German and was constantly attended by
the Austrian military. Effie seemed blissfully unaware that her
handsome young Austrians were professional men of violence who
had just waged a brutal and bloody campaign across Northern

Italy, had besieged and shelled Venice and were regarded by the defeated Venetians as their bitter enemies. Thun in particular had received several wounds, some in hand-to-hand street fighting in Milan, and had been awarded a bravery medal. Consorting with the forces of a violent occupation had to be done diplomatically when your house servants were the ones being occupied. Effie, however, even had a dress made in the Austrian colours of orange and black. Her young Italian music master made it very clear to her that he did not enjoy teaching her when she was wearing it, nor would he have appreciated being asked by Effie to play music by German composers.[30] The cook too seems to have become disaffected with life at the Casa Wetzlar. On 12th April Effie told her mother that she was once more in Rawdon Brown's good books and that he had warned her that his servant Joan suspected that Nani the shared cook was poisoning the food. Brown himself had been made ill by Nani's food, as had his servant. Nani had been seen buying strong drugs. On reflection Effie too decided she had been made ill by meals he had prepared and intended to dismiss him, particularly since he had been giving them very careless and badly cooked dinners. Curiously, John does not seem to have been affected at all.

As if this was not enough, there had also been a number of thefts from the Casa Wetzlar. On 26th April Effie wrote that the previous week a pound in zwanziggers had been stolen from her locked desk. Beppo, being the only person who had access to the house, was the prime suspect but she was puzzled because she always carried the keys with her. He was not dismissed. Then an old woman, a sort of itinerant seller of curiosities, had called at the Casa Wetzlar and offered to sell a beautiful antique fan to her which turned out to be Effie's own which had disappeared from the house without her noticing. This, she wrote, was 'very disagreeable for the other servants and we don't know that things of more value might not disappear.'[31]

On 6th April Effie had told her brother George that 'Venice is so tempting just now at night that it is hardly possible not to be imprudent.'[32] Falkenhayn, Foster, Thun and Diller had continued to be Effie's close companions and dancing partners at picnics and parties, but by the end of the month many of Effie's acquaintances who had overwintered in Venice were beginning to leave.[33] The Russians who had been in residence for four months all left, taking Wrbna with them. Cheney had also decided to sell up and return to England for good. The weather, a combination of hot sun, cold east wind and little rain, continued to hold back the spring grass and cause food prices to rise. Effie was 'sorry every day as one thing after another shows me that we must leave Venice.'[34]

On 15th May, two days before the lease expired, John and Effie left the Casa Wetzlar and moved into a hotel on the Piazza San Marco with a view over the square to St. Mark's. They were both delighted with the change. They enjoyed the bustle of the square and the music; now the weather improved enough for John and Effie to sleep with the windows open. Effie did however mention to her mother that she and John slept in different rooms.[35] Count Thun seems to have been a regular visitor to the Ruskins' suite, as was Mr. Foster, accompanied by his two dogs: a setter and a terrier he had trained to do tricks and which Thun called Mr. Punch.[36] In April Effie had described the mysterious Foster as 'an honest, well bred Englishman of the right thinking kind. The only fault John has to him is being too fond of horses. He spent a year in the desert in Algeria and tells us curious stories of his Life there.'[37] Count Festitics, who had been in Hungary for some time, had apparently resolved his differences with her. He paid a call in the last week of May and invited Effie to ride with him in Vicenza but she declined his offer pleading lack of time. Even Brown had sullenly returned to the fold after he had been forced to ask Effie to intervene with the Austrians on his behalf. With society and visiting long since at an end, Effie took to bathing from two till five at the Lido from a tent constructed by her gondoliers from old sails provided by Brown. The sea was now warm but the beach still deserted.

On 1st June the Ruskins were in Verona again because John had to finish some work there. According to John they were 'excessively petted' by the Austrians. John put this down to the fact that there were no women at all there willing to fraternise. Relations between the Austrians and the Italian peasantry seemed better there than at Venice but the upper classes were distinctly hostile. Radetzky sent Effie a signed picture of himself, and his chief of staff put his carriage at their disposal which was smartly escorted on trips into the surrounding countryside by Thun, Diller and another officer (possibly Foster) on horseback. On the 5th Thun invited them to a lavish breakfast with yet another bouquet 'a yard and a half round and half a yard high.'[38]

The Ruskins returned to Venice and began to prepare for their departure on the 12th. There was last minute shopping and a round of calls to say farewells, but on the day of their leaving, with the hotel bill paid and most of their bags already packed, they were dramatically forced to postpone their departure.

CHAPTER XVII

SCANDAL

⁊

On the following day John wrote to his father a terse account of what had happened: 'I am unluckily detained here for a couple of days by a robbery committed on Effie's jewellery as she was packing – a very strange one – requiring me to make declarations in order to free several of the servants of the inn from suspicion, but I will not be after my time, D. V. at home'[1] Effie who had begun a letter to her mother within hours of the robbery gave more detail about what had happened.

> Today I got all my things spread out in my little room and began packing up to go away by the 4 o'clock train. Yesterday Ct. Carl Morosini having brought his sister Ctsse. Venier to see me, although it poured with rain I had promised to return her visit, and proceeded to see them and moreover was curious to see the Ménage of a young Venetian Lady descended from such an illustrious house as they never come into society and I only made acquaintance with the brother by chance.
>
> Before going I told Mary to stay in the room as everything was lying about and I would be in in half an hour. I went and Mdme Venier received me most kindly and showed me her atelier, as she is a great artist, and her hair the most splendid I ever saw and quite fair. They were so sorry to let me go, and made me write my name in her Almanac and overwhelmed me with amiabilities and I was home in less than an hour. I began to pack and took up the case with the Major's bracelet

in it. I felt it very light; I opened it – it was gone! I rang for Mary; she knew nothing. All my Jewels were lying together and all my best things gone – my Serpent – my Diamond bird and heart – John's Diamond studs and several other things. Whoever took them must be most experienced, for my money was left, my other bracelets left and a number of trinkets. The Master of the Café and all the house were instantly in the greatest consternation. The Police came and set their agents to work and I hope something may come of it, but the thing is most mysterious for nobody saw anybody come in or go out, and after I left, Mary locked the door and only opened it for John, who however left it open for ten minutes, not more, before I came in. The Police have desired us to stay till Monday.[2]

In the event the Ruskins were to be held up far beyond the 14th of June. Over the next few days Effie found out that other items of jewellery had also been taken. After taking statements the Italian police had focussed their suspicions not on some anonymous Italian petty criminal but, sensationally, on an officer serving with the Emperor's own regiment.

The identity of the suspect quickly became public knowledge as being none other than the mysterious Englishman Mr. Foster, although both John and Effie carefully omitted mentioning his name in their correspondence. From being 'an honest, well-bred Englishman of the right thinking kind,' Effie now described Foster as a not particularly 'bien élevé' person whom she had never liked. John recalled Foster's irreligion, his constant attacks on the clergy and his never going to church. According to Effie the Italian police had told the master of the café on the day after the robbery that they had already recovered the jewels at a 'certain house' and named Foster as having taken them there. Brown and Cheney, who seemed suspiciously well informed, had advised John and Effie to get out of Venice as soon as they could and before the affair began to escalate into a diplomatic incident. They also expressed the opinion that the Austrians would pay the police to cover up the stain on their honour and by the 16th the police had indeed retracted their story. In such cases the Austrian army had been known to sue the local police for defamation and with the country still in a state of siege and under martial law the Italians were not in a strong position.

Effie was in no doubt that Foster was the culprit and there was a strong body of circumstantial evidence against him. Three days before the robbery Foster had asked to see Effie's jewellery after admiring a brooch she was wearing. Effie told him that they were not worth the trouble of unlocking the bureau and that anyway Mary had the key. He then asked when the Ruskins were leaving and if he could come to say good-bye. Effie booked him in at 11.30 on the morning of their departure, but when he arrived he did not talk to her but picked up a Bible lying among her jewel boxes and appeared to read it. He asked her how much he should spend on a present from Venice which he intended to send to a lady. Foster then left the rooms with Effie who was on her way to a 12.00 am appointment with Mme. Venier. Ten minutes later Foster returned to the rooms and made Mary unlock the door so that he could write a line to John. He was in the room fifteen minutes but only wrote seven lines. Mary waited impatiently for him to leave. Foster called her and handed her the letter which later turned out to be asking John to send him some razors from London. Mary locked the door and handed the key to the waiter. Some time afterwards John arrived and then left again 'on various business in the town' leaving the key in the door. Effie returned between ten and twenty minutes later. Mary did not hear anyone else in the passage during the hour Effie was away. Effie's Spitz dog Zoë, a present from Count Thun, was trained to bark at intruders but never made a sound. Foster subsequently told two different people that he had not seen the Ruskins since the previous Friday and went pale when told that they were still in Venice. Nor did he make any attempt to contact them until John wrote him a note. Even then he made unconvincing excuses for not seeing them.[3]

The jewellery was not so valuable, worth perhaps a hundred pounds at most, but the social fallout was immense. Effie blamed Mary for her stupidity in not taking enough care with the key. John blamed Effie for her carelessness in always leaving her jewels lying about but admitted that it would have been an open and shut case had he not left the key in the door. Foster's regiment had by now taken over the investigation and the Ruskins were yet again prevented from leaving. Although Foster was confined to barracks the Austrians had rejected the findings of the Italians and demanded more evidence. John and Effie were being questioned each day for two or three hours in order to pick up on any discrepancies. Count Thun, one of Effie's most loyal admirers over the past year, had taken Foster's side and now expressed personal enmity towards the Ruskins. The weather having turned very warm, Effie spent her spare time bathing at the Lido or catching the cool breeze in a boat on the lagoon.

John and Effie were told they could leave on the 16th but with all their bags packed and a gondola waiting at the door, the Governor ordered them not to leave until Foster had been examined. The new departure date was set for the 19th. At this stage John still expected to get back the jewels and that Foster would be escorted out of Venice under guard. What in fact happened was that the affair dragged on and on until the British Consul felt compelled to formally demand their passport from the authorities. They finally left for Verona on the 29th. By that time Foster was still confined to barracks and the jewels had still not been returned.

Both Cheney and the British Consul had advised the Ruskins not to wait for any trial and to get out of Austrian territory as quickly as they could. The Austrian army were not averse to violent attacks on foreign civilians and the previous December a nineteen-year-old English boy had been sabre-slashed across the head merely for trying to cross the road through Austrian troops. From the beginning of the affair Cheney had been advising John on how to give his evidence carefully and in order not to provoke a duel. He even advised them to ask Radetzky for a military escort to Switzerland. On the 24th John had told his father that all danger of a duel was entirely over. Nevertheless, when they reached Verona, John received a hostile visit from one of Thun's fellow officers. Thun's representative asked John to provide answers to two questions: first, why he was leaving Venice (before the trial), and secondly, whether he was ready to deny having any suspicion of Mr. Foster's honour. If he failed to answer these questions he should choose his weapons for a duel with Count Thun. John answered that he sought no man's life and had no intention of risking his own, whereupon he was told that in that case Thun would consider John to be 'très peu honorable' and motivated by 'basse vengeance.'[4] Effie, in bed, overheard the conversation from an adjoining room and was 'a little put off her sleep by it' which further delayed their planned 6 am departure from Verona.[5]

Taking Cheney's advice they hired an expensive carriage in Verona and posted to the frontier, only stopping after they reached Airolo, the first settlement on the southern side of the St. Gothard pass. Travelling via Brescia, Bergamo, Como, Lugano, Bellinzona and Brasca, they managed the journey in only three days. The Ruskin family usually took a week. John, George and Mary were delighted to be out from under the Austrian shadow. George, who hated the Austrians, waved goodbye with his Calabrian hat, a form of headgear banned by the occupying forces as a symbol of resistance. Effie, on the other hand, writing to her mother from Airolo on the 4th, professed herself unable to see why they had had to flee and thought the affair proved the fine order and discipline of the Austrian army, who were incapable of believing their comrade to be dishonest, and were as perfect in their behaviour as it was possible to be.[6] Given the circumstances this was a very bizarre point of view.

John was delighted to be back in the Alps and again asked Effie if this might not be the right sort of life for them. Effie, already pining for Venice, declined the offer. She told Brown that Swiss air made her miserable:

> I know what happiness it would be to John if I could love this mountainous country as he does however he thinks I am very contented and I only whisper on paper, my heresy to you, because you know how many I have and one more won't shake you.[7]

The robbery and its aftermath caused increased tensions between the married couple. On the way back to England the Ruskins travelled apart. John remained in Strasburg with the Catholic converts Lord and Lady Feilding in order to see a holy woman; Effie took an overnight train to Paris, travelled seventeen hours, slept three and went shopping.[8]

Effie and John arrived back in London on Tuesday July 13th.

They stayed at Denmark Hill for a few days and Effie told her mother about Mr. Ruskin's fury with Foster and the Austrians when he heard about the affair. For once he had been supported by Effie who now thought his reaction quite natural. Effie must have been very miserable at this time. Before the couple moved to their new home at Herne Hill, Effie's in-laws gave her some token pieces of jewellery to replace what had been lost. Mr. Ruskin, who had been going over the accounts, also suggested to Effie that she take entire care of the couple's money and give John an allowance of £200 a year for all his expenses. According to Effie this was because John was 'far too Liberal' and could not save.

By the time Effie wrote to her brother on the 18th of July she had heard from Venice that no new evidence had been brought forward and Foster was to be freed. This she regarded as a successful whitewash by the Austrians. She still thought Foster was the guilty party but protested that because he had hid his real character she and John could not be blamed for having such an acquaintance. She warned George not to speak about the affair and above all not to malign Foster or even hint that he was arrested.[9] By the 26th Effie was relieved to have heard from Cheney who was in Vienna that the story was unknown there. Brown however warned John to prepare a full written account of all that had happened just in case it should resurface.

If they thought that the scandal had been left behind in Venice they were very much mistaken. On the 21st of July the *Morning Chronicle* published the story, making out that it was John and not the police who had accused Foster. Several other papers picked up the story including the *Church and State Gazette* on the 23rd, and the newspaper section of *The Gardener's Chronicle* on the 24th which gave John's full name.[10] These accounts were suspiciously identical in their wording and all related that the jewels had been given to the sentry at Foster's door by 'an unknown hand.' The general impression was that John had acted out of jealousy.[11] The worst account appeared in the *Globe* on the 27th which gave Foster's name and described him sympathetically as a captain in the 'Kaiser' regiment of the Austrian army, a very distinguished soldier, twice decorated for service in the Italian as well as the Hungarian campaigns. According to their account 'the regiment was so fully impressed by the high character of their English comrade in arms that they have clubbed their dollars, and offer a large reward for the detection of the true robber.' Even if Foster was acquitted by the court martial he would, according to their source, be forced to resign his commission unless the true thief could be found. The article ended ominously: 'Many duels are anticipated.'[12]

Effie told her mother on the 30th that six papers had already run versions of the story and that it was being spoken of at clubs and dinner parties. Mr. Ruskin feared Society gossiping that Effie had dropped her jewels whilst visiting the barracks and that John had acted out of jealousy or even that Effie had given her jewels to Foster for services rendered.[13] From Venice Mr. Dawkins wrote that Thun's friends now thought he had acted unwisely, that because of other suspicions Foster was likely to lose his commission, but that the affair was no longer a subject of conversation there. On the 2nd of August Effie heard from Brown that on the day of the robbery a woman of the town had been caught in possession of some of the jewellery and arrested on the 6th or 7th (either Brown or Effie got these dates wrong – the robbery was not until the 12th) and that both the woman and Foster were still being held, but that in the meantime the chief of police had either resigned or been sacked and been replaced by a military man. This he thought tended to corroborate the first account they had heard of what happened.[14]

In England the speculation was such that by the 31st John was forced to write a letter to *The Times* to protect his reputation. This appeared on the 2nd of August. John again pointed out that he and Effie had accused no-one. If any accusations had been made then it was either by the police who had evidence or the hoteliers who wanted to divert suspicion from themselves. With regard to the story that Effie had dropped the jewels into the hand of the sentry at the officer's door, John pointed out that since the jewels had never been recovered this was 'mere fable.'[15]

By the time Effie wrote to Brown on the 20th of August she could tell him that the story had vanished from the papers and that the gossip about the affair appeared to be over. She was however still asked from time to time whether she had ever got her jewels back. Mr. Ruskin meanwhile had made enquiries about where the stories had originated. He believed the source of the original article had either been a Mr. Mudie, a banker in Venice, or Foster himself. The second paper to run the story had sent someone to Venice 'to make the story more interesting' by finding out the names.[16]

Effie had received invitations from Lady Davy and the Eastlakes immediately after the story first appeared in the papers and had visited John Lockhart in September. At least one of these people was present in a semi-professional capacity. In August Lady Eastlake had accepted Effie's return invitation to dinner at Denmark Hill and reported what she discovered back to her publisher John Murray. She then visited Venice and met Brown. From Venice, in 'evident glee' according to George Paston, she sent another long account of the affair to John Murray in which she described Thun as a young *vaurien* of twenty two years old who bullied John mercilessly. She too mentioned a Venetian lady accomplice of low reputation and a mysterious box, purported to contain the jewels, which Thun was sending to Effie.[17] The East-lakes were of course the first to cut the Ruskins socially by preventing them from attending an Academy function. This was probably an early indication of Lady Eastlake's feral dislike of John. But there were signs that the Ruskins might be excluded by other fair-weather Society friends.

Also in November Effie heard from Lady Sorell that Foster, who had been acquitted and had kept his commission, was coming back to England. Astonishingly Effie did not warn John or his father even though she already knew from Brown what would inevitably happen when Foster was freed. Sure enough in March 1853 John was surprised at breakfast by another challenge on Foster's behalf, this time from a man called Gibson who had served with Foster for eighteen months on the continent. According to Effie, Foster was accusing John of jealousy (!) and herself of all sorts of calumnies. Effie does not explain what these 'all sorts of calumnies' were, just as she never really explained what caused the fatal duel in Verona, but it is interesting to note that, unlike the previous challenge, this time Effie herself was involved. Gibson gave John the first full account of what Foster was saying about them in Venice. John of course refused to give Foster satisfaction in the affair and read Gibson the written statement he had prepared on the advice of Brown. According to Effie, Gibson was astonished to discover that Foster had told him an entirely different story and after retracting the message he had brought, went off to find out the truth of the matter.[18] Later that same day Mr. Gibson delivered a letter to Herne Hill.

I am desired by Mr. F. to communicate to you that his

sentiments as read to you by me this morning, are still and will continue unchanged. As to the reports on which I spoke so strongly this morning, as Mr. Foster is not their originator, he does not wish to assert them or enter into any discussion respecting them, and is about immediately to join his regiment at Venice. I have therefore to close any further communication with you on this or any other topic.

There can be no doubt that the 'reports' mentioned here are identical with the 'calumnies' that Effie wrote about. It became clear from John's subsequent comments to Brown that Foster's 'strong words' concerned Effie's behaviour in Venice.

I was not pleased at the idea of this rascal proclaiming to his brother officers that he had not proceeded in the affair in mercy to Mrs. Ruskin's reputation. Effie was at once so kind and so prudent in all her intercourse with these Austrian gentlemen that I did not believe it possible they could allow any scandalous reports to go abroad respecting her, whatever views they might be disposed to take of my conduct.[19]

Had Effie's intercourse with Foster in Venice been a little too kind and encouraged him to have hopes? Millais was later to give an interesting postscript to this little drama by telling Effie's mother: 'I believe she used to speak with him in the interesting manner that she charmed [illeg. Swinton of Swinton?] when in Edinburgh, and hence induced him to return to his native land.' After Foster turned up again in London at the time of the annulment, Millais joked that he might follow John to Switzerland and strangle him in a forest or carry Effie off to a continental dungeon. These very odd ideas suggest that Foster was indeed emotionally involved with Effie.[20]

Neither would Effie have forgotten the threats made by Festitics and Wrbna to have their revenge by calumnies. It was at this time that Mme. Pallavicini also began to behave 'rudely' to Effie, which Effie thought might have been because her countrymen must have put ideas into her head. This falling out was permanent. Effie's reputation was now an issue with both Austrians and Italians.

Taking into consideration all the available evidence on this Venetian episode, the facts seem to be these. Because of the difficult nature of her relationship with her husband and because of the mismatch of their two characters, Effie was left in a tricky social limbo which her flirtatious character made even more dangerous. The peculiar circumstances of the Venetian occupation surrounded her with lots of young men short of dancing partners and accustomed to solving problems with violence. Over time Effie had made several enemies amongst her erstwhile admirers by unintentionally but predictably raising hopes, arousing jealousy and thereby causing unpleasantness, and, less predictably, death and injury. The same political naïvety which endeared Effie to the Austrians also made her unpopular with the locals and with her servants. Petty thefts had already occurred.

Foster was a mercenary, an unpleasant character, and possibly an imposter. Mr. Ruskin checked his story that he was the younger son of a Stourbridge ironmaster, but John was never contacted by any of his family or friends. Much later it transpired that someone very well acquainted with the Fosters of Stourbridge had never heard of him. Prior to his posting to Venice, Foster had formerly been stationed in Florence and was a visitor to the establishments of expatriates in Florence where property had gone missing. He had asked to be transferred from Florence to Venice. He arrived in possession of substantial funds. Effie was careless with her jewellery and possessions. Foster was such a blatant suspect that it is difficult to believe that he had made any serious attempt to cover his tracks. He was almost certainly infatuated with Effie and may well have been amenable to the idea of disposing of John by deliberately provoking a duel.

Effie and her many male friends generally despised and ridiculed John and his work. Cheney and Brown, who may well have been in Venice acting for British interests in some unofficial capacity, also did not like John but were obliged to help him in order to prevent a diplomatic incident. The Austrians could have been predicted to carry out a whitewash to protect their reputation and, even if acquitted, Foster would have had to challenge John in order to preserve his good name. If he had not left Venice when he did, John might well have been compelled to fight a duel he would not have survived.[21] After John left Austrian territory it would have been more difficult to force him to fight. The Austrians deliberately delayed the Ruskins in Venice as long as they could.

Effie loved Venice and did not want to return to Herne Hill. Cheney told Mr. Ruskin that he had urged them to leave before they were stopped but that Effie had not wanted to leave Venice immediately. Had she done so there would have been no unpleasantness. Thun, Effie's most loyal admirer and a close friend of Foster, was not obliged to challenge John on Foster's behalf. He was however stationed in Verona and in a position to intercept the Ruskins' escape. A duel would have satisfied the honour of the regiment and solved Effie's marital problems literally at a stroke whilst leaving her reputation intact. By insisting on her 'day of rest' Effie was again responsible for the delay in Verona.

After the Ruskins returned to London a concerted attempt was made to fan the incident into a major scandal which would damage John's reputation. The scandal was not just that John had accused Foster from jealousy but arose out of Effie's rôle in the affair. Inexplicably Effie did not warn John that Foster was on his way to England even though the newspapers had warned of 'many duels'. After he heard Foster's 'calumnies,' John would have been determined not to let Effie do any more damage to his reputation. The scandal and the challenges would have snuffed out any lingering hopes he might have had of reconciling their characters and saving the marriage.

John and Effie were not happy with the Herne Hill house. They both agreed that, despite the enormous cost, the furniture and decoration was in poor taste if not downright vulgar. At first there were no domestic servants and so they dined, either separately or together, at Denmark Hill where John spent most days working in his old study. Effie did not have a carriage either and could only use the Denmark Hill carriage on Wednesdays. This meant that the very restricted comings and goings of her social life would be reported back to her in-laws.

Almost as soon as she had arrived back in London Effie had linked up with yet another young man. This time it was the son of her old friends from Park Street, Clare Ford. On August 2nd John's father warned Mr. Gray about 'young Ford, a sort of man about town coming calling' on Effie.[22] In 1851 even her brother George had found his sister's conduct with Ford disturbing enough to report it to his parents. At that time Effie had told her father that these stories arose from simple jealousy.[23] Mr. Gray was not convinced.

In an attempt to reassure Mr. Gray, John wrote an extraordinary letter to him that Albert Gray made sure was locked away in the Bodleian until 1968!

But I wished to write to you at present in order, as far as may be, to set your mind at rest respecting the acquaintance of Effie with Mr. [Ford], which she says, appears to cause you considerable uneasiness. I quite agree in all you say of the necessity of great caution in a young/ married/ [added later in margin] lady of Effie's beauty and natural liveliness. but I am happy to be able to assure you that I have never seen the slightest want of caution on her part in the course of her various relations with young men of every character – but on the contrary the greatest shrewdness and quickness in detecting the slightest want of proper feeling on their part, followed by fearless decision in forbidding or otherwise preventing their further intrusion upon her in cases which required such severity – so that she runs much more chance of being found fault with for prudery than coquetry. In Mr. [Ford]'s case I think she has so acted – and is acting – with perfect prudence as well as kindness and I believe she may have more cause to look back with pleasure to the intercourse she has permitted in this instance – than to any other of her London acquaintanceships – for she has done the young man already infinite service – has prevailed upon him to give up his town life – to work in a quiet country place in the Pyrenees for nearly a year – and to prepare himself for a place in the Foreign Office which I trust will be filled by him with credit, when – had it not been for Effie – he would I believe at this moment – have been one of the idlest and most hopeless loungers in the London clubrooms. I am not sanguine as to 'reformations' in general – neither am I in this case – but there is now a chance for the young man – and in the state in which we found him two years ago – there was none – except in the kindness of those whose society pleased him.

That he has worked during the period of our Venetian sojourn, I know – for he has brought us a series of drawings which show great industry as well as great genius – and although I should have thought – and hoped – better of him if he had been led to this execution by his own sense – instead of by the influence of a pretty woman, I do not think the exertion must necessarily be abortive – because in its first origin it was not based on the most profound principles of philosophy – I should also think it great selfishness in any young woman to forego the chance of doing so great a good, merely because it was possible that some ill natured people might laugh at her – On the other hand it is equally necessary that she should distinguish efforts to please her made with an occult motive, from efforts to please her made – as they are daily and innocently made – under the natural influence of womanly tact and gentleness – And I believe that Mr. [Ford] while indeed he is much readier to hear and act upon a lecture from Effie than anybody else is as honourable and upright in all his purposes and feelings respecting her as her admirers of the ages of 70 and 86 – I see nothing whatever likely to cause the slightest harmful talking – in her permitting his occasional visits more especially as I am going to give him some hints about his drawing and shall be at home much more than I was at Park St., but it would cause talk to some extent if she were abruptly to check an intercourse of so long standing.[24]

There is an extraordinary undercurrent of sexual *double-entendre* in this letter which may not have been entirely unintentional. Effie looks back 'with pleasure to the intercourse she has permitted' with Ford, 'an intercourse of long standing' by one 'upright in all his purposes and feelings'. John even suggests that 'to check an intercourse of so long standing' might itself cause talk. Nor does John believe Ford's subsequent exertion must necessarily be 'abortive'. As for working in a 'quiet country place in the Pyrenees' for a year, well, just substitute a 'pair o'knees' and you may suspect more than a hint of music hall naughtiness. Mr. Gray got the message.[25] Effie was escorted back to Perth on the 24th of September (the trip had been delayed by yet another outbreak of illness at Bowerswell) and by November 10th she was back in Herne Hill with a contingent of chaperones, namely, her sisters and their governess. Her father visited shortly afterwards. For the time being, young men ceased to be a problem.

It was clear by now that Effie had acquired a reputation. Effie's notoriety was so widespread that Millais, writing to Mrs. Gray a year later, admitted that he had heard about her even before he met John. Arguing the need for chaperones just after the return from Scotland in 1853 he advised her mother to ensure that:

> she would not be left by herself to receive strangers, and
> gallant rakes, who can always find an excuse for calling, and
> who look upon Ruskin as a kind of milksop. I have met many
> of these fellows even before I knew Ruskin, and have heard
> them circulating over dinner tables the most unwarrantable
> insinuations.[26]

The novelist Mrs. Gaskell had also heard about Effie in Venice: 'I know that he [John] forgave her many scrapes at Venice, and so many stories were told falsely 2 years ago about them.'[27] What Mrs. Gaskell wrote in her letter may well have been hearsay, but the point is that she had heard it said. On hearing rumours of a divorce in May 1854 Jane Carlyle also wrote that

'I have always pitied Mrs. Ruskin, while people generally blame her, – for love of dress and company and flirtation. She was too young and pretty to be so left to her own devices.'[28] Even Effie's mother had felt it necessary on several occasions to advise her daughter to be careful.

Previous biographers have always assumed that John's postponement of consummation was only an excuse for his incapacity to fulfil his marital obligations. I have argued that he refrained from intercourse because he had discovered the contrived nature of his marriage. It is difficult to know exactly what was in his mind at the time, but is there any evidence that he intended to honour his promise? John's account is surprisingly consistent with the facts. He claimed that the delay was necessary because he had to work and that he had to travel in order to complete that work. Effie accepted that he did not 'wish any children to interfere with his plans of studies.'[29] In the event the five years until Effie's 25th birthday were extended to include the year when she was 25. The technical deadline for keeping his promise then being her 26th birthday on May 7th 1854. In fact he needed almost exactly these six years to complete his work on the two central books of his life: *The Seven Lamps of Architecture* (begun in 1846 and published in 1849) and *The Stones of Venice* (1851-53). These architectural volumes occupied all his creative energies during the period of his marriage and required extended periods of residence on the continent, particularly in Venice. On his own admission John wrote *The Stones of Venice* to an identical deadline.[30] Back in December 1851 he had outlined his future plans to his father. At that time he was three years into his marriage and repeatedly mentioned to his father a further two years necessary to finish his writing, even at one time asserting that after those two years he would give up writing altogether.[31] In 1852 he had asked his

349

father to rent a house for him for only two or three years and when considering the effect on Effie of living in a cottage at Norwood spoke of it quite specifically as the loss of her life from 24 to 27.[32] These dates are suspiciously close to the original deadline of 'when she was 25.'

Volume 2 of *The Stones of Venice* came out in July 1853 and was already in the shops while the couple were on their final holiday together in Scotland. The third volume was only delayed by the work on the eighty-page index which John finished at the end of August whilst he was at Glenfinlas and in time for it to appear in October, just before he left the Highlands. He had fulfilled his literary agenda. Was there any evidence that he intended to honour his promise and start a family with Effie? Prior to their returning from Venice in 1852, John and Effie did not have a permanent home in London. They had begun their married life at John's parents' house at Denmark Hill, before moving to 31 Park Street, Mayfair, on which John's father had taken out a three-year lease after they came back from Effie's first continental tour. Park Street was only ever intended as a means of launching John into Society and was as temporary as the carriage which went with it, the idea being that the couple could spend the social season there. In fact the greater part of their married life was not spent at Park Street but on the continent and in Effie's case without John at Bowerswell for nearly eight months in 1849. The last time they stayed at Park Street was in August 1851 before they went to Venice. When they returned in July 1852 it was to an entirely different establishment: the small suburban house at 30 Herne Hill, Camberwell, close to John's parents at Denmark Hill. Back in January 1852 John had specifically and repeatedly asked his father to arrange economical furnished 'lodgings' within walking distance of Denmark Hill for two or three years, in other words just until the non-consummation period was over. John intended that after that he would give up writing and settle somewhere permanent.

In the event and with John's acquiescence, his father had taken out a thirty-four year lease on this house. At the time Ruskin senior had hinted heavily that Denmark Hill was getting to be too much for the old parents and that they might take over the lease and furniture of 30 Herne Hill for themselves when John moved on. But the Herne Hill house was ideal for quite a different purpose. Both John and his father knew this from personal experience since it was next door to the identical house in which John had spent his childhood from the age of four. If Effie insisted that he fulfil his promise to consummate the marriage then she could not argue that it was not a suitable place to bring up children.

CHAPTER XVIII

UNTYING THE KNOT

ల

John had naïvely believed that whatever the circumstances attending his marriage, his wife might grow to love him in time. One of the reasons for delaying consummation until Effie was 25 was in order to allow this to happen. As time passed he realised that his wife's feelings of affection toward him appeared gradually to have been extinguished.[1] He found that he was living a lie with a wife who did not love or respect either him or his work and whose carefree behaviour constituted a continued danger for both their reputations. He had already been within an inch of losing his reputation in a major scandal. His life had been threatened twice, and the newspapers hinted at more duels. Now his deadline was fast approaching. John had promised to delay consummation until Effie was twenty-five.[2] It was now five years since he made that promise; a promise which technically had to be fulfilled before the 7th of May 1854: Effie's 26th birthday. By now, and certainly by her 25th birthday, it was a promise he no longer wanted to fulfil.

The course of a marriage begun in such inauspicious circumstances was predictable; its ending was not. For respectable people moving in high society there was to all intents and purposes no way out of a failed marriage. In England the only permanent solution to failed marriages was Parliamentary Divorce. This was so damaging and difficult that even George IV failed to divorce his wife Caroline and was unpopular for the rest of his reign as a result. For women it was to be avoided at almost any cost whether or not they were the guilty party. It was possible for a woman to procure a judicial separation in an ecclesiastical court but remarriage was then not possible. Separation and divorce were unthinkable for respectable couples such as the Ruskins. For either of these young people to even consider dissolving their marriage or separating, the situation would have to be so threatening as to make ending the marriage the lesser of the two evils.

Far from being threatening, the marriage had hitherto had its compensations for a young woman of Effie's formidable socialising talents and appetite for high society entertainments. Which other respectable woman of her age could boast of such an unchaperoned round of high society living, unencumbered by the daily duties of a large household, without even having the sexual duties of a wife and therefore without the dangers and obligations of childbirth?

John on the other hand found himself threatened from the outset. Having sexual relations with a woman who had offered herself in a desperate attempt to secure financial security for her family would always be a morally indefensible activity for him. Greville MacDonald reported that John told his father George that 'he was not the man to claim intimate relations, to him most sacred, without the only justification for them, namely that of loving the woman beyond anything in heaven and earth.'[3] Furthermore no matter where they lived Effie's naturally flirtatious manner had attracted one young man after another who usually became regular visitors to the Ruskin home. No matter how innocent the pleasures Effie took in these relationships, there was always the danger of scandal and worse.

John was a man with a mission. Like many of his contemporaries he believed that art and society were mutual shaping forces; that a deformed society could corrupt art; that great art could improve society; and that the moral nature of the artist could be read in his art. He could therefore argue that the greatest artists were nothing less than prophets of God. He saw his writing as an almost religious duty to persuade his contemporaries to step back from the moral and æsthetic abyss which lay before them. Because his writing had such a strong moral and ethical basis, his reputation was a precious asset to him. Any hint of scandal would result in his being excluded by the circle of influential people for whom his early books were written: those who had the power and influence to shape society. His wealth had meant that he had never had to compromise his principles. For example when he discovered that his adverse criticism of a book in a periodical review had been censored because the author was under contract to John Murray, the publisher of the periodical, he practically stopped reviewing books.[4]

Nearly all Ruskin's biographers have accepted that it was Effie who wanted to end the marriage. This point of view is based on the Gray family's version of events and the fact that Effie was the one who applied for the annulment. After all, there can be no doubt that Effie had fallen in love with Millais and John's reputation was so damaged by the accusations of impotency that it seemed inconceivable that he might have conspired to bring about his own downfall in this way. There is however not a shred of evidence that Effie wanted to end the marriage at any time in its first five years; indeed quite the reverse appears to be the case. She was not happy in the marriage and once expressed a wish that she had been 'the boy' in the family, but, like any Victorian wife, she wanted to avoid marriage breakdown at all costs.

When in 1849 Ruskin's father had heard a report that she was 'so unhappy with John that proceedings were instituted for a separation,' she related this news to her mother as 'a capitle joke.'[5] In the letter to her father which is generally assumed to be the beginning of her rôle in the formal annulment process and usually but wrongly assumed to be the first time her father knew what had been going on, Effie told her father quite unequivocally that 'I have never made any formal complaint to you'[6] and that she had 'always resisted the idea of a separation and would take no steps in the matter.'[7] Even when the marriage was in its death throes, Effie's threat to take John to law in Edinburgh was only an attempt to get him to treat her 'in a becoming manner,'[8] not to force consummation and certainly not to end the marriage. It was only after the Scottish holiday had come to an end that Effie came to express extreme antipathy to life with John. Even after John had complained of her behaviour to her parents she told him that she was prepared to modify her behaviour to avoid unpleasantness.

On the other hand there is no shortage of evidence to show that, even before Effie's young men began to threaten his life, John wanted to get out of the marriage on almost any terms that would leave his reputation intact. In April 1854, after she had left him, Effie wrote of his 'desire to get rid of me in any manner consistent with his own safety and comparative freedom.'[9] She also mentions that 'once years before' the annulment, John had 'offered me £800 a year to allow him to retire into a monastery and retain his name – that I declined. He was then under the influence of Manning.'[10] Privately arranged separations of this kind became increasingly popular in the 1840s, as evidenced by the way in which they were covered in the legal textbooks of the time. They were by far the best way of dissolving marriages which did not involve adultery or cruelty. Effie and John would have been able to live separate lives but Effie would not have been free to re-marry and any children she produced would be illegitimate and might end her alimony. Whilst planning his return from Venice John mentioned that he had 'always, before, had some faint idea of becoming a clergyman either abroad or at home.'[11] At the eleventh hour of his marriage John wrote to his father that 'Perhaps for my health it might be better that I should declare at once I wanted to be a Protestant monk: separate from my wife and go and live in that hermitage above Sion which I have always rather envied.'[12] More than once Effie mentions John offering to take all the blame in a separation. In the letter to her father on 7th March 1854 she claimed to have threatened him with law in Edinburgh and he said: 'Well and if I was to take all the blame?' At that time she commented, 'I think he might not oppose my protest.'[13] However, in a letter she wrote to Mrs. Ruskin on April 25th 1854 after she had left John, his words had become 'Well what if I do take all the blame, you would make a great piece of work for your Father and go home and lose your position,' as if John resisted the idea.[14] Of course this later letter would have been vetted by her legal team and they would have advised her to avoid any suggestion of an agreement between the two spouses not to contest the suit. Collusion of this nature would be a reason for the court to dismiss the case. ('Taking the blame' here must be in the context of an annulment, since the man's adultery without aggravating circumstances such as bigamy or incest was not a ground for divorce in England, and by this time John was not interested in a mere legal separation. In any case there could be absolutely no question of John committing or even admitting adultery. His reputation and influence would have been utterly destroyed.[15]) Of course these were mostly remarks made by Effie in the acrimonious atmosphere of a marital breakdown, but there is a considerable body of circumstantial evidence to show that John was not such a passive partner in the whole of the marriage as he has been painted. Indeed there is convincing evidence that he was the one who engineered its end.

If John had indeed decided to inquire into the prospects of ending his marriage after he and Effie returned to England, he could not have chosen a better time to do it. *The First Report of the Commissioners appointed by her Majesty to Enquire into the Law of Divorce and more particularly into the Mode of obtaining Divorces A Vinculo matrimonii,* published in May 1853, is a comprehensive and lucid account of marital litigation in Britain before the first divorce act. It is made clear in the opening remarks that the English state conspired against all forms of marriage dissolution and had done so since the seventeenth century:

> with regard to Divorces which rescind the marriage contract, it is to be observed that, strictly speaking, that contract is indissoluble, and when once it has been constituted in a legal manner, there are no means of putting an end to it in any of our courts.[16]

However Parliament had stepped in to open loopholes intended to deal with problems of inheritance specific to the landed gentry. The remedy was an exceptional law made for each individual case. In 1830 the Solicitor General had described Parliamentary divorce as intended 'in the first instance to secure the descent of property in high and mighty families.'[17] The first problem in 'high and mighty families' was the inability of the wife to provide sons and heirs; the second, and more widely relevant, the problem of 'spurious issue' or false heirs. If there was any danger of the wife bearing another man's children, then the husband must be able to get rid of her. To understand this is to understand why the woman's adultery was grounds for divorce and the man's not. His adulterous offspring did not interfere with the inheritance and did not become a charge on the wife. As the ancient Roman jurist had noted: 'Maternity is a fact, paternity is a matter of opinion.'[18]

The procedure in Parliamentary divorce was that the husband first applied in an ecclesiastical court for a judicial separation on the grounds of the wife's adultery. This was the so-called 'separation from bed and board', *a mensa et thoro*. Written depositions were handed into the court by officials who had visited the parties and their witnesses months previously. If granted, this separation allowed the parties to live separately and the wife to receive alimony. But they were not free to re-marry. The husband next went to a common law court and sued the lover for 'criminal conversation' with his wife. The whole aim of this was to recover damages. The lover could deny the charge or claim that the wife was of low reputation, or he could collude and admit the charges for a percentage of the damages. So-called 'Crim. Con.' trials were disastrous for women. No one other than the lover would marry her afterwards. Finally the actual divorce would require a private Act of Parliament. A Private Bill had to be entered into the Lords and there the whole evidence would be re-heard. The Lords would satisfy themselves that the grounds were just and the Bill then moved to the Commons where the financial settlement was sorted out.

By this time the husband might have spent anything between £1,000 and £10,000 and three years on the process. His entire private life would be public knowledge and the case would probably have been featured along with pornographic illustrations in the many magazines such as *Trials for Adultery*, or *The Crim. Con. Gazette* which fed on adultery trials and were sold everywhere on the streets. No wonder that in the ten years before 1853 there had been only forty-three divorce bills, an average of four per year.

Women only very rarely separated from their husbands in this way. Of the 325 Parliamentary divorces between 1670 and 1857 all but four were initiated by men.

Although by going to the ecclesiastical courts a wife could obtain a separation from bed and board for the husband's adultery, in the 156 years of Parliamentary divorces only four women ever obtained a full divorce that way and that was with extra aggravating circumstances. The first in 1801 involved a husband who was travelling in Scotland with his sister-in-law. The wife successfully petitioned for divorce on the grounds of his adultery with incest. In 1850 adultery with bigamy became additional grounds. No matter how blatant, cruel or perverted a husband's behaviour, some blame was always attributed to the wife. No woman's reputation could survive the process. It is worth bearing in mind that for a woman the threat of divorce was a thing to be taken extremely seriously and to be avoided at almost any cost. The wife had to make absolutely sure her behaviour gave no grounds for suspicion of infidelity.[19]

Effie of course was extremely vulnerable on this count but probably regarded John's desire to keep his own reputation as being her guarantee. Whether in fact she was correct in this belief is debatable. According to F. J. Furnivall, when John and Effie were in Venice: 'Ruskin had hoped that she would elope with an Italian Count who had stayed in the house; but it was the Count who eloped, not with Mrs. Ruskin, but with all her jewels instead.'[20] Furnivall has to be taken seriously since in August 1854 John told him that he was one of only three people to whom an entire history of his married life was due.[21] If Furnivall was right, there may indeed have been an Italian Count (or a Count in Italy) subsequently expunged from the records, or alternatively it might explain why it was Count Thun who challenged John to a duel, it being not on Foster's behalf but on his own. One of the few extra-judicial options available to a wife wanting to rid herself of a husband was of course for a lover to kill the husband in a duel. As we have seen there is no evidence prior to the Scottish holiday that Effie wanted to risk her reputation on any form of public legal separation whatsoever.

The 1853 Select Committee Report included a substantial body of evidence from the Lord Advocate of Scotland. The glaring disparities between English and Scottish matrimonial law posed a major problem for English legislators. From the evidence in the Report it is clear that for an English husband, determined to end his marriage as quickly and with as little fuss as possible, there was only one place to go: Scotland. Even the Lord Advocate was forced to admit that this was the case:

> Q. Are you aware that English persons have in repeated instances gone to Scotland for the purposes of divorce?
> A. I think so. I have known English parties go to Scotland where I could assign no other reason for their doing so.[22]

Scotland not only had the laxest marriage laws: it also had the simplest divorce law. After fulfilling the forty-day residence qualification and either husband or wife having committed the requisite adultery, the court would assume jurisdiction and divorce proceedings might only take a matter of days. It was consequently much cheaper than any English equivalent. In England it might be anything from £120 to £140 and two months just for an unopposed judicial separation *a mensa et thoro* without freedom to remarry.[23] An uncontested Scottish divorce *a vinculo matrimonii* ('from the bonds of marriage' – that is, an absolute dissolution) cost £20.[24] However the Scottish divorce required a high degree of collusion between the parties. Typically the adulterous couple holidayed in the Highlands until they fulfilled the forty-day residence qualification and then the other party, usually the wife, sued for divorce in a Scottish court.[25] Many petitions which failed in London were later granted in Edinburgh. The first two women's parliamentary divorce petitions in England both had Scottish connections. The first was a counter-petition to the husband's Scottish divorce application, the second, which failed in England, was granted when the husband, the mistress and the wife all went to Scotland and tried again there. Scotland was so notoriously lax in its divorce law that even Louis Clovis, son of Prince Louis-Lucien Bonaparte, went there after his mistress's 1885 English divorce suit failed on the grounds of collusion. She got her divorce.[26]

For John Ruskin there were barriers to this tempting prospect. First, he could not be the adulterous party or he would lose his reputation; and secondly, Effie would certainly not collude for fear of losing hers. In fact even if Effie was the guilty party, John's reputation might not emerge unscathed. But there can be no doubt about who would have suffered more if such proceedings had been begun.

If John had thoroughly investigated the whole area of divorce law in England, he would have discovered something rather unique and firmly within his area of interest. As a Protestant country England did not benefit from the edicts of the Council of Trent which had swept away the mediæval canon laws to do with marriage in all Catholic countries. Nor had it introduced a modern divorce law in line with all other Protestant countries. England was unique in the whole of Europe in preserving its mediæval canon law structure to deal with marital breakdown.[27] This was a Gothic survival almost as important as the Ducal Palace in Venice. Indeed there was a Venetian connection that John would almost certainly have known about. John's copy of the *Complete Works of Lord Byron* came with explanatory footnotes. Referring to the stanza in Marino Falieri, Doge of Venice: 'Vice without splendour, sin without relief / Even from the gloss of love to smooth it o'er', Note C was entitled 'Venetian Society and Manners'. It consisted of a long extract from Daru's *Histoire de la République de Venise*, one of John's main resources for *The Stones of Venice*:

> That freedom of manners, which had long been boasted of as the principal charm of Venetian society, had degenerated into scandalous licentiousness: the tie of marriage was less sacred in that Catholic country, than among those nations where the laws and religion admit of its being dissolved. Because they could not break the contract, they feigned that it had not existed; and the ground of nullity immodestly alleged by the married pair, was admitted with equal facility by priests and magistrates, alike corrupt. These divorces, veiled under another name, became so frequent that the most important act of civil society was discovered to be amenable to a tribunal of exceptions, and to restrain the open scandal of such proceedings became the office of the police. In 1782 the Council of Ten decreed, that every woman who should sue for a dissolution of her marriage should be compelled to await the decision of the judges in some convent to be named by the court. Soon afterwards the same council summoned all causes of that nature before itself.[28]

The Venetian courts may not have been so amenable to unhappy spouses in 1852, but the English ecclesiastical courts were. Not only that, but the church courts involved in this process were in the news in 1853 because they featured prominently in the

Parliamentary *Report on the Law of Divorce* published in that year. As a consequence the need for their reform was debated in Parliament. Criticism of the church courts increased significantly following the publication of the report and, in succeeding years, divorce reform Bills were repeatedly brought before Parliament. The ecclesiastical lawyers had a reputation for being a 'closed shop' and keeping their mysteries to themselves. It had been sarcastically suggested that, like the Talmudists among the Jews, they dealt only in oral traditions or secret writing.[29] There is a strong argument that the 1857 Matrimonial Causes Act was made law less because of concern with the plight of unhappily married women than because of a desire of the legal establishment to defeat the canon lawyers and sweep away the mediæval pantomime of the church courts.

The place of business of the ecclesiastical court in London was known as Doctors' Commons from its offices at St. Benet's Hill, Upper Thames Street. It was also in the public eye for another reason. Charles Dickens had worked there as a shorthand reporter in his teens and he mentions it in several of his novels.[30] In 1850 it was described in some detail in *David Copperfield*:

> Doctors' Commons was approached by a little low archway. Before we had taken many paces down the street beyond it, the noise of the city seemed to melt, as if by magic, into a softened distance. A few dull courts and narrow ways brought us to the sky-lighted offices of Spenlow and Jorkins; in the vestibule of which temple, accessible to pilgrims without the ceremony of knocking, three or four clerks were at work as copyists.[31]

Dickens description of Spenlow's room illustrates the variety of legal work dealt with by the various Courts:

The furniture of the room was old-fashioned and dusty, and the green baize on the top of the writing table had lost all its colour, and was as withered and pale as an old pauper. There were a great many bundles of papers on it, some endorsed as Allegations, and some (to my surprise) as Libels, and some as being in the Consistory Court, and some in the Arches Court, and some in the Prerogative Court, and some in the Admiralty Court, and some in the Delegates Court; giving me occasion to wonder much how many Courts there might be in the gross, and how long it would take to understand them all. Besides these, there were sundry immense manuscript Books of Evidence taken on affidavit, strongly bound, and tied together in massive sets, a set to each cause, as if every cause were a history in ten or twenty volumes.[32]

Dickens also described one of the Courts:

Mr. Spenlow conducted me through a paved courtyard formed of grave brick houses, which I inferred from the Doctors' names upon the doors, to be the official abiding-places of the learned advocates [...] and into a large dull room, not unlike a chapel to my thinking, on the left hand. The upper part of this room was fenced off from the rest; and there, on the two sides of a raised platform of the horseshoe form, sitting on easy old-fashioned dining-room chairs, were sundry gentlemen in red gowns and grey wigs, whom I found to be the Doctors aforesaid. Blinking over a little desk like a pulpit desk, in the curve of the horseshoe was an old gentleman whom, if I had seen him in an aviary, I should certainly have taken for an owl, but who, I learned, was the presiding judge. In the space within the horseshoe lower than these –

that is to say, on about the level of the floor – were sundry
other gentlemen of Mr. Spenlow's rank, and dressed like
him in black gowns with white fur upon them, sitting at a
long green table. [...] The public, represented by a boy with
a comforter, and a shabby-genteel man secretly eating crumbs
out of his coat pockets, was warming itself at a stove in the
centre of the Court. [...] Altogether, I have never on any occasion, made one at such a cozy, dozy, old-fashioned, time
forgotten, sleepy-headed little family-party in all my life;
and I felt it would be quite a soothing opiate to belong to it
in any character – except perhaps as a suitor.[33]

John read every book by Dickens as it came out. He even had
Dickens' latest novels posted to him in Venice. He referred to
himself as Mr. Jingle from *Pickwick Papers* in one of his engagement letters to Effie, and *David Copperfield* appeared in *The Stones
of Venice* which he was working on in 1850.[34] From March 1852
Bleak House, with its withering attack on the Court of Chancery,
was appearing in serial form and John sent to Perth for the final
episode whilst he was at Glenfinlas.[35] Then, even as the Ruskin
case went through the courts, *Hard Times*, pointing out the
blatant unfairness of English matrimonial law and the hideous
circumstances attending upon the impossibility of the poor
getting a divorce, was being serialised in *Household Words*.

In fact John also knew about Doctors' Commons first-hand,
because he had been there in connection with the painter Turner's
will on August 24th 1852.[36] This was of course after the couple
returned from Venice in July; after they had moved into Herne
Hill; after the scandal in the papers in that month and John's reply
in *The Times* in August; and after Clare Ford had begun calling
on Effie once more. At Herne Hill John and Effie did not have

their own carriage and Effie did not like to use the Ruskin parents' carriage, perhaps because her visits might have been reported back to Denmark Hill by the old coachman. John could have borrowed the carriage at any time but most unusually he took the omnibus into town. John's personal diary for 1851-3 is very short and almost devoid of personal memoranda and dates. Quite a few pages have been cut out. The dated personal material restarts with the beginning of his Glenfinlas diary on 20th July 1853.[37]

It is fascinating to note that by 1852 John had also collected a knot of legal minds about him. The publication in 1851 of *Notes on the Construction of Sheepfolds* had resulted in a correspondence with Frederick Denison Maurice who was chaplain to Lincoln's Inn and who later founded the Working Man's College. It was Maurice who introduced Ruskin to F. J. Furnivall who had come down from Cambridge in 1846 to read for the Bar and eventually went into the chambers of the reformist lawyer Bellenden Kerr. By the time of the annulment Furnivall was one of John's closest friends. Another lawyer and old friend was John Pritchard, the MP who had accompanied John and Effie from Champagnole to Chamonix on their second journey to Venice in 1851.[38]

If John had consulted an ecclesiastical lawyer at Doctors' Commons he would have discovered that there were several important differences between canon law and common law. The first and most important of these concerned the nature of evidence. Plaintiffs, defendants and witnesses did not have to appear in person. The written interrogatories which were used instead were much criticised for their incapacity to reveal the truth.[39] Proctors appointed by the court would visit the parties and write down their statements which would later be presented to the judge. Because of this practice there could be no cross-examination of witnesses by barristers in open court, no grinning jury to face and even more important no salacious press coverage. In addition the court accepted circumstantial evidence 'such as would lead the guarded discretion of a reasonable and just man to the conclusion' (for instance in separation cases that adultery had occurred): actual visual evidence of precise dates and places was not essential.[40] As a consequence the church courts were also noted for the rapidity of their proceedings.[41] The ecclesiastical lawyers deliberately made things as easy as possible for their clients in order to boost the falling number of litigants.[42]

Unfortunately the ecclesiastical court could not grant divorces, only judicial separations. The only permanent solution to marriage breakdown it could grant was annulment in cases where the marriage was not legally sound. If John could prove that the marriage never was, then he would be free of Effie and she would apparently be free to marry again. Apart from contractual irregularities, there were very few grounds for annulment. These were bigamy, incest, kidnap, under-age marriage without permission, and non-consummation due to incurable impotence in the man or mental or physical inaptitude of either party. Only non-consummation of the marriage was an option in John and Effie's case since none of the others could be claimed or faked. Non-consummation in itself was not sufficient reason for annulment because the spouse could have wilfully abstained from sexual intercourse. Therefore incurable incapacity had to be proved. This could be due to madness or mental instability of either partner dating from before the marriage, actual physical deformity or obstruction of the genitals, or incurable impotency of the man. We know already that John had offered to take all the blame in order to get out of the marriage. We can now see that an undefended annulment on the grounds of his impotence was the only practicable way in which he could do that. John would have left the lawyer's office with only one problem: how to force an unwilling Effie to petition for annulment on this ground. From this moment onwards almost every action that John took would be determined by the marriage laws of England and Scotland.

John had ample opportunity to take legal advice at the beginning of August 1852. Effie wrote to her mother on the 3rd that John was in London nearly every day from morning to five or six and that she had absolutely no idea what he was doing.[43] At the time both John's and Effie's parents were frantic about the constant calling of Clare Ford. In the meantime John's man-servant George had left the Ruskins' employ and a new young man had been engaged.[44] His name was Frederick Crawley. We know that Effie travelled to Hampstead to interview him, but he did not start work until after she had left for Perth. This was an event of some significance since for obvious reasons the servants' testimony was almost invariably called upon in marriage litigation. The men-servants usually sided with the husband; maid-servants with the wife.[45] Whereas Hobbs had been a Ruskin family retainer and owed some loyalty to John's father, Crawley was from the outset loyal to John alone and remained loyal to him for the rest of his life. John could not have had a better potential witness. Even Effie noted Crawley's staunch refusal to pass on details of John's life at Herne Hill to the Ruskin parents.[46] After Hobbs left, Mr. and Mrs. Ruskin had little idea what was really happening at Herne Hill.

Ruskin at Glenfinlas *by J. E. Millais 1853-4*
John had an extensive knowledge of geology and probably chose this site because of the gneiss rock. He wrote at some length about this hard and primitive rock type. Rich in colour and flora, gneiss was contorted and mysterious in its origin. The formation of gneiss was also relevant to the ongoing debate between the Vulcanists and the Neptunists as to the volcanic or diluvial origin of landscape. John would also have been well aware that the Great Highland-Lowland fault line ran through the area

Effie Ruskin *by J. E. Millais 1853*
Whilst she and John were staying with the Trevelyans on the way to Scotland, Millais
did this portrait for Lady Trevelyan. When finished he thought it was too good,
so kept it and did another for his hostess

John Ruskin *by J. E. Millais 1853*
Also done for Lady Trevelyan at Wallington

John Everett Millais *by William Holman Hunt 1853*
Hunt did this portrait for Thomas Woolner just before the Highland holiday

CHAPTER XIX

A HIGHLAND HOLIDAY

❧

In late February 1853 Effie reassured her mother about her social behaviour: 'I shall think over what you say of my visiting [,] Lady Eastlake quite thinks with you and advises me to try and see some of my particular friends when I can but not to go out without John [,] to keep to my point about that.'[1] Effie's chaperones returned to Perth on March 2nd 1853. Little more than a fortnight later another young man appeared in her letters home.[2] 'These last days I have been sitting to Millais from immediately after breakfast to dinner, thru all the afternoon till dark.'[3] Clare Stuart Wortley claimed that Effie first met John Everett Millais at Ewell Castle, the Gadesdens' place, when she was 17 and he was 16 and there is every reason to suspect that they had kept in some form of contact with each other ever since.[4] Effie might even have been instrumental in John's intervention on behalf of Millais and the Pre-Raphaelites. John and Effie had visited him at Gower Street after Millais and Hunt wrote to thank John for his supportive letters in *The Times* published in May 1851. By July 2nd that year Millais had already dined and taken breakfast with the Ruskins, and had even been invited to accompany them to Switzerland.[5] At that precise date Millais was at work on the background of his *Ophelia* which Effie told her mother was painted in one of Mr. Gadesden's fields at Ewell. She also noted that the lover in Millais' *The Huguenot* was 'one of the Lemprières' – surely insider information.[6] The Gadesdens and the Lemprières who also lived close by, were of course mutual friends of Millais and Effie from

before she was married. Effie told her mother that she had originally also been intended as the model for *The Proscribed Royalist.*[7]
Live modelling for the full female figure in this painting took place
in November 1852. At that time Effie had just returned from Perth
with her sisters and her father was visiting London.[8] As with *The
Huguenot* the official model was Anne Ryan, but the face is so
like Effie's as to suggest either that Millais demonstrated his
legendary ability to catch a likeness from memory or that Effie
did in fact pose but was unwilling to be identified with the
Puritan woman with a secret (Catholic) lover.[9] Millais was at work
on the *Royalist* between June 1852 and March-April 1853.

There is evidence that Millais employed a similar *modus
operandi* with *The Order of Release,* on which he was also working from October 1852. Early studies show that Anne Ryan was
probably used again for the early figure compositions, whilst
Effie posed later for the face. Exactly how or when Effie came to
be modelling for Millais is therefore not certain and although
Millais does not appear in her letters home until March there is
evidence that the sittings may have begun as early as January when
Effie first agreed to pose.[10] According to Effie Millais painted
'slowly and finely' and on such a major Academy piece ('half a year's
work') the longer timescale would be the more plausible. On 11th
November he mentioned that he was drawing the figures 'at
night from nature': hence Effie's later reference to sitting 'till
dark'. The last sitting was definitely at his studio and, given that
the other figures had been painted at Gower Street, there is every
possibility that Effie was drawn there too.

The painting itself became bizarrely prophetic. First called *The
Ransomed* or, according to Effie, *The Ransom,* at the last minute
it became *The Order of Release* probably because the ransom in such
cases traditionally involved the woman sacrificing her virtue for

money, a shadow which the replacing of the original purse by a document did not entirely dispel in the minds of an audience familiar with Shakespeare's *Measure for Measure*. Holman Hunt's *Claudio and Isabella* was in fact exhibited at the 1853 Royal Academy at the same time as Millais' painting. There are some curious aspects of *The Order of Release*, not least the fact that the English red-coat jailer appears to be standing inside the cell (the lock being on the outside of the door) whilst the woman, for whom Effie was the model, is handing the document to him.[11] Contemporary critics also noted that the prisoner had been freed without the guard having to read the order of release! More remarkable is that the jailer is a very fair likeness of John with his characteristic sideburns and rumpled lip, albeit made to look older.[12] The highlander's face is hidden, but the babe-in-arms might well be an infant Millais with his characteristic 'cockatoo' curls, clearly not derived from the mother whose hair was deliberately made blacker than Effie's auburn. Though Millais was famous for his ability to catch a likeness after only a brief acquaintance, I strongly suspect that John's appearance in this picture is evidence of his direct involvement in the whole project, particularly since he then became Millais' major patron for the next twelve months. Although the subject of the painting fitted well into a series of paintings of lovers divided by circumstances which included *The Huguenot, The Proscribed Royalist* and later *The Black Brunswicker*, the Scottish subject matter is strongly suggestive of Sir Walter Scott's Waverley novels. Scott was a favourite Ruskin author and Effie was very sympathetic to the Jacobite story line.[13] On the other hand neither Scott nor the eighteenth century were ever part of the Pre-Raphaelite ethos.[14] John was later to note Millais' unwillingness to read Scott. In fact he seems to have been rather unwilling to read anything other than letters.

The last sitting for Millais took place on 26th March 1853. By this time Effie would have had ample time to more than renew her aquaintance with her former teenage admirer. Her formidable talents for charming and entangling young men would have had their effect on the young artist. Millais was not noted for maturity or worldliness. At the Academy he was known as 'the child'. Effie, the older woman, called the Millais brothers 'the boys' and, according to Acland, Millais was 'a grown up Baby – and does and says in mere exuberant childishness now just what a very [...] and boisterous child would do and say.'[15] With hindsight John later described the painter to his father: 'I saw he was uneducated – little able to follow out a train of thought – proud and impatient'. It was like trying to 'teach [...] a mountain stream.'[16] He was clearly ideal for what John had in mind.

On 31st March Effie wrote to her mother in obvious delight at a sudden transformation that had overtaken John. He had decided to spend the entire month of May going out into Society and making as many acquaintances as he could, and then, after he had given a paper at Oxford, they were to travel via the Trevelyans' house in Northumberland to Scotland where they would visit Bowerswell not once but twice.[17] Inverness, Elgin and the North were mentioned, by which Effie assumed nice invitations would be forthcoming. Even better, John's parents were off to Paris for a month and so would not accompany them. 'Is not John coming out!!' she wrote excitedly.[18] Suffice it to say that John hated Society, hated socialising, and hated Scotland.

John abandoned the Oxford plan on April 21st claiming to be too tired.[19] On that same 21st of April a breakthrough impotency annulment case was judged in camera by Stephen Lushington in the Consistory Court.[20] After reading an ambivalent physicians' report on an impotency test, Judge Lushington had noted that even if the man had no apparent defect he might still be impotent. Moreover, since the physicians clearly could not determine with any certainty whether or not the man was in fact impotent, it was up to the court to decide. Since the woman in the case was still a virgin, the couple had lived together for two years and nature had not taken its course, Lushington ruled nullity on the grounds that although the law had hitherto presumed impotence after a triennial cohabitation without consummation, the three years was an arbitrary period and not followed in Scottish law. Since neither the physicians nor the court could prove whether the man was 'impotent universally, or impotent *quod hanc*,'[21] there was a possibility that the church might find itself to have been deceived if the man should re-marry and have children. Nevertheless Lushington affirmed that the annulment rendered the marriage not just at an end but never having existed. Having never existed the marriage could not be revived, which meant that both parties were free to contract legal marriages with legitimate offspring. A careful reading of his judgement reveals that he not only denied the 1731 judgement in *Welde v. Welde* with regard to the strict application of the three-year co-habitation, on the grounds that ordering the wife to 'go back and try again' might have serious consequences for her health, but also went beyond the alternative judgement in Bury's case which had decreed the second marriage legal but voidable.[22] After this case the presumption was that the second marriage would not be deemed voidable.

This neatly tied up some loose ends in annulment case law. John's solicitor Mr. Rutter recognized its importance twelve months later:

The other and more important Case A falsely called B v. A was also decided in the Consist. [Court] in camera by Dr.

MARRIAGE OF INCONVENIENCE

Lushington so lately as the 21st April last year 'a Medical Certificate of the Husband's impotency [illeg.] was held sufficient' [illeg. who?] possibly can say that such a man is necessarily impotent to all Women? It may be so or it may not – there is no evidence to establish the affirmative, the utmost that can be said is that a man [illeg.] would be impotent as to all – this however is inference and not proof – after a triennial cohabitation without consummation the law presumes impotence [illeg.] in this case the Marre. was declared null and void by reason of the Husband's impotence notwithstanding there had not been triennial cohabitation and there was no visible defect in the Husband.[23]

In other words a man with no physical defect who had lived for less than three years continuously with a woman without consummating the marriage would be presumed impotent with that woman, and the law would infer his incurable impotence with all other women even though that could not be proved. His marriage would be annulled but, astonishingly, would not be re-activated if he subsequently married and proved potent. If John needed any final assurance that his plan would solve his problem this seemed to be it.

However, if he wanted to annul his marriage quietly and anonymously in the ecclesiastical court he also had a deadline. On May 23rd *The Times* reported the publication of the commissioners' report on divorce and outlined its main recommendations. These included that 'a new tribunal shall be constituted to try all questions of divorces' and that 'all matrimonial questions also, which are now determined in the ecclesiastical courts, shall be transferred to the same tribunal.' In addition 'the evidence shall be oral and taken down in the presence of the parties' and 'the rules of evidence shall be the same as those which prevail in the temporal courts of the kingdom' which meant that 'the judges shall have the power of examining the parties, and also of ordering any witnesses to be produced who in their opinion may throw light on the question.' He was now in a race against time. Lord Cranworth introduced a Divorce Bill based on the commissioners' report the very next year.

May 7th 1853 had been Effie's 25th birthday. A year later she told both her father and Mrs. Ruskin in surprisingly similar terms that she had spoken at this time with John about his promise to consummate the marriage when she was 25, and asked him on what terms they were to live. The discussion had not been amicable. John had said that she did not love or respect him, indeed, she disliked him so much that 'it would be sinful to enter into such a connection', and that she was quite unfit to bring up children because if not actually wicked she was at least insane. Despite John's 'perpetual neglect' and despite what must have been a very acrimonious confrontation she claims to have told him that she 'never would refuse to gratify his wishes'. John had responded by telling her that he was going to try to induce her to leave him.[24] The very next day Effie's brother George wrote to his father to tell him that John and Effie intended that John Everett Millais would accompany them to Scotland. Other important plans were being laid at this time for what John and Effie would do the following summer (1854). By the 1st June it had already been agreed that Effie would travel with a friend to a German spa whilst John went separately to Switzerland with his parents.[25]

That same May John most uncharacteristically rented a house in town for the season. From her new base at 6 Charles Street, Berkeley Square, Effie plunged herself once more into the social

whirl she so loved and her letters are full of parties, carriages, aris-
tocrats, and 'chance' meetings with Millais. Her eye was clearly
not on the ball as the arrangements for the holiday were repeatedly changed. On 8th May she asked her father to find a place
where the holiday party could stay in Scotland which he duly did.
The fact that Johnny Millais, whom both John and Effie referred
to as Everett to avoid confusion, would definitely be accompanying them to Scotland does not emerge in Effie's correspondence
with her father until the 30th May, probably because Mr. Ruskin
was becoming increasingly suspicious about her relations with the
young painter who, it seemed, was already besotted with her.[26]
It was on the 30th May that John apparently changed his mind
about the holiday and a new house had to be found. At that time
Effie asked her father to book rooms for the end of the first week
in July and told him that they would be spending the whole holiday in one place.[27] By this time the party was to be John, Effie
and Crawley, Everett Millais, his brother William, and the painter
William Holman Hunt. By June 13th Mr. Gray had dutifully
booked another house for one month with the option of extend-
ing their stay. Holman Hunt had dropped out by the 20th by
which time John had decided to give a course of lectures in
Edinburgh before returning at Christmas.[28] The day before they
left, Effie wrote to her mother 'Millais is so extremely handsome,
besides his talents, that you may fancy how he is run after.'[29] One
of the places to which she ran after him, unchaperoned either by
John or her brother George, who was in London on a visit, was
the home of the Monckton Milnes. Perhaps it is not insignificant
that they took John's side after the annulment.[30] At the very last
moment Mr. Gray, who had booked a house at Dalreach for the
holiday, heard from his son George that, 'Dalreach is all up. John
wrote me a note to stop all arrangements.'[31] From that moment

onwards John was in total control of the holiday, especially since he had decided to avoid the railways in Scotland where possible and travel by carriage.

After the Royal Academy exhibition had opened on May 2nd, Millais' painting had become a runaway success and Millais was now a celebrity. *The Order of Release* was the first painting ever to need police and a barrier for the crowds and it received fulsome praise in the press; except that is for Blackwood's *Edinburgh Magazine* which commented, 'if it be true he had a certain model [...] Instead of tenderness she is the hardest looking creature you can imagine,' adding sardonically: 'A friend of ours said aloud, "I would rather remain in prison all my life, or even be hanged, than go out of prison to live with that woman."'[32] Luckily the review appeared whilst the holiday party was in the Highlands.[33]

John, Effie and Everett Millais left London on June 21st. Their first stop was the Trevelyans' house at Wallington Hall in Northumberland where William Millais would join them later. Pauline Trevelyan was an old friend of John's whom Effie had met before the wedding. Pauline admired John so much she usually referred to him as her 'Master' in her diaries. Whilst in London in March, April and May she had often visited the Ruskins at Herne Hill and even dined with John's parents at Denmark Hill. She had become very close to Effie whom she thought 'very nice.' On the 2nd of April when John had been entertaining Lady James and her husband, 'a terrible bore' according to Pauline, she and Effie escaped and went for a stroll down to Camberwell together. On the 20th of April Pauline and Effie had their photograph taken together (Effie's did not come out owing to her restless movements and had to be taken again). On the 9th of May Pauline called on Effie to do some shopping. She also met John

Everett Millais several times whilst visiting the Ruskins and was sufficiently impressed by his youth to record his age in her diary. The invitation for John, Effie and the Millais brothers to stay at Wallington was the natural result.

The Trevelyans were among John's closest and staunchest friends. John told Pauline Trevelyan that her husband Sir Walter and Henry Acland were the only people besides his parents that he would trust with a full account of his marriage.[34] Now as the Highland holiday began they were able to witness Effie's behaviour at first hand, possibly the whole purpose of the visit. As a result they were always to stand by John. After the annulment Effie bombarded Lady Trevelyan with letters every other day to try and win her over, but she refused to answer or even read them: she had seen what she had seen.[35] There is no reference in her diaries to anything untoward in the Ruskin marriage whilst the party was staying at Wallington. However, it is plain to any one who reads her diaries that it was not her habit to record personal criticisms or scandal of any kind. From her diary it is clear that in the main John and Effie amused themselves separately at Wallington. John, who was ill on arrival, was more often away in the company of Lady Pauline, whilst Effie, who was ill towards the end of the stay, spent some time with Everett Millais posing for not one but two portraits by him. Everett's brother William arrived on the 24th in time for an evening party. 'Effie looked lovely with some Stephanotis in her hair. [...] William Millais sang beautifully [...] Mr. Ruskin read *The Tempest*. John Millais had a bad headache.'[36] In William Bell Scott's autobiographical notes we have an account, albeit second-hand and not from a friendly source, of events unfolding at Wallington.

Already apparently before they reached Northumberland,

the handsome hero had won the heart of the unhappy Mrs.
Ruskin, whose attentions from her husband had it seems
consisted in his keeping a notebook of the defects in her
carriage or speech. More than that the lovers had evidently
come to an understanding with each other, founded apparently on loathing of the owner of the notebook. Mrs. Ruskin
used to escape after breakfast, and joined by Millais was not
heard of until the late hour of dinner. Lady Trevelyan hinted
remonstrance, took alarm in fact, but not caring to speak
confidentially to the lady who acted so strangely in her
house, got Sir Walter to rouse the apparently oblivious
husband.

Bell Scott recounted that Lady Trevelyan had quickly seen what
was going on between the lovers and 'mystified by Ruskin's inexplicable sillyness' with regard to his wife's conduct with Millais,
got Sir Walter to talk to him about it. John 'poo-poohed him' and
'did not see what harm they could do: they were only children!
He had often tried to keep her in order.' Years later, having
thought the matter over, Sir Walter 'was inclined to conclude that
John Ruskin wanted to get rid of his wife; had it been any other
man he would have so concluded.'[37] There is no mention of any
of this in Pauline Trevelyan's diary for 1853. Bell Scott, a lifelong
friend of the Trevelyans, must have asked them for their impressions with hindsight. Pauline Trevelyan was famous for her
remarkable memory.

By this time John was indeed keeping an evidential diary on
Effie's behaviour. This was exactly what a lawyer would have
advised him to do in a situation where the wife was suspected of
infidelity. A week later on June 29th the party crossed the Scottish border. They stopped over briefly in Edinburgh where both

Le Postillon s'arrête en route, by William Millais, 30 June 1853. From Wallington they were accompanied by Sir Walter Trevelyan and Miss Mackenzie for the first nine miles across the moor in a howling gale. Effie travelled in Sir Walter's dog cart with Everett. Left to right: John Everett Millais (his brother called him 'Jack'); Sir Walter; Effie, hidden behind Miss Mackenzie; the postillion, too drunk to drive, holding the horses; William Millais, on the carriage holding the reins with a kerchief round his head; and John, leaning out of the carriage

Effie and Everett Millais had to be treated by Dr. Simpson for identical sore throats. In her letter of 1st July to Brown, Effie wrote that Simpson agreed that Everett had the same symptoms as her and that he gave her chloroform pills and told her to feed them to Everett.[38] They seem to have taken the train to Stirling where Mr. Gray spent a couple of hours with the party before they took another carriage to Dunblane and he caught the train back to Perth. Between Dunblane and Callander, Effie and the Millais brothers visited Doune Castle. John did not accompany them because of a sprained ankle.

In 1854 *The Stirling Journal and Advertiser* commented that the twice daily coaches from Stirling to the two Trossachs hotels were generally full of passengers because 'there is perhaps no drive more appreciated than that to the romantic scenery referred to.' 'The Bridge of Turk hotel, which is first reached, comes abruptly on the view, and is an elegant building amidst an amphitheatre of hills in the immediate neighbourhood of Glenfinglas.'[39]

John and his party reached the remote Brig o'Turk on July 3rd and settled into the 'New Trossachs and Bridge of Turk Hotel'. On the same day Everett had told Charlie Collins that the Trossachs were the place they intended 'finally stopping at.' The hotel had been newly built in 1851 as a speculative venture by the Earl of Moray and was then leased out first to a Mr. McIntyre and then to a Mr. Sinclair. It was not included in the

Effie Ruskin by a window at Doune Castle, with two portraits of James Simpson from memory. From Millais's Glenfinlas sketchbook. The Millais brothers and Effie visited Doune Castle without John who had sprained his ankle. Everett conceived an idea for a portrait of Effie looking out from a window as a pendant to his portrait of John. This is the only surviving record of the proposed painting which was never begun

McIntyre's New Trossachs and Bridge of Turk Hotel in 1853, *by W. B. Banks of Edinburgh. On the left is the Bridge of Michael with Loch Achray beyond. This must have been the view from Ben Ledi slightly to the east of the schoolmaster's cottage. One of the twice daily coaches from Stirling is at the door*

census held on 30th March 1851 and must therefore have been completed late in that year. The hotel's first newspaper advertisements would therefore have appeared in anticipation of the 1852 season. This would have been precisely at the time John began to consider his options with regard to his marriage. It seems highly likely that John always knew exactly where they were going. A letter of the 30th June from Melrose reveals that John had already arranged with his father to pick up his post from Callander close to Brig o'Turk. This arrangement would have had to have been organised some time in advance. There was no postal service to Brig o'Turk. Letters for posting had to be given to the unreliable driver of the daily coach as it passed by. Incoming letters could be collected from Callander. From Doune on July 2nd John informed his father that the party was 'going on to Brig of Turk where there is a new inn'.

In fact the New Trossachs Inn was not the sort of hotel to drop in at without a reservation.[40] Tourism in the Trossachs area increased throughout the 1850's to the extent that *The Stirling Journal* published a pull-out supplement of distinguished visitors to the area. In 1854 it noted that both hotels had a number of such visitors and the coaches were generally full. Certainly by 1864 the available hotel space was insufficient for the demand.[41] In the days before telephones, John could very well have made the reservations by post before the party left London. The impression is given that they were the only guests at this expensive hotel. However on July 6th Everett told his friend Charlie Collins that they were already looking out for an empty cottage where they could put in some furniture and temporary bedding. This also seems to have been planned as early as the 2nd of June when John had told the Rev. W. L. Brown that he was going to Scotland for 'a couple of months' with the Pre-Raphaelites with whom he had 'a kind of brotherly feeling' on account of his defence of them in the papers. He added: 'We are also going to study Economy. Effie is to cook and we are to catch trout.'[42]

In the 1851 census Brig o'Turk had a population of fifty souls in nine households. Nine buildings appear on the 1863 Ordnance Survey map. In 1851 the first tiny cottage on the track up the glen was occupied by the schoolmaster, the Rev. Mr. Alexander Stewart, and his wife, their niece, a 16-year-old girl servant and two boarders. One of the boarders was the Rev. William

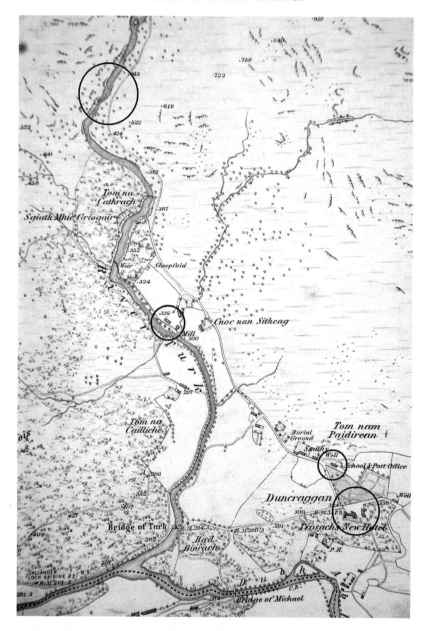

The 1862-3 Ordnance Survey Map showing right to left the re-modelled 'Trosachs New Hotel', the schoolmaster's cottage, the mill cottage, and the portrait site. The present day reservoir was constructed just above the portrait site

*Detail of the 1862-3 map show-
ing the 'New Trosachs Hotel'
after the two new wings and the
coach house had been added. By
1863 the schoolmaster's cottage
had become the school and post
office. The adjacent dwellings
and smithy had been recorded
in the 1851 census. The boggy
area in between the hotel and
the cottage had been converted
into a garden in 1854*

Monteath, the 25-year-old minister for the local Church of
Scotland. In the mornings Stewart taught at least nine children
between five and fifteen years old who appear on the census form
as 'scholars'. The next two recorded households were occupied
by labourers, their wives and children, the eldest two of whom
worked as servants. The third cottage was that of the blacksmith,
his wife and six children. Three other widely spaced cottages off
the track up the glen were occupied by labourers, shepherds, a
tailor, a former soldier and a 'landed proprietor,' their wives and
families. At the far end of the glen was a meal mill where the
miller Mr. John Stewart lived with his wife and three children
next to two other cottages.

By July 10th John had rented accommodation in the schoolmaster's tiny cottage a few minutes walk away from the hotel
which cost the lodgers £1 a week each instead of the £13 for the
hotel.[43] John confirmed the new arrangement in a letter to his
father on July 17th claiming that Effie, himself and Crawley
were now living on £14 per month including extras. However the
cottage had only two bedrooms. Since the Millais brothers were
paying for their own accommodation this might have saved
them some money if they had both moved into the cottage. In
fact only Everett moved into the cottage; William remained at

Brig o'Turk in 1882, after a painting by George Henry in Kelvingrove Art Gallery.
If one of the closer buildings is the smithy then the rebuilt schoolmaster's cottage
should be the gable on the right of the composition

the hotel all the time he was at Glenfinlas. Once Effie had moved into the cottage with Everett there is no evidence she ever returned to the hotel. According to Effie's only surviving letter to her mother from Glenfinlas, sent on Sunday 10th July:

> Crawley I fancy sleeps amongst the Peats but is charmed wherever his bedroom is. John Millais and I have each two little dens where we have room to sleep and turn in but no place whatever to put anything in, there being no drawers, but I have established a file of nails from which my clothes hang and John sleeps on the Sofa in the Parlour. At the other end is the day school and at the kitchen end a nice large room where the clergyman lives, an excellent Preacher who however is not here today as it is the sacrament in Callander. I think we shall do very well and the Cooking is excellent and the people a very respectable old pair.[44]

Everett's letter of the same date described his own accommodation: 'This new residence is the funniest thing you ever saw, my bedroom is not much larger than a snuffbox. I can open the window, shut the door and shave all without getting out of bed.'[45]

Owing to the continual heavy rain of that season the small triangular piece of rough ground in front of the cottage had turned into a bog which overflowed onto the track up the glen and made it into a quagmire. This made the hotel difficult to access from the

My feet ought to be against the wall. *From Millais's Glenfinlas sketchbook. Everett did two versions of this sketch intended to illustrate the tiny dimensions of his bedroom. He claimed that he could open the window, shut the door and shave all without getting out of bed. Note that the door and window face each other*

The Scottish bog exercise. *From Millais's Glenfinlas sketchbook. William Millais, John, Crawley and Effie's dog Zoë struggle through a bog*

glen after dark. Everett was not as specific about the sleeping arrangements of the others as Effie had been, but on the 4th of August he told Mr. Combe that: 'Finding all my friends writing letters, I have just crossed the bog that separates us from them to send you a bulletin of our health and doings.'[46] Who he meant by 'us' and 'them' is an interesting question.

There can be little doubt that the schoolmaster's cottage was their address from July 9th onwards. This was almost certainly the building labelled 'school and post office' on the 1863 OS map. Effie's letter to her mother on July 10th was headed 'care of Mr. Alex Stewart Teacher Bridge of Turk' and Millais headed his letter of July 17th: 'At Mr. Stewart's, Teacher, Bridge of Turk.' There is still a building on that site today but the original cottage seems to have been demolished and rebuilt in 1875. Effie described it as being three minutes walk from the hotel, as indeed it still is. As the first cottage in the hamlet from the road it was recorded as the first household on the 1851 census form. Mr. Stewart, who took care of their mail, could very well have done so for the whole community. Hence the later designation as a post office. In 1851 there were six people living there: the Stewarts, their nine-year-old niece Mary McIntyre, a maid-servant of sixteen called Henrietta Fergusson, the Rev. William Monteath 'Minister of the Church of Scotland at the Trosachs', and a lodger from Dundee. In April 1852 the Stewart household had apparently moved to nearby Aberfoyle leaving only Monteath behind.[47] It seems likely that the Stewarts regularly let out their cottage to visitors in the tourist season. Ann Stewart the schoolmaster's wife was most probably the 'buxom landlady' who greeted Everett every morning for the first month, but she didn't live in the cottage whilst Everett and Effie were there.[48] According to Effie, Mr. Monteath lived in the kitchen, she and Millais occupied the two bedrooms and John used the sofa in the parlour. Presumably, Mr. and Mrs. Stewart would have slept together when at the cottage, so why did John not sleep with Effie?

It has generally been supposed that the accounts of all those in the Ruskin party at Glenfinlas coincide. However on 9th March 1898 Albert Gray set a series of questions to William Millais, the other eyewitness, with the specific intention of finding out about the holiday. His questions and William's answers and validating signature have survived:

1. Can you remember the date at which you went to stay with John Ruskin at Glenfinlas?
In summer of 1853 after the ptg. of the Order of Release Ruskin

ECG and JEM started in Wallington (Sir Walter Trevelyan) where I joined them + after a stay of a few days we all started on the Carter Fell in Melrose Stirling (where I first met your father) + then on to Glenfinlas.

2. Can you describe the cottage or house at Glenfinlas?
The cottage Ruskin took was the Schoolmaster's (Stewart) just across a little bog opposite the New Trossachs Hotel or Inn.

3. How long were you a guest there? Who were the other guests if any?
I was there for more than a month as I painted a large oil picture at the same time JEM was at work at Ruskin's portrait – + also two water colour drawings – no other guests. Dr. Acland paid a short visit afterwards.[49]

4. Was JEM [Everett] there when you left?
This has been answered [See Q.12]

5. How many bedrooms were there available for Ruskin's party?
The accommodation was one sitting room + and a bedroom on either side with a recessed bed in the sitting room where Crawley, Ruskin's man servant slept.

William Millais' sketch of the sleeping arrangements in the schoolmaster's cottage. Crawley's recess is presumably at the top

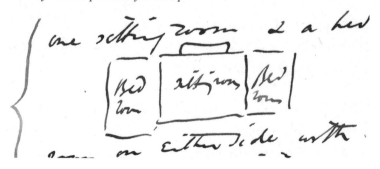

6. How were they occupied at night when you were there?
JEM in one room ECG the other Crawley in the recess.

7. Where did you and Ruskin sleep?
Ruskin and I walked across the bog every night to New Trossachs Inn + slept there + and he had a room there for his work.

8. At what time in the evening did you usually go there?
Ten or eleven o'clock.

9. Had JR occupied a room in the cottage before JEM arrived? And did he give up his room to JEM?
This has been answered. [See Q. 6-7]

10. Did Dr. Acland come to Glenfinlas after you were there? If so where did he sleep?
Yes for about a week he must have slept at the Hotel.

11. Did you escort ECG to Perth + did JR not go to Perth?
12. Did he and JEM go to Edinburgh together for the lectures?
When we had finished our respective works. I accompanied ECG to Bowerswell (Perth) + JEM and Ruskin went off to Edinburgh to lectures I believe.

13. Did you go to Edinburgh for the lectures and did you take ECG there?
No. I went straight home from Perth + never saw JEM or Ruskin afterwards.

[…] Referring to no. 13
I must have gone to Edinburgh on my way home with ECG as I dined with her at Sherriff Jameson's – but didn't see JEM or Ruskin there.[50]

Why Effie's brother and Millais' brother should have deliberately conspired to record an account of the holiday which
reflects so negatively on the judgement of both Effie and Everett
Millais is a mystery. It may have been to prove that John connived
at their entanglement or to establish a story that their bedrooms
were separated by the parlour and Crawley. As with the reminiscences of his grand-aunt and Effie's niece, Albert Gray obviously
considered this affidavit to be prime evidence and deliberately
caused it to be preserved after his death. Once again the question is, if he wanted to know the facts, why did he ask William
Millais then and not his sister Effie or her husband John Everett
while they were still alive? They, after all, were the people in the
cottage. Unfortunately, William Millais was recalling a time over
forty years previously and his memory seems not to have been
reliable about some of the details. Effie in fact returned to Glenfinlas without him and would not have had time to divert via
Edinburgh. As William was sleeping in the hotel he may not have
been familiar with the layout and sleeping arrangements in the
cottage. As a visitor, he might have assumed that the two internal doors opening off the parlour led to the two bedrooms. If
Crawley was indeed sleeping in the recess then surely Effie would
have known about it. Furthermore, his description and drawing
of the sleeping arrangements do not tally with all the other
evidence of the layout of the cottage.

Everett's sketch of his room indicates a distance of about 6 feet
from window catch to door knob which face each other, whereas
William's sketch shows the bedrooms as the full width of the
cottage which would mean the doors opened into the sitting room
and could not have faced the windows. John later described and
sketched the cottage rented by the party. If this was an accurate
representation, the garden was 18 by 10 feet and so from the

John's sketch of a cottage at Glenfinlas from a letter to his father September 30th 1853. If this is the schoolmaster's where are the other cottages? What would have been visible in the odd cut-out at lower right?

sketch the full width of the cottage was at least 10 feet and probably more. This would allow room for a passage at the back into which the bedroom and schoolroom doors opened. The single oblong chimney stack must have had a double flue to serve both the kitchen and the sitting room.[51] This firmly fixes the kitchen end at the left of the frontage and the sitting room adjacent to it, accessible through the left hand door. Lutyens perhaps assumed that the kitchen was on the right because in the letter of 30th September John described the clump of bushes at the right as a 'kitchen garden', but even she located the parlour door on the left.

A Wet Day's Pastime *From Millais's Glenfinlas sketchbook. William and John or Henry Acland playing battledore and shuttlecock in the schoolroom. In the foreground Everett with bandaged hand waits his turn. Effie's nickname of the Countess may have arisen either from her rôle as the scorekeeper in the game or from her handling of the domestic accounts. Effie stands probably with Monteath in the doorway to the accommodation. The rectangular shape behind her could be either a bookcase or a window. Under the table is a tub for water similar to the one on the right of John's sketch of the cottage*

Effie clearly described the sitting room or 'parlour' as being at the other end of the building from the schoolroom. The schoolroom must therefore be on the right in the illustration and accessible from the small fenced yard through the right-hand door. In Millais' sketch of the battledore and shuttlecock game, Effie is standing in the doorway from the schoolroom to the accommodation (impossible if the bedroom occupied the full width of

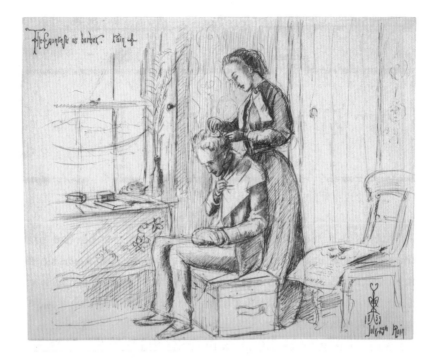

The Countess as Barber. Rain. *From Millais's Glenfinlas sketchbook, dated 25 July 1853. Effie cutting Everett's hair showing the relation of the parlour window (with view) and door. This might not have been quite such an intimate activity had Everett sat on the chair. The newspaper is* The Witness. *John met the editor later at Edinburgh*

the house). The left hand door in the frontage led into the parlour and is clearly visible on Everett's sketch of Effie cutting his hair in the cottage, as is the window which is the one to the right of the door on John's sketch. In the more finished sketch of the cottage the openings from left to right are therefore kitchen window(s), parlour door, parlour window, bedroom window, bedroom window, schoolroom door and schoolroom window (only visible on the Furnivall letter, see page 402). There were probably windows in the back wall too.

Combining the two accounts the most probable ground plan

of the cottage would therefore have been something like this:

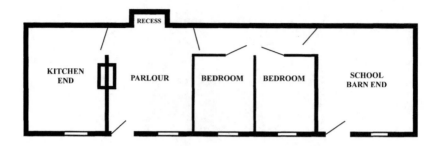

If this is a true account of the situation during the first months of the holiday at Glenfinlas then Everett Millais was sleeping in a tiny cottage inaccessible after dark without a guide with a lamp and separated only by a flimsy partition from another man's wife with whom he was hopelessly in love.[52] The husband was sleeping in another building on the other side of a bog. William Millais clearly remembered crossing a bog to the hotel with John at ten or eleven o'clock every night and Everett recalled a little girl lighting their way across a bog with a big lantern.[53] John and William even attempted to divert a stream to facilitate the regular late-night crossing of this bog without the little girl's aid. Since John and William were in the hotel, Effie's only possible chaperone was John's man-servant sleeping, according to William Millais, in the (probably curtained) parlour recess. If Crawley was indeed in the parlour he was apparently so discreet that Effie told her mother she had no idea where he was sleeping. Either that or she did not take the trouble to find out. As John's personal servant, Crawley would have had to rise before John did at 6 am and while it was still dark. He would only have returned to the cottage after John had gone to bed. As he would then have had to negotiate the bog alone, it would seem highly unlikely that he slept in the cottage at all. Crawley would have been John's witness in any legal action and indeed stayed loyal to John throughout. In her letter to her mother Effie had commented that: 'Crawley thinks Mrs. Ruskin would be awfully horrified if she saw our dwelling.' I believe that Mrs. Gray would also have been horrified had she been told what was going on. Effie had told her mother that John slept on the sofa; she had not said that John slept on the sofa *at night* nor *every night*. Quite what Mrs. Gray thought about John and Effie sleeping separately remains a puzzle because Effie destroyed all her letters. On August 14th Everett mentioned John having his bed made up again in the parlour of the cottage because of 'shortage of room,' but it is clear that John mostly if not always slept in the hotel. He was after all still working against time on his book and according to William Millais he had booked an additional hotel room to work in as he had done in Venice.[54] On the 28th June his father had confirmed that John was half way through the third volume of *The Stones* and complained about having to send parcels 'as big as portmanteaus' into the far North after him.[55] John might have vacated one of his rooms in the hotel when Acland arrived because when Acland left on the 1st of August, Everett took over his room, suggesting that it was booked for the whole holiday. After William and Effie left for Perth on the 18th of August Everett also moved into his brother's former hotel room.

However, looking at all the evidence there is something not quite right about the various descriptions of the cottage, its layout and its location. Everett and Effie's accounts from the very beginning of the holiday were from 'Brig o'Turk', John's description and sketches were sent much later in two letters headed 'Glenfinlas', one to his father on September 30th, the other to Furnivall on the 16th October. As the holiday wore on John rarely

The cottage from John's letter to Furnivall, 16 October 1853. The site of John's portrait is marked 'A'. See the 1863 OS map on p. 404 for the sight line to 'A'

indicated an address on his letters, but from the 14th and 15th August he wrote 'Glenfinlas' instead of 'Bridge of Turk' as formerly. Both John's letters contained similar sketches of the cottage where they were then staying viewed from the south, although there is an extra window on his father's version and the chimney seems to have wandered. The sketch by William Millais does not seem to tally with either of these. There are a number of curious details in these sketches. The cottages in John's letters do not have the same window arrangement as the present cottage and the single chimney is in a different place to the present two chimney stacks. This could of course be explained by later building alterations, but moving windows and chimney stacks would be quite major operations for such a humble building. The two adjacent cottages to the north might also have been just out of

Millais up to his armpits in a fictitious attempt to cross the bog to the hotel at night by lantern light; heading to a letter. Hotel on the left; unknown buildings on the right

sight or omitted in all three of John's sketches. Artists who painted the cottages painted the view from the north which clearly showed the three buildings close together in a line.[56] In the one surviving crude sketch of the hotel by Millais, the hotel is on the left and there is an indistinct group of low buildings on the right usually taken to be the cottage. This is very difficult to reconcile with the topography. If Millais sketched the hotel from the schoolmaster's cottage, these buildings might have been the public house at Duncraggan but seem too close and out of scale. What is even more difficult to explain is the fact that the cottage in the Furnivall letter appears to have a line of sight to the place 'in the distance' where Everett was painting John's portrait, clearly marked with an 'A'. The site of the portrait is in fact about a mile up the glen from the present cottage. In John's sketch it appears to be much closer. In 1853 there was only one building which could have had that line of sight and that was a cottage

Mr. Stewart's meal mill (by 1862-3 a pirn bobbin mill) and the cottages at the far end of the glen. The stream still discharges into pasture land today creating an impassable bog in winter. The arrow indicates the direction of the portrait site

on the river bank next to the mill, situated about half a mile up the glen. That cottage was identical in size to the schoolmaster's and it was on a sloping bank. Unfortunately it is the only building of the nine on the 1864 map that has been demolished without being replaced.[57] Did Everett and Effie have to leave the schoolmaster's at the end of the holiday season and move to another cottage? By the end of September were Effie and Everett actually living together not three minutes walk from the hotel with the Rev. Mr. Monteath but half a mile away on their own? The cottage by the mill would certainly have been more convenient for Everett's daily trudge to the portrait site, particularly since he had to catch the brief interludes between downpours. John told Furnivall: 'We have been since 5th July living in this kind of house with a little garden about eighteen feet long by ten wide, sloping down the bank in front.'[58] When he wrote 'this kind of house' was he disguising the fact that they had not actually been living in 'this house' for the whole holiday? John was always meticulous with the truth particularly where his father was concerned.[59]

John headed his later letters 'Glenfinlas.' Was that a more correct address than 'Brig o'Turk'? There are a number of puzzling comments in the later letters which suggest a location other than the schoolmaster's cottage. The evidence is tantalisingly inconclusive.[60]

John of course continued to be delighted with the arrangements. The husband, his wife and her lover had embarked on a Scottish holiday. It remained only to fulfil the forty-day residence qualification and see what developed. Given Effie's character and situation, given Everett's naïvety, what followed was almost inevitable.

CHAPTER XX

POETIC JUSTICE

❦

Whilst the Ruskin party was with the Trevelyans, Lady Trevelyan had noted in her diary that on the evening of the 24th June, John had read Shakespeare's *The Tempest* to them. Effie looked lovely with flowers in her hair. There is a cryptic reference to something Everett, who had a bad headache, had said about one of the pictures he had painted of Ferdinand and Miranda, the lovers from the play. In the light of what was about to happen it is impossible not to suspect that John saw himself as the controlling Prospero secretly and benignly manipulating the romance between Effie and Everett by means of his magical books. The opening of Act 4 Scene 1 has particular resonance in that it is there that Prospero gives Ferdinand 'this my rich gift' of Miranda but with a warning proviso that:

> If thou dost break her virgin-knot before
> All sanctimonious ceremonies may
> With full and holy rite be minister'd,
> No sweet aspersion shall the heavens let fall
> To make this contract grow; but barren hate,
> Sour-ey'd disdain and discord shall bestrew
> The union of your bed with weeds so loathly
> That you shall hate it both: therefore take heed,
> As Hymen's lamps shall light you.

It was vital to the success of John's plan that the single and only necessary piece of evidence for an annulment should remain intact until the 'full and holy rite' of the ecclesiastical court annulment. Everett, like Ferdinand, had to be warned not to get carried away. In the play Ferdinand pledges to wait until after the nuptials whereupon Prospero tells him: 'Sit, then, and talk with her; she is thine own.' The effect of this upon the besotted Everett Millais can only be imagined. Might John even have cajoled Effie and Everett into reading the parts of the enchanted lovers? The play ends with an epilogue by Prospero:

> release me from my bands
> With the help of your good hands.
> Gentle breath of yours my sails
> Must fill, or else my project fails,
> Which was to please. Now I want
> Spirits to enforce, Art to enchant;
> And my ending is despair,
> Unless I be reliev'd by prayer
> Which pierces so, that it assaults
> Mercy itself, and frees all faults.
> As you from crimes would pardon'd be,
> Let your indulgence set me free.

The sentiment of this passage has an obvious relevance to John's own desire to be released from his marital bands and to be set free, and his dependence upon Everett and Effie to play their indulgent parts in his own project. No wonder Everett got a headache.[1]

Once the party left Wallington and crossed the border into Scotland, Shakespeare was replaced by the native spirit of the place. It is difficult to overestimate the influence of Sir Walter Scott and his works on the Ruskin family. John read Scott's novels by choice constantly as a child. He opened his autobiography with a declaration that he was 'a violent Tory of Walter Scott's school' and that Scott and Homer were his two masters. It would be fair to say that Scott permeated his thoughts. Whilst John was courting Charlotte Lockhart, his father was reading Lockhart's biography of Scott. John may well have seen Charlotte in terms of her grandfather's poetic fictions.[2] The choice of Brig o'Turk and Glenfinlas as the holiday destination could not have been accidental and there is every indication that John always intended the holiday to be there. For John's generation, brought up on the poems and novels of Sir Walter Scott, the whole area around had magical resonance.

In 1796 a new road had been built from Callander to Brig o' Turk and sixteen years later a new bridge was built over the river. Following the publication of Scott's *The Lady of the Lake* in 1810, tourism to Loch Katrine and the Trossachs had increased five-fold overnight. To cope with the increasing tourist trade two new hotels had been built, one at Loch Katrine, the other more recently at Duncraggan by Brig o' Turk. By 1854 the Trossachs New Hotel at Brig o' Turk had an elegant signboard on which a huntsman was represented following the hounds. There were also two quotations from *The Lady of the Lake*, one on each side:

> And when the Brig o' Turk was won
> The headmost horseman rode alone
>
> Then through the dell his horn resounds
> From vain pursuit to call the hounds.[3]

Although in one of the very first letters he wrote from Brig o' Turk Everett told Collins that *The Lady of the Lake* had been set thereabouts,[4] John told his father on the 10th of July, 'I could not get him to read the Lady of the Lake at all.'[5] Which is a pity since Everett might then have been more aware. As it was he had to listen to John reading Scott's *Guy Mannering* aloud to him each evening.[6]

The tiny hamlet of Brig o' Turk (*tuirc* was Gaelic for a wild boar) also achieved celebrity for its rôle in Scott's *Glenfinlas*, his very first original poem.[7] Glenfinlas had been a celebrated Royal Forest but by 1853 according to Everett there was not enough wood to make a walking stick because the poor had cut down all the large trees and there was nothing but underwood. Pamplin the botanist described it in 1857 as 'a desolate tract of ten miles in extent.'[8]

Both of Scott's poems mention 'Glenfinlas', but hardly as the sort of destination for a fun holiday: 'Many a shrieking ghost walks there' in 'Glenfinlas shade':[9]

> Woe to Moneira's sullen rills!
> Woe to Glenfinlas' dreary glen! [...]
> E'en the tired pilgrim's burning feet
> At noon shall shun that sheltering den
> Lest, journeying in their rage he meet
> The wayward Ladies of the Glen.[10]

The core myth of Glenfinlas would have had a deep resonance for John. Two Highland hunters pass the night in a solitary bothy (a primitive hunting lodge) and, whilst making merry over their whisky and venison, one of them expresses a wish that they had pretty lasses with them. No sooner has he spoken the words than two beautiful young women, dressed in green, enter the hut dancing and singing. One of the hunters is seduced into leaving the hut by the siren who had attached herself particularly to him. The other hunter is suspicious, continues playing hymns to the Virgin and refuses the remaining siren's advances. At dawn the woman vanishes and when the hunter searches for his friend he finds that he has been torn to pieces and devoured by the fiend who had seduced him. Henceforth the place was called the Glen of the Green Women.[11] John would not have over-looked the analogy here with the trip to Macdonald's rather more splendid hunting lodge at Crossmount and the subse-quent seduction by Effie Gray which had torn his life to pieces. Would history repeat itself with Everett Millais as the victim?

These green Glenfinlas women were probably elves or fairies who in Scottish legends were vicious, dangerous and cruel. Like Effie they were 'saucy – wicked – witching – malicious', 'unspeak-ably to be feared and fled'. They were also addicted to dancing and midnight revels and serious consequences attended those who interrupted them. Note XLIX to *Lady of the Lake* contains yet more elvish lore. *The Elfin Gray* is a dire warning against offending the fairies with a title blatantly relevant to John's predicament. The elves and fairies wore green habits and they were generally supposed to take offence when any mortals ventured to assume their favourite colour:

> [...] who may dare on wold to wear
> The fairies' fatal green?[12]

Scott pointed out that 'from some reason which has been perhaps, originally a general superstition, green is held in Scot-land to be unlucky to particular tribes and counties.'[13] This was particularly true of the Graeme clan who feature in Lady of the Lake. We know that John bought Effie a green glengarry for the holiday and in every picture that was made at Glenfinlas she has a prominent green collar on her dress. According to Lutyens, Millais' luck was proverbial.[14] When the presentation copies of *The Stones of Venice* arrived at Denmark Hill John wrote from Glen-finlas to his father: 'I should like both the volumes bound in dark

Illustration by Richard Westall for Scott's Glenfinlas, *published 1812. The dog cowers shivering as the green woman enters the solitary cabin to seduce the seer minstrel Moy. 'An huntress maid, in beauty bright, all dropping wet her robes of green, All dropping wet her garments seem; Chill'd was her cheek, her bosom bare, As bending o'er the dying gleam, she wrung the moisture from her hair.'*

green, strongly, for Millais.'[15] Perhaps Ruskin was attempting to enlist the aid of the supernatural. After all, in *The Tempest*, the spirits conjured by Prospero to do his magic were 'Ye elves of hills, brooks, standing lakes and groves.'[16] Five days later Everett Millais was nursing a suspected broken nose and a crushed thumb, both inflicted by the landscape.[17]

Even the holiday cottage they were using had echoes of Scott:

> In grey Glenfinlas' deepest nook
> The solitary cabin stood,
> Fast by Moneira's sullen brook,
> Which murmurs through that lonely wood.[18]

On the 14th of July John mentioned 'a portrait of Effie with foxgloves in her hair'. This too had links to Scott's poetry. In *The Lady of the Lake* the lone horseman who rides beyond the Brig of Turk (1.6) into 'the deep Trosachs' wildest nook' (1.8) found:

> Fox-glove and night-shade, side by side,
> Emblems of punishment and pride,[19]

The portrait was done for John, but he never asked for it. He did however make sure that Effie, who had been receiving tuition from Everett, helped him make a copy of it.[20] Perhaps she too should have read the poem, then she might have realised what John was doing, and why he was leaving a trail of clues for fellow poetry-lovers. Interestingly John used this very quotation in his next major work as an example of 'Scott's habit of drawing a slight moral from every scene…'[21]

John having spent much of the holiday working in the hotel, Effie and Everett had been much together. Everett's letters to his friend Charlie Collins have been heavily censored with black ink probably as a consequence.[22] He also suggested to Holman Hunt that he had 'much that I could tell you but cannot in a letter.'[23] He destroyed all Hunt's letters immediately after he had read them and advised Hunt to do likewise. On July 6th he noted that he and Mrs. Ruskin were going to blow bubbles which they had wanted to do some days back but could not get clean pipes.[24] On July 10th the letter he wrote to Mrs. Collins ends abruptly: 'You

Effie with foxgloves in her hair
*This portrait was made by Everett for John but he never asked for it and it remained
with Everett. John helped Effie make a careful copy of it which Effie kept.
Effie's pose is repeated in* The Waterfall *reproduced pp. 416-7 below*

Two Masters and their Pupils. *From Millais's Glenfinlas sketchbook. Effie and Everett in another intimate pose. Effie reads aloud, probably from Dante, whilst Everett works on his portrait of John. The top right hand corner has been cut out, possibly to remove John, the other 'master'*

really have cause to be jealous of Mrs. Ruskin for a more delightful creature never breathed if I could meet with her…' The last sheet has been 'mislaid.'[25] Again on the 4th August: 'Mrs. Ruskin draws beside me and reads aloud Dante [...] Some of the images are awful, particularly that one in which he speaks of souls confined under water the surface of which is disturbed by ever bursting bubbles from their sighing.'[26] Every evening Everett took a walk with Effie leaving 'Will and Ruskin' to labour with spade and pickaxe at making a canal across a bed of stones.'[27] William Millais confirmed this activity:

NB I may say that I think that Ruskin did not act wisely in

putting JEM + ECG continually together – Every afternoon by way of exercise Ruskin + I spent our time with pickaxe and barrow + spade to try to cut a canal across a bend in the river and whilst he proposed that ECG should roam the hills with JEM and frequently they did not return till quite late – Ruskin's remark to me was 'How well your brother and my wife get on together' – a very dangerous experiment – and had it not been for their integrity evil consequences must have ensued. I may add that JEM returned home hopelessly in love with ECG.[28]

On Monday July 25th John's third staunch friend Henry

Wayside Refreshment. *From Millais's Glenfinlas sketchbook. Everett (?) offering Effie a drink from a river or loch whilst the Stirling coach passes by. For the road to be so close to the water this must have been some distance from the cottage*

The Waterfall, *an outdoor study painted from another set of falls just below the spot chosen for John's portrait; Effie is the seated figure on the right. On 8th July John told his father: 'We have been out all day again sitting on the rocks – painting and singing and fishing [...] Millais himself is doing a bit for practice [...] beautiful thing it will be when done.'*

The next day they moved to the schoolmaster's cottage from where on the 10th Everett described how 'Every day that is fine we go to paint at a rocky waterfall and take our dinner with us. Mrs Ruskin brings her work and her husband draws with us. Nothing could be more delightful.'

A sheet from Millais's Glenfinlas sketchbook. Left: The Idle and the Industrious Painter. *Effie standing close to Everett crouched over his canvas whilst William catches trout for breakfast in the distance. Right:* Henry Acland, *warming himself at the hotel fireplace*

Acland arrived. John's planned paper at Oxford would almost certainly have involved a visit to Acland and may well have been cancelled when John discovered that his friend would be visiting Edinburgh. Everett began his portrait of Ruskin at Glenfinlas shortly afterwards with Acland holding the canvas brought from London.[29] John wrote about it to his father: 'It is getting on beautifully – but terribly slowly: indeed I saw as soon as it were begun that it would take two months at least.'[30] In other words time enough to fulfil the 40 day residence qualification and preclude a visit to Bowerswell before the planned Edinburgh lectures at the beginning of November. Acland stayed until 1st August, which also gave him ample opportunity to see what was going on. He too was to stay loyal to John throughout.

As the rain continued to pour down on poor Everett in his

cramped 'rocky dingle' John attempted to keep him dry enough to keep painting. Standing over him with an umbrella was a temporary solution. Eventually he provided Everett with a small tent complete with portable iron stove. As Effie often shared Everett's very private and secluded dingle, she must also have shared this cosy tent which hid them from all onlookers. John recorded in his diary the hours Everett spent on the painting. They gradually lessened as the holiday wore on.

Effie went to Perth to visit her family on the 18th of August accompanied not by her husband but by William Millais and by Mrs. Stewart the schoolmaster's wife who would act as her chaperone for the return journey. William did not return to Glenfinlas

Highland Shelter. *From Millais's Glenfinlas sketchbook. Everett and Effie arm in arm under a highland plaid. Much of the sketchbook seems to have been his personal memoranda of intimate if not erotic moments with Effie*

Effie Ruskin in natural ornament. *From Millais's Glenfinlas sketchbook. While at Glenfinlas John persuaded Everett to try his hand at practical design. One result was this drawing. The bracket under the cabinet at the left depicts a mouse captured by an owl, surely an allegory of John and Effie, particularly since Effie's tiara is also a mouse with corn stalks. The lizards on her forearm and shoulder recall John's description of her as a salamander, because she thrives in destructive elements. The red squirrels on her breasts may also have had some allegorical significance*

but went straight home. John had suggested that Everett should go with Effie to Bowerswell so as to accompany her return early the following week but he had refused. After William and Effie left for Perth, Everett moved back into the hotel so as to paint the fine view from the window of his brother's old room. Effie returned on the 22nd but Everett was still at the hotel on the 29th. It is not clear whether or when he moved back into the cottage. He complained bitterly to Hunt about having to leave the cottage at night and go back to the hotel. Perhaps he was missing his 'little emigrant crib, Ruskin, his lady and me, all talking whilst dressing.'³¹ Whether at the cottage or the hotel John would in any case have been up and about every morning before Everett. In a letter to his mother John spoke of having to hurry home to let Millais have his breakfast in proper time. Effie was of course a notoriously late riser.³²

By this time John's notebook must have been bulging with the antics of Everett and Effie. One incident in particular would have been enough to start an action, and the very fact that Effie wrote about it in detail in a letter to Rawdon Brown indicates that she was concerned about establishing an alternative narrative for this. Just before October 10th, Effie and Everett arrived home after

Cruel Treatment of a Master to his Pupil. *From Millais's Glenfinlas sketchbook. Everett teases Effie with a frond of bracken whilst John looks on*

Cruel treatment of a Master to his Pupil   July 31ʰ 1853

dark with Effie's dress covered in mud:

> but the other evening you would have been sorry for me. I was returning home with Millais and coming to a very dirty mud bank I asked his help, it was quite dark and he told me to walk on the edge of the grass and I thought I was getting home nicely he had fast hold on my arm when my foot went from under me and down I fell into a cold mud bath, he fell too partly upon me but thereby saved himself but when I got pulled up I found by my weight how much it had been added to by my fall and on reaching home I found myself in such a state my frock could not be brushed for two days.[33]

Lutyens thought the incident would have made good material for a romantic novelist. In the 1850's it would have made better material for a lawyer. Divorce cases had been won on such circumstantial evidence since the law as it then stood did not require direct evidence of the fact of adultery.[34]

In the 'General Facts' which John gave to his lawyer in April 1854 he stated that it was at precisely this time 'about the end of September or beginning of October, 1853, we being then in Scotland,' that Effie had told him that the pains of eternal torment could not be worse to her than going home to live at Herne Hill with him. This seems to indicate a serious confrontation and breakdown in relations.[35] By this time Effie and Everett's behaviour must have become fairly blatant. In a letter to Hunt on October 8th Everett mentioned that Michael Halliday, one of his pupils, had arrived at Glenfinlas. After the split Halliday told Hunt that from what he had seen at that time he had guessed nearly everything that Millais later confessed to him.[36] Already in September Everett had mentioned his 'dreadful wakefulness and the most miserable forebodings' and inability to sleep at night

Ascent of Ben Ledi *From Millais's Glenfinlas sketchbook. Effie and Everett arm in arm accompanied by Effie's dog Zoë. John in the far distance on the left (identifiable by his hat)*

commenting: 'I should feel considerably better for a wife in Scotland. There is such a want of humanity. These chilling mountains make one love little soft, warm, breathing bodies.'[37] Following Halliday's visit Everett took to lying in bed weeping openly. This was ostensibly because Hunt had told him he was leaving for the Holy Land, but the increasingly blatant illicit love affair he was conducting with Effie must have been causing him a good deal of mental anguish. He was supposed to remain behind in Glenfinlas to finish the painting, but in fact he followed the Ruskins to Edinburgh before returning to London on November 10th.[38]

The Edinburgh lectures were a great public success. Over a thousand people crammed into the Philosophical Institution at

4 Queen Street; even overflowing into the lobbies. It was so crowded that people fainted and were carried out. Mr. and Mrs. Gray came to hear their son-in-law and to bathe with Effie in his celebrity. After this triumph John was as well known in Scotland as in England. Pauline Trevelyan was there and met both the Grays and Sherriff Jameson. John caught a chill but this did not stop Effie, her little sister and Everett calling on Pauline. Meanwhile Mrs. Gray had fallen ill and Effie herself had to visit Dr. Simpson suffering from nervous exhaustion, 'tossing in my bed without sleep.' This had probably been caused by some kind of further confrontation with her husband because she later told her father that she had threatened John with law whilst at Edinburgh but didn't really know anything about the law.[39] Effie went on ahead to Perth on the 21st of November: John remained behind in Edinburgh undergoing massage treatment for a throat infection. During this time he wrote some deeply reflective letters to his father. On 6th November he told him that he had had much to think about during the holiday in studying Everett, himself and Effie. His own character had, he thought, remained exactly the same as when he was a boy. So had Effie's. When they married 'I expected to change her. She expected to change me. Neither have succeeded, and both are displeased.' Millais too had proved a disappointment. His conclusion was that 'one cannot make a silk purse out of a sow's ear'. On the 11th of November he told his father that 'perhaps for my health it might be better that I should declare at once that I wanted to be a Protestant monk: separate from my wife and go and live in that hermitage above Sion which I have always rather envied.'[40] The direction his thoughts were taking was unmistakable: separation and Switzerland. Eventually he arrived at Perth on the 10th of December. Those few days John spent at Bowerswell ended his marriage.

CHAPTER XXI

THE TRAP SPRUNG

%

Effie's letter to Rawdon Brown from Bowerswell on the 30th of November had not a hint of impending disaster. Indeed it contained her recollection of a rather pleasant domestic vignette of John pausing in his work to hear her read a letter from Brown and then talking about it. At about the same time, John's mother sent Effie five shillings for each of her little sisters to buy a book.[1] His father sent his love to Effie and referred to Millais in glowing terms as 'the painter of the age', 'greater in one way than Turner.'[2] Relations between the two sets of parents were extremely cordial as a letter of 3rd November shows.[3] Millais had returned to London on the 4th of November and was delighted to be elected the youngest Associate of the Royal Academy shortly afterwards.[4] He dined happily with Ruskin's father in early December, returning 'a little tired and sleepy' from what must have been a pleasant evening with exceptionally fine beverages.[5] There is no trace of any personal disturbance in his letters at the time.

Back in Perth however, events had reached their inevitable conclusion. By the time John left Bowerswell on the 15th of December, Effie was 'in a state of resolute anger'[6] and had developed a nervous facial tic which was to last for several months. She herself said that this tic appeared only when she was 'excited by any distress.'[7] John had a number of other visits to make before returning home. Mr. Gray had already decided that Effie should take her little sister Sophie back to Herne Hill with her again. John and Effie travelled separately to the Blackburns at Glasgow, then split up again. Effie claimed that it was because of her tic and problems the Duke of Hamilton was having with his marriage that she stayed with his sister at Pollock while John visited the Duke's palace to look at missals. It is far more likely that she was so furious that she could not bear her husband's company. Because Mr. Ruskin would not send the coachman out on Christmas day, John and Effie spent the 25th in Durham and had planned to return together on the 26th. Effie however, always a late riser, could not get up in time for the 9 o'clock train so John left her behind. She eventually rolled up at midnight. Crawley had been waiting for her in the freezing snowy weather since 7 o'clock.

Even before Effie left Bowerswell on the 17th, her mother was writing urgent warning letters to Everett in London, although she had only met him for the first time in Edinburgh. There can be no doubt whatsoever that it was by these letters that Everett discovered for the first time that he was a potential co-respondent in a legal action. His state of utter panic shows clearly in the chaotic handwriting in his letter to Mrs. Gray of the 19th December. By the 20th December he was writing about not being suicidal.[8] He had a miserable Christmas, ate no dinner and strolled about London between church services, although he was not a regular church-goer.[9] By January 17th he was planning to join Hunt at Cairo to 'begin a new life, or rather try and end this one.'[10] John Everett Millais was a very frightened young man.

This sudden change is only explicable if John had threatened Effie with separation or divorce. We know from Millais' panicky reply to Mrs. Gray that she had told him about the evidential notebook and warned him not to communicate with Effie. Apart from anything else this is irrefutable evidence that John had produced the notebook to the Grays and that what it contained was to be taken very seriously indeed. Millais was convinced that John had

Millais' handwriting. (Left) Letter of the 19th December.
(Right) His more normal handwriting on 21st December

conspired against Effie. 'If he is such a plotting and scheming fellow, as to take notes secretly to bring against his wife, such a quiet scoundrel ought to be ducked in a millpond. His conduct is so provokingly gentle that it is folly to kick against such a man. From this time, I will never write again to his wife.'[11] Millais explained that not writing was so that John would have no excuse for further complaining: 'though sufficient has past [sic]' he added ominously, 'to enable him to do so, at any time he may think fit.' This, I would argue, is as clear an admission of Millais' guilt in the matter as anyone could wish. Millais declaring that 'I shall not write to her again' and after the annulment telling Effie that it was 'good to see your writing again' would also tend to indicate a regular correspondence prior to the Glenfinlas holiday.

These were probably the letters Effie later asked him to destroy. John knew that Millais was sending letters to Effie.[12] Had he intercepted a more than friendly letter from Millais to Effie and had this given him the idea of the Highland holiday?

In the letter of the 19th and in the less frantic letter of the following day, Millais went on to suppose that John conspired to 'the end that has come about' and had 'appeared purposely to connive at the result.'[13] John's 'Inquisitorial practice of noting down everything which could forward an excuse for complaining against his own wife,' is once more referred to. There can be absolutely no doubt that the 'result,' 'the end that has come about' was a Scottish divorce petition he was threatening 'to bring against his wife'. There is quite simply no other explanation. The popular version of events is that Effie didn't even tell her father and mother until 7th March that the marriage had not been consummated. Given the seriousness of the situation this is completely implausible.

It was not only Everett Millais in his panicky letter of the 19th December, who was inclined to think that John's 'absence in the Highlands seemed purposely to give me the opportunity of being in his wife's society' and that John had done this deliberately so as to bring about what happened. With hindsight William Millais, who knew his brother better than anyone, also thought that John had conducted a risky experiment in putting Everett and Effie continually together at Glenfinlas. For his part, Effie's brother George, who seems to have known his sister's character all too well, always and unwaveringly maintained that John, after conspiring throughout the marriage to engineer entanglements for Effie, had deliberately set up the Highland holiday with Millais in order to get Effie into trouble and get rid of her. Jane Boswell, no doubt judging by what she heard from her friend Effie, also 'never doubted the taking John [Everett] Millais to the Highlands was a regular deep laid scheme which doubtless JR [illegible: assumed?] could not fail judging the world by his own wicked self.'[14] Even John's close friends needed reassurance on this count. John's replies are forceful, but not categorical denials. The letter of 19th August 1854 to Furnivall is typical:

> As to the accusation of having thrown my late wife in Mr. Millais' way with the view supposed by Lady Eastlake, I should as soon think of simply denying an accusation of murder. Let those who say I have committed murder – prove it – let those who believe I have committed it without proof, continue to believe it.[15]

This is not a denial but a challenge to produce evidence. Later in the same letter he also denied having used persuasion on Effie to 'change the position which we held towards each other' since she hated him so much that 'no persuasion of late times would have availed'. After seeing what happened at Wallington, even Sir Walter Trevelyan, if Bell Scott is credible, was inclined to believe that John Ruskin wanted to get rid of his wife and if it had been any other man he would have come to that conclusion.[16] That John did indeed want to get rid of his wife at almost any cost seems beyond doubt. For her part Effie later regarded the sequence of events leading to her release from marriage as supernatural: 'having come entirely from God,' 'the chastisement of an everlasting protector' and 'the dispensations of a generous providence,' because 'everything went so rightly.'[17] This could hardly have been her opinion had she organized the thing herself.

Following the nullity decree Millais wrote about John's visit to Bowerswell at this time. After stating his refusal to believe that John desired Effie's 'fall', he continues: 'There was an amount of cool impudence about his visiting Bowerswell in spite of his insane conduct to Effie, which at once declares him to be inhuman, – no man could have face enough to confront the family of the girl he had so awfully ruined.'[18] This is indeed a revealing passage since John had been congratulated and fêted by the Grays in Edinburgh less than a month previously: he was at Bowerswell as their famous son-in-law paying a long-planned and much anticipated visit. Millais talks of a 'fall', a confrontation and of a girl 'so awfully ruined'. A girl did not get awfully ruined by her husband complaining privately to her father, with or without notes. Only the threatened legal action could do that.

All the evidence suggests that during the visit to Bowerswell, John, who had had ample time to visit a lawyer whilst he was alone in Edinburgh undergoing 'throat massage,' confronted Mr. Gray, a lawyer himself, with an ultimatum: persuade Effie to petition for an annulment of the marriage or he would petition for a public divorce at Edinburgh on the strength of his 'Notes' and the testimony of his loyal friends and servants. As I shall point out later, Frederic Harrison, one of John's early biographers, had heard about an action in a Scotch court whilst he was at Oxford in 1854 and even suggested that John's Edinburgh Lectures were delivered whilst he was a party to a matrimonial suit. It would have been reasonable for him to assume that this was the annulment which, because the marriage had been celebrated in Scotland, should have been heard by a Scotch court. However given the specific date this could only have been a pending Scottish divorce suit.

It has been argued that John would never have done such a thing to Millais as naming him as co-respondent in such a case. Millais was after all his protégé. John's letters home from Glenfinlas refer to Millais in such warm and avuncular terms that at first sight it is difficult to reconcile this with what was actually going on. It is however important to understand the subtlety of John's plan. Furnivall, who was given a full account, later claimed that John: 'was anxious that his wife should leave him, but he did not wish Millais to be the co-respondent.'[19] Nor did he need to, since Scottish law did not require the naming of the lover in the judgement, indeed this was avoided since it was theoretically forbidden for the adulterer to marry the wife notwithstanding that no-one else would.[20] Neither was there such a thing as a Crim. Con. action in Scotland. As the actual device for ending the marriage was to be an annulment, Millais would not have been involved and need never have known anything until it was over. If Millais had really been an innocent party to the whole affair and if the Grays had not been so desperate to acquire him as a replacement son-in-law there was no reason why he should ever have been involved.[21] Of course the purpose of their correspondence, besides avoiding scandal, was to entangle Millais by amassing evidence in case he decided to back out. This was not only because Effie might have had difficulty finding a spouse afterwards, but since Mr. Gray had only John and Effie's word that Effie was *virgo intacta*, it might be necessary to get her married as quickly as possible after the annulment to take the matter beyond dispute. Millais duly obliged. Not only did he all but admit in writing to what had been going on but, terrified of a scandal, he placed himself entirely in the hands of the Grays. George Gray stored the letters away safely with John's. John had no idea whether or what the Grays were writing to Millais. This would explain both why John carried on as normal with Millais and perhaps why Millais was so baffled and furious with him.

John could never have had any actual intention of proceeding with a divorce case. It was a calculated bluff. He would never have risked his reputation in that way. But the Grays could not take the risk. Even if the marriage had indeed never been consummated and their daughter had therefore successfully defended the case, the divorce proceedings would have ruined Effie's reputation. This was because not only the Glenfinlas episode would have been revealed in open court but probably also the Venetian débâcle, and she would in any case have had to defend herself by a counter claim of non-consummation because of impotency. It was a classic defence for childless wives.[22] If she called John's bluff and sat tight she could only look forward to a lonely lifetime in suburban Herne Hill. Mr. Gray would have had no doubt that a divorce would have catastrophic effects not just on Effie but on the whole Gray family, no longer just an obscure lawyer's family at Perth but, since November, known and recognised in the best Edinburgh society because of their famous son-in-law's lectures there.

Without further evidence coming to light there can be no way of knowing for certain exactly what happened during John's final visit to Bowerswell. John must have already instructed a solic-itor to draw up a writ in Edinburgh for Effie to appear in a divorce hearing at some future date; or he might simply have shown George Gray a draft writ and a letter instructing a solicitor.[23] If within a specified time Gray agreed to bring about annulment proceedings in London, the case would be withdrawn. I have been unable to find any such petition in the Scottish archives, but all the original legal papers to do with the English annulment have also disappeared, and there appears to be no published record of that important case, even though it went all the way to judge-ment. Whatever John said to Mr. Gray came as a sudden and terrible shock to him. He would have needed time to consider his options. The ultimate decision was therefore not made whilst his son-in-law was at Perth. Although all the family were aware that John had complained about Effie to her father and threatened to take action, it would seem to me that John's annulment ultimatum would have been delivered to Mr. Gray alone. Effie could not have been included in any arrangement for fear of accusations of collusion when the case came to court. If Effie was still a virgin, collusion was the only obstacle to a successful outcome. If she was ignorant of any arrangement she would not have to lie to the court.

John had failed in every attempt to get out of the marriage and Effie had come to hate him so much that it was impossible for him to persuade her to do anything. Even if he had managed to persuade her, that too would have left them open to accusations of collusion. For the marriage to be annulled she had to be the one to initiate legal proceedings. The only way she could be persuaded to do any such thing was if she was convinced that she was in imminent danger of a far, far worse sequence of events. Her father would have to convince her that 'the Ruskins' were plotting to disgrace her and that the only way to avoid their machinations was a pre-emptive annulment. However, first Mr. Gray would have had to think about John's proposal. This was not an everyday legal case. The commissary courts in Edinburgh had been abolished so if the annulment case had been heard in an open Scottish court there might have been reporters. This raises another question. The marriage had been celebrated in Scotland and according to the most basic principles of international law it should have been annulled according to Scots law. Why then did Mr. Gray, a qualified Scottish lawyer, bring the action in an archaic and obscure English court four hundred miles away? As will become apparent, the annulment was to raise almost as many questions as the wedding had.

Of course none of the Gray parents' correspondence with Effie from this whole period leading up to the annulment has entered the public domain. However, when John and Effie returned to Herne Hill a final letter from Mrs. Gray was waiting for her son-in-law. John answered it with a cryptic note:

> My dear Mrs. Gray – I had your kind note with the green pebble, which is excessively pretty and I am very much obliged to you for sending me this clear piece. I will write you word of Effie's health; but I fear I shall have little cheering information to give you. She passes her days in sullen melancholy, and nothing can help her but an entire change of heart. With sincere regards to Mr. Gray and George believe me affectionately yours[24]

Mrs. Gray's letter must have been sent after Effie and John left Bowerswell. It would seem to have been a very odd communication. Mrs. Gray was no geologist and the idea of this rather stolid woman tramping the wintry Trossachs at such a traumatic time in order to find a 'pretty' specimen for John who was extremely competent in things geological is utterly incredible. It was most probably a cryptic token from the Grays of their 'clear' acceptance of John's terms. It would have had to be cryptic to avoid any written evidence of collusion, or of Effie getting wind of what was going on. The 'entire change of heart' would follow in due course. The green pebble was a Ruskinian touch, but whether he saw it as an elfin-stone, or a reminder of the woman taken in adultery is beyond knowing.[25] He was about to get his order of release. There was a further letter to Mr. Gray important enough to be recorded in John's diary for January 1st 1854 but this has never come to light. Given the legal implications it is not surprising that there is very little other evidence that any kind of agreement was reached between John and Mr. Gray. Albert Gray in his dispute with Collingwood about the first Ruskin biography stated that it was his belief that a pact of silence had been agreed between the families. It is a fact that neither John nor Mr. Gray ever said a public word about the case. Effie on the other hand, not being privy to any deal, was not bound to keep quiet.[26] After the legal papers were served, John's father also aired his views on the subject most vociferously both in public and in private. If there was indeed a pact of silence it was not between the families at all, but only between the collusive parties: John and Mr. Gray. Given the purported facts of the case, and their widespread dissemination, it might well be worth asking: why the need for a pact of silence at all, unless to cover up something not in the public domain?

That the annulment was John's idea seems certain if only for the reason that no lawyer would have recommended Mr. Gray to pursue such a course of action. In the first place it would cost Effie the income on the £10,000 settled on her by Mr. Ruskin which would have to be repaid. This was a slightly unusual state of affairs. Normally it was the impotent husband who had to pay back the dowry, but Effie had not brought one. Nor would Effie get a penny in alimony. This was because a settlement made dependant upon the solemnization of marriage would no longer be valid if that marriage was declared void.[27] Nor could there be any question of damages because impotency was not something that could reasonably have been detected or even suspected prior to the marriage.[28] Moreover, impotency annulments were so rare that if John and Effie annulled their marriage and then re-married other partners, they would be sailing into fairly uncharted waters. In law the impotency had to be incurable for the marriage to be annulled. But even as recently as April 1853 the law had

435

re-affirmed that the most that could be proved was that the man was impotent in that particular marriage and with that particular woman.[29] Thus the wife was indeed free to re-marry, but so also was the man. If subsequently the man had children by his second wife then this could have been regarded as clear evidence that the church had been deceived, with consequences for Effie's reputation. However, by 1854, as the case law then stood, the man's second marriage was legal and his children legitimate. The marriage might possibly still be voidable but this recent case had put even this into doubt.[30] If an interested party had attempted to void the second marriage on the grounds that the church had been deceived and that as a result the first marriage still stood, it could only have been on the grounds of collusion. But as with divorce law, only an interested party could initiate legal action. The reason this unsatisfactory situation had not been resolved was that this unlikely possibility had never yet been attempted. Because the situation was so rare, there was little relevant case law. What would have been terrifying for Effie was that if John married a second time and his second wife had children, this might have the effect of raising the suspicion that Effie's second marriage was bigamous and all her offspring illegitimate. Society would reach its own conclusions about the legitimacy of the annulment and all concerned. For John, re-marriage and children would at least repair the damage to his personal reputation as a man.

John and Effie had travelled back to London separately. That Effie came back at all would seem to indicate that either some form of legal proceedings for divorce had indeed been initiated in Scotland or a deal had been struck, since in English law at least, allowing an adulterous wife back into the matrimonial home might otherwise have constituted 'condonation,' and been seen as evidence of reconciliation. This rule was intended to prevent a husband holding evidence of past adultery over the wife's head for years and years. As it was, John spent a good deal of his time at his parents' house. The final letter from John's father to Mr. Gray on the 16th February would seem to confirm that neither he nor John's mother knew anything at all of what was going on.[31] None of Effie's letters home between January 1 and February 27th have yet turned up. The last before the break reveals a new Effie trying her best not to annoy 'the Ruskins.' Chaperoned once more by ten-year-old Sophie, she was obviously under strict instructions from her father not to do anything which might upset John and cause him to start proceedings:

> When we came home I told John I wished to have a conversation with him as I did not wish to begin another year in this uncomfortable state and that I merely wished him to know that one of his objections to my conduct was not helping him in his work and that he must understand that I was quite ready to do anything he might desire and help him in his work – I took all the hard things he said to me [...] You may be quite sure I will try my best with them.[32]

Although she was clearly cowed by the threat of legal action, there is still no evidence that she was contemplating any of her own. If an agreement had been made between her father and John then she was certainly ignorant of it. Both Effie and John were at this time going to and from Millais' studio. John went for his Glenfinlas portrait and Effie to take Sophie for hers. By the 27th of February and clearly terrified of 'getting into any scrapes' she is refusing to entertain any young man in the evening while John is out of the house and even wrote to Clare Ford to end the correspondence between them. In the same letter and according to Sophie, John had threatened to write a book about Effie's conduct and get a divorce from her. Effie described John reading to her sister from 'the Notes' which contained some of Effie's conversations from the Highlands and then commenting on them. Effie thought him 'a perfect villain to make such a systematic plan of deception.'[33] This is yet more evidence that John had planned the whole thing. By the 28th she is explaining to friends that she cannot dine out alone with them. This new lifestyle must have been very noticeable to the servants. Effie's maid Mary had departed on the previous day.[34] Mary had of course been with Effie in Venice so would have been able to give some account of what had been going on there. Mary's departure meant that both of the servants who had been in Venice had now gone. Did she leave of her own accord, was she dismissed or had she been paid to disappear? According to Effie, Mary was not very bright and not very good at lying. Having dismissed her, Effie could always argue that Mary's evidence was vindictive falsehood. After the annulment case had begun, Effie gloomily supposed that 'the Ruskins' would send for Mary and question her.[35] This would seem to indicate that she still feared a legal action from 'the Ruskins.' This was almost certainly what she believed on 27th February when she wrote: 'I suppose by Autumn something will be done by the R's – do not think any manifestation will come from me. It is impossible for me to tell you all until I am obliged to seek my Father's advice.' At this time she was still planning to go with Jane Boswell to Oxford and then abroad and was convinced that the summer would 'come and go without anything.'[36]

In another letter Effie reported Crawley telling Sophie, 'what I am so afraid of is these [Denmark Hill] servants gossiping and their speaking of my Master and Mistress all over Camberwell.'[37] Effie's little sister Sophie, who was Effie's chaperone at Herne Hill, had a habit of confiding in her French governess Delphine and had written a letter to her that Effie failed to intercept.[38] Delphine, who had been Sophie's governess for three years and who had been at Herne Hill from September 1852 to March 1853, was also dismissed in March 1854 by the Grays. Delphine had to go because Sophie was going to tell her everything on her return from London. The dismissal of Delphine had obviously been the subject of one of Mr. Gray's letters that went missing around the 20th March. This almost certainly fell into John's hands because on 2nd April he told Sophie privately that he was sure that Effie and her mother were determined to prevent her meeting Delphine again.[39] Even by the 9th of May Effie was still worrying about the servants giving evidence. In the event none of the Ruskins' servants left and Crawley remained loyal to John after the marriage ended.[40] Even Effie's dog Zoë, a gift from Count von Thun, stayed behind with John, who subsequently called it 'Wisie.' Effie was particularly worried about being closely associated with gifts received from men friends. Various pictures by Millais are mentioned as causing her particular problems.

The first time there is evidence of Effie mentioning a separation was on 3rd March after her mother had apparently suggested that she must do something. Effie's response was 'towards winter' 'if they do not behave better.'[41] Once again it should be noted that she is only concerned about being treated in a becoming manner and her complaint is not even specific to John but includes the whole Ruskin family who were clearly not yet involved. On the same day Millais too was manœuvred into position by the Grays. 'I shall now be more careful than ever,' he wrote after reading a letter from Perth and 'something must be done by you [...] I think you should enquire into the matter'.[42] According to Effie writing again later the same day, Millais had perfectly understood advice or instructions from the Grays 'and will be off as soon as possible'.[43] Millais too was worried that the Ruskins might be 'bent on obtaining a separation' in which case the Grays would be obliged to consent for Effie's sake.[44] (The informed reader might well ask on what grounds Millais thought such a separation might be possible!)

On Thursday March 2nd Effie had sought to allay her mother's fear that the Ruskins might open her letters, which would suggest that Effie was destroying them after they had been read just as she had done in Venice.[45] It is important to remember that all Mr. and Mrs. Gray's correspondence with her of this period is missing. There is therefore a whole important sub-text completely absent from the story. In particular Mr. Gray's initial manœuvering and his later advice and practical instructions which would have been relayed to Effie through her mother's letters are not there. Examining the surviving letters from Effie and Millais to Mrs. Gray it becomes clear that if John was using the threat of divorce as a means of forcing an annulment of the marriage, not only was Effie ignorant of this but Millais knew even less about what was really going on. The Ruskin parents, with regard to whom Effie was so paranoid, knew absolutely nothing at all. Given Effie's adamant refusal to be persuaded by John into any kind of separation, and given the distressed state Effie was in at Bowerswell and afterwards, Mr. Gray could not have trusted her to keep silent. Any hint that there was an agreement would be dangerous since this would be evidence of collusion and that would be grounds for the court to dismiss the annulment case.[46] Hence Effie's letters survived the subsequent purges as prime evidence of her innocence in the matter.

It is in the light of all this that Effie's letter to her father on 7th March must be read. Some authors have assumed that this letter dropped like a bombshell on an unsuspecting Gray family. This was not the case. Her father had of course already manœuvered Effie into position and offered to give her his legal advice.[47] As Effie had to be the one to initiate the annulment proceedings, Mr. Gray must have been enormously relieved to hear that she was finally giving him permission to proceed on her behalf.[48] That Mr. Gray was in fact already involved is clear from her opening remarks. She had just received letters from Bowerswell communicating her parents' approval for the course of conduct she was about to take. That meant they already knew what she intended to do. Effie herself made it clear that this was her first formal complaint. However, as far as Effie was concerned this letter was the beginning of the legal process leading to a possible separation. The actual nature of the process still remained unclear to her: even by the 20th she was still only talking about a separation. Of course the only grounds for any kind of separation on her part had to be to do with non-consummation since she could not start an action on the grounds of her own alleged adultery! She was beginning to realise that the non-consummation, if it was ever the problem, was also the solution. 'I do not think I am John Ruskin's wife at all,' she wrote. But it would be wrong to assume that this letter of Effie's was the first time George Gray heard about his daughter's failed marriage.[49] She admitted to having bared her soul to her father at Bowerswell and told him how unhappy she was. If the unconventional nature of the marriage had not previously been discussed with her mother in the six childless years since the wedding, it is almost inconceivable that the subject would not have come up at that time. In her letter of 27th February Effie had written quite unecquivocally that 'were it not for the pain of exposure' John was 'most completely in my power.' This could only have been a reference to the non-consummation. After reading letters from her mother, Millais had advised her on the 3rd that she ought to have her father's advice, and we can reconstruct that advice from her letters: 'Let me see what I can do for you before the Ruskins get you into a scrape, and in case they get wind of what is happening and go for divorce or separation themselves. Above all don't say a word to anybody.' We can detect her father's guiding hand in her written response to him:

> the necessity for acting in concert with you might, by being longer delayed, cause you and others connected with my life greater sorrow in the end.

She had realised the immediate necessity of the course of action her father was proposing because she had already been convinced that if she delayed any longer something much worse might happen.[50] She would not have entreated her father to assist her 'unless matters had become so sad for me as to threaten my Life.' On the flap of the envelope belonging to this letter Effie wrote:

> Return me Lady E's letter.[it had been enclosed with Effie's] I have sent a box to Mama today which she will be so good as to put in her storeroom for me. It contains my Dairies [sic] and things she thought I had better send.[51]

She had obviously been advised by her London confidante Lady Eastlake to get all incriminating evidence out of the way just in case and tellingly her Venetian diaries must have been the first things she thought of. Not surprisingly they were never seen again.

In this letter to her father Effie admitted that she had unfortunately already told Lord Glenelg and Lady Eastlake about her troubles before she received the answer to her letter of the 3rd of March, because at that time she was still unwilling to ask her father to act for her until she believed that trouble was unavoidable.[52] Effie had been so anxious and ill with worry that she had already sought informal legal advice. She had asked Lady Eastlake to enquire 'How English Law would treat such a case as mine.'[53] As we shall see, her telling Lady Eastlake was to cost John dear. It is interesting that she almost invariably referred to the 'Ruskins' as her opponents rather than John alone, even though John's parents clearly knew nothing at all about what was going on. Perhaps this shows that she still saw her marriage as an arrangement between two families rather than a relationship between two people. Effie later admitted that:

> I had no idea I could get away up to within a month of leaving him, which I did under the care of my parents and entirely without his knowledge by the advice of lawyers.[54]

This places her very first thoughts of a separation in the last week of March because she left on the 25th April. It is only barely plausible that Effie would have rushed from first thoughts of separation to service of the writ of annulment in only four weeks when the legal and social implications were so great and so complex. In fact she had absolutely no idea what to do or what her father was planning to do as late as the 30th of March. On the 20th she had asked her mother:

> What does my Father think of doing now? and has he been thinking over the fact of my marriage being solemnized in the Scotch form. Is the Scotch marriage Law different and [are]

the laws about dissolving separating parties the same there as here aught not this to be enquired into and has Papa no friend in Edin who could give him some of the necessary details privately – I do not think I shall be able to see Lord G he does not understand the case you see and does not like to inter-fere – Perhaps he will help me yet but you must be considering what to do as Lady E says it aught to be settled before they go to Switzerland [...] and as I have not got any opinion yet it is unfortunate perhaps Lady E will put me up to something.[55]

This letter clearly shows that it was her father who was handling the case, not the bewildered Effie or her London friends.[56] If her father had indeed been researching her case he was certainly not sharing any details with his daughter. As Effie was no legal expert, her questions to her father must have arisen from those she had tried to consult in London who would have pointed out to her that since the marriage was celebrated in Scotland that was where it should be examined. In fact Effie was entirely correct in pointing out that Scottish marriage law was relevant in her case. According to the interpretation of interna-tional law then current, there was indeed a question of whether the annulment should have been effected in a Scottish court or at least according to Scots law. Her father was a Scottish lawyer and she would soon be living in Perth. That the annulment case was in fact held in an English court is probably the most impor-tant piece of evidence that John had organised the whole thing. Possibly as a result, Effie's London connections seem to have wanted nothing to do with her dilemma. She had hoped that Lord Glenelg, Dr. Twiss (Vicar General of the Archbishop of Canter-bury and advocate in the consistory courts), Stephen Lushington (a famous consistory court judge) or even Dean Milman might have helped her with the case, but she was to be disappointed. By the 23rd of March Lady E. had still not put her up to anything and Effie was still in the dark. She wrote a letter to her mother telling her that:

> I have heard nothing from Ld. Glenelg and I do not think I will he has a good deal of bother himself now and I will not write to him again what will Papa do in the absence of any help of this kind – I will see lady E tonight and see what she says! [...] It is a great pity I cannot get at Dr. Twiss but I have no male friend of the age and character that would at all do for a confidence of the kind I suspect we must act without it [...] [She?] and I have ransacked our brains to think of some-one else to get at Dr. Twiss but without effect as yet but he is I suppose the person Papa would go to when he comes – I shall approve of whatever he thinks proper.[57]

After discussing the situation with Lady Eastlake and Rawdon Brown, Effie begged her father not to think she 'undervalued his talents, ability, desire to relieve' her. She was being careful not to offend her father, but with the time shortening and her father still in Perth she was worried about all of these. For his part, Mr. Gray was extraordinarily sanguine and did not think Dr. Twiss's opin-ion was 'of so much consequence.' which was just as well since by the 30th Effie told her mother that she did not see any hope of getting it.[58] By this time she was already making plans for her father's visit to London. Effie's solo trip to Germany had been cancelled in favour of a visit to her parents. Now of course the trip was to be one-way.

It was about this time that Effie began to complain of threats of cruelty by John, usually to start in the autumn when he returns from Switzerland and she returns to Herne Hill from her separate holiday. Again these complaints only appear after the return from the Glenfinlas holiday. Even at Edinburgh John had apparently been so agreeable that Effie's friend Jane Boswell, who had previously disliked John intensely, changed her opinion of him.[59] John mentioned Effie telling him in October 1853 that 'if she were to suffer the pains of eternal torment, they could not be worse to her than going home to live at Herne Hill with me.' It is not clear whether it was Herne Hill or John which caused her the most pain. But it was only from the moment that she arrived there at Christmas that her hatred became 'resolute anger.'[60] It was of course standard practice for husbands wanting a separation to behave in such an unreasonable manner as to drive the wife out of the marital home, which would put her legally at a disadvantage in any future proceedings. Effie accused John of threatening to do this to her 'he should try and break my spirit and enduce me to leave him and return to Perth as I bored him'. She also accused him of threatening her with 'personal cruelty',[61] daily heaping one insult upon another, accusing her of insanity, and even of saying that she needed 'a good beating with a common stick.'[62] This last was not merely an amusing Effie-ism. John had obviously referred to the commonly held, but by 1854 erroneous, belief that disciplining your wife was legal up to certain limits which had to do with the size of the stick. Mrs. Gaskell wrote about a lady friend who visited the Ruskins that Christmas and reported furious rows and John's bad temper.[63] This was very much out of character for John whom even Millais referred to as 'provokingly gentle'. At this time Effie wrote to her mother that Rawdon Brown thought John 'may have a method in his madness.'[64] Brown of course had been in Venice when Effie was there and was to return at the time of the annulment. Probably in this case John was simply getting worried that she might decide not to do anything at all and therefore he was applying more pressure to make her leave. Although he was rumoured to have a temper there is no evidence that John ever lifted his hand in anger to any other human being. There is of course Effie's strange letter to her mother of the 29/30th March with the page torn out leaving the enigmatic unfinished sentence 'for John has found a new method ...' and continuing after the break ' ... what did he mean by this?'[65] John's strategy seems to have had the desired effect. In a later letter Effie revealed that she had not complained about her marriage, even to her mother, 'until he forced me to reveal it by trying to get rid of me in every way his Jesuitical mind could devise – It has certainly been all his own doing – had he been tolerably kind instead of absolutely cruel I never would have exposed myself to such unenviable notoriety.'[66] John seems also to have employed Crawley to deliver one other threat before Effie left: that he was going to visit Rome, with the intention of converting.[67]

John need not have worried. Mr. Gray and his wife arrived on the Dundee boat on the evening of Friday 14th April. In a letter Effie wrote that day to Rawdon Brown, we discover that she had asked Crawley to meet the Grays when they got off the steamer but he had pleaded illness and sent a substitute. Crawley was and remained totally loyal to John. He would have been John's main witness in any legal proceedings. Had he met the Grays on this occasion it might have compromised his independence and possibly given rise to allegations of duplicity if not collusion. Since the Grays' arrival was kept secret from John, this one comment confirmed that she had confided in Crawley and he knew exactly what Effie was planning. Whether or not John knew exactly what was going on at this time depended entirely on where Crawley's loyalty lay.[68]

Effie met her parents 'secretly' the next day. It seems almost incredible that Mr. Gray should have allowed himself so little time to sort out the legal position. April 14th was Good Friday, followed by the Easter weekend and Easter Monday. Would ecclesiastical lawyers really have worked on this religious weekend? According to Effie's note to Rawdon Brown on Easter Monday (the 17th) Mr. Gray had already discovered the relevant case heard the previous year and decided to leave for Perth on Wednesday 19th, and this with regard to 'matters quite beyond the common run of Life' which Effie had been advised 'must be treated by people accustomed to extreme cases and who have had the same passing under their eyes before.'[69] The gossip spread about by Lady Eastlake that John had wanted to sue for a separation (in England) but that clever Mr. Gray had forestalled him by the nullity action was uninformed and malicious. John could not have brought such an action in England so long after he had become aware of the adultery and after he had taken Effie back into the matrimonial home. This threat could only have originated in a Scottish court whilst they were there. If John had wanted he could have continued his divorce action in Scotland and had his divorce within days. Why would he wait for months and have his suit for separation in England thrown out for condonation or become time-expired? He was in any case never interested in a mere separation. More to the point, if George Gray was anxious to forestall John why did he wait so long and even delay service of the writ in the nullity suit to allow John time to get abroad and out of the reach of the court? Lady Eastlake could only have had one source for her gossip: Effie. Effie believed that the nullity action would forestall a suit for separation. She believed it because her father had told her so.

There is an important point to be considered here. Effie's

letters throughout this period show that she firmly expected John to sue for a separation sooner or later. Either she did not have the slightest idea of English matrimonial law, or she knew that the only possible ground her husband could use for instituting a separation was her own adultery and that she therefore considered herself to be vulnerable on that count. Lady Eastlake was not doing Effie's reputation any favours by spreading the rumour that Mr. Gray had forestalled a suit for separation. However it must be assumed that Effie was still a virgin and had known for some time that the non-consummation of the marriage had put John in an equally vulnerable position with regard to his reputation. By 27th February John had however raised the stakes by threatening her with a public divorce. Even though she could probably have successfully defended such a suit, her behaviour during the marriage would have been entered into the court record and if word had got out her reputation would have suffered terribly. If she had won the case she would have returned to Herne Hill as John's wife. At some stage she would still have had to counter-sue for an annulment of the marriage and that would have had to be on the grounds of John's incurable impotence. Her father would have pointed out to her that it would be far better just to go for the annulment and avoid the public disgrace of a suit for adultery altogether. It was fear of this 'pain of exposure' that Effie wanted to avoid at all costs and which, as Lutyens noted, drove her to the brink of derangement and hysteria in the weeks before she left for Scotland. John had her in checkmate. [70]

Effie's departure was postponed by a week on the advice of the lawyers, almost certainly to ensure that John was out of reach of the court at the relevant time. Effie dined with John at Denmark Hill for the last time on April 23rd. The Grays had planned to leave for Perth on Wednesday 26th but the departure was brought forward to Tuesday 25th April so that George Gray would be able to save money by catching the Wednesday steamboat to Dundee. Effie's luggage which, given her extensive trousseau, must have been substantial, had already been sent on in advance. John had watched it leave apparently without comment.[71] The night before she left for Scotland, John even recalled that she had told him that 'she had laid her plans, and was too clever to be beaten by me.– I never condescended to enquire into her plans; but saw her to the railroad the next morning.'[72] On the day of departure John took his wife, her sister Sophie and Crawley, who was to travel with them to Perth, to the railway station. John strode up and down the platform, spoke to an acquaintance, but did not utter a single word to her. As the train left the station he threw his purse into her lap.[73]

Mr. and Mrs. Gray were waiting for Effie at the first stop down the line. Sophie got out, Mrs. Gray got in. Effie gave her father a parcel containing her wedding ring, the household accounts and the house keys and, still accompanied by Crawley, continued to Perth. Mr. Gray took the parcel back to London and gave it to the lawyers.

CHAPTER XXII

A MEDIÆVAL PANTOMIME

୧୨

No-one has thought to ask why, on first hearing about John and Effie's marital difficulties, George Gray didn't simply go to John James Ruskin, one of his very oldest friends, to discuss the problem.[1] Likewise, Effie's 'escape' has been presented as such a triumph of deceit and subterfuge that there has been scarcely a pause to ask why on earth it had to be so dramatic. Everybody knew she was going to Scotland, no-one was planning to stop her. Her luggage was already on its way, John took her to the station and she was even to be accompanied in the train to Perth by John's personal manservant. Once she was safely in Scotland her father would have had all the time in the world to take care of the final legal necessities; unless of course the drama was not for John's benefit but for Effie's. In order to persuade her to go for annulment George Gray had needed to convince her that she was in real and imminent danger of some kind of divorce or separation attempt by 'the Ruskins' or even a belated consummation by John. There could be no last-minute change of mind.

Another question that subsequently perplexed legal minds was that of why the annulment was pursued in an English court when the marriage had been celebrated in Scotland, Effie had moved back to Scotland and George Gray was a member of the Scottish legal profession. Many years afterwards the celebrated British jurist and historian Frederic Harrison published a life of Ruskin in which he referred to an action in a 'Scotch Court' to do with the marriage. He also commented that John's Edinburgh

Lectures were at a moment ill-chosen for a public appearance 'whilst he was a party to a matrimonial dispute.' He was immediately taken to task for this by E. T. Cook, who pointed out that the annulment proceedings had in fact been in the Commissary Court of Surrey, and was most anxious that the reference to a Scotch court be removed from subsequent editions. On receiving Cook's letter Harrison was at first incredulous; he had after all been a member of the Bar since 1858 (the year the Matrimonial Causes Act came into effect) and a professor of jurisprudence and international law for twelve years. He had worked on the codification of the law with Lord Westbury and from 1869-70 was secretary to the commission for the digest of the law. A correspondence followed in which Harrison claimed to have heard about the proceedings in a Scotch court whilst he was at Oxford. Moreover:

> If it was in the Diocese of Rochester or Winchester or anywhere in England – all I can say as a lawyer and expert in international law, the nullification of the Marriage was ultra vires, invalid, and of no effect. – An English Court cannot decree the nullity of a marriage in Scotland – If that be so, the Ruskin Marriage was never nullified, and the Millais Marriage was invalid. See what all this means – including the Millais baronetcy. What is the authority for the assertion that the nullity suit was in an English Court?[2]

Harrison had meanwhile consulted the eminent jurist Professor A. Dicey who had argued quite logically in his standard work *Conflict of Laws* that nullity could only be properly decreed by the court of the country where the marriage had been celebrated:

> Really – in 1853, the law was quite unsettled, and there ought to have been proceedings in some Scotch Court as I was told

there had been. When Dicey first wrote to me in the country and in the absence of his books he was inclined to think, as I did, that the Courts of the Celebrating Country had exclusive jurisdiction.[3]

Here then are at least two eminent experts on international law with decades of experience still convinced in 1904-5 that the general rule was that divorce suits must be brought in the court of the domicile of the husband, whilst nullity suits must be brought in the court of the country where the marriage ceremony took place.[4] Harrison then asked Dicey for a formal opinion, with his books, whereupon Dicey reversed his previous position:

I understand that the decree of nullity was made in 1853 by what was then a proper English Court. If this be so, was and is, in my judgment valid. It is true that the English Courts have apparently assumed jurisdiction to pronounce a decree of nullity on the ground that the marriage was celebrated in England (Dicey Conflict pp. 276-277 + esp. Linke v. Van Aerde 1894 IO Times L.R. 426) and apparently are inclined to concede jurisdiction to the Courts of a foreign country where the marriage was celebrated. (Conflict p. 394-5, Sinclair v. Sinclair, I Hagg. Const. p. 297) But the jurisdiction of the country where a marriage is celebrated is not exclusive and English courts or perhaps rather British Courts, seem now to claim jurisdiction on the grounds that parties are resident, tho' not, it may be domiciled in the country of the Court pronouncing the decree. (see Williams v. Dormer [1852] 2 Rob.505. Roberts v. Brennan P. 1902 p. 148 + Johnson v. Coates Irish L.R. (1898) QBD 130 as also Westlake 3rd. Edn p. 82)[5]

Dicey seems to be saying that if the Surrey court was a proper and legal court and it had assumed to itself jurisdiction in this case then, even if it had exceeded its theoretical competence, that in itself would make the annulment legal and provide a precedent for subsequent cases, even though it was apparently in violation of the then generally accepted ground rules of international law.[6] Dicey demurred to the opinion of a third expert: John Westlake, who had been called to the bar in 1854, was professor of international law at Cambridge for twenty years, representing Britain at the Hague Court from 1900 to 1906, and was author of three standard works on international law.[7] By the time Dicey and Westlake were consulted in 1905 the situation had changed radically from that in 1853.[8] Not only had the law been unsettled in 1853 but the entire jurisdiction of the Commissary Court of Surrey in such matters was abolished just six years later. What seems quite clear from this exchange of letters is that in 1853-4 it was by no means usual for Scotch marriages to be annulled in English courts and that if the leading English experts in international conflicts of laws were unaware fifty years later that a British court had assumed jurisdiction in such cases so early, then which Scottish lawyer in 1854 would have advised Mr. Gray to risk bringing the suit in England? It could well be that the Ruskin case was one of the very first instances with all that would imply.[9] That such an important case was not included in either the *Ecclesiastical Reports* or the *Digest* for 1854 seems rather suspicious.

The papers were served on John and his father at six o'clock on the same evening that Effie left. In his letter to his solicitor John confessed he 'was surprised to receive the citation to court the same afternoon.'[10] Surprised and delighted I would think, since that meant that the annulment case was then unstoppable. The citation essentially required John to appear personally or by his Proctor on the 3rd day after service on the 25th. The following day John's father consulted his solicitor and the case was managed between the two of them. Although Mr. Ruskin dealt with the annulment it would have been entirely against his character. He hated going to law and would do almost anything to avoid it. It had taken him so long to persuade George Gray to conclude his (paid) work on the Richardson inheritance that the case brings to mind Dickens' *Jarndyce v. Jarndyce*.[11] Because the nullity suit was to be undefended, John of course could not play any active rôle without risking accusations of collusion. In fact providing that Effie could come up with a doctor who would say she was a virgin, collusion was the only reason the case could fail. The overwhelming majority of undefended divorce cases were in fact collusive.[12] In undefended annulments of this sort, the wife's virginity was considered proof enough of non-consummation and as John said later: 'it was assumed necessarily in my declining to give any answer to this charge that I was impotent.'[13] This suited John since he did not have to tell any untruths about his ability to consummate. The husband in such cases nearly always moved out of the reach of the court to avoid being called in for examination and so the court had in past times decided that it would be unfair if the wife's suit should be thus halted by the husband's absence. John was in Switzerland when the case was heard on 15th July. He had booked this continental holiday without Effie even before he went to the Highlands and whenever he thought she wanted to change any of the arrangements he became angry.[14] On the 13th December, whilst still at Perth, John told his father that he could not make any engagements that spring and asked him to confirm the plans for the start of the Swiss holiday.[15] The Ruskins left London on the 8th and the original planned date of departure from England of 9th May was never altered. May 8th was of course the day after Effie's 26th birthday, the technical deadline for John's promise to consummate the marriage when she was twenty five. May 9th was also the very day that John should have made his personal appearance in Court and, 'not appearing', was declared in contempt and the case continued without him.

Alexander Wedderburn managed to locate and study the entire file of legal documents pertaining to the case and made notes on its progress. The general legal business would have been carried out at Doctors' Commons, the original court proceedings were at the Vicar General's offices at 3, Creed Lane, Ludgate Hill. The subsequent proceedings were in the Commissary Court of Surrey, held in St. Saviour's Church just south of the river in Southwark. This was because the couple's domicile at Herne Hill was in Surrey which fell under the diocese of Winchester and St. Saviour's was the closest church in that diocese. The same legal personnel were employed at all the locations because only the 'civilians' at Doctors' Commons had a Bar and jurisprudence. Effie's Proctor Mr. Glennie presented the '*exhibit principi*' and returned the citation on 29th April. On 9th May, the day the Ruskins caught the boat for France, John was declared in contempt by the court. On 10th May Glennie brought in the 'Libel and exhibit', essentially the allegations and evidence. Effie and Mr. Gray had returned from Perth to London by sea on 24th May. Strangely, Mrs. Gray did not come with them. Lutyens has suggested that this was to save money, but as a shareholder, George Gray travelled free on the Dundee boat. Moreover Mr. Ruskin later paid all the Grays' travel and accommodation along with the court costs. The Grays stayed in rented rooms in Bury Street which was where Effie's solicitor Mr. Webster took down her deposition. Father and daughter having given their depositions to the court at Doctors' Commons, Effie attended St. Saviour's, Southwark on 30th May 'to swear' in a private room. She did not have to enter a courtroom. Mr. Gray only had to swear that the couple had lived together until Effie left. The Libel was also admitted to court on 30th May and the medical experts Robert Lee and Charles Locock were instructed to examine both Effie and John. Mr. Gray and Effie returned to Perth on the 31st May. On the 7th June and in the continued absence of the defendant John, the court moved to publication of the decree and, after two subsequent non-appearances by John, evidence was closed on 4th July and sentence pronounced on July 15th.

The Libel and exhibits contained two accounts of the marriage as perceived by the Gray side. One was by George Gray, the other by Effie. The courtship and marriage were described and the marriage certificate presented. In the first deposition John was said to be 30 years old and Effie 20 when they wed.[16] The honeymoon had commenced on the 10th April at Blair Atholl and then they had visited the Highlands. They had co-habited but not consummated. Wedderburn uses a fairly transparent code to indicate that they were naked together in the same bed and this is later confirmed.[17] They continued to cohabit in the same bed but John had never attempted to consummate and Effie was still a virgin. According to the Libel this was because John's 'parts were not normal' and he was irremediably incapable. This situation had affected Effie's health and the Complaint at the end, though almost illegible in Wedderburn's notes, seems to allege that this was due to the natural impotency and infirmity of John Ruskin. More detail emerged in another more accurate account provided by Effie herself in which the court was told that the courtship had lasted six months;[18] the marriage was according to the Scotch Kirk; and John was 29 and Effie 19 at the time of the marriage. Their health was good. The honeymoon had also extended to Keswick and they arrived in London on April 22nd. They first lived in Denmark Hill and then in Park Street for three years. Their final London address was Herne Hill until April 1854. During the marriage they spent six months in Normandy, visited Venice twice, and between February and October 1849 Effie was ill in Scotland with her mother and John was abroad with his parents. Effie was also occasionally in Scotland with her parents but without John. Effie's health had failed from distress.[19] The court also heard that John had abstained from consummation owing to a great dislike of children but had promised to consummate the marriage when Effie was 25. Effie was at first an innocent and remained a virgin. This fact was confirmed by an internal examination by Drs. Lee and Locock whose detailed medical report was appended. From Wedderburn's cursory notes it would appear that this report not only confirmed an intact hymen but also the lack of other evidence that intercourse had ever taken place. According to Wedderburn the report was signed by Lee and dated 2nd June. However, Sir Albert Gray also made notes from the court papers and he claimed that the report was signed on the 30th May, but he may have been confused because he also noted that the doctors had been appointed on the same day. According to Sir Albert the doctors' report stated that 'we find the usual signs of virginity are perfect and that she is naturally and perfectly formed and there are no impediments on her part to the proper consummation of the marriage'.[20] Wedderburn commented quite rightly that such evidence was most inconclusive and any modern doctor would confirm that Effie's condition was not necessarily inconsistent with John's virility.

The Libel had contained two charges: incapacity and abnormality. Since John did not appear as the court had ordered on 30th May and could not therefore be examined, there was no evidence whatever of any physical abnormality and therefore no finding. Wedderburn thought it was probably common practice to allege this in impotency cases. In any event the annulment case already mentioned of April 21st 1853 had ruled that physical abnormality was not a necessary condition. The charge of incapacity being similarly impossible to prove medically in the absence of the accused, the finding was, as was usual in such cases, presumed from the condition of Effie who, according to the papers, had been medically examined.

For Effie's part she had only had to obtain confirmation by two doctors of an intact hymen and that she was *apta et habilis*. The medical examination could be privately conducted at the doctor's own rooms. When John was questioned by proxy on whether Effie was 'a pure virgin', he never expressed any doubts for obvious reasons. 'The Lady's conduct has been without reproach',[21] he answered and 'her case will stand any examination':[22] which once again is not the same as saying 'yes'. Certainly John had never reproached her for her conduct and the second phrase only refers to the examination and not its outcome. I also cannot help seeing in the second phrase a slight double-entendre. In any case, having allegedly never consummated the marriage, how would he know whether Effie was or was not a virgin? In the event at least one of the doctors in the case was not as neutral as he should have been. According to Mrs. Gray, Dr. Lee expressed extreme antipathy to John right from the outset. She told her son that Lee 'had read John's books and thought him a Jesuit – but now thinks him mad.' This is hardly the impartiality expected from a professional man, particularly when he had in the past been employed by both the Ruskin family and their solicitor Mr. Rutter.[23] Dr. Lee had already been consulted on 24th April, a week before the papers were served.[24] It is doubtful whether he could have been appointed by the court at that time. It would seem that the court accepted his competence later and whilst Effie was in Perth. On May 28th Effie confirmed that Dr. Locock had been appointed by the court. The first official mention of his appointment was when the Libel was admitted by the court on 30th May. According to Wedderburn's notes the doctors seem to have been instructed by the court on that same day to examine both spouses. Quite when Effie's 'examination' took place is also uncertain. Lutyens thinks that the examination was part of the legal activity on 30th May but at that time Effie's mother was in Perth. It is almost inconceivable that Effie would have submitted to such an intimate examination without her mother present and indeed she did not mention it in her itinerary of that day. The only 'examinations' she mentions having undergone were taking an oath with the doctors in St. Saviour's church and being questioned by a lawyer in a private room. The medical doctors returned home with her but her father remained at Doctors' Commons for more questioning.[25] The Grays left for Perth the next day. The only other option is prior to 24th April when the doctors are first mentioned. Given the importance of the doctor's opinion to the legal proceedings this may well have been Mr Gray's very first priority. At that time Lee was reported as 'giving an opinion in the highest degree satisfactory' and saying that he would be 'at once backed by Dr. Locock at the proper time.'[26] Dr. Locock was only appointed by the court whilst Effie was in Perth. Interestingly Dr. Locock had also been employed by the Ruskins in 1849 to treat Mary Bolding *née* Richardson.[27] On the day before Effie's examination and oath taking at St. Saviour's, she wrote that 'Dr. Locock has been appointed by the court. On being told to wait on me and some details mentioned, he said he knew the case – Lord Lansdowne had been talking to him about it.'[28] If this was true and he only knew of the case secondhand up until the day before the legal questioning and oath taking took place, then it would appear that Locock merely took the word of his colleague. Otherwise it would all tend to suggest either that Effie had been examined by Doctor Lee prior to his being appointed by the court (which appointment must have been after Effie left for Perth) or that there was no examination at all and the whole thing went through on the nod. Effie herself told her mother that on the 30th she only had to swear to the fact with the doctors.[29] Lee and Locock's report was apparently commissioned by the court on 25th April but when submitted it was apparently signed and dated 2nd June.[30]

Collusion was the only danger as far as John was concerned. Usually the prime evidence of collusion was if the wife's legal bills were paid for her by the husband. In the event Ruskin senior paid both sets of lawyers. Effie was not entitled to damages but she was awarded court costs.[31] This did not indicate any punitive measure against John. The husband always paid the costs in divorce cases unless the wife could be proved to have a separate estate and income.[32] Collusion could also be detected when the husband and wife agreed not to fight in court. Hence John's lawyer pointed out to him 'the expedience of allowing the case to proceed without hindrance merely giving sufficient opposition to allow the Lady to obtain her decree without the appearance of collusion.'[33] John replied that he certainly wished 'the case to proceed with as little hindrance as possible.' It is partly for this reason that an adversarial tone had crept into the proceedings. John had already hinted to his solicitor that Effie was suffering from a 'slight nervous affection of the brain' and that 'there were certain circumstances in her person which completely checked' his physical passion.[34]

This is the proper context in which John's 'new' reason for not consummating the marriage should be examined. According to Effie, John first mentioned this other reason at some time in 1853. Given the similarity of the accounts she gave to her father and Mrs. Ruskin, this was almost certainly during the heated discussion around the time of her 25th birthday. This was after John had suddenly decided on a Highland holiday and just days after the crucial judgement in the Consistory Court which would have reinforced John's conviction that an uncontested impotency annulment could set him free. On the 7th March 1854 Effie had told her father that apart from the reasons John had given on the honeymoon for not consummating the marriage:

> finally this last year he told me his true reason (and this to me as villainous as all the rest), that he had imagined women were quite different to what he saw I was, and that the reason he did not make me his Wife was that he was disgusted with my person the first evening 10th April.

This statement has caused a storm of uninformed speculation as to what exactly John meant. It is however necessary to point out here that most of the conjecture which has been attached to Effie using John's word 'person' in this statement is just that. Note that John did not use this reason for non-consummation at the time of the honeymoon, but only much later when he desperately wanted to end the marriage. Nor did he only blurt out these words during an argument. He used an almost identical form of words as an integral part of the account of the 'General Facts' and 'Details' of his marriage given to his solicitor. Fortunately these documents survived attempts by Albert Gray illegally to acquire and destroy them.

The two documents headed 'General Facts' and 'Mr. Pott's

questions and Mr. J. Ruskin's Answers' were provided to John's solicitor Rutter during the annulment proceedings and as information for his proctor Mr. Pott. Mr. Pott was only appointed as proxy after John had left the jurisdiction of the court and was already in Switzerland. In the Statement John confirmed that immediately after the marriage there was an agreement not to consummate the marriage 'for some little time' owing to the distress and anxiety of both newlyweds. This period was later extended to 'when she was twenty-five'. The stated intention was to avoid Effie becoming pregnant which would have disrupted his plans for travel and field research on the Continent. After five years they would be 'settled for good' and the marriage would be consummated. John claimed that he married Effie for companionship rather than from passion, which given that his passion for Effie had been cruelly disappointed by his discovery of the true nature of the marriage, might be an indication of how he had adjusted his expectations. John then suggests several reasons why Effie grew to hate him. The first of which were to do with her antipathy to his parents, his distance from hers and his unwillingness to find her brother a job in the City. John further asserted that he was not impotent, could prove this at once by medical examination, but did not want Effie back in his house. After the annulment the papers remained in Rutter's safe and on his death passed into the possession of his partner Veitch. Veitch's widow then offered them for sale. Sir Albert Gray bought them intending to destroy them. Alexander Wedderburn as one of Ruskin's executors had a prior legal claim to the papers and managed to wrest them back from Gray. The papers were published by Whitehouse as *Vindication of Ruskin* in 1950.

In the 'General Facts' John was quite specific that it was 'points in her character which caused me to regard with excessive pain any idea of having children with her'. In the 'Details' he expanded on this statement:

> It may be thought strange that I could abstain from a woman who to most people was so attractive. But though her face was beautiful, her person was not formed to excite passion. On the contrary there were certain circumstances in her person which completely checked it.[35]

John used the the word 'person' instead of 'body' because it has two meanings: it can also signify personality or character and that, I believe, is the sense in which he used it. This was almost certainly a deliberate equivocation of a kind for which John was notorious in his writings.[36] The statistics from a search of the Library Edition of his complete works indicate that when John wanted to indicate the human physical form he almost always used the word 'body'.[37] In fact John straightaway used the word 'person' of himself too: 'I did not think, either that there could be anything in my own person particularly attractive to her, but believed that she loved me as I loved her with little mingling of desire.' Can anyone with the slightest sense of period and place really believe that John was here referring to Effie's desire for his body? Particularly since he then immediately uses the word 'body' in the unequivocal context of lovemaking:

> Had she treated me as a kind and devoted wife would have done, I should soon have longed to possess her, body and heart.[38]

Note that his physical desire is dependent upon Effie's kindness and devotion, that is to say on personality traits and not on any physical attributes.

To understand why in 1853-4 John should have suddenly

come up with a different reason for the non-consummation it is necessary to understand the legal grounds for an impotency annulment. Not only was mere non-consummation an insufficient ground for annulment, but a mutual agreement not to consummate the marriage, or even a decision by the man not to consummate was regarded as 'wilful non-consummation' and might fatally undermine the claim of incurable impotency. Effie, the complainant and only witness, had to be convinced that the honeymoon non-consummation agreement was merely an excuse not to consummate and that the 'real' reason was that there was something about her 'person' that completely checked John's passion and made him impotent with regard to her.

All this must be taken into account when judging the lurid speculations about the 'certain circumstances in her person.' The strange authorial fantasies that never having seen a naked woman he was repelled by her pubic hair, that she was menstruating, or that she suffered from body odour, have no basis in what John and Effie actually wrote. They also fly in the face of the clear evidence presented in earlier chapters that in the first period of the marriage they slept together naked in a shared bed and that far from being repelled by her physical body he actually found her attractive and looked forward both to taking her clothes off and holding her naked in his arms.

The responsibility for the whole of this field of conjecture lies, as does so much else, with the family polemic of Admiral James in *The Order of Release* who in 1946 claimed that the *sight* of Effie's *body* on their wedding night disgusted John.[38] However, that is not what John said according to Effie in her letter to her father, nor was it what John wrote in his statement to his solicitor. At the time of writing his book James was assumed to be in privileged possession of evidence for what he wrote and since

Whitehouse did not publish his *Vindication of Ruskin* until 1950, no-one could argue with him and the mud stuck. Lutyens, who had initially accepted the James version and suggested that John was repelled by Effie because he had never before seen a woman's pubic hair, was forced to recant in a subsequent work after it was discovered that John had in fact seen pornographic pictures whilst at Oxford.[40] All this conjecture is of course based on the assumption that John actually *saw* Effie naked on their wedding night. Scotland in April is not California. They had just driven 34 miles in a carriage – a very considerable distance. In those days before central heating and electric light, people dressed for bed and slept in the dark. John's first experience of Effie's body may well have been purely tactile.No-one involved in this academic wild goose chase ever seems to have paused to consider how few men in the history of the world must ever have been made impotent on discovering their lover's pubic hair! As for the menstruation, John had had an adopted older sister from the age of ten, and throughout the marriage seemed totally unconcerned about Effie's periodic 'rest days'. His old friend Henry Acland was a physician and Lee's Reader in Anatomy at Oxford. Both John and Acland were responsible for the introduction of the study of natural history to the Oxford curriculum for those taking holy orders. None of the speculations about the 'certain circumstances in her person' has any basis in the evidence; but the form of words John used did have a function in the legal context. It was vitally important to establish a credible absence of physical desire specifically towards Effie.

Annulment cases were unusual in that supplementary allegations were sometimes, albeit reluctantly, allowed. The only valid additional grounds would be if performance of the act was prevented either by a bodily deformity which physically prevented entry or a by a pre-nuptial mental disability. John could not allege the former and was advised against suggesting the latter. Any other complaints would have had no legal force. With John in Switzerland Effie could have alleged bodily deformity, but apart from this she could only allege madness dating from before the marriage. She would therefore have mentioned the sad case of John's grandfather as often as she could to anyone who would listen. Since madness was regarded as inheritable at that time this was potentially a very damaging allegation.[41]

John's statement of 27th April 1854 for his solicitor Mr. Rutter is often cited as his 'defence'. This is simply wrong. The statement was never intended to be entered into the court proceedings. Had the court seen it then the whole case might have been thrown into disarray, since keeping back a just defence, or permitting a false case to be substantiated were collusive actions.[42] In this private document for his solicitor John stated categorically that he was not impotent, a fact which he said could have been ascertained by medical examination: 'I can prove my virility at once, but I do not wish to receive back into my house this woman who has made such a charge against me.'[43] The medical examination would indeed have constituted a defence, but John had no intention whatsoever of defending this case. He had worked far too long and hard to bring it about. He therefore had ensured he would be out of the jurisdiction of the court at the relevant time. John could never subsequently be accused of having misled his solicitor. Since this document was never intended to be made public it is indeed a reputable source. No wonder Albert Gray went to such lengths to acquire and destroy it. As a lawyer he understood how important it was as evidence.

The doctors were appointed by the court to inspect the persons of both parties.[44] Lutyens tried to argue that had Ruskin taken the potency test it would not have materially affected the case. She is again quite simply wrong. The legal ground was not non-consummation but incurable impotency and any hint that he was not in fact impotent would have meant the case was thrown out, whether or not Effie was still a virgin. The April 1853 ruling had shown that it was not always possible for physicians to prove impotency but proving potency would have been relatively simple for John. Because John had moved beyond the reach of the court, examination was impossible, impotence was assumed, and, although any demonstration of potency subsequent to the case could technically be evidence of his having deceived the church, a second marriage was no longer voidable on that ground.[45]

There is also circumstantial evidence that Effie, who had shared a bed with John for several years, was well aware that he was not impotent. Before she fled Herne Hill she wrote 'I did not abuse him for not having married me as just at present he might worry me more than he does.'[46] This would seem to indicate that she was afraid that John might attempt a last minute consummation. Effie apparently stated in her deposition that she 'was living with him occupying the same bed for [near?] upon a year after I had [achieved?] 25 yrs of age but it was the same after that as before.'[47] Mary Lutyens explained Mrs. Gray's curiously jubilant reaction to the final break-up of her daughter's marriage as a release of tension after months of doubt and anxiety that John might make a last minute attempt to exercise his conjugal rights, which would have instantly destroyed their case.[48] So much for John's impotence! There are also hints that Effie was deliberately making herself unattractive for the same reason. She was well known as a stylish dresser and had a substantial wardrobe. The amounts she spent on clothes caused some consternation to John's parents, yet in the same letter she mentions dressing only to appear clean 'as I think a woman under no circumstances should be dirty, but all my things would require looking over and renewing.'[49] There is also the extraordinary incident she mentioned on April 3rd of John's mother treating John and Sophie to a graphic description of 'how she washed her Body in the morning.'[50] Perhaps Mrs. Ruskin had got wind of Effie's ploy and was dropping hints on personal hygiene! Effie's paranoia peaked on April 10th when her friend Jane Boswell was about to leave: 'It would be most improper for me to be here alone as I am quite afraid of John and you do not know what he might not do.'[51] If indeed she knew that John was not impotent, then this is more evidence that John set up the annulment, since her father would never have taken the risk of annulling the marriage if there was the slightest chance that John might contest it. On the same day Effie produced an extraordinarily naïve document for John to sign which would have alerted even the most obtuse husband to the fact that his wife was planning to leave him. It was written in legal language and concerned with gifts from Millais which she had received, was intending to keep and which might have been mentioned in subsequent legal proceedings. She refers to her husband John throughout the document as 'Mr. J. Ruskin'.[52] Of course he signed without demur. She even asked him for the letters he had written to her before the marriage.[53] She also settled all her household accounts, paid her debts to John and even took the keys and the domestic account books with her when she left!

In the event the proceedings were expedited by agreement between the two sets of lawyers. Instead of having to wait until November after the holidays, an extra court day was granted and the case was heard on 15th July 1854. Various reasons were suggested for this. Effie's proctor Mr. Glennie suggested to

George Gray that it was to avoid the 'Cruelty of your daughter being kept in suspense for some months for a sentence she must ultimately have obtained,'[54] and to Mr. Rutter that it was 'to put an end to the painful position in which Miss Gray is now placed.'[55] John's solicitor also pointed out pragmatically to Mr. Ruskin that if the proceedings were delayed Effie might run up debts for John.[56] However, the new date also meant that both John and Effie had a very lucky escape. On July 24th, just nine days after Effie's case was heard in St. Saviour's, a 'Bill to improve the taking of evidence in Ecclesiastical Courts' was passed and a short act came into force:

> That in any suit or proceeding depending in any Ecclesiastical Court in England and Wales, the Court (if it shall think fit) may summon before it and examine or cause to be examined witnesses by word of mouth, and either before or after examination by deposition or affidavit, and notes of such evidence shall be taken down in writing by the Judge or Registrar or by such other person or persons and in such manner as the Court shall direct.[57]

If the case had been held over until November and any problems had arisen in the meantime, Effie, John, and witnesses could have been instructed to give verbal evidence in open court with all the scandal that would entail. Otherwise, as an undefended case, there was only one piece of relevant evidence: that of Dr. Lee. Even so it would have been an anxious wait.

Effie's proctor Glennie had contacted Rutter to ask his agreement to the extra court day. The Ruskin side had however not yet been provided with a copy of the Libel and exhibits despite twice having asked for them. Now John was being asked to agree to the court sitting prematurely – still without his solicitor

ever having seen the charges against him! Rutter took the opportunity to bargain with the Gray team. The Libel and exhibits were
finally sent to Rutter who edited them on minor points.[58] When
Mr. Ruskin saw the depositions he noted that there had been
suppression of the truth. Rutter agreed and added that there was
also actual falsehood since, 'the father has sworn positively where
he could not swear properly otherwise than to his belief.'[59]
Because John did not of course intend to appear in the case, a
Proxy had to be signed in order for his proctor Frederick Pott to
appear at the final court day on his behalf. This was signed in
Lausanne on 5th July 1854 and witnessed by his valet Crawley, his
father and the courier who had brought it. According to Wedderburn's notes Pott was authorised 'to confess the marriage' but
otherwise 'to give a negative issue' and 'to abide for me until a
final decree given.'[60]

On July 15th John Haggard, doctor of Laws and Commissary
of the Bishop of Winchester declared Definitive Sentence or
final Decree in the Commissary Court of Surrey held in the Lady
Chapel of St. Saviour's.[61] Rutter described the extraordinary
scene to Mr. Ruskin:

> nothing could be more privately done – all the persons
> present were Dr. Haggard the Judge Dr. Bayford and Robt.
> Phillimore. her Counsel and a Clerk of the former. the Regis-
> trar and his Assistant, the Court [Keeper? Ledger?] Mr.
> Glennie her Proctor Mr Pott and myself none of those
> present Judge Counsel Proctor or others had on either Wig
> or Gown and when the business began it was more like
> a Consultation than otherwise in and about a sort of
> Communion Table covered with green baize in the Lady
> Chapel I suggested to Mr. Pott and he concurred that we

should employ no Counsel – the Counsel present did not open their mouths – the Judge, Registrar and proctors only spoke and in so low a tone that nothing could be heard a yard from the Judge – no Reporter was present – it has not been noticed in the Times nor do I believe it has been in any other paper.[62]

A handwritten copy of the entire text of the decree extracted from the registry of that court is in the Morgan Library.[63] The salient points of the verdict are that the court believed that Effie's proctor had sufficiently found and proved the intention deduced in the libel with exhibit on behalf of Euphemia Chalmers Gray and that nothing had been accepted, deduced, alleged, exhibited, propounded or proved by or on behalf of John Ruskin to defeat, prejudice or weaken such intention. The court therefore pronounced, deemed and declared that John Ruskin had contracted a pretended marriage with Euphemia Chalmers Gray but that the said marriage was had and celebrated whilst the said John Ruskin was incapable of consummating the same due to incurable impotency. No mention was made of any abnormality. The marriage was thus null and void from the beginning and the said Euphemia Chalmers Gray was free of all bond of marriage with the said John Ruskin.[64]

On 20th August Mr. Ruskin had received copies of the depositions on the Libel and Exhibit and the office copy Sentence, with the advice not to allow John to read them.[65] Rutter the solicitor commented that 'a more fortunate quiet and inexpensive Release from such a Woman – I never in the whole course of my legal experience ever heard or heard of.'[66]

CHAPTER XXIII

AFTERMATH

❧

Before John left for Switzerland on May 8th there had been a final
flurry of indignation in the Effie camp when John's letter about
Holman Hunt's painting *The Light of the World* appeared in *The
Times* of May 5th. John had merely defended in very innocuous
terms what Lady Eastlake inexplicably referred to as 'Hunt's
odious picture' against public incomprehension. Lady Eastlake,
whose hatred of the Pre-Raphaelites had hitherto bordered on the
pathological, nevertheless wrote to Effie: 'What man of the
slightest heart, losing even a bad wife, could have written such
a disgusting farrago not ten days after.'[1] Lady Eastlake's antipathy, only to be explained by personal bile, must have turned
to apoplexy when she read John's second letter in *The Times* of
25th May, this time defending Hunt's *The Awakening Conscience*
which Hunt intended to be seen as a pendant to *The Light of the
World*. In *The Light of the World* Christ knocks on the door of the
human soul; in *The Awakening Conscience* the sinful soul responds.
The subject matter of this modern moral subject was considered
indecorous enough even before it was connected to the Ruskin
case. A kept woman, en dishabille, without a wedding ring, and
in the company of her lover, experiences the descent of the
saving judgment in a St. John's Wood love-nest. In writing about
this tremendous painting John had however mistakenly identified the print on the wall as *The Woman taken in Adultery*, a
subject excruciatingly relevant to his present circumstances,
when in fact the print was almost certainly *Cross Purposes* by Frank

Stone, a contemporary artist being lampooned by Hunt. The second letter was written from Switzerland and John may well have misremembered some of the detail, but there is also a strong possibility that the mistake was deliberate. Millais thought Ruskin had definitely got the story wrong. Holman Hunt himself thought it was an excellent letter.

Whilst he was waiting at Dover for the boat to the Continent, John wrote a revealing letter to Pauline Trevelyan:

Dear lady Trevelyan

I received your little line with deep gratitude – fearing that even you might for a little while have been something altered to me by what has happened. I do not know what Effie has written of me. I am thankful that neither by word nor look of mine, at least voluntarily, any evil was ever spoken of her – She has now put it out of my power to shelter or save her from the consequences of the indulgence of her unchastised will. For me you need not be in pain. All the worst to me – has been long past. I have had no wife for several years – only a shadow – and a duty.

I will write you a long letter soon – at least to Sir Walter. There are only two people beside my parents whom I mean to acquaint with the whole circumstances of this matter – those are Dr Acland, and your husband. The world must talk as it will. I cannot give it the edifying spectacle of a husband and wife challenging each others truth. Happily I have long been accustomed to do without the world – and am as able to do so as I ever was. But I will not give my two best friends the pain of having to trust me in ignorance.

I am very very sorry you have been ill – but it was no wonder. I am sure you loved Effie – it must have been a cruel shock to you to receive her letter – whatever it said.

I hope to be in France to morrow – in Switzerland in a fortnight – my father & mother are with me – I will write again speedily. Be assured all is for the best: and take my earnest thanks for your steady trust in me at a time when I most need it. For indeed Effie has said such things to me that sometimes I could almost have begun to doubt of myself – and what then might my friends do. I hope Hunt's picture will make you quite well again. It might comfort any grief, I think – I mean the 'light of the World'. I cannot write more this evening – but I hope I have said enough to put you out of fear for me –

Ever affectionately Yours

J Ruskin

Best love to Sir Walter.[2]

Geneva, 5th June [1854]

Dear lady Trevelyan

Your kind letter – received last night – was one of great comfort to my father & mother as well as to myself. So far from drawing back from sympathy – and distrusting my friends – I never felt the need of them so much. I am only afraid of their distrusting me. For indeed that a young wife – in Effies position, should leave her husband in this desperate way, might well make the world inclined to believe that the husband had treated her most cruelly. It is impossible for people not to think so – who do not know me, and though I am as independent of the world as most people, I am not used to be looked upon as Effie will make some people look upon me – and am very grateful to my unshaken friends.

Indeed I am most ready to admit I may have been wrong

in several ways – about Effie – but assuredly, I did all I could
for her to the best of my judgement – except where I must
have sacrificed not only my own but my parents entire happiness if I had yielded to her. As for controlling her – I never
felt myself a judge of what was right for her to do or not to
do – and I had so much steady resistance to make to her in
one or two great things that I could not bear to thwart her
in less ones – I used to express my wishes to her very often
– that she would be less with certain people, and more with
others: but, except only with you and Miss Fortescue – it was
generally sure that Effie would take a dislike to the people
whom I liked best. I had no capacity for watching flirtations
– I might as well have set myself to learn a new science, as
to guess at peoples characters and meanings. I should never
have had any peace of mind, if I had been always thinking
how far Effie was going – with this person or that. I knew her
to be clever – and for a long time believed she loved me – I
thought her both too clever – & too affectionate – to pass the
bounds of what was either prudent for herself or kind to me.
I also was induced to believe that her influence over several
young men whom she got about her was very useful to them
– I used to hear her giving good advice like an old lady –
which I thought it possible – from the young lady – might
be listened to – In the last instance (which indeed at present
gives me the most anxiety of all things connected with this
calamity) I trusted as much to the sense – honour – & principle of my friend [Millais] as to Effie's. The honour &
principle failed not. But the sense did – to my infinite astonishment – (for I supposed he must have passed through all
kinds of temptations: – and fancied, besides, his ideal quite
of another kind). But he lost his sense – and this is the worst

of the whole matter at this moment. He never has seen Effie since November, but I don't know what thoughts may come into his head when he hears of this.

The whole matter is strange – complicated – full of difficulty and doubt. I cannot in Effie distinguish art from blindness when she said what was not true I never could tell how far she herself believed it. She never – during the whole course of our married life – once admitted having been wrong in anything. I believe she truly thinks herself conscientious – unselfish and upright – It was in this she was so like Miss Edgeworths lady Olivia. I do not know what she might have been – had she been married to a person more of her own disposition. She is such a mass of contradiction that I pass continually from pity to indignation – & back again – But there was so much that was base and false in her last conduct that I cannot trust to anything she ever said or did. How did she make you believe she was so fond of me? and how, by the bye – came you to think that I was not fond of her? I am not demonstrative in my affections – – but I loved her dearly. Much however of the show and gloss of the affection was taken off by hard wear. Effie never did anything for me. No gratitude was ever mingled with my love. She never praised me nor sympathized in my work – but always laughed at me – I can bear being laughed at as well as most people – but it is not the way in which a wife is likely to increase her husbands regard for her. Finally she drew from my affection all she could – and was perpetually demanding more – and trying to shake me in my settled purposes & principles. No wonder that a cord – so hardly strained, should seem to hang loose sometimes. But it was not broken – nay is not even yet so broken – in spite of much contempt being added to

477

anger – and wounded pride – all contending with the ancient affection – but that I earnestly desire her happiness and should rejoice to hear that she had found some 'way of peace.' That I ever should receive her again as my wife is impossible, because I could never be certain that her repentance was sincere – or if sincere, likely to be permanent, and I believe I have that to do in the world which must not be impeded by indulgences to one who – however much to be pitied now, would in all probability remain pitiable, whatever I sacrificed for her.

I am much grieved to hear of Sir Walter's illness – how kind of him to write to me when he was just recovering from his attack – and how like him to say– nothing about it.

I have been made excessively uncomfortable for the last fortnight by finding restorations going on at Chartres – Rouen – & Amiens – the three best Gothic cathedrals, I believe in the world – I was like to have got quite ill – and was obliged to come away. The sight of the Alps has put me to rights again. I never thought them so beautiful. I am drawing vignettes, which I am rather proud of and which I think you will like, and writing – at present only dismissing arrears of letters – but I shall soon get to my third volume. I will write again in a fortnight or so – to tell you more about our doings – but this letter must go to night – little as there is in it.

I am so glad you like your Hunt. But literally all that I said to him was that I didn't think he was painting up to his own mark, and that I saw a good deal in a withered leaf which he had missed out of it. He is so modest that he never knows whether what he does is his own doing, I believe. I think he has a vague idea that it comes on the paper by accident.

Best love to Sir Walter.

Ever affectionately Yours

J Ruskin

I forgot this was to be addressed to you at Henry Aclands
– my love to them both.[3]

The long letter to Acland, duly forwarded to Walter Trevelyan,
was probably the most complete written account of his marriage
that John ever gave to anyone. He took great pains to soften the
sharp edges.

Gisors, 16th May 1854

My dear Acland

You have probably expected my promised letter with
anxiety. I have been resting a little – after a period of much
trouble – and keeping my mind as far as possible on other
subjects – but I cannot delay longer telling you what you must
wish to know.

I married because I felt myself in need of a companion –
during a period when I was overworked & getting despondent — I found Effie's society [could] refresh me & make me
happy. I thought she loved me – and that I could make of her
all that I wanted a wife to be. I was very foolish in thinking
so – but I knew little of the world – and was unpracticed in
judging of the expression of faces, except on canvas. I was especially deceived in the characters of her parents, whom I
thought straightforward & plain kind of people, but who
were in reality mean, and designing. A fortnight before our
marriage – her father told me he was a ruined man, – having
lost all he possessed by railroads, and being some thousands
of pounds in debt. I never expected any fortune with Effie
– but I was surprised to hear this; and the fortnight spent in

Edinburgh and at her fathers house before marriage was one of much suffering and anxiety – for her especially – who saw her father in the greatest misery about his future prospects, and was about to leave him, with a man for whom as it has since appeared, she in reality had no affection. I did what I could to support them all; but Effie appeared sadly broken by this distress, and I had no thought in taking her away but of nursing her – I never attempted to make her my wife the first night – and afterwards we talked together – and agreed that we would not, for some time consummate marriage; as we both wanted to travel freely – and I particularly wanted my wife to be able to climb Alps with me, and had heard many fearful things of the consequences of bridal tours.

But, before three months had passed – I began to discover that I had been deceived in Effies character. I will not attempt to analyse it for you – it is not necessary for you to know it nor is it easy for me to distinguish between what was definitely wrong in her – and what was disease – for I cannot but attribute much of her conduct to literal nervous affection of the brain – brought on chiefly I believe by mortification at finding that she could not entirely bend me to all her purposes. From the first moment when we married, she never ceased to try to withdraw me from the influence of my father & mother – and to get me to live either in Scotland – or in Italy – or any where but near them – and being doubtless encouraged in this by her parents & finding herself totally incapable of accomplishing this set purpose, mortification gradually induced hatred of my parents, and, at last, of me, to an extent which finally became altogether ungovernable, and which is now leading her into I know not what extremes.

I do not think that many husbands could look back to their

married life with more security of having done all they could
for the sake of their wives than I. Most men, I suppose, find
their wives a comfort, – & a help. I found mine perpetually
in need of comfort – & in need of help, and as far as was in
my power, I gave her both. I found however that the more I
gave, the less I was thanked – and I would not allow the main
work of my life to be interfered with. I would not spend my
days in leaving cards, nor my nights in leaning against the walls
of drawing rooms. Effie found my society not enough for her
happiness – and was angry with me for not being entertaining, when I came to her to find rest. Gradually the worst part
of her character gained ground – more especially a self-will
quite as dominant as my own – and – I may say it certainly
without immodesty – less rational. I found with astonishment
& sorrow, that she could endure my anger without distress –
and from that moment gave up the hope of ever finding in
marriage the happiness I had hoped. Still until very lately I
thought something might happen to make her if not happy
in her lot – at least patient in it; I thought her too proud, and
too clever, to sacrifice her position in any way, and was content
to allow her to find what enjoyment she could with the
acquaintances or friends who were willing to take her society
without mine; or with those whom she chose to invite to the
house – so long as my own room was left quite to me. The
disappointment was no sudden shock – but a gradual diminu-
tion of affection on both sides – soon leaving on her's, none,
– on mine, nothing but a patient determination to fulfil my
duty to her & to be as kind to her as I could – We still, at intervals, had some happy times – and when Effie was with people
whom she liked, she made herself agreeable – so that the
world thought we got on pretty well. I was desirous it should

think so – if possible – and would have borne – and have borne much, in order to prevent Effie from exposing herself – but all in vain.

– The loss of my wife – for such – indeed it was, did not tell upon me as it would upon another man. I married because I wanted amusement, not support: I was prepared to protect & cherish my wife but I never leaned on her – the staff proved rottenness without staggering me – My real sorrows were of another kind. Turner's death – and the destruction of such & such buildings of the 13th century, were worse to me, a hundredfold, than any domestic calamity. I am afraid there is something wrong in this – but so it is; I felt, and feel – that I have work to do which cannot be much helped by any other hand, and which no domestic vexation ought to interrupt. – & I have always had the power of turning my mind to its main work & throwing off the grievousness of the hour. But one thing tormented me much: The more I saw of my wife – the more I dreaded the idea of having children by her, and yet I felt it my duty to consummate the marriage whenever she wished. I straitly charged her to tell me if she thought her health suffered by the way in which we lived: – but it fortunately happened that at first she dreaded rather than desired consummation – and at last, seemed to have no feeling for me but that of hatred. For my own part I had no difficulty in living as we did, for her person – so far from being attractive, like her face, was in several respects displeasing to me.

During the last year, however, the evil came to its head. Provoked beyond measure at finding that she could not change me – mortified at the passing away of her first beauty – and incapable of finding any enjoyment in the life she was compelled to lead, her passions seem entirely to have conquered her reason, and a fixed mania to have taken possession of her – a resolution to get quit of me some way or another – and to revenge herself upon me at the same time – for all the suffering which her own self-will had caused her. I hardly could have believed in the existence of ingratitude so absolute – so unconscious of itself – so utterly shameless and horrible. I said I would not analyse her character to you. But it is perhaps right that you should know the impression which it has left on my own mind – Have you ever read Miss Edgeworths Leonora? – Effie was, as far as I could judge – the 'Lady Olivia' of that novel – (with less refinement) – mingled with the Goneril in King Lear: – (always excepting actual criminality – of which I do not in the least suspect her).[4] False herself – she could not in the least understand my character, and mistook my generosity for simplicity, and my frankness for cunning. Casting about for some means of obtaining her liberty, she seems to have fancied that my offers to consummate marriage were mere hypocrisies – and that I was incapable of fulfilling the duties of a husband. She never informed me of this suspicion – but having arranged with me to pass this summer in Scotland with her father & mother, told me the evening before she left that 'she had laid her plans, and was too clever to be beaten by me.' – I never condescended to enquire into her plans; but saw her to the railroad the next morning. That afternoon, I received a citation to the ecclesiastical court in her name, on a charge of impotence. – and discovered that her father & mother had been in London for some time, arranging the plan with her. She sent back her marriage ring to my mother the same afternoon.

I at first intended simply to state these facts in court; but I have on reflection come to a different conclusion – I have given you my entire confidence – you are at a liberty to tell Mrs Acland if you wish, But no one else – excepting Sir Walter Trevelyan – from whom also I have no secrets. But as respects the courts – I mean to make no answer and see what they can do. If Effie can escape with some fragment of honour – let her; – so that I am not forced to speak, I will not expose her; But I do not know what the issue may be. The one thing which is of course decided is that I receive her no more. I believe she is informing every one who will believe her that I am a villain – so at least I hear from Scotch friends. Let her do her worst. I shall go on with my work – whether people speak ill or well of me – and time will do the rest.

I am writing in the Hotel d'Angleterre at Rouen. Tomorrow I hope to be at work at – ½-past six, drawing the cathedral south transept. I am going on to Switzerland; I hope to be in England early in the autumn. Meantime – when you have time to send me a line, I shall be grateful.

Her father – as you may perhaps know – is a lawyer – and she has probably given him such accounts of herself and of me as may have led him to hope to get large damages – which would be very useful to him. I am sorry to have even to occupy your thoughts with these mean and miserable things – but whatever pain it may give you to hear them – do not vex yourself about me. It is well for me to have seen this side of human nature. It has not made me less trustful of other kinds of human nature – nor I hope, has it lowered my own habits of feeling. On the contrary, I see now that many things which I was disposed before to look upon as innocent are in reality dangerous or criminal, and I hope I have gained from the last six years of my life, knowledge which will be useful for me till its close.

One thing you ought to know – I need not caution you respecting the necessity of silence respecting it – but I think half confidences are no confidences. I have, myself, no doubt that Effies sudden increase of impatience and anger – and the whole of her present wild proceeding is in consequence of her having conceived a passion for a person whom, if she could obtain a divorce from me, she thinks she might marry. It is this which has led her to run all risks, and encounter all opprobrium. If you write to me, direct to 7 Billiter St. it will be forwarded.

My sincerest regards to Mrs Acland.

Believe me always affectionately yours,

J Ruskin

[On the envelope] I have omitted to say that Effie had no excuse, such as some daughters in law might have had – in the conduct of my parents to her. They exercised the most admirable kindness & forbearance towards her throughout aiming only at making her happy & good – if possible, and restraining her in nothing that it was in their power to grant her. I am going to write to Sir Walter Trevelyan but I want to give him just the information I have given you – It would save me the trouble & pain of writing another letter like this to him if you would send this to him at Wallington, Morpeth, for him to read.[5]

Whenever John was emotionally upset he had a resurgence of his consumption. This had happened when he had lost Adèle Domecq, when he had been forbidden to propose to Effie, at his wedding and at Salisbury. It was also to happen later when he lost Rose La Touche. However neither the service of the writ nor the pronouncement of the annulment decree caused him to become ill. The obvious conclusion to be drawn from this is that it was not an unpleasant surprise nor did it disturb him emotionally in the way that those other traumatic events had done. All the letters he wrote at the time show clearly that the annulment was not the unexpected catastrophe for him that the Grays made it out to be. From Chartres on the 27th May John had also written to his friend Mr. C. H. Woodd:

> You need not be so grieved for me, for I have never known what it was to have the love of a wife – my sorrow and disappointment were gradual and therefore subdued, and all their bitterness is long passed. It came in the first six months after marriage – since that time I have been content to bear the punishment of folly in the choice of a companion, to do my duty as if she had been all to me that she ought to have been, and to seek for comfort in my various occupations when it was refused to me by my wife – The catastrophe was not to be averted by either patience or indulgence. The more I endured and the more I permitted, the less I seemed to be loved, in truth I never had been and all my loss is of what I once had hoped, not of what I ever possessed. One result of my married life is alone worth much suffering. It has taught me to know the worth of true affection and true friendship.[6]

His father was extremely shocked and angry about the annulment, but John was not. When Effie was under severe stress, her hair began to fall out, as it did now. That John did not tell even his very closest friends that he had had anything more than a passive rôle in the annulment proceedings is not surprising. To have done so would have been an admission of collusion and have risked reversing the decision of the court. This was probably also why he had sworn a pact of silence with George Gray.

John's father was not quite so restrained in his explanations to friends.

> My Son caught by a pretty face married contrary to his parents Judgement but not to their commands and Miss G. concealed the embarrassed circumstances of her Father – courted my Son and was united in her Father's house at Perth, none of his own Friends attending the Ceremony – he found at once that the woman had no Love for him and he lived with her accordingly – She soon filled his house with men of her own finding till he could not get a single hour for studying without stealing away to his Father's house [...] she wasted my property in the most ruthless manner making away with £15000 in six years [...] she told the World that those men whom she had forced on my Son destroying his domestic quiet, were brought by him and left with her for improper ends, the basest and most preposterous falsehood ever invented by the most abandoned of women.[7]

The annulment should have been a completely private affair. With Effie in Perth, Millais in Glenfinlas and John abroad, Society would have had nothing on which to exercise its curiosity. As Albert Gray pointed out, cases in the ecclesiastical courts were not reported in *The Times* at all.[8] In John and Effie's case the public were made so aware of the alleged nature of the marriage that even the absence of press reporting became a subject of gossip. To understand why the affair blew up into the full blown scandal which John had tried so hard to avoid and why it was so damaging to him, it is necessary to look into the shadowy background picture against which John was posed.

By the time of the annulment John had already begun to make powerful enemies. His penchant for pursuing the truth wherever it led him had started establishment alarm bells ringing in many quarters. He was regarded as especially dangerous because his personal wealth allowed him to bypass the book industry censorship process. Strong measures were deemed necessary when his fame and influence grew to the extent that, despite severe periodical criticism, his enormous power over public opinion remained unaffected and, which was more important, uncontrolled. Unfortunately for John his first clash with the business of bookselling had also involved one of its most important and powerful clans. It was doubly unfortunate that the clash was not merely professional but also had a personal dimension. When *Modern Painters I* was ready, John's father had approached the publisher John Murray II who rejected the book without looking at it, advising John that 'the public cared little about Turner' and anxious to curry favour with the Prince Albert faction advised him to write on the Nazarenes (a modern German school) instead. Mr. Ruskin took the book to Smith, Elder and Co. The rest, as they say, is history. Except that in March 1846 Murray's *Quarterly Review* which had ignored John's book, published a review commissioned by Murray III, of a German art exhibition called 'Modern German Paintings' which championed a rival area of modern art clearly ignored by John's book, but essential to those wishing to ingratiate themselves with the Prince Albert faction.[9] The author of this review was a young woman named Elizabeth Rigby, who had been a creature of the John Murray media empire since 1841. After moving to Edinburgh in 1842, she had on her own admission rather close relations with John Lockhart, the editor of the *Quarterly Review,* who had recently lost his wife. For a while it seemed that they might marry. By 1844 she was sufficiently intimate with the Murray family to stay for three months with the recently widowed Mrs. Murray II and her son John Murray III in London.[10] Elizabeth was not only a great friend of the Murrays but connected to them by marriage. Her youngest sister Mathilda married Mrs. Murray's brother, James Smith.[11] She was thus positioned right at the heart of what John called the 'old Scott and John Murray circle'.[12]

This was the circle that John had entered in 1846 when his celebrity as the author of *Modern Painters II* earned him an invitation to the house of Lady Davy in Park Lane. For John it would have been enough that 'the literary and scientific men who had once known Abbotsford' gathered there.[13] Despite having had his first book rejected and ignored by John Murray, the Ruskins seem to have had cordial relations with the Murrays until at least 1852. Besides the two *Quarterly* articles, John wrote corrections for the 'Handbook' travel guides published by Murray. Mr. Ruskin asked John Murray for introductions for John on the Continent and they were duly given. John was fêted by Lady Davy and, although his father politely declined invitations to Albemarle Street, Murray sent hard-to-find books to John. Whether the romantic entanglement with Charlotte Lockhart caused any lasting resentment is not clear. But with hindsight, John's behaviour with Effie at the French theatre where Charlotte's father was in the audience may well have been seen as being in bad taste in the way that Ruskin senior feared.[14] The *Quarterly* review that John wrote for her father occasioned more conflict. Lockhart censored John's review of Lindsay's *Sketches of the History of Christian Art* so severely that it made John permanently distrustful of both bookselling and reviewing.[15]

Lockhart was not a man to turn the other cheek. He had begun life as a lawyer but his inaptitude for public speaking led to him becoming a contributor to *Blackwood's Magazine*, notorious for literary reviews of such personal venom that they had violent consequences. In 1821 Lockhart had responded to criticism of *Blackwood's* by duelling with the editor of the *London Magazine*. The *London* editor was shot dead by Lockhart's second after he had declined Lockhart's challenge. Recognising this exceptional talent, John Murray recruited Lockhart as editor of the *Quarterly*, a Tory mouthpiece, where he kept a much lower personal profile. There was little in his family life to mellow him. He lost his first son in 1831, his wife in 1837, a profligate son in 1852 after a public humiliation, and he himself had to retire in 1853 for his health. He died in 1854 and his beloved Charlotte, who had married in 1847, only survived him by four years, dying in childbirth after already losing two children in infancy.

Thus John entered into his fateful marriage to Effie having had two unpleasant experiences with the Murray circle and having somehow 'annoyed' the beloved daughter of the irascible editor of the *Quarterly Review*. Now in his rôle as artistic conscience of the nation, John's unrestrained opinions led him into conflict with the art establishment and with one of its rising stars. Charles Lock Eastlake had begun his career as a humble RA of limited talent. He then became secretary of the Fine Arts Commission, and bolstered by the patronage of Prince Albert, was appointed Keeper of the National Gallery before being elected President of the Royal Academy and obtaining a knighthood in 1850. It had however not been plain sailing. In 1847 he had almost had to resign in disgrace over his disastrous picture cleaning policy at the National Gallery. John had intervened in the furore by writing to *The Times* in January 1847. His letter was judicious and restrained but linked Eastlake with the permanent damage done to a Rubens. Eastlake may have been upset, but not enough to stop him recommending John as a reviewer for his new book in June that year.[16] He was however his third choice. In 1851 John was fiercely critical of Eastlake's acquisition policy for the Gallery. This was too much for a man of limited forgiveness. Professional rivalry turned to personal animosity despite John's positive *Quarterly* review of Eastlake's book in 1848.[17] George Paston wrote that: 'There was no love lost between the Eastlakes and the Ruskins, who represented different schools of artistic criticism.'[18] As President of the Royal Academy, Eastlake headed a closed guild that resented any criticism of its members. Before long John's opinion was so respected that an adverse remark by him could render a painter unsaleable. There is ample evidence that artists saw his criticisms as personal attacks.[19] Unfortunately for John, in 1849, Eastlake, a regular visitor at the Murray's, married none other than Elizabeth Rigby. They had first met in Edinburgh in 1843 when Eastlake was a prospective John Murray author, and they had maintained the contact afterwards at Lady Davy's in London. 'Lofty Lucy', as Elizabeth was known,[20] was to be as fiercely loyal to her diminutive husband as she was to Murrays II and III. An intimately connected knot of opposition to John's influence was now in place.

The trigger for the assault on John's reputation was the scandal in Venice of 1852. It was a scandal of both the printed word and Society gossip. Lady Eastlake, as she now was, was adept at both. Having made a special detour from Germany to Venice that year, and being a fluent German speaker, she would have discovered that there was more to the story than a mere jewel robbery. Once back in England she inveigled herself into Effie's intimate acquaintance, even dining at Denmark Hill and reporting back to Murray III. She played an active rôle in the ensuing scandal which John only just managed to contain. The Eastlakes had been the first to snub John by refusing him an invitation to the Royal Academy. As we have seen from Effie's letter of 7th March 1854,[21] Lady Eastlake, herself childless[22] and twenty years older than Effie, had found out that the Ruskin marriage was in trouble and taken an active rôle in the assault on John's reputation and character which accompanied the annulment. George Gray had advised silence. Even Albert Gray admitted that in those days people did not talk about such annulments: 'public sentiment did not require verbatim reports of cases such as this.'[23] As a result of Lady Eastlake's deliberate propaganda campaign the annulment became public and the whole John Murray clique would side with Effie at the time of the annulment. There can be no doubt where the gossip was coming from. John Lockhart wrote to his daughter in April 1854:

> I am not surprised but sorry to hear whispers of a separation between Effie Ruskin & her virtuoso whose neglects have at last exhausted her patience: But I shall have particulars whenever I meet the Eastlakes & till then mum.[24]

Lady Eastlake was anxious to spread the annulment story as widely as possible:

> Sir Chas. [Eastlake] will probably see Mr. Murray in my absence & make him acquainted with the subject [...] for his shop is the great rendezvous of report and rumours and I would like them to find him prepared with the truth.[25]

She also told Lady Davy to spread the information to 'Lady Westminster and her niece', only begging 'her not to let anyone think that they were admitted to this knowledge for the sake of gossip but for the sacred privilege of assisting a much injured and

Elizabeth Rigby
(Lady Eastlake)
*by David Hill and
Robert Adamson,*
c. 1845

long suffering fellow creature.'[26] She followed this with a long list
of other contacts including Boxall, the Milmans, Lockhart and
Murray. The Cheneys were also primed and waiting. The
campaign continued unabated until the 27th when she told
Effie's mother 'I continue to tell the tale whenever and wherever
I think the truth can do good.'[27] On the same day she wrote pages
to Effie outlining the virulent campaign of gossip she was
conducting: she had sent a letter to Lockhart referring him for
particulars to John Murray, Lady Lewis was 'greedy for information, thinks of nothing else,' and yet another almanac of
gossip followed the next day. Millais wrote that 'Lady Eastlake
thinks much worse of him [Ruskin] than any other person I have
met.'[28]

If Lady Eastlake's pathological hatred of John was primarily a personal vendetta, it seems certain that there was also a political background to the opposition campaign. Elizabeth Rigby's political leanings were well known. As the anonymous author of a notorious *Quarterly* review of Thackeray's *Vanity Fair* and Charlotte Brontë's *Jane Eyre* she had expressed unabashed admiration for the diabolical Becky Sharp but only vitriolic criticism of the meek Jane Eyre as 'anti-Christian' and fostering rebellion and Chartism. [29] As Lady Eastlake she seems to have viewed the destruction of John's reputation as being more important than the success of Britain's imperial military strategy; at the same time as she was conducting her hate campaign against John she told Effie:

> Still, as I had not received the agreed note from your Father
> I was glad to rest from any mention of it on the Fast day when
> you divided my prayers much more than half with our fleets
> and armies. [30]

There is also Millais' curious reply to Mrs. Gray about John on 17th January 1854: 'in his sitting he has scarcely alluded to Socialism.' It would be interesting to know the back story to that little gem. Who was accusing John of political radicalism? It must not be forgotten that John had just begun to write on politics and economics. In his final letter to Everett, John suggested that Everett might have been 'concerned in machinations which have for a long time been entered into against my character and fortune.' [31] Even the false rumours that John was planning to go over to Rome would have had a political dimension: anti-Catholicism was as much a political as a religious standpoint. [32] In spreading Brown's joke about John becoming 'another Pope Joan' was Lady Eastlake pandering to those reactionaries who regarded allegiance to Rome as a permanent threat to the state?

Not all the connections in this prospective vendetta were family or business. Rawdon Brown, Effie's duplicitous confidante in Venice and the recipient of one of the only two surviving letters of hers from the Glenfinlas holiday, had on a number of occasions urged Effie to claim damages from the Ruskins. When it became clear that she was not entitled to any, he even suggested she should employ a form of blackmail while old Mr. Ruskin was still in a state of shock.[33] Brown had been at Charterhouse with Murray III.[34] Indeed it was Murray III who introduced him to John. Despite all the help and encouragement John had given him with his book, Brown too would stab John in the back. He was in London at the time of the legal case, as indeed was Edward Cheney, another Charterhouse boy. Even Foster, the sinister English mercenary with the Austrian army, was in town.[35] It would seem that had the annulment turned into any kind of contest, the witnesses for the prosecution were all mysteriously at hand.

The antipathy did not end with the decree of annulment. In June 1854 Lady Eastlake and her husband entertained a large party to dinner at Fitzroy Square which included the Bishop of Edinburgh and John Lockhart. Lockhart had retired the year before and was not a well man but 'growled out his indignation' at John for innocently answering a letter sent to him by Sir Charles. The conversation, initiated by Lockhart and Lady Eastlake, turned to John's books. All present expressed 'their long detestation of the writings' and 'said they would all cut him – Lady E. is gay and happy'.[36] By this time *Blackwood's Magazine* had already launched an attack on John which even Millais thought 'very impudent and vulgar.'[37] That social relations between John and Murray III were seriously broken is evidenced by Murray's hypocritical attempt at reconciliation at Christmas 1855. John's reply speaks for itself:

My dear Murray,

So you want to make it up with me on Christmas day?
Well. I wish you a happy Christmas – no man a sad one, and
– if you are penitent. I am very truly yours

J Ruskin[38]

Nor was this all, for in 1856 when John brought out *Modern Painters III* and *IV* and *Academy Notes*, Lady and Sir Charles Eastlake were involved in a John Murray combined critical assault on his work, ideas and morals. Eastlake's biographer Robertson wrote that on the 30th January John Murray had to dinner both Henry Reeve, new editor of the *Edinburgh Review* and Whitwell Elwin,[39] new editor of the *Quarterly Review*. Lady Eastlake (a second cousin of Reeve's mother) was there on both occasions. Robertson at least is convinced that Ruskin's admirers might well suspect some sort of cabal had taken place.[40] A visitor to John Murray's in April was told of the two articles and commented: 'It is a pity that persons competent to the task have not before now interfered to prevent so seductive a writer from obtaining any authority in matters of art.'[41] This despite the fact that *Blackwood's Magazine*, John's longstanding enemy, had already launched an attack on John in the previous December. The Murrays often used *Blackwood's* contributors and the Murray dynasty had at one time or another interests in all these magazines. Besides owning the *Quarterly*, Murray II had had a half share in *Blackwood's* till 1819, and Lockhart who had been its editor before coming to the *Quarterly*, continued to supply articles afterwards. Murray II published the London issue of the *Edinburgh* from 1807. All three publications involved seem to have co-operated regularly in various ventures. Both these new articles, appearing in March 1856, viciously attacked John's work. The most vituperative of the two was by Lady Eastlake herself and appeared anonymously in the *Quarterly*. Beside the extremely dubious theoretical criticism there was a barely veiled personal attack which questioned both John's morals and his potency:

> Mr. Ruskin's intellectual powers are of the most brilliant description; but there is, we deliberately aver, not one single great moral quality in their application [...] Mr. Ruskin's writings have all the qualities of premature old age – its coldness, callousness, and contraction.[42]

There was a general feeling at the time that the article had gone too far. Lady Eastlake, who always reviewed anonymously, may even have tried to deny her authorship through Ralph Wornum, keeper of the National Gallery, who in 1857 was working with John on the Turner Bequest. He is on record as trying to convince John that she had not been the author.[43] Lady Eastlake was to remain one of John's most implacable enemies. The *Quarterly* consistently opposed John's views on art, and Lady Eastlake was an active agent.[44] Her letter to Murray of March 1862 is revealing in this respect:

> There is a gentleman who writes for Blackwood + who attracted some for his review of Harford's 'Michael Angelo' Mr. J Brassington Atkinson Rosehill Cotham Park Bristol also your papa in Blackwood on the Nat: Gallery. He has ability. The only question is whether he knows what an artist wd. say + think on Turner. He was Ruskin bitten at one time + wd. have to be cautioned on that point.[45]

She even went so far as to accompany Effie, pregnant with her fifth child, to one of John's lectures in 1861. The stunt miscarried, as did Effie. Carlyle blamed 'that termagant of a woman called Lady Eastlake' but thought that the chaotic talk which John gave after he put aside his notes was better than all the neat ones he had heard there.[46]

The establishment opposition to John's ideas redoubled after the publication of his architectural books. He had not only alienated bigots at both ends of the Christian spectrum, he had also offended certain narrow guilds and fraternities, whose members included architects and painters, by making the mysteries of their craft a subject of public interest. As if this was not enough, there was at the very heart of *The Stones of Venice II* a telling demolition of one of the major pillars of Adam Smith's *Wealth of Nations*, the Bible of entrepreneurial capitalism. John's father was justifiably alarmed by this trespassing into the realm of politics and economics, particularly when John later became unjustly linked in the public mind with socialist and even communist ideas. There is every reason to think that John's writing on political economy made him an establishment target. Were his letters from Venice intercepted? After the unrest of 1848, European governments were rabidly paranoid about radical movements of all kinds. How else could one explain Elizabeth Rigby's condemnation of *Jane Eyre* because it questioned God's appointment of the rich and the poor and was therefore an incitement to Chartism?[47] When John had started to write about the relation of art to political economy in 1852 he was putting himself in opposition to the dominant ideology of the day. Not many authors have done that with impunity. One thing is certain: if the establishment thought that the assault on his reputation would stifle his ideas of social justice, they were sadly mistaken. Almost as soon as he returned from Switzerland, he began his philanthropic work with the Working Men's

College, using the income from Effie's marriage settlement to finance the enterprise.[48]

CHAPTER XXIV

ROSE LA TOUCHE

In January 1858 John met Maria La Touche's daughter Rose for the first time, when he was invited to their Mayfair home.[1] Maria was the Evangelical daughter of the widowed and re-married Countess of Desart (in Co. Kilkenny) and her half-brother had been at Christ Church with John. She had married an Irish banker who had at first led a wild hunting and drinking existence but then had suddenly become a Baptist convert. After producing a couple of minor novels Maria fled her husband's provincial philistinism to seek out the culture of London. She became one of John's most ardent supporters and had persuaded him to give drawing lessons to her daughters. The course of John's acquaintance with Rose La Touche was therefore very similar to that with both Charlotte and Effie, both of whom he knew as children before falling for them as young women. John met Rose when she was ten years old and he was thirty-eight. Over the next three years John became extremely fond of the pious child and she of him. John seems to have made a pet of her in the same way as his auntie Bridget had of him. Rosie even wrote letters to him when he was away. There is good reason to suspect that her mother Maria was lonely and believed Ruskin was interested in her as a kindred spirit. In August 1861 John visited their home at Harristown and for the first time confessed his lack of religious orthodoxy to a shocked Maria. Soon after he left, Rose developed the first symptoms of a mysterious illness which would plague her intermittently throughout her short life. Between 1862 and

1865 there was no direct contact between John and the La Touches, who had decided they did not approve of the relationship. They had a more conventional suitor in mind for their daughter who was already showing signs of a sort of wayward wilfulness. John and Rose were however still able to communicate through a number of go-betweens. In 1863 Mrs. La Touche referred to Rosie's 'mysterious brain attacks': 'At present she cannot bear a gleam of light or a whisper, nor can she admit any of us except one, her brain is so terribly sensitive that all impressions give pain.' Mrs. La Touche thought Rosie's condition was possibly self-inflicted or psychosomatic, and wrote 'I am afraid she has *thought* herself into this illness.'[2] The fact that Rose seemed able to predict what would happen to her throughout the coming day and indeed weeks ahead would tend to confirm this diagnosis. However, Rose exhibited classic symptoms of brain damage by reverting to infancy and taking a fortnight to recover something of her adult mind. Even then she could not read or think properly. In the same year John, who hadn't seen her for over twelve months, mentioned 'over-excitement of the brain, causing occasional loss of consciousness, and now she seems only half herself, as if partly dreaming.'[3]

When John next saw Rose she was eighteen years old and seemed to have made a complete recovery. The La Touches came to London in December 1865 and on the strength of the renewed relationship he proposed marriage in January 1866. There was even a hint of knight errantry in the proposal. John, who had described Rose as going half-mad with religion and nearly dying, saw himself as rescuing her from the toils of her father's narrow Evangelical morality. Mr. La Touche was horrified both by John's religious apostasy and his age and John was convinced that Mrs. La Touche was blinded by jealousy when she realised that her daughter had supplanted her in John's affections.[4] It would also seem to have been the case that Rose never received any real emotional warmth and sympathy from her parents and was unhappy living with them in Ireland.[5] In the meantime the devoutly pious Rose had been told about John's unorthodox religious views prompting her to ask him if he was really a pagan. Although John's 'paganism' presented a serious obstacle for Rose it did not cause her to break with him entirely. The La Touche parents, shocked both by John's proposal and the fact that Rose seemed not disinclined to accept him, insisted she ask him to wait three years till she was of age. John was convinced that he could cure Rosie and make her happy; Rosie was sure she could cure John of his unbelief.

In May 1868, nine months before she became twenty one, Rosie wrote a letter to John which prompted him to assume that he had won her heart and she would accept his proposal. A few days later another note arrived telling him that her parents had forbidden her to write to him. It is almost certain that the La Touches' prime motive in opposing the marriage was to avoid scandal since Mrs. La Touche then contacted Effie and John Everett Millais, who had married in 1855.[6] This first letter and Effie's reply of the 19th May 1868 have not surfaced. Effie may have already been alerted to John's marriage proposal by the perfidious Rawdon Brown before Mrs. La Touche contacted her. She certainly would have seen the correspondence as a means of stopping the marriage ever taking place. Effie's letter to Mrs. La Touche did not provide much personal detail about her marriage to John but it did contain a threat. 'If the Banns of Marriage are proclaimed I shall feel obliged in justice to my own character to give it (the Decree) publicity.'[7] The contents of this letter may have caused the La Touches to consult a solicitor, a copy of whose legal opinion was included in

a letter to Mrs. Cowper Temple, John's go-between. The legal opinion, if such it was, asserted in the most lurid and misleading terms
that in the case of John and Effie's annulled marriage, any second
marriage by John would be a nullity unless the second wife had
children in which case he would be a bigamist and the marriage
void for that reason. In order to escape such a charge the second
wife would have to admit to adultery by claiming that her children were not her husband's. For these reasons, in the opinion of
the 'solicitor', no clergyman who knew about the annulment
would perform the marriage although he could not be sanc-
tioned for performing the ceremony.[8]

How Mrs. La Touche received her legal opinion is a mystery
since it was in fact both out of date and wrongly interpreted.[9] As
the law then stood John's first marriage had been ruled never to
have existed, his second marriage would therefore have been as
entirely legal as Effie's. Even if John really had been incurably
impotent his second marriage would not have been a nullity from
the outset. It would have been voidable on that ground but only
by Rose. Had she done so it would not have affected Effie's
second marriage in any way whatsoever. In fact it would have
vindicated her. Even if John was indeed not impotent, and Rose
had children, then those children would also be legitimate.
Because the first marriage had been declared a nullity and the
second marriage was entirely legal, there was absolutely no way
John could ever have been the subject of an action for bigamy.
Indeed had such an action been possible it would have been immediately followed by a similar action against Effie because it
depended entirely upon re-asserting the validity of the first
marriage! Publishing the Annulment Decree when the Banns
were proclaimed would not therefore have constituted any legal
grounds for a priest to refuse to perform the ceremony, it might

however have caused something of a scandal from which neither the La Touches nor the Millais family would have emerged unscathed.

For her part Mrs. La Touche was very clear that it was not John's alleged impotence but his assertion of potency that was the main obstacle to the marriage. She told Mrs. Cowper Temple:

> You mistake me in thinking I have only physical infirmity to lay to Mr. R's charge – the truth is far otherwise. I am sure that he thought himself cured – but that makes no difference – you see by the legal opinion I sent you that under no circumstances could a second marriage of his be legal – or any children he may have legitimate.[10]

Two years after the first exchange of letters between the Millais and the La Touches, John met Rose by chance in London. They kept their reconciliation secret but her parents found out and Mrs. La Touche contacted the Millais' again. For his part Millais, who seems to have initially tried to shield Effie from the La Touches, had only the haziest grasp of the legal case and seemed entirely taken in by all this legal flummery. He was uncertain of the year of the annulment, got the number of doctors wrong and gave the wrong name for Effie's proctor. After the La Touches had asked that the 'fiercest light' be thrown on John's past history he declined such an 'indelicate' enquiry on his wife's behalf by asserting that, 'the facts are known to the world solemnly sworn to us in God's House.' Of course Millais had not been there in St. Saviour's, Southwark and so nothing had been sworn to him. He must have been well aware that the only people who swore were Effie, her father and the doctors, and that the doctors only swore to the fact that Effie was a virgin, a fact never disputed by John. Only Effie could have had any knowledge of John's intimate physiognomy but had never had to swear to its efficacy. She had only had to swear that John had not consummated the marriage. Millais also went along with the strange and erroneous La Touche belief that John would have to set aside the decree in order to contract a second marriage when in fact the marriage would only be possible if the decree held. Millais even asked if John would now submit to a medical examination, although that would not have solved anything and might even have called Millais' own marriage into question![11]

This second flurry of correspondence between the La Touches and the Millais' contained even more false legal advice. This time it was 'an eminent lawyer' advising Mrs. La Touche that John would have to prove that he was not impotent in order to 'set aside the decree and contract a legal marriage.' This is palpably absurd. If John 'set aside the decree' (which was impossible since not only had the appeal term expired but the court itself had been done away with) his previous marriage would be re-instated and he would find himself married, not to Rose, but to Effie whose marriage to Millais would then be bigamous!

In her reply to Mrs. La Touche Effie accused John of behaving insanely towards her in a wicked, impure, discreditable, dishonourable, inhuman, peculiar and unnatural manner, but without specifying any incident or action. She even claimed that he afterwards excused himself from consummating the marriage 'by saying that I had an internal disease.'[12] She denied that the marriage had been in any way arranged or that John had connived at her leaving him and then, to prove her point, naïvely referred to the marriage as a family affair, as she had done ever since the wedding, by asserting that 'it was a great shock to them all.'[13] Her denying that John connived at her separation from him indicated that he had told Mrs. La Touche that this had indeed been the case.

The Gray family, August 1855. Standing back row, left to right: George jnr., Jeannie the family nurse holding baby Everett, Effie's father, Sophie, Millais; front row: John, Albert, Effie's mother, Alice, Melville, Effie

By this time John had begun to defend himself against Effie's accusations. The La Touches claimed that he had told them, using Mrs. Cowper Temple as an intermediary, that his earlier marriage had been arranged without any profession or idea of love; that he had nevertheless tried to make Effie happy but had refrained from consummation on account of there being no love on either side. He was not impotent and had never breathed a word to that effect. Indeed, all the accusations came from Effie's side. For his part, realising that he and Effie were incompatible, that she did not love him and desired to be rid of him, he had offered no resistance in the court case, had not read the depositions, made no statements to the court and allowed her to secure her freedom and happiness at the cost of his own reputation.

In 1871 John, having been wrongly informed by Mr. La Touche that he could not contract a legal second marriage, set about the task of finding out for himself whether the annulment was in any way unsafe. John instructed his cousin W. G. Richardson, who had been a lawyer, 'to obtain whatever interpretation of the decree may be final from the proper sources.'[14] Richardson instructed J. P. Martineau to seek out and copy the court papers. Both Richardson and Martineau agreed that the decree was entirely valid, but a further opinion was sought from legal counsel. Dr. T. H. Tristram concurred with them. The decree was the sentence of a competent court and although there had been a right of appeal to the Court of Arches, that right had expired one year later after which the decree, however it had been arrived at, became binding and unquestionable. Neither John nor Effie could impeach the decree, nor could any other person unless they could provide conclusive evidence of collusion by both parties. Richardson noted significantly that such evidence could only be given by John.[15] There was a very remote possibility that a third party could still attempt to impeach the decree but they would have to prove that they had been pecuniarily damaged by the annulment and again that there was collusion by both John and Effie. Since the evidence of collusion could still only have been provided by John it was almost inconceivable that a third party could succeed in bringing such an action. The conclusion was that for all practical purposes John was free to marry again.

It is clear from his letter of 18th June 1871 that John had already supplied William Cowper Temple with all the legal documents in his possession, including an account of the whole affair written by his father, lawyers' letters which proved that he had never seen the Gray depositions, a copy of the judgement, and, most interestingly of all, a physician's letter from John Simon:

My dearest William, Yesterday evening I made search, at once, and found the documents which I send you herewith; you may perhaps like to see my Father's account of the matter; and if you will glance at the passages underlined now, by me, in the lawyers letters, they will also help you form at least your own conclusions more pleasantly. You will see that the lawyers advised me not to look at the depositions, and I did not – and have no copy of the judgement but of course that is easily obtained. I have also written to John Simon today, to come and determine my bodily health. I have just spoken to my mother about it – in respect of mere age and feebleness – she says my blood is so pure that I should have perfectly healthy children – having never touched a woman, and being of pure descent, (especially my mother's constitution being strangely vigourous).[16]

Note that he is even concerned about the effect that his age might have on his ability to consummate the marriage! From his letter of 23rd July it would seem that the physician had reached a favourable conclusion:

Dear William,

I sent by yesterday's post the final legal opinion, for your support. By today's post, I have written straight and simply to R. [Rose] herself telling her all is ascertained and safe, and that you and Phile, and her aunt – and others – if she chooses will tell her that I deserve her trust.[17]

John was convinced that he had the evidence to clear his name, and the path to marriage. He most probably was right. Unfortunately, Mr. and Mrs. La Touche never allowed Rose to see any of it. Greville MacDonald gave a rough draft of a letter which his father George had written to John:

> You speak of explanations. Not one of those ever reached her.
> Mr. C. T. [Cowper Temple] wrote to her father, probably; you
> sent letters to her aunt. The former was never mentioned to
> her. The latter she has only seen within the last fortnight or
> so and they were interpreted to her, in her girlish ignorance,
> by the livid light of Mrs. …'s [Millais?] letters to her mother
> as confirming the worst things in them … Surrounded with
> false and devilish representation and those coming from the
> lips of another, hearing no defence of you, or anything you
> said to rebut the charges.[18]

It is easy to work out how Rose would have been hood-
winked by her parents. They had shown her legal opinions that
argued entirely falsely that John would have to overturn the
decree in order to marry her. In order to show her that he was
free to marry, John had provided indisputable evidence that the
decree was not overturnable.

In reality the marriage would have been completely legal and
any children legitimate unless and until an interested party
successfully challenged it, a circumstance so unlikely as to be
entirely discounted.[19] If John was incurably impotent the second
marriage would indeed be voidable on that ground, but even
then it would still have to be annulled by the second wife just as
his first marriage had been by Effie. Mrs. La Touche clearly did
not understand, or was unwilling to accept, the difference
between 'voidable' and 'void'. However as I have already pointed
out, it was the judgment of Society and not just the law courts
that Effie and Mrs. La Touche feared. Most of all it was John's
potency and not his impotency that they feared. If John had
married Rose and had children, Society would have drawn its

own conclusions about the annulment and about the Millais marriage.

John had believed that by being entirely passive in the original court case his integrity would not have been called into question, but only his manhood, which could easily be re-asserted later. He had made no false statements to the court; indeed he had made no statements at all. He had read no specific accusations so could not be accused of withholding a defence. He had not colluded with Effie. He had merely allowed her to gain her freedom. Effie for her part had never had to make any false statements about John's potency but merely had to prove that she was still a virgin and that the marriage had not been consummated. It was the court that assumed impotency from the circumstantial evidence. This was important for John. He never wanted to destroy Effie's reputation or force her to perjure herself. Effie had however shared a bed with John for years and would have had no doubts about whether he was impotent or not. If her silence in court when the sentence was read out had indeed allowed a false case to be concluded and if John subsequently had children it would be Effie's integrity that suffered.

The annulment was a far more serious problem than John had thought because he had not understood the social implications. Effie's warning to Mrs. La Touche that she would publish the annulment decree when the banns were called was almost certainly a bluff. The decree would have no legal force in stopping the marriage and the Millais family would be the ones most affected in the ensuing scandal. However even the threat of scandal was a potent deterrent to members of the social élite such as the La Touches. This alone would have made them adamant in their opposition to the marriage. The La Touches and the Millais thus had a combined interest in preventing the marriage.

Effie's intervention to prevent John's marriage to Rose La Touche is strong evidence that John was not impotent. By this time, Effie's husband Millais was a successful society painter on his way to the presidency of the Academy and a baronetcy. Even the suspicion of scandal would have brought his world crashing about his ears. As it was, they had suffered years of social slights and the Queen had been advised not to receive Effie at Court. John's supposed impotence would have had no effect on her marriage to Millais or her reputation. What really worried Effie was that Rose might have children. If John had given Rose a child then everybody would know that he was not incurably impotent, the Church had been deceived and this meant the annulment had been a sham and both second marriages were suspect. Otherwise there was no reason why she should have worried about the marriage at all.

However inconceivably remote the possibility that an attempt might be made by a disgruntled Millais legatee to void Effie's second marriage on the grounds that evidence had been suppressed and there had been collusion between John and Effie over the annulment of the first, if it succeeded this would not only unmake John's second marriage, but it would revalidate his first marriage, make Effie a bigamist, her second marriage void and her children illegitimate. She and her family would be utterly destroyed. Collingwood, who had access to the complete paperwork at Brantwood for his biography, knew full well that the legitimacy of the Millais children was the nub of the matter, and used this knowledge to reply to the bullying pomposity of Albert Gray:

> In preparing the book, I had before me the well-known points you mention, and I gave full weight to the legal proceedings and their result. But I had also a great deal of

information of which you may be unaware, which very considerably modified the popular verdict on the affair, represented in your letter. That information consisted in papers and letters of the period and the personal testimony of people who were intimately connected with the parties at the time.

Mr. Ruskin himself made no direct contributions to my book; he never has made any charges against his wife since the decree: but I cannot agree with you that his biographer must be bound by his reticence.

What binds me is the respect we all owe to the name of Millais. For the sake of Millais and his children, I was careful to suppress anything but the barest hint at painful facts already known, but for the sake of Mr. Ruskin I was bound to hint as much as I did. […] I think you are wise in preventing your relatives from re-opening the question.[20]

In the light of this situation, the lengths to which Effie, her family and her relatives would go in order to prevent John marrying can be imagined.

Although Rose gradually became a very ill young woman there can be no doubt that her condition was exacerbated by the desperate measures her parents took to prevent the marriage and avoid a scandal. John firmly believed that the young girl had been driven mad by her Evangelical father and that only he, John, could save her. In 1867 Lily Armstrong, one of John's ex-pupils from Winnington School, had visited Rose on John's behalf in a nursing home only to discover that she had been strapped down to her bed. In 1874 Mr la Touche attempted to have Rosie locked up with a doctor in Dublin, whence she begged John to deliver her.[21] There can also be no doubt that John and Rose had a real love affair. It might be worth comparing the so-called love letters from Effie to John in chapter 8 with this 1870 letter from Rose to John:

> I will trust you.
>
> I do love you. I have loved you, & shall love you always, always – & you can make this mean what you will.
>
> I have doubted your love, I have wished not to love you. I have thought you unworthy, yet – as surely as I believe God loves you, as surely as my trust is in His Love.
>
> I love you – still and always.
>
> Do not doubt this any more.
>
> I believe God meant us to love each other, yet life – and it seems God's will has divided us.
>
> My father & my mother forbid my writing to you, and I cannot continue to do so in secret. It seems to be God's will that we should be separated, and yet – 'thou art ever with me'. If my love can be any sunshine to you – take – and keep it. And now – may I say God bless you? God, who is love – lead – guide, & bless us both.[22]

After she came of age she more than once spent time with John against the wishes of her parents. Though the marriage never took place John and Rosie continued to make contact until she became too ill and she died in 1875 aged twenty-seven. The fact that John remained passionately devoted to Rose right to the end of her life when she was a grown woman tends to undermine the insinuations of child molestation that have been repeatedly attached to him with regard to this affair.[23] There is of course no evidence at all that John ever 'molested' anybody. Although the delight he took in the company of young girls in later life is certainly curious to modern sensibilities, its influence seems to have been entirely benign. Many of the girls with whom he interacted in his educational activities continued to be very fond of him as grown women. One of his teenage protégées was the fifteen-year-old Octavia Hill. She also began with drawing lessons, but with John's encouragement and generous financial help she became secretary to the Working Men's College, established schools and accommodation for poor women and improved slum dwellings. She went on to train other women to manage housing projects, worked on smoke abatement and helped set up the National Trust.[24]

I have mentioned that at the time of the annulment three of John's closest friends, the Trevelyans, Acland and Furnivall, were given accounts of the marriage. He provided his cousin W. Richardson with an 'an exact narrative of the facts [...] the real truth' and the Cowper Temples must also have been let in on the secret.[25] One other person who was given the full story later was George MacDonald, whom Mrs. La Touche introduced to John in 1863.[26] MacDonald was a saintly poet, novelist and theologian with a large family growing larger. Mrs. La Touche who had left her home in Ireland in search of the cultured life, spent many happy hours with Rose at the MacDonald home in London where it seems both she and her daughter discovered what an informal happy family life was really like. When John entered the MacDonald circle he was in desperate need of friends, particularly after the death of his father in March 1864. He and MacDonald had a lot in common. MacDonald had however heard the rumours and gossip which had persisted since the end of the marriage. He was determined to know the truth before he let John anywhere near his personal life. MacDonald's son Greville remembered the beginning of the friendship:

From my father, too, I had the full story of Ruskin's relations with his wife, whose marriage with him was annulled. For my father had insisted upon knowing all about this event before he would help his friend to his heart's desire. The story reflects nothing but honour upon Ruskin – unless he lied to my father, or my father to me – one supposition as utterly incredible as the other.[27]

Greville MacDonald later published an account of his father's talk with John.

'Was it true that you were incapable?' my father asked point blank. Ruskin laughed merrily and denied it unconditionally.

'Then why,' pursued my father, 'did you not defend yourself?'

'Do you think, if she wanted to be rid of me, I would put any obstacle in her way? I never loved Euphie before I married her; but I hoped I might and ought to, if only for her beauty.'[28]

Nor were the MacDonalds so unworldly as to not be troubled by John's fixation with the sixteen-year-old Rose, particularly as it had led to a rift with the La Touches. George MacDonald must have asked John the questions on the lips of all Ruskin scholars since. John gave a poignant answer:

She is the only living thing – since my white dog died – that I care for – and I very nearly died myself when she got too old to be made a pet of any more – which was infinitely ridiculous; but I never had any right people to care for – and one can't get on with stones only – unless one shuts oneself right up at the Great St. Bernard.[29]

Greville MacDonald also remembered John visiting their house in Hammersmith:

> My own personal memory of Ruskin, especially in those days when he used to visit Rose La Touche [...] although forbidden by her parents to meet him, and when I had opportunities for doing trifling services both to the great man whom I just loved to shake hands with, and to the frail, strangely beautiful, sweetly smiling girl, urges me to tell some day all I know of that wonderful love-story, if only that the world shall realise how honourable and pure-hearted the man was, and what a saintly person Rose La Touche had been all through childhood and girlhood, till she began to die of heartbreak – acute neurasthenia as, I think, the case would now be diagnosed. Thus I have a remarkable series of her mother's intimate letters to my mother, and of Rose's to my father.[30]

According to Greville it was the MacDonalds who in 1872 finally brought the two lovers together in their home for three days: three days which John declared he would have bought with the rest of his life.[31]

There can be no arguing with the fact that both John and Rose were damaged people. Both were deeply imprinted with religion from an early age. Both had their childhoods stolen by a strict Evangelical upbringing. Both were doted upon by their parents and brought up in luxurious isolation. Both had developed strong altruistic tendencies. Both were thwarted in love by parental objections. But such people often find each other. That having found each other they were then torn apart seems to have caused both their minds to break. The tragedy was compounded in that even those of John's true friends who knew what had really happened in his private life could not utter a public word on the subject during his lifetime for fear of the damage such revelations might do to what was left of his reputation. Anyone who successfully defended John's virility against calumny might inadvertently revalidate his nightmarish marriage to Effie in the public mind if not in legal actuality. After John was dead most of his devotees preferred to let sleeping dogs lie. Even Ruskin's literary executors conspired with the Gray and Millais families to suppress the facts of the affair.

EPILOGUE

The John Ruskin revealed in this book is not the John Ruskin who has long been familiar to his serious students. The passive, saintly, slightly fey Ruskin persona which has been built up over the last century is so familiar to Ruskin scholars that we find it difficult to believe that the Ruskin we know could have acted in such an apparently worldly and duplicitous manner as I suggest. However it is clear that his literary executors, albeit with the best of motives, deliberately and systematically censored out much of the true John Ruskin. It is also becoming increasingly clear that the Ruskin we have all come to know is a fiction.

I happen to believe that the real John Ruskin is much more interesting and no less virtuous for having sorted out the horrific situation in which both he and his wife found themselves. Besotted with the flirtatious Effie, he had been easily entrapped into a marriage proposal. Even her own family never tried to argue that she ever had any real love for John. She agreed to the marriage, perhaps on her father's orders, but certainly in the hope of saving both herself and her family from immediate financial ruin. She quickly realised that Mr. Ruskin had been too clever with the marriage settlement and was far too shrewd to be manipulated in money matters. John could not help because he too had no real independent income and did not want to be estranged from his ageing parents. Her sacrifice had been utterly futile. Eventually her bitter resentment against Mr. Ruskin grew to include John.

John had tried everything in his marriage: giving Effie time to grow into love, giving her extraordinary freedom in society, adopting Continental mores with regard to her men friends, offering her a substantial private income, even offering to become a monk; all to no avail. The couple grew apart. Effie's amusement at his eccentricities turned to ridicule; ridicule to disdain; disdain to implacable hatred. When John's reputation and even his life were threatened by Effie's relentless socialising, he had to act. The forced annulment was not just his last resort, it was his only resort. For Effie, even though she had to be compelled to do it, it was certainly the best solution. She kept her reputation, married a handsome talented man of her own age and choosing, had lots of children, became Lady Millais and lived the high society life she had always wanted. Unfortunately the blatant subterfuge of the annulment hung over them both for the rest of their lives. Thanks mainly to Lady Eastlake, what had always been a mere device to end a failed marriage became a subject of public prurience and speculation.

John had offered to take all the blame in the marriage breakdown. He was a man of his word. No matter what lurid calumnies were levelled against him he kept a dignified silence on the subject and never defended himself publicly. The sustained anger expressed by Effie, her second husband and their families after the marriage ended also supports the argument that John initiated the annulment. According to his in-laws' official version of events, John's only crime was to be incurably impotent, a condition which by its very nature would have been beyond his control and which in those repressed days he could not possibly have foreseen. However, that he should have used the law to obtain his freedom would have been a blow to the professional pride of the Gray family. That it should also have cost them in financial terms was rubbing salt in their wounds, but that he should have put Effie in a position where the very legitimacy of her second marriage and offspring might be called into question would have added fear and desperation into an already potent mix. It would be difficult to explain such sustained anger as the result of actions they had themselves instigated of their own free will and with full foreknowledge of the consequences.[1]

John's supporters have generally exercised restraint with regard to his ill-fated marriage. Ruskinians are generally interested in the man's ideas and usually see the public amusement with his private life as an annoying distraction. The world stands in need of original thinkers and John Ruskin's ideas are far too important to be neglected because of old family quarrels. Perhaps it is now time for the calumnies to be scotched and the truth to be accepted.

General Facts.

I was married - in her father's house - to Euphemia Chalmers Gray, on the 10th April. 1848. She entered her 21st year on the 7th May in that year Immediately after our marriage, we agreed that we would not consummate it, at all events for some little time; in order that my wife's state of health might not interfere with a proposed journey on the Continent.

Soon afterwards we agreed that the marriage should not be consummated until my wife was five and twenty.

Before that period had arrived. I had become aware of points in her character which caused me to regard with excessive pain any idea of these having children by her. and therefore, neither before nor after that period, either pressed or forced consummation. but I offered it again and again; and whenever I offered it, it was refused by her.

Her feelings of affection towards me appeared gradually to become extinguished; and were at last replaced by a hatred so great that she told me, about the end of September or beginning of October, 1853, we being then in Scotland, that if she ever were to suffer the pains of eternal torment, they could not be worse to her than going home to live at Herne Hill with me.

I took her home, nevertheless. We arrived in London on the day after Christmas day. 1853. From that time to this she has remained in a resolute anger - venting itself in unexplained insults; and rejecting every attempt of mine to caress her as if I had been a wild beast.

She informed me some days ago - about the 14th or 15th of April, that she intended to go down to Scotland on Tuesday the 25th. To which proposal I assented; understanding that she was to stay with her parents for three months, while I went to Switzerland with my father and mother. I saw her depart by the railway at the post of 9 on a Tuesday morning. and was surprised to receive the citation to meet her the same afternoon.

John Ruskin's General Facts

APPENDIX

❧

Interested readers may like to have the full text of Effie's letter of 6-7th March 1854 to her father, her letter of 25th April 1854 to Mrs. Ruskin and John's various statements to his legal team.

EFFIE'S LETTER TO HER FATHER

Herne Hill 7th March [in fact 6th]

My dearest Father – I have received my Mother's and George's kind letters this morning and feel very thankful that I have your and their approval in the course of conduct I have been endeavouring to pursue for some time – and in fact unless matters had become so sad for me as to threaten my Life I should not have on any account, but feeling that the necessity for acting in concert with you might by being longer delayed cause you and others connected with my Life greater sorrow in the end. I therefore, as I feel now so ill and in perpetual nervous distress, and feel that perhaps I may be adding to yours by a silence which I have kept on John Ruskin's conduct to me ever since I left your care, although I have lately and on my last visit home shown you how very unhappy I was.

You are aware that since 1848 to this last year I have never made any formal complaint to you. There were many reasons for my silence, the principal being of course my great love for you and my dear Mother – fearing to trouble you when you were in great difficulties yourselves, when I tried to look on my unfortunate position as one where, whatever I internally suffered, at least removed me from being a burthen on you – and I resolved that no annoyance which I suffered should give you any. I pass over all other discussions and reasons at present till I see you as I could fill Volumes. To come to the present moment, when even now I was unwilling to tell you all, fearing your anger against John Ruskin who has so illtreated and abused me, and his Parents who have so seconded him, although so far they are innocent, not knowing the gravity of the offence with which I charge him and from which proceeds all the rest. But they have been most guilty in the education they have given him and ought not to have treated me as they have done. I wish neither to be uncharitable nor to take advantage of any of them but I am so ruined and nervous in both mind and body that as they are so anxious to get rid of me, and I have not the satisfaction of feeling that anyone is the least the better for my forbearance and suffering, I have duly considered the step I am about to take in telling you all. Feeling very ill last week and in the greatest perplexity about my duty to you – I went and consulted Lady Eastlake and also partly Lord Glenelg, the two persons in London for whom I have most respect. I did not open my mind to the latter as I did to the former but as I could perfectly rely on their prudence and wisdom I took the advice of Lady E to permit her to make the necessary enquiries of How English Law would treat such a case as mine.* You may perhaps at first wonder that I should apply to anyone in preference to yourself – but I was still unwilling to ask you to act for me until I saw I could not avoid giving you trouble and that of a most serious nature. I enclose Lady

E's most kind and noble letter, it will best show you what she is, as well as perhaps help you, although cases of this description may have come under your own knowledge in the course of your Life. I have therefore simply to tell you that I do not think I am John Ruskin's Wife at all – and I entreat you to assist me to get released from the unnatural position in which I stand to Him. To go back to the day of my marriage the 10th of April 1848. I went as you know away to the Highlands. I had never been told the duties of married persons to each other and knew little or nothing about their relations in the closest union on earth. For days John talked about this relation to me but avowed no intention of making me his Wife. He alleged various reasons, Hatred to children, religious motives, a desire to preserve my beauty, and finally this last year told me his true reason (and this to me is as villainous as all the rest), that he had imagined women were quite different to what he saw I was, and that the reason he did not make me his Wife was because he was disgusted with my person the first evening 10th April. After I began to see things better I argued with him and took the Bible but he soon silenced me and I was not sufficiently awake to what position I was in. Then he said after 6 years he would marry me, when I was 25. This last year we spoke about it. I did say what I thought in May. He then said, as I professed quite a dislike to him, that it would be <u>sinful</u> to enter into such a connexion, as if I was not very <u>wicked</u> I was at least insane and the responsibility that I might have children was too great, as I was quite unfit to bring them up. These are some of the facts. You may imagine what I have gone through – and besides all this the temptations his neglect threw me in the way of. If he had only been kind, I might have lived and died in my maiden state, but in addition to this brutality his leaving me on every occasion – his threats for the future of a wish to break my spirit – and only last night when he wished to put his arm round me (for I believe he was cold) I bade him leave me, he said he had a good mind to beat me and that he had never admired Romanism so much, as if he had a Confessor for me he would soon bring me to my senses. I don't think, poor creature, he knows anything about human creatures – but he is so gifted otherwise and so cold at the same time that he never thinks of people's feelings and yet with his eloquence will always command admiration. I cannot bear his presence and something you will feel is imperative. Once this year I did threaten him with Law, but I really did not know myself about it, as it was in Edinburgh and he said, 'Well, and if I was to take all the blame?' I think he might not oppose my protest – In point of fact, could He?

I should not think of entering your House excepting as free as I was before I left it. All this you must consider over and find out what you can do. Thank God for all his good-ness to me which has enabled me to Live up to this time in his fear and in I trust a virtuous Life – the glory is all his and under him I have been kept from sin by the remembrance of the example you and my dear Mother have ever shown me. If I have not written you clearly enough you must put it down to illness and agitation, for you will hardly wonder this keep-ing up of appearances makes me often sick.

Yr affectionate Daughter Effie Gray

EFFIE'S LETTER TO MRS. RUSKIN

Herne Hill

April 25 – 1854

~~My~~ dear Mrs Ruskin

You have doubtless been wondering why I did not, as was usual with me, pay you a visit at Denmark Hill to bid you goodbye before going to Scotland, but I felt that owing to the circumstances which induce my addressing you this letter that rendered it not only impossible for me to see you now or indeed ever again – but also required that I should state to you the reasons of my sending you my Keys, House Book wherein will be found a statement of this year's account together with an explanation of the money received and spent by me, and also you will find enclosed my marriage ring which I return by this means to your son, with whom I can never hold farther intercourse or communication.

You are aware that I was married by the Scottish form in my father's house on the 10th of April 1848.

From that day to this, your son has never made me his wife, or wished to do so, as he at first overcame my judgment, which was ignorant on such points, by a variety of arguments which even showing him the words of Scripture did not refute or cause him to change his opinions in the least about. Whilst we were at Salisbury, when you caused me to be put in another room on account of an illness, which he told me his Father supposed to arise from his recent connexion with me, he used to laugh and say his Father was imagining things very different to what they were. His conduct and manner went from bad to worse until I felt I could no longer submit to his threats of personal cruelty and desires to get rid of me in any manner consistent with <u>his own</u> safety and comparative freedom. I always resisted the idea of a <u>separation</u> and would take no steps in such a matter, and threatened him with the course I have now pursued if he did not treat me in a becoming manner. He said, 'Well what if I do take all the blame, you would make a great piece of work for your Father and go home and lose your position.'

I have gone through this winter and thought at last that I must either die or consult my parents to take proper steps to ascertain what relief could be got, since your son almost daily heaps one insult upon another, more especially accusing me of <u>Insanity</u>. My Father and Mother came instantly they knew what I suffered to Town and are only sorry I have lived in such an unnatural position so long. I believe you have been all along in total ignorance of this behaviour of your son's. The Law will let you know what I have demanded, and I put it to you and Mr Ruskin to consider what a very great temporal loss, in every point of view, your son's conduct has entailed upon me for these best six years of my life. Your son first said he would marry me when <u>I</u> was <u>25</u> – then on arriving at that age last year – I enquired on what terms we were to live, he said I was quite <u>mad</u>, quite unfit to bring up children, and beside did not love or respect him sufficiently. I said <u>that</u> was quite <u>impossible</u> after his perpetual <u>neglect</u> – but that I never would refuse to gratify his wishes. He then put it off again and said he should try and break my spirit to enduce me to leave him and return to Perth as I bored him. I think <u>he</u> will be glad I have taken this step. I hear that our affairs are perfectly known in London society; and nothing more will be said, since the fact of our marriage not having been consummated was known to <u>many</u> and your son's personal neglect of me <u>notoriously condemned</u> – this has likewise been the case in Perth. My parents have entirely approved of the steps I have taken and my Mother accompanies me to Scotland. All accounts besides the House Books will be found filed in the store-room and any things at Herne Hill amongst the glass, furniture &c that your son considers my property you will, I feel assured, be good enough [to] send after me.

I remain yours truly

Euphemia C. Gray

JOHN'S STATEMENT TO HIS PROCTOR

General Facts.

I was married – in her father's house – to Euphemia Chalmers Gray on the 10th April, 1848. She entered her 21st year on the 7th May in that year. Immediately after our marriage we agreed that we would not consummate it, at all events for some little time, in order that my wife's state of health might not interfere with a proposed journey on the continent.

Soon afterwards we agreed that the marriage should not be consummated untill my wife was five and twenty.

Before that period had arrived I had become aware of points in her character which caused me to regard with excessive pain any idea of having children by her, and therefore, neither before nor after that period, either pressed or forced consummation, but I offered it again and again; and whenever I offered it, it was refused by her.

Her feelings of affection towards me appeared gradually to become extinguished; and were at last replaced by a hatred so great that she told me, about the end of September or beginning of October, 1853, we being then in Scotland, that if she ever were to suffer the pains of eternal torment, they could not be worse to her than going home to live at Herne Hill with me.

I took her home nevertheless. We arrived in London on the day after Christmas Day, 1853. From that time to this she has remained in resolute anger – venting itself in unexplained insults; and rejecting every attempt of mine to caress her as if I had been a wild beast.

She informed me some days ago-about the 14th or 15th of April that she intended to go down to Scotland on Tuesday the 25th to which proposal I assented; understanding that she was to stay with her parents for three months, while I went to Switzerland with my father and mother. I saw her depart by the railway at $^1/_2$ past 9 on Tuesday morning and was surprised to receive the citation to court the same afternoon.

Details relating to the above statement

1st. Reasons for our agreement not to consummate the marriage.

I offered marriage by letter to Miss Gray in the autumn of 1847 and was accepted. Letters passed between us almost daily from that time until I went to Scotland in March 1848 to marry her. I met her at her uncle's, Mr. Sheriff Jameson's at Edinburgh. There, some fortnight before our proposed marriage, Miss Gray informed me that her father "had lost immense sums by railroads" and Mr. Gray, coming over himself, told me he was entirely ruined and must leave his house immediately. His distress appeared very great: and the fortnight or ten days preceding our marriage were passed in great suffering both by Miss Gray and myself – in consequence of revelations of ruin – concealed at that time, at least from *me*.

The whole family rested on me for support and encouragement – Mr. Gray declaring I was their "sheet anchor". But no effort whatever was made to involve me in their embarrassments – nor did I give the slightest hope of being able to assist Mr. Gray who, I believed, must assuredly have become bankrupt. But I expressed no surprise or indignation at the concealment of his affairs from me, although it had entirely destroyed the immediate happiness of my marriage.

Miss Gray appeared in a most weak and nervous state in consequence of this distress – and I was at first afraid of subjecting her system to any new trials. My own passion was also much subdued by anxiety; and I had no difficulty in refraining from consummation on the first night. On speaking to her on the subject the second night we agreed that it would be better to defer consummation for a little time. For my own part, I married in order to have a companion – not for passion's sake; and I was particularly anxious that my wife should be well and strong in order that she might be able to climb Swiss hills with me that year. I had seen much grief arise from the double excitement of possession and marriage travelling and was delighted to find that my wife seemed quite relieved at the suggestion. We tried thus living separate for some little time and then agreed that we would continue to do so till my wife should be five and twenty, as we wished to travel a great deal and thought that in five years we should be settled for good. The letters written to Miss Gray before our marriage are all in my possession and will show that I had no intention of this kind previously. My wife asked me to give her these letters some days ago. I fortunately refused, thinking she would mislay them, as she did not now care about them; but she doubtless intended to destroy them.

2. Reasons for the aversion felt by my wife towards me.

This aversion had nothing to do with our mode of living together. It arose first from my steady resistance to the endeavours of my wife to withdraw me from the influence of my parents, and to get me into close alliance with her own family. She tried to get me to persuade my Father to put her brother into his counting house; and was much offended at my refusal to do so: she then lost no opportunity of speaking against both of my parents, and, every day, was more bitterly mortified at her failure in influencing me. On one occasion, she having been rude to my mother, I rebuked her firmly; and she never forgave either my mother or me.

I married her, thinking her so young and affectionate that I might influence her as I chose, and make of her just such a wife as I wanted. It appeared that <u>she</u> married <u>me</u> thinking she could make of me just the <u>husband she</u> wanted. I was grieved and disappointed at finding I could not change her, and she was humiliated and irritated at finding she could not change me.

I have no doubt she felt at first considerable regard for me, but never a devoted or unselfish one. She had been indulged in all her wishes from her youth; and now felt all restraint an insult. She sometimes expressed doubts of its being <u>right</u> to live as we were living; but always continuing to express her wish to live so. I gravely charged her to tell me if she thought she would be happier in consummating marriage or healthier, I being willing at any time to consummate it; but I answered to her doubts of its being <u>right</u>, that many of the best characters in Church history had preserved virginity in marriage, and that it could not be wrong to do for a time what they had done through life.

It may be thought strange that I <u>could</u> abstain from a woman who to most people was so attractive. But though her face was beautiful, her person was not formed to excite passion. On the contrary there were certain circumstances in her person which completely checked it. I did not think, either, that there could be anything in my own person particularly attractive to <u>her</u>, but believed that she loved me as I loved her, with little mingling of desire.

Had she treated me as a kind and devoted wife would have done, I should soon have longed to possess her, body and heart. But every day that we lived together, there was less sympathy between us, and I soon began to observe characteristics which gave me so much grief and anxiety that I wrote to her father saying they could be accounted for in no other way than by supposing that there was slight nervous affection of the brain. It is of no use to trace the progress of alienation. Perhaps the principal cause of it – next to her resolute effort to detach me from my parents, was her always thinking that I ought to attend <u>her</u>, instead of <u>herself</u> attending me. When I had drawing or writing to do instead of sitting with me as I drew or wrote, she went about on her own quests and then complained that "I left her alone."

For the last half year, she seems to have had no other end in life than the expression of her anger against me and my parents: and having destroyed her own happiness, she has sought wildly for some method of recovering it, without humbling her pride. This it seems, she thinks she can effect by a separation from me, grounded on an accusation of impotence. Probably she now supposes this accusation a just one – and thinks I deceived her in offering consummation. This can of course be ascertained by medical examination, but after what has now passed, I cannot take her to be my wife or to bear me children. This is the point of difficulty with me. I can prove my virility at once, but I do not wish to receive back into my house the woman who has made such a charge against me.

27 April, 1854.

JOHN RUSKIN.

Mr. Pott's Questions and Mr. J. Ruskin's Answers.

P. First question as to the validity of the marriage, when and where solemnized and whether any flaw can be found in that marriage so as to try the case as a nullity on some other ground rather than that proposed by the Citation.

R. As far as I know the marriage is valid.

P. Second, whether the facts upon which the present proceedings are founded if true were in existence at the time the marriage was solemnized or whether they have arisen since the marriage. And positively state whether the marriage has ever been consummated or not.

R. They are not in all respects true, and, so far as they are true, were not in existence before the marriage was solemnized. The marriage has never been consummated.

P. Third, has the lady's conduct been of that nature as to induce a supposition or belief that she is not at this moment a pure virgin, and what are the facts if any to induce such belief.

And also would the lady's case be likely to stand the test of an examination by competent medical and surgical authorities and query how would the party proceeded against feel personally in this particular.

To the first part R. The lady's conduct has been without reproach.

To the last part R. I have no doubt her case will stand every examination.

P. Fourth, the lady's conduct having given rise to so much disagreement and her habits being of so extravagant a nature, to consider the expediency of allowing the case to proceed without hindrance, merely giving a sufficient opposition to allow the lady to obtain her decree without the appearance of collusion.

R. I certainly wish the case to proceed with as little hindrance as possible.

P. Fifth. As the first step taken in cases of this description is usually of the utmost importance it must be fully understood and determined upon as to how the proceedings are to be commenced by the Proctor for the defence.

R. [no further comment].

ACKNOWLEDGEMENTS

Embarking on this project was only possible due to the help and professional skill of my wife. Her conviction that the key to the Ruskin marriage conundrum lay in the dusty volumes of nineteenth century Scottish and English matrimonial law led me to the legal facts of the Ruskin marriage and confirmed my suspicions about the accepted account. Professor Jim Spates of Hobart & William Smith Colleges, NY, gave me invaluable support and advice, particularly with regard to the letter archives in the Morgan Library, New York. The Morgan Library, whilst closed after 2001, very kindly allowed me to spend six weeks researching their archive whilst it was in the impressive underground vault of the Morgan Bank on Fifth Avenue. I am particularly grateful to Inge Dupont and the staff of the Morgan who were untiringly helpful and knowledgeable. I am also grateful to John and Virginia Murray for access to the John Murray archive whilst it was still at Albemarle Street. Julie Sheldon helped me with Lady Eastlake's correspondence and John Batchelor pointed me to the copy of the Trevelyan diaries in the Robinson Library in Newcastle. Sally Phillips gave me guidance in the Law Library at the Royal Courts of Justice in London. Rhoda Fothergill helped me with the history of Bowerswell House. I would also like to thank Derek Baker of the William Morris Society for convincing me that accurate chronology was crucial to proper historical understanding. Institutions which accommodated me included New York Public Library, Princeton University Library, the Bodleian at Oxford, Cambridge University Library, the Ruskin Library at Lancaster University, the Scottish Record Office, the National Library of Scotland, Perth Library, Stirling Council Archives, the British Newspaper Library at Hendon and Essex University Library. The many publishers and institutions which generously gave their permission to reproduce copyright material are credited in the text and footnotes. General support and encouragement has been provided by many Ruskinians but most notably James Dearden of the Guild of St. George and Stephen Wildman of Lancaster University. Last but by no means least I would like to thank Alexander Fyjis-Walker for his encouragement, good judgement and hard work in making such a fine book of it all.

ILLUSTRATIONS

Half-title and Frontispiece: The Order of Release, 1746, 1852-3, *by J. E. Millais, (1829-96). Oil on canvas, 102.9 x 73.7 cm. Presented to the Tate Gallery, London, by Sir Henry Tate in 1898. Photo Credit: ©Tate, London 2013.*

p. 4: Euphemia Ruskin, *by Thomas Richmond, 1851. Oil on board, arched top, 81 x 53 cm, National Portrait Gallery, London. Photograph copyright National Portrait Gallery*

p. 7: Sketch of Ruskin for the Glenfinlas portrait, *by J. E. Millais, 1853, Pencil on blue paper 19.7 x 12.7 cm. Ashmolean Museum, Oxford. Photograph copyright Ashmolean Museum*

p. 8: John Ruskin *by George Richmond, c. 1857. Black and white chalk on coloured paper, 42.5 x 35.6 cm), National Portrait Gallery, London. Photograph copyright National Portrait Gallery*

p. 11: Euphemia Ruskin, *by John Ruskin, 1848 or 1850. Pencil and wash, 26 x 20.4 cm. Ashmolean Museum, Oxford. Photograph copyright Ashmolean Museum*

p. 16: Flos Florum Rosa ['Rose, the flower of flowers']: Portrait of Rose La Touche *by John Ruskin c. 1872-4. Pencil, wash and bodycolour, 49.5 x 33 cm. Ruskin Library, Lancaster University (Ruskin Foundation)*

p. 22: Bowerswell House as originally built (after a water colour formerly at Bowerswell)

p. 29: Bowerswell House as rebuilt by George Gray, photograph by the author

p. 32: The house at 54 Hunter St. where John Ruskin was born; subsequently demolished: photograph Ruskin Library, Lancaster University (Ruskin Foundation)

p. 34: Margaret Ruskin, *1825, by James Northcote. Oil on canvas, 75 x 62.2 cm, Ruskin Library, Lancaster University (Ruskin Foundation)*

p. 35: John James Ruskin, *1848, by George Richmond. Chalk, wash and bodycolour, 52.4 x 39.9 cm Ruskin Library, Lancaster University (Ruskin Foundation)*

p. 41: 28 Herne Hill, *probably by John Ruskin. Pencil and ink, 37 x 44.5 cm, Ruskin Library, Lancaster University (Ruskin Foundation)*

p. 54: Charlotte Lockhart *by David Hill and Robert Adamson. Calotype print, 19.8 x 14.8 cm, National Museums of Scotland*

p. 68: Avonbank School at Stratford-upon-Avon. Glass plate negative of a watercolour. By permission of the Shakespeare Birthplace Trust.

p. 72 Euphemia Chalmers Gray in 1847, aged 19, *by George Richmond R.A. From Mary Lutyens, Effie in Venice (reprinted 2013). Current location unknown.*

p. 73 'The Author of Modern Painters', *photogravure after watercolour of 1843 by George Richmond (original destroyed by fire). Photograph courtesy of the Ruskin Library, Lancaster University (Ruskin Foundation)*

p. 75: 163 Denmark Hill, *by Arthur Severn (husband of Ruskin's cousin and later companion, Joan, née Agnew). Pencil and wash, 22 x 28 cm. Ruskin Library, Lancaster University (Ruskin Foundation) p. 145:* The Gray family, *by J. E. Millais. Sepia ink on paper, 26 x 18.5 cm. Private collection, photograph courtesy Robert Dalrymple, Dalrymple Press*

p. 168: The Marriage Certificate. The Pierpont Morgan Library, New York. (MA 1338 E01)

p. 271. The Riva degli Schiavoni in the third quarter of the 19th century. With thanks to the Hotel Danieli

p. 303 The Casa Wetzlar in 1852, lithograph. From Mary Lutyens, Effie in Venice *(reprinted 2013).*

p. 319:Count Franz von Thun Hohenstein: left, lithograph by August Prinzhofer made after 1885 from a painting by Schrotzberg, c. 1849; right,photograph c. 1860.

p. 369: Ruskin at Glenfinlas *by J.E. Millais, 1853-4. Oil on canvas, 78.7 x 68 cm, arched top. Ashmolean Museum Oxford; photograph copyright National Portrait Gallery*

p. 370: Effie Ruskin *by J. E. Millais 1853, Pencil and watercolour, 33 x 25.4 cm. Private collection. Photograph courtesy the collector*

p. 371: John Ruskin, *by J. E. Millais 1853. Pencil and watercolour, 33 x 25.4 cm. Ruskin Library, Lancaster University (Ruskin Foundation)*

p. 372: J. E. Millais *by William Holman Hunt, 1853. Coloured chalks on coloured paper, 33.2 x 24.8 cm. National Portrait Gallery, London. Photograph copyright National Portrait Gallery*

p. 384: Le Postillon s'arrête en route, *by William Millais, 30 June 1853. Reproduced in* Millais, Life and Letters, *location of original unknown.*

p. 385: Effie Ruskin by a window at Doune Castle, with two portraits of James Simpson from memory. *From Millais's Glenfinlas sketchbook, 1853.22.5 x 18.4 cm. Pen and sepia ink on paper. Birmingham City Museums and Art Gallery. Photograph courtesy Robert Dalrymple, Dalrymple Press*

p. 386: McIntyre's New Trossachs and Bridge of Turk Hotel in 1853, *engraving by W. B. Banks of Edinburgh. Courtesy of University of St. Andrews Library Dept of Special Collections (msDA865.C2/ms1699).*

p. 388 and 389: Ordnance Survey map 1862-3. Stirling Council Archive

p. 390: Brig o'Turk in 1882, sketch by the author after an oil painting of 1882 by George Henry in Kelvingrove Art Gallery

p. 391: 'My feet ought to be against the wall.' *From Millais's Glenfinlas sketchbook, 1853. 22.6 x 17.4. Pen and sepia ink on paper. Private collection, photograph courtesy of the collector*

p. 392: The Scottish bog exercise. *From Millais's Glenfinlas sketchbook, 1853. 17.3 x 11.3 cm. Pen and sepia ink on paper. Private collection. Photograph courtesy Robert Dalrymple, Dalrymple Press*

p. 394: Sketch of the sleeping arrangements in the schoolmaster's cottage, by William Millais, 1898. The Bodleian Libraries, The University of Oxford (MS.Eng.lett. C.228)

p. 397: Sketch of the cottage at Glenfinlas, by John Ruskin. From letter to John James Ruskin dated 30.9.1853. Yale University Beinecke Rare Book and Manuscript Library

p. 398: 'A Wet Day's Pastime.' *From Millais's Glenfinlas sketchbook, 1853. 18.7 x 23 cm. Pen and sepia ink on paper. The Athanæum. Photograph courtesy Robert Dalrymple, Dalrymple Press*

p. 399: 'The Countess as Barber. Rain.' *From Millais's Glenfinlas sketchbook, 1853. 23.2 x 18.7. Pen and sepia ink on paper. Pierpont Morgan Library New York (1968.7) Purchased on the Fellows Fund.*

p. 400: Sketch plan of the cottage by the author

p. 402: Sketch of the cottage at Glenfinlas, by John Ruskin. From a letter to Furnivall 16.10.1853 (NYPL Berg Collection) Image reproduced in the Library Edition of Ruskin's Works

p. 403: Self-portrait, crossing the bog, *by J. E. Millais, from letter reproduced by Malcolm Warner and Mary Lutyens,* Rainy Days at Brig o'Turk,*(1983), no reference. Photograph courtesy Robert Dalrymple, Dalrymple Press*

p. 404: Detail of Ordnance Survey map 1862-3. Stirling Council Archive

p. 411: Illustration to Scott's Glenfinlas by Richard Westall, engraved by R. Golding, 1812

p. 413: Effie with foxgloves in her hair, *by J. E. Millais, 1853. Oil on millboard, 22.5 x 20.5 cm. .The Mander Collection, Wightwick Manor. Image by permission of The National Trust*

p. 414: Two Masters and their Pupils. *From Millais's Glenfinlas sketchbook, 1853. 18.7 x 23.5. Pen and sepia ink on paper. Private collection. Photograph courtesy Robert Dalrymple, Dalrymple Press*

p. 415: Wayside Refreshment. *From Millais's Glenfinlas sketchbook, 1853. 18.7 x 23.3 cm. Pen and sepia ink on paper. Private collection. Photograph courtesy Robert Dalrymple, Dalrymple Press*

p. 416: The Idle and the Industrious Painter *and* Henry Acland. *Sheet from Millais's Glenfinlas sketchbook, 1853. 18.6 x 23.7 cm. Pen and sepia ink on paper. Private c ollection. Photograph courtesy Robert Dalrymple, Dalrymple Press*

p. 417: Highland Shelter. *From Millais's Glenfinlas sketchbook, 1853. 18.7 x 23.3 cm. Pen and sepia ink on paper. Private collection. Photograph courtesy Robert Dalrymple, Dalrymple Press*

pp. 418-419: The Waterfall: Effie by the waters of Glenfinlas, *by J. E. Millais, 1853. Oil on paper board, 29.2 x 39 cm. Delaware Art Museum, Samuel and Mary R. Bancroft Memorial. Image courtesy Bridgeman Art*

p. 420: Effie Ruskin in natural ornament *From Millais's Glenfinlas sketchbook, 1853. 18.7 x 23.7 cm. Pen and sepia ink on paper. Birmingham City Museums and Art Gallery. Photograph copyright Birmingham Museums Trust*

p. 421: Cruel Treatment of a Master to his Pupil. *From Millais's Glenfinlas sketchbook, 1853. 18.6 x 21.5 cm. Pen and sepia ink on paper. Private collection. Photograph courtesy Robert Dalrymple, Dalrymple Press*

p. 423: Ascent of Ben Ledi. *From Millais's Glenfinlas sketchbook, 1853. 18.5 x 23.7 cm. Pen and sepia ink on paper. Private collection. Photograph courtesy Robert Dalrymple, Dalrymple Press*

p. 427: Two letters by J. E. Millais The Pierpont Morgan Library, New York (MA 1338 101 & 102)

p. 492: Elizabeth Rigby (Lady Eastlake) *by David Hill and Robert Adamson, c. 1845. Calotype print 20.6 x 14.7 cm. National Museums of Scotland.*

p. 506: The Gray family, August 1855. Photograph. *From Mary Lutyens,* Millais and the Ruskins, *(reprinted 2013). Current location unknown.*

p. 522: John Ruskin's General Facts, 1854. *Photograph Ruskin Library, Lancaster University (Ruskin Foundation)*

NOTES

Abbreviations for main correspondents

JR	John Ruskin
JJR	John James Ruskin, his father.
MR	Margaret Ruskin his mother.
CR	Catherine Ruskin, John Ruskin's grand-mother
ECG	Euphemia Chalmers Gray
SMG	Sophia Gray, her mother.
GG	George Gray, her father.
GGJr.	Her brother George Gray
JEM	John Everett Millais
CSW	Clare Stuart Wortley

Abbreviations have been used for books in the footnotes as follows:

LE	Library Edition of the Works of John Ruskin
Diaries	J. Evans & J. H. Whitehouse: *The Ruskin Family Letters*, 3 vols. (1956-59)
EinV	Mary Lutyens *Effie in Venice* (1965, republished 1996 and 2013)
M&R	Mary Lutyens *Millais and the Ruskins* (1967, republished 2013)
R&G	Mary Lutyens *The Ruskins and the Grays* (1972, republished 2013)
RFL	Van Akin Burd: *The Ruskin Family Letters*, 2 Vols. (1973)
LFV	J. L. Bradley: *Ruskin's Letters from Venice 1851-2*, (1955)

Other frequently cited books are:

1853 Report: *The First Report of the Commissioners appointed by her Majesty to Enquire into the Law of Divorce and more particularly into the Mode of obtaining Divorces A Vinculo matrimonii* (1853)

J. L. Bradley, *Letters from John Ruskin to Lord and Lady Mount Temple* (1964)

Collingwood, *Life of Ruskin* (date): W. G. Collingwood, *Life of John Ruskin,* 1893 in two volumes; also abridged and revised 8th edition, 1911

Cook, *Life*: E. T. Cook, *The Life of Ruskin* (1911)

Gray, *Marriage:* Sir Albert Gray, *Marriage of John Ruskin*, Bodleian MS. Eng. misc. d.653. There are two copies of this account in the Bodleian with different ancillary material. The other is MS. Eng. misc. d.652.

Hilton, *Early Years*: Tim Hilton, *John Ruskin, the Early Years* (1985)

James, *Order of Release*: Admiral Sir William James, *The Order of Release* (1948)

Leon, *Great Victorian*: Derrick Leon, *Ruskin, The Great Victorian* (1949)

MacDonald, *George Macdonald:* Greville MacDonald, *George Macdonald and his Wife* (1924)

MacDonald, *Reminiscences*: Greville MacDonald, *Reminiscences of a Specialist,* (1932)

J. G Millais, *The Life and Letters of Sir John Everett Millais,* (1899)

Paston, *At John Murray's*: G. Paston (pseudonym of Emily Morse Symonds) *At John Murray's: Records of a Literary Circle 1843-1892,* (1932)

Robertson, *Eastlake*: David Robertson, *Charles Eastlake and the Victorian Art World,* (1978)

Shelford, *Treatise*: Leonard Shelford, *A Practical Treatise of the Law of Marriage and Divorce and registration as altered by the recent statutes containing also the mode of proceeding on divorces in the Ecclesiastical Courts and in Parliament. The Right to the custody of children, voluntary separation between husband and wife. The husband's liability to the wife's debts and the conflict between the laws of England and Scotland with an appendix of statutes,* (1841)

Stone, *Broken Lives*: Lawrence Stone: *Broken Lives* (1993)

Stone, *Road to Divorce*: Lawrence Stone. *Road to Divorce* (1990)

Surtees, *Reflections*: Virginia Surtees, *Reflections of a Friendship* (1979)

Whitehouse, *Vindication*: J. H. Whitehouse, *Vindication of Ruskin*, London (1950)

HGV is Helen Gill Viljoen (Papers in PML)

PML is the Pierpont Morgan Library in New York City.

NLS is the National Library of Scotland.

Introduction pp. 9-20

1. A view expressed by the author of a pamphlet entitled *Something on Ruskinism, with a 'Vestibule' in Rhyme by an Architect* (1851) See Collingwood, *Life* (1893) Vol. 1 p. 150. 'Readers who are not reviewers by profession can hardly fail to perceive that Ruskinism is violently inimical to *sundry existing interests.*'

2. Sophia Gray's father Andrew Jameson was Sheriff of Fife and his son, her brother Andrew, became Sheriff of Aberdeeenshire. Sophia's younger brother Melville Jameson was a partner in George Gray's legal firm. George Gray himself was Writer to the Signet and his son George qualified as a lawyer in 1852, working for the legal firm of Farrier and Murray. His younger son Albert Gray rose to become Counsel to the Chairman of Committees in the House of Lords.

3. See R. Brownell, 'John Ruskin: Patron or Patriarch?' in *The Journal of the William Morris Society* Vol XIV No. 1, Autumn 2000, p. 44

4. Addressed by the 1870 Married Woman's Property Act

5. For the story behind the 1839 Infant Custody Act see A. Chedzoy, *A Scandalous Woman: The Story of Caroline Norton* (1992) p. 179

1: Scottish Roots pp. 21-30

1. Greyfriars Burial Book

2. Saisine of 20.8.1828. James in *The Order of Release* was therefore simply wrong to state (p. 12) that George Gray bought the house from John James Ruskin.

3. Greyfriars Burial Book

4. *Præterita* 1.1.10 (LE 35.19)

5. Gray, *Marriage*. See also *R&G* n. 6 p. 268.

6. She married Andrew in 1811 and he died in 1848. She died in XII.1877 aged 91. Her reminiscences, signed and dated 1.9.1877, were written down by Sir Albert Gray for Gray, *Marriage*. The original signed notes are in Bodleian MS. Eng. lett. c.228,

pp. 23-4

7. Gray, *Marriage*, p. 8

8. JJR to CR 13.4.1815 RFL (23) p. 76

9. JJR to CR 30.6.1815 RFL (25) p. 78

10. John Thomas Ruskin might also have been one of the countless victims of the eruption of Mt. Tambora in 1815 which put so much dust and sulphur dioxide into the atmosphere that weather patterns were affected world-wide. Turner recorded the strange sunsets. In 1816, known as 'the year without a Summer' at least 200,000 died in Europe from cold and famine followed by a typhus epidemic. There were food riots in France and Switzerland and unaffordable food prices in London caused more rioting. In southwest England it rained 142 days out of 153 and countrywide the crops rotted in the fields. The Lake District had snow in July and in London the lakes froze in September. Bizarrely, Scotland was one of the only areas in Western Europe to see the sun that summer; however the bad weather hit Scotland with a vengeance in October of that year. A great hurricane and snowstorm caught the crops still in the fields causing much distress amongst the poor. The following year, 1817, was disastrous right across Scotland with a wet summer and early continual frosts delaying and then damaging the harvest. The resulting distress and hardship caused by the successive crop failures would have hit the Ruskin family hard from all sides. Food would have been scarce and expensive, customers desperate and penniless. This might explain the parlous nature of John Thomas's finances and his unfortunate end.

11. Lancaster T148. Clare Stuart Wortley's introductory notes

12. *Præterita* p. 57 1.III.74 (LE 35:66)

13. JJR to GG 28.4.47: PML MA 1338 (C.02)

14. *Præterita* pp. 57-8 1.III.74 (LE 35:67)

15. *R&G* facing p. 66

16. Sophia Gray to GG 7.1843: PML MA 1338 (B.73)

17. CSW notes 'the family tradition that the new house was built onto or round the old one, and that the family lived in it all the time the building was being done.' Lancaster T148 note to copy ALS SMG to GG 21.7.1843

2: The Boy John, pp. 31-49

1. *Præterita* I.I.19-20 (LE 35:24) See the astrologer's advice in the introduction to Scott's *Guy Mannering*.
2. JR to Miss [Sarah?] Corlass dated 11 February (no year) RFL (34) p. 101 *n.* 7
3. *Præterita* I.I.211 (LE 35:25)
4. JR Diary 2.5.1841.
5. *Præterita* I.II.46 (LE 35:40)
6. *ibid.* I.II.48 (LE 35:43)
7. *ibid.* I.II.23 (LE 35:26)
8. *ibid.* I.II.38-9 (LE 35:36)
9. *ibid.* I.II.49 (LE 35:44)
10. *ibid.* I.I.13-14 (LE 35:20)
11. *ibid.* I.I.32 (LE 35:32)
12. *ibid.* I.III.64 (LE 35:57)
13. JR to JJR 15.3.1823 *RFL* (47) pp. 127-8
14. JR to JJR 19.1.1829 *RFL* (66) p. 172
15. JJR to MR 24.2.1822 *RFL* (43) p. 118
16. *Præterita* I.I.13 (LE 35:20). In *Fors* letter 46 (LE 28.171) he notes that both his mother and aunt attended Mrs. Rice's school but that his aunt absolutely refused the Evangelical principles taught there and laughed at her beloved older sister for accepting them.
17. *Præterita* I.I.35 (LE 35:33)
18. *ibid.* I.III.70 (LE 35:63)
19. *ibid.* I.III.72 (LE 35:65) The reference is to the Oracle at Dodona in Greece founded by an Egyptian priestess abducted by merchants, mythologised as a dove, and whose successors were called 'doves'.
20. *ibid.* I.III.73-4 (LE 35:66)
21. MR to JJR 11.2.1822, *RFL* (42) p. 116
22. *Præterita* I.I.11 (LE 35:19)
23. *ibid.* I.II.41 (LE 35:37)
24. MR to JJR 25.5.1826: *RFL* (55) p. 148
25. *Præterita* I.V.96 (LE 35:87)
26. *ibid.* I.VII.150-1 (LE 35:130-1)

27. *ibid.* I.I.28 (LE 35:28)
28. *ibid.* I.V.116 (LE 35:101-2)
29. *ibid.* I.II.52 (LE 35:45-6)
30. *ibid.* I.II.41 (LE 35: 37)
31. *ibid.* I.II.49 (LE 35:44)
32. MR to JJR 10.4.1820: *RFL* (33) p. 98
33. MR to JJR 2.4.1821: *RFL* (34) p. 100
34. *Præterita* I.II.53 (LE 35:46)
35. *ibid.* I.V.100 (LE 35:89)
36. *ibid.* I.V.109 (LE 35:96)
37. *RFL* n. 2 p. 276. JJR account books: 'John's expenses Oxford [...] Archery £2 Fencing £5/13/0d' (Lancaster MS.28)
38. *Præterita* I.II.50 (LE 35:44-5)
39. *ibid* I.V.97 (LE 35:88)
40. JR to JJR 15.3.1823: *RFL* (47) pp. 127-8
41. JJR to JR 24.2.1832: *RFL* (100) p. 264
42. *Præterita* I.II.50 (LE 35:44-5)
43. *ibid.* I.I.9 (LE 35:18)
44. MR to JJR 19.2.1831: *RFL* (82) p. 217
45. JR to JJR 20.2.1832: *RFL* (99) p. 262

3: First Loves, pp. 50-55

1. *Præterita* I.III.71 (LE 35:65)
2. *ibid.* I.IV.81 (LE 35: 81-2). The 'Angel in the House' was Coventry Patmore's future wife Emily Augusta Andrews and the inspiration for his poem of that name. Rev. Mr. Andrews was the minister at the Ruskin family chapel in Walworth. In *Fors* Ruskin describes Sybilla Dowie whom he also met when he was twelve and she was twenty as 'certainly the most beautiful girl of the pure English-Greek type I ever saw.' (LE 29.426)
3. Joan Severn to Lucia Alexander 17.11. 1886: PML F. J. Sharp coll. MA 3451
4. *Præterita* I.X.206 (LE 35:179) The fifth and eldest daughter Diana had just married.
5. JJR to GG 28.4.1847: PML MA 1338 (C.02)
6. *Præterita* I.XII.247-9 (LE 35:221-2)
7. *ibid.* I.XII.257-9 (LE 35:229-232)
8. *ibid.* II.X.39. (LE 35:277)
9. *ibid.* II.II.192. (LE 35:422)
10. ECG to SMG 20.10.1851: PML MA 1338 (N.13). The median age of single persons entering into a first marriage in 1851 was

about 25 for both men and women. However the upper classes married much later than the lower.

4: The Dark Shadow, pp. 56-66

1. JJR to William Alexander 14.12.1854: PML MA 1571 (156)
2. Collingwood, *Life* (1893), Vol. 1, pp. 60-1
3. MR to JJR 7-8.5.1826: *RFL* (53) pp. 141-2
4. MR to JJR 25.5.1826: *RFL* (55) p. 149
5. *Præterita* I.III.70 (LE 35:63). Like the glover-Grays the tanner-Richardsons may have developed a resistance to tuberculosis through natural selection which Patrick's children by an outsider did not share.
6. John Richardson to GG 28.5.1830: Bodleian MS. Eng. lett. d.227, p. 43
7. JJR to GG 25.6.1835: Bodleian MS. Eng. lett. d.227, p.101. George Gray's son John had just died of whooping cough.
8. JJR to Melville Jameson: *R&G*, p. 14 (no date: no reference)
9. JR Diary 7.12.1840
10. JR Diary 12.3.1841
11. *Præterita* II.1.16-7 (LE 35.259)
12. *ibid.* II.1.17 (LE 35.259) & LE 1.418 *n*.2
13. Draft letter ECG to Mrs. La Touche 10.10.1870: PML MA 1338 (XYZ.04). See also Lutyens: 'The Millais – La Touche Correspondence', *Cornhill Magazine*, Spring 1967, p. 13
14. Collingwood, *Life*, Vol. 1, pp. 94-5. See JR to JJR 23.11.1853 re. Dr. Beveridge: 'His cures of various <u>spine</u> and nervous complaints are stated to be miraculous' [JR's emphasis]. Lancaster transcripts T110; original Yale.
15. *Edinburgh Guardian* 19.11.1853; 'walking, too, with a slight stoop', Collingwood, *Life* (1893), Vol. 1, p. 169
16. *Præterita* II.III.52 (LE 35:290-1)
17. See ECG to Rawdon Brown 27.4.1854: PML MA 1338 (T.47): 'Rome [...] he nearly died there once'.
18. LE 1.447 LCF Venice 16.5.1841.
19. All the dates mentioned are diary entries

20. JJR to GG 24.5.1841: PML MA 1338 (B.56a) quoted *R&G* p. 16 (no ref.)
21. Andrew Jameson to his sister 7.6.1841, quoted *R&G* p. 15 (no ref.)
22. Diary of Mary Richardson, 29.5.1841, p. 252. Unpublished typescript: Lancaster T49
23. JJR to JR 7.10.1841: *RFL* (244) p. 691
24. Collingwood, *Life*, (1893), Vol. 1, pp. 94-5
25. *Præterita* I.V.97 (LE 35:88)
26. JR to ECG 28.6.1849: PML MA 1338 (H.35)
27. *Præterita* I.V.96 (LE 35:87)
28. George Sand noted that Chopin, another tuberculosis victim, also experienced hallucinations and depression as a result of the disease.
29. MS: Lancaster L66
30. It has been noted recently that illegal immigrants to the UK often suffer a resurgence of latent tuberculosis owing to the stress of their journeys.
31. The question arises of why Effie did not contract the infection from John either before or during the marriage. The answer might be found in the occupation of her great-grandfather. He was also in the leather trade as a 'glover of Perth' and if this had been the family business for any length of time, a rather severe form of natural selection may well have operated in which only those resistant to the disease would have survived. Although the Grays lost many children through a variety of diseases, none of them succumbed to tuberculosis. A similar severe selective effect was observed in the enclosed society of historical Jewish ghettoes among whose members tuberculosis also became relatively rare.

5: The Fair Maid of Perth, pp. 67-91

1. JJR to William Alexander 14.12.1854: PML MA 1571 (156)
2. Clare Stuart Wortley: summary of school letters in Lancaster T148
3. Lutyens added punctuation to her transcripts of Effie's letters in order to make

them readable, and in the interests of clarity the present author was reluctantly compelled to adopt the same practice, even though this gives a rather misleading impression of Effie as a lady of letters.

4. Melville Jameson to SMG, 27.7.1841, from Grindelwald: PML MA 1338 (B.65)

5. Melville Jameson to GG. 12.8.1841: PML MA 1338 (B.67), R&G p. 17 (no ref.)

6. Melville Jameson to Andrew Jameson 17.7.1841: PML MA 1338 (B.64)

7. JJR to William Alexander Leith 14.12.1854: PML MA 1571 (156)

8. JJR to GG 10.12.1851: PML MA 1338 (N.26)

9. JJR to GG 16.2.1854: PML MA 1338 (T.09)

10. Lutyens omitted many of the references to dress and fashion.

11. JR to ECG 30.11.1847: PML MA 1338 (E.06)

12. Gray, *Marriage*, p. 19

13. James, *Order of Release*, p. 19. Clare Stuart Wortley is also certain that Effie was at Avonbank in 1847: see Lancaster T148 summary of school letters p. 3

14. JR to ECG 11.11.1847: PML MA 1338 (E.03)

15. Mrs. Gaskell to John Forster 18.5.1854: NLS MS.2262 f.35-40. Letter 195 in *The Letters of Mrs. Gaskell,* ed. J. Chapple & A. Pollard (1966). Mrs Gaskell may have had some inside information since Charlotte Ker, who accompanied the Ruskin's on their first trip to Venice, was 'a poor Scottish girl, the niece of some friends of mine'. Gaskell also knew Effie's old schoolmistress who she said four years previously had prophesied the precise (end) of it all, given Effie's high temper and love of admiration. The schoolmistress, who had stayed over a week with the Ruskins at Christmas 1853, claimed that Effie had been spoiled from her childhood and was now being spoiled by John who couldn't bear to thwart her even though he disapproved of her excess of visiting. Gaskell also quoted a Miss Wedgewood, a relation of the Byerleys who had founded the school, as having the same ideas and the same fears about Effie.

16. JJR to William Alexander 14.12.1854: PML MA 1571 (156)

17. Copy JJR to GG London 28.4.1847: PML MA 1338 (C.02)

18. JR to ECG Folkestone 30.11.1847: PML MA 1338 (E.06)

19. Copy JJR to GG 28.4.1847: PML MA 1338 (C.02)

20. GG to JJR Perth 1.5.1847: PML MA 1338 (C.03)

21. JEM to SMG 15.7.54: PML MA 1338 (UV.69)

22. ECG to SMG 11.3.1850: PML MA 1338 (K.24). 'I am very sorry I have had to cross my letter but I daresay Mama will read it entirely to you as I know you don't like crossed letters and it is bad for your eyesight reading these and even although I believe all gentlemen have the same dislike to them, but John tells me I write plainer than I used to which I hope is the case.'

23. ECG to SMG 5.5.1847: PML MA 1338 (C.07), R&G p. 35, James, *Order of Release,* p. 30

24. ECG to SMG Denmark Hill Fri. 7.5. 1847: PML MA 1338 (C.08)

25. ECG to SMG Denmark Hill 14.5.1847: PML MA 1338 (C.10)

26. ECG to SMG Ewell Castle 27.5.1847: PML MA 1338 (C.13)

27. JJR to GG 31.8.1848: PML MA 1338 (G.08)

28. JJR to ECG 21.11.1847: PML MA 1338 (D.09) 'I never saw the lady in question, I cannot therefore say I admired her.'

29. *Præterita* II.x.192 (LE 35:422)

30. *ibid.* II.x.198 (LE 35:428)

31. ECG to SMG 1[3].6.1849: PML MA 1338 (C.21)

32. JRR to JR 13/14.9.1847: Lancaster 1996 L01749

33. JRR to JR 2.9.1847: Lancaster 1996 L01744

34. JR to Lady Davy 13.8.1847: PML MA 2007 Misc. Eng. 1847-9

35. Lockhart to Murray, Milton 9.11.1846: John Murray Archive uncatalogued at Albemarle Street, now NLS MS.1566.

36. Lockhart to Charlotte Lockhart 30.12. 1846: NSL MS.1556 f.142-3. There is another interesting letter from Lockhart to Maria Edgeworth dated 2.5.1847 in which he tells her 'Charlotte is still my Charlotte'. James Hope's proposal appears on 21.7.1847 some time after Lockhart had dined with Mr. Ruskin at Denmark Hill. See A. Lang, *Life and Letters of J. G. Lockhart*, 1897, pp. 296, 299.

37. C. E. Norton: 'The Complete Ruskin', *New York Times,* 4.6.1904. Whether it was to be near her or to escape what had become an emotional impasse is not clear. Whilst he was there he wrote the article for her father's magazine. Had his suit been successful he was thinking of taking a house there.

38. LE 12.xl & 8.xxiv. Lockhart took exception to John's attack on Gally Knight – a John Murray author.

39. JJR to GG 3.5.1847: PML MA 1338 (C.04)

40. ECG to SMG 28.4.1847: PML MA 1338 (C.05)

41. ECG to SMG 28.4.1847: PML MA 1338 (C.05)

42. ECG to GGJr. 29.4.1847: PML MA 1338 (C.06)

43. ECG to SMG 5.5.1847: PML MA 1338 (C.07). Lutyens elided the description of Mrs. Liddell's dress.

44. JJR to JR 4.10.1847: Yale. LE 36:xviii-ix (part); Cook, *Life*, 1, p. 216 (part) PML HGV Box D ch. X (unpub.)

45. JJR to JR 2.9.1847: (Lancaster 1996 L01744), quoted *R&G* pp. 49-50

46. ECG to SMG 5.5.1847: PML MA 1338 (C.07)

47. Quoted from *Literary World*, 19.5.1893 by Collingwood, *Life,* (1911 ed), p. 117*n*.

48. See the note from Mary Millais to Clare Stuart Wortley 29.11.1939 about transcript letter ECG to GG Jr. 17.6.1847; Lancaster T148. Most of the references to these young men are red-pencilled (editor unknown) on the copy letters.

6: Strange Courtship, pp. 92-104

1. JR to ECG 23.2.1848: PML MA 1338 (E.19)

2. ECG to GG 15.6.1847: PML MA 1338 (C.22)

3. JR to ECG 30.11.1847: PML MA 1338 (E.06)

4. *Præterita* II.x.194 (LE 35.423)

5. ECG to SMG 7.6.1847: PML MA 1338 (C.20)

6. See JR to SMG, Crossmount, 1.9.1847: PML MA 1338 (D.04). 'PS. Mr. Macdonald begs to be most kindly brought to Miss Gray's remembrance (No mere matter of form this!)'.

7. JJR to JR 5.7.1845, Edinburgh, quoted: PML HGV Box 50, year file for 1845. 'MacDonald writes me a long letter anxious to bring you over to admire Scotland.'

8. *Præterita* II.x.196. 'William MacDonald took to me and got me to promise, that autumn, to come to me at Crossmount.' See also ECG to SMG, 12.6.1847, PML MA 1338 (C.21): 'I think he intends being at Crossmount to visit Mr. MacDonald.' See LE 39.78: 'Crossmount Lodge – a very small whitewashed house, with a little projecting square tower covered with ivy above the door, dining room and drawing-room, and a little library on the ground floor, and some six or seven small bedrooms above.'

9. ECG to SMG 18.6. 1847: PML MA 1338 (C.24)

10. *Præterita* II.x.198 (LE 35.428)

11. JR to SMG 15.9.1847: PML MA.1338 (D.05)

12. *Præterita* II.x.196 (LE 35.425)

13. JR to JJR 25.8.1847: LE 36.75

14. See JJR to William Alexander Leith, 14.12.1854, PML MA 1571 (156): 'my Son proposed Marriage to which, fearful of another blow to his Constitution, we consented.'

15. *R&G* pp. 48-9 ref: Unpublished: Stuart Wortley.

16. JJR to JR 2.9.1847: Lancaster 1996 L01744, quoted *R&G* pp. 49-50. The Revd. Thomas Dale had taught Ruskin in his Camberwell school, and had apparently said that that there were 74 girls in love

with him.

17. JJR to JR 8.9.1847: Lancaster 1996 L01746, quoted *R&G,* pp. 54-5

18. JJR to JR 13/14.9.1847: Lancaster 1996 L01749, quoted *EinV* pp. 11-3, no ref.

19. JJR to JR 4.10.1847: quoted Viljoen PML HGV Papers Box D ch. X (unpub). Ref LE 36.xviii-ix (part); Cook, *Life,* I, p. 216 (part):

20. JJR to William Alexander Leith, 14.12. 1854: PML MA 1571 (156)

21. MR to JR 11.9.1847: Whitehouse, *Vindication,* p. 37

22. JR to SMG 15.9.1847: PML MA 1338 (D.05)

7: The Proposal, pp. 105-114

1. JR to William Macdonald 5.10.1847: Lancaster L25

2. JR to SMG 10.10.1847: Bodleian MS. Eng. lett. c.228, p. 1-2 (and copy in: PML MA 1338 (D.07)). Sir Albert Gray felt that this letter was so problematical that he forbade the Bodleian to make it available to the public for thirty years after his death in 1928 (he had wanted an unprecedented eighty years), and then only to approved readers. On the same day JR wrote to John Murray asking for a two-week extension for his review of Eastlake's *Materials.* See John Murray Archive uncatalogued at Albemarle Street, now NLS. On 2.12.1847 he told Macdonald that 'I passed a most miserable Sunday at Berwick': *Nineteenth Century and After,* 5.1919, pp. 943-955. (Lancaster T30). On 13.3.1848 John wrote to Effie: 'But what a frightful place to stop at – Berwick – the very saddest and darkest town I ever – But then I had just parted from you, and that was perhaps the reason Edinburgh looked so ill': PML MA 1338 (E.25). See also the letter JR to Dr. John Brown 8.12.1847: 'Things had happened to cross me very much, and I was in a bad humour and ill', quoted HGV notes; original: Yale.

3. ECG to SMG 8.5.1847: PML MA 1338 (C.08)

4. James, *Order of Release,* p. 33

5. JR to ECG n.d. (probably 11.1847), first page missing: PML MA 1338 (E.04)

6. JR to ECG 2.11.1847: Private Collection, published M. Lutyens, 'From Ruskin to Effie Gray,' *Times Literary Supplement* 3.3.1978, quoted Hilton, *Early Years,* p. 115

7. Ruskin's statement to his lawyer: Whitehouse, *Vindication,* p. 13.

8. Gray, *Marriage,* pp. 20-1

9. JR to SMG 9.12.1847: PML MA 1338 (E.07)

10. JR to ECG 19.12.1847: PML MA 1338 (E.10)

11. JR to ECG 19.12.1847: PML MA 1338 (E.10); James, *Order of Release,* pp. 76-77; *R&G,* p. 74n.

12. See *R&G* p. 65 inter alia.

13. Andrew Jameson to GG: PML MA 1338 (D.10)

14. JR to ECG 15.12.1847: PML MA 1338 (E.08)

15. In a November letter (E.03) John promised to visit her in February. On January 3rd he reminded her 'only one whole month between us now.' (E.12) This visit never took place. It was in February that political events in France rendered George Gray's railway shares all but worthless. The opening paragraph of *R&G* ch. 9, p. 80, seems to elide February altogether.

8: A Very Sufficient and Entire Man-Trap pp. 115-143

1. JR to Rev. F. A. Malleson 28.11.1872: quoted *R&G* p. 67; transcript at Lancaster, original F. L. Malleson.

2. Mrs. Gaskell to John Forster 18.5.1854 NLS MS.2262 f.35-40. *The Letters of Mrs. Gaskell* ed. Chapple and Pollard (1966) p. 287

3. *The Brantwood Diary of John Ruskin,* ed Helen Gill Viljoen (1971) p. 369

4. *Daily Telegraph* 15.10.1932: Letter from Miss Violet Hunt

5. Lutyens identified William Kelty MacLeod, her suitor and favourite polka partner, as the son of Lt-Col. Alexander MacLeod, a

neighbour at Greenbank, Kinnoull. See
R&G p. 66.

6. JR to ECG Thursday n.d. (11.11?): PML MA
1338 (E.03)

7. JR to ECG 30.11.1847: PML MA 1338 (E.06)

8. JR to ECG 19.12.1847: PML MA 1338 (E.10).
There is an unmarked elision in John's
letter of December 19th as it appears in
James, and Lutyens separated the elided
material from its context in a rather
confusing manner. This is the full text of
that part of the letter.

9. There are also red-pencilled references to
Prizie, a Perth neighbour of the Grays,
in the copy letters at Lancaster. See
Lancaster T148 copy letter ECG to SMG
28.4.1847 and note by CSW 'a young man
whose admiration of Effie reached the
first stages of courtship with the approval
of her parents; but who does not seem
ever to have got any further, doubtless
because John Ruskin was preferred.' In a
letter of 29.4.1847, PML MA 1338 (C.06), to
George from Denmark Hill Effie also
mentions 'Brooks' as a potential rival to
Prizie and hopes 'Prizie will call on me
after the 18th if he is in town.' He did. See
ECG to SMG 2.6.1847, PML MA 1338
(C.16) [red-pencilled]. 'Snob' Gardner also
gets two mentions in her letters 'on horseback, he is much improved in appearance
and seems very proud of being now six
feet' 7.5.1847, PML MA 1338 (C.08) [all
passages marked in copy letters in
Lancaster T148]

10. JR to ECG 11.9.1847: PML MA 1338 (E.04)

11. JR to ECG 9.1.1848: PML MA 1338 (E.13)

12. JR to ECG Thursday n.d. (11.11): PML MA
1338 (E.03)

13. ECG to SMG 15.5.1850: PML MA 1338
(L.06)

14. JR to ECG 15.12.1847: PML MA 1338 (E.08)

15. JR to ECG 9.11.1847: PML MA 1338 (E. 02)

16. ECG to JR 8.2.1848: PML MA 1338 (E.16)

17. JR to ECG 15.12.1847: PML MA 1338
(E.08). Dante, *Inferno,* Canto IX. The
tower is the home of Medusa, the queen

of endless woe and her three attendants
Megæra, Alecto and Tisiphone, hellish
furies stained with blood. It was perhaps
fortunate that Effie was very unlikely to
have understood the reference.

18. JR to ECG Thursday n.d. [11.11.1847]:
PML MA 1338 (E.03)

19. MR to JJR 17.3.1831: *RFL* (95) p. 251

20. MR to JR 27.11.1847: *R&G* p. 71 ref.
CSW; also Whitehouse, *Vindication*, pp.
40-1.

21. JJR to ECG 21.11.47: PML 1338 (D.09)

22. PML MA 1338 (E.16)

23. PML MA 1338 (E.17). The ending is an
imitation of John's scrawl.

24. PML MA 1338 (E.18). Catalogued as 20th
February.

25. MR to JJR 3.2.48: *R&G* p.83-4; Lancaster
1997 LO2159

26. ECG to SMG 27.2.1854: PML MA 1338
(T.10)

27. JR to ECG 3.1.1848: PML MA 1338 (E.12)

28. JR to ECG 23.2.1848: PML MA 1338 (E.19)

29. JR to ECG 21.11.1847: PML MA 1338 (E.05)

30. JR to ECG 30.11.1847: PML MA 1338 (E.05)

31. JR to ECG 30.11.1847: PML MA 1338 (E.06)

32. JR to ECG 15.12.1847: PML MA 1338 (E.08)

33. JR to ECG 15.12.1847: PML MA 1338 (E.08)

34. JR to ECG 23.2.1848: PML MA 1338 (E.19)

35. JR to ECG 23.2.1848: PML MA 1338 (E.19)

36. JR to ECG 28.2.1848: PML MA 1338 (E.21)

37. ECG to SMG 19.3.1848: PML MA 1338
(E.26); *R&G*, p. 95 no ref.

38. JR to ECG 14.3.1848: PML MA 1338 (E.25)

39. JR to ECG 6.3.1848: private collection,
quoted, Hilton, *Early Years,* pp. 116-7

9: A Speculative Man, pp. 144-166

1. JJR to JR 8.9.1847: *R&G,* p. 54; Lancaster
LO1746

2. JJR to JR 2.9.1847: *R&G* p. 50; Lancaster
1996 LO1744

3. JJR to GG 22.3.1848: PML MA 1338 (E.31)

4. GGJr. to SMG before July 1843: PML MA
1338 (B.74). See also SMG to GG 'I would
fain think you had a long enough head for
the Americans, clever as they are at helping

themselves.' Copy Lancaster T148

5. JJR to GG 17.11.1849: PML MA 1338 (1J.18)

6. JJR to GG 26.7.1849: PML MA 1338 (H.15)

7. JJR to GG 17.3.1848: PML MA 1338 (E.29) Elided by Lutyens.

8. MR to JR Denmark Hill 11.9.1847, quoted Whitehouse: *Vindication,* p. 36. See also Viljoen year file 1847: PML HGV Box 50. Second sentence an unmarked elision in James, p. 44, also elided in Lutyens.

9. JR to JJR 22.7.1848: *R&G* p.156; original Yale.

10. As for example the Brontës. See Rebecca Fraser: *Charlotte Brontë* (1988), p. 248. For more general information about the speculation and the economic history of this period see: Andrew Odlyzko: *Collective Hallucinations and Inefficient Markets: the British railway mania of the 1840's* (Minnesota, 2010) p. 32; D. M. Evans: *The Commercial Crisis, 1847-1848 Being Facts and Figures* (1849) pp. 77-83; M. D. Bordo & A. J. Schwartz, eds.: *A Retrospective on the Classical Gold Standard* (Chicago 1984), pp. 233-276

11. She was still looking out for young George's interest a year later. See ECG to GG & SMG 11.4.1848: PML MA 1338 (F.01)

12. ECG to SMG 27.5.1847: PML MA 1338 (C.16)

13. JJR to GG 23.2.1848: PML MA 1338 (E.20)

14. JR to ECG (n.d., 11.1847): PML MA 1338 (E.04)

15. JJR to GG 17.3.1848: PML MA 1338 (E.29) The elision in this quotation was quoted earlier in the chapter (p. 144; see fn. 7).

16. JR to GG 17.3.1848: PML MA 1338 (E.28)

17. JJR to GG 22.3.1848: PML MA 1338 (E.31)

18. Ruskin's Statement to his Proctor in Whitehouse, *Vindication,* p. 13. See also PML MA 1571 (156) JJR to William Alexander Leith 14.12.1854: 'it was only after settlements were signed that Mr. Gray told the young Couple at Sheriff Jameson's House in Edinr. in April 1848 that he was a ruined Man – his House and Furniture not being his own.'

19. Whitehouse, *Vindication,* p. 14

20. MR to JR 27.11.1847: Whitehouse, *Vindication,* pp. 40-1

21. JJR to GG 23.2.1848: PML MA 1338 (E.20)

22. ECG to Pauline Trevelyan 6.4.1848: quoted Surtees, *Reflections of a Friendship,* p. 4. Since none of John's friends attended it is not clear who these 'mutual friends' were.

23. Andrew Jameson to SMG 30.3.1848: PML MA 1338 (E.33)

24. Whitehouse, *Vindication,* p. 13

25. JJR to GG 28.3.1848: PML MA 1338 (E.32)

26. Whitehouse, *Vindication,* pp. 13-14

27. This was technically true since although JJR had been told that George Gray was facing financial ruin even before the settlements were signed, it was only a matter of days before the wedding that John heard first from Effie and then from Mr. Gray himself that Bowerswell House and its furniture had been seized, by which time it was far too late to stop the marriage, which indeed had been frantically brought forward by the Grays. See: PML MA 1571 (156): JJR to William Alexander Leith 14.12.1854

28. JJR to GG 22.3.48: PML MA 1338 (E.31)

29. JJR to GG 28.3.48: PML MA 1338 (E.32)

30. JR to JJR 27.9.48: *R&G* pp. 155-6, ref.: unpublished Yale

31. See JJR to GG 19.5.1849: PML MA 1338 (H.29); Lancaster transcript T147

32. PML MA 1571 (156): JJR to William Alexander Leith 14.12.1854 'I did not go to the Marriage but I told my Son that out of respect for him I would settle £10,000 on her.'

33. JJR Account book, Lancaster MS.30, 'My entire property on the 1st April 1850.'

34. JJR accounts 1845-63, Lancaster MS.29. In the accounts for April 1848 there is a payment of £24. 12/5d to Rutter the solicitor for 'John's settlement' and £7. 9/- for 'John's settlement transfer'.

35. JJR accounts 1826-52, Lancaster MS.30. In 1853 Mr. Ruskin was worth £81,592. 15/2d. By the time of his death this had doubled

to a colossal £161,416. 0/18d.

36. JJR Accounts 1845-63, Lancaster MS.29.

37. J. C. Rutter to JJR 20.8.1854: PML MA 1571 (167). The 10,000 3¼%'s 'formerly John's' were converted to new 3%'s on 10 April 1855.

38. Nor did the Ruskins ask for repayment of the income Effie had received from the settlement during the marriage although they had a legal right to do so. The story put about by Charles Augustus Howell (W. Rossetti, *Rossetti Papers,* pp. 196, 225) that Mr. Ruskin gave Effie £40,000 on her marriage and that the sum remained with her after the annulment and was still maintaining her father and mother in 1867 is entirely unfounded and is disproved by the accounts both financial and epistolary. It was also categorically denied by Sir Albert Gray (see Gray, *Marriage,* App. 3)

39. *R&G* p. 104 and Brantwood Diary p. 369.

40. See Whitehouse: *Vindication* p. 33, where W. G. Collingwood is quoted referring to the 'disappointment and disillusioning of a young girl who found herself married, by parental arrangement, to a man with whom she had nothing in common.' The parents who did the arranging were the Grays.

10: The Wedding, pp. 167-180

1. See National Archives of Scotland CH2299/80 *A Bill intituled An Act to amend the Law of Scotland affecting the constitution of Marriage.* 'Whereas the law of Marriage in Scotland has by reason of its great Uncertainty been found to be attended with serious Evils, and it is otherwise expedient that the same be amended as regards the Constitution of Marriage in that country'.

2. 'It is a sad disappointment to me Lizzie Cockburn not being able to be my bridesmaid; now she is obliged to go with Lord Cockburn on the Circuit.' ECG to Pauline Trevelyan 6.4.1848, quoted Surtees, *Reflections of a Friendship,* p. 4.

3. See JR to Mrs. Buckland 23.4.1848 (Bodleian Eng. misc. c.215): 'we sent cards to no-one – I found my wife's acquaintance and mine was too numerous to be received en masse at Denmark Hill.'

4. See *Nineteenth Century and After Magazine,* Vol. 85, May 1919, pp. 943-955; J. H. Whitehouse: 'Ruskin and an early friendship' (William Macdonald corr.) There was some friction between them on religious matters but the 'personal note' John included in his letter of 2.12.1847 was almost certainly announcing his secret engagement to Effie and probably asking him to be best man. However, John did not attend Macdonald's wedding (Effie went alone) and refused to congratulate him on his son's birth, claiming that he was not his friend, ECG to SMG 8.2.52: PML MA 1338 (0.09). His changed attitude was sufficient to prompt an enquiry from Macdonald's mother whether there was any coolness between John and her son. John denied that there was (see *LFV* 27, 2.10.1851) and in later correspondence John was perfectly affable with Macdonald (see undated ALS, a reply to a query on the subject of stained glass probably written in the early years of his marriage, Princeton CO.199 series A 47813)

5. JJR to GG 13.6.49: PML MA 1338 (H.31)

6. James, *Order of Release,* p. 95

7. Gray, *Marriage,* App. 1, p. 39

8. Another, unlikely, alternative is that they suspected that marriage with a weak man might be short-lived.

9. Sir Henry Newbolt: *My World as in my Time: Memoirs 1862-1932,* (1932), pp. 221-2

10. See also E. C. Gaskell to Mr. Foster 18.5.1854, NLS MS.2262 f.35-40. Even Mrs. Gaskell had heard the gossip, 'so many stories were told falsely 2 years ago about them – one was that while abroad they travelled in separate carriages' which, she explained, they did, but not for the reasons people supposed. Mrs Gaskell insisted that she *knew* all this because Charlotte

Ker was 'the neice of some friends of mine' and had therefore heard an eye witness account."

11. ECG to Mrs. La Touche 10.10.1870: PML MA 1338 (XYZ.04)

12. Jeannie Boswell relayed the Scottish gossip to ECG on 10.7.1854, PML MA 1338 (UV.66): 'I hear that a number of people say this is what might have been expected for your marrying JR as you, your father and mother all agreed to his condition as to how you and he were to live together. Now I am sure this is untrue: then that all the Perth people knew long ago the terms you lived on, and so they go on – wondering yr. mother ever permitted the marriage.'

13. PML MA 1338 (T.51-58) Notes in handwriting of Charles Stuart-Wortley (a KC and MP, husband of Effie's daughter Alice) on a conversation with Eliza Jameson 9.1.1925. *M&R* p. 186 n. 3.

14. Lady Eastlake to ECG 3.5.1854: PML MA 1338 (UV.13)

15. JJR to Charles Collins 28.12.1854: PML MA 1571 (156)

16. ECG to Rawdon Brown 9.5.1854: PML MA 1338 (UV.20)

17. George Gray's will in the Perth Library mentions that prints of Hogarth's *Marriage à la Mode* were hung on the stairs at Bowerswell! Gray & Jameson family papers 1847-1949 MS.126

18. W. G. Collingwood to Albert Gray 6.2.1893: Gray, *Marriage*, pp. 55-6 (11-12)

19. John's statement to his solicitor 27.4.54: Whitehouse, *Vindication*, p. 14

20. See the correspondence between Whitehouse and Sir Albert Gray and particularly the letters of 15.1.1925 and 20.1.1925. Also the correspondence between Sir Albert Gray and the representative of Mrs. Veitch whose husband had inherited the papers and letters from Ruskin's solicitor: Bodleian MS. Eng. lett. c.228 (118-132) (134-169). The sequence of events was described by Whitehouse in *Vindication*,

pp. 10-11. Mrs. Veitch thought she could make some money from the letters that had come to her and contacted John Murray, who contacted Gray. The letters were however the property and copyright of John Ruskin. They should have been returned by his solicitor and therefore ownership passed to Ruskin's executors on his death. As they were confidential correspondence with his solicitor Rutter there was also the question of a breach of professional confidence. Gray strung out the correspondence for months in the knowledge that Whitehouse was seriously ill. He only surrendered Ruskin's statements to his solicitor after Whitehouse finally threatened legal action. As a lawyer Gray knew he would lose. No-one but Mrs. Veitch (Rutter's successor's widow) and Gray saw the letters hinted at in their correspondence and mentioned by Ruskin himself in the Statements and elsewhere as proof that he had no intention of not consummating the marriage beforehand and proof of Effie's duplicity prior to the marriage. Gray flatly denied that they had come into his possession and Whitehouse, having never seen them, could not prove Gray a liar. Gray kept an illegal copy of the Statements despite Whitehouse's protests. Gray had told Mrs Veitch that he intended to burn the letters and this is almost certainly what happened to them.

21. JR to ECG 30.11.1847: PML MA 1338 (E.06)

22. JR to Miss Wedderburn 2.3.1848: Wedderburn transcript p. 289, Bodleian MS. Eng. lett. c.32

23. SMG to MR 4.11.48, quoted *R&G* p. 106

24. Quoted Whitehouse, *Vindication*, p. 40

25. John's statement to his solicitor 27.4.54: Whitehouse, *Vindication*, p. 14

26. JR to Mary Russell Mitford 21.4.1853, LE 36.85. John claimed that this depression began some two months previously. This was when the Bourbon monarchy fell and George Gray was financially ruined.

27. Sir Albert Gray to Collingwood 16.3.1893

where he is extremely agitated about 'a passage from a letter of Mr. Ruskin to Miss Mitford [see cutting in d.652], written eleven days later, which shows Mr. Ruskin in some distress of mind, and the impression is conveyed as seems to have been intended, that the writer was suffering the natural distress of a man who has been led into a marriage de convenance.' Gray, *Marriage*, App. 1, p. 62-3; original in Bodleian MS. Eng. lett. c.228

28. ECG to GG 7.3.1854: PML MA 1338 (T.17)

29. MacDonald: *Reminiscences*, p. 100

30. Roderick Phillips: *Putting Asunder* (1988) quoting M. Girouard: *The Return to Camelot* (1981), pp. 200-3

31. Restraint was not the only explanation. Contemporaries refer to 'French tricks and German vices' involved in childless marriages.

32. JR to ECG 19.1.1848: PML MA 1338 (E.13)

11: The Newly-weds, pp. 181-210

1. ECG to SMG 11.4.1848: PML MA 1338 (F.02)

2. ECG to SMG 13.4.1848: PML MA 1338 (F.03)

3. ECG to SMG 19.4.1848: PML MA 1338 (F.06)

4. ECG to Pauline Trevelyan from Dover 24.6.1848, quoted Surtees: *Reflections of a Friendship,* p. 6. Had John been having sleepless nights?

5. JR to JJR 13.4.1848: unpublished letter from Tarbert in Yale University Library quoted Leon, *Great Victorian*, p. 117.

6. A non-consummation pact would have been seen as wilful non-consummation and undermined the whole case.

7. ECG to SMG 28.4.1848: PML MA 1338 (F.08)

8. JJR to GG 28.4.1848: PML MA 1338 (F.09)

9. ECG to SMG 29.4.1848: 1.5.1848 (F.10)

10. ECG to GG 3.5.1848: PML MA 1338 (F.11)

11. ECG to SMG 8.5.1848: PML MA 1338 (F.13)

12. JJR to GG 24.5.1848: PML MA 1338 (F.20)

13. Effie's very first letter home after the wedding had expressed a hope that the family's financial affairs might not be as bad as they anticipated and that some of their former property might eventually be returned to them, but that if they lost the whole world they should count their blessings and trust in God. 'Tell dear George I will not forget his interests and I think they are in no danger we plan to see about [illeg.] as soon as we possibly can.' ECG to GG & SMG 11.4.1848: PML MA 1338 (F.02)

14. JR to SMG 12.5.1848: PML MA 1338 (F.16)

15. ECG to SMG 29.5.1848: PML MA 1338 (F.21)

16. ECG to SMG 7.6.1848: PML MA 1338 (F.24)

17. ECG to SMG 7.6.1848: PML MA 1338 (F.31). Quoted *R&G* p. 124, no ref.

18. ECG to SMG 10.7.1848: PML MA 1338 (F.32)

19. SMG to JJR 11.1849: (IJ.12) NB: This is a copy.

20. JR to ECG 30.11.1847: PML MA 1338 (E.06)

21. JR to ECG 23.2.1848: PML MA 1338 (E.19)

22. JR to SMG 9.12.1847: PML MA 1338 (E.07)

23. JR to ECG 3.1.1848: PML MA 1338 (E.12)

24. JJR to W. H. Harrison 20.7.1848: 'I find it very slow hanging about here'.

25. ECG to MR 25.4.1854: PML MA 1338 (T.43) NB: this is a copy.

26. ECG to SMG 20.7.1848: PML MA 1338 (F.34)

27. JJR to GG 4.7.1849: PML MA 1338 (H.36)

28. JR to GG 5.7.1849: PML MA 1338 (H.38)

29. ECG to 'Papa & Mama' 11.4.1848: PML MA 1338 (F.02)

30. ECG to GG 22.4.1848: PML MA 1338 (F.07)

31. ECG to SMG 23.7.1848: PML MA 1338 (F.35)

32. ECG to SMG 30.7.1848: PML MA 1338 (F.37)

33. ECG to GG 3.8.1848: PML MA 1338 (F.38)

34. JR to MR 20.8.1848: quoted *R&G* pp.

133-4; original: Yale.

35. JR to JJR 10.9.1848: quoted J. G. Links: *The Ruskins in Normandy*, (1968) pp. 46-7, no ref.; original: probably Yale.

36. JR to ECG 22.4.1849: PML MA 1338 (H.19)

37. GG to ECG 28.8.1848 PML MA 1338 (G.06) & JJR to GG 24.8.1848 PML MA 1338 (G.04)

38. JR to JJR 4.9.1848: quoted *R&G* p. 140; original: Yale.

39. JR to JJR 9.9.1848: quoted *R&G* p. 140; original: Yale.

40. JR to JJR 5.10.1848: quoted *R&G* p. 160; original: Yale.

41. ECG to SMG 5.10.1848: PML MA 1338 (G.19)

42. ECG to GG 10.10.1848: PML MA 1338 (G.20)

43. ECG to SMG 23-4.10.1848: PML MA 1338 (G.24)

44. JR to JJR 11.9.1848: quoted *R&G* p. 152. Original: Yale

45. JR to GG 5.7.1849: PML MA 1338 (H.38)

46. ECG to SMG 27.10.1848, PML MA 1338 (G.25) John was presumably in the Gentlemen's cabin for the short crossing.

12: Keeping House, pp. 211-256

1. JR to GG 5.7.1849: PML MA 1338 (H.38)

2. ECG to SMG 27.10.1848: PML MA 1338 (G.25)

3. ECG to SMG 27.10.1848: PML MA 1338 (G.25)

4. ECG to SMG 28.10.1848: PML MA 1338 (G.27)

5. ECG to SMG 1.11.1848: PML MA 1338 (G.28)

6. *EinV* p. 26n. no ref.

7. JJR to GG 6.11.1848: PML MA 1338 (G.29)

8. JJR to GG 6.11.1848: PML MA 1338 (G.29) and ECG to SMG 9.11.1848: PML MA 1338 (G.30)

9. ECG to SMG 12.11.1848: PML MA 1338 (G.32)

10. ECG to SMG 5.12.1848: PML MA 1338 (G.38)

11. JJR to GG 16.2.1854: PML MA 1338 (T.09)

'They have had from me 15,500 and spent all except a short lease of house and value of furniture.'

12. JR to GG 5.7.1849: PML MA 1338 (H.38)

13. GG to SMG 25.1.1849: PML MA 1338 (H.10)

14. MR to JJR 5.2.1849: Lancaster 1996 L02165. In the event Effie stayed with the Macdonalds at St. Martins near Perth and, besides the horse exercise, she went for dinner with the Farquharsons at Ayr and visited Edinburgh.

15. JJR to GG 19.5.1849: PML MA 1338 (H.29)

16. JR to ECG 3.5.1849: PML MA 1338 (H.26)

17. MR to JJR 5.2.1849: Lancaster 1996 L02165. Mr. Ruskin insisted John and Effie keep accounts when they were in Venice and examined them carefully when they returned.

18. Diary for 1849, p. 2: Wedderburn transcripts, Bodleian Eng. misc. c.215

19. JJR to GG 4.3.1849: PML MA 1338 (H.16)

20. JR to ECG 22.4.1849: PML MA 1338 (H.19)

21. JR to ECG 24.4.1849: PML MA 1338 (H.20). At the time of the annulment Effie declared in her statement that they had been naked in bed together. This was a necessary proof condition of the charge of impotence but in the light of these declarations there is no reason not to believe her.

22. JR to ECG 27.4.1849: PML MA 1338 (H.21)

23. He had already made a similar comment to Dr. J. Brown in a letter written from Folkestone on 15.4.1849: 'I trust that she is now gaining strength and that when she is restored to me, or as I feel almost inclined to say, when we are married next time, I hope to take better care of her.' Wedderburn transcript. Bodleian MS. Eng. lett. c.33.

24. JR to ECG 29.4.1849: PML MA 1338 (H.22)

25. JR to ECG 2.5.1849: PML MA 1338 (H.25)

26. JR to ECG 10.5.1849: PML MA 1338 (H.27)

27. JJR to GG 19.5.1849: PML MA 1338 (H.29) See Lady Violet Greville: *Ladies in the Field: Sketches of Sport*, London (1894):

'The healthful, exhilarating feeling caused by rapid movement through the air, and the sense of power conveyed by the easy gallop of a good horse, tends greatly to moral and physical well-being and satisfaction. Riding improves the temper, the spirits and the appetite; black shadows and morbid fancies disappear from the mental horizon...' quoted J. Trollope: *Britannia's Daughters* (1983), p. 205.

28. *R&G* p. 209

29. James Young Simpson: *Answer to the Religious Objections Advanced against the Employment of Anæsthetic Agents in Midwifery and Surgery,* December 1847. It has never been clear where these supposed religious objections originated.

30. Pauline Trevelyan: diary for 19.11.1853. I am grateful to John Batchelor for directing me to the microfilm of Lady Trevelyan's diary for the period in Newcastle University library. After returning from Venice Effie supplied chloroform to her former physician there. In her December 1848 review of *Vanity Fair* and *Jane Eyre* Elizabeth Rigby spoke of taking 'ether with our fellow-Christians for a twelve-month', *Quarterly Review*, p. 153.

31. JR to ECG 27.5.1849: PML MA 1338 (H.29a)

32. JJR to GG 4.6.1849: PML MA 1338 (H.30)

33. JJR to GG 13.6.1849: PML MA 1338 (H.31)

34. GG to JJR draft letter 22.6.1849: PML MA 1338 (H.33)

35. JR to ECG 15.6.1849: PML MA 1338 (H.32)

36. JR to ECG 24.6.1849: PML MA 1338 (H.34)

37. JJR to GG 4.7.1849: PML MA 1338 (H.36)

38. ECG to SMG 13.11.1849: PML MA 1338 (IJ.17)

39. GG to JJR (fragment) 22.6.1849: PML MA 1338 (H.37)

40. JR to GG 5.7.1849: PML MA 1338 (H.38)

41. ECG to SMG 8.11.1849: PML MA 1338 (IJ.15)

42. ECG to GG 6-9.1.1850: PML MA (K.02)

43. See JR to JJR 15.1.1852, *LFV* 115: 'I don't think Effie will stay in Scotland this time—

she did not find it so pleasant before—and besides people made so many impertinent remarks to her, and talked so much scandal that I don't much wonder at her not choosing to do it a second time.'

44. JJR to GG 7.8.1849: PML MA 1338 (H.39)

45. JR to ECG 2.9.1849: PML MA 1338 (H.41)

46. JR to ECG 8.9.1849: PML MA 1338 (H.42)

13: Ocean's Lovely Daughter, pp. 257-283

1. JJR to JR 26.9.1849: Lancaster 1996 LO1771)

2. ECG to SMG 30.9.1849: PML MA 1338 (H.44)

3. ECG to SMG 30.9.1849: PML MA 1338 (H.44)

4. JR to Lady Davy 25.10.1849: PML MA 2007 Misc. Eng. 1847-9

5. JJR to GG 20.10.1849: PML MA 1338 (IJ.06)

6. JJR to William Alexander, Leith 14.12.1854: PML MA 1571 (156)

7. ECG to SMG 6.10.1849: PML MA 1338 (IJ.01)

8. ECG to GG 9.10.1849: PML MA 1338 (IJ.03)

9. ECG to SMG 17.10.1849: PML MA 1338 (IJ.05)

10. ECG to GG 27.10.1849: PML MA 1338 (IJ.08)

11. ECG to GG 28.10.1849: PML MA 1338 (IJ.09)

12. ECG to SMG 4.11.1849: PML MA 1338 (IJ.14)

13. ECG to SMG 8.11.1849: PML MA 1338 (IJ.15)

14. ECG to SMG 8.11.1849: PML MA 1338 (IJ.15)

15. ECG to SMG 13.11.1849: PML MA 1338 (IJ.17)

16. ECG to GG Jr. 15(18?).11.1849: PML MA 1338 (IJ.19)

17. ECG to SMG 19.11.1849: PML MA 1338 (IJ.21)

18. JJR to GG 17.11.1849: PML MA 1338 (IJ.18)

19. ECG to SMG 13.11.1849: PML MA 1338 (IJ.17); 19.11.1849 (IJ.21); 27.11. 1849 (IJ.24)

20. ECG to SMG 27.11.1849: PML MA 1338 (IJ.24)

21. ECG to SMG 24.11.1849: PML MA 1338 (IJ.22)

22. ECG to SMG 19.11.1849: PML MA 1338 (IJ.21)

23. ECG to SMG 24.11.1849: PML MA 1338 (IJ.22)

24. Brown seems to have taken an extraordinary interest in the Austrian siege even to the extent of making himself an observation post up a tree within the field of fire of a gun firing 900lb shells.

25. Mrs. Gray and Millais first met Brown at the time of the annulment. Millais wrote: 'I was astonished to find Mr. Brown such a youthful gentleman – I had conceived in my mind (I don't know why) that he was slightly infirm in appearance, and paternal in character, but I think Mr. Brown will have a young wife yet. He is very nervous and quaint.' JEM to SMG 6.5.1854: PML MA 1338 (UV.17). I was amused to note that Tim Hilton also misapprehended Brown as a 'shrewd old man': *Early Years,* p. 148.

26. ECG to SMG 30.12.1849: PML MA 1338 (IJ.31)

27. ECG to SMG 22.12.1849: PML MA 1338 (IJ.29)

28. ECG to SMG 18.1.1850: PML MA 1338 (K.08). The end of the letter is filed as K.12.

29. ECG to SMG 22.12.1849: PML MA 1338 (IJ.29)

30. ECG to SMG 9.2.1850: PML MA 1338 (K.16)

31. ECG to SMG 22.12.1849: PML MA 1338 (IJ.29)

32. ECG to Rawdon Brown 29.12.1849: PML MA 1338 (IJ.30)

33. ECG to GGJr 13-16(?).1.1850: PML MA 1338 (K.04)

34. ECG to SMG 27.1.1850: PML MA 1338 (K.12)

35. ECG to SMG 24.2.1850: PML MA 1338 (K.20)

36. ECG to SMG 24.2.1850: PML MA 1338 (K20). Elided by Lutyens.

37. ECG to SMG 3.2.1850: PML MA 1338 (K.14)

38. ECG to SMG 11.3.1850: PML MA 1338 (K.23). 'I had another long letter to George which if you think proper you can send to him.'

39. Although even his mother had gone to see Taglioni in his youth. In *Præterita* she has 'faultless genius' and 'stainlessly simple character' (LE 35.176).

40. ECG to SMG 24.2.1850: PML MA 1338 (K.20)

41. ECG to SMG 24.11.1849: PML MA 1338 (IJ.22)

42. ECG to SMG 18.1.1850: PML MA 1338 (K.08)

43. ECG to Rawdon Brown 22.2.1849 (error for 1850): PML MA 1338 (K.19)

14: Hiatus, pp. 284-299

1. ECG to GG 10.12.1849: PML MA 1338 (IJ.27)

2. ECG to SMG 22.12.1849: PML MA 1338 (IJ.29)

3. ECG to SMG 11.3.1850: PML MA 1338 (K.23)

4. ECG to SMG 18.4.1850: PML MA 1338 (K.31)

5. ECG to SMG 7.4.1850: PML MA 1338 (K.28)

6. ECG to SMG 21.4.1850: PML MA 1338 (L.01)

7. ECG to SMG 10.5.1850: PML MA 1338 (L.05). Quite where she got this money is unclear.

8. In a letter to Rawdon Brown dated 2.7.1850 Effie, pining for Venice, wrote: 'how sorry I am for some people having not seen half what I have and not many have enjoyed themselves more': PML MA 1338 (L.23).

9. ECG to Rawdon Brown 4.1850: PML MA 1338 (L.02). There are definite echoes of Baron Béthune's marriage here.

10. ECG to SMG 15.5.1850: PML MA 1338 (L.06). This may well be the same Newton who was later to turn up in Venice. He was

afterwards arrested for spying (sketching the fortifications) at Verona, put in jail and then ignominiously expelled from the Austrian territories. See *The Gardener's Chronicle Newspaper* 28.8.1852.

11. GGJr to SMG 28.5.1850: PML MA 1338 (L.08)

12. GGJr to SMG 12.6.1850: PML MA 1338 (L.15)

13. ECG to SMG 24.5.1850: PML MA 1338 (L.08)

14. ECG to Rawdon Brown 2.7.1850: PML MA 1338 (L.23)

15. ECG to Rawdon Brown 18?.8.1850: PML MA 1338 (L.39)

16. ECG to Rawdon Brown 2.7.1850: PML MA 1338 (L.23)

17. See ECG to SMG 9.2.1850: 'As usual I danced considerably with Troubetzkoi.' This despite his having cleverly made love to her earlier: PML MA 1338 (K.16)

18. ECG to SMG 3/5.7.1850: PML MA 1338 (L.24); and ECG to Rawdon Brown 2.7.1850: PML MA 1338 (L.23)

19. ECG to Rawdon Brown incomplete letter n.d. (18.8?): PML MA 1338 (L.39)

20. ECG to Rawdon Brown: PML MA 1338 (L.39)

21. ECG to SMG 26.10.1850: PML MA 1338 (L.40)

22. ECG to Rawdon Brown 11.12.1850: PML MA 1338 (L.48)

23. JR to SMG n.d. 29?.12.1850, (Copy): PML MA 1338 (L.45)

24. Although the city began to fill with the social élite from February onwards I assume John meant the main Season from Easter to July. The first volume of *The Stones* was published in March.

25. John had met the Pritchards through his old Oxford tutor the Rev. Osborne Gordon. John Pritchard, a trained lawyer, was MP for Bridgnorth at the time.

26. JR Diary 1.5.1851.

27. It had an expensive ornamental binding. She mentioned it on 24.11.1849 but was uncertain if that was the book on

which John was then working. PML MA 1338 (IJ.22)

28. ECG to Rawdon Brown 2.6.1851: PML MA 1338 (M.32)

29. ECG to SMG 8.1851: PML MA 1338 (M.38)

30. George Gray to his niece Mrs. Stuart Wortley 3.5.1910. Lancaster typescript. See also *M&R*, pp. 14 & 233.

15: Queen of Marble and of Mud, pp. 300-314

1. JR to JJR 9.9.1851: *LFV* 6

2. ECG to GGJr 19.9.1851: PML MA 1338 (N.09). A state of affairs entirely approved of by both John and Mr. Ruskin: see *EinV* p. 187 (no ref.).

3. On 18.9.1851 John had worked out that compared with the previous year at the Danieli they saved 7 napoleons a month in rooms, 11 francs a day in food and 5 swansigs a day in gondola expenses: *LFV* 13.

4. ECG to GGJr 19.9.1851: PML MA 1338 (N.09)

5. JR to JJR 19.11.1851: *LFV* 60

6. JJR to GG 10.12.1851: PML MA 1338 (N.26). Including James' unmarked elisions.

7. JR to JJR 21.12.1851: *LFV* 91. Mrs. Ruskin's eyesight was failing.

8. JR to JJR 16.1.1852: *LFV* 117

9. JR to JJR 16.1.1852: *LFV* 117

10. JR to JJR 16.1.1852: *LFV* 117

11. ECG to SMG 17.11.1851: PML MA 1338 (N.20)

12. ECG to SMG 30.11.1851: PML MA 1338 (N.22)

13. ECG to SMG 25.11.1851: PML MA 1338 (N.21). Elided in Lutyens. Also mentioned on 29-30.4 1851.

14. ECG to SMG 20.10.51: PML MA 1338 (N.16). Parts of the letter (wrongly dated) appear in James, *Order of Release*, pp. 184-5, and provide a wonderful example of his mendacious editing. He includes an Effie attack on Mrs. Ruskin for advising her son on his health and diet, but elides a page of Effie complaining to her mother

about drowsiness, excessive sickness, dior-
rhea (sic), constant internal pains, rheu-
matism, shivering, insomnia, fainting and
moaning on the floor, being rescued by
John and the special diet she adopted as a
result. Throughout his dreadful book
James invariably refers to the Casa Wetzlar
as the 'Casa Metzler'. Even Lutyens pointed
out that in fact Mrs. Ruskin's special diet was
intended for Effie not John: *EinV*, p. 213.

15. JR to JJR 8.2.1852: *LFV* 138

16. She told her mother that she also offered
to give up her music lessons with her 24
year old Italian music master but John
would not hear of it.

17. JR to JJR 27.12.1851: *LFV* 96

18. JR to JJR 27.12.1851: *LFV* 96

19. JR to JJR 12.1.1852: *LFV* 112

20. JR to JJR 14.1.1852: *LFV* 114

21. JR to JJR 27.12.1851: *LFV* 96

22. JR to JJR 17.3.1852: *LFV* 176

23. JR to JJR 28.12.1852: *LFV* 97

24. JR to JJR 14.1.1852 : *LFV* 114

25. JR to JJR 27.12.1851: *LFV* 96

26. JR to JJR 17.3.1852: *LFV* 176

27. ECG to SMG 24.2.1852: PML MA 1338
(O.12)

28. JJR to GG 30.3.1852: PML MA 1338 (O.15)

29. JJR to GG 2.4.1852: PML MA 1338 (O.16).
Passage elided in both James and Lutyens.

30. JR to JJR 27.4.1852: *LFV* 217

16: Dancing with Danger, pp. 315-331

1. ECG to JR 8.2.1848: PML MA 1338 (E.16)

2. ECG to SMG 24.11.1851: PML MA 1338
(IJ.22)

3. See ECG to GG 19.1.1852: PML MA 1338
(O.10). 'I wish that I had been the Boy and
never left you – which I believe in the end
might have been better for all parties, for
then the Ruskins wouldn't have had me to
grumble at and I would always have been
with my mother and you and amongst all
the places I shall always love best.'

4. See ECG to SMG 28.12.1851: PML MA
1338 (N.30). 'Ct. Festitics has just been
here and says he would not be the reader

of this crossed letter for anything [...]
I daresay Papa is quite of his opinion but
I hope you don't mind reading it to him
as I can say so much more when I can send
you a long crossed letter and I like to
receive yours so much that I hope you
won't mind mine.'

5. See ECG to SMG 26.4.1852: PML MA 1338
(O.21) 'I always burn yr. letters; you may
always write exactly what you like to me
as I read them over, mark what I have to
answer and then burn your letter.'

6. See ECG to SMG 20.2.1852: PML MA
1338 (O.12). 'I admire yr. prudence about
my letters. Of course I always trust to yr.
discretion in everything I write.'

7. See ECG to SMG 25-27.2.1854: PML MA
1338 (T.10)

8. ECG to GGJr 9.2.1850: PML MA 1338
(O.10).

9. Jane Pallavicini, Irish/Austrian and married
to an Italian, was also in a difficult social
situation with regard to her fellow countrymen who had just fired 60,000 shells at
Venice.

10. Marlay was 20. ECG to SMG 10.10.1851:
PML MA 1338 (N.13)

11. ECG to SMG 30.11.1851: PML MA 1338
(N.22). According to Effie: 'A fine animal
but he is spoiled.'

12. ECG to SMG 20.12.1851: PML MA 1338
(N.28)

13. ECG to SMG 25.11.1851: PML MA 1338
(N.21) Thun was not a tall man. Surviving
photographs (eg the one reproduced on p.
319) show his sabre barely clearing the
ground. Effie was planning to disguise
him in a woman's costume during Carnival. The dark and lonely streets were
probably under curfew as Venice was still
in a state of siege.

Thun went on to have an eventful military career. He commanded the Austrian
land forces in the 1859 war against Italy
and France and led the Österreichische
Frei Korps in Mexico between 1864-6.
The withdrawal of the Austrian and

French troops under US pressure led to the tragic death of Maximilian von Hapsburg (depicted by Manet) for which Thun was later granted the dubious distinction of being the subject of a dream interpretation by Sigmund Freud: 'the arrogant Count Thun involved in the death of a monarch'.

14. ECG to SMG 30.11.1851: PML MA 1338 (N.22)

15. ECG to SMG 4.1.1852: PML MA 1338 (0.01). Effie's popularity as a dancing partner may have had something to do with the difference between the English and the Austrian style of dancing the polka. The English involved close bodily contact: the Austrians held their partners at arms' length.

16. ECG to SMG 1.2.1852: PML MA 1338 (0.08)

17. See JR to JJR 27.1.52, 28.1.52: LFV 127, 128

18. ECG to SMG 1.2.1852: PML MA 1338 (0.08.). This confirms that Effie shut out her admirers very soon after the balls at Verona and Venice. She still met people in the street and when she went out at night.

19. ECG to SMG 8.2.1852: PML MA 1338 (0.09)

20. ECG to SMG [8].2.1852: PML MA 1338 (0.09). Brown later told her that it was 'just in fun.' ECG to SMG 12.4.52: PML MA 1338 (0.19)

21. ECG to SMG 8.2.1852: PML MA 1338 (0.09)

22. ECG to SMG 24.2.1852: PML MA 1338 (0.13). Diller was organising the dancing. Later that same year General Reischach was presented with a pair of duelling pistols made by Mathias Nowotny in Vienna, engraved 'Gevonnen zu Poroenone/ General Baron Reischach/ Zen 12ten October 1852'. This perhaps shows how little the duellers had to fear punishment by their commanders.

23. ECG to SMG 1.2.1852: PML MA 1338 (0.08)

24. ECG to SMG 24/28.2.1852: PML MA 1338 (0.13)

25. ECG to SMG 23.5.1852: PML MA 1338 (0.26)

26. ECG to SMG 20.12.1851: PML MA 1338 (N.28)

27. ECG to SMG 24.2.1852: PML MA 1338 (0.13)

28. ECG to SMG 24.2.1852: PML MA 1338 (0.13). The Austrians spoke French on formal occasions, German in private.

In the libretto of The Barber of Seville the Calumny is introduced thus: 'Così, con buona grazia, bisogna principiare a inventar qualche favola che al pubblico lo metta in male vista, che comparir lo faccia un uomo infame, un'anima perduta… lo, lo vi servirò; fra Quattro giorni, credete a me, Basilio ve lo giura, noi lo farem sloggiar da queste mura.' ('I mean in all politeness that you should give an inkling that there's something suspicious about the Count, to set the people thinking, hint at some base transaction, so that they shun him, believing that he's guilty, I'll help you with a will, Three days at furthest, I stake my word, Basilio's ne'er mistaken and he will be too glad to quit the city'; translation by Natalia MacFarren). Interestingly the target in Rossini is a count who is the female protagonist's secret lover.

29. Ute Frevert, Men of Honour: a social and cultural history of the duel, (1995), pp. 188-9. Especially relevant as Frevert concentrates on the Germanic aspects of duelling.

30. ECG to SMG 4.1.1852: PML MA 1338 (0.01) where Effie mentions Mendelssohn and the music master's reaction to the dress: 'He once hinted that it ought to be burned.'

31. ECG to SMG 26.4.1852: PML MA 1338 (0.21) The incident was omitted in Lutyens.

32. ECG to GGJr. 6.4.1852: PML MA 1338 (0.18)

33. Diller came for a ball given by Madame Wetzlar on the 14th April and spent a couple of evenings with Effie.

34. ECG to SMG 11.5.1852: PML MA 1338 (0.24) Lutyens dated this letter 5.5.1852.

35. ECG to SMG 23.5.1852: PML MA 1338 (0.26)

36. ECG to GGJr 6.4.1852: PML MA 1338 (0.18)

37. ECG to GGJr 6.4.1852: PML MA 1338 (0.18). John later revised his opinion: 'Mr. F. bore the highest possible character – and appeared to us one of the worthiest and frankest persons in the circle in which we moved. He took my fancy more than Effie's – and the only lesson which I can possibly view from the affair is first – never to presume on my own impressions of character' (JR to GG 9.8.1852: Bodleian MS. Eng. lett. d.227 (7)). The French had invaded Algeria for domestic political reasons in 1830 on the pretext that the Dey had struck the French consul with a fly-whisk in an argument over a debt which the French government would not repay. Algiers was assaulted by 675 ships and 37,000 troops who proceeded to loot the city reputed to contain the treasure of the Barbary pirates. The régime of Charles X that had initiated the assault in a blatant attempt to consolidate its rule at home, fell a fortnight afterwards. The new French régime of Louis-Philippe reneged on the initial promise to withdraw after the Dey had been overthrown. Colonisation was promoted, then discouraged, then promoted again. Later on, a well-led resistance emerged and jihad was declared against the French. More troops were sent until by 1847 a third of the entire French army, 108,000 troops, was in Algeria. Between 1842 and 1847, the period in which the 'honest well bred right thinking' Foster would have been serving in Algeria as a soldier of fortune, the French general Bugeaud embarked on a total conquest of the country which entailed virtual eradi-cation of the local population in order to clear land for 50,000 French colonists. The troops burned villages, destroyed crops and orchards, looted granaries and generally laid waste to the country from end to end. No regard was paid to age or sex. Rape was commonplace. A certain Lieutenant-Colonel de Montagnac wrote to a friend in 1841: 'Toutes les populations qui n'acceptent pas nos conditions doivent être rasées. Tout doit être pris, saccagé, sans distinction d'âge ni de sexe: l'herbe ne doit plus pousser où l'armée française a mis le pied. Qui veut la fin veut les moyens, quoiqu'en disent nos philanthropes. Tous les bons militaires que j'au l'honneur de commander pré-venus par moi-même que s'il leur arrive de m'amener un Arabe vivant, ils recevront une volée de coups de plat de sabre [...] Voilà, mon brave ami, comment il faut faire la guerre aux Arabes: tuer tous les hommes jusqu'à l'âge de quinze ans, prendre toutes les femmes et les enfants, en charger les bâtiments, les envoyer aux iles Marquises ou ailleurs. En un mot, anéantir tout ce qui ne rampera pas à nos pieds comme des chiens.' (Lt. Col de Montagnac: *Letters d'un soldat,* Paris 1885, repr 1998, p. 153.) When hundreds of villagers took refuge in caves the French are reputed to have lit fires at the tunnel mouths and asphyxiated them. In 1847 Bugeaud, who had also been heavily engaged in land speculation, was forced to resign for exceeding his orders and Louis-Philippe was overthrown the following year. France's defeat in the Franco-Prussian War of 1870 and the fall of the Third Republic provoked another wave of colonisation and another unsuccessful Arab uprising after which the French controlled all Algerian assets. Between 1830 and 1871 the native population of about 3-4 million had declined by a third.

38. JR to JJR 5.6.1852: *LFV* 255

17: Scandal, pp. 332-351

1. JR to JJR 13.6.1852: *LFV* 262.

2. ECG to SMG 12.6.1852: PML MA 1338 (O.30)

3. ECG to SMG 15/16.6.1852: PML MA 1338 (O.32). Although Zoë the Spitz was a German breed and a present from Thun, Foster was the expert dog trainer and close friend of Thun. If Foster had trained the dog it might not have barked at him. When the Ruskins eventually reached Paris, the dog seriously injured itself leaping out of the hotel window. Effie eventually decided not to take Zoë with her when she left John. John changed the dog's name to 'Wisie.'

4. ECG to Rawdon Brown 4.7.1852: PML MA 1338 (O.37)

5. Edward Cheney to Mr. Dawkins (British Consul) undated, quoted in *EinV* p. 331. See aso JR to Rawdon Brown, *EinV* p. 332. Effie never could manage early rising. The first letter she wrote to her mother about the challenge seems to be missing from the Bowerswell papers. See *EinV* p. 339.

6. ECG to SMG 4.7.1852: PML MA 1338 (O.36)

7. ECG to Rawdon Brown 4.7.1852: PML MA 1338 (O.37). This passage is elided in Lutyens.

8. ECG to SMG 10.7.1852: PML MA 1338 (O.38)

9. ECG to GGJR 18.7.1852: PML MA 1338 (PQ.02)

10. *The Gardener's Chronicle Newspaper* 24.7. 1852, p. 276

11. Almost certainly the result of a single source.

12. *The Globe and Traveller* 27.7.1852

13. JJR to GG 27.7.1852: PML MA 1338 (PQ.07). Effie was not short of male admirers and so the most plausible 'service' that Foster might have rendered would have been to provoke John into a fatal duel, thereby releasing Effie from her *mariage de convenance*.

14. ECG to SMG 2.8.1852: PML MA 1338 (PQ.11)

15. JR to *The Times* 31.7.1852 (published 2.8.1852)

16. JR to GG 2.8.1852: PML MA 1338 (PQ.12); and ECG to Rawdon Brown 20.8.1852: PML MA 1338 (PQ.17) second leaf missing.

17. Paston, *At John Murray's*, pp. 110-11. Effie thought the box might contain a bomb. Lady Eastlake, who had met Brown in Venice, hinted that there was more to the story than she could write. Thun may well have been a 'rotter' but that did not prevent her husband having dealings with him later over the acquisition of paintings for the National Gallery. Thun, having been recommended by the Minister of Foreign Affairs and possibly exceeding his authority, signed the export document for Paul Veronese's *The Family of Darius*. Thun claimed to know the picture well as a fine specimen. Ruskin considered this picture 'the most precious Paul Veronese in the world' (LE 13.552) See Robertson, *Eastlake* p. 167 quoting Sir George Hamilton Seymour to Lord Clarendon 9.7.1856. Thun also seems to have visited Britain since his name was mentioned as a guest of Charlotte (Lockhart) and James Hope.

18. ECG to Rawdon Brown 4.3.53: PML MA 1338 (R.06)

19. JR to Rawdon Brown 6.3.1853: *EinV* pp. 342-3, ref. Cavendish-Bentinck unpublished.

20. JEM to SMG 5.6.1854: PML MA 1338 (UV.45)

21. Duelling was not unknown in England. John Gibson Lockhart's challenge to the editor of the *London Magazine* in 1821 was a prime example. It was however dying out. Andrew Lang, *Life and Letters of J. G. Lockhart*, (1897) p. 337, notes that Lockhart objected to Elwin as editor of the *Quarterly* because a man in orders could not 'go on the ground' if necessary: a reference to duelling. 'In his youth a gentleman had a case of pistols just as he

had a dressing case.'

22. JJR to GG 2.8.52: PML MA 1338 (PQ.12). Ford, John and Effie had dined at Denmark Hill on 11.6.1852.

23. ECG to SMG 8.1851: PML MA 1338 (M.38). Quoted *EinV* p. 175, no ref.

24. JR to GG 8.8.1852: Bodleian, Sir Albert Gray Papers MS. Eng. lett. d.227 (7)

25. See also ECG to SMG 24.8.1852: PML MA 1338 (PQ.19). Where Effie told her mother that Clare Ford was: 'all alone in bed with feverish pains in the head he fell from his horse some years ago on his head And I don't think it will ever be well. He has been working so hard at the Foreign Office that he has brought on one of these attacks of dreadful nervous pains to which he is subject which prevents him sleeping for a week at a time.' She mentioned visiting him again ('I went…') in mid- September when he was recovering.

26. JEM to SMG 21.12.1853: PML MA 1338 (T.02)

27. Mrs. Gaskell to John Forster 18.5.1854 NLS MS.2262 f.35-40. 'Two years ago' was in 1852 and at the time of the Venetian scandal.

28. J. Carlyle to Dr. Carlyle 9.5.1854 in A. Carlyle: *JWC: New Letters and Memorials* (1883)

29. ECG to Rawdon Brown undated [late August 1850]: PML MA 1338 (L.39)

30. JR to JJR 8.2.1852: 'I could not help working against time for the five months'. *LFV* 138.

31. JR to JJR 16.1.1852: *LFV* 117

32. Since John's actual promise was when Effie 'was 25' the technical deadline was Effie's 26th birthday (Effie later admitted that six years had been agreed) but in the unlikely event that he had been forced to keep his promise then she might well have entered confinement at some stage in her 26th year and that would have prevented her from going into Society.

18: Untying the Knot, pp. 352-368

1. John's statement to his solicitor 27.4.1854: Whitehouse, *Vindication*, p. 12

2. Effie confirmed that he agreed to postpone 'marrying' her for six years. She was still not yet 26 years old when she left John.

3. MacDonald: *Reminiscences,* p. 100.

4. *Præterita* II.X.193 (LE 35.423). A notable exception was Eastlake's *Materials &c* which he reviewed for the *Quarterly.*

5. ECG to SMG 30.9.1849 (H.44). The gossip came from the Farquharsons whose son William was John's best man. The Macdonalds were therefore privy to some insider knowledge of the beginning of the marriage.

6. ECG to GG 7.3.1854: PML MA 1338 (T.17)

7. ECG to MR 25.4.1854: PML MA 1338 (T.43)

8. ECG to MR 25.4.1854: PML MA 1338 (T.43)

9. ECG to MR 25.4.1854: PML MA 1338 (T.43)

10. ECG to Mrs. La Touche 10.10.1870: PML MA 1338 (XYZ.04). This offer must have been made in August 1852 when John lunched with Manning. John himself mentions 'my proposed hermitage' at Bonneville in *Præterita* II.XI.206 (LE 35.436)

11. JR to JJR 28.12.1851, *LFV* 97

12. JR to MR 11.11.1853, quoted Leon, *Great Victorian,* p. 191; original: Yale. But then he worries that his work might suffer! He may well have been reading Scott's *The Monastery.*

13. ECG to GG 7.3.1854: PML MA 1338 (T.17)

14. ECG to MR 25.4.1854: PML MA 1338 (T.43)

15. That his reputation was his primary concern is evidenced by the letters he exchanged with the Mount Temples in 1868-71. See Bradley: *Letters … to Lord and Lady Mount Temple,* p. 133: 3.868: 'but if a second time an evil report goes forth about my marriage – my power of doing good by any teaching may be lost – & lost for ever. And this was a fearful question to me – above all personal ones.' Also 23.7.1871 (p. 298): 'My plans are far greater things than my own poor love, now – but if,

wisely, it can now be fulfilled, I think it will help in all my purposes – not least in recovered honour before all the world ...'

16. *First Report of the Commissioners,* p. 3, x.

17. Quoted Stone, *Road to Divorce,* p. 364. There was another important reason why the 'high and mighty' landed aristocracy should be excepted: they still formed the political ruling élite of the country. A spurious heir would not only inherit wealth, but a potential seat in government.

18. Attributed to Gaius or Caius, a second century Roman jurist and author of *Institutes* and *Commentaries,* about whom almost nothing is known.

19. See the excellent accounts in Stone, *Road to Divorce* and Allen Horstman, *Victorian Divorce,* (1985) p. 6

20. William Rothenstein: *Men and Memories i* (1931), pp. 367-8. See Paston, *At John Murray's,* p. 111n. Interestingly after reading Lady Eastlake's long account of the matter, Paston misquotes Rothenstein by claiming it was an Austrian count.

21. JR to Furnivall 19.8.1854 (British Museum Ashley MS.3922) quoted in *An Ill-Assorted Marriage. An Unpublished Letter by John Ruskin Privately printed by Clement Shorter* (1915), quoted *M&R* p. 232.

22. Evidence before 1844 Select Committee in *First Report of the Commissioners,* p. 64, Q.108.

23. *First Report of the Commissioners,* p. 18.

24. *First Report of the Commissioners,* p. 73. 'The average cost of rescinding a marriage in Scotland, is 30*l.* Where there is no opposition 20*l.* will suffice. In one case the entire expenditure was but 15*l.* 17*s.* 6*d.*'

25. See Leonard Shelford, *Practical Treatise,* p. 766.

26. The first action for divorce was instituted in 1885 in London by Rosalie Barlow's husband Mr. Megone on the grounds of her criminal intimacy with Louis Clovis. This was dismissed on the grounds of collusion. A similar suit was then instituted in a Scottish court on the grounds that Louis and Rosalie were living openly as man and wife in Scotland. this was granted on 3.3.1888.

27. Stone: *Broken Lives,* p. 10.

28. *Complete Works of Lord Byron* (1837), note C to p. 392 (p. 719).

29. Preface to *1 Decisions in the High Court of Admiralty: During the time of Sir Geo. Hay and Sir James Marriot* (1801) via A. H. Manchester *Sydney Law Review* vol. 10 no. 1, January 1966 p. 27.

30. *Pickwick Papers* (1836), *David Copperfield* (1850), *Bleak House* (1852)

31. Charles Dickens: *David Copperfield* (1850) Ch. xxiii.

32. *ibid.*

33. *ibid.*

34. LE 9:200 *n*.1

35. JR to JJR 10.9.1853: Lancaster transcript T110, original Yale.

36. ECG to SMG 24.8.1852: PML MA 1338 (PQ.19)

37. See Wedderburn transcripts of JR Diary, Bodleian MS. Eng. misc. c.218; Evans & Whitehouse: *Diaries of John Ruskin II* (1958), p. 478. There is a rogue entry dated June 2nd Sunday in a notebook (10a) which Evans and Whitehouse wrongly ascribed to 1853. June 2nd 1853 was a Thursday. The nearest Sunday June 2nd was in 1855. Another rogue entry for August 11th would also fall plausibly on a Sunday in 1855. There is only one other diary entry for 1855, also for June. Dr. Cumming's church, mentioned in this last diary entry as 'Dr. C', was very close to Doctors' Commons, both St. Benet's Hill and Crown Court being off opposite ends of Queen Victoria St.

38. There were other connections between John and canon law. James Hope who married Charlotte Lockhart was an established ecclesiastical lawyer. Vernon Lushington was the son of the most famous divorce lawyer of the age, Judge Stephen Lushington, who handled the divorce trials of both Queen Caroline and Lady Byron.

Effie tried unsuccessfully to enlist Stephen Lushington's aid in her annulment. Vernon Lushington, himself a noted lawyer, was to become a great champion and supporter of the Pre-Raphaelites and a supporter of the radical social and economic theories of both Carlyle and Ruskin. Vernon was also involved with the Working Man's College which John funded with Effie's marriage settlement after the annulment, and he became the friend and editor of John's father-figure Thomas Carlyle. His address was 8 College Street, Doctors' Commons. He later contributed to the cost of the Oxford Museum, one of the only architectural projects in which John was directly involved. There was another odd later connection. When John was made the first Slade Professor of Art at Oxford it was thanks to a generous endowment by Mr. Felix Slade, a wealthy Proctor in Doctors' Commons. One cannot help wondering if inside knowledge of the court case allowed these men to regard Ruskin and his writings without bias.

39. Stone, *Road to Divorce,* p. 31. The insufficiencies of this system were also described in the 1853 *Report.*

40. Stone, *Road to Divorce,* pp. 197-8

41. Stone, *Road to Divorce,* pp. 184-5

42. Stone, *Road to Divorce,* p. 185n. The Consistory Court only dealt with twelve to fifteen cases per year over the five to six years prior to the compilation of the 1853 *Report.* The majority of these were unopposed (*op. cit.,* p. 28). The *Ecclesiastical Reports* noted 79 nullity suits over the century of which nineteen were for impotence, only ten of which were granted. (A. H. Manchester, 'The Principles and Rules of Ecclesiastical Law and Matrimonial Relief', *Sydney Law Review* 6 (1968) p. 31.)

43. ECG to SMG 3.8.1852: PML MA 1338 (PQ.11)

44. John Hobbs, called George to avoid confusion in a household which already

had two Johns, had been a Ruskin family servant for twelve years. John's constant companion in Venice, he fair-copied John's manuscripts and made daguerreotypes for him. Shortly after the duel at Verona he told John and Effie that he wanted to leave their employ and hoped Mr. Ruskin could find him work in the Docks. In the event he went to Australia, became a JP, a police magistrate and a member of the Lands Department in NSW. He died in 1892. According to John he 'became my body servant in 1842 and left me to push his higher fortune in 1854.' (LE 35.343). According to Effie, who was glad to see him go, he was always relaying gossip back to Denmark Hill. Both the timing of his departure and his subsequent rise to a position of responsibility are perhaps not without significance.

45. Alan Horstman, *Victorian Divorce* (1985), p. 6.

46. ECG to SMG 27.2.54: PML MA 1338 (T.10)

19: A Highland Holiday, pp. 373-405

1. ECG to SMG 26?2.1853 PML MA 1338 (R.05)

2. According to JJR's diary Millais dined at Denmark Hill on 17.3 and 25.3 and three times in April; Lancaster MS. 33

3. ECG to SMG 20.3.1853: PML MA 1338 (R.07)

4. James noted that 'Millais occasionally corresponded with Effie, which was perfectly natural between close friends and Ruskin caused no objection' (p. 125). Lutyens noted that after the marriage break-up Effie wrote to Millais asking him to destroy all her letters to him (*M&R* p. 126). The present author suspects that some of the correspondence may well have fallen into John's hands.

5. LE 12.xviii, quoting J. G. Millais: *Life and Letters of Sir J. E. Millais* Vol. 1, p. 118. The trip did not take place.

6. ECG to SMG 31.8.1852 PML MA 1338

(PQ.22) The Lemprières, like the Millais, were an old Jersey family. Arthur Lemprière was 15 or 16 at the time and only modelled for the head. The female model was Anne Ryan.

7. ECG to SMG 27.3.1853: PML MA 1338 (R.08) Final sheet missing?

8. So the suggestive comment that Millais made about the model in his letter to Hunt of 11.11.1852 could not have involved Effie. 'Today I have been drawing the girl's figure in the landscape. Yesterday it was too small, and today too large. Tomorrow she comes again when I hope to get it between the two sizes*/ * I don't mean her legs.' Quoted from 'HL' in *The Pre-Raphaelites*, Tate exhibition catalogue (1984), p. 105.

9. Ann Ryan definitely posed for the head in the *Huguenot*. Readers should judge for themselves whether the woman in the *Royalist* is the same person.

10. See Hunt, *The Wider Sea* (1982) p. 223 quoting the diary of G. P. Boyce in *The Old Water Colour Society Club 19th. Annual Volume* (1941) p. 17. Or see Surtees, *The Diaries of George Price Boyce* (1980), p. 9. Lutyens (*M&R* p. 28) notes an unusual gap in Effie's letters between 22.1 and 22.2.1853 and ascribes this to her mother having 'preserved very few from this period.' Effie later asked Millais to destroy all her letters to him. She must have meant the earlier ones from 1852-3 as they both stopped writing after Glenfinlas.

11. J. G Millais in *Life and Letters of Sir J. E. Millais* suggested in the interests of delicacy that the room was not in fact outside a 'prison' but was a 'bare waiting room.'

12. Ruskin traced his name etymologically back through 'ruskyn' or 'red skin' (1385) to the 'red-coat' of the squirrel. See LE 35.lxi & fn. The rumpled lip was the result of a dog bite when he was a child.

13. ECG to SMG 20.3.1853: PML MA 1338 (R.07). There is no mention of *The Order*

of Release anywhere in the Library Edition of the complete works.

14. Although Millais was later to paint *Effie Deans* and *The Bride of Lammermoor*. It would be interesting to know what attracted him to paint the flirtatious Effie, connected with an illegitimate birth and a trial for infanticide, rather than the Fair Maid of Perth, the virtuous glover's daughter who was the cause of so much death and violence amongst those contending for her hand.

15. Acland to his wife 27.7.1853, Bodleian MS. Acland d.9 foll.134-5, quoted Hilton, *Early Years,* p. 189. Val Prinsep also spoke of his 'boyish energy' and Ruskin of his 'childish exuberance of conversation.'

16. JR to JJR 6.11.1853: Lancaster transcript T110, original Yale

17. See JR to Rev. W. L. Brown 31.3.1853, Bodleian MS. Eng. lett. c.33: 'We are going to take a trotting tour in a post-chaise – in opposition to Railroads –to the North of Scotland.'

18. ECG to SMG 31.3.1853: PML MA 1338 (R.09)

19. ECG to SMG 21.4.1853: PML MA 1338 (R.12)

20. See Spink's *Ecclesiastical Reports,* Vol.1, p. 14-15: *A falsely called B v. B,* 21.4.1853.

21. 'Impotence *quod hanc*': literally 'impotence because of this.' Nowadays it is acknowledged that a man can suffer psychic impotence with regard to one woman (usually his wife) but be able to perform with another.

22. *Welde v. Welde* (2. Lee 586) of 1731 was the outdated case which would be used by the La Touches which ruled that if the man married again and had children this would re-validate the first marriage.

23. Mr. Rutter to JJR 23.5.1854: PML MA 1571 (1.69)

24. ECG to GG 6-7.3.1854: PML MA 1338 (T.17); & ECG to Margaret Ruskin 25.4.1854: PML MA 1338 (T.43) copy.

25. ECG to SMG 1.1.1854: PML MA 1338

(T.04). 'We talked of the German plan and John peevishly looking up told me not to begin talking of what had been settled six months ago.' (John's trip to Switzerland was planned even before the Scottish holiday.)

26. ECG to SMG 15.4.1853: PML MA 1338 (R.11)

27. ECG to GG 30.5.1853: PML MA 1338 (R.23)

28. LE 12.xix. Realizing the implications for Effie's reputation of being part of an all-male party, Cook and Wedderburn added Pauline Trevelyan's friend 'Miss M'Kenzie' to the party, almost certainly to imply a chaperone for Effie, the only female on the holiday. Miss McKenzie, who was a guest at Wallington, in fact only accompanied the party from Wallington to Melrose.

29. ECG to SMG 20.6.1853: PML MA 1338 (R.30)

30. ECG to SMG 21.5.1853: PML MA 1338 (R.22); and JEM to SMG 30.5.1854: PML MA 1338 (UV.36)

31. GGJr to SMG 25.6.1853: PML MA 1338 (R.33)

32. *Blackwoods Edinburgh Magazine,* July 1853, p. 100: 'The Fine Arts and Public Taste in 1853'. *Blackwoods* criticized the female figure at some length: 'Instead of the eye dimmed even with a tear, it looks defiance, as if she had contested the matter at some previous time with the jailer, and looks triumph, as much to say, "I've won, and so pay me."' The soldier-jailer was praised as 'natural' and 'indifferent.'

33. The painting was bought by the lawyer Joseph Arden for £400.

34. JR to Pauline Trevelyan 8.5.1854 from Dover: Surtees, *Reflections of a Friendship,* p. 81.

35. William Bell Scott's unpublished autobiographical notes, quoted *M&R* p. 212; original: collection Mrs. J. Camp, Troxell, Conn., USA.

36. Pauline Trevelyan's Diary 24.6.1853,

microfilm, Newcastle University Library.

37. William Bell Scott's autobiographical notes quoted *M&R* pp. 276-277; original: collection Mrs. J. Camp, Troxell, Conn., USA.

38. This was not the only time Effie and Millais had synchronised illnesses. On 1.1.1854 Effie complained of 'my eye very frightful with a sty': PML MA 1338 (T.04). On 18.1.1854 Millais told John that he had a rash on his eyelid burned off with acid: PML MA 1338 (T.05).

In addition to being an analgesic and anæsthetic, chloroform also has euphoric effects and can remove inhibitions. It can also cause hallucinations of a sexual nature. If Effie and Everett were feeding each other chloroform pills at Glenfinlas no wonder the holiday took an uninhibited amorous turn. Effie remained dependent on chloroform for most of her life. *M&R* p. 264

39. *Stirling Journal & Advertiser* 4.8.1854 and 25.8.1854

40. JR to JJR 2.7.1853: Lancaster transcript T110, original Yale. G. H. Fleming: *John Everett Millais,* (1998); from his description I suspect, however, that he mistook the Trossachs New Hotel at Brig o'Turk for the Trossachs Hotel overlooking Loch Katrine.

41. *Stirling Journal & Advertiser* 4.8.1854, 2.9.1864 p. 4f. The Trossachs New Hotel after having had wings added to cope with the tourist numbers was entirely destroyed by fire in the early hours of 18.11.1864 and the site was never rebuilt. (*Stirling Journal & Advertiser* 18.11.1864, and 25.11.1864). The stable block survives as Burnt Inn House.

42. JR to Rev. W. L. Brown 2.6.1853: Bodleian MS. Eng. lett. c.33

43. The stay was extended first owing to John having sprained his ankle, then to the portrait. John may have had a secondary motive in moving to the cottage. The term 'domicile' in Scottish divorce cases

did include staying at hotels (see 1853 *Report*, pp. 63-4) but this had become such an acknowledged part of the divorce process that perhaps he was trying to avoid accusations of complicity and collusion. See William Millais account below for the 'no other guests'. Everett however mentions a fellow guest who was called early every morning by the boots. Henry Acland stayed at the hotel and the picture dealer Gambart accompanied by the artist Rosa Bonheur lunched with them there: J. G. Millais: *Life and Letters of Sir J. E. Millais,* pp. 210-11.

44. ECG to SMG 10.7.1853 *M&R* pp. 65-6: PML MA 1338 (s.07). In a letter that was subsequently censored with heavy black ink, Millais also mentioned that 'John is having his bed made in the sitting room': PML MA 1338 (s.13). The 'respectable old pair' were 51 and 48.

45. JEM to Mrs. William Collins 10.7.1853: *M&R* p. 68, PML MA 1338 (s.06)

46. JEM to Mr. Combe 4.8.1853: J. G. Millais, *Life and Letters of Sir J. E. Millais,* p. 201. J. G. Millais erroneously puts the Millais brothers in 'microscopic apartments' in the Trossachs New Hotel while their friends the Ruskins were 'more luxuriously accommodated' at the 'manse' at Brig o'Turk some five hundred yards away'; all nonsense of course: p. 196.

47. The *Stirling Journal* for 16.4.1852 (4e) records the scholars being examined by 'Rev. Mr. Stewart of Aberfoyle and the Rev Mr. Monteith of Brig of Turk'.

48. JEM to Mr. Combe 4.8.1853: J. G. Millais, *Life and Letters of Sir J. E. Millais,* p. 201. Mrs. Stewart unfortunately died of a heart attack shortly after the party left for Edinburgh.

49. William seems to be inferring here and Gray in Q.10 that Acland visited Glenfinlas after he had left. In fact Acland left on 1.8 and William on 18.8 so they would have been sleeping and eating in the hotel together.

50. W. H. Millais to Sir Albert Gray 9.3.1898 Sir Albert Gray Papers, Bodleian MS. Eng. lett.c.228, pp. 67-8. The dinner with Jameson at Edinburgh was in July en route from Wallington to Glenfinlas. See ECG to Rawdon Brown 1.7.1853, *M&R* p.56.

51. The chimney stack appears to have wandered further along the ridge in the earlier letter but sits in the correct place astride the ridge in the later letter. The later sketch must have it in the correct position otherwise the kitchen would be without a fireplace for cooking. The incorrect number of windows in the later letter could be simply because it is a much rougher sketch than the earlier. In the rather curious sketch of the cottage made in 1910 by Miss E. M. B. Warren (published in E. T. Cook, *Homes and Haunts of John Ruskin,* 1912), if this is indeed the same cottage which seems doubtful, then some re-modelling work had clearly been done but the chimneys and therefore the kitchen and parlour are still on the left of the building (a second chimney must have been built onto the kitchen gable of the new higher extension). More difficult to explain are the apparent changes to the landscape and the absence of other cottages.

52. Everett referred to his 'compartment' in the cottage and to his 'little emigrant crib.' Lutyens also referred to 'Effie's little soft warm breathing body so close to him in the next cubicle' *M&R* p. 90.

53. JEM to Hunt 29.8.1853, *M&R* p.88, no ref.

54. Even Lutyens noted that although John had told his father that board and lodging at the schoolmaster's was only £1 per person per week for himself, Effie and Crawley, he nevertheless asked for an extra £70 from his father. See 'Where Did Ruskin Sleep?', *TLS* 2.1.1969, p. 17.

55. JJR to W. H. Harrison, 28.6.1853: PML MA 1338 (1.18)

56. Except for Miss E. M. B. Warren (see note 51 above) who seems to have painted the

wrong landscape. Henry George's painting at Glasgow Kelvingrove shows a view from the north of the first three cottages at Brig o'Turk in 1882 after the bog had been filled in but before the track bed for the light railway used to transport materials to the dam had been built. It is difficult to reconcile this picture with either of John's sketches except that the second furthest house has a small fenced sloping front garden. The middle building appears to be the smithy with metal cartwheel tyres leaning against the wall. Only the gable of the (rebuilt?) schoolmaster's is visible in the right background. Thomas Hodgson Liddell painted the cottages in snow from an almost identical viewpoint that same year (Christies 20.7. 2005; tracing below, gable again in black.)

57. The mill cottage by the mill-lead is the only one of the nine buildings shown on the 1864 OS map of the area to have been subsequently entirely demolished even to the digging out of the foundations and without being replaced by a new building. The broken ground is still clearly visible today in the back garden of the first new house upstream of the mill. In such a desperately poor location, with people living six or seven to a cottage, why would this recently habitable dwelling be demolished and who could have paid for it? By 1864 the Stewart meal mill of 1851 had become the Lockhart pirn bobbin factory turning wooden bobbins for local wool spinners and weavers.

58. JR to F. J. Furnivall 16.10.1853: NYPL Berg Collection 64B 798 m.b.

59. John asked his father several times whether he was thinking of joining them at Brig o'Turk. This may have been a way of checking that he would not arrive unexpectedly whilst the cottage was still being used.

60. See JR to JJR 9.10.1853 'We shall be very sorry to leave our cottage, and I shall especially regret a grassy walk, some twenty yards long, which I walk up and down whenever I want exercise without going too far from home; but it is very beautiful, with a few clusters of brambles twining among the rocks at the side of it, and itself quite a smooth sward, a group of ash trees at the bottom overhanging a rocky stream and the open hills above it' (LE 12. xxii).

The other cottage was part of the mill complex which also belonged to a Mr. Stewart, and it also had an impassable bog in front of it, albeit at the other side of a bridge across the river, the bank of which was beyond the mill-lead or culvert immediately in front of the cottage. The two regular parallel lines running in the foreground in front of the garden in the sketch John sent his father could well be the mill-lead from the weir to the mill, built from dressed stone and still there but now filled in and used as a path. Unfortunately the strange cut-out on the sketch in the letter to JJR would have been where the bridge was and would have made the cottage instantly recognizable. The bog is also still there today and is caused by a stream, clearly indicated on the 1864 map, which discharges into fields still used for pasture land. There is no stream marked on the 1864 map at the schoolmaster's. A letter from JR to JJR of 9.10.1853 describes the smooth grass sward close to the cottage with rocks at the side of it and 'a group of ash trees at the bottom overhanging a rocky stream, and the open hills above it' (LE 12. xxii, original Yale). The bog across from the mill still blocks the way from the site of the old bridge to the track that leads through West Bridge of Turk farm, back to the road and up to the hotel. In the farmhouse at the other side of the bog lived a girl of fourteen. There was one other structure marked on the 1864 map which could have been visible from this cottage. This was a sheepfold which would have been at the foot of the group of trees in the sketch John sent to his father. The low walls are still there today.

20: Poetic Justice, pp. 406-424

1. The fact that *The Tempest* begins with a shipwreck is not irrelevant. The Petrarchan conceit of an unhappy lover as a ship on a stormy sea would have been familiar to John and since at least the seventeenth century Dutch artists had used images of storm-tossed ships to allegorise relationships heading for the rocks. In the nineteenth century Clarkson Stansfield's *The Abandoned* was used in this way by Augustus Egg in his *Past & Present* trilogy which John later reviewed.

2. His biographers certainly thought this way. Effie the glover's daughter became 'The Fair Maid of Perth', and his later love Rose La Touche 'The Bride of Lammermuir.' See also William Scott, Lord Stowell, Judge of the London Consistory Court in *Quarterly Review* 75.149 (1844), p. 49: 'I could furnish a series of stories from the annals of Doctors' Commons which should rival the Waverley novels in interest' (via Stone, *Broken Lives*, p. v).

3. *Stirling Journal & Advertiser* 25.8.1854, p. 3, 4e, quoting Scott, *Lady of the Lake*, canto 1: 6 and 10.

4 JEM to Charlie Collins 3.7.1853: PML MA 1338 (s.04)

5. JR to JJR 10.7.1853: *M&R* p. 64

6. JEM to Charlie Collins 20.7.1853. 'Ruskin has been reading 'Guy Mannering' to us' PML MA 1338 (s.09). Without wanting to

push the point too far, there are some tantalising distant echoes in this book. The romantic lead is called Brown, the mother of his inamorata is Sophia and coquetry and jealousy both come into play, as does a duel over a triviality. There is also the bankruptcy of the father owing to incompetence. Scott was of course a lawyer and wrote several books with legal themes including *Redgauntlet* and *Heart of Midlothian*.

7. See LE 29.542. John also thought it was his very worst.

8. JEM to Collins 6.7.1853: PML MA 1338 (s.08) and William Pamplin: *A Botanical Tour in the Highlands of Perthshire* (1857) pp. 15-16. The trees have since recovered so well that it is impossible to see the profiles of the hills.

9. Scott, *Glenfinlas*, canto 28, and *Lady of the Lake*, canto 11, 26

10. Scott, *Glenfinlas*, cantos 63-4

11. Scott: *Minstrelsy of the Scottish Border* London (1931) p. 641, Introduction to *Glenfinlas*

12. Scott, *Lady of the Lake*, canto IV, 13

13. Scott, *Lady of the Lake*, note LII

14. *M&R* p. 33, no ref.

15. JR to JJR 19.7.1853: *M&R* p. 69

16. Shakespeare, *The Tempest* 5.1.33

17. Millais had not been helping John and William with their task, but had been trying to build a bridge of stones across the brook so that 'Mrs. Ruskin' could reach the other side. See JEM to Charles Collins 24.7.1853. PML MA 1338 (s.10)

18. Scott, *Glenfinlas* canto 13.

19. Scott, *Lady of the Lake* 1.12. Digitalis and atropine are of course the potent toxins secreted in these plants. Picking foxgloves is a highly dangerous pastime, as John knew well. In *Præterita* 1.IV.77 (LE 35.70) he mentions the suspicion that he may have been made seriously ill as a child by picking them. Hence a horror of foxglove dells was added to his horror of river eddies. Both the flower poisons are

extremely potent emblems: the one which stills the heart and the other no less dangerous used by women as an eye cosmetic, hence 'bella donna'. The name was originally 'folk's glove' where the 'folk' were the fairies. Like wearing green, picking foxgloves offends the fairies! John constructed a fascinating matrix of symbolism around the foxglove. It is a 'gay poison' and 'a type of deceit' in *Modern Painters* V (LE 6.68), a 'type of this world' in *Stones of Venice ii* (LE 10.203). He puts foxglove and nightshade together in his draconidæ class of plants in *Proserpina i* and in *Proserpina ii* he writes of 'the legal strictness of a foxglove' and 'that legal order of blossoming…' (LE 25.253).

20. John and Effie worked on the copy together and both signed it. It is illustrated in James, *Order of Release*, p. 120. Note how the flowers are more detailed than the rest.

21. *Modern Painters* III IV.XVI.45 (LE 5.351) Three quotations appear together linking river foam and eddies, foxglove and nightshade, and a woman 'Her dark eye flashed; she paused and sighed; – "Ah, what have I to do with pride!"'.

22. Apocryphally by Holman Hunt. It is however still possible to make out references to Effie through the blacking-out even with the naked eye. Modern technology would surely be able to restore these lost lines. The Bowerswell papers include six letters from Millais from Brig o'Turk/Glenfinlas to the Collins family from this period heavily censored in black ink. See for example Millais to Collins 2.9.1852, PML MA 1338 (PQ.30).

23. JEM to Holman Hunt, undated but after 3.9.1853: *M&R* pp. 89-90, no ref. given

24. JEM to Charles Collins 6.7.1853: PML MA 1338 (S.04)

25. JEM to Mrs. Collins, 10.7.1853: PML MA 1338 (S.06)

26. JEM to Charles Collins PML MA 1338 4.8.1853 (S.13) Dante *Inferno*, Canto VII:

'This too for certain know, that underneath the water dwells a multitude, whose sighs into these bubbles make the surface heave, as thine eye tells thee wheresoe'er it turn. Fix'd in the slime they say: "Sad once were we, in the sweet air made gladsome by the sun, carrying a foul and lazy mist within: now in these murky settlings are we sad."' This was the fifth circle of Hell, reserved for the wrathful and the gloomy who did not enjoy the sun whilst they still had it.

27. JEM to Charles Collins: PML MA 1338 14.8.1853 (S.17)

28. W. H. Millais to Sir Albert Gray 9.3.1898 Bodleian, MS. Eng. lett. c.228 (62-3) (67-9). Jeannie Boswell also 'never doubted the taking John Millais to the Highlands was a regular deep laid scheme which doubtless JR [assumed?] could not fail judging the world by his own wicked self.' To ECG 15.9.54: PML MA 1338 (W.07)

29. Diary 20.7.1853, p. 479. The first canvas from Edinburgh had not been white enough.

30. JR to JJR 18.8.1853 Quoted Leon, *Great Victorian*, pp. 184-5; original: Yale. John kept a time-table of the work for seven weeks. Millais' output gradually decreased.

31. JEM to Holman Hunt 29.8.1853: *M&R* p. 88, no ref.; and JEM to Mrs. Collins *M&R* p. 90, no date given and no ref.

32. JR to MR Glenfinlas 16.10.1853: Bodleian MS. Eng. lett. c.33 (transcript)

33. ECG to Rawdon Brown Brig o'Turk 10.10.1853: PML MA 1338 (S.20). One of only three letters written by Effie at Glenfinlas to surface. After this letter there is another gap until 1.1 broken only by another letter to Brown on 30.11.

34. 'Putting on a green gown' was a common euphemism applied to country women who engaged in illicit naughtiness between the sexes. Middleton vs. Middleton 1793. Hannah the maid noticed that her mistress's dress was 'wet and dirty all up the back', and on another occasion noticed

her 'muslim robe all down the back stained with green'. Lord Kenyon the judge said that 'a secret withdrawal to a secluded spot by two adults of the opposite sex was sufficient evidence that adultery had taken place', Stone, *Broken Lives,* pp. 190-201. See also Whitehouse, *Vindication,* p. 30: 'It is now known that Ruskin could have won an easy victory in the Divorce Court.' See also F. J. N Rogers, *A Practical Arrangement of Ecclesiastical Law* (1840) p. 327: 'Adultery being an act of darkness, and of great secrecy, can hardly be proved by any direct means; therefore in relation to the proof by reason of such difficulty, it happens that presumptive evidence alone is sufficient proof... Facts need not be so specially proved as to produce the conclusion that the fact of adultery was committed at a particular hour, or in a particular room (2 Hag.Con.4), statements of a general, loose, and unduly familiar conduct are sufficient to establish a high and undue degree of familiarity between parties. Isolated facts may lead to a conclusion of crime: for the proper way to consider this evidence is not to take them separately, but in conjunction; they mutually interpret each other; their constant repetition gives them a determinate character; and such habits, when continued in public, lead to the inference that the parties would go greater lengths if opportunities of privacy occurred.' (2. Hag. Con. 228)

35. Whitehouse, *Vindication,* p. 12

36. See *M&R* p. 93: JEM to Hunt 5.5.1854, Burt Collection

37. JEM to Charles Collins 25.9.1853: PML MA 1338 (S.19)

38. Thereby inexplicably missing John's lecture on 'Pre-Raphaelitism' on the 11th.

39. ECG to Rawdon Brown 30.11.1853: PML MA 1338 (S.23); and ECG to GG 7.3.1854: PML MA 1338 (T.17)

40. JR to JJR 6.11.1853 and 11.11.1853. He cancelled his engagements for the spring and asked his father to confirm the start

date of the Swiss trip whilst he was at Bowerswell on 13.12.1853: Lancaster transcript T110, original Yale.

21: The Trap Sprung, pp. 425-450

1. JR to MR 5.12.1853, quoted Leon: *Great Victorian,* p. 192; original: Yale.

2. JJR to JR 14.12.1853: Lancaster 1996 L01916

3. JJR to SMG 3.11.1853: PML MA 1338 (S.22)

4. He had already been elected once before but when it was found out that he was under age his membership had been rescinded.

5. JEM to Mr. Combe, Thursday, December (no date) 1853, quoted J. E. Millais: *The Life and Letters of Sir J. E. Millais,* Vol. 1, p. 221.

6. John's statement to his solicitor 27.4.1854 'I took her home nevertheless. She has remained in resolute anger, venting itself in unexplained insults.' Whitehouse: *Vindication,* p. 13.

7. ECG to Rawdon Brown 4.2.1854: PML MA 1338 (T.19)

8. JEM to SMG 21.12.1853: PML MA 1338 (T.02)

9. JEM to Mr. Combe 26.12.1853 quoted J. G. Millais: *Life and Letters of Sir J. E. Millais,* Vol. 1, p. 221. Sir Albert Gray commented that 'the church attendance is remarkable, for Millais, though one of the best of men, was throughout his life "parcus deorum cultor et infrequens"'. Bodleian MS. Eng. misc. d.653.

10. JEM to SMG 17.1.1854: PML MA 1338 (T.06). Millais was in an awkward position. He spent an entire day at the British Museum with John on 6.1 and John sat for him on 12.1 and 19.1. JR Diaries II p. 488.

11. JEM to SMG 19.12.1853: PML MA 1338 (T.01)

12. JEM to SMG 19.12.1853: PML MA 1338 (T.01). 'I should never have written to your daughter had not Ruskin been cognisant to the correspondence'.

13. JEM to SMG 20.12.1853: PML MA 1338 (T.02)

14. J. D. Boswell to ECG 15.9.1854: PML MA 1338 (W.07)

15. JR to Furnivall 18.8.1854: British Library Ashley Ms. 3922. Quoted in *An Ill-Assorted Marriage. An Unpublished Letter by John Ruskin* (privately printed, 1915)

16. William Bell Scott's autobiographical notes, quoted *M&R* pp. 276-277. Original collection Mrs. J. Camp Troxell, Conn., USA.

17. ECG to Rawdon Brown 8.6.1854: PML MA 1338 (UV.48)

18. JEM to GG 27.7.1854: PML MA 1338 (UV.78)

19. Sir W. Rothenstein: *Men and Memories* London (1931) pp. 367-8, referred to by Paston, *At John Murray's*, p. 111n.

20. Had John or his legal advisor read the 1853 *Report* p. 67 he would have known this: 'Q. 171   Is there a Scotch law passed in the year 1600, whereby the party divorced by reason of adultery is prohibited from intermarrying with the paramour? – There is; from intermarrying with the person with whom she is declared by the sentence of divorce to have committed the crime. Q. 176.   Does not it depend upon whether the name of the person with whom the adultery is committed is mentioned in the Bill of Divorce – I have known cases where the accusation was, having committed adultery or cohabited with a person known, not the husband; but the name of such party was not discoverable.' See also Stone, *Road to Divorce*, p. 357

21. One of the devices whereby the prohibition on marriage to the adulterous party was circumvented was re-marriage in England. See *The First Report of the Commissioners*, 1853, p. 67

22. See Stone: *Broken Lives*, pp. 133-134, *Beaufort v. Beaufort*

23. Scott's *Bride of Lammermuir* opens with a discussion of a not irrelevant quote from Levitical Law.

24. JR to SMG 27.12.1853: PML MA 1338 (T.03) The first sentence of this letter was elided in James. According to his diary John wrote to 'Mr. Gray' and Alice on Jan. 1st (Diaries II p. 487). Curiously this was not the first time Mrs. Gray had sent John a geological sample. See ECG to SMG 14.11.1850: 'I gave John the piece of rock you sent for him for which he is [illeg.] obliged.'

25. There are also some Shakespearean references in *Two Gentlemen of Verona*: 'Give her no token but stones; for she's as hard as steel' (1.1) and 'He is a stone, a very pebble stone' (11.3)

26. A receipt for 'a box returned' by The Scottish Central Railway Company from Perth Station for John Ruskin Esq. London on 3.7.1855 also presents a bit of an enigma. John never spent much time in Perth so it is difficult to understand what the Grays might have had to send him. He already had his love letters to Effie, perhaps as part of the deal he had sent hers to the Grays who then returned the empty box. The three which turned up in the auction at Brantwood in 1931 might just have been left behind or mislaid. The 3rd July was the day Effie married Millais and caught the train from Perth to Glasgow, but Millais was certainly in no condition to send parcels. I doubt very much that it was either a wedding present or a piece of the bride cake. Could the box originally have contained his evidential notebooks? Given the public acrimony between the parties, this could well be evidence of collusion. PML MA 1338 (W.29)

27. See Shelford, *Practical Treatise*, p. 592. No alimony will be allotted ... in the case of some legal impediment whereby the marriage was null and void *ab initio*. (b) Godolph. Abr. 509. See also J. Rutter to JJR 23.5.1854, PML MA 1571 (169): 'you need not fear from them in consequence an Action for damages and I consider the Marriage Settlement (of which I am one of the Trustees) would then be void and the Trust Money yours.'

28. See Spink's *Ecclesiastical Reports* Vol. 1, p. 248, *B-n v. B-n* [female incapacity]: 'these marriages are in themselves, *ab initio*, void. There is no injury to complain of when the marriage is pronounced null and void; the injury had been previously inflicted by one or other of the parties; sometimes perhaps knowingly; sometimes in utter ignorance of his or her state at the date of the marriage.'

29. See Shelford, *Practical Treatise*, p. 207-8 and the description of the case of Lady Essex, which is however suspect since 'it is said that the countess, under a pretence of modesty, having obtained leave to put on a veil when she was inspected, introduced a young woman of her age and stature dressed in her clothes, to be searched in her place, and deceived the jury of matrons and the Court.'

30. See Shelford, *Practical Treatise*, p. 207: OF IMPOTENCE Effect of the sentence of separation. – By the canon law, the marriage is not absolutely dissolved; the parties are separated; and if the Church is deceived, the former marriage is to be renewed; and if a second marriage is contracted it becomes null and void.' But on p. 208: 'If a man divorced by reason of perpetual impotence in himself marries again, the issue of the second marriage is legitimate. The wife of one Bury was divorced from him on account of frigidity, it appearing that for three years after the marriage she remained *virgo intacta* on account of the husband's impotency, and that he was *inaptus ad generandum*. The husband afterwards married again, and his wife had children. The question was whether they were legitimate or not? And it was decided they were; for by the divorce *causa frigidatis* the marriage was dissolved *a vinculo matrimonii*, and consequently each of them might marry again; and admitting the second marriage to be voidable, yet it continued a marriage until it was dissolved, and consequently the issue of such

marriage was legitimate, if no divorce was obtained during the lifetime of the parties. (Bury's case Dyer, 179, a; 5Rep.98 b.) Also Thomas Poynter: *A Concise view of the Doctrine and Practice of Ecclesiastical Courts to Marriage and Divorce* (1824) p. 126: 'Bury's case is in point. The marriage was dissolved by reason of his impotency, he married and had issue; upon which it was urged that the church being evidently deceived as to his perpetual impotency, the divorce thereupon was null; and if so, that the second marriage was unlawful, and the issue illegitimate. But the Court resolved, that since there had been divorce for frigidity or impotency, it was clear that each of them might marry again; and though it should be allowed that the church appearing to have been deceived is the foundation of their sentence, the second marriage was voidable yet till it should be dissolved, it remained a marriage, and the issue during coverture lawful' 5Rep.98; Mo 225; Dyer, 179. By April 1853 even the voidability of the second marriage had been called into question. See Spink's *Ecclesiastical Reports* vol. 1 p.14 fn. (a)

31. The new work being done on John's problematical relationship with his father might put an additional level of interpretation on the whole affair (see James L. Spates, 'John Ruskin's Dark Star' in *The Bulletin of the John Rylands University of Manchester* Vol. 82, No. 1, spring 2000). But it would seem that getting married and getting unmarried were the two major occasions on which John went against his father's will. Both proved disastrous for him.

32. ECG to SMG 1.1.1854: PML MA 1338 (T.04)

33. ECG to SMG 27.2.1854: PML MA 1338 (T.10)

34. See ECG to Rawdon Brown 18.3.1854: PML MA 1338 (T.19). Effie's implausible excuse was that Mary left her because she was tired of the dull, quiet life at Herne

Hill. See ECG to Rawdon Brown 18.3.1854: PML MA 1338 (T.19).

35. ECG to Rawdon Brown 9.5.1854: PML MA 1338 (UV.20)

36. ECG to SMG 27.2.1854: PML MA 1338 (T.10)

37. ECG to SMG 27.2.1854: PML MA 1338 (T.10)

38. ECG to SMG 20.3.1854: PML MA 1338 (T.20)

39. ECG to SMG 3.4.1854: PML MA 1338 (T.25)

40. ECG to SMG 20.3.1854: PML MA 1338 (T.20)

41. ECG to SMG 2-3.3.1854: PML MA 1338 (T.13); in other words after John returned from Switzerland.

42. JEM to SMG 3.3.1854: PML MA 1338 (T.15)

43. ECG to SMG 3.3.1854: PML MA 1338 (T.14). In fact he left May 23rd for Glenfinlas.

44. JEM to SMG 3.3.1854: PML MA 1338 (T.14)

45. ECG to SMG 2.3.1854: PML MA 1338 (T.13)

46. See Shelford, *Practical Treatise,* p. 737: 'In actions of divorce […] there must not appear the slightest indication of an improper understanding between them.'

47. Gray, *Marriage*, p. 32

48. Even Lutyens noticed that Mrs. Gray was curiously jubilant about the marriage break-up after the flight to Perth. It was probably relief that the alternative scenario had not come about. *M&R* p. 181.

49. Albert Gray asserted that Mr. Gray had sprung into immediate legal action when Lady Eastlake told Mr. Gray the marriage was unconsummated and that Effie was involved with Millais (see Gray *Marriage*, p. 32) but the Grays already knew that Millais was involved with Effie. John had told them at Bowerswell. Otherwise they would not have sent him warning letters.

50. After Effie confided in Lady Eastlake, she too was of the same opinion. See Lady

Eastlake to SMG 29.4.1854 PML MA 1338 (UV.06): 'I am convinced that you have only forestalled him in the act of separation and that if Mr. Gray had not acted with such excellent promptitude and prudence now, he might have had a far more difficult task to perform a year hence.' That John did in fact have grounds to act seems to have been taken for granted!

51. ECG to GG 7.3.1854: PML MA 1338 (T.17). When she was in Venice Effie had told her mother that she had thought of writing a book about all the Austrians she met. After she sent her Venetian diaries she also sent away a 'paper parcel put away amongst my things' on 3.4.1854: PML MA 1338 (T.25)

52. ECG to GG 7.3.1854: PML MA 1338 (T.17)

53. ECG to GG 7.3.1854: PML MA 1338 (T.17)

54. ECG to Mrs. La Touche 10.10.1870: PML MA 1338 (XYZ.04) Effie goes on 'So far from his conniving at my leaving him it was a great shock to them all' naïvely appending the statement that he once offered her £800 a year to allow him to retire into a monastery! It was certainly a shock to his parents, who knew nothing whatsoever about what was going on, but as she never saw John for years after she left and as nobody wrote any first hand accounts about him being shocked, it is difficult to know how she came to this conclusion. All the surviving accounts seem to express outrage that John carried on exactly as normal. Everett Millais certainly believed that John's 'absence in the Highlands seemed purposely to give me an opportunity of being in his wife's society' and he seemed 'purposely to connive at the result', JEM to SMG 19.12 and 20.12.1853.

55. ECG to SMG 20.3.1854: PML MA 1338 (T.20) last sheet missing.

56. See Albert Gray's account of the marriage: 'my father's mind was soon made up. The marriage must be annulled at any cost. It

was first necessary to explain the nature of the contemplated proceedings to Mrs. Ruskin and to obtain her concurrence.' Gray, *Marriage*, p. 33. It is interesting to note that Mr. Gray did not know Millais ('a poor and struggling artist at best') personally at this time. They had met briefly only twice.

57. ECG to SMG 23.3.1854: PML MA 1338 (T.21)

58. ECG to SMG 29[30].3.1854: (T.23)

59. ECG to SMG 23.3.1854: PML MA 1338 (T.21)

60. JR statement to lawyer 27.4.1854: Whitehouse: *Vindication* (1950) p. 13

61. ECG to MR 25.4.1854: PML MA 1338 (T.43), James, *Order of Release*, pp. 225-6.

62. ECG to SMG 23.3.1854: PML MA 1338 (T.21)

63. Mrs. Gaskell to John Forster 18.5.1854 NLS MS2262 f.35-40. Letter 195 in *The Letters of Mrs. Gaskell*, ed. J. Chapple & A. Pollard (1966). There is some slight confusion in this source as to which Mr. and Mrs. Ruskin are being referred to at any given time, the parents or the children.

64. ECG to SMG 10.4.1854: PML MA 1338 (T.30)

65. ECG to SMG 29/30.3.1854: PML MA 1338 (T.23)

66. Copy ? ECG to Mrs. (Lizzie) Cleghorn (an old school friend) n.d. (Jul/Aug 1854) PML MA 1338 (UV.73)

67. See also PML MA 1338 (T.51-58). Admiral James wrote: 'I believe they would have made the best of a bad job if some streak of madness in JR had not caused his indifference to Effie to turn to harsh treatment of her': James, *Order of Release*, p. 6

68. According to Effie on 4.2.1854 'Crawley is the most careful and interested of men to do anything I tell him for Mr. Brown of Venice': PML MA 1338 (T.08) See also ECG to Brown 27.4.1854, PML MA 1338 (T.47), where Crawley told her brother George that he was going to take the first opportunity to leave John's employ. He

never did. John and Crawley became very close; indeed he did many of the things Effie should have done to help John with his work, eventually moving with his wife into a cottage next to Brantwood and becoming curator of the Ruskin drawing school at Oxford.

69. ECG to Rawdon Brown 17.4.1854: PML MA 1338 (T.35); and ECG to SMG undated but prob. 7.4.1854: PML MA 1338 (T.26). *M&R*, p. 169.

70. ECG to SMG 25/27.2.1854: PML MA 1338 (T.10) and *M&R*, p. 138.

71. GGJr. to SMG 22.4.1854: PML MA 1338 (T.39)

72. JR to Acland 16.5.1854: Surtees: *Reflections of a Friendship*, pp. 270-4

73. ECG to Rawdon Brown 27.4.1854: PML MA 1338 (T.47). Joan Severn later told Lucia Alexander that almost the last words Effie spoke to John had been 'Can't you give me some more money?' 17.11.1886: PML MA 3451.

22: A Mediæval Pantomime, pp. 451-472

1. See ECG to GG 3.4.1854: PML MA 1338 (T.25) 'I should like to see you and hear your opinion before you meet Mr. R.' See also Andrew Jameson to SMG 27 April: PML MA 1338 (UV.03) 'I almost wish Mr. Gray had taken his first plan and seen his [John's] father before resorting to the last remedy. However it has been done on the best advice.' I wonder, whose advice would that have been?

2. F. Harrison to E. T. Cook 20.12.1904. Correspondence between Cook and Harrison re points of law on Ruskin marriage, Lancaster L67. The book in question is F. Harrison, *John Ruskin*, London 1902, pp. 57 and 83.

3. F. Harrison to E. T. Cook 16.1.1905 Lancaster 67 2003 L05827. Albert Venn Dicey, *A Digest of the Law of England with reference to the Conflict of Laws* (1896), the first and still the standard text on the subject: 'the prince of legal textbooks.'

Dicey was also the author of *The Law of Domicil* (1879). Dicey was for some time the Principal of the Working Men's College set up by Ruskin using the money that previously had served as his marriage allowance. See JJR Account book 1855 Lancaster MS.29.

4. Even Effie had been advised that the fact that the marriage had been celebrated in Scotland was relevant. See previous chapter. Lutyens did not mention the reference to the Scotch marriage although she quoted from the same letter.

5. Correspondence between E. T. Cook and F. Harrison re points of law on Ruskin marriage, 16.1.1905: Lancaster L67 2003 L05823. Note the slide from English to British courts. In the second edition Harrison did change the form of words in his 'vailed' reference to the marriage on p. 57. 'Scotch Court' was deleted and now reads ambiguously: 'the wife left her husband and returned to her parents. A suit in the local court for nullity was brought by the wife...'; p. 83 now reads '...followed by a matrimonial suit'. Dicey thought the crucial issue was that of domicile, particularly of the defendant. The 1852 case of *Williams v. Dormer* did not provide an exact precedent for the Ruskin case. The Williams' marriage was an English one, they lived in England until in November 1838 the wife brought a nullity suit on the grounds of an invalid licence (Curteis' *Ecclesiastical Reports* 1. Curt. 870). This having failed she then succeeded in a judicial separation from bed and board. On 15.4.1852 the husband subsequently attempted a nullity suit on the same grounds but the court declined jurisdiction on the grounds that the wife (the defendant) did not share domicile with the man. Normally the wife's legal domicile was with the husband but owing to the judicial separation of the Williams this had ceased to be the case. Moreover in a nullity case where the marriage was

alleged to have never existed a shared domicile could not be assumed. However, the judge did assert that jurisdiction was sufficiently founded in nullity cases if the defendant (John in *Ruskin v. Ruskin*) was resident in England, not on a visit or as a traveller, and not having taken up that residence for the purpose of the suit (Spink's *Ecclesiastical Reports* 2.Rob.505).

6. Still the case in 2001. See J. G. Collier, *Conflict of Laws*, 2001, in which he explains that choice of applicable law is based on a very few general rules. The first example he gives is that the formal validity of a marriage is governed by the law of the place of celebration. Where this involves the contractual basis of marriage this indeed still applies but where incapacity is involved the situation was always more complicated. See also J. H. C. Morris, *Conflict of Laws* (3rd. ed., 1984), p. 207: 'Before 1974 the jurisdiction of the English courts to entertain petitions for nullity of marriage was one of the most vexed and difficult questions in the whole of the English conflict of laws.' This would not necessarily preclude the Ruskin case being heard in an English court but the case would have to be judged with reference to Scottish law. *R. v Povey* for bigamy in 1852 (1 Pearce (cc) 32) had established that 'In order to establish the fact of a marriage in Scotland some witness conversant with the law of Scotland as to marriage must be called.' (H. Jeremy, *An Analytical Digest of the Reports of Cases [...] in the Ecclesiastical Courts &c.* (1854)) As the case was heard in an ecclesiastical court, the equivalent of which had been abolished in Scotland, this might indeed raise questions of competency.

7. His works, classics in their field, included *A Treatise on Private International Law* (1858; second edition, rewritten, 1880; fifth edition, 1912), *Chapters on the Principles of International Law* (1894), *International Law* (two volumes, 1904-07; second

edition, 1910-13).

8. The Matrimonial Causes Act of 1857 did not mention the conditions of competence of the court with regard to divorce *a vinculo* (absolute divorce as opposed to judicial separation from bed and board). The Parliamentary divorces had been too few in number to establish any definite system. In the following years there was a gradual adoption of the so-called rule of matrimonial domicile in divorce cases. In 1861 the original rule that the validity of a marriage depended on the law of the place of celebration was qualified when the House of Lords distinguished between the formalities of marriage, governed by the *lex loci celebrationis,* and the capacity to marry, governed by each party's antenuptial domicile (Westlake, *A Treatise on Private International Law* (6th ed., 1905), p. 149; *Brook v. Brook* 9 H.L.C. 193). But even as late as *Niboyet v. Niboyet* (1878) the jurisdiction of the English court in divorce cases where the matrimonial domicile was in England did not extend to annulment cases: 'It applies therefore, as it seems to me, to suits for judicial separation and to suits for restitution of conjugal rights. I do not think it does apply to suits for a declaration of nullity of marriage' (Westlake, *op. cit.*, p. 90). The rules with regard to divorce jurisdiction were only officially established in 1895 after *Le Mesurier v. Le Mesurier* at which time the judges pointed out that 'when carefully examined, neither the English nor the Scottish decisions are in their lordships' opinion sufficient to establish the proposition that, in either of these countries, there exists a recognized rule of general law to the effect that a so-called rule of matrimonial domicile gives jurisdiction to dissolve marriage' (Westlake, *op. cit.*, p. 85). The judges ruled that 'It is both just and reasonable therefore that the differences of married people should be adjusted in accordance with the laws of the community to which they

belong and be dealt with by the tribunals which alone can administer those laws' (Westlake, *op. cit.,* p. 86). By 1905 mere residence in England was sufficient to claim the jurisdiction of the English court in both divorce and annulment cases.

9. I have been unable to find an exact precedent for the Ruskin case, but it would seem that John had been well advised. See F. J. N. Rogers, *A Practical Arrangement of Ecclesiastical Law* (1840). Rogers admits that English law is inapplicable when considering the validity of foreign marriages, which must be judged according to the law of the country where the marriage took place (p. 573). With regard to the contractual and formal nature of the marriage this was fairly accepted practice; incapacity to marry is however less straightforward. Nevertheless he asserts the exclusive right of the ecclesiastical court to pronounce a binding and effectual judgement on the legality of a marriage. 'The judgements of that court are also binding on questions of marriages of British subjects contracted in foreign countries, and of aliens, if necessary, and this must be in order to prevent a failure of justice; and there is the less difficulty in doing so, from the knowledge that the principles which regulate English marriages are such as are generally applicable to the marriages of Christian foreign countries; the marriage law of England being founded on the same general principles and having, like them, the ancient canon law for its basis' (p. 551).

10. Whitehouse, *Vindication*, p. 13.

11. See the correspondence JJR to GG, Bodleian MS. Eng. lett. d.227, particularly 1.10.1830 and 6. 9 1831.

12. Stone, *Road to Divorce*, p. 31: 'it has to be remembered that the undefended cases which were the large majority were undoubtedly collusive and in others the defence was perfunctory and deliberately misleading'. In Church courts in separation

cases where written interrogatories were the rule, uncontested suits could not be investigated and other witnesses could not be called.

13. JR to William Cowper Temple 20.9.1870: PML MA 1571 (164)

14. ECG to SMG 1.1.1854: PML MA 1338 (T.04). 'We talked of the German plan and John peevishly looking up told me not to begin talking of what had been settled six months ago' (thus even before the Scottish holiday).

15. JR to JJR 13.12.1853: Lancaster transcript T110, original Yale. Lushington was asked by the Select Committee how long a Consistorial Court divorce would take. He replied two to three months but: 'It depends of course upon the period of the year at which it commences, If it is just before the long vacation they would lose three months, in which nothing is done. Supposing it commences in November they would get a divorce by Easter Term with the greatest of ease.' 1853 *Report* p. 38. This might account for the rather inexplicable timing of the Scottish holiday which extended into autumn and early winter. Scotland has not the climate of Tuscany. In the event the case did in fact run out of time but an extra court day was added in order to prevent the carry over to November. July 15th was the day of St. Swithun, the patron saint of Winchester Cathedral and thus of the relevant diocese. Given the 'forty days of rain' at Glenfinlas, St. Swithun seems to have had quite a hand in the case.

16. The age of the parties could be an important consideration if older people were involved.

17. See Richardson to JR 4.7.1871: PML MA 1571 (155). John's lawyer cousin W. G. Richardson confirmed that the Court had evidence that he 'occupied the same apartment and bed as his wife *solus cum sola, nudus cum nuda* and yet that she remained *virgo intacta.*' It was essential for the success of the suit to state the fact of being naked in bed together. Separate beds might have indicated wilful non-consummation and therefore not the incurable impotence necessary for annulment.

18. Albert Gray also made notes on the legal papers and recorded both the use of the first person and the phrase 'George Gray swears'. Bodleian, MS. Eng. lett. c.228, p. 21.

19. The evidence of a medical man that the woman's health was seriously impaired by distress of mind owing to the non-consummation had been taken into consideration by Lushington in the important 1853 case. Lushington used this effect on the health of the wife as a reason for not enforcing further cohabitation. See Spink's *Ecclesiastical Reports* Vol. 1 p.16. [*A falsely called B v. B*].

20. Bodleian MS. Eng. lett c.228, p. 21

21. In fact this was exactly as Bell Scott reported. John never reproached Effie for her conduct with Millais at the Trevelyan house.

22. Whitehouse, *Vindication,* p. 17.Probably written at about the same time as the 27th April statement. Lutyens confused this document with the Legal Proxy sent by Rutter to Lausanne on 7th July. That document was merely an authorisation for a proctor to make an appearance on John's behalf 'say nothing and hear Sentence pronounced': PML MA 1571 (165)

23. SMG to GGJr 24.4.1854: PML MA 1338 (T.42). See also Rutter to JJR 1.7. 1854: PML MA 1571 (168). Lee had delivered all John's solicitor's children. Strange that despite the supposed need for absolute secrecy George Gray should have employed a doctor so connected with both the Ruskins and their family solicitor!

24. SMG to GGJr 24.4.1854: PML MA 1338 (T.42)

25. ECG to SMG 30.5.1854: PML MA 1338 (UV.35)

26. SMG to GGJr 24.4.1854: PML MA 1338 (T.42)

27. JR to ECG 27.5.1849: PML MA 1338 (H.29a)

28. ECG to SMG 28.5.1854: PML MA 1338 (UV.34)

29. ECG to SMG 28.5.1854: PML MA 1338 (UV.34)

30. It has been argued that since Charles Locock was the Queen's doctor, his reputation was a guarantee in such a case. However, like Dr. Simpson in Edinburgh, Locock may also have had a darker side. There is a persistent rumour that he secretly delivered an illegitimate son for Princess Louise Caroline Alberta and arranged for him to be adopted by his own son. Attempts by descendants to have confirmatory DNA tests carried out after exhumation were refused by Rochester Consistory Court as recently as 2002.

31. JJR account book for 1854 records John's law expenses as £257/15/10d: Lancaster Ms.29. Effie's costs were £139/16/2d which included 20gns for the doctors and £44 for the Grays' travel and accommodation: Rutter to JJR 19.6.1854, PML MA 1571 (166). John's proctor Mr. Pott waived his fee 'in this peculiar case' (he had not had to do anything except appear) but accepted £50 'compensation': PML MA 1571 (167).

32. See Shelford, *Practical Treatise*, p. 533. The husband would have to appeal to the Court of Arches. Married women could not have separate bank accounts as Murray found out when he sent Lady Eastlake crossed cheques. See Paston, *At John Murray's*, p. 164.

33. JR's answers to Mr. Pott apptd. 5.7.1854: Whitehouse, *Vindication*, p. 18

34. JR statement to his proctor 27.4.1854: Whitehouse, *Vindication*, p. 15

35. He also used an almost identical phrase in his letter to Acland on 16.5.1854 quoted in the following chapter.

36. Equivocation and double meanings of words were the subject of a continuing contemporary debate between 1843 and 1864. Charles Kingsley wrote of equivocation being justified on the grounds that 'then we do not deceive our neighbour but allow him to deceive himself.' Given her *amour propre* John knew which definition Effie would assume. See R. Brownell, *A Torch at Midnight* (2013) particularly chapter 3, and ed. R. Brownell, *Contemporary Reviews of The Seven Lamps of Architecture* (2013).

37. Whitehouse, *Vindication*, pp. 15-6. In fact when John unequivocally meant the physical body he almost invariably used the word 'body'. There are 1619 uses of the word in the Library Edition of his complete works and, other than where he used the word in its other senses such as 'a body of men' or a 'body of work', the overwhelming number of these uses refer straightforwardly to the physical human body. The word 'person' may also however definitely have the meaning of 'body' and John did use it in his writing in that sense albeit very rarely. However, of the 1168 uses of the word 'person' fewer than 20 can be said to refer exclusively to the physical body as being separate from all other aspects of the person, and of these only a handful can be taken in no other way. Perhaps the least equivocal use is where he described a man being forced 'back till his person forms an arch' (LE 25.169). Another is in *Ariadne Florentina* where he discusses Botticelli's portrait of Simonetta Vespucci, mistress of Giuliano de Medici: 'Now I think she must have been induced to let Sandro draw from her whole person undraped, more or less.'(LE 22.483-4) However, when he wrote that 'In Michelangelo the person is everything, the dress nothing,' (LE 22.499) 'person' certainly meant 'the physical appearance of the whole body,' but a nude by Michelangelo is so much more than a mere life study. In the overwhelming number of John's uses of the word 'person,' it cannot be taken as an exact

synonym for 'body' and this is for a very cogent reason, explained at some length and repeatedly throughout his work. He believed quite firmly that the opposition of body to soul was a monkish error and that the beauty of the person was determined by everything that person thought, did or experienced. Thus in *Munera Pulveris*: 'Every right action and true thought sets the seal of beauty on person and face, every wrong action and foul thought its seed of distortion' (LE 17.149) and a footnote sends the reader back to *The Art of England* where he had asserted that 'On all the beautiful features of men and women throughout the ages, are written the solemnities and majesty of the law they knew.' Again, 'the pursuit of Justice [regulates] dignity of person as of mind' (LE 20.229). That is why in many cases where the word 'person' could well be taken as synonymous with 'body' it is also invested with moral qualities such as dignity (LE 12.154), honesty (LE 29.157), and nobility (LE 17.150). For John the beauty or ugliness of physical human form was always fused with moral or spiritual considerations. His 'person' is usually a much richer notion than his 'body'.

38. Whitehouse, *Vindication*, p.16.

39. James, *Order of Release*, p. 96: 'It was not till five years later, when his strange love had turned to persecution, that he told his wife that until he saw her body, he imagined women were quite different and that the sight of her on their wedding night disgusted him.' James' book was published in 1948 and immediately preceded the introduction of media and particularly television advertising on a mass scale. Much of this advertising was directed specifically at women and, in order to sell consumer products to them, was intended to increase their anxieties with regard to their bodies. It is perhaps no coincidence that those particular US preoccupations, body odour, body hair and 'female

hygiene' should all have been proposed as reasons why John found Effie unattractive. In empathising with Effie, might not writers have been projecting their own 20th-century anxieties about their bodies wholly inappropriately onto a 19th-century world which showed little concern for such issues. Right up to the 1970's the legacy of the Hayes Code seems to have resulted in a situation in the US where pornography was defined by whether or not pubic hair was depicted. This seems to have compounded the suspicion that female body hair was 'dirty'. By the time Lutyens published, female depilation was almost *de rigueur* for US actresses. That the 'horror of hair' was subsequently replaced by 'crypto-pædophilia' as the century wore on only serves to confirm that fashionable modern anxieties were being projected onto the Ruskin/Gray story. It seems there are fashions even in smears!

40. *R&G* p. 108*n* quoting JR to JJR 12.8.1862; Van Akin Burd, *The Winnington Letters* (1969), p. 369. See also *R&G* pp. 108-9 where Lutyens suggest John 'may have trumped up this reason in order to hurt Effie, for he did not tell her this until there was hatred and bitterness between them'. There was much uninformed speculation amongst JR's early biographers. Frederic Harrison wrote to Cook in 1904 that he believed that the marriage was arranged by the parents and that he knew 'nothing to show that she or [even] he had from the other anything normally called love (of the person). He was apparently as innocent as a baby. It would be quite natural that, both being [illeg.] virgin and physically cool, marriage was not consummated when they were first put to bed. A dangerous illness of his followed and he was an invalid for some time. She perhaps never encouraged him, possibly never suffered him, to make further trial, and they lapsed into habitual separation and easy indifference. This I know to be

the fact about Thomas Carlyle [...] Mrs. C. died *intacta*. I know a healthy vigorous young couple, who for four months never could find how babies were made.' F. Harrison to E. T. Cook 20.12.1904, Lancaster L67.

41. Rutter dissuaded Mr. Ruskin snr. from alleging 'irritation of the woman's brain' because she might argue that it had arisen from the non-consummation, 23.5.1854: PML MA 1571 (169). Effie's restlessness and inability to sit quietly alone for any length of time were often noted. Mr. Ruskin disliked 'the restless undomestic character of the Girl' from the start, and noted that 'She was never one day quiet or satisfied without the House being full of Company or going to Plays and Concerts Nightly': PML MA 1571 (156). Apart from the compulsive dancing Pauline Trevelyan noted how Effie had to sit three times for her photograph because she kept moving. Perhaps there was indeed some very slight dysfunction. In those days the extreme form of such behaviour was sometimes referred to as St. Vitus' Dance, a term often used incorrectly for restless children, particularly girls. Today we would probably ascribe it to mild autism, hyperactivity or ADD. Could this have been one of the circumstances in Effie's person that repelled John?

42. 1853 *Report* p. 47. See 23.5.1854, PML MA 1571 (169), where Rutter also cautioned Mr. Ruskin to be as passive as possible, even to the extent of not being represented in court, 'I feel disposed to help them so far as not to lay your son open to the charges of Collusion,' in order to obtain the 'so much to be desired release.'

43. There is evidence that he repeated this statement to George Allen claiming that he could have defended the suit but that had he done so he would have been 'saddled with that woman for life': Leon, *Great Victorian*, p. 404. In fact John had even been advised by his lawyer that he could

have forced Effie to return if he promised to fulfil his duty as a husband! John did not exercise that option. Joan Severn noted 'his Lawyer asked if he'd have her back saying he could oblige her to come provided he would live with her as other Husbands – he said "never".' Severn to Alexander 17.11.1886: PML MA 3451

44. See Albert Gray's notes extracted from the depositions (Bodleian MS. Eng. lett. c.228, p.21)

45. See Spink's *Ecclesiastical Reports,* Vol. 1, p. 14-15, *A falsely called B v. B* 21.4.1853. As described on p. 373 above, Lushington's judgement denied *Welde v. Welde* (2. Lee 586) 1731 which was the case used by the La Touches which ruled that if the man married again and had children this would re-validate the first marriage, and also *Bury v. Bury.*

46. ECG to SMG 30.3.1854: PML MA 1338 (T.23)

47. See Sir Albert Gray's notes extracted from the depositions (Bodleian MS. Eng. lett. c.228, p.21)

48. *M&R* p.181. Lutyens also came to the conclusion that John was not impotent: see *M&R,* p. 193. Note the double standards in Lady Eastlake's comments on JJR 'Nothing can be more indecent and vulgar than the affected glee at a catastrophe so disgraceful to their wretched son.'

49. ECG to SMG 30.3.1854: PML MA 1338 (T.23)

50. ECG to SMG 3.4.1854: PML MA 1338 (T.25)

51. ECG to SMG 10.4.1854: PML MA 1338 (T.30)

52. Document 'devised and written' by ECG 10.4.1854: PML MA 1338 (T.29a)

53. See Whitehouse, *Vindication,* p. 14. 'The letters written to Miss Gray before our marriage are all in my possession [...] My wife asked me to give her these letters some days ago.' John's refusal could well be more evidence of planning. Why were these letters in his possession?

54. Mr. Glennie to GG 15.7.1854, copied in ECG to Rawdon Brown 20.7.1854: PML MA 1338 (UV.70)

55. Mr. Glennie to Mr. Rutter 26.6.1854: PML MA 1571 (168)

56. Rutter to JJR 1.7.54: PML MA 1571 (168)

57. *The Times* 29.7.1854. The first case under the new rules seems to have been *Fyler v. Fyler* on 6.12.1854. The proctor Phillimore asked the court for direction. Lushington granting permission noted that *viva voce* evidence was optional but if either party desired it, the other party must concede unless there was good cause not to (Spink's *Ecclesiastical Reports*, vol. 1, pp. 69-70).

58. Rutter to JJR 1.7.1854: PML MA 1571 (168). The minor points almost certainly included the reference to bodily deformity on John's part.

59. Rutter to JJR 20.8.1854: PML MA 1571 (167). Such things happened when there was no cross-examination of witnesses. See also PML MA 1571 (155) where W. G. Richardson also pointed out that 'it appears to me undoubted that there was fraud practised' in the court.

60. Wedderburn notes on Ruskin Proxy 5.7.1854: Lancaster L67

61. The Lady Chapel at St. Saviour's, Southwark had been renovated in 1832. St. Saviour was a corruption of San(cta) Salvator or Holy Liberator/Redeemer, the original name of St. John Lateran in Rome. St. Saviour's also had a chapel of St. John. St. Saviour's was accustomed to play-acting; it was the local church for Shakespeare's Globe and other theatres and was known as the actors' church.

62. Rutter to JJR 19.7.1854: PML MA 1571 (166). Although the Ruskin annulment was certainly unusual enough to be of legal interest it did not appear in Spink's *Ecclesiastical Reports* for 1854 even in the usual anonymous form. Nor did it appear in any of the Analytical Digests covering that period. This would tend to suggest

some kind of official cover-up.

63. There is also a copy of the Sentence in the Kirk Session Book for Kinnoull 30.7.1854: Minute engrossing Extract of Disannulling of Marriage p. 224, NLS CH2/948/7

64. PML MA 1571 (162)

65. So long as John did not read the court papers he was not aware of the specific accusations made against him and therefore could not be accused of collusion by withholding a just defence.

66. Rutter to JJR. 20.8.1854: PML MA 1571 (167)

23: Aftermath, pp. 473-499

1. Lady Eastlake to ECG 9.5.1854: PML MA 1338 (UV.21). The present author has long pored over John's letter to *The Times* in an attempt to discover what might possibly have caused Lady Eastlake to refer to it as a 'disgusting farrago.' The only sentence remotely applicable to John and Effie concerns 'an apple shaken from one of the trees of the orchard, thus marking that the entire awakening of the conscience is not merely to committed, but to hereditary guilt' (LE 12.330). This subtle reference to Original Sin and to Eve's apple might conceivably have been seized upon by the rabid imagination of Lady Eastlake as a veiled attack on Effie. Although it was a religious commonplace, Hunt considered the orchard background to be so important that he had timed his work to catch it in the proper season (LE 12.331). The apple is also a symbol of St Swithun, whose feast day is July 15, the day on which the annulment case came to judgment.

2. JR to Pauline Trevelyan 8.5.1854: Surtees: *Reflections of a Friendship*, pp. 78-9

3. JR to Pauline Trevelyan 5.6.1854: Surtees: *Reflections of a Friendship*, pp. 81-3

4. It is not difficult to see the parallels between Effie and Lady Olivia in Edgeworth's *Leonora*. e.g. 'Full of life and spirits, with a heart formed for all the

enthusiasm, for all the delicacy of love, I married early, in the fond expectation of meeting a heart suited to my own. Cruelly disappointed, I found – merely a husband. My heart recoiled upon itself; true to my own principles of virtue, I scorned dissimulation. I candidly confessed to my husband, that my love was extinguished. I proved to him, alas! too clearly, that we were not born for each other. The attractive moment of illusion was past – never more to return; the repulsive reality remained. The living was chained to the dead, and, by the inexorable tyranny of English laws, that chain, eternally galling to innocence, can be severed only by the desperation of vice. Divorce, according to our barbarous institutions, cannot be obtained without guilt. Appalled at the thought, I saw no hope but in submission. Yet to submit to live with the man I could not love was, to a mind like mine, impossible. My principles and my feelings equally revolted from this legal prostitution. We separated. I sought for balm to my wounded heart in foreign climes.' 'Lady Olivia is just returned to England. Scandal, imported from the continent, has had such an effect in prejudicing many of her former friends and acquaintance against her, that she is in danger of being excluded from that society of which she was once the ornament and the favourite.' 'Nothing would tempt you to associate with those who have avowed themselves regardless of right and wrong; but I must warn you against another, and a far more dangerous class, who professing the most refined delicacy of sentiment, and boasting of invulnerable virtue, exhibit themselves in the most improper and hazardous situations; and who, because they are without fear, expect to be deemed free from reproach. Either from miraculous good fortune, or from a singularity of temper, these adventurous heroines may possibly escape with what they call perfect

innocence. So much the worse for society. Their example tempts others, who fall a sacrifice to their weakness and folly. I would punish the tempters in this case more than the victims, and for them the most effectual species of punishment is contempt. Neglect is death to these female lovers of notoriety. The moment they are out of fashion their power to work mischief ceases.'

Goneril plotted against her virtuous husband's life offering her bed to her accomplice.

5. JR to Acland 16.5.1854: Surtees: *Reflections of a Friendship*, pp. 270-4

6. Wedderburn transcripts p. 152: Bodleian MS. Eng. lett. c.33

7. Copy AL JJR to W. Collins December 1854: PML MA 1571 (156). 'He (John) will neither say nor write as word in his own defence.'

8. The marriage between the actress Ellen Terry and G. F. Watts, the painter of Effie's 1851 portrait, was annulled entirely discreetly a year after they were married in 1864 and did not affect the careers of either.

9. Robertson, *Eastlake*, p. 100 *n.2*. John had it seems good reason not to include German painters in his magnum opus. Rigby wrote to Murray from Düsseldorf: 'I am almost afraid to speak of the Dusseldorf artists – I was so terribly disappointed in them. There never was such a mistake as that school altogether – not tolerable in any department, and I saw them all' (quoted in Paston, *At John Murray's*, p. 57). The title of her article 'Modern German Paintings' (*Quarterly Review*, vol. 77, March 1846, pp. 323-48) was an obvious spoiler for John's book. She seems to have had a rather mercenary attitude to art criticism.

10. Robertson, *Eastlake*, pp. 100 & 106

11. Robertson, *Eastlake*, p. 170.

12. *Præterita*, II.x.192, LE 35.421

13. *Præterita*, II.x.192, LE 35.422

14. June 10th (?) 1847. JJR to JR September 1847, Lancaster 1996 LD1749, quoted *Ein V*, p. 12

15. LE 12.xl and 8.xxiv. Lockhart took exception to John's attack on Gally Knight, a John Murray author.

16. C. L. Eastlake to John Murray 14.6.1847: John Murray Archive uncatalogued at Albemarle Street, now NLS

17. *Quarterly Review* Mar 1848.

18. G. Paston, *At John Murray's*, p. 110.

19. *Punch* published a poem by a 'Perfectly Furious Academician': 'I takes and paints, Hears no complaints, And sells before I'm dry; Till Savage Ruskin He sticks his tusk in, Then nobody will buy. N.B. Confound Ruskin: only that won't come into poetry – but it's true.' LE 14.xxvii.

20. Lockhart had given her this nickname.

21. ECG to GG 7.3.1854: PML MA 1338 (T.17)

22. She miscarried in June 1851.

23. Gray: *Marriage*, pp. 1-2

24. NLS MS 1557 ff.179-80

25. Lady Eastlake to SMG 18.4.1854: PML MA 1338 (T.36)

26. Lady Eastlake to ECG 18.4.1854: PML MA 1338 (T.37)

27. Lady Eastlake to SMG 29.4.1854: PML MA 1338 (UV.06). The 'truth' seems to be her euphemism for Ruskin's alleged impotence. See later in the same letter: 'He [Millais] had known nothing of the truth and asked me with painful blushes if I had.' Can it really be true that Millais did not know that the marriage was unconsummated at this late stage?

28. JEM to SMG 5.5.1854: PML MA 1338 (UV.14)

29. *Quarterly Review*, vol. 84, December 1848, pp. 153-185. Anti-Christian because it challenged the divinely ordained position of the rich and the poor; so vitriolic that one of Charlotte's uncles came over from Ireland to give its anonymous author a good thrashing. See Robertson, *Eastlake*, p. 106 (quoting W. Wright: *The Brontës in*

Ireland (1893) p. xxix). *Jane Eyre* was published on 16.10.1847 at the height of the October Crisis. In the same month Karl Marx began writing *The Communist Manifesto*. Charlotte Brontë had of course lost money in the collapse of the railway bubble and was a Ruskin enthusiast.

30. Lady Eastlake to ECG 27.4.1854: PML MA 1338 (UV.05)

31. JR to JEM 20.12.1854: PML MA 1338 (W.11)

32. See Robert Hewison, *Ruskin on Venice* (2009) p. 48.

33. Rawdon Brown to ECG 1.5.1854: PML MA 1338 (UV.07)

34. Robertson, *Eastlake*, p. 170.

35. See JEM to SMG 5.6.1854. Effie had seen Foster in town and Millais asked Mrs. Gray if he had recognised Effie.

36. Lady Eastlake to ECG 25.6.54: PML MA 1338 (UV.56); and ECG to Rawdon Brown 14.7.1854: PML MA 1338 (UV.68)

37. JEM to SMG 15.7.1854: PML MA 1338 (UV.69)

38. John Murray Archive Box 36 not catalogued at Albemarle Street, now NLS

39. Elwin was a country parson with a talent for elegant prose who was elevated to the dizzy heights of editorship when Lockhart retired. Paston writes 'Elwin wrote to Murray nearly every day for advice and suggestions.' Murray's replies were all destroyed. *Op.cit.* p. 129

40. Robertson, *Eastlake*, p. 383 *n*.122. Ruskin himself already suspected something of the kind. In the preface to his 1856 *Academy Notes* John noted his steady refusal to write for 'that once respectable periodical' the *Quarterly* and the account of his private life which had lately appeared in that magazine 'as a consequence'.

41. Sir Frederick Pollock: *Personal Remembrances* (1877) II, pp. 44-5, quoted in Robertson, *Eastlake*, p. 383.

42. *Quarterly Review*, vol. 98, March 1856, pp. 384-433; quoted Robertson, *Eastlake*, p. 384

43. Hilton: *Early Years,* p. 243-4.

44. Lady Eastlake's correspondence with John Murray between 1849 and 1857 is so sparsely represented in the John Murray archive as to be almost noteworthy by its absence. Even after Ruskin died the John Murray of the time was involved in the transaction which put the *Vindication* documents illegally in the hands of Sir Albert Gray, who was only prevented from destroying them by the threat of legal action. 'Before going to see her [Mrs. Veitch, wife of Rutter's successor] I went to see John Murray, to ask him whether, during his conversation with Mr. Thornhill he had formed any opinion as to whether there was any intention to drive a hard bargain': Bodleian MS. Eng. lett. c.228 (146)

45. Lady Eastlake to John Murray 9.3.1862 John Murray archive uncatalogued at Albemarle Street, now NLS

46. LE 7. lix

47. *Quarterly Review,* vol. 84, December 1848, pp. 153-185.

48. JJR Accounts 1845-63 Lancaster Ms. 29. In the outgoings for 1855 Mr. Ruskin notes 'paid John 1 yr. 8 months being from 1 May 1854 the same as agreed for Marriage Allowance being now wanted for Workmen £500'.

24: Rose La Touche, pp. 500-517

1. The love affair between John and Rose is not the main subject of this book and is only cursorily dealt with in so far as it bears upon his marriage. Interested readers should turn to *John Ruskin and Rose La Touche: Her Unpublished Diaries of 1861 and 1867,* ed. Van Akin Burd (1979).

2. Mrs. La Touche to Mrs. MacDonald 15.10. 1863, quoted Leon, *Great Victorian,* p. 359

3. JR to C. E. Norton 10.3.1863: LE 36.436

4. JR to Georgiana Cowper Temple 15.9. 1866: unpublished original with Mrs. Detmar Blow, quoted Leon, *Great Victorian,* p. 368. See also correspondence between JR and Maria La Touche in Lancaster. Just before Rose died Mrs. La Touche allowed John and Rose to meet several times and there was a later reconciliation between John and her mother.

5. See Whitehouse, *Vindication,* p. 50

6. They had married as soon as decently possible after the decree. With the exception of his brother William, none of the Millais family and none of his friends came to the wedding: JEM to Hunt 22.5.1855, PML MA 1338 (W.20). His parents moved out of their Gower St. home, possibly because of the scandal. Following her marriage to Everett and despite for many years presenting him annually with a child, Effie continued to spend much time in Perth with her mother. She also continued to show symptoms of neurotic illness. Although she seems to have enjoyed her life with Millais and was supportive of him in his work, the impression given by her later letters is more of her interest in financial and social aspects of her husband's career than personal or æsthetic aspirations. It has been noted that in later years there did not seem to be any deep emotional bond between them. She became obsessed with the 'Problem of Being Presented at Court' and thereby achieving the same social status she had enjoyed with John. She always suspected the Ruskins of plotting against her in this matter. Millais' later work was perhaps best summarised by William Morris: 'A great talent squandered.'

7. Mrs. La Touche to ECG 8.10.1870: PML MA 1338 (XYZ.03). A copy of the solicitor's opinion survived. The authority consulted seems to have been R. Burns, *Ecclesiastical Law,* 2 vols., (1763, but regularly updated; the 9th edition, corrected by R. Phillimore, appeared in 1842). The edition used by the La Touche solicitor is unknown. See Leon, *Great Victorian,* pp. 402-4.

8. Sent by Mrs. La Touche to Mrs. Cowper,

quoted Leon, *Great Victorian,* p. 403. The legal opinion may well have been based on *Welde v. Welde* (2. Lee 586) of 1731 in which the Court is reported to have said 'If the parties should be divorced, and both should marry again, and he should have children by the second marriage, these second marriages must be by law set aside and the first declared valid; for when the Church appears to have been deceived, the sentence must be revoked' (quoted Spink's *Ecclesiastical Reports,* Vol. 1, p. 14). This had generally been ignored in favour of the Bury case (5 Rep. 98b) and had been entirely overturned by Lushington in 1853. Was Ireland such a legal backwater?

9. Comprehensively demolished by Leon, *Great Victorian,* pp. 402-4 and even Lutyens admitted it was both incorrect and incorrectly passed on. See *Cornhill Magazine,* Spring 1967, p. 10.

10. Mrs. La Touche to Mrs. Cowper Temple, December 1868: unpublished. Leon, *Great Victorian,* p. 416. Note her fear of children being born!

11. Copy JEM to Mr. La Touche 10.10.1870: PML MA 1338 (XYZ.05). G. H. Fleming has noted an abrupt cooling of passion between Millais and Effie in August 1867 just before her correspondence with Mrs. La Touche began. This coincided with the conception of Effie's eighth and final child. Although this would have been reason enough for any woman to close the bedroom door in those days before contraception became respectable, the rumours that her ex-husband was proposing to marry must have put her under extra stress. For Millais at least it may well have been the first time he learned the full truth about the Ruskin marriage and the legal implications of the annulment. If that was so, then it might have been the first time he realised that his own marriage was suspect. It may also been the first

time he fully contemplated his own involvement by the Grays.

12. ECG to Mrs. La Touche 10.10.1870: PML MA 1338 (XYZ.04). John may have been referring to Effie's ongoing health problems and extended stay at Perth.

13. ECG to Mrs. La Touche 10.10.1870: PML MA 1338 (XYZ.04)

14. Bradley, *Letters... to Lord and Lady Mount Temple,* Letter 1.7.1871.

15. W. Richardson to JR 21.7.1871: PML MA 1571 (157). Was this a hint that John had arranged everything with Mr. Gray?

16. Bradley, *Letters... to Lord and Lady Mount Temple,* p. 296, letter of 18.7.1871 from Denmark Hill. Sir John Simon was one of the top medical men in the land. He specialised in infectious diseases.

17. Bradley, *Letters... to Lord and Lady Mount Temple,* p. 298, letter 23.7.1871.

18. MacDonald, *Reminiscences,* pp. 115-16.

19. See Shelford, *Practical Treatise,* p. 208. Also Thomas Poynter, *A Concise View of the Doctrine and Practice of Ecclesiastical Courts to Marriage and Divorce* (1824) p. 126.

20. ALS W. G. Collingwood to Sir Albert Gray 28.1.1898. Bodleian MS. Eng. lett. c. 228 (39-40) and Gray, *Marriage,* App. 2 (73-4) (30 yr. hold)

21. JR to C. E. Norton 28.12.1874: *Letters of John Ruskin to Charles Eliot Norton* (2 vols, 1904-5), p .349, quoted Hewison, *Ruskin, Turner and the Pre-Raphaelites* (2000), p. 260.

22. JR to Georgiana Mount Temple 20.3. 1870: Bradley, *Letters... to Lord and Lady Mount Temple,* pp. 273-4.

23. Any reader tempted to impose modern ideas and values retrospectively on the Victorian era should also be aware that in the year of Rosie's death the age of consent for young girls was raised – from 12 to 13 years old.

24. See R. L. Brownell: 'John Ruskin: Patron or Patriarch?', *The Journal of the William*

Morris Society, Vol. XIV, No.1, autumn 2000

25. W. G. Richardson to JR 4.7.1871: PML MA 1571 (155)

26. Maria La Touche to MacDonald (no date) 1863, quoted by William Raeper: *George MacDonald* (1986), p. 215 *n.*2.

27. MacDonald, *George MacDonald,* p. 331.

28. MacDonald, *Reminiscences,* p. 100. The account continues: 'Then he proceeded to explain his deplorable foolishness; how over persuaded by his parents, he proposed to a girl whom he only admired. Curiously ignorant he presumed that the necessary love would follow marriage, as he had been assured it would.' Perhaps somehow the accounts of Ruskin's relations with Charlotte Lockhart and Effie Gray have been mixed together here since there can be no doubt that John's parents were initially against the marriage and his letters to Effie before the wedding indicate that

he was completely besotted with her.

29. JR to G. MacDonald 13.2.1865, quoted in MacDonald, *George MacDonald,* p. 333. John's father and mother were still alive.

30. MacDonald, *George MacDonald,* p. 331.

31. MacDonald, *George MacDonald,* p. 336.

Epilogue, pp. 519-521

1. See Leon, *Great Victorian,* p. 406: 'The young members of the Gray family were brought up to think of Ruskin with abhorrence [...] the Millais children were deliberately hostile in their attitude to him [...] Many years later, Holman Hunt's daughter Gladys, met Mary Millais unexpectedly in the High St. Kensington, and was both shocked and surprised at a diatribe against Ruskin that she poured out at length for no apparent reason whatever [...] most hostile of all was the attitude of Millais himself.'

INDEX

Acland, Henry 98, 190, 197, 376, 382, 394, 395, *398*, 401, 415-8, *418*, 466, 474, 479, 484, 485, 514

Albano 62

Alboni 186

Alexander, William 56

Andrews, Miss 50

Andrews, Rev. E. 50

Angoulême, Duchess of 302

Armstrong, Lily 512

Avonbank School 67, *68*, 71, 72, 89, 141

Bayford, Dr. 471

Beresford Chapel, Walworth 50

Berry, Duchess of 302

Berwick 105

Blackwood's Magazine 381, 490, 495, 496

Blaikie, David 58

Blair Atholl 176, 181, 457

Bodichon, Barbara 68

Boswell, Jane 225, 241, 428, 438, 446, 469

Boucheret, Jessie 69

Bowerswell House early history 21, *22;* as built 23, 24; as rebuilt 28, *29*, 30; horrific events at 25-7, 88; John avoids 94-95, 97; John calls to propose 104-5, 108-9, 111-114; Effie at 117; parties at 141, *145*; John arrives for wedding 144, 150, 171, 175; 146, 150, 154-5, 158, 165, 167, 190, 200; Gadesden visits 203; Effie returns to 218; John arrives to collect Effie 256, 258; John arrives and departs,Effie stays 292-3; gas lighting installed 306; illness at 348, 350; proposed visits to 376; William Millais visits 395, 419-20; John's final visit 424-6, 429-30, 432, 434, 440-1

Brig o'Turk 385, *386,* 387, *388, 389,* 390, 392, 401, 402, 405, 408, 409, 412

Brontë, family 57, 145

Brontë, Charlotte 494; *Jane Eyre* 494

Brown, Ford Madox, 296

Brown, Rawdon Lubbock, 274, 275, 277, 278, 279, 280, 281, 283, 288, 291, 293, 294, 297, 299, 300. 301, 302, 316, 318, 319, 320, 322, 325, 326, 329, 331, 334, 337, 338, 339, 340, 341, 342, 344, 384, 387, 421, 425, 445, 446, 447, 448, 494, 495, 502, warns Effie about behaviour, 280-1, 291

Bunyan, John, *Pilgrim's Progress* 260

Byerley, Fanny, Maria & Anne 68

Byron, Lord 48
  Complete Works 362,
Marino Falieri, Doge of Venice 362

Calderidge, second Master of Eton 186

Callander 384, 386, 387, 390, 408

Carlyle, Jane 180, 348

Carlyle, Thomas 180, 498

Chamonix (Chamouni) 125, 237, 252, 255, 258, 264

Charlemont, Lady 288

Charles Ferdinand, Archduke 321

Charles Street 379

Charterhouse 208, 495

Church and State Gazette 338

Clark, Sir James 60
  Treatise on Pulmonary Consumption 61

Cockburn, Lizzie 141, 168

Cockburn, Lord 141-2

Collingwood, W. G. 26, 56, 61, 63, 170, 174, 435, 511
  The Life of John Ruskin, 26, 56, 61, 63, 174, 435, 511

Collins, Charlie 385, 387, 408, 412,

Collins, Mrs. 412

Combe, Thomas,392

Cook, E. T. 452

Cowper, Georgina, later Cowper-Temple, later Lady Mount-Temple, *née* Tollemache 53, 503, 504, 506, 514

Cowper, William, later Cowper-Temple, later Barone Temple 507, 509, 514

Cox, David 186

Craigmillar Castle 152

Crawley, Frederick, 368, 380, 389, 390, *392*, 394, 395, 396, 400, 401, 426, 438, 439, 447, 450, 471

Crossmount, Pitlochrie, 94, 95, 96, 104, 109, 250, 410

Croydon, 37, 38, 39, 40, 44, 45, 46, 58, 63, 64

Danieli, Hotel, 270, *271*, 279, 281, 297, 301, 302, 317

Dante 122, *414*

Daru, Pierre Antoine Noel, Count
Histoire de la République de Venise 362

Davy, Lady 83, 84, 96, 186, 215, 257, 262, 270, 284, 340, 489, 491, 492

Dawkins, Mr. 339

Denmark Hill, 69, *75*, 87, 91, 92, 93, 95, 96, 97, 105, 107, 108, 111, 112, 113, 115, 120, 123, 168, 183, 184, 185, 189, 202, 203, 211, 212, 214, 216, 217, 218, 220, 238, 240, 241, 255, 258, 259, 287, 288, 290, 294, 297, 304, 309, 310, 312, 313, 326, 338, 340, 345, 350, 351, 366, 381, 410, 438, 449, 458, 491, 527

Desart, Countess of 500

Dicey, A. 452, 453, 454
Conflict of Laws, 452

Dickens, Charles, works in Doctors Commons, 363
Bleak House, 365, 445
David Copperfield, 363-4, 365
Hard Times, 365
Pickwick Papers, 365

Dijon 225, 254, 255, 263

divorce law 20; ecclesiastical 359, 361-3, 366-7, 376-8, 451-472; Venetian 362; Parliamentary divorce 352, 357-9, 361; Scottish 360-1, 405, 426, 430-1, 452; reform of 19, 378, 379; *The First report of the Commissioners (on Divorce)* (1853) 357, 360, 363, 378

Doctors' Commons 363, 365, 366, 456, 460

Domecq, Adèle Clotilde 51, 52, 53, 55, 56, 60, 66, 74, 76, 159, 163, 173, 211, 285, 485
marriage to baron Duquesne, 53, 285

Domecq, Caroline (Countess Bethune) 53, 163, 211, 212, 285

Domecq, Cécile (Countess de Chabrillan) 163, 285, 286

Domecq, Diana (Countess Maison), 163, 285

Domecq, Elise (Countess de Roys) 163, 285

Domecq, John Pedro 53, 232

Domecq, Pedro 28, 51, 53, 76,

Dufferin, Lord 302, 318

Dunblane 384

Dundee 93, 393, 447, 450, 456

Dunkeld 24, 96, 97

Dürer, Albrecht 303

Durham 426

Eastlake, Charles Lock, 14, 340, 341, 491, 492, 496

Eastlake, Lady (Elizabeth Rigby), 131, 340, 341, 373, 429, 442, 443, 445, 448, 449, 473, 490, 491, 492, (493), 494, 495, 496, 497, 498, 520, 524

Edgeworth, Maria 477, 483

Edinburgh, 21, 95, 106, 114, 131, 141, 142, 152, 157, 158, 173, 208, 209, 213, 214, 218, 226, 227, 228, 250, 252, 261, 342, 355, 356, 361, 380, 383, *386*, 395, 396, *399*, 418, 423, 424, 426, 430, 432, 433, 446, 451, 480, 488, 491, 495, 526, 530

Edinburgh Review 496

Edinburgh, Bishop of 495

Elwin, Whitwell 496

Esterhazy, Countess 302, 322, 327, 328

Ewart, Francis 204

Feilding, Lord and Lady 337

Fielding, Copley 186

Findlay, Rev. John 27

Folkestone, 109, 127, 190, 220, 221, 263

Furnivall, F. J. 299, 359, 366, *399*, *402*, 403, 404, 429, 431, 514

Gadesden, Mr & Mrs William 79, 187, 203, 204, 373

Gardener's Chronicle 338

Gardner, Mr & Mrs William 92, 93, 147, 187, 290

Gardner, 'Snob' 91

Gaskell, Elizabeth, 68, 74, 113, 115, 315, 348, 446, at Avonbank School, 68

Geneva 125, 224, 225, 236, 263, 475

Glenelg, Lord 302, 443, 444, 445, 524

Glenfinlas 7, 61, 169, 350, 365, 366, *369*, 385, *388*, 389, 390, 393, 394, 395, 396, *397*, 400, 401, 402, 403, 404, 405, 408, 409, 410, 412, *416-7*, 418, 419, 422, 423, 427, 428, 430, 432, 437, 446, 487, 495

Glennie, J. I. 456, 469, 470, 471

Globe 339

Gordon, Murphy & Co 28

Gorzkowski, Governor 322

Gray, (Sir) Albert, 23, 24, 25, 26, 27, 109, 169, 171, 175, 177, 293, 345, 393, 396, 435, 458, 462, 463, 467, 487, 492, *506*, 511

Gray, Alice, 107, 236, *506*

Gray, Euphemia Chalmers 2, *4*, 9, *11*, 13, 15, 18, 21, 23, 55; birth 67; death of younger brothers 71; death of younger sisters 71; education at Avonbank School 67, 68, 71, 72, 89, 141; handwriting 69, 80, 138, 194, 317; visits Herne Hill 69; visits Denmark Hill, 69, 75, 95; start of affair with John 66; romantic parting at Denmark Hill 92; refuses John's proposal 105-7; accepts John's proposal 108; acting under orders 99, 100, 144; 'love letters' to John 131-7; marriage settlement 151, 162, 163, 164-5, 173, 435, 499, 519; wedding 167; honeymoon 175, 176, 181, 182, 190, 201, 223, 261, 457, 462, 465, 525, 529, 531; unsupported speculation with regard to attitude to pubic hair and personal hygiene 13, 178, 465-6; first trip abroad 204-210; death of brother Robert 218, 221; provides for family 201, 212-3, 215, 218, 244, 276, 287, 306-7; returns to Perth 95, 218, 348, 419, 420, 424, 450; horse riding 90, 133-4, 224, 226, 228, 229, 231, 244, 252, 257, 290; scathing about John's illness 197-8; illness 93, 137, 199, 210, 211, 216-7, 218, 221, 224, 225-9, 241, 243, 244, 245, 247, 248, 252, 255-6, 261, 263, 274, 276-8, 382,

Gray, Euphemia Chalmers *continued* 384, 424; sea-sickness 93, 204, 263; facial tic 425; hair falling out 137, 138, 207, 208, 486; dress in Austrian colours 322, 329; takes charge of accounts 301, 338; shopping 206, 263, 271, 272, 274, 287, 293, 301, 302, 305, 331, 337, 381; meets the Béthunes 211-2; gossip, 9, 13, 81, 90-1, 169, 171, 249, 250-1, 260-2, 291, 299, 327, 338-9, 438, 487, 492-3; and William Kelty MacLeod 115, 116, 117, 143, 215, 315, 316; and 'Prizie' Tasker 91, 117, 118, 124, 143, 215, 270, 315, 316; and 'Captn. C.' 118, 290; and Jessie Jameson's three brothers 118, 315; and William Macdonald 93, 94, 115, 117, 135, 158, 261; and 'Snob' Gardner 91; and Parker Howell 91; and Brooks 91; and Brinsley Marlay 318; and Charles Newton 289; and Dr. Purvis 273; and Frederick Gibbs 318; and Mr. Valentine 272, 277; and Edward Cheney 289, 292, 295, 297, 302, 318, 319, 330, 334, 336, 338, 344, 493, 495; and Lord Dufferin 302, 318; and Mr. Blumenthal 277; and Sir Francis Scott 318; and Count Alphonse Wimpffen 269, 272, 274; and Charles Paulizza 274, 275, 277, 278, 279, 280, 281, 283, 292, 299, 300, 316, 318; and Prince Troubetzkoi 279, 280, 281, 292, 317; and Count Thun 318, 320, 321, 323, 324, 325, 329, 330, 331, 335, 336, 339, 340, 341, 344, 359, 439; and Baron Diller 321, 323, 324, 325, 330, 331; and Count Falkenhayn 302, 318, 320, 321, 328, 330; and Count Festitics 318, 321, 326, 327, 328, 330, 343; and Count Nugent 318, 320, 321, 323; and Baron Reischach 302, 323; and Count Wrbn 318, 320, 321, 322, 323, 325, 326, 327, 328, 330, 343; and General Duodo, 320; and Mr. Foster 318, 320, 321, 323, 330, 331, 333, 334, 335, 336, 338, 339, 340-5, 360, 495; and Clare Ford, 289, 298, 299, 316, 345, 346, 347, 348, 365, 368, 437; modelling for Millais 373-375, 382, *385*, *413*, *418-9*; modelling for *Order of*

Gray, Euphemia Chalmers *continued*
Release 373-5; *398, 399, 413, 414, 415, 416-7, 418, 419, 420, 421, 423, 506;* Highland holiday 9, 361, 376, 380-405, 406-424, 425-6; leaves John, 450; writes to her father 336, 441-2, 523-6; writes to John's mother 356. 527-30; examined by lawyers, 456-7; marriage annulled 471-2; marriage to Millais, 502; writes to Mrs La Touche, 502, 504-5

Gray, George Snr. (Effie's father) 15, 21, 24, 27, 29, 55, 59, 62, 67, 75, 78, 80, 87, 89, 103, 117, 131, 144, *145,* 146-166, 170, 171, 173, 174, 176, 184, 185, 190, 198, 201, 206, 207, 208, 209, 214, 216, 218, 219, 220, 221, 226, 229, 233, 236, 238, 244, 247, 249, 251, 262, 304, 306, 307, 313, 345, 348, 380, 384, 424, 425, 430-5, 437, 439, 440, 441, 445, 447-451, 454- 457, 460, 470, 487,492, *506,* 530, 531; and Richardsons 24, 67, 455; marriage, 27, 55; buys Bowerswell House 21; rebuilds Bowerswell House, 29, 146; early difficulties: with railroads, 145; and with Australasian Banks, 144; and with California gold mines, 144; and with land speculation in U.S.A., 144; caught in Railway shares crash, 144-166, 190, 209; entirely ruined, 157; financial difficulties, 88, 103, 131, 133-4, 137, 144-166, 170, 190, 200, 206, 249; objects to Swiss trip, 103; correspondence with John James Ruskin 219-222, 226-235, 238-244, 249-251, 262, 304-7, 313-4, 345, 437; books house for Highland holiday 380; meets Millais in Stirling 384; at Edinburgh Lectures 424; talk with John at Bowerswell 430-3; pact of silence 10, 26-7, 434-5, 487, 492; advises Effie 439-451; and annulment proceedings 454-457, 460, 470

Gray, George Jnr. (Effie's brother) 88, 140, *145,* 147, 159, 187-8, 190, 200-6, 212-5, 217, 218, 279, 280-1, 287, 296, 298-9, 301, 330, 345, 379, 380, 428, 463, *506,* 532; concern about Effie's behaviour, 280-1, 316, 345

Gray, Melville, 267, 306, *506*
Gray, Mrs. Andrew, 23-6, 30
Gray, Sophia Maria (Effie's mother) 15, 27, 30, 55, 67, 78, 80, 81, 84, 88, 92, 96, 105-7, 109-13, 130, 134, 138, 139, 140, 141, 143, (*145*), 149, 152-4, 158-9, 160-1, 176, 184, 187-9, 191, 200, 211-2, 217-8, 227-8, 231, 233, 238, 243, 247, 248-9, 259, 264, 272-6, 279-281, 285, 293-4, 296, 298-9, 302, 306, 313, 316, 317, 327-9, 332, 337-9, 342, 348, 373, 376, 380, 390, 401, 424, 426, 434, 440, 442, 444-5, 447, 450, 456, 459, 460, 468, *506;* gives birth 27, 109; warns Effie about behaviour, 276, 316, 368, 373; warns Everett 426

Gray, Sophie *145,* 425, 437, 438-9, 450, 469, *506;* portrait by Millais 437
Grays of Camberwell 42, 46
Great Exhibition 290, 295, 296-7
Grisi 186
Haggard, John 471
Hallam, Henry 186
Halliday, Michael 422-3
Hamilton, Duke of 426
Harrison, Frederic 430, 451-3
Herne Hill 35, 39, 40, *41,* 47, 51, 52, 58, 61, 68, 69, 311, 313, 314, 338, 341, 344, 345, 348, 350, 351, 365, 368, 381, 422, 413, 425, 432, 434, 439, 445, 446, 449, 456, 458, 468, 523, 527, 529, 530
Hill, Octavia, 514
Hobbs, John (known as George) 104, 122, 198, 221, 260, 262, 264, 271, 272, 301, 321, 323, 325, 326, 328, 337, 368,
Hohenloe, Princess 302
Hope, James 84
Hope, Lady France, 186
Hunt, Violet Holman 115
Hunt, William Holman 170-2, 296, *372,* 373, 375, 380, 412, 420, 422-3, 426, 473-5, 478; *Claudio and Isabella* 375; *The Light of the World* 473, 475; *The Awakening Conscience* 473
Hunter Street 31, *32,* 35, 40
Jablonowska, Princess 320
James, Sir Walter & Lady 381

Jameson, Andrew 63, 114, 158, 395, 424, 530

Jameson, Eliza Tucket 27, 172

Jameson, Jessie 118, 209, 211, 315

Jameson, Melville 70, 106

Jeffrey, Lord 141

Jephson, Dr. 63, 93

Keir, Patrick Small 21

Ker, Charlotte 248, 257-60, 262, 264, 266, 269, 270-5, 277, 279, 280-1, 283, 306, 317

Kerr, Bellenden 366

Keswick 126, 182, 457

La Touche, John 500-2, 507-8, 512, 514

La Touche, Maria 500-5, 508-510; writes to Effie 502, 504

La Touche, Rose, 15, 16, 65, 486, 500-517, falls ill 500; recovers from illness 501; suspected tuberculosis 65; love letter to John Ruskin 513; death, 65, 513

Landseer, Sir Edwin 186

Leamington 63, 93

Lee, Robert 457-9, 460-1, 470

Leeds 106, 108, 114, 155, 259, 295

Lemprière family 373

Lewis, Lady 493

Liddell, Mr & Mrs 88, 98, 121, 186, 289

Lind, Jenny 186

Lindsay, Lord, *Sketches of the History of Christian Art* 86, 489

Lockhart, Charlotte, 53, *54*, 55, 83-6, 89,92, 95, 100-1, 186, 408, 489, 490, 500

Lockhart, John, 53, 54, 84, 86, 99, 102, 186, 215, 340, 408, 488-90, 492-3, 495-6; *Life of Sir Walter Scott* 103, 408

Locock, Charles 457-8, 460-1

London Magazine 490

Louis-Philippe, King of France, abdication 150

Lushington, Stephen 376-8, 444

MacDonald, George 57, 66, 179, 353, 509, 514-6; and tuberculosis 57; and Rose La Touche and John 514-6

MacDonald, Greville 353, 508, 502-4

Macdonald, William 93, 94, 96, 105, 109, 115, 117, 135, 143, 158, 168, 250, 261, 410; best man at wedding, 115, 168

Mackenzie, Olive 65

Magazine of Natural History 49

Manning, Cardinal H. E. 355

Marmont, Marshall 302

Martineau, Harriet 68

Martineau, J. P. 507

Matrimonial Causes Act (1857) 363, 452

Maurice, Frederick Denison 366

McEwen, John 21

McEwen, Margaret 21

Milan 265, 267, 268, 269, 329

Millais, John Everett, *2, 7*, 80, *145*, 170, 171, 274, 296, 297, 342, 348, 354, 373-376, 379-384, 389-394, 396, 400, 401, 403, 406-412, 428, *414, 415, 418, 419, 420, 421, 422, 423*, 424, 425-7, *427*, 428-31, 437, 439-440, 442, 469, 474, 487, 493, 494, 495, 502, 504-5, *506*, 511, 512; Highland holiday 361, *369, 370, 371*, 376, 380-405, *384, 385, 391, 392, 398, 399, 404*, 406-424, 425-6, 438; moves into schoolmaster's cottage, 389; elected ARA, 425; panic, 426-7, *427*; marriage to Effie, 502; PAINTINGS: *Ophelia* 373; *The Huguenot* 373-5; *The Proscribed Royalist* 374-5; *The Order of Release*, *2*, 374-6, 381; *The Black Brunswicker* 375; *Ruskin at Glenfinlas*, *7*, *369, 385*, 394, 404, 418-9, 423; *Effie with foxgloves in her hair* 412, *413*; *The Water-fall at Glenfinlas 416-7*,

Millais, William, 380, 381, 382, *384*, 389, 393, *394*, 396, *398*, 400, 401, 402, 414, *418,* 419, 420, 428; statement to Albert Gray 393-5

Milman, Dean 444, 493

Milman, Henry Hart 186

Milnes, Richard Monckton (Lord Houghton) 380

Mitford, Mary Russell 90, 177

Monteath, Rev. William 387, 393, *398*, 404

Morning Chronicle 338

Morosini, Count 332

Mount-Temple, see Cowper-Temple

Mudie, Mr. 340

Murray, John 83, 84, 85, 86, 141, 186, 215, 340, 354, 488-93, 495-7

Murray, Lady 141, 186

Naples 63

New Hall School, Chelmsford 52

Newbolt, Sir Henry 170

Nisbett, Mr. 85

North Inch 39

Norton, Charles Eliot 86

Norwich, Bishop of 186

Oliphant family 57

Oliphant, Henry 186

Otway, Lady 266, 267

Oxford 16, 33, 49, 93, 95, 169, 190, 197, 199,
    251, 376, 415, 430, 438, 452, 466

Paget, Mrs. Charles 79, 92

Pallavicini, Countess 302, 318, 319, 320,
    343

Palmerston, Viscountess, 186

Paris, 10, 51, 77, 125, 150, 190, 205, 207,
    209, 211, 221, 224, 255, 258, 261, 263, 285,
    287, 288, 300, 305, 337, 376,

Park Street 83, 202, 214-7, 220, 258-9, 261,
    270, 287-9, 292, 294, 296-9, 304, 306,
    309, 316, 345, 347, 350, 458

Paston, George (alias of Emily Morse
    Symonds) 340, 491

Perth Courier 21

Perth 9, 21-28, 38, 39, 42, 47, 58, 67, 70, 71,
    77-9, 91, 94, 95, 97, 103, 106, 107, 109,
    111, 114, 115, 117, 120-1, 125, 130, 143-4,
    148-50, 152-3, 155-7, 160-1, 163, 169, 171-3,
    187, 203-4, 215-6, 218, 220, 222, 225-6,
    228-9, 231, 249-52, 254, 258, 261-2, 270,
    307, 315, 348, 365, 368, 373-4, 384, 395,
    401, 419, 420, 424, 425, 432-3, 439, 444-
    6, 448, 450-1, 455-7, 460-1, 487, 528-9;
    Rose Terrace 39

Phillimore, Robert 471

Pott, F. W. 462-3, 471, 534

Priestley, Joseph 68

Pritchard, John, MP 295, 366

Prout, Samuel, 186

Quarterly Review 53, 86, 186, 488-491, 494,
    496, 497

Radetzky, Marshal 265-6, 268-9, 318, 321-5,
    331, 336

Reeve, Henry 496

Reischach, Baron, 302, 323

Richardson, Bridget 38, 40, 46, 500; love
    for John 37; death, 40, 64

Richardson, Charles 45-6

Richardson, James 58; death, 59

Richardson, Jessie (formerly Ruskin, Janet),
    21, 24, 26, 28, 38, 39, 58, 67, early days in
    Perth, 21; forced to marry Patrick, 67;
    John's memories of 38-9; death of chil-
    dren 22-3, 39, 59; death, 28, 59, 67

Richardson, Jessie (Jnr) 39, 50; death, 39, 59

Richardson, Margaret 63-4

Richardson, Mary 38, 39, 59, 63, 134-5, 136,
    242, 251, 460; childhood in Perth, 39;
    adopted by Ruskins 39; death, 237

Richardson, Moll 24

Richardson, Patrick 67; death, 59, 67

Richardson, W. G. 507, 514

Richardson, William 208

Richmond, George *8, 35, 72, 73,* 98

Richmond, Thomas *4,* 296

Rigby, Mathilda 489

Rigby, Elizabeth *see* Eastlake, Lady

Roberts, David 186

Rogers, Samuel 186

Rome 14, 53, 61, 62, 447, 494

Rossie Castle 158

Royal Academy Exhibition, 184, 296, 375, 381

Ruskin, Catherine arrives in Perth, 21; dies
    of stroke, 22

Ruskin, John, *8, 16, 73,* birth, 23, 31, *32,*
    childhood 31-49; religious education 31-
    4; toys 36-8; pets 38, 43, 45, 126, 189, 330,
    335, *392, 423,* 439, 515; early education
    48-9; visits Perth 28, 38-9; given dancing
    and fencing lessons 46; first symptoms
    of chest disease 59; declared consumptive
    56; illness 53, 56-66, 87, 90, 96, 176, 197,
    216, 224, 241, 250, 384, 424; Lake
    District Tour 49, 59; European tour
    1840, 60-3; Welsh Tour 63; European
    tour 1846 74; at Oxford 49, 53, 60;
    coughs blood at Oxford 60; wins
    Newdigate Poetry Prize 49; meets Effie
    as a child 67; and Miss Andrews, 50; and
    Adèle Clotilde Domecq, 51, 52, 53, 55, 56,
    60, 66, 74, 76, 159, 163, 173, 211, 285, 485;

Ruskin, John *continued*
and Charlotte Lockhart, 53, *54*, 55, 76-
86, 89, 92, 95, 100-1, 186, 408, 489, 490,
500; and Miss Wardell, 52, 89; and
Charlotte Withers, 52, 89 romantic parting from Effie at Denmark Hill 92;
parents object to engagement with Effie
93; parents agree to engagement 96-103;
visits Bowerswell 104-5, 167-175, 256, 258,
292, 424-6; proposal refused 105-7;
proposal accepted 108; love letters to
Effie 123-30; realises true state of Gray's
financial affairs 173; wedding 167; honeymoon 176-9, 181-2, 525, 529, 531;
unsupported speculation with regard to
attitude to pubic hair and personal
hygiene 13, 178, 465-6; English Cathedrals tour 191, 197, 200-3; Normandy
tour 203-210; work regime 206; Swiss
tour 220-255; *Modern Painters* 9, 69, 82,
183, 222, 296, 309, 488, 489, 496; *The
King of the Golden River* 71, 296; *The
Seven Lamps of Architecture* 9, 17, 191,
205, 220, 224, 257, 349; *Notes on the
Construction of Sheepfolds* 296, 366; *Pre-
Raphaelitism* 296; *The Stones of Venice* 9,
10, 257, 258, 282, 294-6, 308-9, 349-50,
362, 365, 401, 410, 498; *Academy Notes*,
64, 496; *Præterita*, 31, 40, 43, 46-7, 51-2,
62-4, 83, 93, 96; first trip to Venice
263ff; behaviour in Venice 282-3; attitude to Effie 281; second trip to Venice
300ff; expenses in Venice 303f; jewel
robbery 332-7 challenged to a duel 336,
341; scandal 338-340; letters to *The Times*
340, 373, 473-4; at Doctors' Commons
365; Highland holiday 7, 9, 169, 350, 361,
365, *369*, *371*, 376, 380-405,406-424, *384*,
392, *397*, *398*, *402*, *421*, *423*, 425-6, 428,
429, 438, 455, 462; evidential notebook,
383, 421, 426, 427, 430, 438; Edinburgh
Lectures 380, 423, 424, 430, 432, 452;
statement to his proctor 462-5, 467, 522,
529; marriage annulled 469-472; and
Rose La Touche 500-517; proposes to
Rose La Touche, 501; mental illness 66

Ruskin, John James, 21-8, *35*, 38-41, 43, 45-
6, 48, 51-3, 55, 56-63, 67, 69-71, 74-8,
80-4; sent to London at 16, 21; early
career in wine trade 28; marries Margaret
Cox 27; works with Gray on Richardson
trust fund 67, 455; complains about Effie
to George Gray 75; gives permission for
proposal 98-103; marriage settlement 151,
162-5, 173, 243, 435, 499; decides not to
attend wedding ceremony 148; congratu-
lates Effie on engagement 128-30;
concerned about Effie's health 226
Ruskin, John Thomas, 21, 24-7, 29-30, 64,
467; arrives in Perth 21; death 22-3, 25,
64-5; reports of suicide, 23, 30; burial, 23
Ruskin, Margaret, 21-30, *30*, 31-41, 43-9, 51-
2, 58,60, 75-7, 79-82, 87, 97-9, 102-3,
124, 127-30, 134, 137, 145, 148, 158, 176,
183-5, 191, 197-8, 200, 202-3, 205, 218,
220, 227-8, 230, 232, 234-5, 238-245, 249-
51, 259, 261, 287, 305, 309, 356, 368, 379,
401, 462, 469, 523, 527; enters Ruskin
household in Perth 22; death of father
47 engagement to John James Ruskin
22; marriage, 23, 2 visits to Perth, 2
superstitious dread of Bowerswell, 28,
157; superstitious dread of Perth, 28, 77,
94-5, 103, 157, 251; gives approval for
proposal 97, 103; relations with Effie
238-243; refuses to have Effie at
Denmark Hill 309
Ruskin, Telford and Domecq 28, 52, 88,
147, 165, 208
Rutter, J. G. 163-4, 377, 459, 463, 467, 470- 2
Ryan, Anne 374
Salisbury 191, 197-8, 200, 202, 241, 251, 486,
527
Samoilow, Princess 269
Sartoris, Mr and Mrs. 186
Scott, Sir Walter, 53-4, 83, 103, 375, 407-
411, *411*, 489; *Rhymer's Glen* 54;
Glenfinlas 409-412, *411*; *Guy Mannering*
409; *Lady of the Lake* 408-412
Scott, Sophia 53
Scott, William Bell 382-3, 429
Severn, Joan, 51, 115, 164-5

Shakespeare, William, *Cymbeline* 254; *King Lear*, 239, 483; *The Tempest* 382, 406-7, 411; *Measure for Measure* 375

Shelburn, Lord & Lady 186

Simpson, Dr. James 227-8, 243, 248, 261-2, 293, 384, *385*, 424

Sismondi, J. C. L. S. de, *Histoire des Républiques Italiennes au Moyen Age* 225, 257

Smith, Adam, *Wealth of Nations* 498

Smith, James 489

Smith, Julia Leigh 68

Sorell, Lady 302, 318-20, 341

Spain, Infanta of 302

Stanfield, Clarkson 186

Stewart, Alexander 387, 389, 392-394, 419

Stewart, Mrs Ann 387, 393, 419

Stirling 384, *386*, 387, 394, 415

Stirling Journal and Advertiser 380, 387

Stone, Frank 473-4

Strachan, Ann 221

Stuart Wortley, Clare 27, 373

Switzerland, 103, 105, 186, 220, 226, 236, 237, 250, 263, 297, 308, 312, 336, 342, 373, 379, 424, 444, 445, 455, 463, 467, 473-475, 484, 498, 530

Taglioni 264, 280-1

Tayler, Patrick 21

Telford, Henry 28, 41

Thackeray, William, 145; *Vanity Fair* 494

The Times 296, 340, 365, 373, 378, 472-3, 487, 490

Touche, Rev. John Edward 167

Trevelyan, Pauline, Lady 158, 181, 189, 227, *370*, *371*, 381, 382, 383, 406, 424, 474, 475

Trevelyan, Sir Walter 382, 383, *384*, 394, 406, 429, 475, 479, 484-5, 514,

Tristram, T. H. 507

Trossachs New Hotel 385, (386), 387, *388*, *389*, 390-6, 400, 401, 403, *404*, 408, 412, *418*, 420

tuberculosis 56-66, 173, 198, 251

Turin 63

Turner, J. M. W. 54, 88, 95, 186, 207, 289, 309, 365, 425, 482, 488, 497

Tweedale, John 58

Twiss, Sir Travers 444

Venice 9, 10, 61, 62-3, 88, 171, 215, 216, 237, 248, 253, 257-83, 284, 286, 288-299, 300-314, 315-331, 332- 6, 338-344, 348-350, 356, 359, 361, 362, 365-6, 401, 410, 438, 440, 446, 458, 491, 495, 498

Venier, Countess 332, 334

Verona 268, 274, 285, 318, 321, 323-6, 331, 336, 341, 344

Vevay 59, 125, 236

Vicenza,326, 331

Wardell, Miss 52, 89

Waterford, Louisa Countess of 179

Watts, G. F. 296

Wedderburn, Alexander 456-460, 463, 471

Westlake, John 453, 454

Westminster, Lady 492

Wetzlar, Baroness 297, 300

Wetzlar, Casa 297, 300, 302, *303*, 308, 312, 317-8, 320-2, 326-7, 329-30

Whewell, William 295

Wigram, Sir James 186

Windus, William Lindsay 64

Withers, Charlotte 52, 89

Wordsworth, William 86

Working Men's College 164, 366, 498, 514

Wornum, Ralph, 497

ABOUT THE AUTHOR

ↀↀ

After writing his doctoral dissertation on John Ruskin,
Rob Brownell taught art history for twenty years across a
wide range of educational institutions. His main focus of
interest was Victorian Britain and particularly John Ruskin,
William Morris, and the Pre-Raphaelites. This led him
inevitably into the wider fields of nineteenth century
economics and science, and deeper into the historical
background. As a result he has developed a
supplementary interest in seventeenth century Holland
and in the art of the middle ages. He is the author
of books, articles and conference papers on
nineteenth century art and architecture.

ALSO BY ROBERT BROWNELL
FROM PALLAS ATHENE

A TORCH AT MIDNIGHT

A study of Ruskin's
The Seven Lamps of Architecture

ISBN 978 1 84368 077 2

THE CONTEMPORARY REVIEWS
OF JOHN RUSKIN'S
THE SEVEN LAMPS OF ARCHITECTURE

A study of Ruskin's
The Seven Lamps of Architecture

ISBN 978 1 84368 079 6

First published 2013 by
Pallas Athene (Publishers) Ltd,
Studio 11B, Archway Studios,
25-27 Bickerton Road,
London N19 5JT

www.pallasathene.co.uk

The publisher would like to pay special
thanks, as always, to Stephen Wildman,
for his unstinting help and support, to
Robert Hewison, to Sir Geoffroy Millais,
and to Holly-Blue Ross for proof-reading

ISBN 978-1-84368-076-5

Printed on FSC certified paper in
England by T. J. International, Padstow,
with colour sections printed by
Park Lane Press, Corsham, using fully
sustainable, vegetable oil-based inks,
power from 100% renewable resources
and waterless printing technology